SOFTWARE ENGINEERING

Ninth Edition

Ian Sommerville

Addison-Wesley

Boston   Columbus   Indianapolis   New York   San Francisco   Upper Saddle River
Amsterdam   Cape Town   Dubai   London   Madrid   Milan   Munich   Paris   Montreal   Toronto
Delhi   Mexico City   São Paulo   Sydney   Hong Kong   Seoul   Singapore   Taipei   Tokyo

Editorial Director: Marcia Horton
Editor in Chief: Michael Hirsch
Acquisitions Editor: Matt Goldstein
Editorial Assistant: Chelsea Bell
Managing Editor: Jeff Holcomb
Senior Production Project Manager: Marilyn Lloyd
Director of Marketing: Margaret Waples
Marketing Coordinator: Kathryn Ferranti
Senior Manufacturing Buyer: Carol Melville
Text Designer: Susan Raymond
Cover Art Director: Elena Sidorova
Front Cover Photograph: © Jacques Pavlovsky/Sygma/Corbis
Interior Chapter Opener: © graficart.net/Alamy
Full-Service Project Management: Andrea Stefanowicz, GGS Higher Education Resources,
    a Division of PreMedia Global, Inc.
Composition and Illustrations: GGS Higher Education Resources, a Division of PreMedia Global, Inc.
Printer/Binder: Edwards Brothers
Cover Printer: Lehigh-Phoenix Color/Hagerstown

Library of Congress Cataloging-in-Publication Data

Sommerville, Ian
    Software engineering / Ian Sommerville. — 9th ed.
        p. cm.
    Includes index.
    ISBN-13: 978-0-13-703515-1
    ISBN-10: 0-13-703515-2
    1. Software engineering.   I. Title.
    QA76.758.S657 2011
    005.1—dc22

                                                        2009053058

10 9 8 7 6 5 4 3 2 1–EB–14 13 12 11 10

ISBN 10:   0-13-703515-2
ISBN 13: 978-0-13-703515-1

PREFACE

As I was writing the final chapters in this book in the summer of 2009, I realized that software engineering was 40 years old. The name 'software engineering' was proposed in 1969 at a NATO conference to discuss software development problems—large software systems were late, did not deliver the functionality needed by their users, cost more than expected, and were unreliable. I did not attend that conference but, a year later, I wrote my first program and started my professional life in software.

Progress in software engineering has been remarkable over my professional lifetime. Our societies could not function without large, professional software systems. For building business systems, there is an alphabet soup of technologies—J2EE, .NET, SaaS, SAP, BPEL4WS, SOAP, CBSE, etc.—that support the development and deployment of large enterprise applications. National utilities and infrastructure—energy, communications, and transport—all rely on complex and mostly reliable computer systems. Software has allowed us to explore space and to create the World Wide Web, the most significant information system in the history of mankind. Humanity is now faced with a new set of challenges—climate change and extreme weather, declining natural resources, an increasing world population to be fed and housed, international terrorism, and the need to help elderly people lead satisfying and fulfilled lives. We need new technologies to help us address these problems and, for sure, software will play a central role in these technologies.

Software engineering is, therefore, a critically important technology for the future of mankind. We must continue to educate software engineers and develop the discipline so that we can create more complex software systems. Of course, there are still problems with software projects. Software is still sometimes late and costs more than expected. However, we should not let these problems conceal the real successes in software engineering and the impressive software engineering methods and technologies that have been developed.

Software engineering is now such a huge area that it is impossible to cover the whole subject in one book. My focus, therefore, is on key topics that are fundamental to all development processes and topics concerned with the development of reliable, distributed systems. There is an increased emphasis on agile methods and software reuse. I strongly believe that agile methods have their place but so too does 'traditional' plan-driven software engineering. We need to combine the best of these approaches to build better software systems.

Books inevitably reflect the opinions and prejudices of their authors. Some readers will inevitably disagree with my opinions and with my choice of material. Such disagreement is a healthy reflection of the diversity of the discipline and is essential for its evolution. Nevertheless, I hope that all software engineers and software engineering students can find something of interest here.

Integration with the Web

There is an incredible amount of information on software engineering available on the Web and some people have questioned if textbooks like this one are still needed. However, the quality of available information is very patchy, information is sometimes presented badly and it can be hard to find the information that you need. Consequently, I believe that textbooks still have an important role to play in learning. They serve as a roadmap to the subject and allow information on method and techniques to be organized and presented in a coherent and readable way. They also provide a starting point for deeper exploration of the research literature and material available on the Web.

I strongly believe that textbooks have a future but only if they are integrated with and add value to material on the Web. This book has therefore been designed as a hybrid print/web text in which core information in the printed edition is linked to supplementary material on the Web. Almost all chapters include specially written 'web sections' that add to the information in that chapter. There are also four 'web chapters' on topics that I have not covered in the print version of the book.

The website that is associated with the book is:

http://www.SoftwareEngineering-9.com

The book's web has four principal components:

1. *Web sections* These are extra sections that add to the content presented in each chapter. These web sections are linked from breakout boxes in each chapter.

2. *Web chapters* There are four web chapters covering formal methods, interaction design, documentation, and application architectures. I may add other chapters on new topics during the lifetime of the book.

3. *Material for instructors* The material in this section is intended to support people who are teaching software engineering. See the "Support Materials" section in this Preface.

4. *Case studies* These provide additional information about the case studies used in the book (insulin pump, mental health-care system, wilderness weather system)

as well as information about further case studies, such as the failure of the Ariane 5 launcher.

As well as these sections, there are also links to other sites with useful material on software engineering, further reading, blogs, newsletters, etc.

I welcome your constructive comments and suggestions about the book and the website. You can contact me at ian@SoftwareEngineering-9.com. Please include [SE9] in the subject of your message. Otherwise, my spam filters will probably reject your mail and you will not receive a reply. I do not have time to help students with their homework, so please don't ask.

Readership

The book is primarily aimed at university and college students taking introductory and advanced courses in software and systems engineering. Software engineers in the industry may find the book useful as general reading and as a means of updating their knowledge on topics such as software reuse, architectural design, dependability and security, and process improvement. I assume that readers have completed an introductory programming course and are familiar with programming terminology.

Changes from previous editions

This edition has retained the fundamental material on software engineering that was covered in previous editions but I have revised and updated all chapters and have included new material on many different topics. The most important changes are:

1. The move from a print-only book to a hybrid print/web book with the web material tightly integrated with the sections in the book. This has allowed me to reduce the number of chapters in the book and to focus on core material in each chapter.

2. Complete restructuring to make it easier to use the book in teaching software engineering. The book now has four rather than eight parts and each part may be used on its own or in combination with other parts as the basis of a software engineering course. The four parts are an introduction to software engineering, dependability and security, advanced software engineering, and software engineering management.

3. Several topics from previous editions are presented more concisely in a single chapter, with extra material moved onto the Web.

4. Additional web chapters, based on chapters from previous editions that I have not included here, are available on the Web.

5. I have updated and revised the content in all chapters. I estimate that between 30% and 40% of the text has been completely rewritten.

6. I have added new chapters on agile software development and embedded systems.

7. As well as these new chapters, there is new material on model-driven engineering, open source development, test-driven development, Reason's Swiss Cheese model, dependable systems architectures, static analysis and model checking, COTS reuse, software as a service, and agile planning.

8. A new case study on a patient record system for patients who are undergoing treatment for mental health problems has been used in several chapters.

Using the book for teaching

I have designed the book so that it can be used in three different types of software engineering courses:

1. *General introductory courses in software engineering* The first part of the book has been designed explicitly to support a one-semester course in introductory software engineering.

2. *Introductory or intermediate courses on specific software engineering topics* You can create a range of more advanced courses using the chapters in Parts 2–4. For example, I have taught a course in critical systems engineering using the chapters in Part 2 plus chapters on quality management and configuration management.

3. *More advanced courses in specific software engineering topics* In this case, the chapters in the book form a foundation for the course. These are then supplemented with further reading that explores the topic in more detail. For example, a course on software reuse could be based around Chapters 16, 17, 18, and 19.

More information about using the book for teaching, including a comparison with previous editions, is available on the book's website.

Support materials

A wide range of support material is available to help people using the book for teaching software engineering courses. This includes:

- PowerPoint presentations for all of the chapters in the book.

- Figures in PowerPoint.

- An instructor's guide that gives advice on how to use the book in different courses and explains the relationship between the chapters in this edition and previous editions.

- Further information on the book's case studies.

- Additional case studies that may be used in software engineering courses.

- Additional PowerPoint presentations on systems engineering.

- Four web chapters covering formal methods, interaction design, application architectures, and documentation.

All of this material is available free to readers of the book from the book's website or from the Pearson support site below. Additional material for instructors is available on a restricted basis to accredited instructors only:

- Model answers to selected end-of-chapter exercises.

- Quiz questions and answers for each chapter.

All support material, including restricted material, is available from:
http://www.pearsonhighered.com/sommerville/

Instructors using the book for teaching may obtain a password to access restricted material by registering at the Pearson website, by contacting their local Pearson representative, or by requesting a password by e-mail from computing@aw.com. Passwords are not available from the author.

Acknowledgments

A large number of people have contributed over the years to the evolution of this book and I'd like to thank everyone (reviewers, students, and book users) who have commented on previous editions and made constructive suggestions for change.

I'd particularly like to thank my family (Anne, Ali, and Jane) for their help and support while the book was being written. A big thank-you especially to my daughter, Jane, who discovered a talent for proofreading and editing. She was tremendously helpful in reading the entire book and did a great job spotting and fixing a large number of typos and grammatical errors.

Ian Sommerville
October 2009

Contents at a glance

CONTENTS

PART 1

Introduction to Software Engineering

My aim in this part of the book is to provide a general introduction to software engineering. I introduce important concepts such as software processes and agile methods, and describe essential software development activities, from initial software specification through to system evolution. The chapters in this part have been designed to support a one-semester course in software engineering.

Chapter 1 is a general introduction that introduces professional software engineering and defines some software engineering concepts. I have also written a brief discussion of ethical issues in software engineering. I think that it is important for software engineers to think about the wider implications of their work. This chapter also introduces three case studies that I use in the book, namely a system for managing records of patients undergoing treatment for mental health problems, a control system for a portable insulin pump and a wilderness weather system.

Chapters 2 and 3 cover software engineering processes and agile development. In Chapter 2, I introduce commonly used generic software process models, such as the waterfall model, and I discuss the basic activities that are part of these processes. Chapter 3 supplements this with a discussion of agile development methods for software engineering. I mostly use Extreme Programming as an example of an agile method but also briefly introduce Scrum in this chapter.

The remainder of the chapters in this part are extended descriptions of the software process activities that will be introduced in Chapter 2. Chapter 4 covers the critically important topic of requirements engineering, where the requirements for what a system should do are defined. Chapter 5 introduces system modeling using the UML, where I focus on the use of use case diagrams, class diagrams, sequence diagrams, and state diagrams for modeling a software system. Chapter 6 introduces architectural design and I discuss the importance of architecture and the use of architectural patterns in software design.

Chapter 7 introduces object-oriented design and the use of design patterns. I also introduce important implementation issues here—reuse, configuration management, and host-target development and discuss open source development. Chapter 8 focuses on software testing from unit testing during system development to the testing of software releases. I also discuss the use of test-driven development—an approach pioneered in agile methods but which has wide applicability. Finally, Chapter 9 presents an overview of software evolution issues. I cover evolution processes, software maintenance, and legacy system management.

1

Introduction

Objectives

The objectives of this chapter are to introduce software engineering and to provide a framework for understanding the rest of the book. When you have read this chapter you will:

- understand what software engineering is and why it is important;

- understand that the development of different types of software systems may require different software engineering techniques;

- understand some ethical and professional issues that are important for software engineers;

- have been introduced to three systems, of different types, that will be used as examples throughout the book.

Contents

We can't run the modern world without software. National infrastructures and utilities are controlled by computer-based systems and most electrical products include a computer and controlling software. Industrial manufacturing and distribution is completely computerized, as is the financial system. Entertainment, including the music industry, computer games, and film and television, is software intensive. Therefore, software engineering is essential for the functioning of national and international societies.

Software systems are abstract and intangible. They are not constrained by the properties of materials, governed by physical laws, or by manufacturing processes. This simplifies software engineering, as there are no natural limits to the potential of software. However, because of the lack of physical constraints, software systems can quickly become extremely complex, difficult to understand, and expensive to change.

There are many different types of software systems, from simple embedded systems to complex, worldwide information systems. It is pointless to look for universal notations, methods, or techniques for software engineering because different types of software require different approaches. Developing an organizational information system is completely different from developing a controller for a scientific instrument. Neither of these systems has much in common with a graphics-intensive computer game. All of these applications need software engineering; they do not all need the same software engineering techniques.

There are still many reports of software projects going wrong and 'software failures'. Software engineering is criticized as inadequate for modern software development. However, in my view, many of these so-called software failures are a consequence of two factors:

1. *Increasing demands* As new software engineering techniques help us to build larger, more complex systems, the demands change. Systems have to be built and delivered more quickly; larger, even more complex systems are required; systems have to have new capabilities that were previously thought to be impossible. Existing software engineering methods cannot cope and new software engineering techniques have to be developed to meet new these new demands.

2. *Low expectations* It is relatively easy to write computer programs without using software engineering methods and techniques. Many companies have drifted into software development as their products and services have evolved. They do not use software engineering methods in their everyday work. Consequently, their software is often more expensive and less reliable than it should be. We need better software engineering education and training to address this problem.

Software engineers can be rightly proud of their achievements. Of course we still have problems developing complex software but, without software engineering, we would not have explored space, would not have the Internet or modern telecommunications. All forms of travel would be more dangerous and expensive. Software engineering has contributed a great deal and I am convinced that its contributions in the 21st century will be even greater.

History of software engineering

The notion of 'software engineering' was first proposed in 1968 at a conference held to discuss what was then called the 'software crisis' (Naur and Randell, 1969). It became clear that individual approaches to program development did not scale up to large and complex software systems. These were unreliable, cost more than expected, and were delivered late.

Throughout the 1970s and 1980s, a variety of new software engineering techniques and methods were developed, such as structured programming, information hiding and object-oriented development. Tools and standard notations were developed and are now extensively used.

http://www.SoftwareEngineering-9.com/Web/History/

1.1 Professional software development

Lots of people write programs. People in business write spreadsheet programs to simplify their jobs, scientists and engineers write programs to process their experimental data, and hobbyists write programs for their own interest and enjoyment. However, the vast majority of software development is a professional activity where software is developed for specific business purposes, for inclusion in other devices, or as software products such as information systems, CAD systems, etc. Professional software, intended for use by someone apart from its developer, is usually developed by teams rather than individuals. It is maintained and changed throughout its life.

Software engineering is intended to support professional software development, rather than individual programming. It includes techniques that support program specification, design, and evolution, none of which are normally relevant for personal software development. To help you to get a broad view of what software engineering is about, I have summarized some frequently asked questions in Figure 1.1.

Many people think that software is simply another word for computer programs. However, when we are talking about software engineering, software is not just the programs themselves but also all associated documentation and configuration data that is required to make these programs operate correctly. A professionally developed software system is often more than a single program. The system usually consists of a number of separate programs and configuration files that are used to set up these programs. It may include system documentation, which describes the structure of the system; user documentation, which explains how to use the system, and websites for users to download recent product information.

This is one of the important differences between professional and amateur software development. If you are writing a program for yourself, no one else will use it and you don't have to worry about writing program guides, documenting the program design, etc. However, if you are writing software that other people will use and other engineers will change then you usually have to provide additional information as well as the code of the program.

Question	Answer
What is software?	Computer programs and associated documentation. Software products may be developed for a particular customer or may be developed for a general market.
What are the attributes of good software?	Good software should deliver the required functionality and performance to the user and should be maintainable, dependable, and usable.
What is software engineering?	Software engineering is an engineering discipline that is concerned with all aspects of software production.
What are the fundamental software engineering activities?	Software specification, software development, software validation, and software evolution.
What is the difference between software engineering and computer science?	Computer science focuses on theory and fundamentals; software engineering is concerned with the practicalities of developing and delivering useful software.
What is the difference between software engineering and system engineering?	System engineering is concerned with all aspects of computer-based systems development including hardware, software, and process engineering. Software engineering is part of this more general process.
What are the key challenges facing software engineering?	Coping with increasing diversity, demands for reduced delivery times, and developing trustworthy software.
What are the costs of software engineering?	Roughly 60% of software costs are development costs; 40% are testing costs. For custom software, evolution costs often exceed development costs.
What are the best software engineering techniques and methods?	While all software projects have to be professionally managed and developed, different techniques are appropriate for different types of system. For example, games should always be developed using a series of prototypes whereas safety critical control systems require a complete and analyzable specification to be developed. You can't, therefore, say that one method is better than another.
What differences has the Web made to software engineering?	The Web has led to the availability of software services and the possibility of developing highly distributed service-based systems. Web-based systems development has led to important advances in programming languages and software reuse.

Figure 1.1 Frequently asked questions about software

Software engineers are concerned with developing software products (i.e., software which can be sold to a customer). There are two kinds of software products:

1. *Generic products* These are stand-alone systems that are produced by a development organization and sold on the open market to any customer who is able to

buy them. Examples of this type of product include software for PCs such as databases, word processors, drawing packages, and project-management tools. It also includes so-called vertical applications designed for some specific purpose such as library information systems, accounting systems, or systems for maintaining dental records.

2. *Customized (or bespoke) products* These are systems that are commissioned by a particular customer. A software contractor develops the software especially for that customer. Examples of this type of software include control systems for electronic devices, systems written to support a particular business process, and air traffic control systems.

An important difference between these types of software is that, in generic products, the organization that develops the software controls the software specification. For custom products, the specification is usually developed and controlled by the organization that is buying the software. The software developers must work to that specification.

However, the distinction between these system product types is becoming increasingly blurred. More and more systems are now being built with a generic product as a base, which is then adapted to suit the requirements of a customer. Enterprise Resource Planning (ERP) systems, such as the SAP system, are the best examples of this approach. Here, a large and complex system is adapted for a company by incorporating information about business rules and processes, reports required, and so on.

When we talk about the quality of professional software, we have to take into account that the software is used and changed by people apart from its developers. Quality is therefore not just concerned with what the software does. Rather, it has to include the software's behavior while it is executing and the structure and organization of the system programs and associated documentation. This is reflected in so-called quality or non-functional software attributes. Examples of these attributes are the software's response time to a user query and the understandability of the program code.

The specific set of attributes that you might expect from a software system obviously depends on its application. Therefore, a banking system must be secure, an interactive game must be responsive, a telephone switching system must be reliable, and so on. These can be generalized into the set of attributes shown in Figure 1.2, which I believe are the essential characteristics of a professional software system.

1.1.1 Software engineering

Software engineering is an engineering discipline that is concerned with all aspects of software production from the early stages of system specification through to maintaining the system after it has gone into use. In this definition, there are two key phrases:

1. *Engineering discipline* Engineers make things work. They apply theories, methods, and tools where these are appropriate. However, they use them selectively

Product characteristics	Description
Maintainability	Software should be written in such a way so that it can evolve to meet the changing needs of customers. This is a critical attribute because software change is an inevitable requirement of a changing business environment.
Dependability and security	Software dependability includes a range of characteristics including reliability, security, and safety. Dependable software should not cause physical or economic damage in the event of system failure. Malicious users should not be able to access or damage the system.
Efficiency	Software should not make wasteful use of system resources such as memory and processor cycles. Efficiency therefore includes responsiveness, processing time, memory utilization, etc.
Acceptability	Software must be acceptable to the type of users for which it is designed. This means that it must be understandable, usable, and compatible with other systems that they use.

Figure 1.2 Essential attributes of good software

and always try to discover solutions to problems even when there are no applicable theories and methods. Engineers also recognize that they must work to organizational and financial constraints so they look for solutions within these constraints.

2. *All aspects of software production* Software engineering is not just concerned with the technical processes of software development. It also includes activities such as software project management and the development of tools, methods, and theories to support software production.

Engineering is about getting results of the required quality within the schedule and budget. This often involves making compromises—engineers cannot be perfectionists. People writing programs for themselves, however, can spend as much time as they wish on the program development.

In general, software engineers adopt a systematic and organized approach to their work, as this is often the most effective way to produce high-quality software. However, engineering is all about selecting the most appropriate method for a set of circumstances so a more creative, less formal approach to development may be effective in some circumstances. Less formal development is particularly appropriate for the development of web-based systems, which requires a blend of software and graphical design skills.

Software engineering is important for two reasons:

1. More and more, individuals and society rely on advanced software systems. We need to be able to produce reliable and trustworthy systems economically and quickly.

2. It is usually cheaper, in the long run, to use software engineering methods and techniques for software systems rather than just write the programs as if it was a personal programming project. For most types of systems, the majority of costs are the costs of changing the software after it has gone into use.

The systematic approach that is used in software engineering is sometimes called a software process. A software process is a sequence of activities that leads to the production of a software product. There are four fundamental activities that are common to all software processes. These activities are:

1. Software specification, where customers and engineers define the software that is to be produced and the constraints on its operation.

2. Software development, where the software is designed and programmed.

3. Software validation, where the software is checked to ensure that it is what the customer requires.

4. Software evolution, where the software is modified to reflect changing customer and market requirements.

Different types of systems need different development processes. For example, real-time software in an aircraft has to be completely specified before development begins. In e-commerce systems, the specification and the program are usually developed together. Consequently, these generic activities may be organized in different ways and described at different levels of detail depending on the type of software being developed. I describe software processes in more detail in Chapter 2.

Software engineering is related to both computer science and systems engineering:

1. Computer science is concerned with the theories and methods that underlie computers and software systems, whereas software engineering is concerned with the practical problems of producing software. Some knowledge of computer science is essential for software engineers in the same way that some knowledge of physics is essential for electrical engineers. Computer science theory, however, is often most applicable to relatively small programs. Elegant theories of computer science cannot always be applied to large, complex problems that require a software solution.

2. System engineering is concerned with all aspects of the development and evolution of complex systems where software plays a major role. System engineering is therefore concerned with hardware development, policy and process design and system deployment, as well as software engineering. System engineers are involved in specifying the system, defining its overall architecture, and then integrating the different parts to create the finished system. They are less concerned with the engineering of the system components (hardware, software, etc.).

As I discuss in the next section, there are many different types of software. There is no universal software engineering method or technique that is applicable for all of these. However, there are three general issues that affect many different types of software:

1. *Heterogeneity* Increasingly, systems are required to operate as distributed systems across networks that include different types of computer and mobile devices. As well as running on general-purpose computers, software may also have to execute on mobile phones. You often have to integrate new software with older legacy systems written in different programming languages. The challenge here is to develop techniques for building dependable software that is flexible enough to cope with this heterogeneity.

2. *Business and social change* Business and society are changing incredibly quickly as emerging economies develop and new technologies become available. They need to be able to change their existing software and to rapidly develop new software. Many traditional software engineering techniques are time consuming and delivery of new systems often takes longer than planned. They need to evolve so that the time required for software to deliver value to its customers is reduced.

3. *Security and trust* As software is intertwined with all aspects of our lives, it is essential that we can trust that software. This is especially true for remote software systems accessed through a web page or web service interface. We have to make sure that malicious users cannot attack our software and that information security is maintained.

Of course, these are not independent issues. For example, it may be necessary to make rapid changes to a legacy system to provide it with a web service interface. To address these challenges we will need new tools and techniques as well as innovative ways of combining and using existing software engineering methods.

1.1.2 Software engineering diversity

Software engineering is a systematic approach to the production of software that takes into account practical cost, schedule, and dependability issues, as well as the needs of software customers and producers. How this systematic approach is actually implemented varies dramatically depending on the organization developing the software, the type of software, and the people involved in the development process. There are no universal software engineering methods and techniques that are suitable for all systems and all companies. Rather, a diverse set of software engineering methods and tools has evolved over the past 50 years.

Perhaps the most significant factor in determining which software engineering methods and techniques are most important is the type of application that is being developed. There are many different types of application including:

1. *Stand-alone applications* These are application systems that run on a local computer, such as a PC. They include all necessary functionality and do not need to

be connected to a network. Examples of such applications are office applications on a PC, CAD programs, photo manipulation software, etc.

2. *Interactive transaction-based applications* These are applications that execute on a remote computer and that are accessed by users from their own PCs or terminals. Obviously, these include web applications such as e-commerce applications where you can interact with a remote system to buy goods and services. This class of application also includes business systems, where a business provides access to its systems through a web browser or special-purpose client program and cloud-based services, such as mail and photo sharing. Interactive applications often incorporate a large data store that is accessed and updated in each transaction.

3. *Embedded control systems* These are software control systems that control and manage hardware devices. Numerically, there are probably more embedded systems than any other type of system. Examples of embedded systems include the software in a mobile (cell) phone, software that controls anti-lock braking in a car, and software in a microwave oven to control the cooking process.

4. *Batch processing systems* These are business systems that are designed to process data in large batches. They process large numbers of individual inputs to create corresponding outputs. Examples of batch systems include periodic billing systems, such as phone billing systems, and salary payment systems.

5. *Entertainment systems* These are systems that are primarily for personal use and which are intended to entertain the user. Most of these systems are games of one kind or another. The quality of the user interaction offered is the most important distinguishing characteristic of entertainment systems.

6. *Systems for modeling and simulation* These are systems that are developed by scientists and engineers to model physical processes or situations, which include many, separate, interacting objects. These are often computationally intensive and require high-performance parallel systems for execution.

7. *Data collection systems* These are systems that collect data from their environment using a set of sensors and send that data to other systems for processing. The software has to interact with sensors and often is installed in a hostile environment such as inside an engine or in a remote location.

8. *Systems of systems* These are systems that are composed of a number of other software systems. Some of these may be generic software products, such as a spreadsheet program. Other systems in the assembly may be specially written for that environment.

Of course, the boundaries between these system types are blurred. If you develop a game for a mobile (cell) phone, you have to take into account the same constraints (power, hardware interaction) as the developers of the phone software. Batch processing systems are often used in conjunction with web-based systems. For example, in a company, travel expense claims may be submitted through a web application but processed in a batch application for monthly payment.

You use different software engineering techniques for each type of system because the software has quite different characteristics. For example, an embedded control system in an automobile is safety-critical and is burned into ROM when installed in the vehicle. It is therefore very expensive to change. Such a system needs very extensive verification and validation so that the chances of having to recall cars after sale to fix software problems are minimized. User interaction is minimal (or perhaps nonexistent) so there is no need to use a development process that relies on user interface prototyping.

For a web-based system, an approach based on iterative development and delivery may be appropriate, with the system being composed of reusable components. However, such an approach may be impractical for a system of systems, where detailed specifications of the system interactions have to be specified in advance so that each system can be separately developed.

Nevertheless, there are software engineering fundamentals that apply to all types of software system:

1. They should be developed using a managed and understood development process. The organization developing the software should plan the development process and have clear ideas of what will be produced and when it will be completed. Of course, different processes are used for different types of software.

2. Dependability and performance are important for all types of systems. Software should behave as expected, without failures and should be available for use when it is required. It should be safe in its operation and, as far as possible, should be secure against external attack. The system should perform efficiently and should not waste resources.

3. Understanding and managing the software specification and requirements (what the software should do) are important. You have to know what different customers and users of the system expect from it and you have to manage their expectations so that a useful system can be delivered within budget and to schedule.

4. You should make as effective use as possible of existing resources. This means that, where appropriate, you should reuse software that has already been developed rather than write new software.

These fundamental notions of process, dependability, requirements, management, and reuse are important themes of this book. Different methods reflect them in different ways but they underlie all professional software development.

You should notice that these fundamentals do not cover implementation and programming. I don't cover specific programming techniques in this book because these vary dramatically from one type of system to another. For example, a scripting language such as Ruby is used for web-based system programming but would be completely inappropriate for embedded systems engineering.

1.1.3 Software engineering and the Web

The development of the World Wide Web has had a profound effect on all of our lives. Initially, the Web was primarily a universally accessible information store and it had little effect on software systems. These systems ran on local computers and were only accessible from within an organization. Around 2000, the Web started to evolve and more and more functionality was added to browsers. This meant that web-based systems could be developed where, instead of a special-purpose user interface, these systems could be accessed using a web browser. This led to the development of a vast range of new system products that delivered innovative services, accessed over the Web. These are often funded by adverts that are displayed on the user's screen and do not involve direct payment from users.

As well as these system products, the development of web browsers that could run small programs and do some local processing led to an evolution in business and organizational software. Instead of writing software and deploying it on users' PCs, the software was deployed on a web server. This made it much cheaper to change and upgrade the software, as there was no need to install the software on every PC. It also reduced costs, as user interface development is particularly expensive. Consequently, wherever it has been possible to do so, many businesses have moved to web-based interaction with company software systems.

The next stage in the development of web-based systems was the notion of web services. Web services are software components that deliver specific, useful functionality and which are accessed over the Web. Applications are constructed by integrating these web services, which may be provided by different companies. In principle, this linking can be dynamic so that an application may use different web services each time that it is executed. I cover this approach to software development in Chapter 19.

In the last few years, the notion of 'software as a service' has been developed. It has been proposed that software will not normally run on local computers but will run on 'computing clouds' that are accessed over the Internet. If you use a service such as web-based mail, you are using a cloud-based system. A computing cloud is a huge number of linked computer systems that is shared by many users. Users do not buy software but pay according to how much the software is used or are given free access in return for watching adverts that are displayed on their screen.

The advent of the web, therefore, has led to a significant change in the way that business software is organized. Before the web, business applications were mostly monolithic, single programs running on single computers or computer clusters. Communications were local, within an organization. Now, software is highly distributed, sometimes across the world. Business applications are not programmed from scratch but involve extensive reuse of components and programs.

This radical change in software organization has, obviously, led to changes in the ways that web-based systems are engineered. For example:

1.   Software reuse has become the dominant approach for constructing web-based systems. When building these systems, you think about how you can assemble them from pre-existing software components and systems.

2. It is now generally recognized that it is impractical to specify all the requirements for such systems in advance. Web-based systems should be developed and delivered incrementally.

3. User interfaces are constrained by the capabilities of web browsers. Although technologies such as AJAX (Holdener, 2008) mean that rich interfaces can be created within a web browser, these technologies are still difficult to use. Web forms with local scripting are more commonly used. Application interfaces on web-based systems are often poorer than the specially designed user interfaces on PC system products.

The fundamental ideas of software engineering, discussed in the previous section, apply to web-based software in the same way that they apply to other types of software system. Experience gained with large system development in the 20th century is still relevant to web-based software.

1.2 Software engineering ethics

Like other engineering disciplines, software engineering is carried out within a social and legal framework that limits the freedom of people working in that area. As a software engineer, you must accept that your job involves wider responsibilities than simply the application of technical skills. You must also behave in an ethical and morally responsible way if you are to be respected as a professional engineer.

It goes without saying that you should uphold normal standards of honesty and integrity. You should not use your skills and abilities to behave in a dishonest way or in a way that will bring disrepute to the software engineering profession. However, there are areas where standards of acceptable behavior are not bound by laws but by the more tenuous notion of professional responsibility. Some of these are:

1. *Confidentiality* You should normally respect the confidentiality of your employers or clients irrespective of whether or not a formal confidentiality agreement has been signed.

2. *Competence* You should not misrepresent your level of competence. You should not knowingly accept work that is outside your competence.

3. *Intellectual property rights* You should be aware of local laws governing the use of intellectual property such as patents and copyright. You should be careful to ensure that the intellectual property of employers and clients is protected.

4. *Computer misuse* You should not use your technical skills to misuse other people's computers. Computer misuse ranges from relatively trivial (game playing on an employer's machine, say) to extremely serious (dissemination of viruses or other malware).

Software Engineering Code of Ethics and Professional Practice

ACM/IEEE-CS Joint Task Force on Software Engineering Ethics and Professional Practices

PREAMBLE
The short version of the code summarizes aspirations at a high level of the abstraction; the clauses that are included in the full version give examples and details of how these aspirations change the way we act as software engineering professionals. Without the aspirations, the details can become legalistic and tedious; without the details, the aspirations can become high sounding but empty; together, the aspirations and the details form a cohesive code.

   Software engineers shall commit themselves to making the analysis, specification, design, development, testing and maintenance of software a beneficial and respected profession. In accordance with their commitment to the health, safety and welfare of the public, software engineers shall adhere to the following Eight Principles:

1. PUBLIC — Software engineers shall act consistently with the public interest.
2. CLIENT AND EMPLOYER — Software engineers shall act in a manner that is in the best interests of their client and employer consistent with the public interest.
3. PRODUCT — Software engineers shall ensure that their products and related modifications meet the highest professional standards possible.
4. JUDGMENT — Software engineers shall maintain integrity and independence in their professional judgment.
5. MANAGEMENT — Software engineering managers and leaders shall subscribe to and promote an ethical approach to the management of software development and maintenance.
6. PROFESSION — Software engineers shall advance the integrity and reputation of the profession consistent with the public interest.
7. COLLEAGUES — Software engineers shall be fair to and supportive of their colleagues.
8. SELF — Software engineers shall participate in lifelong learning regarding the practice of their profession and shall promote an ethical approach to the practice of the profession.

Figure 1.3 The ACM/IEEE Code of Ethics (© IEEE/ACM 1999)

Professional societies and institutions have an important role to play in setting ethical standards. Organizations such as the ACM, the IEEE (Institute of Electrical and Electronic Engineers), and the British Computer Society publish a code of professional conduct or code of ethics. Members of these organizations undertake to follow that code when they sign up for membership. These codes of conduct are generally concerned with fundamental ethical behavior.

Professional associations, notably the ACM and the IEEE, have cooperated to produce a joint code of ethics and professional practice. This code exists in both a short form, shown in Figure 1.3, and a longer form (Gotterbarn et al., 1999) that adds detail and substance to the shorter version. The rationale behind this code is summarized in the first two paragraphs of the longer form:

Computers have a central and growing role in commerce, industry, government, medicine, education, entertainment and society at large. Software engineers are those who contribute by direct participation or by teaching, to the analysis, specification, design, development, certification, maintenance and testing of software systems. Because of their roles in developing software systems, software engineers have significant opportunities to do good or cause harm, to enable others to do good or cause harm, or to influence others to do good or cause harm. To ensure, as much as possible, that their efforts will be used for good, software engineers must commit themselves to making software engineering a beneficial and respected profession. In accordance with that commitment, software engineers shall adhere to the following Code of Ethics and Professional Practice.

The Code contains eight Principles related to the behaviour of and decisions made by professional software engineers, including practitioners, educators, managers, supervisors and policy makers, as well as trainees and students of the profession. The Principles identify the ethically responsible relationships in which individuals, groups, and organizations participate and the primary obligations within these relationships. The Clauses of each Principle are illustrations of some of the obligations included in these relationships. These obligations are founded in the software engineer's humanity, in special care owed to people affected by the work of software engineers, and the unique elements of the practice of software engineering. The Code prescribes these as obligations of anyone claiming to be or aspiring to be a software engineer.

In any situation where different people have different views and objectives you are likely to be faced with ethical dilemmas. For example, if you disagree, in principle, with the policies of more senior management in the company, how should you react? Clearly, this depends on the particular individuals and the nature of the disagreement. Is it best to argue a case for your position from within the organization or to resign in principle? If you feel that there are problems with a software project, when do you reveal these to management? If you discuss these while they are just a suspicion, you may be overreacting to a situation; if you leave it too late, it may be impossible to resolve the difficulties.

Such ethical dilemmas face all of us in our professional lives and, fortunately, in most cases they are either relatively minor or can be resolved without too much difficulty. Where they cannot be resolved, the engineer is faced with, perhaps, another problem. The principled action may be to resign from their job but this may well affect others such as their partner or their children.

A particularly difficult situation for professional engineers arises when their employer acts in an unethical way. Say a company is responsible for developing a safety-critical system and, because of time pressure, falsifies the safety validation records. Is the engineer's responsibility to maintain confidentiality or to alert the customer or publicize, in some way, that the delivered system may be unsafe?

The problem here is that there are no absolutes when it comes to safety. Although the system may not have been validated according to predefined criteria, these criteria may be too strict. The system may actually operate safely throughout its lifetime. It is also the case that, even when properly validated, the system may fail and cause an accident. Early disclosure of problems may result in damage to the employer and other employees; failure to disclose problems may result in damage to others.

You must make up your own mind in these matters. The appropriate ethical position here depends entirely on the views of the individuals who are involved. In this case, the potential for damage, the extent of the damage, and the people affected by the damage should influence the decision. If the situation is very dangerous, it may be justified to publicize it using the national press (say). However, you should always try to resolve the situation while respecting the rights of your employer.

Another ethical issue is participation in the development of military and nuclear systems. Some people feel strongly about these issues and do not wish to participate in any systems development associated with military systems. Others will work on military systems but not on weapons systems. Yet others feel that national security is an overriding principle and have no ethical objections to working on weapons systems.

In this situation, it is important that both employers and employees should make their views known to each other in advance. Where an organization is involved in military or nuclear work, they should be able to specify that employees must be willing to accept any work assignment. Equally, if an employee is taken on and makes clear that they do not wish to work on such systems, employers should not put pressure on them to do so at some later date.

The general area of ethics and professional responsibility is becoming more important as software-intensive systems pervade every aspect of work and everyday life. It can be considered from a philosophical standpoint where the basic principles of ethics are considered and software engineering ethics are discussed with reference to these basic principles. This is the approach taken by Laudon (1995) and to a lesser extent by Huff and Martin (1995). Johnson's text on computer ethics (2001) also approaches the topic from a philosophical perspective.

However, I find that this philosophical approach is too abstract and difficult to relate to everyday experience. I prefer the more concrete approach embodied in codes of conduct and practice. I think that ethics are best discussed in a software engineering context and not as a subject in their own right. In this book, therefore, I do not include abstract ethical discussions but, where appropriate, include examples in the exercises that can be the starting point for a group discussion on ethical issues.

1.3 Case studies

To illustrate software engineering concepts, I use examples from three different types of systems throughout the book. The reason why I have not used a single case study is that one of the key messages in this book is that software engineering practice depends on the type of systems being produced. I therefore choose an appropriate example when discussing concepts such as safety and dependability, system modeling, reuse, etc.

The three types of systems that I use as case studies are:

1. *An embedded system* This is a system where the software controls a hardware device and is embedded in that device. Issues in embedded systems typically

include physical size, responsiveness, power management, etc. The example of an embedded system that I use is a software system to control a medical device.

2. *An information system* This is a system whose primary purpose is to manage and provide access to a database of information. Issues in information systems include security, usability, privacy, and maintaining data integrity. The example of an information system that I use is a medical records system.

3. *A sensor-based data collection system* This is a system whose primary purpose is to collect data from a set of sensors and process that data in some way. The key requirements of such systems are reliability, even in hostile environmental conditions, and maintainability. The example of a data collection system that I use is a wilderness weather station.

I introduce each of these systems in this chapter, with more information about each of them available on the Web.

1.3.1 An insulin pump control system

An insulin pump is a medical system that simulates the operation of the pancreas (an internal organ). The software controlling this system is an embedded system, which collects information from a sensor and controls a pump that delivers a controlled dose of insulin to a user.

People who suffer from diabetes use the system. Diabetes is a relatively common condition where the human pancreas is unable to produce sufficient quantities of a hormone called insulin. Insulin metabolises glucose (sugar) in the blood. The conventional treatment of diabetes involves regular injections of genetically engineered insulin. Diabetics measure their blood sugar levels using an external meter and then calculate the dose of insulin that they should inject.

The problem with this treatment is that the level of insulin required does not just depend on the blood glucose level but also on the time of the last insulin injection. This can lead to very low levels of blood glucose (if there is too much insulin) or very high levels of blood sugar (if there is too little insulin). Low blood glucose is, in the short term, a more serious condition as it can result in temporary brain malfunctioning and, ultimately, unconsciousness and death. In the long term, however, continual high levels of blood glucose can lead to eye damage, kidney damage, and heart problems.

Current advances in developing miniaturized sensors have meant that it is now possible to develop automated insulin delivery systems. These systems monitor blood sugar levels and deliver an appropriate dose of insulin when required. Insulin delivery systems like this already exist for the treatment of hospital patients. In the future, it may be possible for many diabetics to have such systems permanently attached to their bodies.

A software-controlled insulin delivery system might work by using a micro-sensor embedded in the patient to measure some blood parameter that is proportional to the sugar level. This is then sent to the pump controller. This controller computes the sugar level and the amount of insulin that is needed. It then sends signals to a miniaturized pump to deliver the insulin via a permanently attached needle.

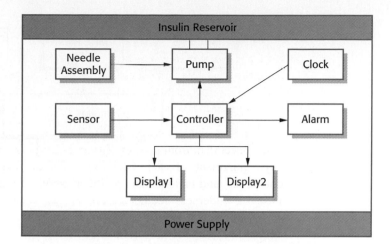

Figure 1.4 Insulin
pump hardware

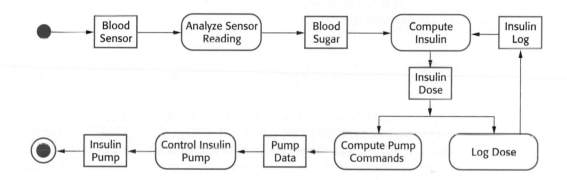

Figure 1.5 Activity
model of the insulin
pump

Figure 1.4 shows the hardware components and organization of the insulin pump. To understand the examples in this book, all you need to know is that the blood sensor measures the electrical conductivity of the blood under different conditions and that these values can be related to the blood sugar level. The insulin pump delivers one unit of insulin in response to a single pulse from a controller. Therefore, to deliver 10 units of insulin, the controller sends 10 pulses to the pump. Figure 1.5 is a UML activity model that illustrates how the software transforms an input blood sugar level to a sequence of commands that drive the insulin pump.

Clearly, this is a safety-critical system. If the pump fails to operate or does not operate correctly, then the user's health may be damaged or they may fall into a coma because their blood sugar levels are too high or too low. There are, therefore, two essential high-level requirements that this system must meet:

1. The system shall be available to deliver insulin when required.

2. The system shall perform reliably and deliver the correct amount of insulin to counteract the current level of blood sugar.

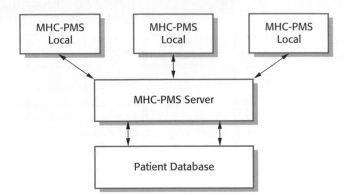

Figure 1.6 The organization of the MHC-PMS

The system must therefore be designed and implemented to ensure that the system always meets these requirements. More detailed requirements and discussions of how to ensure that the system is safe are discussed in later chapters.

1.3.2 A patient information system for mental health care

A patient information system to support mental health care is a medical information system that maintains information about patients suffering from mental health problems and the treatments that they have received. Most mental health patients do not require dedicated hospital treatment but need to attend specialist clinics regularly where they can meet a doctor who has detailed knowledge of their problems. To make it easier for patients to attend, these clinics are not just run in hospitals. They may also be held in local medical practices or community centers.

The MHC-PMS (Mental Health Care-Patient Management System) is an information system that is intended for use in clinics. It makes use of a centralized database of patient information but has also been designed to run on a PC, so that it may be accessed and used from sites that do not have secure network connectivity. When the local systems have secure network access, they use patient information in the database but they can download and use local copies of patient records when they are disconnected. The system is not a complete medical records system so does not maintain information about other medical conditions. However, it may interact and exchange data with other clinical information systems. Figure 1.6 illustrates the organization of the MHC-PMS.

The MHC-PMS has two overall goals:

1. To generate management information that allows health service managers to assess performance against local and government targets.

2. To provide medical staff with timely information to support the treatment of patients.

The nature of mental health problems is such that patients are often disorganized so may miss appointments, deliberately or accidentally lose prescriptions and medication, forget instructions, and make unreasonable demands on medical staff. They may drop in on clinics unexpectedly. In a minority of cases, they may be a danger to themselves or to other people. They may regularly change address or may be homeless on a long-term or short-term basis. Where patients are dangerous, they may need to be 'sectioned'—confined to a secure hospital for treatment and observation.

Users of the system include clinical staff such as doctors, nurses, and health visitors (nurses who visit people at home to check on their treatment). Nonmedical users include receptionists who make appointments, medical records staff who maintain the records system, and administrative staff who generate reports.

The system is used to record information about patients (name, address, age, next of kin, etc.), consultations (date, doctor seen, subjective impressions of the patient, etc.), conditions, and treatments. Reports are generated at regular intervals for medical staff and health authority managers. Typically, reports for medical staff focus on information about individual patients whereas management reports are anonymized and are concerned with conditions, costs of treatment, etc.

The key features of the system are:

1. *Individual care management* Clinicians can create records for patients, edit the information in the system, view patient history, etc. The system supports data summaries so that doctors who have not previously met a patient can quickly learn about the key problems and treatments that have been prescribed.

2. *Patient monitoring* The system regularly monitors the records of patients that are involved in treatment and issues warnings if possible problems are detected. Therefore, if a patient has not seen a doctor for some time, a warning may be issued. One of the most important elements of the monitoring system is to keep track of patients who have been sectioned and to ensure that the legally required checks are carried out at the right time.

3. *Administrative reporting* The system generates monthly management reports showing the number of patients treated at each clinic, the number of patients who have entered and left the care system, number of patients sectioned, the drugs prescribed and their costs, etc.

Two different laws affect the system. These are laws on data protection that govern the confidentiality of personal information and mental health laws that govern the compulsory detention of patients deemed to be a danger to themselves or others. Mental health is unique in this respect as it is the only medical speciality that can recommend the detention of patients against their will. This is subject to very strict legislative safeguards. One of the aims of the MHC-PMS is to ensure that staff always act in accordance with the law and that their decisions are recorded for judicial review if necessary.

As in all medical systems, privacy is a critical system requirement. It is essential that patient information is confidential and is never disclosed to anyone apart from authorized medical staff and the patient themselves. The MHC-PMS is also a safety-critical

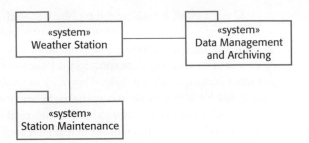

Figure 1.7 The weather station's environment

system. Some mental illnesses cause patients to become suicidal or a danger to other people. Wherever possible, the system should warn medical staff about potentially suicidal or dangerous patients.

The overall design of the system has to take into account privacy and safety requirements. The system must be available when needed otherwise safety may be compromised and it may be impossible to prescribe the correct medication to patients. There is a potential conflict here—privacy is easiest to maintain when there is only a single copy of the system data. However, to ensure availability in the event of server failure or when disconnected from a network, multiple copies of the data should be maintained. I discuss the trade-offs between these requirements in later chapters.

1.3.3   A wilderness weather station

To help monitor climate change and to improve the accuracy of weather forecasts in remote areas, the government of a country with large areas of wilderness decides to deploy several hundred weather stations in remote areas. These weather stations collect data from a set of instruments that measure temperature and pressure, sunshine, rainfall, wind speed, and wind direction.

Wilderness weather stations are part of a larger system (Figure 1.7), which is a weather information system that collects data from weather stations and makes it available to other systems for processing. The systems in Figure 1.7 are:

1. *The weather station system* This is responsible for collecting weather data, carrying out some initial data processing, and transmitting it to the data management system.

2. *The data management and archiving system* This system collects the data from all of the wilderness weather stations, carries out data processing and analysis, and archives the data in a form that can be retrieved by other systems, such as weather forecasting systems.

3. *The station maintenance system* This system can communicate by satellite with all wilderness weather stations to monitor the health of these systems and provide reports of problems. It can update the embedded software in these systems. In the event of system problems, this system can also be used to remotely control a wilderness weather system.

In Figure 1.7, I have used the UML package symbol to indicate that each system is a collection of components and have identified the separate systems, using the UML stereotype «system». The associations between the packages indicate there is an exchange of information but, at this stage, there is no need to define them in any more detail.

Each weather station includes a number of instruments that measure weather parameters such as the wind speed and direction, the ground and air temperatures, the barometric pressure, and the rainfall over a 24-hour period. Each of these instruments is controlled by a software system that takes parameter readings periodically and manages the data collected from the instruments.

The weather station system operates by collecting weather observations at frequent intervals—for example, temperatures are measured every minute. However, because the bandwidth to the satellite is relatively narrow, the weather station carries out some local processing and aggregation of the data. It then transmits this aggregated data when requested by the data collection system. If, for whatever reason, it is impossible to make a connection, then the weather station maintains the data locally until communication can be resumed.

Each weather station is battery-powered and must be entirely self-contained—there are no external power or network cables available. All communications are through a relatively slow-speed satellite link and the weather station must include some mechanism (solar or wind power) to charge its batteries. As they are deployed in wilderness areas, they are exposed to severe environmental conditions and may be damaged by animals. The station software is therefore not just concerned with data collection. It must also:

1. Monitor the instruments, power, and communication hardware and report faults to the management system.

2. Manage the system power, ensuring that batteries are charged whenever the environmental conditions permit but also that generators are shut down in potentially damaging weather conditions, such as high wind.

3. Allow for dynamic reconfiguration where parts of the software are replaced with new versions and where backup instruments are switched into the system in the event of system failure.

Because weather stations have to be self-contained and unattended, this means that the software installed is complex, even though the data collection functionality is fairly simple.

KEY POINTS

■ Software engineering is an engineering discipline that is concerned with all aspects of software production.

■ Software is not just a program or programs but also includes documentation. Essential software product attributes are maintainability, dependability, security, efficiency, and acceptability.

■ The software process includes all of the activities involved in software development. The high-level activities of specification, development, validation, and evolution are part of all software processes.

■ The fundamental notions of software engineering are universally applicable to all types of system development. These fundamentals include software processes, dependability, security, requirements, and reuse.

■ There are many different types of systems and each requires appropriate software engineering tools and techniques for their development. There are few, if any, specific design and implementation techniques that are applicable to all kinds of systems.

■ The fundamental ideas of software engineering are applicable to all types of software systems. These fundamentals include managed software processes, software dependability and security, requirements engineering, and software reuse.

■ Software engineers have responsibilities to the engineering profession and society. They should not simply be concerned with technical issues.

■ Professional societies publish codes of conduct that set out the standards of behavior expected of their members.

FURTHER READING

'No silver bullet: Essence and accidents of software engineering'. In spite of its age, this paper is a good general introduction to the problems of software engineering. The essential message of the paper still hasn't changed. (F. P. Brooks, *IEEE Computer,* **20** (4), April 1987.) http://doi.ieeecomputersociety.org/10.1109/MC.1987.1663532.

'Software engineering code of ethics is approved'. An article that discusses the background to the development of the ACM/IEEE Code of Ethics and that includes both the short and long form of the code. (*Comm. ACM*, D. Gotterbarn, K. Miller, and S. Rogerson, October 1999.) http://portal.acm.org/citation.cfm?doid=317665.317682.

Professional Issues in Software Engineering. This is an excellent book discussing legal and professional issues as well as ethics. I prefer its practical approach to more theoretical texts on ethics. (F. Bott, A. Coleman, J. Eaton and D. Rowland, 3rd edition, 2000, Taylor and Francis.)

IEEE Software, March/April 2002. This is a special issue of the magazine devoted to the development of Web-based software. This area has changed very quickly so some articles are a little dated but most are still relevant. (*IEEE Software,* **19** (2), 2002.) http://www2.computer.org/portal/web/software.

'A View of 20th and 21st Century Software Engineering'. A backward and forward look at software engineering from one of the first and most distinguished software engineers. Barry Boehm identifies timeless software engineering principles but also suggests that some commonly used practices are obsolete. (B. Boehm, *Proc. 28th Software Engineering Conf.,* Shanghai. 2006.) http://doi.ieeecomputersociety.org/10.1145/1134285.1134288.

'Software Engineering Ethics'. Special issue of IEEE Computer, with a number of papers on the topic. (*IEEE Computer,* **42** (6), June 2009.)

EXERCISES

1.1. Explain why professional software is not just the programs that are developed for a customer.

1.2. What is the most important difference between generic software product development and custom software development? What might this mean in practice for users of generic software products?

1.3. What are the four important attributes that all professional software should have? Suggest four other attributes that may sometimes be significant.

1.4. Apart from the challenges of heterogeneity, business and social change, and trust and security, identify other problems and challenges that software engineering is likely to face in the 21st century (Hint: think about the environment).

1.5. Based on your own knowledge of some of the application types discussed in section 1.1.2, explain, with examples, why different application types require specialized software engineering techniques to support their design and development.

1.6. Explain why there are fundamental ideas of software engineering that apply to all types of software systems.

1.7. Explain how the universal use of the Web has changed software systems.

1.8. Discuss whether professional engineers should be certified in the same way as doctors or lawyers.

1.9. For each of the clauses in the ACM/IEEE Code of Ethics shown in Figure 1.3, suggest an appropriate example that illustrates that clause.

1.10. To help counter terrorism, many countries are planning or have developed computer systems that track large numbers of their citizens and their actions. Clearly this has privacy implications. Discuss the ethics of working on the development of this type of system.

REFERENCES

Gotterbarn, D., Miller, K. and Rogerson, S. (1999). Software Engineering Code of Ethics is Approved. Comm. ACM, **42** (10), 102–7.

Holdener, A. T. (2008). *Ajax: The Definitive Guide*. Sebastopol, Ca.: O'Reilly and Associates.

Huff, C. and Martin, C. D. (1995). Computing Consequences: A Framework for Teaching Ethical Computing. Comm. ACM, **38** (12), 75–84.

Johnson, D. G. (2001). *Computer Ethics*. Englewood Cliffs, NJ: Prentice Hall.

Laudon, K. (1995). Ethical Concepts and Information Technology. Comm. ACM, **38** (12), 33–9.

Naur, P. and Randell, B. (1969). Software Engineering: Report on a Conference sponsored by the NATO Science Committee, Garmisch, Germany. 7th to 11th October 1968.

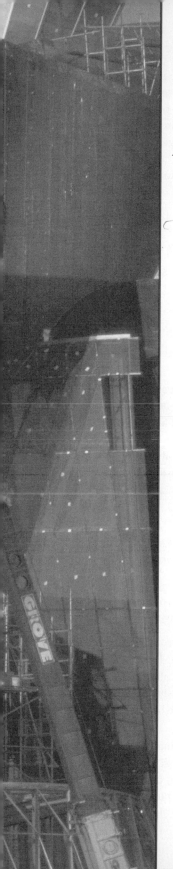

2

Software processes

Objectives

The objective of this chapter is to introduce you to the idea of a software process—a coherent set of activities for software production. When you have read this chapter you will:

- understand the concepts of software processes and software process models;

- have been introduced to three generic software process models and when they might be used;

- know about the fundamental process activities of software requirements engineering, software development, testing, and evolution;

- understand why processes should be organized to cope with changes in the software requirements and design;

- understand how the Rational Unified Process integrates good software engineering practice to create adaptable software processes.

Contents

A software process is a set of related activities that leads to the production of a software product. These activities may involve the development of software from scratch in a standard programming language like Java or C. However, business applications are not necessarily developed in this way. New business software is now often developed by extending and modifying existing systems or by configuring and integrating off-the-shelf software or system components.

There are many different software processes but all must include four activities that are fundamental to software engineering:

1. *Software specification* The functionality of the software and constraints on its operation must be defined.

2. *Software design and implementation* The software to meet the specification must be produced.

3. *Software validation* The software must be validated to ensure that it does what the customer wants.

4. *Software evolution* The software must evolve to meet changing customer needs.

In some form, these activities are part of all software processes. In practice, of course, they are complex activities in themselves and include sub-activities such as requirements validation, architectural design, unit testing, etc. There are also supporting process activities such as documentation and software configuration management.

When we describe and discuss processes, we usually talk about the activities in these processes such as specifying a data model, designing a user interface, etc., and the ordering of these activities. However, as well as activities, process descriptions may also include:

1. Products, which are the outcomes of a process activity. For example, the outcome of the activity of architectural design may be a model of the software architecture.

2. Roles, which reflect the responsibilities of the people involved in the process. Examples of roles are project manager, configuration manager, programmer, etc.

3. Pre- and post-conditions, which are statements that are true before and after a process activity has been enacted or a product produced. For example, before architectural design begins, a pre-condition may be that all requirements have been approved by the customer; after this activity is finished, a post-condition might be that the UML models describing the architecture have been reviewed.

Software processes are complex and, like all intellectual and creative processes, rely on people making decisions and judgments. There is no ideal process and most organizations have developed their own software development processes. Processes have evolved to take advantage of the capabilities of the people in an organization and the specific characteristics of the systems that are being developed. For some systems, such as critical systems, a very structured development process is required. For business systems, with rapidly changing requirements, a less formal, flexible process is likely to be more effective.

Sometimes, software processes are categorized as either plan-driven or agile processes. Plan-driven processes are processes where all of the process activities are planned in advance and progress is measured against this plan. In agile processes, which I discuss in Chapter 3, planning is incremental and it is easier to change the process to reflect changing customer requirements. As Boehm and Turner (2003) discuss, each approach is suitable for different types of software. Generally, you need to find a balance between plan-driven and agile processes.

Although there is no 'ideal' software process, there is scope for improving the software process in many organizations. Processes may include outdated techniques or may not take advantage of the best practice in industrial software engineering. Indeed, many organizations still do not take advantage of software engineering methods in their software development.

Software processes can be improved by process standardization where the diversity in software processes across an organization is reduced. This leads to improved communication and a reduction in training time, and makes automated process support more economical. Standardization is also an important first step in introducing new software engineering methods and techniques and good software engineering practice. I discuss software process improvement in more detail in Chapter 26.

2.1 Software process models

As I explained in Chapter 1, a software process model is a simplified representation of a software process. Each process model represents a process from a particular perspective, and thus provides only partial information about that process. For example, a process activity model shows the activities and their sequence but may not show the roles of the people involved in these activities. In this section, I introduce a number of very general process models (sometimes called 'process paradigms') and present these from an architectural perspective. That is, we see the framework of the process but not the details of specific activities.

These generic models are not definitive descriptions of software processes. Rather, they are abstractions of the process that can be used to explain different approaches to software development. You can think of them as process frameworks that may be extended and adapted to create more specific software engineering processes.

The process models that I cover here are:

1. *The waterfall model* This takes the fundamental process activities of specification, development, validation, and evolution and represents them as separate process phases such as requirements specification, software design, implementation, testing, and so on.

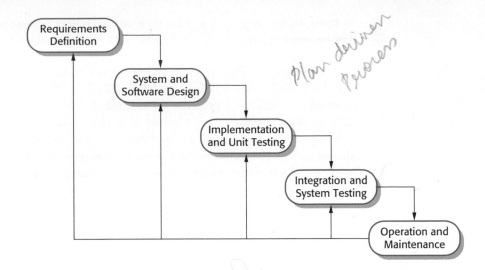

Figure 2.1 The
waterfall model

2. *Incremental development* This approach interleaves the activities of specification, development, and validation. The system is developed as a series of versions (increments), with each version adding functionality to the previous version.

3. *Reuse-oriented software engineering* This approach is based on the existence of a significant number of reusable components. The system development process focuses on integrating these components into a system rather than developing them from scratch.

These models are not mutually exclusive and are often used together, especially for large systems development. For large systems, it makes sense to combine some of the best features of the waterfall and the incremental development models. You need to have information about the essential system requirements to design a software architecture to support these requirements. You cannot develop this incrementally. Sub-systems within a larger system may be developed using different approaches. Parts of the system that are well understood can be specified and developed using a waterfall-based process. Parts of the system which are difficult to specify in advance, such as the user interface, should always be developed using an incremental approach.

2.1.1 The waterfall model

The first published model of the software development process was derived from more general system engineering processes (Royce, 1970). This model is illustrated in Figure 2.1. Because of the cascade from one phase to another, this model is known as the 'waterfall model' or software life cycle. The waterfall model is an example of a plan-driven process—in principle, you must plan and schedule all of the process activities before starting work on them.

The principal stages of the waterfall model directly reflect the fundamental development activities:

1. *Requirements analysis and definition* The system's services, constraints, and goals are established by consultation with system users. They are then defined in detail and serve as a system specification.

2. *System and software design* The systems design process allocates the requirements to either hardware or software systems by establishing an overall system architecture. Software design involves identifying and describing the fundamental software system abstractions and their relationships.

3. *Implementation and unit testing* During this stage, the software design is realized as a set of programs or program units. Unit testing involves verifying that each unit meets its specification.

4. *Integration and system testing* The individual program units or programs are integrated and tested as a complete system to ensure that the software requirements have been met. After testing, the software system is delivered to the customer.

5. *Operation and maintenance* Normally (although not necessarily), this is the longest life cycle phase. The system is installed and put into practical use. Maintenance involves correcting errors which were not discovered in earlier stages of the life cycle, improving the implementation of system units and enhancing the system's services as new requirements are discovered.

In principle, the result of each phase is one or more documents that are approved ('signed off'). The following phase should not start until the previous phase has finished. In practice, these stages overlap and feed information to each other. During design, problems with requirements are identified. During coding, design problems are found and so on. The software process is not a simple linear model but involves feedback from one phase to another. Documents produced in each phase may then have to be modified to reflect the changes made.

Because of the costs of producing and approving documents, iterations can be costly and involve significant rework. Therefore, after a small number of iterations, it is normal to freeze parts of the development, such as the specification, and to continue with the later development stages. Problems are left for later resolution, ignored, or programmed around. This premature freezing of requirements may mean that the system won't do what the user wants. It may also lead to badly structured systems as design problems are circumvented by implementation tricks.

During the final life cycle phase (operation and maintenance) the software is put into use. Errors and omissions in the original software requirements are discovered. Program and design errors emerge and the need for new functionality is identified. The system must therefore evolve to remain useful. Making these changes (software maintenance) may involve repeating previous process stages.

Cleanroom software engineering

An example of a formal development process, originally developed by IBM, is the Cleanroom process. In the Cleanroom process each software increment is formally specified and this specification is transformed into an implementation. Software correctness is demonstrated using a formal approach. There is no unit testing for defects in the process and the system testing is focused on assessing the system's reliability.

The objective of the Cleanroom process is zero-defects software so that delivered systems have a high level of reliability.

http://www.SoftwareEngineering-9.com/Web/Cleanroom/

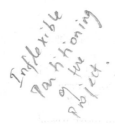

The waterfall model is consistent with other engineering process models and documentation is produced at each phase. This makes the process visible so that managers can monitor progress against the development plan. Its major problem is the inflexible partitioning of the project into distinct stages. Commitments must be made at an early stage in the process, which makes it difficult to respond to changing customer requirements.

In principle, the waterfall model should only be used when the requirements are well understood and unlikely to change radically during system development. However, the waterfall model reflects the type of process used in other engineering projects. As is easier to use a common management model for the whole project, software processes based on the waterfall model are still commonly used.

An important variant of the waterfall model is formal system development, where a mathematical model of a system specification is created. This model is then refined, using mathematical transformations that preserve its consistency, into executable code. Based on the assumption that your mathematical transformations are correct, you can therefore make a strong argument that a program generated in this way is consistent with its specification.

Formal development processes, such as that based on the B method (Schneider, 2001; Wordsworth, 1996) are particularly suited to the development of systems that have stringent safety, reliability, or security requirements. The formal approach simplifies the production of a safety or security case. This demonstrates to customers or regulators that the system actually meets its safety or security requirements.

Processes based on formal transformations are generally only used in the development of safety-critical or security-critical systems. They require specialized expertise. For the majority of systems this process does not offer significant cost-benefits over other approaches to system development.

2.1.2 Incremental development

Incremental development is based on the idea of developing an initial implementation, exposing this to user comment and evolving it through several versions until an adequate system has been developed (Figure 2.2). Specification, development, and

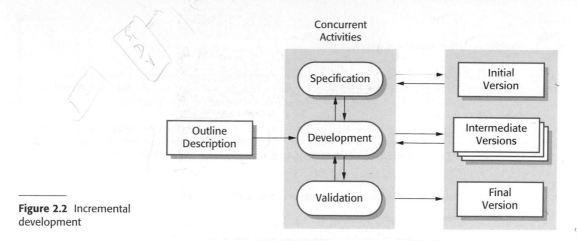

Figure 2.2 Incremental
development

validation activities are interleaved rather than separate, with rapid feedback across
activities.

Incremental software development, which is a fundamental part of agile
approaches, is better than a waterfall approach for most business, e-commerce, and
personal systems. Incremental development reflects the way that we solve problems. We rarely work out a complete problem solution in advance but move toward
a solution in a series of steps, backtracking when we realize that we have made a
mistake. By developing the software incrementally, it is cheaper and easier to make
changes in the software as it is being developed.

Each increment or version of the system incorporates some of the functionality
that is needed by the customer. Generally, the early increments of the system include
the most important or most urgently required functionality. This means that the
customer can evaluate the system at a relatively early stage in the development to see
if it delivers what is required. If not, then only the current increment has to be
changed and, possibly, new functionality defined for later increments.

Incremental development has three important benefits, compared to the waterfall
model:

1. The cost of accommodating changing customer requirements is reduced. The
   amount of analysis and documentation that has to be redone is much less than is
   required with the waterfall model.

2. It is easier to get customer feedback on the development work that has been
   done. Customers can comment on demonstrations of the software and see how
   much has been implemented. Customers find it difficult to judge progress from
   software design documents.

3. More rapid delivery and deployment of useful software to the customer is possible, even if all of the functionality has not been included. Customers are able to
   use and gain value from the software earlier than is possible with a waterfall
   process.

Problems with incremental development

Although incremental development has many advantages, it is not problem-free. The primary cause of the difficulty is the fact that large organizations have bureaucratic procedures that have evolved over time and there may be a mismatch between these procedures and a more informal iterative or agile process.

Sometimes these procedures are there for good reasons—for example, there may be procedures to ensure that the software properly implements external regulations (e.g., in the United States, the Sarbanes-Oxley accounting regulations). Changing these procedures may not be possible so process conflicts may be unavoidable.

http://www.SoftwareEngineering-9.com/Web/IncrementalDev/

Incremental development in some form is now the most common approach for the development of application systems. This approach can be either plan-driven, agile, or, more usually, a mixture of these approaches. In a plan-driven approach, the system increments are identified in advance; if an agile approach is adopted, the early increments are identified but the development of later increments depends on progress and customer priorities.

From a management perspective, the incremental approach has two problems:

1. *The process is not visible.* Managers need regular deliverables to measure progress. If systems are developed quickly, it is not cost-effective to produce documents that reflect every version of the system.

2. *System structure tends to degrade as new increments are added.* Unless time and money is spent on refactoring to improve the software, regular change tends to corrupt its structure. Incorporating further software changes becomes increasingly difficult and costly.

The problems of incremental development become particularly acute for large, complex, long-lifetime systems, where different teams develop different parts of the system. Large systems need a stable framework or architecture and the responsibilities of the different teams working on parts of the system need to be clearly defined with respect to that architecture. This has to be planned in advance rather than developed incrementally.

You can develop a system incrementally and expose it to customers for comment, without actually delivering it and deploying it in the customer's environment. Incremental delivery and deployment means that the software is used in real, operational processes. This is not always possible as experimenting with new software can disrupt normal business processes. I discuss the advantages and disadvantages of incremental delivery in Section 2.3.2.

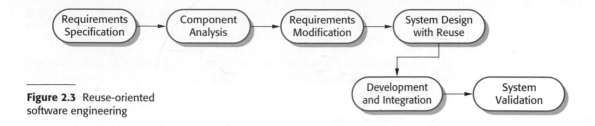

Figure 2.3 Reuse-oriented software engineering

2.1.3 Reuse-oriented software engineering

In the majority of software projects, there is some software reuse. This often happens informally when people working on the project know of designs or code that are similar to what is required. They look for these, modify them as needed, and incorporate them into their system.

This informal reuse takes place irrespective of the development process that is used. However, in the 21st century, software development processes that focus on the reuse of existing software have become widely used. Reuse-oriented approaches rely on a large base of reusable software components and an integrating framework for the composition of these components. Sometimes, these components are systems in their own right (COTS or commercial off-the-shelf systems) that may provide specific functionality such as word processing or a spreadsheet.

A general process model for reuse-based development is shown in Figure 2.3. Although the initial requirements specification stage and the validation stage are comparable with other software processes, the intermediate stages in a reuse-oriented process are different. These stages are:

1. *Component analysis* Given the requirements specification, a search is made for components to implement that specification. Usually, there is no exact match and the components that may be used only provide some of the functionality required.

2. *Requirements modification* During this stage, the requirements are analyzed using information about the components that have been discovered. They are then modified to reflect the available components. Where modifications are impossible, the component analysis activity may be re-entered to search for alternative solutions.

3. *System design with reuse* During this phase, the framework of the system is designed or an existing framework is reused. The designers take into account the components that are reused and organize the framework to cater for this. Some new software may have to be designed if reusable components are not available.

4. *Development and integration* Software that cannot be externally procured is developed, and the components and COTS systems are integrated to create the new system. System integration, in this model, may be part of the development process rather than a separate activity.

There are three types of software component that may be used in a reuse-oriented process:

1. Web services that are developed according to service standards and which are available for remote invocation.

2. Collections of objects that are developed as a package to be integrated with a component framework such as .NET or J2EE.

3. Stand-alone software systems that are configured for use in a particular environment.

Reuse-oriented software engineering has the obvious advantage of reducing the amount of software to be developed and so reducing cost and risks. It usually also leads to faster delivery of the software. However, requirements compromises are inevitable and this may lead to a system that does not meet the real needs of users. Furthermore, some control over the system evolution is lost as new versions of the reusable components are not under the control of the organization using them.

Software reuse is very important and I have dedicated several chapters in the third part of the book to this topic. General issues of software reuse and COTS reuse are covered in Chapter 16, component-based software engineering in Chapters 17 and 18, and service-oriented systems in Chapter 19.

2.2 Process activities

Real software processes are interleaved sequences of technical, collaborative, and managerial activities with the overall goal of specifying, designing, implementing, and testing a software system. Software developers use a variety of different software tools in their work. Tools are particularly useful for supporting the editing of different types of document and for managing the immense volume of detailed information that is generated in a large software project.

The four basic process activities of specification, development, validation, and evolution are organized differently in different development processes. In the waterfall model, they are organized in sequence, whereas in incremental development they are interleaved. How these activities are carried out depends on the type of software, people, and organizational structures involved. In extreme programming, for example, specifications are written on cards. Tests are executable and developed before the program itself. Evolution may involve substantial system restructuring or refactoring.

2.2.1 Software specification

Software specification or requirements engineering is the process of understanding and defining what services are required from the system and identifying the constraints on the system's operation and development. Requirements engineering is a

Software development tools

Software development tools (sometimes called Computer-Aided Software Engineering or CASE tools) are programs that are used to support software engineering process activities. These tools therefore include design editors, data dictionaries, compilers, debuggers, system building tools, etc.

Software tools provide process support by automating some process activities and by providing information about the software that is being developed. Examples of activities that can be automated include:

■ The development of graphical system models as part of the requirements specification or the software design

■ The generation of code from these graphical models

■ The generation of user interfaces from a graphical interface description that is created interactively by the user

■ Program debugging through the provision of information about an executing program

■ The automated translation of programs written using an old version of a programming language to a more recent version

Tools may be combined within a framework called an Interactive Development Environment or IDE. This provides a common set of facilities that tools can use so that it is easier for tools to communicate and operate in an integrated way. The ECLIPSE IDE is widely used and has been designed to incorporate many different types of software tools.

http://www.SoftwareEngineering-9.com/Web/CASE/

particularly critical stage of the software process as errors at this stage inevitably lead to later problems in the system design and implementation.

The requirements engineering process (Figure 2.4) aims to produce an agreed requirements document that specifies a system satisfying stakeholder requirements. Requirements are usually presented at two levels of detail. End-users and customers need a high-level statement of the requirements; system developers need a more detailed system specification.

There are four main activities in the requirements engineering process:

1. *Feasibility study* An estimate is made of whether the identified user needs may be satisfied using current software and hardware technologies. The study considers whether the proposed system will be cost-effective from a business point of view and if it can be developed within existing budgetary constraints. A feasibility study should be relatively cheap and quick. The result should inform the decision of whether or not to go ahead with a more detailed analysis.

2. *Requirements elicitation and analysis* This is the process of deriving the system requirements through observation of existing systems, discussions with potential users and procurers, task analysis, and so on. This may involve the development of one or more system models and prototypes. These help you understand the system to be specified.

3. *Requirements specification* Requirements specification is the activity of translating the information gathered during the analysis activity into a document that

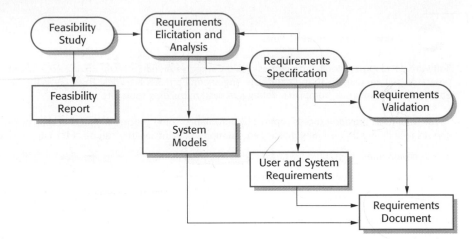

Figure 2.4 The
requirements
engineering process

defines a set of requirements. Two types of requirements may be included in this
document. User requirements are abstract statements of the system requirements for the customer and end-user of the system; system requirements are a
more detailed description of the functionality to be provided.

4. *Requirements validation* This activity checks the requirements for realism, consis-
    tency, and completeness. During this process, errors in the requirements document
    are inevitably discovered. It must then be modified to correct these problems.

Of course, the activities in the requirements process are not simply carried out in a
strict sequence. Requirements analysis continues during definition and specification and
new requirements come to light throughout the process. Therefore, the activities of
analysis, definition, and specification are interleaved. In agile methods, such as extreme
programming, requirements are developed incrementally according to user priorities and
the elicitation of requirements comes from users who are part of the development team.

2.2.2 Software design and implementation

The implementation stage of software development is the process of converting a
system specification into an executable system. It always involves processes of software design and programming but, if an incremental approach to development is
used, may also involve refinement of the software specification.

A software design is a description of the structure of the software to be implemented,
the data models and structures used by the system, the interfaces between system components and, sometimes, the algorithms used. Designers do not arrive at a finished
design immediately but develop the design iteratively. They add formality and detail as
they develop their design with constant backtracking to correct earlier designs.

Figure 2.5 is an abstract model of this process showing the inputs to the design
process, process activities, and the documents produced as outputs from this process.

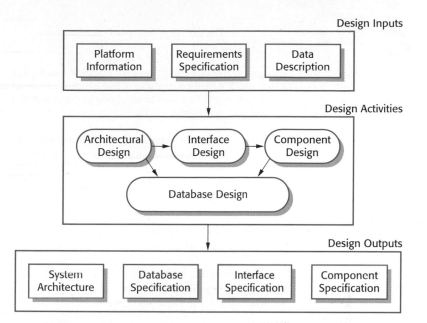

Design Inputs

| Platform Information | Requirements Specification | Data Description |

Design Activities

Architectural Design → Interface Design → Component Design

Database Design

Design Outputs

| System Architecture | Database Specification | Interface Specification | Component Specification |

Figure 2.5 A general model of the design process

The diagram suggests that the stages of the design process are sequential. In fact, design process activities are interleaved. Feedback from one stage to another and consequent design rework is inevitable in all design processes.

Most software interfaces with other software systems. These include the operating system, database, middleware, and other application systems. These make up the 'software platform', the environment in which the software will execute. Information about this platform is an essential input to the design process, as designers must decide how best to integrate it with the software's environment. The requirements specification is a description of the functionality the software must provide and its performance and dependability requirements. If the system is to process existing data, then the description of that data may be included in the platform specification; otherwise, the data description must be an input to the design process so that the system data organization to be defined.

The activities in the design process vary, depending on the type of system being developed. For example, real-time systems require timing design but may not include a database so there is no database design involved. Figure 2.5 shows four activities that may be part of the design process for information systems:

1. *Architectural design,* where you identify the overall structure of the system, the principal components (sometimes called sub-systems or modules), their relationships, and how they are distributed.

2. *Interface design,* where you define the interfaces between system components. This interface specification must be unambiguous. With a precise interface, a component can be used without other components having to know how it is implemented. Once interface specifications are agreed, the components can be designed and developed concurrently.

Structured methods

Structured methods are an approach to software design in which graphical models that should be developed as part of the design process are defined. The method may also define a process for developing the models and rules that apply to each model type. Structured methods lead to standardized documentation for a system and are particularly useful in providing a development framework for less-experienced and less-expert software developers.

http://www.SoftwareEngineering-9.com/Web/Structured-methods/

3. *Component design,* where you take each system component and design how it will operate. This may be a simple statement of the expected functionality to be implemented, with the specific design left to the programmer. Alternatively, it may be a list of changes to be made to a reusable component or a detailed design model. The design model may be used to automatically generate an implementation.

4. *Database design,* where you design the system data structures and how these are to be represented in a database. Again, the work here depends on whether an existing database is to be reused or a new database is to be created.

These activities lead to a set of design outputs, which are also shown in Figure 2.5. The detail and representation of these vary considerably. For critical systems, detailed design documents setting out precise and accurate descriptions of the system must be produced. If a model-driven approach is used, these outputs may mostly be diagrams. Where agile methods of development are used, the outputs of the design process may not be separate specification documents but may be represented in the code of the program.

Structured methods for design were developed in the 1970s and 1980s and were the precursor to the UML and object-oriented design (Budgen, 2003). They rely on producing graphical models of the system and, in many cases, automatically generating code from these models. Model-driven development (MDD) or model-driven engineering (Schmidt, 2006), where models of the software are created at different levels of abstraction, is an evolution of structured methods. In MDD, there is greater emphasis on architectural models with a separation between abstract implementation-independent models and implementation-specific models. The models are developed in sufficient detail so that the executable system can be generated from them. I discuss this approach to development in Chapter 5.

The development of a program to implement the system follows naturally from the system design processes. Although some classes of program, such as safety-critical systems, are usually designed in detail before any implementation begins, it is more common for the later stages of design and program development to be interleaved. Software development tools may be used to generate a skeleton program from a design. This includes code to define and implement interfaces, and, in many cases, the developer need only add details of the operation of each program component.

Programming is a personal activity and there is no general process that is usually followed. Some programmers start with components that they understand, develop these, and then move on to less-understood components. Others take the opposite

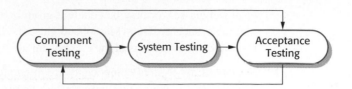

Figure 2.6 Stages
of testing

approach, leaving familiar components till last because they know how to develop them. Some developers like to define data early in the process then use this to drive the program development; others leave data unspecified for as long as possible.

Normally, programmers carry out some testing of the code they have developed. This often reveals program defects that must be removed from the program. This is called debugging. Defect testing and debugging are different processes. Testing establishes the existence of defects. Debugging is concerned with locating and correcting these defects.

When you are debugging, you have to generate hypotheses about the observable behavior of the program then test these hypotheses in the hope of finding the fault that caused the output anomaly. Testing the hypotheses may involve tracing the program code manually. It may require new test cases to localize the problem. Interactive debugging tools, which show the intermediate values of program variables and a trace of the statements executed, may be used to support the debugging process.

2.2.3 Software validation

Software validation or, more generally, verification and validation (V&V) is intended to show that a system both conforms to its specification and that it meets the expectations of the system customer. Program testing, where the system is executed using simulated test data, is the principal validation technique. Validation may also involve checking processes, such as inspections and reviews, at each stage of the software process from user requirements definition to program development. Because of the predominance of testing, the majority of validation costs are incurred during and after implementation.

Except for small programs, systems should not be tested as a single, monolithic unit. Figure 2.6 shows a three-stage testing process in which system components are tested then the integrated system is tested and, finally, the system is tested with the customer's data. Ideally, component defects are discovered early in the process, and interface problems are found when the system is integrated. However, as defects are discovered, the program must be debugged and this may require other stages in the testing process to be repeated. Errors in program components, say, may come to light during system testing. The process is therefore an iterative one with information being fed back from later stages to earlier parts of the process.

The stages in the testing process are:

1. *Development testing* The components making up the system are tested by the people developing the system. Each component is tested independently, without other system components. Components may be simple entities such as functions

or object classes, or may be coherent groupings of these entities. Test automation tools, such as JUnit (Massol and Husted, 2003), that can re-run component tests when new versions of the component are created, are commonly used.

2. *System testing* System components are integrated to create a complete system. This process is concerned with finding errors that result from unanticipated interactions between components and component interface problems. It is also concerned with showing that the system meets its functional and non-functional requirements, and testing the emergent system properties. For large systems, this may be a multi-stage process where components are integrated to form sub-systems that are individually tested before these sub-systems are themselves integrated to form the final system.

3. *Acceptance testing* This is the final stage in the testing process before the system is accepted for operational use. The system is tested with data supplied by the system customer rather than with simulated test data. Acceptance testing may reveal errors and omissions in the system requirements definition, because the real data exercise the system in different ways from the test data. Acceptance testing may also reveal requirements problems where the system's facilities do not really meet the user's needs or the system performance is unacceptable.

Normally, component development and testing processes are interleaved. Programmers make up their own test data and incrementally test the code as it is developed. This is an economically sensible approach, as the programmer knows the component and is therefore the best person to generate test cases.

If an incremental approach to development is used, each increment should be tested as it is developed, with these tests based on the requirements for that increment. In extreme programming, tests are developed along with the requirements before development starts. This helps the testers and developers to understand the requirements and ensures that there are no delays as test cases are created.

When a plan-driven software process is used (e.g., for critical systems development), testing is driven by a set of test plans. An independent team of testers works from these pre-formulated test plans, which have been developed from the system specification and design. Figure 2.7 illustrates how test plans are the link between testing and development activities. This is sometimes called the V-model of development (turn it on its side to see the V).

Acceptance testing is sometimes called 'alpha testing'. Custom systems are developed for a single client. The alpha testing process continues until the system developer and the client agree that the delivered system is an acceptable implementation of the requirements.

When a system is to be marketed as a software product, a testing process called 'beta testing' is often used. Beta testing involves delivering a system to a number of potential customers who agree to use that system. They report problems to the system developers. This exposes the product to real use and detects errors that may not have been anticipated by the system builders. After this feedback, the system is modified and released either for further beta testing or for general sale.

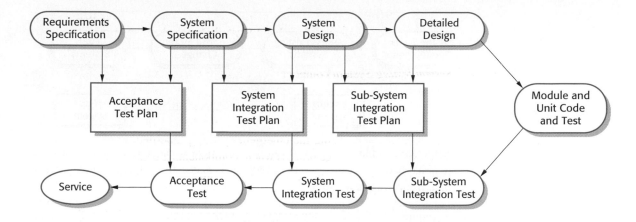

Figure 2.7
Testing phases
in a plan-driven
software process

2.2.4 Software evolution

The flexibility of software systems is one of the main reasons why more and more software is being incorporated in large, complex systems. Once a decision has been made to manufacture hardware, it is very expensive to make changes to the hardware design. However, changes can be made to software at any time during or after the system development. Even extensive changes are still much cheaper than corresponding changes to system hardware.

Historically, there has always been a split between the process of software development and the process of software evolution (software maintenance). People think of software development as a creative activity in which a software system is developed from an initial concept through to a working system. However, they sometimes think of software maintenance as dull and uninteresting. Although the costs of maintenance are often several times the initial development costs, maintenance processes are sometimes considered to be less challenging than original software development.

This distinction between development and maintenance is increasingly irrelevant. Hardly any software systems are completely new systems and it makes much more sense to see development and maintenance as a continuum. Rather than two separate processes, it is more realistic to think of software engineering as an evolutionary process (Figure 2.8) where software is continually changed over its lifetime in response to changing requirements and customer needs.

2.3 Coping with change

Change is inevitable in all large software projects. The system requirements change as the business procuring the system responds to external pressures and management priorities change. As new technologies become available, new design and implementation possibilities emerge. Therefore whatever software process model is used, it is essential that it can accommodate changes to the software being developed.

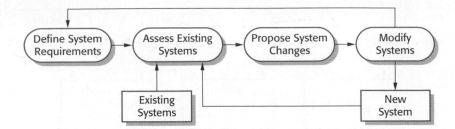

Figure 2.8 System evolution

Change adds to the costs of software development because it usually means that work that has been completed has to be redone. This is called rework. For example, if the relationships between the requirements in a system have been analyzed and new requirements are then identified, some or all of the requirements analysis has to be repeated. It may then be necessary to redesign the system to deliver the new requirements, change any programs that have been developed, and re-test the system.

There are two related approaches that may be used to reduce the costs of rework:

1. Change avoidance, where the software process includes activities that can anticipate possible changes before significant rework is required. For example, a prototype system may be developed to show some key features of the system to customers. They can experiment with the prototype and refine their requirements before committing to high software production costs.

2. Change tolerance, where the process is designed so that changes can be accommodated at relatively low cost. This normally involves some form of incremental development. Proposed changes may be implemented in increments that have not yet been developed. If this is impossible, then only a single increment (a small part of the system) may have to be altered to incorporate the change.

In this section, I discuss two ways of coping with change and changing system requirements. These are:

1. System prototyping, where a version of the system or part of the system is developed quickly to check the customer's requirements and the feasibility of some design decisions. This supports change avoidance as it allows users to experiment with the system before delivery and so refine their requirements. The number of requirements change proposals made after delivery is therefore likely to be reduced.

2. Incremental delivery, where system increments are delivered to the customer for comment and experimentation. This supports both change avoidance and change tolerance. It avoids the premature commitment to requirements for the whole system and allows changes to be incorporated into later increments at relatively low cost.

The notion of refactoring, namely improving the structure and organization of a program, is also an important mechanism that supports change tolerance. I discuss this in Chapter 3, which covers agile methods.

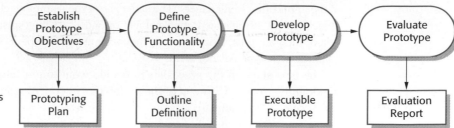

Figure 2.9 The process
of prototype
development

2.3.1 Prototyping

A prototype is an initial version of a software system that is used to demonstrate
concepts, try out design options, and find out more about the problem and its possible solutions. Rapid, iterative development of the prototype is essential so that costs
are controlled and system stakeholders can experiment with the prototype early in
the software process.

A software prototype can be used in a software development process to help
anticipate changes that may be required:

1. In the requirements engineering process, a prototype can help with the elicitation and validation of system requirements.

2. In the system design process, a prototype can be used to explore particular software solutions and to support user interface design.

System prototypes allow users to see how well the system supports their work.
They may get new ideas for requirements, and find areas of strength and weakness in
the software. They may then propose new system requirements. Furthermore, as the
prototype is developed, it may reveal errors and omissions in the requirements that
have been proposed. A function described in a specification may seem useful and well
defined. However, when that function is combined with other functions, users often
find that their initial view was incorrect or incomplete. The system specification may
then be modified to reflect their changed understanding of the requirements.

A system prototype may be used while the system is being designed to carry out
design experiments to check the feasibility of a proposed design. For example, a
database design may be prototyped and tested to check that it supports efficient data
access for the most common user queries. Prototyping is also an essential part of the
user interface design process. Because of the dynamic nature of user interfaces, textual descriptions and diagrams are not good enough for expressing the user interface
requirements. Therefore, rapid prototyping with end-user involvement is the only
sensible way to develop graphical user interfaces for software systems.

A process model for prototype development is shown in Figure 2.9. The objectives of prototyping should be made explicit from the start of the process. These may
be to develop a system to prototype the user interface, to develop a system to validate
functional system requirements, or to develop a system to demonstrate the feasibility

of the application to managers. The same prototype cannot meet all objectives. If the objectives are left unstated, management or end-users may misunderstand the function of the prototype. Consequently, they may not get the benefits that they expected from the prototype development.

The next stage in the process is to decide what to put into and, perhaps more importantly, what to leave out of the prototype system. To reduce prototyping costs and accelerate the delivery schedule, you may leave some functionality out of the prototype. You may decide to relax non-functional requirements such as response time and memory utilization. Error handling and management may be ignored unless the objective of the prototype is to establish a user interface. Standards of reliability and program quality may be reduced.

The final stage of the process is prototype evaluation. Provision must be made during this stage for user training and the prototype objectives should be used to derive a plan for evaluation. Users need time to become comfortable with a new system and to settle into a normal pattern of usage. Once they are using the system normally, they then discover requirements errors and omissions.

A general problem with prototyping is that the prototype may not necessarily be used in the same way as the final system. The tester of the prototype may not be typical of system users. The training time during prototype evaluation may be insufficient. If the prototype is slow, the evaluators may adjust their way of working and avoid those system features that have slow response times. When provided with better response in the final system, they may use it in a different way.

Developers are sometimes pressured by managers to deliver throwaway prototypes, particularly when there are delays in delivering the final version of the software. However, this is usually unwise:

1. It may be impossible to tune the prototype to meet non-functional requirements, such as performance, security, robustness, and reliability requirements, which were ignored during prototype development.

2. Rapid change during development inevitably means that the prototype is undocumented. The only design specification is the prototype code. This is not good enough for long-term maintenance.

3. The changes made during prototype development will probably have degraded the system structure. The system will be difficult and expensive to maintain.

4. Organizational quality standards are normally relaxed for prototype development.

Prototypes do not have to be executable to be useful. Paper-based mock-ups of the system user interface (Rettig, 1994) can be effective in helping users refine an interface design and work through usage scenarios. These are very cheap to develop and can be constructed in a few days. An extension of this technique is a Wizard of Oz prototype where only the user interface is developed. Users interact with this interface but their requests are passed to a person who interprets them and outputs the appropriate response.

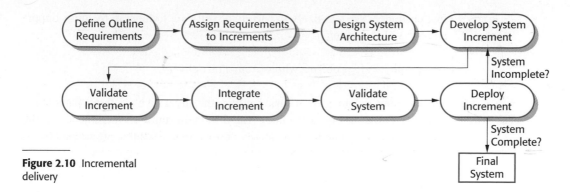

Figure 2.10 Incremental delivery

2.3.2 Incremental delivery

Incremental delivery (Figure 2.10) is an approach to software development where some of the developed increments are delivered to the customer and deployed for use in an operational environment. In an incremental delivery process, customers identify, in outline, the services to be provided by the system. They identify which of the services are most important and which are least important to them. A number of delivery increments are then defined, with each increment providing a sub-set of the system functionality. The allocation of services to increments depends on the service priority, with the highest-priority services implemented and delivered first.

Once the system increments have been identified, the requirements for the services to be delivered in the first increment are defined in detail and that increment is developed. During development, further requirements analysis for later increments can take place but requirements changes for the current increment are not accepted.

Once an increment is completed and delivered, customers can put it into service. This means that they take early delivery of part of the system functionality. They can experiment with the system and this helps them clarify their requirements for later system increments. As new increments are completed, they are integrated with existing increments so that the system functionality improves with each delivered increment.

Incremental delivery has a number of advantages:

1. Customers can use the early increments as prototypes and gain experience that informs their requirements for later system increments. Unlike prototypes, these are part of the real system so there is no re-learning when the complete system is available.

2. Customers do not have to wait until the entire system is delivered before they can gain value from it. The first increment satisfies their most critical requirements so they can use the software immediately.

3. The process maintains the benefits of incremental development in that it should be relatively easy to incorporate changes into the system.

4. As the highest-priority services are delivered first and increments then integrated, the most important system services receive the most testing. This means

that customers are less likely to encounter software failures in the most important parts of the system.

However, there are problems with incremental delivery:

1. Most systems require a set of basic facilities that are used by different parts of the system. As requirements are not defined in detail until an increment is to be implemented, it can be hard to identify common facilities that are needed by all increments.

2. Iterative development can also be difficult when a replacement system is being developed. Users want all of the functionality of the old system and are often unwilling to experiment with an incomplete new system. Therefore, getting useful customer feedback is difficult.

3. The essence of iterative processes is that the specification is developed in conjunction with the software. However, this conflicts with the procurement model of many organizations, where the complete system specification is part of the system development contract. In the incremental approach, there is no complete system specification until the final increment is specified. This requires a new form of contract, which large customers such as government agencies may find difficult to accommodate.

There are some types of system where incremental development and delivery is not the best approach. These are very large systems where development may involve teams working in different locations, some embedded systems where the software depends on hardware development and some critical systems where all the requirements must be analyzed to check for interactions that may compromise the safety or security of the system.

These systems, of course, suffer from the same problems of uncertain and changing requirements. Therefore, to address these problems and get some of the benefits of incremental development, a process may be used in which a system prototype is developed iteratively and used as a platform for experiments with the system requirements and design. With the experience gained from the prototype, definitive requirements can then be agreed.

2.3.3 Boehm's spiral model

A risk-driven software process framework (the spiral model) was proposed by Boehm (1988). This is shown in Figure 2.11. Here, the software process is represented as a spiral, rather than a sequence of activities with some backtracking from one activity to another. Each loop in the spiral represents a phase of the software process. Thus, the innermost loop might be concerned with system feasibility, the next loop with requirements definition, the next loop with system design, and so on. The spiral model combines change avoidance with change tolerance. It assumes that

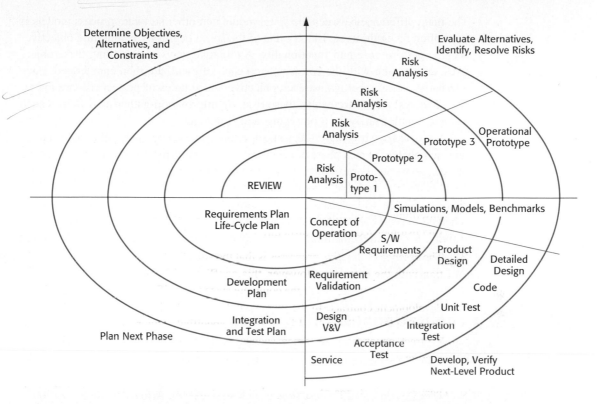

Determine Objectives,
Alternatives, and
Constraints

Evaluate Alternatives,
Identify, Resolve Risks

Risk
Analysis

Risk
Analysis

Risk
Analysis

Operational
Prototype 3   Prototype

Prototype 2

Risk
Analysis   Proto-
type 1

REVIEW

Requirements Plan
Life-Cycle Plan

Concept of
Operation

Simulations, Models, Benchmarks

S/W
Requirements   Product
Design   Detailed
Design

Development
Plan

Requirement
Validation

Code

Unit Test

Plan Next Phase

Integration
and Test Plan

Design
V&V

Integration
Test

Acceptance
Test

Service

Develop, Verify
Next-Level Product

Figure 2.11 Boehm's
spiral model of the
software process
(©IEEE 1988)

changes are a result of project risks and includes explicit risk management activities to reduce these risks.

Each loop in the spiral is split into four sectors:

1. *Objective setting* Specific objectives for that phase of the project are defined. Constraints on the process and the product are identified and a detailed management plan is drawn up. Project risks are identified. Alternative strategies, depending on these risks, may be planned.

2. *Risk assessment and reduction* For each of the identified project risks, a detailed analysis is carried out. Steps are taken to reduce the risk. For example, if there is a risk that the requirements are inappropriate, a prototype system may be developed.

3. *Development and validation* After risk evaluation, a development model for the system is chosen. For example, throwaway prototyping may be the best development approach if user interface risks are dominant. If safety risks are the main consideration, development based on formal transformations may be the most appropriate process, and so on. If the main identified risk is sub-system integration, the waterfall model may be the best development model to use.

4. *Planning* The project is reviewed and a decision made whether to continue with a further loop of the spiral. If it is decided to continue, plans are drawn up for the next phase of the project.

The main difference between the spiral model and other software process models is its explicit recognition of risk. A cycle of the spiral begins by elaborating objectives such as performance and functionality. Alternative ways of achieving these objectives, and dealing with the constraints on each of them, are then enumerated. Each alternative is assessed against each objective and sources of project risk are identified. The next step is to resolve these risks by information-gathering activities such as more detailed analysis, prototyping, and simulation.

Once risks have been assessed, some development is carried out, followed by a planning activity for the next phase of the process. Informally, risk simply means something that can go wrong. For example, if the intention is to use a new programming language, a risk is that the available compilers are unreliable or do not produce sufficiently efficient object code. Risks lead to proposed software changes and project problems such as schedule and cost overrun, so risk minimization is a very important project management activity. Risk management, an essential part of project management, is covered in Chapter 22.

2.4 The Rational Unified Process

The Rational Unified Process (RUP) (Krutchen, 2003) is an example of a modern process model that has been derived from work on the UML and the associated Unified Software Development Process (Rumbaugh, et al., 1999; Arlow and Neustadt, 2005). I have included a description here, as it is a good example of a hybrid process model. It brings together elements from all of the generic process models (Section 2.1), illustrates good practice in specification and design (Section 2.2) and supports prototyping and incremental delivery (Section 2.3).

The RUP recognizes that conventional process models present a single view of the process. In contrast, the RUP is normally described from three perspectives:

1. A dynamic perspective, which shows the phases of the model over time.

2. A static perspective, which shows the process activities that are enacted.

3. A practice perspective, which suggests good practices to be used during the process.

Most descriptions of the RUP attempt to combine the static and dynamic perspectives in a single diagram (Krutchen, 2003). I think that makes the process harder to understand, so I use separate descriptions of each of these perspectives.

The RUP is a phased model that identifies four discrete phases in the software process. However, unlike the waterfall model where phases are equated with process activities, the phases in the RUP are more closely related to business rather than technical concerns. Figure 2.11 shows the phases in the RUP. These are:

1. *Inception* The goal of the inception phase is to establish a business case for the system. You should identify all external entities (people and systems) that will

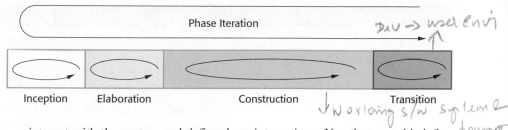

Figure 2.12 Phases in the Rational Unified Process

[handwritten: Dev → used envi]

[handwritten: Working s/w system & docum~]

[handwritten: Inception, Elaboration, construction, Transition]

interact with the system and define these interactions. You then use this information to assess the contribution that the system makes to the business. If this contribution is minor, then the project may be cancelled after this phase.

2. *Elaboration* The goals of the elaboration phase are to develop an understanding of the problem domain, establish an architectural framework for the system, develop the project plan, and identify key project risks. On completion of this phase you should have a requirements model for the system, which may be a set of UML use-cases, an architectural description, and a development plan for the software.

3. *Construction* The construction phase involves system design, programming, and testing. Parts of the system are developed in parallel and integrated during this phase. On completion of this phase, you should have a working software system and associated documentation that is ready for delivery to users.

4. *Transition* The final phase of the RUP is concerned with moving the system from the development community to the user community and making it work in a real environment. This is something that is ignored in most software process models but is, in fact, an expensive and sometimes problematic activity. On completion of this phase, you should have a documented software system that is working correctly in its operational environment.

Iteration within the RUP is supported in two ways. Each phase may be enacted in an iterative way with the results developed incrementally. In addition, the whole set of phases may also be enacted incrementally, as shown by the looping arrow from Transition to Inception in Figure 2.12.

The static view of the RUP focuses on the activities that take place during the development process. These are called workflows in the RUP description. There are six core process workflows identified in the process and three core supporting workflows. The RUP has been designed in conjunction with the UML, so the workflow description is oriented around associated UML models such as sequence models, object models, etc. The core engineering and support workflows are described in Figure 2.13.

The advantage in presenting dynamic and static views is that phases of the development process are not associated with specific workflows. In principle at least, all of the RUP workflows may be active at all stages of the process. In the early phases of the process, most effort will probably be spent on workflows such as business modelling and requirements and, in the later phases, in testing and deployment.

Workflow	Description
Business modelling	The business processes are modelled using business use cases.
Requirements	Actors who interact with the system are identified and use cases are developed to model the system requirements.
Analysis and design	A design model is created and documented using architectural models, component models, object models, and sequence models.
Implementation	The components in the system are implemented and structured into implementation sub-systems. Automatic code generation from design models helps accelerate this process.
Testing	Testing is an iterative process that is carried out in conjunction with implementation. System testing follows the completion of the implementation.
Deployment	A product release is created, distributed to users, and installed in their workplace.
Configuration and change management	This supporting workflow manages changes to the system (see Chapter 25).
Project management	This supporting workflow manages the system development (see Chapters 22 and 23).
Environment	This workflow is concerned with making appropriate software tools available to the software development team.

Figure 2.13 Static workflows in the Rational Unified Process

The practice perspective on the RUP describes good software engineering practices that are recommended for use in systems development. Six fundamental best practices are recommended:

1. *Develop software iteratively* Plan increments of the system based on customer priorities and develop the highest-priority system features early in the development process.

2. *Manage requirements* Explicitly document the customer's requirements and keep track of changes to these requirements. Analyze the impact of changes on the system before accepting them.

3. *Use component-based architectures* Structure the system architecture into components, as discussed earlier in this chapter.

4. *Visually model software* Use graphical UML models to present static and dynamic views of the software.

5. *Verify software quality* Ensure that the software meets the organizational quality standards.

6. *Control changes to software* Manage changes to the software using a change management system and configuration management procedures and tools.

The RUP is not a suitable process for all types of development, e.g., embedded software development. However, it does represent an approach that potentially combines the three generic process models discussed in Section 2.1. The most important innovations in the RUP are the separation of phases and workflows, and the recognition that deploying software in a user's environment is part of the process. Phases are dynamic and have goals. Workflows are static and are technical activities that are not associated with a single phase but may be used throughout the development to achieve the goals of each phase.

KEY POINTS

■ Software processes are the activities involved in producing a software system. Software process models are abstract representations of these processes.

■ General process models describe the organization of software processes. Examples of these general models include the waterfall model, incremental development, and reuse-oriented development.

■ Requirements engineering is the process of developing a software specification. Specifications are intended to communicate the system needs of the customer to the system developers.

■ Design and implementation processes are concerned with transforming a requirements specification into an executable software system. Systematic design methods may be used as part of this transformation.

■ Software validation is the process of checking that the system conforms to its specification and that it meets the real needs of the users of the system.

■ Software evolution takes place when you change existing software systems to meet new requirements. Changes are continuous and the software must evolve to remain useful.

■ Processes should include activities to cope with change. This may involve a prototyping phase that helps avoid poor decisions on requirements and design. Processes may be structured for iterative development and delivery so that changes may be made without disrupting the system as a whole.

■ The Rational Unified Process is a modern generic process model that is organized into phases (inception, elaboration, construction, and transition) but separates activities (requirements, analysis, and design, etc.) from these phases.

FURTHER READING

Managing Software Quality and Business Risk. This is primarily a book about software management but it includes an excellent chapter (Chapter 4) on process models. (M. Ould, John Wiley and Sons Ltd, 1999.)

Process Models in Software Engineering. This is an excellent overview of a wide range of software engineering process models that have been proposed. (W. Scacchi, *Encyclopaedia of Software Engineering,* ed. J.J. Marciniak, John Wiley and Sons, 2001.) http://www.ics.uci.edu/~wscacchi/Papers/SE-Encyc/Process-Models-SE-Encyc.pdf.

The Rational Unified Process—An Introduction (3rd edition). This is the most readable book available on the RUP at the time of this writing. Krutchen describes the process well, but I would like to have seen more on the practical difficulties of using the process. (P. Krutchen, Addison-Wesley, 2003.)

EXERCISES

2.1. Giving reasons for your answer based on the type of system being developed, suggest the most appropriate generic software process model that might be used as a basis for managing the development of the following systems:

A system to control anti-lock braking in a car

A virtual reality system to support software maintenance

A university accounting system that replaces an existing system

An interactive travel planning system that helps users plan journeys with the lowest environmental impact

2.2. Explain why incremental development is the most effective approach for developing business software systems. Why is this model less appropriate for real-time systems engineering?

2.3. Consider the reuse-based process model shown in Figure 2.3. Explain why it is essential to have two separate requirements engineering activities in the process.

2.4. Suggest why it is important to make a distinction between developing the user requirements and developing system requirements in the requirements engineering process.

2.5. Describe the main activities in the software design process and the outputs of these activities. Using a diagram, show possible relationships between the outputs of these activities.

2.6. Explain why change is inevitable in complex systems and give examples (apart from prototyping and incremental delivery) of software process activities that help predict changes and make the software being developed more resilient to change.

2.7. Explain why systems developed as prototypes should not normally be used as production systems.

2.8. Explain why Boehm's spiral model is an adaptable model that can support both change avoidance and change tolerance activities. In practice, this model has not been widely used. Suggest why this might be the case.

2.9. What are the advantages of providing static and dynamic views of the software process as in the Rational Unified Process?

2.10. Historically, the introduction of technology has caused profound changes in the labor market and, temporarily at least, displaced people from jobs. Discuss whether the introduction of extensive process automation is likely to have the same consequences for software engineers. If you don't think it will, explain why not. If you think that it will reduce job opportunities, is it ethical for the engineers affected to passively or actively resist the introduction of this technology?

REFERENCES

Arlow, J. and Neustadt, I. (2005). *UML 2 and the Unified Process: Practical Object-Oriented Analysis and Design (2nd Edition)*. Boston: Addison-Wesley.

Boehm, B. and Turner, R. (2003). *Balancing Agility and Discipline: A Guide for the Perplexed*. Boston: Addison-Wesley.

Boehm, B. W. (1988). 'A Spiral Model of Software Development and Enhancement'. *IEEE Computer*, **21** (5), 61–72.

Budgen, D. (2003). *Software Design (2nd Edition)*. Harlow, UK.: Addison-Wesley.

Krutchen, P. (2003). *The Rational Unified Process—An Introduction (3rd Edition)*. Reading, MA: Addison-Wesley.

Massol, V. and Husted, T. (2003). *JUnit in Action*. Greenwich, Conn.: Manning Publications Co.

Rettig, M. (1994). 'Practical Programmer: Prototyping for Tiny Fingers'. *Comm. ACM*, **37** (4), 21–7.

Royce, W. W. (1970). 'Managing the Development of Large Software Systems: Concepts and Techniques'. IEEE WESTCON, Los Angeles CA: 1–9.

Rumbaugh, J., Jacobson, I. and Booch, G. (1999). *The Unified Software Development Process*. Reading, Mass.: Addison-Wesley.

Schmidt, D. C. (2006). 'Model-Driven Engineering'. *IEEE Computer*, **39** (2), 25–31.

Schneider, S. (2001). *The B Method*. Houndmills, UK: Palgrave Macmillan.

Wordsworth, J. (1996). *Software Engineering with B*. Wokingham: Addison-Wesley.

3

Agile software development

Objectives

The objective of this chapter is to introduce you to agile software development methods. When you have read the chapter, you will:

■ understand the rationale for agile software development methods, the agile manifesto, and the differences between agile and plan-driven development;

■ know the key practices in extreme programming and how these relate to the general principles of agile methods;

■ understand the Scrum approach to agile project management;

■ be aware of the issues and problems of scaling agile development methods to the development of large software systems.

Contents

Businesses now operate in a global, rapidly changing environment. They have to respond to new opportunities and markets, changing economic conditions, and the emergence of competing products and services. Software is part of almost all business operations so new software is developed quickly to take advantage of new opportunities and to respond to competitive pressure. Rapid development and delivery is therefore now often the most critical requirement for software systems. In fact, many businesses are willing to trade off software quality and compromise on requirements to achieve faster deployment of the software that they need.

Because these businesses are operating in a changing environment, it is often practically impossible to derive a complete set of stable software requirements. The initial requirements inevitably change because customers find it impossible to predict how a system will affect working practices, how it will interact with other systems, and what user operations should be automated. It may only be after a system has been delivered and users gain experience with it that the real requirements become clear. Even then, the requirements are likely to change quickly and unpredictably due to external factors. The software may then be out of date when it is delivered.

Software development processes that plan on completely specifying the requirements and then designing, building, and testing the system are not geared to rapid software development. As the requirements change or as requirements problems are discovered, the system design or implementation has to be reworked and retested. As a consequence, a conventional waterfall or specification-based process is usually prolonged and the final software is delivered to the customer long after it was originally specified.

For some types of software, such as safety-critical control systems, where a complete analysis of the system is essential, a plan-driven approach is the right one. However, in a fast-moving business environment, this can cause real problems. By the time the software is available for use, the original reason for its procurement may have changed so radically that the software is effectively useless. Therefore, for business systems in particular, development processes that focus on rapid software development and delivery are essential.

The need for rapid system development and processes that can handle changing requirements has been recognized for some time. IBM introduced incremental development in the 1980s (Mills et al., 1980). The introduction of so-called fourth-generation languages, also in the 1980s, supported the idea of quickly developing and delivering software (Martin, 1981). However, the notion really took off in the late 1990s with the development of the notion of agile approaches such as DSDM (Stapleton, 1997), Scrum (Schwaber and Beedle, 2001), and extreme programming (Beck, 1999; Beck, 2000).

Rapid software development processes are designed to produce useful software quickly. The software is not developed as a single unit but as a series of increments, with each increment including new system functionality. Although there are many approaches to rapid software development, they share some fundamental characteristics:

1. The processes of specification, design, and implementation are interleaved. There is no detailed system specification, and design documentation is minimized or generated automatically by the programming environment used to

implement the system. The user requirements document only defines the most important characteristics of the system.

2. The system is developed in a series of versions. End-users and other system stakeholders are involved in specifying and evaluating each version. They may propose changes to the software and new requirements that should be implemented in a later version of the system.

3. System user interfaces are often developed using an interactive development system that allows the interface design to be quickly created by drawing and placing icons on the interface. The system may then generate a web-based interface for a browser or an interface for a specific platform such as Microsoft Windows.

Agile methods are incremental development methods in which the increments are small and, typically, new releases of the system are created and made available to customers every two or three weeks. They involve customers in the development process to get rapid feedback on changing requirements. They minimize documentation by using informal communications rather than formal meetings with written documents.

3.1 Agile methods

In the 1980s and early 1990s, there was a widespread view that the best way to achieve better software was through careful project planning, formalized quality assurance, the use of analysis and design methods supported by CASE tools, and controlled and rigorous software development processes. This view came from the software engineering community that was responsible for developing large, long-lived software systems such as aerospace and government systems.

This software was developed by large teams working for different companies. Teams were often geographically dispersed and worked on the software for long periods of time. An example of this type of software is the control systems for a modern aircraft, which might take up to 10 years from initial specification to deployment. These plan-driven approaches involve a significant overhead in planning, designing, and documenting the system. This overhead is justified when the work of multiple development teams has to be coordinated, when the system is a critical system, and when many different people will be involved in maintaining the software over its lifetime.

However, when this heavyweight, plan-driven development approach is applied to small and medium-sized business systems, the overhead involved is so large that it dominates the software development process. More time is spent on how the system should be developed than on program development and testing. As the system requirements change, rework is essential and, in principle at least, the specification and design has to change with the program.

Dissatisfaction with these heavyweight approaches to software engineering led a number of software developers in the 1990s to propose new 'agile methods'. These allowed the development team to focus on the software itself rather than on its design and documentation. Agile methods universally rely on an incremental approach to software specification, development, and delivery. They are best suited to application development where the system requirements usually change rapidly during the development process. They are intended to deliver working software quickly to customers, who can then propose new and changed requirements to be included in later iterations of the system. They aim to cut down on process bureaucracy by avoiding work that has dubious long-term value and eliminating documentation that will probably never be used.

The philosophy behind agile methods is reflected in the agile manifesto that was agreed on by many of the leading developers of these methods. This manifesto states:

We are uncovering better ways of developing software by doing it and helping others do it. Through this work we have come to value:

Individuals and interactions over processes and tools

Working software over comprehensive documentation

Customer collaboration over contract negotiation

Responding to change over following a plan

That is, while there is value in the items on the right, we value the items on the left more.

Probably the best-known agile method is extreme programming (Beck, 1999; Beck, 2000), which I describe later in this chapter. Other agile approaches include Scrum (Cohn, 2009; Schwaber, 2004; Schwaber and Beedle, 2001), Crystal (Cockburn, 2001; Cockburn, 2004), Adaptive Software Development (Highsmith, 2000), DSDM (Stapleton, 1997; Stapleton, 2003), and Feature Driven Development (Palmer and Felsing, 2002). The success of these methods has led to some integration with more traditional development methods based on system modelling, resulting in the notion of agile modelling (Ambler and Jeffries, 2002) and agile instantiations of the Rational Unified Process (Larman, 2002).

Although these agile methods are all based around the notion of incremental development and delivery, they propose different processes to achieve this. However, they share a set of principles, based on the agile manifesto, and so have much in common. These principles are shown in Figure 3.1. Different agile methods instantiate these principles in different ways and I don't have space to discuss all agile methods. Instead, I focus on two of the most widely used methods: extreme programming (Section 3.3) and Scrum (Section 3.4).

Agile methods have been very successful for some types of system development:

1. Product development where a software company is developing a small or medium-sized product for sale.

2. Custom system development within an organization, where there is a clear commitment from the customer to become involved in the development process and where there are not a lot of external rules and regulations that affect the software.

Principle	Description
Customer involvement	Customers should be closely involved throughout the development process. Their role is provide and prioritize new system requirements and to evaluate the iterations of the system.
Incremental delivery	The software is developed in increments with the customer specifying the requirements to be included in each increment.
People not process	The skills of the development team should be recognized and exploited. Team members should be left to develop their own ways of working without prescriptive processes.
Embrace change	Expect the system requirements to change and so design the system to accommodate these changes.
Maintain simplicity	Focus on simplicity in both the software being developed and in the development process. Wherever possible, actively work to eliminate complexity from the system.

Figure 3.1 The principles of agile methods

As I discuss in the final section of this chapter, the success of agile methods has meant that there is a lot of interest in using these methods for other types of software development. However, because of their focus on small, tightly integrated teams, there are problems in scaling them to large systems. There have also been experiments in using agile approaches for critical systems engineering (Drobna et al., 2004). However, because of the need for security, safety, and dependability analysis in critical systems, agile methods require significant modification before they can be routinely used for critical systems engineering.

In practice, the principles underlying agile methods are sometimes difficult to realize:

1. Although the idea of customer involvement in the development process is an attractive one, its success depends on having a customer who is willing and able to spend time with the development team and who can represent all system stakeholders. Frequently, the customer representatives are subject to other pressures and cannot take full part in the software development.

2. Individual team members may not have suitable personalities for the intense involvement that is typical of agile methods, and therefore not interact well with other team members.

3. Prioritizing changes can be extremely difficult, especially in systems for which there are many stakeholders. Typically, each stakeholder gives different priorities to different changes.

4. Maintaining simplicity requires extra work. Under pressure from delivery schedules, the team members may not have time to carry out desirable system simplifications.

5. Many organizations, especially large companies, have spent years changing their culture so that processes are defined and followed. It is difficult for them to move to a working model in which processes are informal and defined by development teams.

Another non-technical problem—that is a general problem with incremental development and delivery—occurs when the system customer uses an outside organization for system development. The software requirements document is usually part of the contract between the customer and the supplier. Because incremental specification is inherent in agile methods, writing contracts for this type of development may be difficult.

Consequently, agile methods have to rely on contracts in which the customer pays for the time required for system development rather than the development of a specific set of requirements. So long as all goes well, this benefits both the customer and the developer. However, if problems arise then there may be difficult disputes over who is to blame and who should pay for the extra time and resources required to resolve the problems.

Most books and papers that describe agile methods and experiences with agile methods talk about the use of these methods for new systems development. However, as I explain in Chapter 9, a huge amount of software engineering effort goes into the maintenance and evolution of existing software systems. There are only a small number of experience reports on using agile methods for software maintenance (Poole and Huisman, 2001). There are two questions that should be considered when considering agile methods and maintenance:

1. Are systems that are developed using an agile approach maintainable, given the emphasis in the development process of minimizing formal documentation?

2. Can agile methods be used effectively for evolving a system in response to customer change requests?

Formal documentation is supposed to describe the system and so make it easier for people changing the system to understand. In practice, however, formal documentation is often not kept up to date and so does not accurately reflect the program code. For this reason, agile methods enthusiasts argue that it is a waste of time to write this documentation and that the key to implementing maintainable software is to produce high-quality, readable code. Agile practices therefore emphasize the importance of writing well-structured code and investing effort in code improvement. Therefore, the lack of documentation should not be a problem in maintaining systems developed using an agile approach.

However, my experience of system maintenance suggests that the key document is the system requirements document, which tells the software engineer what the system is supposed to do. Without such knowledge, it is difficult to assess the impact of proposed system changes. Many agile methods collect requirements informally and incrementally and do not create a coherent requirements document. In this respect, the use of agile methods is likely to make subsequent system maintenance more difficult and expensive.

Agile practices, used in the maintenance process itself, are likely to be effective, whether or not an agile approach has been used for system development. Incremental delivery, design for change and maintaining simplicity all make sense when software is being changed. In fact, you can think of an agile development process as a process of software evolution.

However, the main difficulty after software delivery is likely to be keeping customers involved in the process. Although a customer may be able to justify the full-time involvement of a representative during system development, this is less likely during maintenance where changes are not continuous. Customer representatives are likely to lose interest in the system. Therefore, it is likely that alternative mechanisms, such as change proposals, discussed in Chapter 25, will be required to create the new system requirements.

The other problem that is likely to arise is maintaining continuity of the development team. Agile methods rely on team members understanding aspects of the system without having to consult documentation. If an agile development team is broken up, then this implicit knowledge is lost and it is difficult for new team members to build up the same understanding of the system and its components.

Supporters of agile methods have been evangelical in promoting their use and have tended to overlook their shortcomings. This has prompted an equally extreme response, which, in my view, exaggerates the problems with this approach (Stephens and Rosenberg, 2003). More reasoned critics such as DeMarco and Boehm (DeMarco and Boehm, 2002) highlight both the advantages and disadvantages of agile methods. They propose a hybrid approach where agile methods incorporate some techniques from plan-driven development may be the best way forward.

3.2 Plan-driven and agile development

Agile approaches to software development consider design and implementation to be the central activities in the software process. They incorporate other activities, such as requirements elicitation and testing, into design and implementation. By contrast, a plan-driven approach to software engineering identifies separate stages in the software process with outputs associated with each stage. The outputs from one stage are used as a basis for planning the following process activity. Figure 3.2 shows the distinctions between plan-driven and agile approaches to system specification.

In a plan-driven approach, iteration occurs within activities with formal documents used to communicate between stages of the process. For example, the requirements will evolve and, ultimately, a requirements specification will be produced. This is then an input to the design and implementation process. In an agile approach, iteration occurs across activities. Therefore, the requirements and the design are developed together, rather than separately.

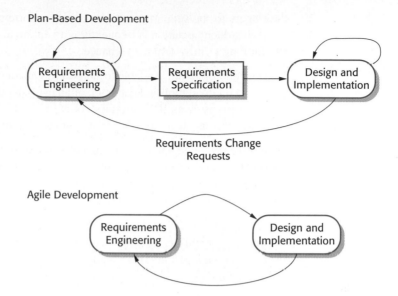

Figure 3.2 Plan-driven and agile specification

A plan-driven software process can support incremental development and delivery. It is perfectly feasible to allocate requirements and plan the design and development phase as a series of increments. An agile process is not inevitably code-focused and it may produce some design documentation. As I discuss in the following section, the agile development team may decide to include a documentation 'spike', where, instead of producing a new version of a system, the team produce system documentation.

In fact, most software projects include practices from plan-driven and agile approaches. To decide on the balance between a plan-based and an agile approach, you have to answer a range of technical, human, and organizational questions:

1. Is it important to have a very detailed specification and design before moving to implementation? If so, you probably need to use a plan-driven approach.

2. Is an incremental delivery strategy, where you deliver the software to customers and get rapid feedback from them, realistic? If so, consider using agile methods.

3. How large is the system that is being developed? Agile methods are most effective when the system can be developed with a small co-located team who can communicate informally. This may not be possible for large systems that require larger development teams so a plan-driven approach may have to be used.

4. What type of system is being developed? Systems that require a lot of analysis before implementation (e.g., real-time system with complex timing requirements) usually need a fairly detailed design to carry out this analysis. A plan-driven approach may be best in those circumstances.

5. What is the expected system lifetime? Long-lifetime systems may require more design documentation to communicate the original intentions of the system

developers to the support team. However, supporters of agile methods rightly argue that documentation is frequently not kept up to date and it is not of much use for long-term system maintenance.

6. What technologies are available to support system development? Agile methods often rely on good tools to keep track of an evolving design. If you are developing a system using an IDE that does not have good tools for program visualization and analysis, then more design documentation may be required.

7. How is the development team organized? If the development team is distributed or if part of the development is being outsourced, then you may need to develop design documents to communicate across the development teams. You may need to plan in advance what these are.

8. Are there cultural issues that may affect the system development? Traditional engineering organizations have a culture of plan-based development, as this is the norm in engineering. This usually requires extensive design documentation, rather than the informal knowledge used in agile processes.

9. How good are the designers and programmers in the development team? It is sometimes argued that agile methods require higher skill levels than plan-based approaches in which programmers simply translate a detailed design into code. If you have a team with relatively low skill levels, you may need to use the best people to develop the design, with others responsible for programming.

10. Is the system subject to external regulation? If a system has to be approved by an external regulator (e.g., the Federal Aviation Authority [FAA] approve software that is critical to the operation of an aircraft) then you will probably be required to produce detailed documentation as part of the system safety case.

In reality, the issue of whether a project can be labelled as plan-driven or agile is not very important. Ultimately, the primary concern of buyers of a software system is whether or not they have an executable software system that meets their needs and does useful things for the individual user or the organization. In practice, many companies who claim to have used agile methods have adopted some agile practices and have integrated these with their plan-driven processes.

3.3 Extreme programming

Extreme programming (XP) is perhaps the best known and most widely used of the agile methods. The name was coined by Beck (2000) because the approach was developed by pushing recognized good practice, such as iterative development, to 'extreme' levels. For example, in XP, several new versions of a system may be developed by different programmers, integrated and tested in a day.

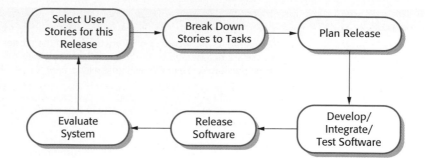

Figure 3.3 The extreme programming release cycle

In extreme programming, requirements are expressed as scenarios (called user stories), which are implemented directly as a series of tasks. Programmers work in pairs and develop tests for each task before writing the code. All tests must be successfully executed when new code is integrated into the system. There is a short time gap between releases of the system. Figure 3.3 illustrates the XP process to produce an increment of the system that is being developed.

Extreme programming involves a number of practices, summarized in Figure 3.4, which reflect the principles of agile methods:

1. Incremental development is supported through small, frequent releases of the system. Requirements are based on simple customer stories or scenarios that are used as a basis for deciding what functionality should be included in a system increment.

2. Customer involvement is supported through the continuous engagement of the customer in the development team. The customer representative takes part in the development and is responsible for defining acceptance tests for the system.

3. People, not process, are supported through pair programming, collective ownership of the system code, and a sustainable development process that does not involve excessively long working hours.

4. Change is embraced through regular system releases to customers, test-first development, refactoring to avoid code degeneration, and continuous integration of new functionality.

5. Maintaining simplicity is supported by constant refactoring that improves code quality and by using simple designs that do not unnecessarily anticipate future changes to the system.

In an XP process, customers are intimately involved in specifying and prioritizing system requirements. The requirements are not specified as lists of required system functions. Rather, the system customer is part of the development team and discusses scenarios with other team members. Together, they develop a 'story card' that encapsulates the customer needs. The development team then aims to implement that scenario in a future release of the software. An example of a story card for the mental

Principle or practice	Description
Incremental planning	Requirements are recorded on Story Cards and the Stories to be included in a release are determined by the time available and their relative priority. The developers break these Stories into development 'Tasks'. See Figures 3.5 and 3.6.
Small releases	The minimal useful set of functionality that provides business value is developed first. Releases of the system are frequent and incrementally add functionality to the first release.
Simple design	Enough design is carried out to meet the current requirements and no more.
Test-first development	An automated unit test framework is used to write tests for a new piece of functionality before that functionality itself is implemented.
Refactoring	All developers are expected to refactor the code continuously as soon as possible code improvements are found. This keeps the code simple and maintainable.
Pair programming	Developers work in pairs, checking each other's work and providing the support to always do a good job.
Collective ownership	The pairs of developers work on all areas of the system, so that no islands of expertise develop and all the developers take responsibility for all of the code. Anyone can change anything.
Continuous integration	As soon as the work on a task is complete, it is integrated into the whole system. After any such integration, all the unit tests in the system must pass.
Sustainable pace	Large amounts of overtime are not considered acceptable as the net effect is often to reduce code quality and medium term productivity
On-site customer	A representative of the end-user of the system (the Customer) should be available full time for the use of the XP team. In an extreme programming process, the customer is a member of the development team and is responsible for bringing system requirements to the team for implementation.

Figure 3.4 Extreme programming practices

health care patient management system is shown in Figure 3.5. This is a short description of a scenario for prescribing medication for a patient.

The story cards are the main inputs to the XP planning process or the 'planning game'. Once the story cards have been developed, the development team breaks these down into tasks (Figure 3.6) and estimates the effort and resources required for implementing each task. This usually involves discussions with the customer to refine the requirements. The customer then prioritizes the stories for implementation, choosing those stories that can be used immediately to deliver useful business support. The intention is to identify useful functionality that can be implemented in about two weeks, when the next release of the system is made available to the customer.

Of course, as requirements change, the unimplemented stories change or may be discarded. If changes are required for a system that has already been delivered, new story cards are developed and again, the customer decides whether these changes should have priority over new functionality.

Prescribing Medication

Kate is a doctor who wishes to prescribe medication for a patient attending a clinic. The patient record is already displayed on her computer so she clicks on the medication field and can select current medication', 'new medication' or 'formulary'.

If she selects 'current medication', the system asks her to check the dose. If she wants to change the dose, she enters the dose and then confirms the prescription.

If she chooses 'new medication', the system assumes that she knows which medication to prescribe. She types the first few letters of the drug name. The system displays a list of possible drugs starting with these letters. She chooses the required medication and the system responds by asking her to check that the medication selected is correct. She enters the dose and then confirms the prescription.

If she chooses 'formulary', the system displays a search box for the approved formulary. She can then search for the drug required. She selects a drug and is asked to check that the medication is correct. She enters the dose and then confirms the prescription.

The system always checks that the dose is within the approved range. If it isn't, Kate is asked to change the dose.

After Kate has confirmed the prescription, it will be displayed for checking. She either clicks 'OK' or 'Change'. If she clicks 'OK', the prescription is recorded on the audit database. If she clicks on 'Change', she reenters the 'Prescribing medication' process.

Figure 3.5 A 'prescribing medication' story.

Sometimes, during the planning game, questions that cannot be easily answered come to light and additional work is required to explore possible solutions. The team may carry out some prototyping or trial development to understand the problem and solution. In XP terms, this is a 'spike', an increment where no programming is done. There may also be 'spikes' to design the system architecture or to develop system documentation.

Extreme programming takes an 'extreme' approach to incremental development. New versions of the software may be built several times per day and releases are delivered to customers roughly every two weeks. Release deadlines are never slipped; if there are development problems, the customer is consulted and functionality is removed from the planned release.

When a programmer builds the system to create a new version, he or she must run all existing automated tests as well as the tests for the new functionality. The new build of the software is accepted only if all tests execute successfully. This then becomes the basis for the next iteration of the system.

A fundamental precept of traditional software engineering is that you should design for change. That is, you should anticipate future changes to the software and design it so that these changes can be easily implemented. Extreme programming, however, has discarded this principle on the basis that designing for change is often wasted effort. It isn't worth taking time to add generality to a program to cope with change. The changes anticipated often never materialize and completely different change requests may actually be made. Therefore, the XP approach accepts that changes will happen and reorganize the software when these changes actually occur.

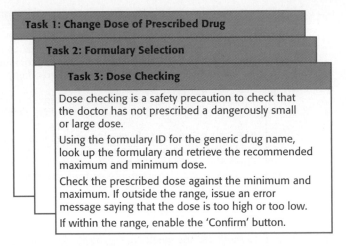

Task 1: Change Dose of Prescribed Drug

Task 2: Formulary Selection

Task 3: Dose Checking

Dose checking is a safety precaution to check that the doctor has not prescribed a dangerously small or large dose.

Using the formulary ID for the generic drug name, look up the formulary and retrieve the recommended maximum and minimum dose.

Check the prescribed dose against the minimum and maximum. If outside the range, issue an error message saying that the dose is too high or too low.

If within the range, enable the 'Confirm' button.

Figure 3.6 Examples of task cards for prescribing medication.

A general problem with incremental development is that it tends to degrade the software structure, so changes to the software become harder and harder to implement. Essentially, the development proceeds by finding workarounds to problems, with the result that code is often duplicated, parts of the software are reused in inappropriate ways, and the overall structure degrades as code is added to the system.

Extreme programming tackles this problem by suggesting that the software should be constantly refactored. This means that the programming team look for possible improvements to the software and implement them immediately. When a team member sees code that can be improved, they make these improvements even in situations where there is no immediate need for them. Examples of refactoring include the reorganization of a class hierarchy to remove duplicate code, the tidying up and renaming of attributes and methods, and the replacement of code with calls to methods defined in a program library. Program development environments, such as Eclipse (Carlson, 2005), include tools for refactoring which simplify the process of finding dependencies between code sections and making global code modifications.

In principle then, the software should always be easy to understand and change as new stories are implemented. In practice, this is not always the case. Sometimes development pressure means that refactoring is delayed because the time is devoted to the implementation of new functionality. Some new features and changes cannot readily be accommodated by code-level refactoring and require the architecture of the system to be modified.

In practice, many companies that have adopted XP do not use all of the extreme programming practices listed in Figure 3.4. They pick and choose according to their local ways of working. For example, some companies find pair programming helpful; others prefer to use individual programming and reviews. To accommodate different levels of skill, some programmers don't do refactoring in parts of the system they did not develop, and conventional requirements may be used rather than user stories. However, most companies who have adopted an XP variant use small releases, test-first development, and continuous integration.

3.3.1 Testing in XP

As I discussed in the introduction to this chapter, one of the important differences between incremental development and plan-driven development is in the way that the system is tested. With incremental development, there is no system specification that can be used by an external testing team to develop system tests. As a consequence, some approaches to incremental development have a very informal testing process, in comparison with plan-driven testing.

To avoid some of the problems of testing and system validation, XP emphasizes the importance of program testing. XP includes an approach to testing that reduces the chances of introducing undiscovered errors into the current version of the system.

The key features of testing in XP are:

1. Test-first development,

2. incremental test development from scenarios,

3. user involvement in the test development and validation, and

4. the use of automated testing frameworks.

Test-first development is one of the most important innovations in XP. Instead of writing some code and then writing tests for that code, you write the tests before you write the code. This means that you can run the test as the code is being written and discover problems during development.

Writing tests implicitly defines both an interface and a specification of behavior for the functionality being developed. Problems of requirements and interface misunderstandings are reduced. This approach can be adopted in any process in which there is a clear relationship between a system requirement and the code implementing that requirement. In XP, you can always see this link because the story cards representing the requirements are broken down into tasks and the tasks are the principal unit of implementation. The adoption of test-first development in XP has led to more general test-driven approaches to development (Astels, 2003). I discuss these in Chapter 8.

In test-first development, the task implementers have to thoroughly understand the specification so that they can write tests for the system. This means that ambiguities and omissions in the specification have to be clarified before implementation begins. Furthermore, it also avoids the problem of 'test-lag'. This may happen when the developer of the system works at a faster pace than the tester. The implementation gets further and further ahead of the testing and there is a tendency to skip tests, so that the development schedule can be maintained.

User requirements in XP are expressed as scenarios or stories and the user prioritizes these for development. The development team assesses each scenario and breaks it down into tasks. For example, some of the task cards developed from the story card for prescribing medication (Figure 3.5) are shown in Figure 3.6. Each task generates one or more unit tests that check the implementation described in that task. Figure 3.7 is a shortened description of a test case that has been developed to check that the prescribed dose of a drug does not fall outside known safe limits.

Test 4: Dose Checking

Input:
1. A number in mg representing a single dose of the drug.
2. A number representing the number of single doses per day.

Tests:
1. Test for inputs where the single dose is correct but the frequency is too high.
2. Test for inputs where the single dose is too high and too low.
3. Test for inputs where the single dose × frequency is too high and too low.
4. Test for inputs where single dose × frequency is in the permitted range.

Output:
OK or error message indicating that the dose is outside the safe range.

Figure 3.7 Test case description for dose checking

The role of the customer in the testing process is to help develop acceptance tests for the stories that are to be implemented in the next release of the system. As I discuss in Chapter 8, acceptance testing is the process where the system is tested using customer data to check that it meets the customer's real needs.

In XP, acceptance testing, like development, is incremental. The customer who is part of the team writes tests as development proceeds. All new code is therefore validated to ensure that it is what the customer needs. For the story in Figure 3.5, the acceptance test would involve scenarios where (a) the dose of a drug was changed, (b) a new drug was selected, and (c) the formulary was used to find a drug. In practice, a series of acceptance tests rather than a single test are normally required.

Relying on the customer to support acceptance test development is sometimes a major difficulty in the XP testing process. People adopting the customer role have very limited available time and may not be able to work full-time with the development team. The customer may feel that providing the requirements was enough of a contribution and so may be reluctant to get involved in the testing process.

Test automation is essential for test-first development. Tests are written as executable components before the task is implemented. These testing components should be stand-alone, should simulate the submission of input to be tested, and should check that the result meets the output specification. An automated test framework is a system that makes it easy to write executable tests and submit a set of tests for execution. Junit (Massol and Husted, 2003) is a widely used example of an automated testing framework.

As testing is automated, there is always a set of tests that can be quickly and easily executed. Whenever any functionality is added to the system, the tests can be run and problems that the new code has introduced can be caught immediately.

Test-first development and automated testing usually results in a large number of tests being written and executed. However, this approach does not necessarily lead to thorough program testing. There are three reasons for this:

1. Programmers prefer programming to testing and sometimes they take shortcuts when writing tests. For example, they may write incomplete tests that do not check for all possible exceptions that may occur.

2. Some tests can be very difficult to write incrementally. For example, in a complex user interface, it is often difficult to write unit tests for the code that implements the 'display logic' and workflow between screens.

3. It difficult to judge the completeness of a set of tests. Although you may have a lot of system tests, your test set may not provide complete coverage. Crucial parts of the system may not be executed and so remain untested.

Therefore, although a large set of frequently executed tests may give the impression that the system is complete and correct, this may not be the case. If the tests are not reviewed and further tests written after development, then undetected bugs may be delivered in the system release.

3.3.2 Pair programming

Another innovative practice that has been introduced in XP is that programmers work in pairs to develop the software. They actually sit together at the same workstation to develop the software. However, the same pairs do not always program together. Rather, pairs are created dynamically so that all team members work with each other during the development process.

The use of pair programming has a number of advantages:

1. It supports the idea of collective ownership and responsibility for the system. This reflects Weinberg's (1971) idea of egoless programming where the software is owned by the team as a whole and individuals are not held responsible for problems with the code. Instead, the team has collective responsibility for resolving these problems.

2. It acts as an informal review process because each line of code is looked at by at least two people. Code inspections and reviews (covered in Chapter 24) are very successful in discovering a high percentage of software errors. However, they are time consuming to organize and, typically, introduce delays into the development process. Although pair programming is a less formal process that probably doesn't find as many errors as code inspections, it is a much cheaper inspection process than formal program inspections.

3. It helps support refactoring, which is a process of software improvement. The difficulty of implementing this in a normal development environment is that effort in refactoring is expended for long-term benefit. An individual who practices refactoring may be judged to be less efficient than one who simply carries on developing code. Where pair programming and collective ownership are used, others benefit immediately from the refactoring so they are likely to support the process.

You might think that pair programming would be less efficient than individual programming. In a given time, a pair of developers would produce half as much code as two individuals working alone. There have been various studies of the productivity of paid programmers with mixed results. Using student volunteers, Williams and her collaborators (Cockburn and Williams, 2001; Williams et al., 2000) found that productivity with pair programming seems to be comparable with that of two people working independently. The reasons suggested are that pairs discuss the software before development so probably have fewer false starts and less rework. Furthermore, the number of errors avoided by the informal inspection is such that less time is spent repairing bugs discovered during the testing process.

However, studies with more experienced programmers (Arisholm et al., 2007; Parrish et al., 2004) did not replicate these results. They found that there was a significant loss of productivity compared with two programmers working alone. There were some quality benefits but these did not fully compensate for the pair-programming overhead. Nevertheless, the sharing of knowledge that happens during pair programming is very important as it reduces the overall risks to a project when team members leave. In itself, this may make pair programming worthwhile.

3.4 Agile project management

The principal responsibility of software project managers is to manage the project so that the software is delivered on time and within the planned budget for the project. They supervise the work of software engineers and monitor how well the software development is progressing.

The standard approach to project management is plan-driven. As I discuss in Chapter 23, managers draw up a plan for the project showing what should be delivered, when it should be delivered, and who will work on the development of the project deliverables. A plan-based approach really requires a manager to have a stable view of everything that has to be developed and the development processes. However, it does not work well with agile methods where the requirements are developed incrementally; where the software is delivered in short, rapid increments; and where changes to the requirements and the software are the norm.

Like every other professional software development process, agile development has to be managed so that the best use is made of the time and resources available to the team. This requires a different approach to project management, which is adapted to incremental development and the particular strengths of agile methods.

The Scrum approach (Schwaber, 2004; Schwaber and Beedle, 2001) is a general agile method but its focus is on managing iterative development rather than specific technical approaches to agile software engineering. Figure 3.8 is a diagram of the Scrum management process. Scrum does not prescribe the use of programming practices such as pair programming and test-first development. It can therefore be used with more technical agile approaches, such as XP, to provide a management framework for the project.

There are three phases in Scrum. The first is an outline planning phase where you establish the general objectives for the project and design the software architecture.

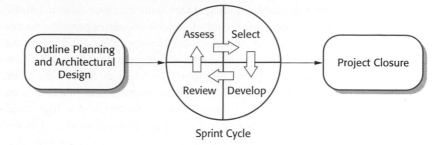

Figure 3.8 The Scrum process

This is followed by a series of sprint cycles, where each cycle develops an increment of the system. Finally, the project closure phase wraps up the project, completes required documentation such as system help frames and user manuals, and assesses the lessons learned from the project.

The innovative feature of Scrum is its central phase, namely the sprint cycles. A Scrum sprint is a planning unit in which the work to be done is assessed, features are selected for development, and the software is implemented. At the end of a sprint, the completed functionality is delivered to stakeholders. Key characteristics of this process are as follows:

1. Sprints are fixed length, normally 2–4 weeks. They correspond to the development of a release of the system in XP.

2. The starting point for planning is the product backlog, which is the list of work to be done on the project. During the assessment phase of the sprint, this is reviewed, and priorities and risks are assigned. The customer is closely involved in this process and can introduce new requirements or tasks at the beginning of each sprint.

3. The selection phase involves all of the project team who work with the customer to select the features and functionality to be developed during the sprint.

4. Once these are agreed, the team organizes themselves to develop the software. Short daily meetings involving all team members are held to review progress and if necessary, reprioritize work. During this stage the team is isolated from the customer and the organization, with all communications channelled through the so-called 'Scrum master'. The role of the Scrum master is to protect the development team from external distractions. The way in which the work is done depends on the problem and the team. Unlike XP, Scrum does not make specific suggestions on how to write requirements, test-first development, etc. However, these XP practices can be used if the team thinks they are appropriate.

5. At the end of the sprint, the work done is reviewed and presented to stakeholders. The next sprint cycle then begins.

The idea behind Scrum is that the whole team should be empowered to make decisions so the term 'project manager', has been deliberately avoided. Rather, the

'Scrum master' is a facilitator who arranges daily meetings, tracks the backlog of work to be done, records decisions, measures progress against the backlog, and communicates with customers and management outside of the team.

The whole team attends the daily meetings, which are sometimes 'stand-up' meetings to keep them short and focused. During the meeting, all team members share information, describe their progress since the last meeting, problems that have arisen, and what is planned for the following day. This means that everyone on the team knows what is going on and, if problems arise, can replan short-term work to cope with them. Everyone participates in this short-term planning—there is no top-down direction from the Scrum master.

There are many anecdotal reports of the successful use of Scrum available on the Web. Rising and Janoff (2000) discuss its successful use in a telecommunication software development environment, and they list its advantages as follows:

1. The product is broken down into a set of manageable and understandable chunks.

2. Unstable requirements do not hold up progress.

3. The whole team has visibility of everything and consequently team communication is improved.

4. Customers see on-time delivery of increments and gain feedback on how the product works.

5. Trust between customers and developers is established and a positive culture is created in which everyone expects the project to succeed.

Scrum, as originally designed, was intended for use with co-located teams where all team members could get together every day in stand-up meetings. However, much software development now involves distributed teams with team members located in different places around the world. Consequently, there are various experiments going on to develop Scrum for distributed development environments (Smits and Pshigoda, 2007; Sutherland et al., 2007).

3.5 Scaling agile methods

Agile methods were developed for use by small programming teams who could work together in the same room and communicate informally. Agile methods have therefore been mostly used for the development of small and medium-sized systems. Of course, the need for faster delivery of software, which is more suited to customer needs, also applies to larger systems. Consequently, there has been a great deal of interest in scaling agile methods to cope with larger systems, developed by large organizations.

Denning et al. (2008) argue that the only way to avoid common software engineering problems, such as systems that don't meet customer needs and budget overruns, is to find ways of making agile methods work for large systems. Leffingwell (2007) discusses which agile practices scale to large systems development. Moore and Spens (2008) report on their experience of using an agile approach to develop a large medical system with 300 developers working in geographically distributed teams.

Large software system development is different from small system development in a number of ways:

1. Large systems are usually collections of separate, communicating systems, where separate teams develop each system. Frequently, these teams are working in different places, sometimes in different time zones. It is practically impossible for each team to have a view of the whole system. Consequently, their priorities are usually to complete their part of the system without regard for wider systems issues.

2. Large systems are 'brownfield systems' (Hopkins and Jenkins, 2008); that is they include and interact with a number of existing systems. Many of the system requirements are concerned with this interaction and so don't really lend themselves to flexibility and incremental development. Political issues can also be significant here—often the easiest solution to a problem is to change an existing system. However, this requires negotiation with the managers of that system to convince them that the changes can be implemented without risk to the system's operation.

3. Where several systems are integrated to create a system, a significant fraction of the development is concerned with system configuration rather than original code development. This is not necessarily compatible with incremental development and frequent system integration.

4. Large systems and their development processes are often constrained by external rules and regulations limiting the way that they can be developed, that require certain types of system documentation to be produced, etc.

5. Large systems have a long procurement and development time. It is difficult to maintain coherent teams who know about the system over that period as, inevitably, people move on to other jobs and projects.

6. Large systems usually have a diverse set of stakeholders. For example, nurses and administrators may be the end-users of a medical system but senior medical staff, hospital managers, etc. are also stakeholders in the system. It is practically impossible to involve all of these different stakeholders in the development process.

There are two perspectives on the scaling of agile methods:

1. A 'scaling up' perspective, which is concerned with using these methods for developing large software systems that cannot be developed by a small team.

2. A 'scaling out' perspective, which is concerned with how agile methods can be introduced across a large organization with many years of software development experience.

Agile methods have to be adapted to cope with large systems engineering. Leffingwell (2007) argues that it is essential to maintain the fundamentals of agile methods—flexible planning, frequent system releases, continuous integration, test-driven development, and good team communications. I believe that the critical adaptations that have to be introduced are as follows:

1. For large systems development, it is not possible to focus only on the code of the system. You need to do more up-front design and system documentation. The software architecture has to be designed and there has to be documentation produced to describe critical aspects of the system, such as database schemas, the work breakdown across teams, etc.

2. Cross-team communication mechanisms have to be designed and used. This should involve regular phone and video conferences between team members and frequent, short electronic meetings where teams update each other on progress. A range of communication channels such as e-mail, instant messaging, wikis, and social networking systems should be provided to facilitate communications.

3. Continuous integration, where the whole system is built every time any developer checks in a change, is practically impossible when several separate programs have to be integrated to create the system. However, it is essential to maintain frequent system builds and regular releases of the system. This may mean that new configuration management tools that support multi-team software development have to be introduced.

Small software companies that develop software products have been amongst the most enthusiastic adopters of agile methods. These companies are not constrained by organizational bureaucracies or process standards and they can change quickly to adopt new ideas. Of course, larger companies have also experimented with agile methods in specific projects, but it is much more difficult for them to 'scale out' these methods across the organization. Lindvall, et al. (2004) discuss some of the problems in scaling-out agile methods in four large technology companies.

It is difficult to introduce agile methods into large companies for a number of reasons:

1. Project managers who do not have experience of agile methods may be reluctant to accept the risk of a new approach, as they do not know how this will affect their particular projects.

2. Large organizations often have quality procedures and standards that all projects are expected to follow and, because of their bureaucratic nature, these are likely to be incompatible with agile methods. Sometimes, these are supported by software

tools (e.g., requirements management tools) and the use of these tools is mandated for all projects.

3. Agile methods seem to work best when team members have a relatively high skill level. However, within large organizations, there are likely to be a wide range of skills and abilities, and people with lower skill levels may not be effective team members in agile processes.

4. There may be cultural resistance to agile methods, especially in those organizations that have a long history of using conventional systems engineering processes.

Change management and testing procedures are examples of company procedures that may not be compatible with agile methods. Change management is the process of controlling changes to a system, so that the impact of changes is predictable and costs are controlled. All changes have to be approved in advance before they are made and this conflicts with the notion of refactoring. In XP, any developer can improve any code without getting external approval. For large systems, there are also testing standards where a system build is handed over to an external testing team. This may conflict with the test-first and test-often approaches used in XP.

Introducing and sustaining the use of agile methods across a large organization is a process of cultural change. Cultural change takes a long time to implement and often requires a change of management before it can be accomplished. Companies wishing to use agile methods need evangelists to promote change. They must devote significant resources to the change process. At the time of writing, few large companies have made a successful transition to agile development across the organization.

KEY POINTS

■ Agile methods are incremental development methods that focus on rapid development, frequent releases of the software, reducing process overheads, and producing high-quality code. They involve the customer directly in the development process.

■ The decision on whether to use an agile or a plan-driven approach to development should depend on the type of software being developed, the capabilities of the development team, and the culture of the company developing the system.

■ Extreme programming is a well-known agile method that integrates a range of good programming practices such as frequent releases of the software, continuous software improvement, and customer participation in the development team.

■ A particular strength of extreme programming is the development of automated tests before a program feature is created. All tests must successfully execute when an increment is integrated into a system.

■ The Scrum method is an agile method that provides a project management framework. It is centered around a set of sprints, which are fixed time periods when a system increment is developed. Planning is based on prioritizing a backlog of work and selecting the highest-priority tasks for a sprint.

■ Scaling agile methods for large systems is difficult. Large systems need up-front design and some documentation. Continuous integration is practically impossible when there are several separate development teams working on a project.

FURTHER READING

Extreme Programming Explained. This was the first book on XP and is still, perhaps, the most readable. It explains the approach from the perspective of one of its inventors and his enthusiasm comes through very clearly in the book. (Kent Beck, Addison-Wesley, 2000.)

'Get Ready for Agile Methods, With Care'. A thoughtful critique of agile methods that discusses their strengths and weaknesses, written by a vastly experienced software engineer. (B. Boehm, *IEEE Computer*, January 2002.) http://doi.ieeecomputersociety.org/10.1109/2.976920.

Scaling Software Agility: Best Practices for Large Enterprises. Although focused on issues of scaling agile development, this book also includes a summary of the principal agile methods such as XP, Scrum, and Crystal. (D. Leffingwell, Addison-Wesley, 2007.)

Running an Agile Software Development Project. Most books on agile methods focus on a specific method but this book takes a different approach and discusses how to put XP into practice in a project. Good, practical advice. (M. Holcombe, John Wiley and Sons, 2008.)

EXERCISES

3.1. Explain why the rapid delivery and deployment of new systems is often more important to businesses than the detailed functionality of these systems.

3.2. Explain how the principles underlying agile methods lead to the accelerated development and deployment of software.

3.3. When would you recommend *against* the use of an agile method for developing a software system?

3.4. Extreme programming expresses user requirements as stories, with each story written on a card. Discuss the advantages and disadvantages of this approach to requirements description.

3.5. Explain why test-first development helps the programmer to develop a better understanding of the system requirements. What are the potential difficulties with test-first development?

3.6. Suggest four reasons why the productivity rate of programmers working as a pair might be more than half that of two programmers working individually.

3.7. Compare and contrast the Scrum approach to project management with conventional plan-based approaches, as discussed in Chapter 23. The comparisons should be based on the effectiveness of each approach for planning the allocation of people to projects, estimating the cost of projects, maintaining team cohesion, and managing changes in project team membership.

3.8. You are a software manager in a company that develops critical control software for aircraft. You are responsible for the development of a software design support system that supports the translation of software requirements to a formal software specification (discussed in Chapter 13). Comment on the advantages and disadvantages of the following development strategies:

a. Collect the requirements for such a system from software engineers and external stakeholders (such as the regulatory certification authority) and develop the system using a plan-driven approach.

b. Develop a prototype using a scripting language, such as Ruby or Python, evaluate this prototype with software engineers and other stakeholders, then review the system requirements. Redevelop the final system using Java.

c. Develop the system in Java using an agile approach with a user involved in the development team.

3.9. It has been suggested that one of the problems of having a user closely involved with a software development team is that they 'go native'; that is, they adopt the outlook of the development team and lose sight of the needs of their user colleagues. Suggest three ways how you might avoid this problem and discuss the advantages and disadvantages of each approach.

3.10. To reduce costs and the environmental impact of commuting, your company decides to close a number of offices and to provide support for staff to work from home. However, the senior management who introduce the policy are unaware that software is developed using agile methods, which rely on close team working and pair programming. Discuss the difficulties that this new policy might cause and how you might get around these problems.

REFERENCES

Ambler, S. W. and Jeffries, R. (2002). *Agile Modeling: Effective Practices for Extreme Programming and the Unified Process.* New York: John Wiley & Sons.

Arisholm, E., Gallis, H., Dyba, T. and Sjoberg, D. I. K. (2007). 'Evaluating Pair Programming with Respect to System Complexity and Programmer Expertise'. *IEEE Trans. on Software Eng.,* **33** (2), 65–86.

Astels, D. (2003). *Test Driven Development: A Practical Guide.* Upper Saddle River, NJ: Prentice Hall.

Beck, K. (1999). 'Embracing Change with Extreme Programming'. *IEEE Computer,* **32** (10), 70–8.

Beck, K. (2000). *extreme Programming explained.* Reading, Mass.: Addison-Wesley.

Carlson, D. (2005). *Eclipse Distilled.* Boston: Addison-Wesley.

Cockburn, A. (2001). *Agile Software Development.* Reading, Mass.: Addison-Wesley.

Cockburn, A. (2004). *Crystal Clear: A Human-Powered Methodology for Small Teams.* Boston: Addison-Wesley.

Cockburn, A. and Williams, L. (2001). 'The costs and benefits of pair programming'. *In Extreme programming examined. (ed.).* Boston: Addison-Wesley.

Cohn, M. (2009). *Succeeding with Agile: Software Development Using Scrum.* Boston: Addison-Wesley.

Demarco, T. and Boehm, B. (2002). 'The Agile Methods Fray'. *IEEE Computer,* **35** (6), 90–2.

Denning, P. J., Gunderson, C. and Hayes-Roth, R. (2008). 'Evolutionary System Development'. *Comm. ACM,* **51** (12), 29–31.

Drobna, J., Noftz, D. and Raghu, R. (2004). 'Piloting XP on Four Mission-Critical Projects'. *IEEE Software,* **21** (6), 70–5.

Highsmith, J. A. (2000). *Adaptive Software Development: A Collaborative Approach to Managing Complex Systems.* New York: Dorset House.

Hopkins, R. and Jenkins, K. (2008). *Eating the IT Elephant: Moving from Greenfield Development to Brownfield. Boston,* Mass.: IBM Press.

Larman, C. (2002). *Applying UML and Patterns: An Introduction to Object-oriented Analysis and Design and the Unified Process.* Englewood Cliff, NJ: Prentice Hall.

Leffingwell, D. (2007). *Scaling Software Agility: Best Practices for Large Enterprises.* Boston: Addison-Wesley.

Lindvall, M., Muthig, D., Dagnino, A., Wallin, C., Stupperich, M., Kiefer, D., May, J. and Kahkonen, T. (2004). 'Agile Software Development in Large Organizations'. *IEEE Computer,* **37** (12), 26–34.

Martin, J. (1981). *Application Development Without Programmers*. Englewood Cliffs, NJ: Prentice-Hall.

Massol, V. and Husted, T. (2003). *JUnit in Action*. Greenwich, Conn.: Manning Publications Co.

Mills, H. D., O'Neill, D., Linger, R. C., Dyer, M. and Quinnan, R. E. (1980). 'The Management of Software Engineering'. *IBM Systems. J.*, **19** (4), 414–77.

Moore, E. and Spens, J. (2008). 'Scaling Agile: Finding your Agile Tribe'. *Proc. Agile 2008 Conference,* Toronto: IEEE Computer Society. 121–124.

Palmer, S. R. and Felsing, J. M. (2002). *A Practical Guide to Feature-Driven Development*. Englewood Cliffs, NJ: Prentice Hall.

Parrish, A., Smith, R., Hale, D. and Hale, J. (2004). 'A Field Study of Developer Pairs: Productivity Impacts and Implications'. *IEEE Software,* **21** (5), 76–9.

Poole, C. and Huisman, J. W. (2001). 'Using Extreme Programming in a Maintenance Environment'. *IEEE Software,* **18** (6), 42–50.

Rising, L. and Janoff, N. S. (2000). 'The Scrum Software Development Process for Small Teams'. *IEEE Software,* **17** (4), 26–32.

Schwaber, K. (2004). *Agile Project Management with Scrum*. Seattle: Microsoft Press.

Schwaber, K. and Beedle, M. (2001). *Agile Software Development with Scrum*. Englewood Cliffs, NJ: Prentice Hall.

Smits, H. and Pshigoda, G. (2007). 'Implementing Scrum in a Distributed Software Development Organization'. Agile 2007, Washington, DC: IEEE Computer Society.

Stapleton, J. (1997). *DSDM Dynamic Systems Development Method*. Harlow, UK: Addison-Wesley.

Stapleton, J. (2003). *DSDM: Business Focused Development, 2nd ed.* Harlow, UK: Pearson Education.

Stephens, M. and Rosenberg, D. (2003). *Extreme Programming Refactored*. Berkley, Calif.: Apress.

Sutherland, J., Viktorov, A., Blount, J. and Puntikov, N. (2007). 'Distributed Scrum: Agile Project Management with Outsourced Development Teams'. 40th Hawaii Int. Conf. on System Sciences, Hawaii: IEEE Computer Society.

Weinberg, G. (1971). *The Psychology of Computer Programming*. New York: Van Nostrand.

Williams, L., Kessler, R. R., Cunningham, W. and Jeffries, R. (2000). 'Strengthening the Case for Pair Programming'. *IEEE Software,* **17** (4), 19–25.

4

Requirements engineering

Objectives

The objective of this chapter is to introduce software requirements and to discuss the processes involved in discovering and documenting these requirements. When you have read the chapter you will:

■ understand the concepts of user and system requirements and why these requirements should be written in different ways;

■ understand the differences between functional and nonfunctional software requirements;

■ understand how requirements may be organized in a software requirements document;

■ understand the principal requirements engineering activities of elicitation, analysis and validation, and the relationships between these activities;

■ understand why requirements management is necessary and how it supports other requirements engineering activities.

Contents

The requirements for a system are the descriptions of what the system should do—the services that it provides and the constraints on its operation. These requirements reflect the needs of customers for a system that serves a certain purpose such as controlling a device, placing an order, or finding information. The process of finding out, analyzing, documenting and checking these services and constraints is called requirements engineering (RE).

The term 'requirement' is not used consistently in the software industry. In some cases, a requirement is simply a high-level, abstract statement of a service that a system should provide or a constraint on a system. At the other extreme, it is a detailed, formal definition of a system function. Davis (1993) explains why these differences exist:

> *If a company wishes to let a contract for a large software development project, it must define its needs in a sufficiently abstract way that a solution is not pre-defined. The requirements must be written so that several contractors can bid for the contract, offering, perhaps, different ways of meeting the client organization's needs. Once a contract has been awarded, the contractor must write a system definition for the client in more detail so that the client understands and can validate what the software will do. Both of these documents may be called the requirements document for the system.*

Some of the problems that arise during the requirements engineering process are a result of failing to make a clear separation between these different levels of description. I distinguish between them by using the term 'user requirements' to mean the high-level abstract requirements and 'system requirements' to mean the detailed description of what the system should do. User requirements and system requirements may be defined as follows:

1. User requirements are statements, in a natural language plus diagrams, of what services the system is expected to provide to system users and the constraints under which it must operate.

2. System requirements are more detailed descriptions of the software system's functions, services, and operational constraints. The system requirements document (sometimes called a functional specification) should define exactly what is to be implemented. It may be part of the contract between the system buyer and the software developers.

Different levels of requirements are useful because they communicate information about the system to different types of reader. Figure 4.1 illustrates the distinction between user and system requirements. This example from a mental health care patient management system (MHC-PMS) shows how a user requirement may be expanded into several system requirements. You can see from Figure 4.1 that the user requirement is quite general. The system requirements provide more specific information about the services and functions of the system that is to be implemented.

User Requirement Definition

1. The MHC-PMS shall generate monthly management reports showing the cost of drugs prescribed by each clinic during that month.

System Requirements Specification

1.1 On the last working day of each month, a summary of the drugs prescribed, their cost, and the prescribing clinics shall be generated.

1.2 The system shall automatically generate the report for printing after 17.30 on the last working day of the month.

1.3 A report shall be created for each clinic and shall list the individual drug names, the total number of prescriptions, the number of doses prescribed, and the total cost of the prescribed drugs.

1.4 If drugs are available in different dose units (e.g., 10 mg, 20 mg) separate reports shall be created for each dose unit.

1.5 Access to all cost reports shall be restricted to authorized users listed on a management access control list.

Figure 4.1 User and system requirements

You need to write requirements at different levels of detail because different readers use them in different ways. Figure 4.2 shows possible readers of the user and system requirements. The readers of the user requirements are not usually concerned with how the system will be implemented and may be managers who are not interested in the detailed facilities of the system. The readers of the system requirements need to know more precisely what the system will do because they are concerned with how it will support the business processes or because they are involved in the system implementation.

In this chapter, I present a 'traditional' view of requirements rather than requirements in agile processes. For most large systems, it is still the case that there is a clearly identifiable requirements engineering phase before the implementation of the system begins. The outcome is a requirements document, which may be part of the system development contract. Of course, there are usually subsequent changes to the requirements and user requirements may be expanded into more detailed system requirements. However, the agile approach of concurrently eliciting the requirements as the system is developed is rarely used for large systems development.

4.1 Functional and non-functional requirements

Software system requirements are often classified as functional requirements or non-functional requirements:

1.   *Functional requirements* These are statements of services the system should provide, how the system should react to particular inputs, and how the system

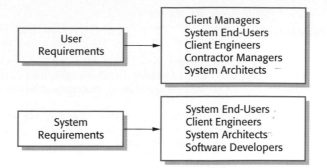

Figure 4.2 Readers of different types of requirements specification

should behave in particular situations. In some cases, the functional requirements may also explicitly state what the system should not do.

2. *Non-functional requirements* These are constraints on the services or functions offered by the system. They include timing constraints, constraints on the development process, and constraints imposed by standards. Non-functional requirements often apply to the system as a whole, rather than individual system features or services.

In reality, the distinction between different types of requirement is not as clear-cut as these simple definitions suggest. A user requirement concerned with security, such as a statement limiting access to authorized users, may appear to be a non-functional requirement. However, when developed in more detail, this requirement may generate other requirements that are clearly functional, such as the need to include user authentication facilities in the system.

This shows that requirements are not independent and that one requirement often generates or constrains other requirements. The system requirements therefore do not just specify the services or the features of the system that are required; they also specify the necessary functionality to ensure that these services/features are delivered properly.

4.1.1 Functional requirements

The functional requirements for a system describe what the system should do. These requirements depend on the type of software being developed, the expected users of the software, and the general approach taken by the organization when writing requirements. When expressed as user requirements, functional requirements are usually described in an abstract way that can be understood by system users. However, more specific functional system requirements describe the system functions, its inputs and outputs, exceptions, etc., in detail.

Functional system requirements vary from general requirements covering what the system should do to very specific requirements reflecting local ways of working or an organization's existing systems. For example, here are examples of functional

Domain requirements

Domain requirements are derived from the application domain of the system rather than from the specific needs of system users. They may be new functional requirements in their own right, constrain existing functional requirements, or set out how particular computations must be carried out.

The problem with domain requirements is that software engineers may not understand the characteristics of the domain in which the system operates. They often cannot tell whether or not a domain requirement has been missed out or conflicts with other requirements.

http://www.SoftwareEngineering-9.com/Web/Requirements/DomainReq.html

requirements for the MHC-PMS system, used to maintain information about patients receiving treatment for mental health problems:

1. A user shall be able to search the appointments lists for all clinics.

2. The system shall generate each day, for each clinic, a list of patients who are expected to attend appointments that day.

3. Each staff member using the system shall be uniquely identified by his or her eight-digit employee number.

These functional user requirements define specific facilities to be provided by the system. These have been taken from the user requirements document and they show that functional requirements may be written at different levels of detail (contrast requirements 1 and 3).

Imprecision in the requirements specification is the cause of many software engineering problems. It is natural for a system developer to interpret an ambiguous requirement in a way that simplifies its implementation. Often, however, this is not what the customer wants. New requirements have to be established and changes made to the system. Of course, this delays system delivery and increases costs.

For example, the first example requirement for the MHC-PMS states that a user shall be able to search the appointments lists for all clinics. The rationale for this requirement is that patients with mental health problems are sometimes confused. They may have an appointment at one clinic but actually go to a different clinic. If they have an appointment, they will be recorded as having attended, irrespective of the clinic.

The medical staff member specifying this may expect 'search' to mean that, given a patient name, the system looks for that name in all appointments at all clinics. However, this is not explicit in the requirement. System developers may interpret the requirement in a different way and may implement a search so that the user has to choose a clinic then carry out the search. This obviously will involve more user input and so take longer.

In principle, the functional requirements specification of a system should be both complete and consistent. Completeness means that all services required by the user should be defined. Consistency means that requirements should not have contradictory definitions. In practice, for large, complex systems, it is practically impossible to achieve requirements consistency and completeness. One reason for this is that it is easy to make mistakes and omissions when writing specifications for complex systems. Another reason is that there are many stakeholders in a large system. A stakeholder is a person or role that is affected by the system in some way. Stakeholders have different—and often inconsistent—needs. These inconsistencies may not be obvious when the requirements are first specified, so inconsistent requirements are included in the specification. The problems may only emerge after deeper analysis or after the system has been delivered to the customer.

4.1.2   Non-functional requirements

Non-functional requirements, as the name suggests, are requirements that are not directly concerned with the specific services delivered by the system to its users. They may relate to emergent system properties such as reliability, response time, and store occupancy. Alternatively, they may define constraints on the system implementation such as the capabilities of I/O devices or the data representations used in interfaces with other systems.

Non-functional requirements, such as performance, security, or availability, usually specify or constrain characteristics of the system as a whole. Non-functional requirements are often more critical than individual functional requirements. System users can usually find ways to work around a system function that doesn't really meet their needs. However, failing to meet a non-functional requirement can mean that the whole system is unusable. For example, if an aircraft system does not meet its reliability requirements, it will not be certified as safe for operation; if an embedded control system fails to meet its performance requirements, the control functions will not operate correctly.

Although it is often possible to identify which system components implement specific functional requirements (e.g., there may be formatting components that implement reporting requirements), it is often more difficult to relate components to non-functional requirements. The implementation of these requirements may be diffused throughout the system. There are two reasons for this:

1. Non-functional requirements may affect the overall architecture of a system rather than the individual components. For example, to ensure that performance requirements are met, you may have to organize the system to minimize communications between components.

2. A single non-functional requirement, such as a security requirement, may generate a number of related functional requirements that define new system services that are required. In addition, it may also generate requirements that restrict existing requirements.

Non functional requirements arise through user needs, because of budget constraints, organizational policies, the need for interoperability with other software or

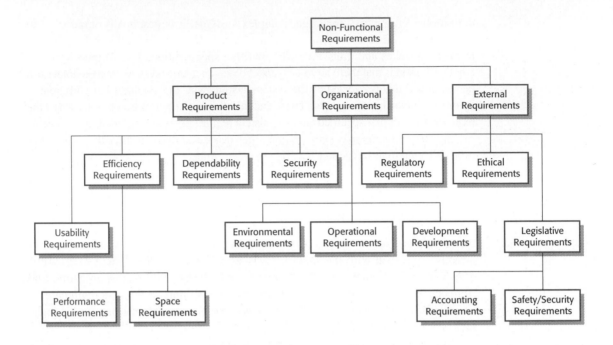

Figure 4.3 Types of non-functional requirement

hardware systems, or external factors such as safety regulations or privacy legisla-tion. Figure 4.3 is a classification of non-functional requirements. You can see from this diagram that the non-functional requirements may come from required charac-teristics of the software (product requirements), the organization developing the soft-ware (organizational requirements), or from external sources:

1. *Product requirements* These requirements specify or constrain the behavior of the software. Examples include performance requirements on how fast the system must execute and how much memory it requires, reliability requirements that set out the acceptable failure rate, security requirements, and usability requirements.

2. *Organizational requirements* These requirements are broad system requirements derived from policies and procedures in the customer's and developer's organiza-tion. Examples include operational process requirements that define how the sys-tem will be used, development process requirements that specify the programming language, the development environment or process standards to be used, and envi-ronmental requirements that specify the operating environment of the system.

3. *External requirements* This broad heading covers all requirements that are derived from factors external to the system and its development process. These may include regulatory requirements that set out what must be done for the sys-tem to be approved for use by a regulator, such as a central bank; legislative requirements that must be followed to ensure that the system operates within the law; and ethical requirements that ensure that the system will be acceptable to its users and the general public.

PRODUCT REQUIREMENT
The MHC-PMS shall be available to all clinics during normal working hours (Mon–Fri, 08.30–17.30). Downtime within normal working hours shall not exceed five seconds in any one day.

ORGANIZATIONAL REQUIREMENT
Users of the MHC-PMS system shall authenticate themselves using their health authority identity card.

EXTERNAL REQUIREMENT
The system shall implement patient privacy provisions as set out in HStan-03-2006-priv.

Figure 4.4 Examples of non-functional requirements in the MHC-PMS

Figure 4.4 shows examples of product, organizational, and external requirements taken from the MHC-PMS whose user requirements were introduced in Section 4.1.1. The product requirement is an availability requirement that defines when the system has to be available and the allowed down time each day. It says nothing about the functionality of MHC-PMS and clearly identifies a constraint that has to be considered by the system designers.

The organizational requirement specifies how users authenticate themselves to the system. The health authority that operates the system is moving to a standard authentication procedure for all software where, instead of users having a login name, they swipe their identity card through a reader to identify themselves. The external requirement is derived from the need for the system to conform to privacy legislation. Privacy is obviously a very important issue in healthcare systems and the requirement specifies that the system should be developed in accordance with a national privacy standard.

A common problem with non-functional requirements is that users or customers often propose these requirements as general goals, such as ease of use, the ability of the system to recover from failure, or rapid user response. Goals set out good intentions but cause problems for system developers as they leave scope for interpretation and subsequent dispute once the system is delivered. For example, the following system goal is typical of how a manager might express usability requirements:

The system should be easy to use by medical staff and should be organized in such a way that user errors are minimized.

I have rewritten this to show how the goal could be expressed as a 'testable' non-functional requirement. It is impossible to objectively verify the system goal, but in the description below you can at least include software instrumentation to count the errors made by users when they are testing the system.

Medical staff shall be able to use all the system functions after four hours of training. After this training, the average number of errors made by experienced users shall not exceed two per hour of system use.

Whenever possible, you should write non-functional requirements quantitatively so that they can be objectively tested. Figure 4.5 shows metrics that you can use to specify non-functional system properties. You can measure these characteristics

Property	Measure
Speed	Processed transactions/second User/event response time Screen refresh time
Size	Mbytes Number of ROM chips
Ease of use	Training time Number of help frames
Reliability	Mean time to failure Probability of unavailability Rate of failure occurrence Availability
Robustness	Time to restart after failure Percentage of events causing failure Probability of data corruption on failure
Portability	Percentage of target dependent statements Number of target systems

Figure 4.5 Metrics for specifying non-functional requirements

when the system is being tested to check whether or not the system has met its non-functional requirements.

In practice, customers for a system often find it difficult to translate their goals into measurable requirements. For some goals, such as maintainability, there are no metrics that can be used. In other cases, even when quantitative specification is possible, customers may not be able to relate their needs to these specifications. They don't understand what some number defining the required reliability (say) means in terms of their everyday experience with computer systems. Furthermore, the cost of objectively verifying measurable, non-functional requirements can be very high and the customers paying for the system may not think these costs are justified.

Non-functional requirements often conflict and interact with other functional or non-functional requirements. For example, the authentication requirement in Figure 4.4 obviously requires a card reader to be installed with each computer attached to the system. However, there may be another requirement that requests mobile access to the system from doctors' or nurses' laptops. These are not normally equipped with card readers so, in these circumstances, some alternative authentication method may have to be allowed.

It is difficult, in practice, to separate functional and non-functional requirements in the requirements document. If the non-functional requirements are stated separately from the functional requirements, the relationships between them may be hard to understand. However, you should explicitly highlight requirements that are clearly related to emergent system properties, such as performance or reliability. You can do this by putting them in a separate section of the requirements document or by distinguishing them, in some way, from other system requirements.

Requirements document standards

A number of large organizations, such as the U.S. Department of Defense and the IEEE, have defined standards for requirements documents. These are usually very generic but are nevertheless useful as a basis for developing more detailed organizational standards. The U.S. Institute of Electrical and Electronic Engineers (IEEE) is one of the best-known standards providers and they have developed a standard for the structure of requirements documents. This standard is most appropriate for systems such as military command and control systems that have a long lifetime and are usually developed by a group of organizations.

http://www.SoftwareEngineering-9.com/Web/Requirements/IEEE-standard.html

Non-functional requirements such as reliability, safety, and confidentiality requirements are particularly important for critical systems. I cover these requirements in Chapter 12, where I describe specific techniques for specifying dependability and security requirements.

4.2 The software requirements document

The software requirements document (sometimes called the software requirements specification or SRS) is an official statement of what the system developers should implement. It should include both the user requirements for a system and a detailed specification of the system requirements. Sometimes, the user and system requirements are integrated into a single description. In other cases, the user requirements are defined in an introduction to the system requirements specification. If there are a large number of requirements, the detailed system requirements may be presented in a separate document.

Requirements documents are essential when an outside contractor is developing the software system. However, agile development methods argue that requirements change so rapidly that a requirements document is out of date as soon as it is written, so the effort is largely wasted. Rather than a formal document, approaches such as Extreme Programming (Beck, 1999) collect user requirements incrementally and write these on cards as user stories. The user then prioritizes requirements for implementation in the next increment of the system.

For business systems where requirements are unstable, I think that this approach is a good one. However, I think that it is still useful to write a short supporting document that defines the business and dependability requirements for the system; it is easy to forget the requirements that apply to the system as a whole when focusing on the functional requirements for the next system release.

The requirements document has a diverse set of users, ranging from the senior management of the organization that is paying for the system to the engineers responsible for developing the software. Figure 4.6, taken from my book with Gerald Kotonya on requirements engineering (Kotonya and Sommerville, 1998) shows possible users of the document and how they use it.

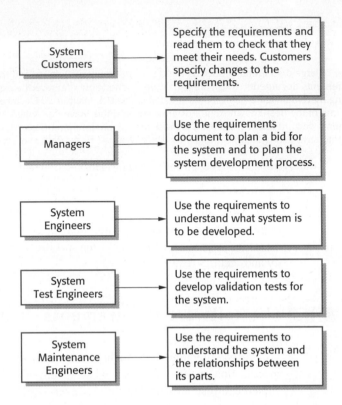

Figure 4.6 Users of a requirements document

The diversity of possible users means that the requirements document has to be a compromise between communicating the requirements to customers, defining the requirements in precise detail for developers and testers, and including information about possible system evolution. Information on anticipated changes can help system designers avoid restrictive design decisions and help system maintenance engineers who have to adapt the system to new requirements.

The level of detail that you should include in a requirements document depends on the type of system that is being developed and the development process used. Critical systems need to have detailed requirements because safety and security have to be analyzed in detail. When the system is to be developed by a separate company (e.g., through outsourcing), the system specifications need to be detailed and precise. If an in-house, iterative development process is used, the requirements document can be much less detailed and any ambiguities can be resolved during development of the system.

Figure 4.7 shows one possible organization for a requirements document that is based on an IEEE standard for requirements documents (IEEE, 1998). This standard is a generic standard that can be adapted to specific uses. In this case, I have extended the standard to include information about predicted system evolution. This information helps the maintainers of the system and allows designers to include support for future system features.

Naturally, the information that is included in a requirements document depends on the type of software being developed and the approach to development that is to be used. If an evolutionary approach is adopted for a software product (say), the

Chapter	Description
Preface	This should define the expected readership of the document and describe its version history, including a rationale for the creation of a new version and a summary of the changes made in each version.
Introduction	This should describe the need for the system. It should briefly describe the system's functions and explain how it will work with other systems. It should also describe how the system fits into the overall business or strategic objectives of the organization commissioning the software.
Glossary	This should define the technical terms used in the document. You should not make assumptions about the experience or expertise of the reader.
User requirements definition	Here, you describe the services provided for the user. The non-functional system requirements should also be described in this section. This description may use natural language, diagrams, or other notations that are understandable to customers. Product and process standards that must be followed should be specified.
System architecture	This chapter should present a high-level overview of the anticipated system architecture, showing the distribution of functions across system modules. Architectural components that are reused should be highlighted.
System requirements specification	This should describe the functional and non-functional requirements in more detail. If necessary, further detail may also be added to the non-functional requirements. Interfaces to other systems may be defined.
System models	This might include graphical system models showing the relationships between the system components, the system, and its environment. Examples of possible models are object models, data-flow models, or semantic data models.
System evolution	This should describe the fundamental assumptions on which the system is based, and any anticipated changes due to hardware evolution, changing user needs, and so on. This section is useful for system designers as it may help them avoid design decisions that would constrain likely future changes to the system.
Appendices	These should provide detailed, specific information that is related to the application being developed; for example, hardware and database descriptions. Hardware requirements define the minimal and optimal configurations for the system. Database requirements define the logical organization of the data used by the system and the relationships between data.
Index	Several indexes to the document may be included. As well as a normal alphabetic index, there may be an index of diagrams, an index of functions, and so on.

Figure 4.7 The structure of a requirements document

requirements document will leave out many of detailed chapters suggested above. The focus will be on defining the user requirements and high-level, non-functional system requirements. In this case, the designers and programmers use their judgment to decide how to meet the outline user requirements for the system.

However, when the software is part of a large system project that includes interacting hardware and software systems, it is usually necessary to define the requirements

Problems with using natural language for requirements specification

The flexibility of natural language, which is so useful for specification, often causes problems. There is scope for writing unclear requirements, and readers (the designers) may misinterpret requirements because they have a different background to the user. It is easy to amalgamate several requirements into a single sentence and structuring natural language requirements can be difficult.

http://www.SoftwareEngineering-9.com/Web/Requirements/NL-problems.html

to a fine level of detail. This means that the requirements documents are likely to be very long and should include most if not all of the chapters shown in Figure 4.7. For long documents, it is particularly important to include a comprehensive table of contents and document index so that readers can find the information that they need.

4.3 Requirements specification

Requirements specification is the process of writing down the user and system requirements in a requirements document. Ideally, the user and system requirements should be clear, unambiguous, easy to understand, complete, and consistent. In practice, this is difficult to achieve as stakeholders interpret the requirements in different ways and there are often inherent conflicts and inconsistencies in the requirements.

The user requirements for a system should describe the functional and non-functional requirements so that they are understandable by system users who don't have detailed technical knowledge. Ideally, they should specify only the external behavior of the system. The requirements document should not include details of the system architecture or design. Consequently, if you are writing user requirements, you should not use software jargon, structured notations, or formal notations. You should write user requirements in natural language, with simple tables, forms, and intuitive diagrams.

System requirements are expanded versions of the user requirements that are used by software engineers as the starting point for the system design. They add detail and explain how the user requirements should be provided by the system. They may be used as part of the contract for the implementation of the system and should therefore be a complete and detailed specification of the whole system.

Ideally, the system requirements should simply describe the external behavior of the system and its operational constraints. They should not be concerned with how the system should be designed or implemented. However, at the level of detail required to completely specify a complex software system, it is practically impossible to exclude all design information. There are several reasons for this:

1. You may have to design an initial architecture of the system to help structure the requirements specification. The system requirements are organized according to

Notation	Description
Natural language sentences	The requirements are written using numbered sentences in natural language. Each sentence should express one requirement.
Structured natural language	The requirements are written in natural language on a standard form or template. Each field provides information about an aspect of the requirement.
Design description languages	This approach uses a language like a programming language, but with more abstract features to specify the requirements by defining an operational model of the system. This approach is now rarely used although it can be useful for interface specifications.
Graphical notations	Graphical models, supplemented by text annotations, are used to define the functional requirements for the system; UML use case and sequence diagrams are commonly used.
Mathematical specifications	These notations are based on mathematical concepts such as finite-state machines or sets. Although these unambiguous specifications can reduce the ambiguity in a requirements document, most customers don't understand a formal specification. They cannot check that it represents what they want and are reluctant to accept it as a system contract.

Figure 4.8 Ways of writing a system requirements specification

the different sub-systems that make up the system. As I discuss in Chapters 6 and 18, this architectural definition is essential if you want to reuse software components when implementing the system.

2. In most cases, systems must interoperate with existing systems, which constrain the design and impose requirements on the new system.

3. The use of a specific architecture to satisfy non-functional requirements (such as N-version programming to achieve reliability, discussed in Chapter 13) may be necessary. An external regulator who needs to certify that the system is safe may specify that an already certified architectural design be used.

User requirements are almost always written in natural language supplemented by appropriate diagrams and tables in the requirements document. System requirements may also be written in natural language but other notations based on forms, graphical system models, or mathematical system models can also be used. Figure 4.8 summarizes the possible notations that could be used for writing system requirements.

Graphical models are most useful when you need to show how a state changes or when you need to describe a sequence of actions. UML sequence charts and state charts, described in Chapter 5, show the sequence of actions that occur in response to a certain message or event. Formal mathematical specifications are sometimes used to describe the requirements for safety- or security-critical systems, but are rarely used in other circumstances. I explain this approach to writing specifications in Chapter 12.

3.2 The system shall measure the blood sugar and deliver insulin, if required, every 10 minutes. (*Changes in blood sugar are relatively slow so more frequent measurement is unnecessary; less frequent measurement could lead to unnecessarily high sugar levels.*)

3.6 The system shall run a self-test routine every minute with the conditions to be tested and the associated actions defined in Table 1. (*A self-test routine can discover hardware and software problems and alert the user to the fact the normal operation may be impossible.*)

Figure 4.9
Example requirements for the insulin pump software system

4.3.1 Natural language specification

Natural language has been used to write requirements for software since the beginning of software engineering. It is expressive, intuitive, and universal. It is also potentially vague, ambiguous, and its meaning depends on the background of the reader. As a result, there have been many proposals for alternative ways to write requirements. However, none of these have been widely adopted and natural language will continue to be the most widely used way of specifying system and software requirements.

To minimize misunderstandings when writing natural language requirements, I recommend that you follow some simple guidelines:

1. Invent a standard format and ensure that all requirement definitions adhere to that format. Standardizing the format makes omissions less likely and requirements easier to check. The format I use expresses the requirement in a single sentence. I associate a statement of rationale with each user requirement to explain why the requirement has been proposed. The rationale may also include information on who proposed the requirement (the requirement source) so that you know whom to consult if the requirement has to be changed.

2. Use language consistently to distinguish between mandatory and desirable requirements. Mandatory requirements are requirements that the system must support and are usually written using 'shall'. Desirable requirements are not essential and are written using 'should'.

3. Use text highlighting (bold, italic, or color) to pick out key parts of the requirement.

4. Do not assume that readers understand technical software engineering language. It is easy for words like 'architecture' and 'module' to be misunderstood. You should, therefore, avoid the use of jargon, abbreviations, and acronyms.

5. Whenever possible, you should try to associate a rationale with each user requirement. The rationale should explain why the requirement has been included. It is particularly useful when requirements are changed as it may help decide what changes would be undesirable.

Figure 4.9 illustrates how these guidelines may be used. It includes two requirements for the embedded software for the automated insulin pump, introduced in Chapter 1. You can download the complete insulin pump requirements specification from the book's web pages.

Insulin Pump/Control Software/SRS/3.3.2

Function	Compute insulin dose: Safe sugar level.
Description	Computes the dose of insulin to be delivered when the current measured sugar level is in the safe zone between 3 and 7 units.
Inputs	Current sugar reading (r2), the previous two readings (r0 and r1).
Source	Current sugar reading from sensor. Other readings from memory.
Outputs	CompDose—the dose in insulin to be delivered.
Destination	Main control loop.
Action	CompDose is zero if the sugar level is stable or falling or if the level is increasing but the rate of increase is decreasing. If the level is increasing and the rate of increase is increasing, then CompDose is computed by dividing the difference between the current sugar level and the previous level by 4 and rounding the result. If the result, is rounded to zero then CompDose is set to the minimum dose that can be delivered.
Requirements	Two previous readings so that the rate of change of sugar level can be computed.
Pre-condition	The insulin reservoir contains at least the maximum allowed single dose of insulin.
Post-condition	r0 is replaced by r1 then r1 is replaced by r2.
Side effects	None.

Figure 4.10
A structured specification of a requirement for an insulin pump

4.3.2 Structured specifications

Structured natural language is a way of writing system requirements where the freedom of the requirements writer is limited and all requirements are written in a standard way. This approach maintains most of the expressiveness and understandability of natural language but ensures that some uniformity is imposed on the specification. Structured language notations use templates to specify system requirements. The specification may use programming language constructs to show alternatives and iteration, and may highlight key elements using shading or different fonts.

The Robertsons (Robertson and Robertson, 1999), in their book on the VOLERE requirements engineering method, recommend that user requirements be initially written on cards, one requirement per card. They suggest a number of fields on each card, such as the requirements rationale, the dependencies on other requirements, the source of the requirements, supporting materials, and so on. This is similar to the approach used in the example of a structured specification shown in Figure 4.10.

To use a structured approach to specifying system requirements, you define one or more standard templates for requirements and represent these templates as structured forms. The specification may be structured around the objects manipulated by the system, the functions performed by the system, or the events processed by the system. An example of a form-based specification, in this case, one that defines how to calculate the dose of insulin to be delivered when the blood sugar is within a safe band, is shown in Figure 4.10.

Condition	Action
Sugar level falling (r2 < r1)	CompDose = 0
Sugar level stable (r2 = r1)	CompDose = 0
Sugar level increasing and rate of increase decreasing ((r2 − r1) < (r1 − r0))	CompDose = 0
Sugar level increasing and rate of increase stable or increasing ((r2 − r1) ≥ (r1 − r0))	CompDose = round ((r2 − r1)/4) If rounded result = 0 then CompDose = MinimumDose

Figure 4.11 Tabular specification of computation for an insulin pump

When a standard form is used for specifying functional requirements, the following information should be included:

1. A description of the function or entity being specified.

2. A description of its inputs and where these come from.

3. A description of its outputs and where these go to.

4. Information about the information that is needed for the computation or other entities in the system that are used (the 'requires' part).

5. A description of the action to be taken.

6. If a functional approach is used, a pre-condition setting out what must be true before the function is called, and a post-condition specifying what is true after the function is called.

7. A description of the side effects (if any) of the operation.

Using structured specifications removes some of the problems of natural language specification. Variability in the specification is reduced and requirements are organized more effectively. However, it is still sometimes difficult to write requirements in a clear and unambiguous way, particularly when complex computations (e.g., how to calculate the insulin dose) are to be specified.

To address this problem, you can add extra information to natural language requirements, for example, by using tables or graphical models of the system. These can show how computations proceed, how the system state changes, how users interact with the system, and how sequences of actions are performed.

Tables are particularly useful when there are a number of possible alternative situations and you need to describe the actions to be taken for each of these. The insulin pump bases its computations of the insulin requirement on the rate of change of blood sugar levels. The rates of change are computed using the current and previous readings. Figure 4.11 is a tabular description of how the rate of change of blood sugar is used to calculate the amount of insulin to be delivered.

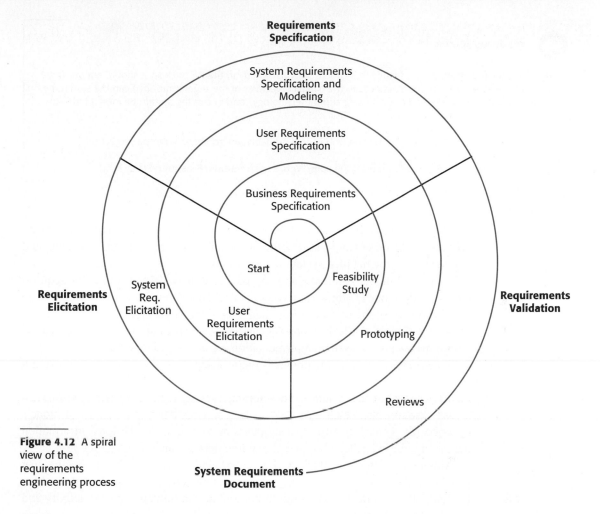

Figure 4.12 A spiral view of the requirements engineering process

4.4 Requirements engineering processes

As I discussed in Chapter 2, requirements engineering processes may include four high-level activities. These focus on assessing if the system is useful to the business (feasibility study), discovering requirements (elicitation and analysis), converting these requirements into some standard form (specification), and checking that the requirements actually define the system that the customer wants (validation). I have shown these as sequential processes in Figure 2.6. However, in practice, requirements engineering is an iterative process in which the activities are interleaved.

Figure 4.12 shows this interleaving. The activities are organized as an iterative process around a spiral, with the output being a system requirements document. The amount of time and effort devoted to each activity in each iteration depends on the stage of the overall process and the type of system being developed. Early in the process, most effort will be spent on understanding high-level business and

Feasibility studies

A feasibility study is a short, focused study that should take place early in the RE process. It should answer three key questions: a) does the system contribute to the overall objectives of the organization? b) can the system be implemented within schedule and budget using current technology? and c) can the system be integrated with other systems that are used?

If the answer to any of these questions is no, you should probably not go ahead with the project.

http://www.SoftwareEngineering-9.com/Web/Requirements/FeasibilityStudy.html

non-functional requirements, and the user requirements for the system. Later in the process, in the outer rings of the spiral, more effort will be devoted to eliciting and understanding the detailed system requirements.

This spiral model accommodates approaches to development where the requirements are developed to different levels of detail. The number of iterations around the spiral can vary so the spiral can be exited after some or all of the user requirements have been elicited. Agile development can be used instead of prototyping so that the requirements and the system implementation are developed together.

Some people consider requirements engineering to be the process of applying a structured analysis method, such as object-oriented analysis (Larman, 2002). This involves analyzing the system and developing a set of graphical system models, such as use case models, which then serve as a system specification. The set of models describes the behavior of the system and is annotated with additional information describing, for example, the system's required performance or reliability.

Although structured methods have a role to play in the requirements engineering process, there is much more to requirements engineering than is covered by these methods. Requirements elicitation, in particular, is a human-centered activity and people dislike the constraints imposed on it by rigid system models.

In virtually all systems, requirements change. The people involved develop a better understanding of what they want the software to do; the organization buying the system changes; modifications are made to the system's hardware, software, and organizational environment. The process of managing these changing requirements is called requirements management, which I cover in Section 4.7.

4.5 Requirements elicitation and analysis

After an initial feasibility study, the next stage of the requirements engineering process is requirements elicitation and analysis. In this activity, software engineers work with customers and system end-users to find out about the application domain, what services the system should provide, the required performance of the system, hardware constraints, and so on.

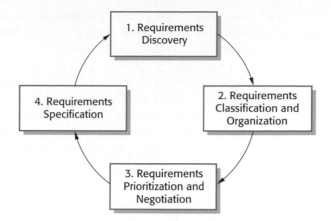

Figure 4.13 The requirements elicitation and analysis process

Requirements elicitation and analysis may involve a variety of different kinds of people in an organization. A system stakeholder is anyone who should have some direct or indirect influence on the system requirements. Stakeholders include end-users who will interact with the system and anyone else in an organization who will be affected by it. Other system stakeholders might be engineers who are developing or maintaining other related systems, business managers, domain experts, and trade union representatives.

A process model of the elicitation and analysis process is shown in Figure 4.13. Each organization will have its own version or instantiation of this general model depending on local factors such as the expertise of the staff, the type of system being developed, the standards used, etc.

The process activities are:

1. *Requirements discovery* This is the process of interacting with stakeholders of the system to discover their requirements. Domain requirements from stakeholders and documentation are also discovered during this activity. There are several complementary techniques that can be used for requirements discovery, which I discuss later in this section.

2. *Requirements classification and organization* This activity takes the unstructured collection of requirements, groups related requirements, and organizes them into coherent clusters. The most common way of grouping requirements is to use a model of the system architecture to identify sub-systems and to associate requirements with each sub-system. In practice, requirements engineering and architectural design cannot be completely separate activities.

3. *Requirements prioritization and negotiation* Inevitably, when multiple stakeholders are involved, requirements will conflict. This activity is concerned with prioritizing requirements and finding and resolving requirements conflicts through negotiation. Usually, stakeholders have to meet to resolve differences and agree on compromise requirements.

4. *Requirements specification* The requirements are documented and input into the next round of the spiral. Formal or informal requirements documents may be produced, as discussed in Section 4.3.

Figure 4.13 shows that requirements elicitation and analysis is an iterative process with continual feedback from each activity to other activities. The process cycle starts with requirements discovery and ends with the requirements documentation. The analyst's understanding of the requirements improves with each round of the cycle. The cycle ends when the requirements document is complete.

Eliciting and understanding requirements from system stakeholders is a difficult process for several reasons:

1. Stakeholders often don't know what they want from a computer system except in the most general terms; they may find it difficult to articulate what they want the system to do; they may make unrealistic demands because they don't know what is and isn't feasible.

2. Stakeholders in a system naturally express requirements in their own terms and with implicit knowledge of their own work. Requirements engineers, without experience in the customer's domain, may not understand these requirements.

3. Different stakeholders have different requirements and they may express these in different ways. Requirements engineers have to discover all potential sources of requirements and discover commonalities and conflict.

4. Political factors may influence the requirements of a system. Managers may demand specific system requirements because these will allow them to increase their influence in the organization.

5. The economic and business environment in which the analysis takes place is dynamic. It inevitably changes during the analysis process. The importance of particular requirements may change. New requirements may emerge from new stakeholders who were not originally consulted.

Inevitably, different stakeholders have different views on the importance and priority of requirements and, sometimes, these views are conflicting. During the process, you should organize regular stakeholder negotiations so that compromises can be reached. It is impossible to completely satisfy every stakeholder but if some stakeholders feel that their views have not been properly considered then they may deliberately attempt to undermine the RE process.

At the requirements specification stage, the requirements that have been elicited so far are documented in such a way that they can be used to help with requirements discovery. At this stage, an early version of the system requirements document may be produced with missing sections and incomplete requirements. Alternatively, the requirements may be documented in a completely different way (e.g., in a spreadsheet or on cards). Writing requirements on cards can be very effective as these are easy for stakeholders to handle, change, and organize.

Viewpoints

A viewpoint is way of collecting and organizing a set of requirements from a group of stakeholders who have something in common. Each viewpoint therefore includes a set of system requirements. Viewpoints might come from end-users, managers, etc. They help identify the people who can provide information about their requirements and structure the requirements for analysis.

http://www.SoftwareEngineering-9.com/Web/Requirements/Viewpoints.html

4.5.1 Requirements discovery

Requirements discovery (sometime called requirements elicitation) is the process of gathering information about the required system and existing systems, and distilling the user and system requirements from this information. Sources of information during the requirements discovery phase include documentation, system stakeholders, and specifications of similar systems. You interact with stakeholders through interviews and observation and you may use scenarios and prototypes to help stakeholders understand what the system will be like.

Stakeholders range from end-users of a system through managers to external stakeholders such as regulators, who certify the acceptability of the system. For example, system stakeholders for the mental healthcare patient information system include:

1. Patients whose information is recorded in the system.

2. Doctors who are responsible for assessing and treating patients.

3. Nurses who coordinate the consultations with doctors and administer some treatments.

4. Medical receptionists who manage patients' appointments.

5. IT staff who are responsible for installing and maintaining the system.

6. A medical ethics manager who must ensure that the system meets current ethical guidelines for patient care.

7. Healthcare managers who obtain management information from the system.

8. Medical records staff who are responsible for ensuring that system information can be maintained and preserved, and that record keeping procedures have been properly implemented.

In addition to system stakeholders, we have already seen that requirements may also come from the application domain and from other systems that interact with the system being specified. All of these must be considered during the requirements elicitation process.

These different requirements sources (stakeholders, domain, systems) can all be represented as system viewpoints with each viewpoint showing a subset of the requirements for the system. Different viewpoints on a problem see the problem in different ways. However, their perspectives are not completely independent but usually overlap so that they have common requirements. You can use these viewpoints to structure both the discovery and the documentation of the system requirements.

4.5.2   Interviewing

Formal or informal interviews with system stakeholders are part of most requirements engineering processes. In these interviews, the requirements engineering team puts questions to stakeholders about the system that they currently use and the system to be developed. Requirements are derived from the answers to these questions. Interviews may be of two types:

1.   Closed interviews, where the stakeholder answers a pre-defined set of questions.

2.   Open interviews, in which there is no pre-defined agenda. The requirements engineering team explores a range of issues with system stakeholders and hence develop a better understanding of their needs.

In practice, interviews with stakeholders are normally a mixture of both of these. You may have to obtain the answer to certain questions but these usually lead on to other issues that are discussed in a less structured way. Completely open-ended discussions rarely work well. You usually have to ask some questions to get started and to keep the interview focused on the system to be developed.

Interviews are good for getting an overall understanding of what stakeholders do, how they might interact with the new system, and the difficulties that they face with current systems. People like talking about their work so are usually happy to get involved in interviews. However, interviews are not so helpful in understanding the requirements from the application domain.

It can be difficult to elicit domain knowledge through interviews for two reasons:

1.   All application specialists use terminology and jargon that are specific to a domain. It is impossible for them to discuss domain requirements without using this terminology. They normally use terminology in a precise and subtle way that is easy for requirements engineers to misunderstand.

2.   Some domain knowledge is so familiar to stakeholders that they either find it difficult to explain or they think it is so fundamental that it isn't worth mentioning. For example, for a librarian, it goes without saying that all acquisitions are catalogued before they are added to the library. However, this may not be obvious to the interviewer, and so it isn't taken into account in the requirements.

Interviews are also not an effective technique for eliciting knowledge about organizational requirements and constraints because there are subtle power relationships between the different people in the organization. Published organizational structures rarely match the reality of decision making in an organization but interviewees may not wish to reveal the actual rather than the theoretical structure to a stranger. In general, most people are generally reluctant to discuss political and organizational issues that may affect the requirements.

Effective interviewers have two characteristics:

1. They are open-minded, avoid pre-conceived ideas about the requirements, and are willing to listen to stakeholders. If the stakeholder comes up with surprising requirements, then they are willing to change their mind about the system.

2. They prompt the interviewee to get discussions going using a springboard question, a requirements proposal, or by working together on a prototype system. Saying to people 'tell me what you want' is unlikely to result in useful information. They find it much easier to talk in a defined context rather than in general terms.

Information from interviews supplements other information about the system from documentation describing business processes or existing systems, user observations, etc. Sometimes, apart from the information in the system documents, the interview information may be the only source of information about the system requirements. However, interviewing on its own is liable to miss essential information and so it should be used in conjunction with other requirements elicitation techniques.

4.5.3 Scenarios

People usually find it easier to relate to real-life examples rather than abstract descriptions. They can understand and criticize a scenario of how they might interact with a software system. Requirements engineers can use the information gained from this discussion to formulate the actual system requirements.

Scenarios can be particularly useful for adding detail to an outline requirements description. They are descriptions of example interaction sessions. Each scenario usually covers one or a small number of possible interactions. Different forms of scenarios are developed and they provide different types of information at different levels of detail about the system. The stories used in extreme programming, discussed in Chapter 3, are a type of requirements scenario.

A scenario starts with an outline of the interaction. During the elicitation process, details are added to this to create a complete description of that interaction. At its most general, a scenario may include:

1. A description of what the system and users expects when the scenario starts.

2. A description of the normal flow of events in the scenario.

3. A description of what can go wrong and how this is handled.

4. Information about other activities that might be going on at the same time.

5. A description of the system state when the scenario finishes.

INITIAL ASSUMPTION:
The patient has seen a medical receptionist who has created a record in the system and collected the patient's personal information (name, address, age, etc.). A nurse is logged on to the system and is collecting medical history.

NORMAL:
The nurse searches for the patient by family name. If there is more than one patient with the same surname, the given name (first name in English) and date of birth are used to identify the patient.

The nurse chooses the menu option to add medical history.

The nurse then follows a series of prompts from the system to enter information about consultations elsewhere on mental health problems (free text input), existing medical conditions (nurse selects conditions from menu), medication currently taken (selected from menu), allergies (free text), and home life (form).

WHAT CAN GO WRONG:
The patient's record does not exist or cannot be found. The nurse should create a new record and record personal information.

Patient conditions or medication are not entered in the menu. The nurse should choose the 'other' option and enter free text describing the condition/medication.

Patient cannot/will not provide information on medical history. The nurse should enter free text recording the patient's inability/unwillingness to provide information. The system should print the standard exclusion form stating that the lack of information may mean that treatment will be limited or delayed. This should be signed and handed to the patient.

OTHER ACTIVITIES:
Record may be consulted but not edited by other staff while information is being entered.

SYSTEM STATE ON COMPLETION:
User is logged on. The patient record including medical history is entered in the database, a record is added to the system log showing the start and end time of the session and the nurse involved.

Figure 4.14 Scenario for collecting medical history in MHC-PMS

Scenario-based elicitation involves working with stakeholders to identify scenarios and to capture details to be included in these scenarios. Scenarios may be written as text, supplemented by diagrams, screen shots, etc. Alternatively, a more structured approach such as event scenarios or use cases may be used.

As an example of a simple text scenario, consider how the MHC-PMS may be used to enter data for a new patient (Figure 4.14). When a new patient attends a clinic, a new record is created by a medical receptionist and personal information (name, age, etc.) is added to it. A nurse then interviews the patient and collects medical history. The patient then has an initial consultation with a doctor who makes a diagnosis and, if appropriate, recommends a course of treatment. The scenario shows what happens when medical history is collected.

4.5.4   Use cases

Use cases are a requirements discovery technique that were first introduced in the Objectory method (Jacobson et al., 1993). They have now become a fundamental feature of the unified modeling language. In their simplest form, a use case identifies

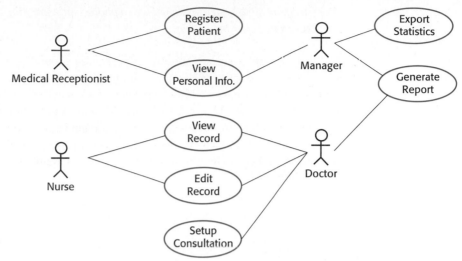

Figure 4.15 Use cases for the MHC-PMS

the actors involved in an interaction and names the type of interaction. This is then supplemented by additional information describing the interaction with the system. The additional information may be a textual description or one or more graphical models such as UML sequence or state charts.

Use cases are documented using a high-level use case diagram. The set of use cases represents all of the possible interactions that will be described in the system requirements. Actors in the process, who may be human or other systems, are represented as stick figures. Each class of interaction is represented as a named ellipse. Lines link the actors with the interaction. Optionally, arrowheads may be added to lines to show how the interaction is initiated. This is illustrated in Figure 4.15, which shows some of the use cases for the patient information system.

There is no hard and fast distinction between scenarios and use cases. Some people consider that each use case is a single scenario; others, as suggested by Stevens and Pooley (2006), encapsulate a set of scenarios in a single use case. Each scenario is a single thread through the use case. Therefore, there would be a scenario for the normal interaction plus scenarios for each possible exception. You can, in practice, use them in either way.

Use cases identify the individual interactions between the system and its users or other systems. Each use case should be documented with a textual description. These can then be linked to other models in the UML that will develop the scenario in more detail. For example, a brief description of the Setup Consultation use case from Figure 4.15 might be:

> *Setup consultation allows two or more doctors, working in different offices, to view the same record at the same time. One doctor initiates the consultation by choosing the people involved from a drop-down menu of doctors who are online. The patient record is then displayed on their screens but only the initiating doctor can edit the record. In addition, a text chat window is created to help*

coordinate actions. It is assumed that a phone conference for voice communication will be separately set up.

Scenarios and use cases are effective techniques for eliciting requirements from stakeholders who interact directly with the system. Each type of interaction can be represented as a use case. However, because they focus on interactions with the system, they are not as effective for eliciting constraints or high-level business and nonfunctional requirements or for discovering domain requirements.

The UML is a de facto standard for object-oriented modeling, so use cases and use case–based elicitation are now widely used for requirements elicitation. I discuss use cases further in Chapter 5 and show how they are used alongside other system models to document a system design.

4.5.5 Ethnography

Software systems do not exist in isolation. They are used in a social and organizational context and software system requirements may be derived or constrained by that context. Satisfying these social and organizational requirements is often critical for the success of the system. One reason why many software systems are delivered but never used is that their requirements do not take proper account of how the social and organizational context affects the practical operation of the system.

Ethnography is an observational technique that can be used to understand operational processes and help derive support requirements for these processes. An analyst immerses himself or herself in the working environment where the system will be used. The day-to-day work is observed and notes made of the actual tasks in which participants are involved. The value of ethnography is that it helps discover implicit system requirements that reflect the actual ways that people work, rather than the formal processes defined by the organization.

People often find it very difficult to articulate details of their work because it is second nature to them. They understand their own work but may not understand its relationship to other work in the organization. Social and organizational factors that affect the work, but which are not obvious to individuals, may only become clear when noticed by an unbiased observer. For example, a work group may self-organize so that members know of each other's work and can cover for each other if someone is absent. This may not be mentioned during an interview as the group might not see it as an integral part of their work.

Suchman (1987) pioneered the use of ethnography to study office work. She found that the actual work practices were far richer, more complex, and more dynamic than the simple models assumed by office automation systems. The difference between the assumed and the actual work was the most important reason why these office systems had no significant effect on productivity. Crabtree (2003) discusses a wide range of studies since then and describes, in general, the use of ethnography in systems design. In my own research, I have investigated methods of

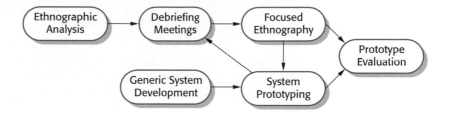

Figure 4.16
Ethnography and
prototyping for
requirements
analysis

integrating ethnography into the software engineering process by linking it with requirements engineering methods (Viller and Sommerville, 1999; Viller and Sommerville, 2000) and documenting patterns of interaction in cooperative systems (Martin et al., 2001; Martin et al., 2002; Martin and Sommerville, 2004).

Ethnography is particularly effective for discovering two types of requirements:

1. Requirements that are derived from the way in which people actually work, rather than the way in which process definitions say they ought to work. For example, air traffic controllers may switch off a conflict alert system that detects aircraft with intersecting flight paths, even though normal control procedures specify that it should be used. They deliberately put the aircraft on conflicting paths for a short time to help manage the airspace. Their control strategy is designed to ensure that these aircrafts are moved apart before problems occur and they find that the conflict alert alarm distracts them from their work.

2. Requirements that are derived from cooperation and awareness of other people's activities. For example, air traffic controllers may use an awareness of other controllers' work to predict the number of aircrafts that will be entering their control sector. They then modify their control strategies depending on that predicted workload. Therefore, an automated ATC system should allow controllers in a sector to have some visibility of the work in adjacent sectors.

Ethnography can be combined with prototyping (Figure 4.16). The ethnography informs the development of the prototype so that fewer prototype refinement cycles are required. Furthermore, the prototyping focuses the ethnography by identifying problems and questions that can then be discussed with the ethnographer. He or she should then look for the answers to these questions during the next phase of the system study (Sommerville et al., 1993).

Ethnographic studies can reveal critical process details that are often missed by other requirements elicitation techniques. However, because of its focus on the end-user, this approach is not always appropriate for discovering organizational or domain requirements. They cannot always identify new features that should be added to a system. Ethnography is not, therefore, a complete approach to elicitation on its own and it should be used to complement other approaches, such as use case analysis.

Requirements reviews

A requirements review is a process where a group of people from the system customer and the system developer read the requirements document in detail and check for errors, anomalies, and inconsistencies. Once these have been detected and recorded, it is then up to the customer and the developer to negotiate how the identified problems should be solved.

http://www.SoftwareEngineering-9.com/Web/Requirements/Reviews.html

4.6 Requirements validation

Requirements validation is the process of checking that requirements actually define the system that the customer really wants. It overlaps with analysis as it is concerned with finding problems with the requirements. Requirements validation is important because errors in a requirements document can lead to extensive rework costs when these problems are discovered during development or after the system is in service.

The cost of fixing a requirements problem by making a system change is usually much greater than repairing design or coding errors. The reason for this is that a change to the requirements usually means that the system design and implementation must also be changed. Furthermore the system must then be re-tested.

During the requirements validation process, different types of checks should be carried out on the requirements in the requirements document. These checks include:

1. *Validity checks* A user may think that a system is needed to perform certain functions. However, further thought and analysis may identify additional or different functions that are required. Systems have diverse stakeholders with different needs and any set of requirements is inevitably a compromise across the stakeholder community.

2. *Consistency checks* Requirements in the document should not conflict. That is, there should not be contradictory constraints or different descriptions of the same system function.

3. *Completeness checks* The requirements document should include requirements that define all functions and the constraints intended by the system user.

4. *Realism checks* Using knowledge of existing technology, the requirements should be checked to ensure that they can actually be implemented. These checks should also take account of the budget and schedule for the system development.

5. *Verifiability* To reduce the potential for dispute between customer and contractor, system requirements should always be written so that they are verifiable. This means that you should be able to write a set of tests that can demonstrate that the delivered system meets each specified requirement.

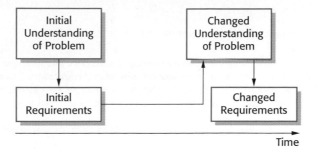

Figure 4.17
Requirements
evolution

There are a number of requirements validation techniques that can be used individually or in conjunction with one another:

1. *Requirements reviews* The requirements are analyzed systematically by a team of reviewers who check for errors and inconsistencies.

2. *Prototyping* In this approach to validation, an executable model of the system in question is demonstrated to end-users and customers. They can experiment with this model to see if it meets their real needs.

3. *Test-case generation* Requirements should be testable. If the tests for the requirements are devised as part of the validation process, this often reveals requirements problems. If a test is difficult or impossible to design, this usually means that the requirements will be difficult to implement and should be reconsidered. Developing tests from the user requirements before any code is written is an integral part of extreme programming.

You should not underestimate the problems involved in requirements validation. Ultimately, it is difficult to show that a set of requirements does in fact meet a user's needs. Users need to picture the system in operation and imagine how that system would fit into their work. It is hard even for skilled computer professionals to perform this type of abstract analysis and harder still for system users. As a result, you rarely find all requirements problems during the requirements validation process. It is inevitable that there will be further requirements changes to correct omissions and misunderstandings after the requirements document has been agreed upon.

4.7 Requirements management

The requirements for large software systems are always changing. One reason for this is that these systems are usually developed to address 'wicked' problems—problems that cannot be completely defined. Because the problem cannot be fully defined, the software requirements are bound to be incomplete. During the software process, the stakeholders' understanding of the problem is constantly changing (Figure 4.17). The system requirements must then also evolve to reflect this changed problem view.

Enduring and volatile requirements

Some requirements are more susceptible to change than others. Enduring requirements are the requirements that are associated with the core, slow-to-change activities of an organization. Enduring requirements are associated with fundamental work activities. Volatile requirements are more likely to change. They are usually associated with supporting activities that reflect how the organization does its work rather than the work itself.

http://www.SoftwareEngineering-9.com/Web/Requirements/EnduringReq.html

Once a system has been installed and is regularly used, new requirements inevitably emerge. It is hard for users and system customers to anticipate what effects the new system will have on their business processes and the way that work is done. Once end-users have experience of a system, they will discover new needs and priorities. There are several reasons why change is inevitable:

1. The business and technical environment of the system always changes after installation. New hardware may be introduced, it may be necessary to interface the system with other systems, business priorities may change (with consequent changes in the system support required), and new legislation and regulations may be introduced that the system must necessarily abide by.

2. The people who pay for a system and the users of that system are rarely the same people. System customers impose requirements because of organizational and budgetary constraints. These may conflict with end-user requirements and, after delivery, new features may have to be added for user support if the system is to meet its goals.

3. Large systems usually have a diverse user community, with many users having different requirements and priorities that may be conflicting or contradictory. The final system requirements are inevitably a compromise between them and, with experience, it is often discovered that the balance of support given to different users has to be changed.

Requirements management is the process of understanding and controlling changes to system requirements. You need to keep track of individual requirements and maintain links between dependent requirements so that you can assess the impact of requirements changes. You need to establish a formal process for making change proposals and linking these to system requirements. The formal process of requirements management should start as soon as a draft version of the requirements document is available. However, you should start planning how to manage changing requirements during the requirements elicitation process.

4.7.1 Requirements management planning

Planning is an essential first stage in the requirements management process. The planning stage establishes the level of requirements management detail that is required. During the requirements management stage, you have to decide on:

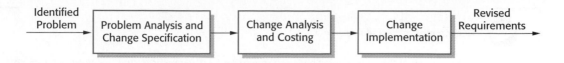

Figure 4.18
Requirements change
management

1. *Requirements identification* Each requirement must be uniquely identified so that it can be cross-referenced with other requirements and used in traceability assessments.

2. *A change management process* This is the set of activities that assess the impact and cost of changes. I discuss this process in more detail in the following section.

3. *Traceability policies* These policies define the relationships between each requirement and between the requirements and the system design that should be recorded. The traceability policy should also define how these records should be maintained.

4. *Tool support* Requirements management involves the processing of large amounts of information about the requirements. Tools that may be used range from specialist requirements management systems to spreadsheets and simple database systems.

Requirements management needs automated support and the software tools for this should be chosen during the planning phase. You need tool support for:

1. *Requirements storage* The requirements should be maintained in a secure, managed data store that is accessible to everyone involved in the requirements engineering process.

2. *Change management* The process of change management (Figure 4.18) is simplified if active tool support is available.

3. *Traceability management* As discussed above, tool support for traceability allows related requirements to be discovered. Some tools are available which use natural language processing techniques to help discover possible relationships between requirements.

For small systems, it may not be necessary to use specialized requirements management tools. The requirements management process may be supported using the facilities available in word processors, spreadsheets, and PC databases. However, for larger systems, more specialized tool support is required. I have included links to information about requirements management tools in the book's web pages.

4.7.2 Requirements change management

Requirements change management (Figure 4.18) should be applied to all proposed changes to a system's requirements after the requirements document has been approved. Change management is essential because you need to decide if the benefits of implementing new requirements are justified by the costs of implementation. The advantage of

Requirements traceability

You need to keep track of the relationships between requirements, their sources, and the system design so that you can analyze the reasons for proposed changes and the impact that these changes are likely to have on other parts of the system. You need to be able to trace how a change ripples its way through the system. Why?

http://www.SoftwareEngineering-9.com/Web/Requirements/ReqTraceability.html

using a formal process for change management is that all change proposals are treated consistently and changes to the requirements document are made in a controlled way.

There are three principal stages to a change management process:

1. *Problem analysis and change specification* The process starts with an identified requirements problem or, sometimes, with a specific change proposal. During this stage, the problem or the change proposal is analyzed to check that it is valid. This analysis is fed back to the change requestor who may respond with a more specific requirements change proposal, or decide to withdraw the request.

2. *Change analysis and costing* The effect of the proposed change is assessed using traceability information and general knowledge of the system requirements. The cost of making the change is estimated both in terms of modifications to the requirements document and, if appropriate, to the system design and implementation. Once this analysis is completed, a decision is made whether or not to proceed with the requirements change.

3. *Change implementation* The requirements document and, where necessary, the system design and implementation, are modified. You should organize the requirements document so that you can make changes to it without extensive rewriting or reorganization. As with programs, changeability in documents is achieved by minimizing external references and making the document sections as modular as possible. Thus, individual sections can be changed and replaced without affecting other parts of the document.

If a new requirement has to be urgently implemented, there is always a temptation to change the system and then retrospectively modify the requirements document. You should try to avoid this as it almost inevitably leads to the requirements specification and the system implementation getting out of step. Once system changes have been made, it is easy to forget to include these changes in the requirements document or to add information to the requirements document that is inconsistent with the implementation.

Agile development processes, such as extreme programming, have been designed to cope with requirements that change during the development process. In these processes, when a user proposes a requirements change, this change does not go through a formal change management process. Rather, the user has to prioritize that change and, if it is high priority, decide what system features that were planned for the next iteration should be dropped.

KEY POINTS

■ Requirements for a software system set out what the system should do and define constraints on its operation and implementation.

■ Functional requirements are statements of the services that the system must provide or are descriptions of how some computations must be carried out.

■ Non-functional requirements often constrain the system being developed and the development process being used. These might be product requirements, organizational requirements, or external requirements. They often relate to the emergent properties of the system and therefore apply to the system as a whole.

■ The software requirements document is an agreed statement of the system requirements. It should be organized so that both system customers and software developers can use it.

■ The requirements engineering process includes a feasibility study, requirements elicitation and analysis, requirements specification, requirements validation, and requirements management.

■ Requirements elicitation and analysis is an iterative process that can be represented as a spiral of activities—requirements discovery, requirements classification and organization, requirements negotiation, and requirements documentation.

■ Requirements validation is the process of checking the requirements for validity, consistency, completeness, realism, and verifiability.

■ Business, organizational, and technical changes inevitably lead to changes to the requirements for a software system. Requirements management is the process of managing and controlling these changes.

FURTHER READING

Software Requirements, 2nd edition. This book, designed for writers and users of requirements, discusses good requirements engineering practice. (K. M. Weigers, 2003, Microsoft Press.)

'Integrated requirements engineering: A tutorial'. This is a tutorial paper that I wrote in which I discuss requirements engineering activities and how these can be adapted to fit with modern software engineering practice. (I. Sommerville, IEEE Software, 22(1), Jan–Feb 2005.) http://dx.doi.org/10.1109/MS.2005.13.

Mastering the Requirements Process, 2nd edition. A well-written, easy-to-read book that is based on a particular method (VOLERE) but which also includes lots of good general advice about requirements engineering. (S. Robertson and J. Robertson, 2006, Addison-Wesley.)

'Research Directions in Requirements Engineering'. This is a good survey of requirements engineering research that highlights future research challenges in the area to address issues such as scale and agility. (B. H. C. Cheng and J. M. Atlee, Proc. Conf on Future of Software Engineering, IEEE Computer Society, 2007.) http://dx.doi.org/10.1109/FOSE.2007.17.

EXERCISES

4.1. Identify and briefly describe four types of requirement that may be defined for a computer-based system.

4.2. Discover ambiguities or omissions in the following statement of requirements for part of a ticket-issuing system:

An automated ticket-issuing system sells rail tickets. Users select their destination and input a credit card and a personal identification number. The rail ticket is issued and their credit card account charged. When the user presses the start button, a menu display of potential destinations is activated, along with a message to the user to select a destination. Once a destination has been selected, users are requested to input their credit card. Its validity is checked and the user is then requested to input a personal identifier. When the credit transaction has been validated, the ticket is issued.

4.3. Rewrite the above description using the structured approach described in this chapter. Resolve the identified ambiguities in an appropriate way.

4.4. Write a set of non-functional requirements for the ticket-issuing system, setting out its expected reliability and response time.

4.5. Using the technique suggested here, where natural language descriptions are presented in a standard format, write plausible user requirements for the following functions:

■ An unattended petrol (gas) pump system that includes a credit card reader. The customer swipes the card through the reader then specifies the amount of fuel required. The fuel is delivered and the customer's account debited.

■ The cash-dispensing function in a bank ATM.

■ The spelling-check and correcting function in a word processor.

4.6. Suggest how an engineer responsible for drawing up a system requirements specification might keep track of the relationships between functional and non-functional requirements.

4.7. Using your knowledge of how an ATM is used, develop a set of use cases that could serve as a basis for understanding the requirements for an ATM system.

4.8. Who should be involved in a requirements review? Draw a process model showing how a requirements review might be organized.

4.9. When emergency changes have to be made to systems, the system software may have to be modified before changes to the requirements have been approved. Suggest a model of a process for making these modifications that will ensure that the requirements document and the system implementation do not become inconsistent.

4.10. You have taken a job with a software user who has contracted your previous employer to develop a system for them. You discover that your company's interpretation of the requirements is different from the interpretation taken by your previous employer. Discuss what you should do in such a situation. You know that the costs to your current employer will increase if the ambiguities are not resolved. However, you have also a responsibility of confidentiality to your previous employer.

REFERENCES

Beck, K. (1999). 'Embracing Change with Extreme Programming'. *IEEE Computer*, **32** (10), 70–8.

Crabtree, A. (2003). *Designing Collaborative Systems: A Practical Guide to Ethnography*. London: Springer-Verlag.

Davis, A. M. (1993). *Software Requirements: Objects, Functions and States*. Englewood Cliffs, NJ: Prentice Hall.

IEEE. (1998). 'IEEE Recommended Practice for Software Requirements Specifications'. In *IEEE Software Engineering Standards Collection*. Los Alamitos, Ca.: IEEE Computer Society Press.

Jacobson, I., Christerson, M., Jonsson, P. and Overgaard, G. (1993). *Object-Oriented Software Engineering*. Wokingham: Addison-Wesley.

Kotonya, G. and Sommerville, I. (1998). *Requirements Engineering: Processes and Techniques*. Chichester, UK: John Wiley and Sons.

Larman, C. (2002). *Applying UML and Patterns: An Introduction to Object-oriented Analysis and Design and the Unified Process*. Englewood Cliff, NJ: Prentice Hall.

Martin, D., Rodden, T., Rouncefield, M., Sommerville, I. and Viller, S. (2001). 'Finding Patterns in the Fieldwork'. *Proc. ECSCW'01*. Bonn: Kluwer. 39–58.

Martin, D., Rouncefield, M. and Sommerville, I. (2002). 'Applying patterns of interaction to work (re)design: E-government and planning'. *Proc. ACM CHI'2002,* ACM Press. 235–42.

Martin, D. and Sommerville, I. (2004). 'Patterns of interaction: Linking ethnomethodology and design'. *ACM Trans. on Computer-Human Interaction,* **11** (1), 59–89.

Robertson, S. and Robertson, J. (1999). *Mastering the Requirements Process*. Harlow, UK: Addison-Wesley.

Sommerville, I., Rodden, T., Sawyer, P., Bentley, R. and Twidale, M. (1993). 'Integrating ethnography into the requirements engineering process'. *Proc. RE'93,* San Diego CA.: IEEE Computer Society Press. 165–73.

Stevens, P. and Pooley, R. (2006). *Using UML: Software Engineering with Objects and Components, 2nd ed*. Harlow, UK: Addison Wesley.

Suchman, L. (1987). *Plans and Situated Actions*. Cambridge: Cambridge University Press.

Viller, S. and Sommerville, I. (1999). 'Coherence: An Approach to Representing Ethnographic Analyses in Systems Design'. *Human-Computer Interaction,* **14** (1 & 2), 9–41.

Viller, S. and Sommerville, I. (2000). 'Ethnographically informed analysis for software engineers'. *Int. J. of Human-Computer Studies,* **53** (1), 169–96.

5

System modeling

Objectives

The aim of this chapter is to introduce some types of system model that may be developed as part of the requirements engineering and system design processes. When you have read the chapter, you will:

- understand how graphical models can be used to represent software systems;

- understand why different types of model are required and the fundamental system modeling perspectives of context, interaction, structure, and behavior;

- have been introduced to some of the diagram types in the Unified Modeling Language (UML) and how these diagrams may be used in system modeling;

- be aware of the ideas underlying model-driven engineering, where a system is automatically generated from structural and behavioral models.

Contents

System modeling is the process of developing abstract models of a system, with each model presenting a different view or perspective of that system. System modeling has generally come to mean representing the system using some kind of graphical notation, which is now almost always based on notations in the Unified Modeling Language (UML). However, it is also possible to develop formal (mathematical) models of a system, usually as a detailed system specification. I cover graphical modeling using the UML in this chapter and formal modeling in Chapter 12.

Models are used during the requirements engineering process to help derive the requirements for a system, during the design process to describe the system to engineers implementing the system and after implementation to document the system's structure and operation. You may develop models of both the existing system and the system to be developed:

1. Models of the existing system are used during requirements engineering. They help clarify what the existing system does and can be used as a basis for discussing its strengths and weaknesses. These then lead to requirements for the new system.

2. Models of the new system are used during requirements engineering to help explain the proposed requirements to other system stakeholders. Engineers use these models to discuss design proposals and to document the system for implementation. In a model-driven engineering process, it is possible to generate a complete or partial system implementation from the system model.

The most important aspect of a system model is that it leaves out detail. A model is an abstraction of the system being studied rather than an alternative representation of that system. Ideally, a representation of a system should maintain all the information about the entity being represented. An abstraction deliberately simplifies and picks out the most salient characteristics. For example, in the very unlikely event of this book being serialized in a newspaper, the presentation there would be an abstraction of the book's key points. If it were translated from English into Italian, this would be an alternative representation. The translator's intention would be to maintain all the information as it is presented in English.

You may develop different models to represent the system from different perspectives. For example:

1. An external perspective, where you model the context or environment of the system.

2. An interaction perspective where you model the interactions between a system and its environment or between the components of a system.

3. A structural perspective, where you model the organization of a system or the structure of the data that is processed by the system.

4. A behavioral perspective, where you model the dynamic behavior of the system and how it responds to events.

These perspectives have much in common with Krutchen's 4 + 1 view of system architecture (Kruchten, 1995), where he suggests that you should document a system's architecture and organization from different perspectives. I discuss this 4 + 1 approach in Chapter 6.

In this chapter, I use diagrams defined in UML (Booch et al., 2005; Rumbaugh et al., 2004), which has become a standard modeling language for object-oriented modeling. The UML has many diagram types and so supports the creation of many different types of system model. However, a survey in 2007 (Erickson and Siau, 2007) showed that most users of the UML thought that five diagram types could represent the essentials of a system:

1. Activity diagrams, which show the activities involved in a process or in data processing.

2. Use case diagrams, which show the interactions between a system and its environment.

3. Sequence diagrams, which show interactions between actors and the system and between system components.

4. Class diagrams, which show the object classes in the system and the associations between these classes.

5. State diagrams, which show how the system reacts to internal and external events.

As I do not have space to discuss all of the UML diagram types here, I focus on how these five key types of diagram are used in system modeling.

When developing system models, you can often be flexible in the way that the graphical notation is used. You do not always need to stick rigidly to the details of a notation. The detail and rigor of a model depends on how you intend to use it. There are three ways in which graphical models are commonly used:

1. As a means of facilitating discussion about an existing or proposed system.

2. As a way of documenting an existing system.

3. As a detailed system description that can be used to generate a system implementation.

In the first case, the purpose of the model is to stimulate the discussion amongst the software engineers involved in developing the system. The models may be incomplete (so long as they cover the key points of the discussion) and they may use the modeling notation informally. This is how models are normally used in so-called 'agile modeling' (Ambler and Jeffries, 2002). When models are used as documentation, they do not have to be complete as you may only wish to develop models for some parts of a system. However, these models have to be correct—they should use the notation correctly and be an accurate description of the system.

The Unified Modeling Language

The Unified Modeling Language is a set of 13 different diagram types that may be used to model software systems. It emerged from work in the 1990s on object-oriented modeling where similar object-oriented notations were integrated to create the UML. A major revision (UML 2) was finalized in 2004. The UML is universally accepted as the standard approach for developing models of software systems. Variants have been proposed for more general system modeling.

http://www.SoftwareEngineering-9.com/Web/UML/

In the third case, where models are used as part of a model-based development process, the system models have to be both complete and correct. The reason for this is that they are used as a basis for generating the source code of the system. Therefore, you have to be very careful not to confuse similar symbols, such as stick and block arrowheads, that have different meanings.

5.1 Context models

At an early stage in the specification of a system, you should decide on the system boundaries. This involves working with system stakeholders to decide what functionality should be included in the system and what is provided by the system's environment. You may decide that automated support for some business processes should be implemented but others should be manual processes or supported by different systems. You should look at possible overlaps in functionality with existing systems and decide where new functionality should be implemented. These decisions should be made early in the process to limit the system costs and the time needed for understanding the system requirements and design.

In some cases, the boundary between a system and its environment is relatively clear. For example, where an automated system is replacing an existing manual or computerized system, the environment of the new system is usually the same as the existing system's environment. In other cases, there is more flexibility, and you decide what constitutes the boundary between the system and its environment during the requirements engineering process.

For example, say you are developing the specification for the patient information system for mental healthcare. This system is intended to manage information about patients attending mental health clinics and the treatments that have been prescribed. In developing the specification for this system, you have to decide whether the system should focus exclusively on collecting information about consultations (using other systems to collect personal information about patients) or whether it should also collect personal patient information. The advantage of relying on other systems for patient information is that you avoid duplicating data. The major disadvantage, however, is that using other systems may make it slower to access information. If these systems are unavailable, then the MHC-PMS cannot be used.

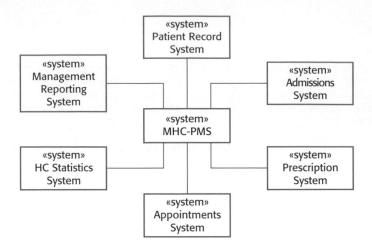

Figure 5.1 The context
of the MHC-PMS

The definition of a system boundary is not a value-free judgment. Social and organizational concerns may mean that the position of a system boundary may be determined by non-technical factors. For example, a system boundary may be deliberately positioned so that the analysis process can all be carried out on one site; it may be chosen so that a particularly difficult manager need not be consulted; it may be positioned so that the system cost is increased and the system development division must therefore expand to design and implement the system.

Once some decisions on the boundaries of the system have been made, part of the analysis activity is the definition of that context and the dependencies that a system has on its environment. Normally, producing a simple architectural model is the first step in this activity.

Figure 5.1 is a simple context model that shows the patient information system and the other systems in its environment. From Figure 5.1, you can see that the MHC-PMS is connected to an appointments system and a more general patient record system with which it shares data. The system is also connected to systems for management reporting and hospital bed allocation and a statistics system that collects information for research. Finally, it makes use of a prescription system to generate prescriptions for patients' medication.

Context models normally show that the environment includes several other automated systems. However, they do not show the types of relationships between the systems in the environment and the system that is being specified. External systems might produce data for or consume data from the system. They might share data with the system, or they might be connected directly, through a network or not connected at all. They might be physically co-located or located in separate buildings. All of these relations may affect the requirements and design of the system being defined and must be taken into account.

Therefore, simple context models are used along with other models, such as business process models. These describe human and automated processes in which particular software systems are used.

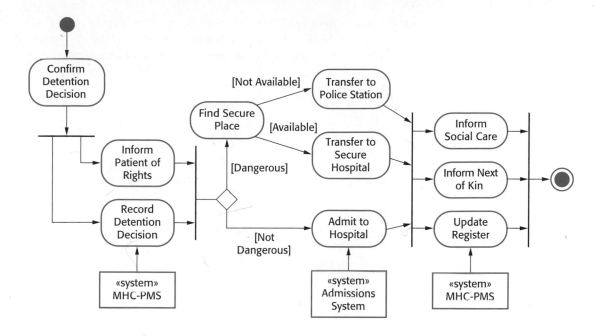

Figure 5.2 Process model of involuntary detention

Figure 5.2 is a model of an important system process that shows the processes in which the MHC-PMS is used. Sometimes, patients who are suffering from mental health problems may be a danger to others or to themselves. They may therefore have to be detained against their will in a hospital so that treatment can be administered. Such detention is subject to strict legal safeguards—for example, the decision to detain a patient must be regularly reviewed so that people are not held indefinitely without good reason. One of the functions of the MHC-PMS is to ensure that such safeguards are implemented.

Figure 5.2 is a UML activity diagram. Activity diagrams are intended to show the activities that make up a system process and the flow of control from one activity to another. The start of a process is indicated by a filled circle; the end by a filled circle inside another circle. Rectangles with round corners represent activities, that is, the specific sub-processes that must be carried out. You may include objects in activity charts. In Figure 5.2, I have shown the systems that are used to support different processes. I have indicated that these are separate systems using the UML stereotype feature.

In a UML activity diagram, arrows represent the flow of work from one activity to another. A solid bar is used to indicate activity coordination. When the flow from more than one activity leads to a solid bar then all of these activities must be complete before progress is possible. When the flow from a solid bar leads to a number of activities, these may be executed in parallel. Therefore, in Figure 5.2, the activities to inform social care and the patient's next of kin, and to update the detention register may be concurrent.

Arrows may be annotated with guards that indicate the condition when that flow is taken. In Figure 5.2, you can see guards showing the flows for patients who are dangerous and not dangerous to society. Patients who are dangerous to society must be detained in a secure facility. However, patients who are suicidal and so are a danger to themselves may be detained in an appropriate ward in a hospital.

5.2 Interaction models

All systems involve interaction of some kind. This can be user interaction, which involves user inputs and outputs, interaction between the system being developed and other systems or interaction between the components of the system. Modeling user interaction is important as it helps to identify user requirements. Modeling system to system interaction highlights the communication problems that may arise. Modeling component interaction helps us understand if a proposed system structure is likely to deliver the required system performance and dependability.

In this section, I cover two related approaches to interaction modeling:

1. Use case modeling, which is mostly used to model interactions between a system and external actors (users or other systems).

2. Sequence diagrams, which are used to model interactions between system components, although external agents may also be included.

Use case models and sequence diagrams present interaction at different levels of detail and so may be used together. The details of the interactions involved in a high-level use case may be documented in a sequence diagram. The UML also includes communication diagrams that can be used to model interactions. I don't discuss these here as they are an alternative representation of sequence charts. In fact, some tools can generate a communication diagram from a sequence diagram.

5.2.1 Use case modeling

Use case modeling was originally developed by Jacobson et al. (1993) in the 1990s and was incorporated into the first release of the UML (Rumbaugh et al., 1999). As I have discussed in Chapter 4, use case modeling is widely used to support requirements elicitation. A use case can be taken as a simple scenario that describes what a user expects from a system.

Each use case represents a discrete task that involves external interaction with a system. In its simplest form, a use case is shown as an ellipse with the actors involved in the use case represented as stick figures. Figure 5.3 shows a use case from the MHC-PMS that represents the task of uploading data from the MHC-PMS to a more general patient record system. This more general system maintains summary data about a patient rather than the data about each consultation, which is recorded in the MHC-PMS.

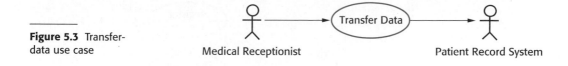

Figure 5.3 Transfer-
data use case

Medical Receptionist   Patient Record System

Notice that there are two actors in this use case: the operator who is transferring the data and the patient record system. The stick figure notation was originally developed to cover human interaction but it is also now used to represent other external systems and hardware. Formally, use case diagrams should use lines without arrows as arrows in the UML indicate the direction of flow of messages. Obviously, in a use case messages pass in both directions. However, the arrows in Figure 5.3 are used informally to indicate that the medical receptionist initiates the transaction and data is transferred to the patient record system.

Use case diagrams give a fairly simple overview of an interaction so you have to provide more detail to understand what is involved. This detail can either be a simple textual description, a structured description in a table, or a sequence diagram as discussed below. You chose the most appropriate format depending on the use case and the level of detail that you think is required in the model. I find a standard tabular format to be the most useful. Figure 5.4 shows a tabular description of the 'Transfer data' use case.

As I have discussed in Chapter 4, composite use case diagrams show a number of different use cases. Sometimes, it is possible to include all possible interactions with a system in a single composite use case diagram. However, this may be impossible because of the number of use cases. In such cases, you may develop several diagrams, each of which shows related use cases. For example, Figure 5.5 shows all of the use cases in the MHC-PMS in which the actor 'Medical Receptionist' is involved.

Figure 5.4 Tabular description of the 'Transfer data' use case

MHC-PMS: Transfer data	
Actors	Medical receptionist, patient records system (PRS)
Description	A receptionist may transfer data from the MHC-PMS to a general patient record database that is maintained by a health authority. The information transferred may either be updated personal information (address, phone number, etc.) or a summary of the patient's diagnosis and treatment.
Data	Patient's personal information, treatment summary
Stimulus	User command issued by medical receptionist
Response	Confirmation that PRS has been updated
Comments	The receptionist must have appropriate security permissions to access the patient information and the PRS.

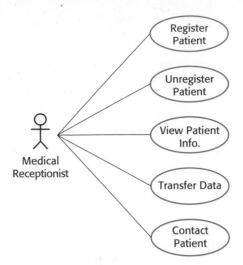

Figure 5.5 Use cases
involving the role
'medical receptionist'

5.2.2 Sequence diagrams

Sequence diagrams in the UML are primarily used to model the interactions between
the actors and the objects in a system and the interactions between the objects themselves. The UML has a rich syntax for sequence diagrams, which allows many different kinds of interaction to be modeled. I don't have space to cover all possibilities
here so I focus on the basics of this diagram type.

As the name implies, a sequence diagram shows the sequence of interactions that
take place during a particular use case or use case instance. Figure 5.6 is an example
of a sequence diagram that illustrates the basics of the notation. This diagram models
the interactions involved in the View patient information use case, where a medical
receptionist can see some patient information.

The objects and actors involved are listed along the top of the diagram, with a dotted line drawn vertically from these. Interactions between objects are indicated by
annotated arrows. The rectangle on the dotted lines indicates the lifeline of the object
concerned (i.e., the time that object instance is involved in the computation). You
read the sequence of interactions from top to bottom. The annotations on the arrows
indicate the calls to the objects, their parameters, and the return values. In this example, I also show the notation used to denote alternatives. A box named alt is used
with the conditions indicated in square brackets.

You can read Figure 5.6 as follows:

1. The medical receptionist triggers the ViewInfo method in an instance P of the
    PatientInfo object class, supplying the patient's identifier, PID. P is a user inter-
    face object, which is displayed as a form showing patient information.

2. The instance P calls the database to return the information required, supplying
    the receptionist's identifier to allow security checking (at this stage, we do not
    care where this UID comes from).

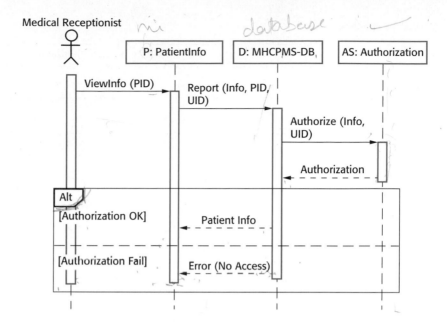

Figure 5.6 Sequence diagram for View patient information

3. The database checks with an authorization system that the user is authorized for this action.

4. If authorized, the patient information is returned and a form on the user's screen is filled in. If authorization fails, then an error message is returned.

Figure 5.7 is a second example of a sequence diagram from the same system that illustrates two additional features. These are the direct communication between the actors in the system and the creation of objects as part of a sequence of operations. In this example, an object of type Summary is created to hold the summary data that is to be uploaded to the PRS (patient record system). You can read this diagram as follows:

1. The receptionist logs on to the PRS.

2. There are two options available. These allow the direct transfer of updated patient information to the PRS and the transfer of summary health data from the MHC-PMS to the PRS.

3. In each case, the receptionist's permissions are checked using the authorization system.

4. Personal information may be transferred directly from the user interface object to the PRS. Alternatively, a summary record may be created from the database and that record is then transferred.

5. On completion of the transfer, the PRS issues a status message and the user logs off.

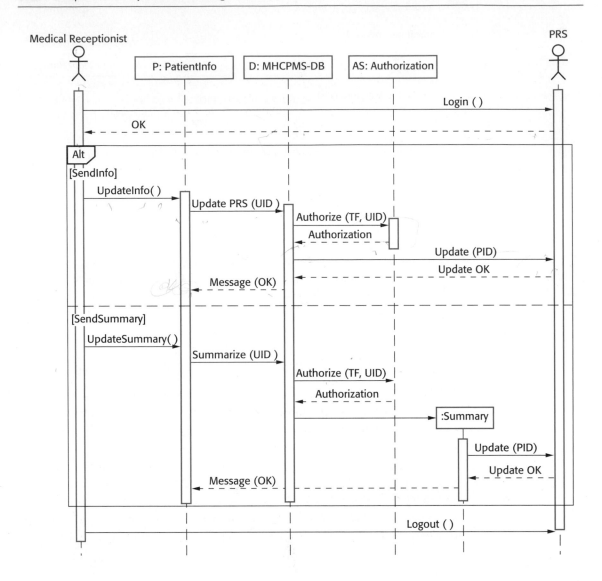

Figure 5.7 Sequence diagram for transfer data

Unless you are using sequence diagrams for code generation or detailed documentation, you don't have to include every interaction in these diagrams. If you develop system models early in the development process to support requirements engineering and high-level design, there will be many interactions which depend on implementation decisions. For example, in Figure 5.7 the decision on how to get the user's identifier to check authorization is one that can be delayed. In an implementation, this might involve interacting with a User object but this is not important at this stage and so need not be included in the sequence diagram.

Object-oriented requirements analysis

In object-oriented requirements analysis, you model real-world entities using object classes. You may create different types of object model, showing how object classes are related to each other, how objects are aggregated to form other objects, how objects interact with other objects, and so on. These each present unique information about the system that is being specified.

http://www.SoftwareEngineering-9.com/Web/OORA/

5.3 Structural models

Structural models of software display the organization of a system in terms of the components that make up that system and their relationships. Structural models may be static models, which show the structure of the system design or dynamic models, which show the organization of the system when it is executing. These are not the same things—the dynamic organization of a system as a set of interacting threads may be very different from a static model of the system components.

You create structural models of a system when you are discussing and designing the system architecture. Architectural design is a particularly important topic in software engineering and UML component, package, and deployment diagrams may all be used when presenting architectural models. I cover different aspects of software architecture and architectural modeling in Chapters 6, 18, and 19. In this section, I focus on the use of class diagrams for modeling the static structure of the object classes in a software system.

5.3.1 Class diagrams

Class diagrams are used when developing an object-oriented system model to show the classes in a system and the associations between these classes. Loosely, an object class can be thought of as a general definition of one kind of system object. An association is a link between classes that indicates that there is a relationship between these classes. Consequently, each class may have to have some knowledge of its associated class.

When you are developing models during the early stages of the software engineering process, objects represent something in the real world, such as a patient, a prescription, a doctor, etc. As an implementation is developed, you usually need to define additional implementation objects that are used to provide the required system functionality. Here, I focus on the modeling of real-world objects as part of the requirements or early software design processes.

Class diagrams in the UML can be expressed at different levels of detail. When you are developing a model, the first stage is usually to look at the world, identify the essential objects, and represent these as classes. The simplest way of writing these is to write the class name in a box. You can also simply note the existence of an association

Figure 5.8 UML
classes and association

by drawing a line between classes. For example, Figure 5.8 is a simple class diagram showing two classes: Patient and Patient Record with an association between them.

In Figure 5.8, I illustrate a further feature of class diagrams—the ability to show how many objects are involved in the association. In this example, each end of the association is annotated with a 1, meaning that there is a 1:1 relationship between objects of these classes. That is, each patient has exactly one record and each record maintains information about exactly one patient. As you can see from later examples, other multiplicities are possible. You can define that an exact number of objects are involved or, by using a *, as shown in Figure 5.9, that there are an indefinite number of objects involved in the association.

Figure 5.9 develops this type of class diagram to show that objects of class Patient are also involved in relationships with a number of other classes. In this example, I show that you can name associations to give the reader an indication of the type of relationship that exists. The UML also allows the role of the objects participating in the association to be specified.

At this level of detail, class diagrams look like semantic data models. Semantic data models are used in database design. They show the data entities, their associated attributes, and the relations between these entities. This approach to modeling was first proposed in the mid-1970s by Chen (1976); several variants have been developed since then (Codd, 1979; Hammer and McLeod, 1981; Hull and King, 1987), all with the same basic form.

The UML does not include a specific notation for this database modeling as it assumes an object-oriented development process and models data using objects and their relationships. However, you can use the UML to represent a semantic data model. You can think of entities in a semantic data model as simplified object classes

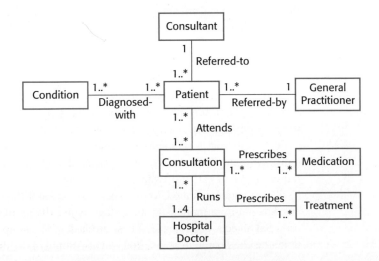

Figure 5.9 Classes
and associations in the
MHC-PMS

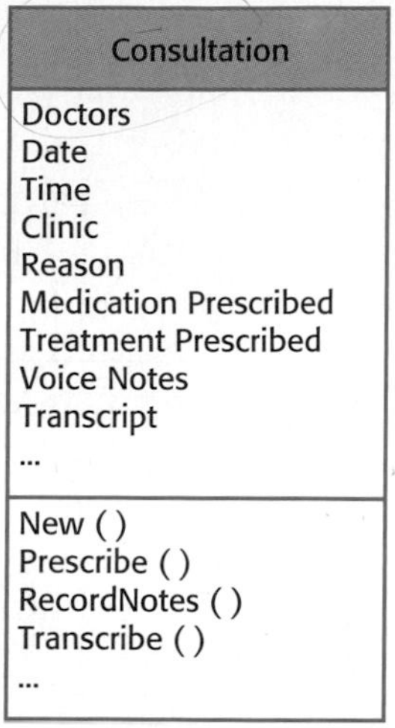

Figure 5.10 The consultation class

(they have no operations), attributes as object class attributes and relations as named associations between object classes.

When showing the associations between classes, it is convenient to represent these classes in the simplest possible way. To define them in more detail, you add information about their attributes (the characteristics of an object) and operations (the things that you can request from an object). For example, a Patient object will have the attribute Address and you may include an operation called ChangeAddress, which is called when a patient indicates that they have moved from one address to another. In the UML, you show attributes and operations by extending the simple rectangle that represents a class. This is illustrated in Figure 5.10 where:

1. The name of the object class is in the top section.

2. The class attributes are in the middle section. This must include the attribute names and, optionally, their types.

3. The operations (called methods in Java and other OO programming languages) associated with the object class are in the lower section of the rectangle.

Figure 5.10 shows possible attributes and operations on the class Consultation. In this example, I assume that doctors record voice notes that are transcribed later to record details of the consultation. To prescribe medication, the doctor involved must use the Prescribe method to generate an electronic prescription.

5.3.2 Generalization

Generalization is an everyday technique that we use to manage complexity. Rather than learn the detailed characteristics of every entity that we experience, we place these entities in more general classes (animals, cars, houses, etc.) and learn the characteristics of

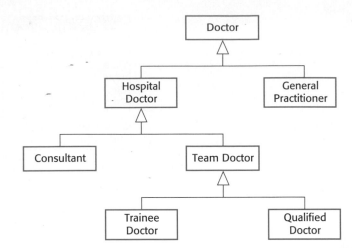

Figure 5.11 A generalization
hierarchy

these classes. This allows us to infer that different members of these classes have some common characteristics (e.g., squirrels and rats are rodents). We can make general statements that apply to all class members (e.g., all rodents have teeth for gnawing).

In modeling systems, it is often useful to examine the classes in a system to see if there is scope for generalization. This means that common information will be maintained in one place only. This is good design practice as it means that, if changes are proposed, then you do not have to look at all classes in the system to see if they are affected by the change. In object-oriented languages, such as Java, generalization is implemented using the class inheritance mechanisms built into the language.

The UML has a specific type of association to denote generalization, as illustrated in Figure 5.11. The generalization is shown as an arrowhead pointing up to the more general class. This shows that general practitioners and hospital doctors can be generalized as doctors and that there are three types of Hospital Doctor—those that have just graduated from medical school and have to be supervised (Trainee Doctor); those that can work unsupervised as part of a consultant's team (Registered Doctor); and consultants, who are senior doctors with full decision-making responsibilities.

In a generalization, the attributes and operations associated with higher-level classes are also associated with the lower-level classes. In essence, the lower-level classes are subclasses inherit the attributes and operations from their superclasses. These lower-level classes then add more specific attributes and operations. For example, all doctors have a name and phone number; all hospital doctors have a staff number and a department but general practitioners don't have these attributes as they work independently. They do however, have a practice name and address. This is illustrated in Figure 5.12, which shows part of the generalization hierarchy that I have extended with class attributes. The operations associated with the class Doctor are intended to register and de-register that doctor with the MHC-PMS.

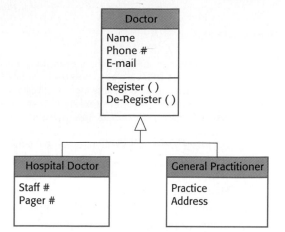

Figure 5.12
A generalization
hierarchy with
added detail

5.3.3 Aggregation

Objects in the real world are often composed of different parts. For example, a study pack for a course may be composed of a book, PowerPoint slides, quizzes, and recommendations for further reading. Sometimes in a system model, you need to illustrate this. The UML provides a special type of association between classes called aggregation that means that one object (the whole) is composed of other objects (the parts). To show this, we use a diamond shape next to the class that represents the whole. This is shown in Figure 5.13, which shows that a patient record is a composition of Patient and an indefinite number of Consultations.

5.4 Behavioral models

Behavioral models are models of the dynamic behavior of the system as it is executing. They show what happens or what is supposed to happen when a system responds to a stimulus from its environment. You can think of these stimuli as being of two types:

1. *Data* Some data arrives that has to be processed by the system.

2. *Events* Some event happens that triggers system processing. Events may have associated data but this is not always the case.

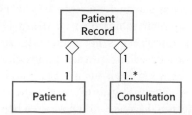

Figure 5.13 The
aggregation association

Data-flow diagrams

Data-flow diagrams (DFDs) are system models that show a functional perspective where each transformation represents a single function or process. DFDs are used to show how data flows through a sequence of processing steps. For example, a processing step could be the filtering of duplicate records in a customer database. The data is transformed at each step before moving on to the next stage. These processing steps or transformations represent software processes or functions where data-flow diagrams are used to document a software design.

http://www.SoftwareEngineering-9.com/Web/DFDs

Many business systems are data processing systems that are primarily driven by data. They are controlled by the data input to the system with relatively little external event processing. Their processing involves a sequence of actions on that data and the generation of an output. For example, a phone billing system will accept information about calls made by a customer, calculate the costs of these calls, and generate a bill to be sent to that customer. By contrast, real-time systems are often event driven with minimal data processing. For example, a landline phone switching system responds to events such as 'receiver off hook' by generating a dial tone, or the pressing of keys on a handset by capturing the phone number, etc.

5.4.1 Data-driven modeling

Data-driven models show the sequence of actions involved in processing input data and generating an associated output. They are particularly useful during the analysis of requirements as they can be used to show end-to-end processing in a system. That is, they show the entire sequence of actions that take place from an input being processed to the corresponding output, which is the system's response.

Data-driven models were amongst the first graphical software models. In the 1970s, structured methods such as DeMarco's Structured Analysis (DeMarco, 1978) introduced data-flow diagrams (DFDs) as a way of illustrating the processing steps in a system. Data-flow models are useful because tracking and documenting how the data associated with a particular process moves through the system helps analysts and designers understand what is going on. Data-flow diagrams are simple and intuitive and it is usually possible to explain them to potential system users who can then participate in validating the model.

The UML does not support data-flow diagrams as they were originally proposed and used for modeling data processing. The reason for this is that DFDs focus on system functions and do not recognize system objects. However, because data-driven systems are so common in business, UML 2.0 introduced activity diagrams, which are similar to data-flow diagrams. For example, Figure 5.14 shows the chain of processing involved in the insulin pump software. In this diagram, you can see the processing steps (represented as activities) and the data flowing between these steps (represented as objects).

An alternative way of showing the sequence of processing in a system is to use UML sequence diagrams. You have seen how these can be used to model interaction but, if

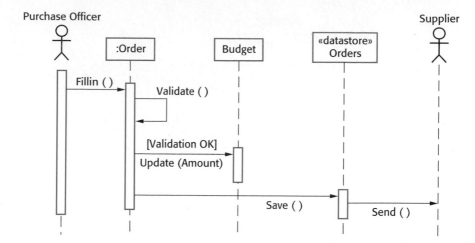

Figure 5.14 An activity model of the insulin pump's operation

you draw these so that messages are only sent from left to right, then they show the sequential data processing in the system. Figure 5.15 illustrates this, using a sequence model of the processing of an order and sending it to a supplier. Sequence models highlight objects in a system, whereas data-flow diagrams highlight the functions. The equivalent data-flow diagram for order processing is shown on the book's web pages.

5.4.2 Event-driven modeling

Event-driven modeling shows how a system responds to external and internal events. It is based on the assumption that a system has a finite number of states and that events (stimuli) may cause a transition from one state to another. For example, a system controlling a valve may move from a state 'Valve open' to a state 'Valve closed' when an operator command (the stimulus) is received. This view of a system is particularly appropriate for real-time systems. Event-based modeling was introduced in real-time design methods such as those proposed by Ward and Mellor (1985) and Harel (1987, 1988).

Figure 5.15 Order processing

The UML supports event-based modeling using state diagrams, which were based on Statecharts (Harel, 1987, 1988). State diagrams show system states and events that cause

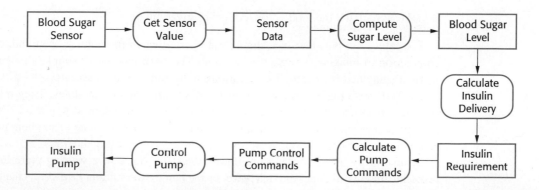

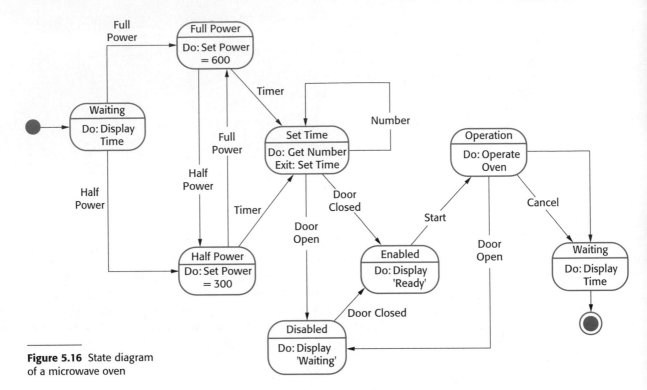

Figure 5.16 State diagram of a microwave oven

transitions from one state to another. They do not show the flow of data within the system but may include additional information on the computations carried out in each state.

I use an example of control software for a very simple microwave oven to illustrate event-driven modeling. Real microwave ovens are actually much more complex than this system but the simplified system is easier to understand. This simple microwave has a switch to select full or half power, a numeric keypad to input the cooking time, a start/stop button, and an alphanumeric display.

I have assumed that the sequence of actions in using the microwave is:

1. Select the power level (either half power or full power).

2. Input the cooking time using a numeric keypad.

3. Press Start and the food is cooked for the given time.

For safety reasons, the oven should not operate when the door is open and, on completion of cooking, a buzzer is sounded. The oven has a very simple alphanumeric display that is used to display various alerts and warning messages.

In UML state diagrams, rounded rectangles represent system states. They may include a brief description (following 'do') of the actions taken in that state. The labeled arrows represent stimuli that force a transition from one state to another. You can indicate start and end states using filled circles, as in activity diagrams.

From Figure 5.16, you can see that the system starts in a waiting state and responds initially to either the full-power or the half-power button. Users can change

State	Description
Waiting	The oven is waiting for input. The display shows the current time.
Half power	The oven power is set to 300 watts. The display shows 'Half power'.
Full power	The oven power is set to 600 watts. The display shows 'Full power'.
Set time	The cooking time is set to the user's input value. The display shows the cooking time selected and is updated as the time is set.
Disabled	Oven operation is disabled for safety. Interior oven light is on. Display shows 'Not ready'.
Enabled	Oven operation is enabled. Interior oven light is off. Display shows 'Ready to cook'.
Operation	Oven in operation. Interior oven light is on. Display shows the timer countdown. On completion of cooking, the buzzer is sounded for five seconds. Oven light is on. Display shows 'Cooking complete' while buzzer is sounding.

Stimulus	Description
Half power	The user has pressed the half-power button.
Full power	The user has pressed the full-power button.
Timer	The user has pressed one of the timer buttons.
Number	The user has pressed a numeric key.
Door open	The oven door switch is not closed.
Door closed	The oven door switch is closed.
Start	The user has pressed the Start button.
Cancel	The user has pressed the Cancel button.

Figure 5.17 States and stimuli for the microwave oven

their mind after selecting one of these and press the other button. The time is set and, if the door is closed, the Start button is enabled. Pushing this button starts the oven operation and cooking takes place for the specified time. This is the end of the cooking cycle and the system returns to the waiting state.

The UML notation lets you indicate the activity that takes place in a state. In a detailed system specification you have to provide more detail about both the stimuli and the system states. I illustrate this in Figure 5.17, which shows a tabular description of each state and how the stimuli that force state transitions are generated.

The problem with state-based modeling is that the number of possible states increases rapidly. For large system models, therefore, you need to hide detail in the

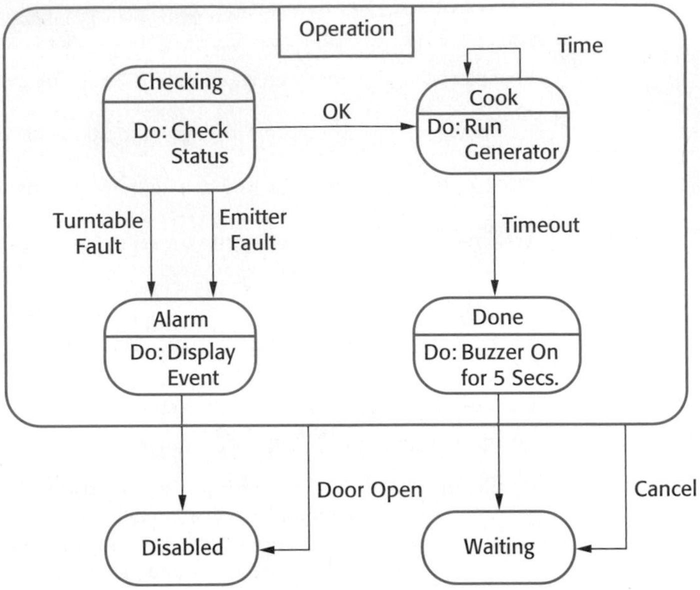

Figure 5.18 Microwave oven operation

models. One way to do this is by using the notion of a superstate that encapsulates a number of separate states. This superstate looks like a single state on a high-level model but is then expanded to show more detail on a separate diagram. To illustrate this concept, consider the Operation state in Figure 5.15. This is a superstate that can be expanded, as illustrated in Figure 5.18.

The Operation state includes a number of sub-states. It shows that operation starts with a status check and that if any problems are discovered an alarm is indicated and operation is disabled. Cooking involves running the microwave generator for the specified time; on completion, a buzzer is sounded. If the door is opened during operation, the system moves to the disabled state, as shown in Figure 5.15.

5.5 Model-driven engineering

Model-driven engineering (MDE) is an approach to software development where models rather than programs are the principal outputs of the development process (Kent, 2002; Schmidt, 2006). The programs that execute on a hardware/software platform are then generated automatically from the models. Proponents of MDE argue that this raises the level of abstraction in software engineering so that engineers no longer have to be concerned with programming language details or the specifics of execution platforms.

Model-driven engineering has its roots in model-driven architecture (MDA) which was proposed by the Object Management Group (OMG) in 2001 as a new software development paradigm. Model-driven engineering and model-driven architecture are often seen as the same thing. However, I think that MDE has a wider scope than

MDA. As I discuss later in this section, MDA focuses on the design and implementation stages of software development whereas MDE is concerned with all aspects of the software engineering process. Therefore, topics such as model-based requirements engineering, software processes for model-based development, and model-based testing are part of MDE but not, currently, part of MDA.

Although MDA has been in use since 2001, model-based engineering is still at an early stage of development and it is unclear whether or not it will have a significant effect on software engineering practice. The main arguments for and against MDE are:

1. *For MDE* Model-based engineering allows engineers to think about systems at a high level of abstraction, without concern for the details of their implementation. This reduces the likelihood of errors, speeds up the design and implementation process, and allows for the creation of reusable, platform-independent application models. By using powerful tools, system implementations can be generated for different platforms from the same model. Therefore, to adapt the system to some new platform technology, it is only necessary to write a translator for that platform. When this is available, all platform-independent models can be rapidly rehosted on the new platform.

2. *Against MDE* As I discussed earlier in this chapter, models are a good way of facilitating discussions about a software design. However, it does not always follow that the abstractions that are supported by the model are the right abstractions for implementation. So, you may create informal design models but then go on to implement the system using an off-the-shelf, configurable package. Furthermore, the arguments for platform independence are only valid for large long-lifetime systems where the platforms become obsolete during a system's lifetime. However, for this class of systems, we know that implementation is not the major problem—requirements engineering, security and dependability, integration with legacy systems, and testing are more significant.

There have been significant MDE success stories reported by the OMG on their Web pages (www.omg.org/mda/products_success.htm) and the approach is used within large companies such as IBM and Siemens. The techniques have been used successfully in the development of large, long-lifetime software systems such as air traffic management systems. Nevertheless, at the time of writing, model-driven approaches are not widely used for software engineering. Like formal methods of software engineering, which I discuss in Chapter 12, I believe that MDE is an important development. However, as is also the case with formal methods, it is not clear whether the costs and risks of model-driven approaches outweigh the possible benefits.

5.5.1 Model-driven architecture

Model-driven architecture (Kleppe, et al., 2003; Mellor et al., 2004; Stahl and Voelter, 2006) is a model-focused approach to software design and implementation that uses a sub-set of UML models to describe a system. Here, models at different

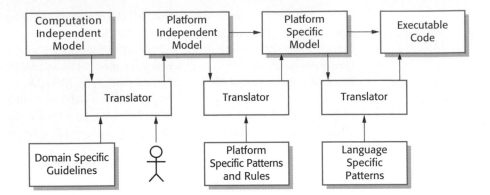

Figure 5.19 MDA transformations

levels of abstraction are created. From a high-level platform independent model it is possible, in principle, to generate a working program without manual intervention.

The MDA method recommends that three types of abstract system model should be produced:

1. A computation independent model (CIM) that models the important domain abstractions used in the system. CIMs are sometimes called domain models. You may develop several different CIMs, reflecting different views of the system. For example, there may be a security CIM in which you identify important security abstractions such as an asset and a role and a patient record CIM, in which you describe abstractions such as patients, consultations, etc.

2. A platform independent model (PIM) that models the operation of the system without reference to its implementation. The PIM is usually described using UML models that show the static system structure and how it responds to external and internal events.

3. Platform specific models (PSM) which are transformations of the platform-independent model with a separate PSM for each application platform. In principle, there may be layers of PSM, with each layer adding some platform-specific detail. So, the first-level PSM could be middleware-specific but database independent. When a specific database has been chosen, a database-specific PSM can then be generated.

As I have said, transformations between these models may be defined and applied automatically by software tools. This is illustrated in Figure 5.19, which also shows a final level of automatic transformation. A transformation is applied to the PSM to generate executable code that runs on the designated software platform.

At the time of writing, automatic CIM to PIM translation is still at the research prototype stage. It is unlikely that completely automated translation tools will be available in the near future. Human intervention, indicated by a stick figure in Figure 5.19, will be needed for the foreseeable future. CIMs are related and part of the translation

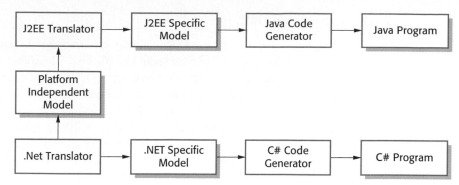

Figure 5.20 Multiple platform-specific models

process may involve linking concepts in different CIMs. For example, the concept of a role in a security CIM may be mapped onto the concept of a staff member in a hospital CIM. Mellor and Balcer (2002) give the name 'bridges' to the information that supports mapping from one CIM to another.

The translation of PIMs to PSMs is more mature and several commercial tools are available that provide translators from PIMs to common platforms such as Java and J2EE. These rely on an extensive library of platform-specific rules and patterns to convert the PIM to the PSM. There may be several PSMs for each PIM in the system. If a software system is intended to run on different platforms (e.g., J2EE and .NET), then it is only necessary to maintain the PIM. The PSMs for each platform are automatically generated. This is illustrated in Figure 5.20.

Although MDA-support tools include platform-specific translators, it is often the case that these will only offer partial support for the translation from PIMs to PSMs. In the vast majority of cases, the execution environment for a system is more than the standard execution platform (e.g., J2EE, .NET, etc.). It also includes other application systems, application libraries that are specific to a company, and user interface libraries. As these vary significantly from one company to another, standard tool support is not available. Therefore, when MDA is introduced, special purpose translators may have to be created that take the characteristics of the local environment into account. In some cases (e.g., for user interface generation), completely automated PIM to PSM translation may be impossible.

There is an uneasy relationship between agile methods and model-driven architecture. The notion of extensive up-front modeling contradicts the fundamental ideas in the agile manifesto and I suspect that few agile developers feel comfortable with model-driven engineering. The developers of MDA claim that it is intended to support an iterative approach to development and so can be used within agile methods (Mellor, et al., 2004). If transformations can be completely automated and a complete program generated from a PIM, then, in principle, MDA could be used in an agile development process as no separate coding would be required. However, as far as I am aware, there are no MDA tools that support practices such as regression testing and test-driven development.

5.5.2 Executable UML

The fundamental notion behind model-driven engineering is that completely automated transformation of models to code should be possible. To achieve this, you have to be able to construct graphical models whose semantics are well defined. You also need a way of adding information to graphical models about the ways in which the operations defined in the model are implemented. This is possible using a subset of UML 2, called Executable UML or xUML (Mellor and Balcer, 2002). I don't have space here to describe the details of xUML, so I simply present a short overview of its main features.

UML was designed as a language for supporting and documenting software design, not as a programming language. The designers of UML were not concerned with semantic details of the language but with its expressiveness. They introduced useful notions such as use case diagrams that help with the design but which are too informal to support execution. To create an executable sub-set of UML, the number of model types has therefore been dramatically reduced to three key model types:

1. Domain models identify the principal concerns in the system. These are defined using UML class diagrams that include objects, attributes, and associations.

2. Class models, in which classes are defined, along with their attributes and operations.

3. State models, in which a state diagram is associated with each class and is used to describe the lifecycle of the class.

The dynamic behavior of the system may be specified declaratively using the object constraint language (OCL) or may be expressed using UML's action language. The action language is like a very high-level programming language where you can refer to objects and their attributes and specify actions to be carried out.

KEY POINTS

■ A model is an abstract view of a system that ignores some system details. Complementary system models can be developed to show the system's context, interactions, structure, and behavior.

■ Context models show how a system that is being modeled is positioned in an environment with other systems and processes. They help define the boundaries of the system to be developed.

■ Use case diagrams and sequence diagrams are used to describe the interactions between user the system being designed and users/other systems. Use cases describe interactions between a system and external actors; sequence diagrams add more information to these by showing interactions between system objects.

■ Structural models show the organization and architecture of a system. Class diagrams are used to define the static structure of classes in a system and their associations.

■ Behavioral models are used to describe the dynamic behavior of an executing system. This can be modeled from the perspective of the data processed by the system or by the events that stimulate responses from a system.

■ Activity diagrams may be used to model the processing of data, where each activity represents one process step.

■ State diagrams are used to model a system's behavior in response to internal or external events.

■ Model-driven engineering is an approach to software development in which a system is represented as a set of models that can be automatically transformed to executable code.

FURTHER READING

Requirements Analysis and System Design. This book focuses on information systems analysis and discusses how different UML models can be used in the analysis process. (L. Maciaszek, Addison-Wesley, 2001.)

MDA Distilled: Principles of Model-driven Architecture .This is a concise and accessible introduction to the MDA method. It is written by enthusiasts so the book says very little about possible problems with this approach. (S. J. Mellor, K. Scott and D. Weise, Addison-Wesley, 2004.)

Using UML: Software Engineering with Objects and Components, 2nd ed. A short, readable introduction to the use of the UML in system specification and design. This book is excellent for learning and understanding the UML, although it is not a full description of the notation. (P. Stevens with R. Pooley, Addison-Wesley, 2006.)

EXERCISES

5.1. Explain why it is important to model the context of a system that is being developed. Give two examples of possible errors that could arise if software engineers do not understand the system context.

5.2. How might you use a model of a system that already exists? Explain why it is not always necessary for such a system model to be complete and correct. Would the same be true if you were developing a model of a new system?

5.3. You have been asked to develop a system that will help with planning large-scale events and parties such as weddings, graduation celebrations, birthday parties, etc. Using an activity diagram, model the process context for such a system that shows the activities involved in planning a party (booking a venue, organizing invitations, etc.) and the system elements that may be used at each stage.

5.4. For the MHC-PMS, propose a set of use cases that illustrates the interactions between a doctor, who sees patients and prescribes medicine and treatments, and the MHC-PMS.

5.5. Develop a sequence diagram showing the interactions involved when a student registers for a course in a university. Courses may have limited enrollment, so the registration process must include checks that places are available. Assume that the student accesses an electronic course catalog to find out about available courses.

5.6. Look carefully at how messages and mailboxes are represented in the e-mail system that you use. Model the object classes that might be used in the system implementation to represent a mailbox and an e-mail message.

5.7. Based on your experience with a bank ATM, draw an activity diagram that models the data processing involved when a customer withdraws cash from the machine.

5.8. Draw a sequence diagram for the same system. Explain why you might want to develop both activity and sequence diagrams when modeling the behavior of a system.

5.9. Draw state diagrams of the control software for:

■ An automatic washing machine that has different programs for different types of clothes.

■ The software for a DVD player.

■ A telephone answering system that records incoming messages and displays the number of accepted messages on an LED. The system should allow the telephone customer to dial in from any location, type a sequence of numbers (identified as tones), and play any recorded messages.

5.10. You are a software engineering manager and your team proposes that model-driven engineering should be used to develop a new system. What factors should you take into account when deciding whether or not to introduce this new approach to software development?

REFERENCES

Ambler, S. W. and Jeffries, R. (2002). *Agile Modeling: Effective Practices for Extreme Programming and the Unified Process*. New York: John Wiley & Sons.

Booch, G., Rumbaugh, J. and Jacobson, I. (2005). *The Unified Modeling Language User Guide, 2nd ed.* Boston: Addison-Wesley.

Chen, P. (1976). 'The entity relationship model—Towards a unified view of data'. *ACM Trans. on Database Systems*, **1** (1), 9–36.

Codd, E. F. (1979). 'Extending the database relational model to capture more meaning'. *ACM Trans. on Database Systems*, **4** (4), 397–434.

DeMarco, T. (1978). *Structured Analysis and System Specification*. New York: Yourdon Press.

Erickson, J. and Siau, K. (2007). 'Theoretical and practical complexity of modeling methods'. *Comm. ACM*, **50** (8), 46–51.

Hammer, M. and McLeod, D. (1981). 'Database descriptions with SDM: A semantic database model'. *ACM Trans. on Database Sys.*, **6** (3), 351–86.

Harel, D. (1987). 'Statecharts: A visual formalism for complex systems'. *Sci. Comput. Programming*, **8** (3), 231–74.

Harel, D. (1988). 'On visual formalisms'. *Comm. ACM*, **31** (5), 514–30.

Hull, R. and King, R. (1987). 'Semantic database modeling: Survey, applications and research issues'. *ACM Computing Surveys,* **19** (3), 201–60.

Jacobson, I., Christerson, M., Jonsson, P. and Overgaard, G. (1993). *Object-Oriented Software Engineering*. Wokingham.: Addison-Wesley.

Kent, S. (2002). 'Model-driven engineering'. Proc. 3rd Int. Conf. on Integrated Formal Methods, 286–98.

Kleppe, A., Warmer, J. and Bast, W. (2003). *MDA Explained: The Model Driven Architecture—Practice and Promise*. Boston: Addison-Wesley.

Kruchten, P. (1995). 'The 4 + 1 view model of architecture'. *IEEE Software*, **11** (6), 42–50.

Mellor, S. J. and Balcer, M. J. (2002). *Executable UML*. Boston: Addison-Wesley.

Mellor, S. J., Scott, K. and Weise, D. (2004). *MDA Distilled: Principles of Model-driven Architecture*. Boston: Addison-Wesley.

Rumbaugh, J., Jacobson, I. and Booch, G. (1999). *The Unified Modeling Language Reference Manual*. Reading, Mass.: Addison-Wesley.

Rumbaugh, J., Jacobson, I. and Booch, G. (2004). *The Unified Modeling Language Reference Manual, 2nd ed.* Boston: Addison-Wesley.

Schmidt, D. C. (2006). 'Model-Driven Engineering'. *IEEE Computer,* **39** (2), 25–31.

Stahl, T. and Voelter, M. (2006). *Model-Driven Software Development: Technology, Engineering, Management.* New York: John Wiley & Sons.

Ward, P. and Mellor, S. (1985). *Structured Development for Real-time Systems.* Englewood Cliffs, NJ: Prentice Hall.

6

Architectural design

Objectives

The objective of this chapter is to introduce the concepts of software architecture and architectural design. When you have read the chapter, you will:

- understand why the architectural design of software is important;

- understand the decisions that have to be made about the system architecture during the architectural design process;

- have been introduced to the idea of architectural patterns, well-tried ways of organizing system architectures, which can be reused in system designs;

- know the architectural patterns that are often used in different types of application system, including transaction processing systems and language processing systems.

Contents

Architectural design is concerned with understanding how a system should be organized and designing the overall structure of that system. In the model of the software development process, as shown in Chapter 2, architectural design is the first stage in the software design process. It is the critical link between design and requirements engineering, as it identifies the main structural components in a system and the relationships between them. The output of the architectural design process is an architectural model that describes how the system is organized as a set of communicating components.

In agile processes, it is generally accepted that an early stage of the development process should be concerned with establishing an overall system architecture. Incremental development of architectures is not usually successful. While refactoring components in response to changes is usually relatively easy, refactoring a system architecture is likely to be expensive.

To help you understand what I mean by system architecture, consider Figure 6.1. This shows an abstract model of the architecture for a packing robot system that shows the components that have to be developed. This robotic system can pack different kinds of object. It uses a vision component to pick out objects on a conveyor, identify the type of object, and select the right kind of packaging. The system then moves objects from the delivery conveyor to be packaged. It places packaged objects on another conveyor. The architectural model shows these components and the links between them.

In practice, there is a significant overlap between the processes of requirements engineering and architectural design. Ideally, a system specification should not include any design information. This is unrealistic except for very small systems. Architectural decomposition is usually necessary to structure and organize the specification. Therefore, as part of the requirements engineering process, you might propose an abstract system architecture where you associate groups of system functions or features with large-scale components or sub-systems. You can then use this decomposition to discuss the requirements and features of the system with stakeholders.

You can design software architectures at two levels of abstraction, which I call *architecture in the small* and *architecture in the large*:

1. Architecture in the small is concerned with the architecture of individual programs. At this level, we are concerned with the way that an individual program is decomposed into components. This chapter is mostly concerned with program architectures.

2. Architecture in the large is concerned with the architecture of complex enterprise systems that include other systems, programs, and program components. These enterprise systems are distributed over different computers, which may be owned and managed by different companies. I cover architecture in the large in Chapters 18 and 19, where I discuss distributed systems architectures.

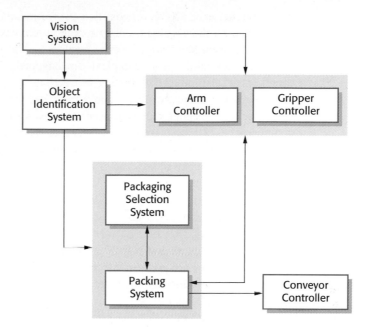

Figure 6.1 The architecture of a packing robot control system

Software architecture is important because it affects the performance, robustness, distributability, and maintainability of a system (Bosch, 2000). As Bosch discusses, individual components implement the functional system requirements. The non-functional requirements depend on the system architecture—the way in which these components are organized and communicate. In many systems, non-functional requirements are also influenced by individual components, but there is no doubt that the architecture of the system is the dominant influence.

Bass et al. (2003) discuss three advantages of explicitly designing and document-ing software architecture:

1. *Stakeholder communication* The architecture is a high-level presentation of the sys-tem that may be used as a focus for discussion by a range of different stakeholders.

2. *System analysis* Making the system architecture explicit at an early stage in the system development requires some analysis. Architectural design decisions have a profound effect on whether or not the system can meet critical require-ments such as performance, reliability, and maintainability.

3. *Large-scale reuse* A model of a system architecture is a compact, manageable description of how a system is organized and how the components interoperate. The system architecture is often the same for systems with similar requirements and so can support large-scale software reuse. As I explain in Chapter 16, it may be possible to develop product-line architectures where the same architecture is reused across a range of related systems.

Hofmeister et al. (2000) propose that a software architecture can serve firstly as a design plan for the negotiation of system requirements, and secondly as a means of structuring discussions with clients, developers, and managers. They also suggest that it is an essential tool for complexity management. It hides details and allows the designers to focus on the key system abstractions.

System architectures are often modeled using simple block diagrams, as in Figure 6.1. Each box in the diagram represents a component. Boxes within boxes indicate that the component has been decomposed to sub-components. Arrows mean that data and or control signals are passed from component to component in the direction of the arrows. You can see many examples of this type of architectural model in Booch's software architecture catalog (Booch, 2009).

Block diagrams present a high-level picture of the system structure, which people from different disciplines, who are involved in the system development process, can readily understand. However, in spite of their widespread use, Bass et al. (2003) dislike informal block diagrams for describing an architecture. They claim that these informal diagrams are poor architectural representations, as they show neither the type of the relationships among system components nor the components' externally visible properties.

The apparent contradictions between practice and architectural theory arise because there are two ways in which an architectural model of a program is used:

1. *As a way of facilitating discussion about the system design* A high-level architectural view of a system is useful for communication with system stakeholders and project planning because it is not cluttered with detail. Stakeholders can relate to it and understand an abstract view of the system. They can then discuss the system as a whole without being confused by detail. The architectural model identifies the key components that are to be developed so managers can start assigning people to plan the development of these systems.

2. *As a way of documenting an architecture that has been designed* The aim here is to produce a complete system model that shows the different components in a system, their interfaces, and their connections. The argument for this is that such a detailed architectural description makes it easier to understand and evolve the system.

Block diagrams are an appropriate way of describing the system architecture during the design process, as they are a good way of supporting communications between the people involved in the process. In many projects, these are often the only architectural documentation that exists. However, if the architecture of a system is to be thoroughly documented then it is better to use a notation with well-defined semantics for architectural description. However, as I discuss in Section 6.2, some people think that detailed documentation is neither useful, nor really worth the cost of its development.

6.1 Architectural design decisions

Architectural design is a creative process where you design a system organization that will satisfy the functional and non-functional requirements of a system. Because it is a creative process, the activities within the process depend on the type of system being developed, the background and experience of the system architect, and the specific requirements for the system. It is therefore useful to think of architectural design as a series of decisions to be made rather than a sequence of activities.

During the architectural design process, system architects have to make a number of structural decisions that profoundly affect the system and its development process. Based on their knowledge and experience, they have to consider the following fundamental questions about the system:

1. Is there a generic application architecture that can act as a template for the system that is being designed?

2. How will the system be distributed across a number of cores or processors?

3. What architectural patterns or styles might be used?

4. What will be the fundamental approach used to structure the system?

5. How will the structural components in the system be decomposed into sub-components?

6. What strategy will be used to control the operation of the components in the system?

7. What architectural organization is best for delivering the non-functional requirements of the system?

8. How will the architectural design be evaluated?

9. How should the architecture of the system be documented?

Although each software system is unique, systems in the same application domain often have similar architectures that reflect the fundamental concepts of the domain. For example, application product lines are applications that are built around a core architecture with variants that satisfy specific customer requirements. When designing a system architecture, you have to decide what your system and broader application classes have in common, and decide how much knowledge from these application architectures you can reuse. I discuss generic application architectures in Section 6.4 and application product lines in Chapter 16.

For embedded systems and systems designed for personal computers, there is usually only a single processor and you will not have to design a distributed architecture for the system. However, most large systems are now distributed systems in which the system software is distributed across many different computers. The choice of distribution architecture is a key decision that affects the performance and reliability of the system. This is a major topic in its own right and I cover it separately in Chapter 18.

The architecture of a software system may be based on a particular architectural pattern or style. An architectural pattern is a description of a system organization (Garlan and Shaw, 1993), such as a client–server organization or a layered architecture. Architectural patterns capture the essence of an architecture that has been used in different software systems. You should be aware of common patterns, where they can be used, and their strengths and weaknesses when making decisions about the architecture of a system. I discuss a number of frequently used patterns in Section 6.3.

Garlan and Shaw's notion of an architectural style (style and pattern have come to mean the same thing) covers questions 4 to 6 in the previous list. You have to choose the most appropriate structure, such as client–server or layered structuring, that will enable you to meet the system requirements. To decompose structural system units, you decide on the strategy for decomposing components into sub-components. The approaches that you can use allow different types of architecture to be implemented. Finally, in the control modeling process, you make decisions about how the execution of components is controlled. You develop a general model of the control relationships between the various parts of the system.

Because of the close relationship between non-functional requirements and software architecture, the particular architectural style and structure that you choose for a system should depend on the non-functional system requirements:

1. *Performance* If performance is a critical requirement, the architecture should be designed to localize critical operations within a small number of components, with these components all deployed on the same computer rather than distributed across the network. This may mean using a few relatively large components rather than small, fine-grain components, which reduces the number of component communications. You may also consider run-time system organizations that allow the system to be replicated and executed on different processors.

2. *Security* If security is a critical requirement, a layered structure for the architecture should be used, with the most critical assets protected in the innermost layers, with a high level of security validation applied to these layers.

3. *Safety* If safety is a critical requirement, the architecture should be designed so that safety-related operations are all located in either a single component or in a small number of components. This reduces the costs and problems of safety validation and makes it possible to provide related protection systems that can safely shut down the system in the event of failure.

4. *Availability* If availability is a critical requirement, the architecture should be designed to include redundant components so that it is possible to replace and update components without stopping the system. I describe two fault-tolerant system architectures for high-availability systems in Chapter 13.

5. *Maintainability* If maintainability is a critical requirement, the system architecture should be designed using fine-grain, self-contained components that may

readily be changed. Producers of data should be separated from consumers and shared data structures should be avoided.

Obviously there is potential conflict between some of these architectures. For example, using large components improves performance and using small, fine-grain components improves maintainability. If both performance and maintainability are important system requirements, then some compromise must be found. This can sometimes be achieved by using different architectural patterns or styles for different parts of the system.

Evaluating an architectural design is difficult because the true test of an architecture is how well the system meets its functional and non-functional requirements when it is in use. However, you can do some evaluation by comparing your design against reference architectures or generic architectural patterns. Bosch's (2000) description of the non-functional characteristics of architectural patterns can also be used to help with architectural evaluation.

6.2 Architectural views

I explained in the introduction to this chapter that architectural models of a software system can be used to focus discussion about the software requirements or design. Alternatively, they may be used to document a design so that it can be used as a basis for more detailed design and implementation, and for the future evolution of the system. In this section, I discuss two issues that are relevant to both of these:

1. What views or perspectives are useful when designing and documenting a system's architecture?

2. What notations should be used for describing architectural models?

It is impossible to represent all relevant information about a system's architecture in a single architectural model, as each model only shows one view or perspective of the system. It might show how a system is decomposed into modules, how the run-time processes interact, or the different ways in which system components are distributed across a network. All of these are useful at different times so, for both design and documentation, you usually need to present multiple views of the software architecture.

There are different opinions as to what views are required. Krutchen (1995), in his well-known 4+1 view model of software architecture, suggests that there should be four fundamental architectural views, which are related using use cases or scenarios. The views that he suggests are:

1. A logical view, which shows the key abstractions in the system as objects or object classes. It should be possible to relate the system requirements to entities in this logical view.

2.   A process view, which shows how, at run-time, the system is composed of inter-acting processes. This view is useful for making judgments about non-functional system characteristics such as performance and availability.

3.   A development view, which shows how the software is decomposed for development, that is, it shows the breakdown of the software into components that are implemented by a single developer or development team. This view is useful for software managers and programmers.

4.   A physical view, which shows the system hardware and how software components are distributed across the processors in the system. This view is useful for systems engineers planning a system deployment.

Hofmeister et al. (2000) suggest the use of similar views but add to this the notion of a conceptual view. This view is an abstract view of the system that can be the basis for decomposing high-level requirements into more detailed specifications, help engineers make decisions about components that can be reused, and represent a product line (discussed in Chapter 16) rather than a single system. Figure 6.1, which describes the architecture of a packing robot, is an example of a conceptual system view.

In practice, conceptual views are almost always developed during the design process and are used to support architectural decision making. They are a way of communicating the essence of a system to different stakeholders. During the design process, some of the other views may also be developed when different aspects of the system are discussed, but there is no need for a complete description from all perspectives. It may also be possible to associate architectural patterns, discussed in the next section, with the different views of a system.

There are differing views about whether or not software architects should use the UML for architectural description (Clements, et al., 2002). A survey in 2006 (Lange et al., 2006) showed that, when the UML was used, it was mostly applied in a loose and informal way. The authors of that paper argued that this was a bad thing. I disagree with this view. The UML was designed for describing object-oriented systems and, at the architectural design stage, you often want to describe systems at a higher level of abstraction. Object classes are too close to the implementation to be useful for architectural description.

I don't find the UML to be useful during the design process itself and prefer informal notations that are quicker to write and which can be easily drawn on a whiteboard. The UML is of most value when you are documenting an architecture in detail or using model-driven development, as discussed in Chapter 5.

A number of researchers have proposed the use of more specialized architectural description languages (ADLs) (Bass et al., 2003) to describe system architectures. The basic elements of ADLs are components and connectors, and they include rules and guidelines for well-formed architectures. However, because of their specialized nature, domain and application specialists find it hard to understand and use ADLs. This makes it difficult to assess their usefulness for practical software engineering. ADLs designed for a particular domain (e.g., automobile systems) may be used as a

Name	MVC (Model-View-Controller)
Description	Separates presentation and interaction from the system data. The system is structured into three logical components that interact with each other. The Model component manages the system data and associated operations on that data. The View component defines and manages how the data is presented to the user. The Controller component manages user interaction (e.g., key presses, mouse clicks, etc.) and passes these interactions to the View and the Model. See Figure 6.3.
Example	Figure 6.4 shows the architecture of a web-based application system organized using the MVC pattern.
When used	Used when there are multiple ways to view and interact with data. Also used when the future requirements for interaction and presentation of data are unknown.
Advantages	Allows the data to change independently of its representation and vice versa. Supports presentation of the same data in different ways with changes made in one representation shown in all of them.
Disadvantages	Can involve additional code and code complexity when the data model and interactions are simple.

Figure 6.2 The model-view-controller (MVC) pattern

basis for model-driven development. However, I believe that informal models and notations, such as the UML, will remain the most commonly used ways of documenting system architectures.

Users of agile methods claim that detailed design documentation is mostly unused. It is, therefore, a waste of time and money to develop it. I largely agree with this view and I think that, for most systems, it is not worth developing a detailed architectural description from these four perspectives. You should develop the views that are useful for communication and not worry about whether or not your architectural documentation is complete. However, an exception to this is when you are developing critical systems, when you need to make a detailed dependability analysis of the system. You may need to convince external regulators that your system conforms to their regulations and so complete architectural documentation may be required.

6.3 Architectural patterns

The idea of patterns as a way of presenting, sharing, and reusing knowledge about software systems is now widely used. The trigger for this was the publication of a book on object-oriented design patterns (Gamma et al., 1995), which prompted the development of other types of pattern, such as patterns for organizational design (Coplien and Harrison, 2004), usability patterns (Usability Group, 1998), interaction (Martin and Sommerville, 2004), configuration management (Berczuk and

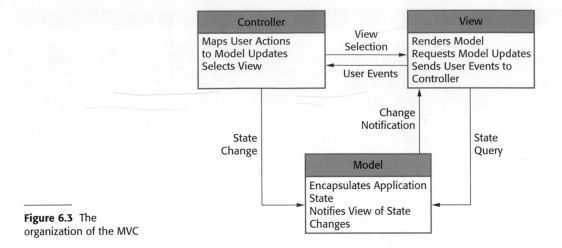

Figure 6.3 The organization of the MVC

Appleton, 2002), and so on. Architectural patterns were proposed in the 1990s under the name 'architectural styles' (Shaw and Garlan, 1996), with a five-volume series of handbooks on pattern-oriented software architecture published between 1996 and 2007 (Buschmann et al., 1996; Buschmann et al., 2007a; Buschmann et al., 2007b; Kircher and Jain, 2004; Schmidt et al., 2000).

In this section, I introduce architectural patterns and briefly describe a selection of architectural patterns that are commonly used in different types of systems. For more information about patterns and their use, you should refer to published pattern handbooks.

You can think of an architectural pattern as a stylized, abstract description of good practice, which has been tried and tested in different systems and environments. So, an architectural pattern should describe a system organization that has been successful in previous systems. It should include information of when it is and is not appropriate to use that pattern, and the pattern's strengths and weaknesses.

For example, Figure 6.2 describes the well-known Model-View-Controller pattern. This pattern is the basis of interaction management in many web-based systems. The stylized pattern description includes the pattern name, a brief description (with an associated graphical model), and an example of the type of system where the pattern is used (again, perhaps with a graphical model). You should also include information about when the pattern should be used and its advantages and disadvantages. Graphical models of the architecture associated with the MVC pattern are shown in Figures 6.3 and 6.4. These present the architecture from different views—Figure 6.3 is a conceptual view and Figure 6.4 shows a possible run-time architecture when this pattern is used for interaction management in a web-based system.

In a short section of a general chapter, it is impossible to describe all of the generic patterns that can be used in software development. Rather, I present some selected examples of patterns that are widely used and which capture good architectural design principles. I have included some further examples of generic architectural patterns on the book's web pages.

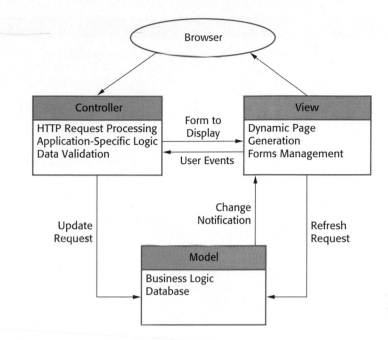

Figure 6.4 Web application architecture using the MVC pattern

6.3.1 Layered architecture

The notions of separation and independence are fundamental to architectural design because they allow changes to be localized. The MVC pattern, shown in Figure 6.2, separates elements of a system, allowing them to change independently. For example, adding a new view or changing an existing view can be done without any changes to the underlying data in the model. The layered architecture pattern is another way of achieving separation and independence. This pattern is shown in Figure 6.5. Here, the system functionality is organized into separate layers, and each layer only relies on the facilities and services offered by the layer immediately beneath it.

This layered approach supports the incremental development of systems. As a layer is developed, some of the services provided by that layer may be made available to users. The architecture is also changeable and portable. So long as its interface is unchanged, a layer can be replaced by another, equivalent layer. Furthermore, when layer interfaces change or new facilities are added to a layer, only the adjacent layer is affected. As layered systems localize machine dependencies in inner layers, this makes it easier to provide multi-platform implementations of an application system. Only the inner, machine-dependent layers need be re-implemented to take account of the facilities of a different operating system or database.

Figure 6.6 is an example of a layered architecture with four layers. The lowest layer includes system support software—typically database and operating system support. The next layer is the application layer that includes the components concerned with the application functionality and utility components that are used by other application components. The third layer is concerned with user interface

Name	Layered architecture
Description	Organizes the system into layers with related functionality associated with each layer. A layer provides services to the layer above it so the lowest-level layers represent core services that are likely to be used throughout the system. See Figure 6.6.
Example	A layered model of a system for sharing copyright documents held in different libraries, as shown in Figure 6.7.
When used	Used when building new facilities on top of existing systems; when the development is spread across several teams with each team responsibility for a layer of functionality; when there is a requirement for multi-level security.
Advantages	Allows replacement of entire layers so long as the interface is maintained. Redundant facilities (e.g., authentication) can be provided in each layer to increase the dependability of the system.
Disadvantages	In practice, providing a clean separation between layers is often difficult and a high-level layer may have to interact directly with lower-level layers rather than through the layer immediately below it. Performance can be a problem because of multiple levels of interpretation of a service request as it is processed at each layer.

Figure 6.5 The layered architecture pattern

management and providing user authentication and authorization, with the top layer providing user interface facilities. Of course, the number of layers is arbitrary. Any of the layers in Figure 6.6 could be split into two or more layers.

Figure 6.7 is an example of how this layered architecture pattern can be applied to a library system called LIBSYS, which allows controlled electronic access to copyright material from a group of university libraries. This has a five-layer architecture, with the bottom layer being the individual databases in each library.

You can see another example of the layered architecture pattern in Figure 6.17 (found in Section 6.4). This shows the organization of the system for mental health-care (MHC-PMS) that I have discussed in earlier chapters.

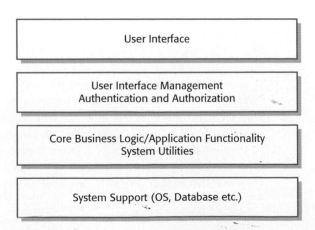

Figure 6.6 A generic layered architecture

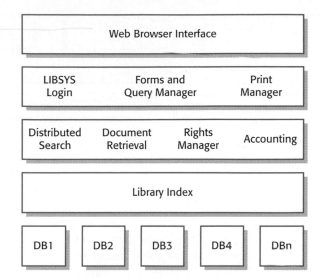

Figure 6.7 The architecture of the LIBSYS system

6.3.2 Repository architecture

The layered architecture and MVC patterns are examples of patterns where the view presented is the conceptual organization of a system. My next example, the Repository pattern (Figure 6.8), describes how a set of interacting components can share data.

The majority of systems that use large amounts of data are organized around a shared database or repository. This model is therefore suited to applications in which

Figure 6.8 The repository pattern

Name	Repository
Description	All data in a system is managed in a central repository that is accessible to all system components. Components do not interact directly, only through the repository.
Example	Figure 6.9 is an example of an IDE where the components use a repository of system design information. Each software tool generates information which is then available for use by other tools.
When used	You should use this pattern when you have a system in which large volumes of information are generated that has to be stored for a long time. You may also use it in data-driven systems where the inclusion of data in the repository triggers an action or tool.
Advantages	Components can be independent—they do not need to know of the existence of other components. Changes made by one component can be propagated to all components. All data can be managed consistently (e.g., backups done at the same time) as it is all in one place.
Disadvantages	The repository is a single point of failure so problems in the repository affect the whole system. May be inefficiencies in organizing all communication through the repository. Distributing the repository across several computers may be difficult.

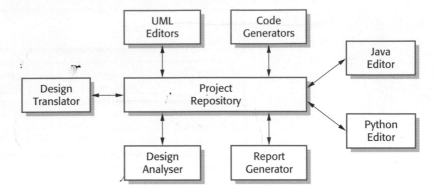

Figure 6.9 A repository architecture for an IDE

data is generated by one component and used by another. Examples of this type of system include command and control systems, management information systems, CAD systems, and interactive development environments for software.

Figure 6.9 is an illustration of a situation in which a repository might be used. This diagram shows an IDE that includes different tools to support model-driven development. The repository in this case might be a version-controlled environment (as discussed in Chapter 25) that keeps track of changes to software and allows rollback to earlier versions.

Organizing tools around a repository is an efficient way to share large amounts of data. There is no need to transmit data explicitly from one component to another. However, components must operate around an agreed repository data model. Inevitably, this is a compromise between the specific needs of each tool and it may be difficult or impossible to integrate new components if their data models do not fit the agreed schema. In practice, it may be difficult to distribute the repository over a number of machines. Although it is possible to distribute a logically centralized repository, there may be problems with data redundancy and inconsistency.

In the example shown in Figure 6.9, the repository is passive and control is the responsibility of the components using the repository. An alternative approach, which has been derived for AI systems, uses a 'blackboard' model that triggers components when particular data become available. This is appropriate when the form of the repository data is less well structured. Decisions about which tool to activate can only be made when the data has been analyzed. This model is introduced by Nii (1986). Bosch (2000) includes a good discussion of how this style relates to system quality attributes.

6.3.3 Client–server architecture

The repository pattern is concerned with the static structure of a system and does not show its run-time organization. My next example illustrates a very commonly used run-time organization for distributed systems. The Client–server pattern is described in Figure 6.10.

Name	Client–server
Description	In a client–server architecture, the functionality of the system is organized into services, with each service delivered from a separate server. Clients are users of these services and access servers to make use of them.
Example	Figure 6.11 is an example of a film and video/DVD library organized as a client–server system.
When used	Used when data in a shared database has to be accessed from a range of locations. Because servers can be replicated, may also be used when the load on a system is variable.
Advantages	The principal advantage of this model is that servers can be distributed across a network. General functionality (e.g., a printing service) can be available to all clients and does not need to be implemented by all services.
Disadvantages	Each service is a single point of failure so susceptible to denial of service attacks or server failure. Performance may be unpredictable because it depends on the network as well as the system. May be management problems if servers are owned by different organizations.

Figure 6.10 The client–server pattern

A system that follows the client–server pattern is organized as a set of services and associated servers, and clients that access and use the services. The major components of this model are:

1. A set of servers that offer services to other components. Examples of servers include print servers that offer printing services, file servers that offer file management services, and a compile server, which offers programming language compilation services.

2. A set of clients that call on the services offered by servers. There will normally be several instances of a client program executing concurrently on different computers.

3. A network that allows the clients to access these services. Most client–server systems are implemented as distributed systems, connected using Internet protocols.

Client–server architectures are usually thought of as distributed systems architectures but the logical model of independent services running on separate servers can be implemented on a single computer. Again, an important benefit is separation and independence. Services and servers can be changed without affecting other parts of the system.

Clients may have to know the names of the available servers and the services that they provide. However, servers do not need to know the identity of clients or how many clients are accessing their services. Clients access the services provided by a server through remote procedure calls using a request-reply protocol such as the http

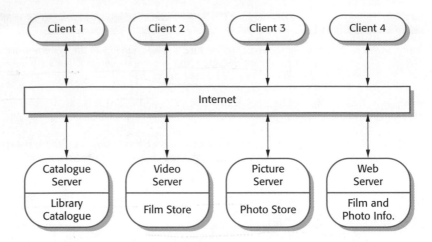

Figure 6.11 A client–server architecture for a film library

protocol used in the WWW. Essentially, a client makes a request to a server and waits until it receives a reply.

Figure 6.11 is an example of a system that is based on the client–server model. This is a multi-user, web-based system for providing a film and photograph library. In this system, several servers manage and display the different types of media. Video frames need to be transmitted quickly and in synchrony but at relatively low resolution. They may be compressed in a store, so the video server can handle video compression and decompression in different formats. Still pictures, however, must be maintained at a high resolution, so it is appropriate to maintain them on a separate server.

The catalog must be able to deal with a variety of queries and provide links into the web information system that includes data about the film and video clips, and an e-commerce system that supports the sale of photographs, film, and video clips. The

Figure 6.12 The pipe and filter pattern

Name	Pipe and filter
Description	The processing of the data in a system is organized so that each processing component (filter) is discrete and carries out one type of data transformation. The data flows (as in a pipe) from one component to another for processing.
Example	Figure 6.13 is an example of a pipe and filter system used for processing invoices.
When used	Commonly used in data processing applications (both batch- and transaction-based) where inputs are processed in separate stages to generate related outputs.
Advantages	Easy to understand and supports transformation reuse. Workflow style matches the structure of many business processes. Evolution by adding transformations is straightforward. Can be implemented as either a sequential or concurrent system.
Disadvantages	The format for data transfer has to be agreed upon between communicating transformations. Each transformation must parse its input and unparse its output to the agreed form. This increases system overhead and may mean that it is impossible to reuse functional transformations that use incompatible data structures.

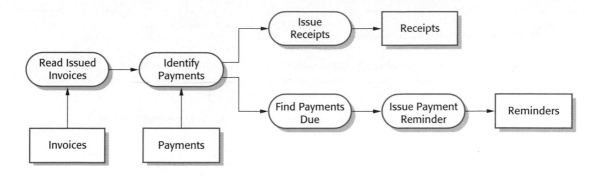

Figure 6.13 An
example of the pipe
and filter architecture

client program is simply an integrated user interface, constructed using a web browser, to access these services.

The most important advantage of the client–server model is that it is a distributed architecture. Effective use can be made of networked systems with many distributed processors. It is easy to add a new server and integrate it with the rest of the system or to upgrade servers transparently without affecting other parts of the system. I discuss distributed architectures, including client–server architectures and distributed object architectures, in Chapter 18.

6.3.4 Pipe and filter architecture

My final example of an architectural pattern is the pipe and filter pattern. This is a model of the run-time organization of a system where functional transformations process their inputs and produce outputs. Data flows from one to another and is transformed as it moves through the sequence. Each processing step is implemented as a transform. Input data flows through these transforms until converted to output. The transformations may execute sequentially or in parallel. The data can be processed by each transform item by item or in a single batch.

The name 'pipe and filter' comes from the original Unix system where it was possible to link processes using 'pipes'. These passed a text stream from one process to another. Systems that conform to this model can be implemented by combining Unix commands, using pipes and the control facilities of the Unix shell. The term 'filter' is used because a transformation 'filters out' the data it can process from its input data stream.

Variants of this pattern have been in use since computers were first used for automatic data processing. When transformations are sequential with data processed in batches, this pipe and filter architectural model becomes a batch sequential model, a common architecture for data processing systems (e.g., a billing system). The architecture of an embedded system may also be organized as a process pipeline, with each process executing concurrently. I discuss the use of this pattern in embedded systems in Chapter 20.

An example of this type of system architecture, used in a batch processing application, is shown in Figure 6.13. An organization has issued invoices to customers. Once a week, payments that have been made are reconciled with the invoices. For

Architectural patterns for control

There are specific architectural patterns that reflect commonly used ways of organizing control in a system. These include centralized control, based on one component calling other components, and event-based control, where the system reacts to external events.

http://www.SoftwareEngineering-9.com/Web/Architecture/ArchPatterns/

those invoices that have been paid, a receipt is issued. For those invoices that have not been paid within the allowed payment time, a reminder is issued.

Interactive systems are difficult to write using the pipe and filter model because of the need for a stream of data to be processed. Although simple textual input and output can be modeled in this way, graphical user interfaces have more complex I/O formats and a control strategy that is based on events such as mouse clicks or menu selections. It is difficult to translate this into a form compatible with the pipelining model.

6.4 Application architectures

Application systems are intended to meet a business or organizational need. All businesses have much in common—they need to hire people, issue invoices, keep accounts, and so on. Businesses operating in the same sector use common sector-specific applications. Therefore, as well as general business functions, all phone companies need systems to connect calls, manage their network, issue bills to customers, etc. Consequently, the application systems used by these businesses also have much in common.

These commonalities have led to the development of software architectures that describe the structure and organization of particular types of software systems. Application architectures encapsulate the principal characteristics of a class of systems. For example, in real-time systems, there might be generic architectural models of different system types, such as data collection systems or monitoring systems. Although instances of these systems differ in detail, the common architectural structure can be reused when developing new systems of the same type.

The application architecture may be re-implemented when developing new systems but, for many business systems, application reuse is possible without re-implementation. We see this in the growth of Enterprise Resource Planning (ERP) systems from companies such as SAP and Oracle, and vertical software packages (COTS) for specialized applications in different areas of business. In these systems, a generic system is configured and adapted to create a specific business application.

Application architectures

There are several examples of application architectures on the book's website. These include descriptions of batch data-processing systems, resource allocation systems, and event-based editing systems.

http://www.SoftwareEngineering-9.com/Web/Architecture/AppArch/

For example, a system for supply chain management can be adapted for different types of suppliers, goods, and contractual arrangements.

As a software designer, you can use models of application architectures in a number of ways:

1. *As a starting point for the architectural design process* If you are unfamiliar with the type of application that you are developing, you can base your initial design on a generic application architecture. Of course, this will have to be specialized for the specific system being developed, but it is a good starting point for design.

2. *As a design checklist* If you have developed an architectural design for an application system, you can compare this with the generic application architecture. You can check that your design is consistent with the generic architecture.

3. *As a way of organizing the work of the development team* The application architectures identify stable structural features of the system architectures and in many cases, it is possible to develop these in parallel. You can assign work to group members to implement different components within the architecture.

4. *As a means of assessing components for reuse* If you have components you might be able to reuse, you can compare these with the generic structures to see whether there are comparable components in the application architecture.

5. *As a vocabulary for talking about types of applications* If you are discussing a specific application or trying to compare applications of the same types, then you can use the concepts identified in the generic architecture to talk about the applications.

There are many types of application system and, in some cases, they may seem to be very different. However, many of these superficially dissimilar applications actually have much in common, and thus can be represented by a single abstract application architecture. I illustrate this here by describing the following architectures of two types of application:

1. *Transaction processing applications* Transaction processing applications are database-centered applications that process user requests for information and update the information in a database. These are the most common type of interactive business systems. They are organized in such a way that user actions can't interfere with each other and the integrity of the database is maintained. This

Figure 6.14 The structure of transaction processing applications

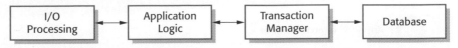

class of system includes interactive banking systems, e-commerce systems, information systems, and booking systems.

2. *Language processing systems* Language processing systems are systems in which the user's intentions are expressed in a formal language (such as Java). The language processing system processes this language into an internal format and then interprets this internal representation. The best-known language processing systems are compilers, which translate high-level language programs into machine code. However, language processing systems are also used to interpret command languages for databases and information systems, and markup languages such as XML (Harold and Means, 2002; Hunter et al., 2007).

I have chosen these particular types of system because a large number of web-based business systems are transaction-processing systems, and all software development relies on language processing systems.

6.4.1 Transaction processing systems

Transaction processing (TP) systems are designed to process user requests for information from a database, or requests to update a database (Lewis et al., 2003). Technically, a database transaction is sequence of operations that is treated as a single unit (an atomic unit). All of the operations in a transaction have to be completed before the database changes are made permanent. This ensures that failure of operations within the transaction does not lead to inconsistencies in the database.

From a user perspective, a transaction is any coherent sequence of operations that satisfies a goal, such as 'find the times of flights from London to Paris'. If the user transaction does not require the database to be changed then it may not be necessary to package this as a technical database transaction.

An example of a transaction is a customer request to withdraw money from a bank account using an ATM. This involves getting details of the customer's account, checking the balance, modifying the balance by the amount withdrawn, and sending commands to the ATM to deliver the cash. Until all of these steps have been completed, the transaction is incomplete and the customer accounts database is not changed.

Transaction processing systems are usually interactive systems in which users make asynchronous requests for service. Figure 6.14 illustrates the conceptual architectural structure of TP applications. First a user makes a request to the system through an I/O processing component. The request is processed by some application-specific logic. A transaction is created and passed to a transaction manager, which is usually embedded in the database management system. After the transaction manager

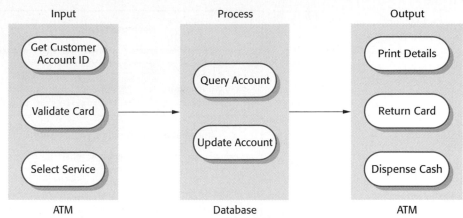

Input | Process | Output

Get Customer Account ID

Validate Card

Select Service

ATM

Query Account

Update Account

Database

Print Details

Return Card

Dispense Cash

ATM

Figure 6.15 The software architecture of an ATM system

has ensured that the transaction is properly completed, it signals to the application that processing has finished.

Transaction processing systems may be organized as a 'pipe and filter' architecture with system components responsible for input, processing, and output. For example, consider a banking system that allows customers to query their accounts and withdraw cash from an ATM. The system is composed of two cooperating software components—the ATM software and the account processing software in the bank's database server. The input and output components are implemented as software in the ATM and the processing component is part of the bank's database server. Figure 6.15 shows the architecture of this system, illustrating the functions of the input, process, and output components.

6.4.2   Information systems

All systems that involve interaction with a shared database can be considered to be transaction-based information systems. An information system allows controlled access to a large base of information, such as a library catalog, a flight timetable, or the records of patients in a hospital. Increasingly, information systems are web-based systems that are accessed through a web browser.

Figure 6.16 a very general model of an information system. The system is modeled using a layered approach (discussed in Section 6.3) where the top layer supports the user interface and the bottom layer is the system database. The user communications layer handles all input and output from the user interface, and the information retrieval layer includes application-specific logic for accessing and updating the database. As we shall see later, the layers in this model can map directly onto servers in an Internet-based system.

As an example of an instantiation of this layered model, Figure 6.17 shows the architecture of the MHC-PMS. Recall that this system maintains and manages details of patients who are consulting specialist doctors about mental health problems. I have

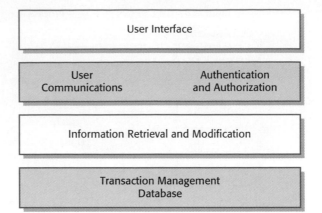

Figure 6.16 Layered
information system
architecture

added detail to each layer in the model by identifying the components that support user communications and information retrieval and access:

1. The top layer is responsible for implementing the user interface. In this case, the UI has been implemented using a web browser.

2. The second layer provides the user interface functionality that is delivered through the web browser. It includes components to allow users to log in to the system and checking components that ensure that the operations they use are allowed by their role. This layer includes form and menu management components that present information to users, and data validation components that check information consistency.

3. The third layer implements the functionality of the system and provides components that implement system security, patient information creation and updating, import and export of patient data from other databases, and report generators that create management reports.

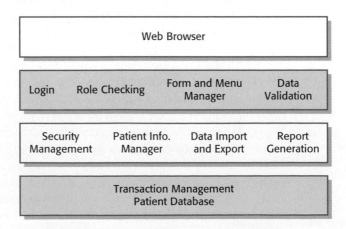

Figure 6.17 The
architecture of the
MHC-PMS

4.   Finally, the lowest layer, which is built using a commercial database management system, provides transaction management and persistent data storage.

Information and resource management systems are now usually web-based systems where the user interfaces are implemented using a web browser. For example, e-commerce systems are Internet-based resource management systems that accept electronic orders for goods or services and then arrange delivery of these goods or services to the customer. In an e-commerce system, the application-specific layer includes additional functionality supporting a 'shopping cart' in which users can place a number of items in separate transactions, then pay for them all together in a single transaction.

The organization of servers in these systems usually reflects the four-layer generic model presented in Figure 6.16. These systems are often implemented as multi-tier client server/architectures, as discussed in Chapter 18:

1.   The web server is responsible for all user communications, with the user interface implemented using a web browser;

2.   The application server is responsible for implementing application-specific logic as well as information storage and retrieval requests;

3.   The database server moves information to and from the database and handles transaction management.

Using multiple servers allows high throughput and makes it possible to handle hundreds of transactions per minute. As demand increases, servers can be added at each level to cope with the extra processing involved.

6.4.3 Language processing systems

Language processing systems translate a natural or artificial language into another representation of that language and, for programming languages, may also execute the resulting code. In software engineering, compilers translate an artificial programming language into machine code. Other language-processing systems may translate an XML data description into commands to query a database or to an alternative XML representation. Natural language processing systems may translate one natural language to another e.g., French to Norwegian.

A possible architecture for a language processing system for a programming language is illustrated in Figure 6.18. The source language instructions define the program to be executed and a translator converts these into instructions for an abstract machine. These instructions are then interpreted by another component that fetches the instructions for execution and executes them using (if necessary) data from the environment. The output of the process is the result of interpreting the instructions on the input data.

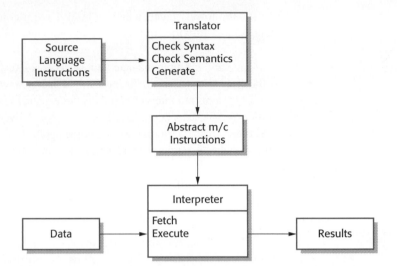

Figure 6.18 The architecture of a language processing system

Of course, for many compilers, the interpreter is a hardware unit that processes machine instructions and the abstract machine is a real processor. However, for dynamically typed languages, such as Python, the interpreter may be a software component.

Programming language compilers that are part of a more general programming environment have a generic architecture (Figure 6.19) that includes the following components:

1. A lexical analyzer, which takes input language tokens and converts them to an internal form.

2. A symbol table, which holds information about the names of entities (variables, class names, object names, etc.) used in the text that is being translated.

3. A syntax analyzer, which checks the syntax of the language being translated. It uses a defined grammar of the language and builds a syntax tree.

4. A syntax tree, which is an internal structure representing the program being compiled.

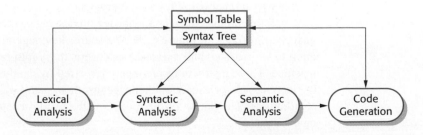

Figure 6.19 A pipe and filter compiler architecture

Reference architectures

Reference architectures capture important features of system architectures in a domain. Essentially, they include everything that might be in an application architecture although, in reality, it is very unlikely that any individual application would include all the features shown in a reference architecture. The main purpose of reference architectures is to evaluate and compare design proposals, and to educate people about architectural characteristics in that domain.

http://www.SoftwareEngineering-9.com/Web/Architecture/RefArch.html

5. A semantic analyzer that uses information from the syntax tree and the symbol table to check the semantic correctness of the input language text.

6. A code generator that 'walks' the syntax tree and generates abstract machine code.

Other components might also be included which analyze and transform the syntax tree to improve efficiency and remove redundancy from the generated machine code. In other types of language processing system, such as a natural language translator, there will be additional components such as a dictionary, and the generated code is actually the input text translated into another language.

There are alternative architectural patterns that may be used in a language processing system (Garlan and Shaw, 1993). Compilers can be implemented using a composite of a repository and a pipe and filter model. In a compiler architecture, the symbol table is a repository for shared data. The phases of lexical, syntactic, and semantic analysis are organized sequentially, as shown in Figure 6.19, and communicate through the shared symbol table.

This pipe and filter model of language compilation is effective in batch environments where programs are compiled and executed without user interaction; for example, in the translation of one XML document to another. It is less effective when a compiler is integrated with other language processing tools such as a structured editing system, an interactive debugger or a program prettyprinter. In this situation, changes from one component need to be reflected immediately in other components. It is better, therefore, to organize the system around a repository, as shown in Figure 6.20.

This figure illustrates how a language processing system can be part of an integrated set of programming support tools. In this example, the symbol table and syntax tree act as a central information repository. Tools or tool fragments communicate through it. Other information that is sometimes embedded in tools, such as the grammar definition and the definition of the output format for the program, have been taken out of the tools and put into the repository. Therefore, a syntax-directed editor can check that the syntax of a program is correct as it is being typed and a prettyprinter can create listings of the program in a format that is easy to read.

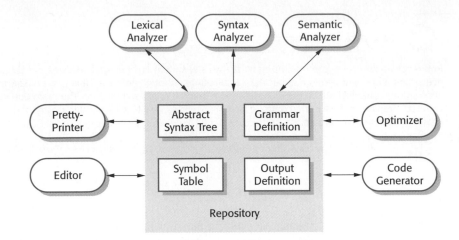

Figure 6.20 A repository architecture for a language processing system

KEY POINTS

■ A software architecture is a description of how a software system is organized. Properties of a system such as performance, security, and availability are influenced by the architecture used.

■ Architectural design decisions include decisions on the type of application, the distribution of the system, the architectural styles to be used, and the ways in which the architecture should be documented and evaluated.

■ Architectures may be documented from several different perspectives or views. Possible views include a conceptual view, a logical view, a process view, a development view, and a physical view.

■ Architectural patterns are a means of reusing knowledge about generic system architectures. They describe the architecture, explain when it may be used, and discuss its advantages and disadvantages.

■ Commonly used architectural patterns include Model-View-Controller, Layered Architecture, Repository, Client–server, and Pipe and Filter.

■ Generic models of application systems architectures help us understand the operation of applications, compare applications of the same type, validate application system designs, and assess large-scale components for reuse.

■ Transaction processing systems are interactive systems that allow information in a database to be remotely accessed and modified by a number of users. Information systems and resource management systems are examples of transaction processing systems.

■ Language processing systems are used to translate texts from one language into another and to carry out the instructions specified in the input language. They include a translator and an abstract machine that executes the generated language.

FURTHER READING

Software Architecture: Perspectives on an Emerging Discipline. This was the first book on software architecture and has a good discussion on different architectural styles. (M. Shaw and D. Garlan, Prentice-Hall, 1996.)

Software Architecture in Practice, 2nd ed. This is a practical discussion of software architectures that does not oversell the benefits of architectural design. It provides a clear business rationale explaining why architectures are important. (L. Bass, P. Clements and R. Kazman, Addison-Wesley, 2003.)

'The Golden Age of Software Architecture' This paper surveys the development of software architecture from its beginnings in the 1980s through to its current usage. There is little technical content but it is an interesting historical overview. (M. Shaw and P. Clements, *IEEE Software,* **21** (2), March–April 2006.) http://dx.doi.org/10.1109/MS.2006.58.

Handbook of Software Architecture. This is a work in progress by Grady Booch, one of the early evangelists for software architecture. He has been documenting the architectures of a range of software systems so you can see reality rather than academic abstraction. Available on the Web and intended to appear as a book. http://www.handbookofsoftwarearchitecture.com/.

EXERCISES

6.1. When describing a system, explain why you may have to design the system architecture before the requirements specification is complete.

6.2. You have been asked to prepare and deliver a presentation to a non-technical manager to justify the hiring of a system architect for a new project. Write a list of bullet points setting out the key points in your presentation. Naturally, you have to explain what is meant by system architecture.

6.3. Explain why design conflicts might arise when designing an architecture for which both availability and security requirements are the most important non-functional requirements.

6.4. Draw diagrams showing a conceptual view and a process view of the architectures of the following systems:

An automated ticket-issuing system used by passengers at a railway station.

A computer-controlled video conferencing system that allows video, audio, and computer data to be visible to several participants at the same time.

A robot floor cleaner that is intended to clean relatively clear spaces such as corridors. The cleaner must be able to sense walls and other obstructions.

6.5. Explain why you normally use several architectural patterns when designing the architecture of a large system. Apart from the information about patterns that I have discussed in this chapter, what additional information might be useful when designing large systems?

6.6. Suggest an architecture for a system (such as iTunes) that is used to sell and distribute music on the Internet. What architectural patterns are the basis for this architecture?

6.7. Explain how you would use the reference model of CASE environments (available on the book's web pages) to compare the IDEs offered by different vendors of a programming language such as Java.

6.8. Using the generic model of a language processing system presented here, design the architecture of a system that accepts natural language commands and translates these into database queries in a language such as SQL.

6.9. Using the basic model of an information system, as presented in Figure 6.16, suggest the components that might be part of an information system that allows users to view information about flights arriving and departing from a particular airport.

6.10. Should there be a separate profession of 'software architect' whose role is to work independently with a customer to design the software system architecture? A separate software company would then implement the system. What might be the difficulties of establishing such a profession?

REFERENCES

Bass, L., Clements, P. and Kazman, R. (2003). Software Architecture in Practice, 2nd ed. Boston: Addison-Wesley.

Berczuk, S. P. and Appleton, B. (2002). Software Configuration Management Patterns: Effective Teamwork, Practical Integration. Boston: Addison-Wesley.

Booch, G. (2009). 'Handbook of software architecture'. Web publication. http://www.handbookofsoftwarearchitecture.com/.

Bosch, J. (2000). Design and Use of Software Architectures. Harlow, UK: Addison-Wesley.

Buschmann, F., Henney, K. and Schmidt, D. C. (2007a). Pattern-oriented Software Architecture Volume 4: A Pattern Language for Distributed Computing. New York: John Wiley & Sons.

Buschmann, F., Henney, K. and Schmidt, D. C. (2007b). Pattern-oriented Software Architecture Volume 5: On Patterns and Pattern Languages. New York: John Wiley & Sons.

Buschmann, F., Meunier, R., Rohnert, H. and Sommerlad, P. (1996). Pattern-oriented Software Architecture Volume 1: A System of Patterns. New York: John Wiley & Sons.

Clements, P., Bachmann, F., Bass, L., Garlan, D., Ivers, J., Little, R., Nord, R. and Stafford, J. (2002). Documenting Software Architectures: Views and Beyond. Boston: Addison-Wesley.

Coplien, J. H. and Harrison, N. B. (2004). Organizational Patterns of Agile Software Development. Englewood Cliffs, NJ: Prentice Hall.

Gamma, E., Helm, R., Johnson, R. and Vlissides, J. (1995). Design Patterns: Elements of Reusable Object-Oriented Software. Reading, Mass.: Addison-Wesley.

Garlan, D. and Shaw, M. (1993). 'An introduction to software architecture'. Advances in Software Engineering and Knowledge Engineering, 1 1–39.

Harold, E. R. and Means, W. S. (2002). XML in a Nutshell. Sebastopol. Calif.: O'Reilly.

Hofmeister, C., Nord, R. and Soni, D. (2000). Applied Software Architecture. Boston: Addison-Wesley.

Hunter, D., Rafter, J., Fawcett, J. and Van Der Vlist, E. (2007). Beginning XML, 4th ed. Indianapolis, Ind.: Wrox Press.

Kircher, M. and Jain, P. (2004). Pattern-Oriented Software Architecture Volume 3: Patterns for Resource Management. New York: John Wiley & Sons.

Krutchen, P. (1995). 'The 4+1 view model of software architecture'. IEEE Software, 12 (6), 42–50.

Lange, C. F. J., Chaudron, M. R. V. and Muskens, J. (2006). 'UML software description and architecture description'. IEEE Software, 23 (2), 40–6.

Lewis, P. M., Bernstein, A. J. and Kifer, M. (2003). Databases and Transaction Processing: An Application-oriented Approach. Boston: Addison-Wesley.

Martin, D. and Sommerville, I. (2004). 'Patterns of interaction: Linking ethnomethodology and design'. ACM Trans. on Computer-Human Interaction, 11 (1), 59–89.

Nii, H. P. (1986). 'Blackboard systems, parts 1 and 2'. AI Magazine, 7 (3 and 4), 38–53 and 62–9.

Schmidt, D., Stal, M., Rohnert, H. and Buschmann, F. (2000). Pattern-Oriented Software Architecture Volume 2: Patterns for Concurrent and Networked Objects. New York: John Wiley & Sons.

Shaw, M. and Garlan, D. (1996). Software Architecture: Perspectives on an Emerging Discipline. Englewood Cliffs, NJ: Prentice Hall.

Usability group. (1998). 'Usability patterns'. Web publication. http://www.it.bton.ac.uk/cil/usability/patterns/.

7

Design and implementation

Objectives

The objectives of this chapter are to introduce object-oriented software design using the UML and highlight important implementation concerns. When you have read this chapter, you will:

■ understand the most important activities in a general, object-oriented design process;

■ understand some of the different models that may be used to document an object-oriented design;

■ know about the idea of design patterns and how these are a way of reusing design knowledge and experience;

■ have been introduced to key issues that have to be considered when implementing software, including software reuse and open-source development.

Contents

Software design and implementation is the stage in the software engineering process at which an executable software system is developed. For some simple systems, software design and implementation is software engineering, and all other activities are merged with this process. However, for large systems, software design and implementation is only one of a set of processes (requirements engineering, verification and validation, etc.) involved in software engineering.

Software design and implementation activities are invariably interleaved. Software design is a creative activity in which you identify software components and their relationships, based on a customer's requirements. Implementation is the process of realizing the design as a program. Sometimes, there is a separate design stage and this design is modeled and documented. At other times, a design is in the programmer's head or roughly sketched on a whiteboard or sheets of paper. Design is about how to solve a problem, so there is always a design process. However, it isn't always necessary or appropriate to describe the design in detail using the UML or other design description language.

Design and implementation are closely linked and you should normally take implementation issues into account when developing a design. For example, using the UML to document a design may be the right thing to do if you are programming in an object-oriented language such as Java or C#. It is less useful, I think, if you are developing in a dynamically typed language like Python and makes no sense at all if you are implementing your system by configuring an off-the-shelf package. As I discussed in Chapter 3, agile methods usually work from informal sketches of the design and leave many design decisions to programmers.

One of the most important implementation decisions that has to be made at an early stage of a software project is whether or not you should buy or build the application software. In a wide range of domains, it is now possible to buy off-the-shelf systems (COTS) that can be adapted and tailored to the users' requirements. For example, if you want to implement a medical records system, you can buy a package that is already used in hospitals. It can be cheaper and faster to use this approach rather than developing a system in a conventional programming language.

When you develop an application in this way, the design process becomes concerned with how to use the configuration features of that system to deliver the system requirements. You don't usually develop design models of the system, such as models of the system objects and their interactions. I discuss this COTS-based approach to development in Chapter 16.

I assume that most readers of this book will have had experience of program design and implementation. This is something that you acquire as you learn to program and master the elements of a programming language like Java or Python. You will have probably learned about good programming practice in the programming languages that you have studied, as well as how to debug programs that you have developed. Therefore, I don't cover programming topics here. Instead, this chapter has two aims:

1.   To show how system modeling and architectural design (covered in Chapters 5 and 6) are put into practice in developing an object-oriented software design.

Structured design methods

Structured design methods propose that software design should be tackled in a methodical way. Designing a system involves following the steps of the method and refining the design of a system at increasingly detailed levels. In the 1990s, there were a number of competing methods for object-oriented design. However, the inventors of the most commonly used methods came together and invented the UML, which unified the notations used in the different methods.

Rather than focus on methods, most discussions now are about processes where design is seen as part of the overall software development process. The Rational Unified Process (RUP) is a good example of a generic development process.

http://www.SoftwareEngineering-9.com/Web/Structured-methods/

2. To introduce important implementation issues that are not usually covered in programming books. These include software reuse, configuration management, and open source development.

As there are a vast number of different development platforms, the chapter is not biased towards any particular programming language or implementation technology. Therefore, I have presented all examples using the UML rather than in a programming language such as Java or Python.

7.1 Object-oriented design using the UML

An object-oriented system is made up of interacting objects that maintain their own local state and provide operations on that state. The representation of the state is private and cannot be accessed directly from outside the object. Object-oriented design processes involve designing object classes and the relationships between these classes. These classes define the objects in the system and their interactions. When the design is realized as an executing program, the objects are created dynamically from these class definitions.

Object-oriented systems are easier to change than systems developed using functional approaches. Objects include both data and operations to manipulate that data. They may therefore be understood and modified as stand-alone entities. Changing the implementation of an object or adding services should not affect other system objects. Because objects are associated with things, there is often a clear mapping between real-world entities (such as hardware components) and their controlling objects in the system. This improves the understandability, and hence the maintainability, of the design.

To develop a system design from concept to detailed, object-oriented design, there are several things that you need to do:

1. Understand and define the context and the external interactions with the system.

2. Design the system architecture.

3. Identify the principal objects in the system.

4. Develop design models.

5. Specify interfaces.

Like all creative activities, design is not a clear-cut, sequential process. You develop a design by getting ideas, proposing solutions, and refining these solutions as information becomes available. You inevitably have to backtrack and retry when problems arise. Sometimes you explore options in detail to see if they work; at other times you ignore details until late in the process. Consequently, I have deliberately not illustrated this process as a simple diagram because that would imply design can be thought of as a neat sequence of activities. In fact, all of the above activities are interleaved and so influence each other.

I illustrate these process activities by designing part of the software for the wilderness weather station that I introduced in Chapter 1. Wilderness weather stations are deployed in remote areas. Each weather station records local weather information and periodically transfers this to a weather information system, using a satellite link.

7.1.1 System context and interactions

The first stage in any software design process is to develop an understanding of the relationships between the software that is being designed and its external environment. This is essential for deciding how to provide the required system functionality and how to structure the system to communicate with its environment. Understanding of the context also lets you establish the boundaries of the system.

Setting the system boundaries helps you decide what features are implemented in the system being designed and what features are in other associated systems. In this case, you need to decide how functionality is distributed between the control system for all of the weather stations, and the embedded software in the weather station itself.

System context models and interaction models present complementary views of the relationships between a system and its environment:

1. A system context model is a structural model that demonstrates the other systems in the environment of the system being developed.

2. An interaction model is a dynamic model that shows how the system interacts with its environment as it is used.

The context model of a system may be represented using associations. Associations simply show that there are some relationships between the entities involved in the association. The nature of the relationships is now specified. You may therefore document the environment of the system using a simple block diagram, showing the entities in the system and their associations. This is illustrated in Figure 7.1, which shows that

Weather station use cases

Report weather—send weather data to the weather information system

Report status—send status information to the weather information system

Restart—if the weather station is shut down, restart the system

Shutdown—shut down the weather station

Reconfigure—reconfigure the weather station software

Powersave—put the weather station into power-saving mode

Remote control—send control commands to any weather station subsystem

http://www.SoftwareEngineering-9.com/Web/WS/Usecases.html

the systems in the environment of each weather station are a weather information system, an onboard satellite system, and a control system. The cardinality information on the link shows that there is one control system but several weather stations, one satellite, and one general weather information system.

When you model the interactions of a system with its environment you should use an abstract approach that does not include too much detail. One way to do this is to use a use case model. As I discussed in Chapters 4 and 5, each use case represents an interaction with the system. Each possible interaction is named in an ellipse and the external entity involved in the interaction is represented by a stick figure.

The use case model for the weather station is shown in Figure 7.2. This shows that the weather station interacts with the weather information system to report weather data and the status of the weather station hardware. Other interactions are with a control system that can issue specific weather station control commands. As I explained in Chapter 5, a stick figure is used in the UML to represent other systems as well as human users.

Each of these use cases should be described in structured natural language. This helps designers identify objects in the system and gives them an understanding of what the system is intended to do. I use a standard format for this description that clearly identifies what information is exchanged, how the interaction is initiated, and

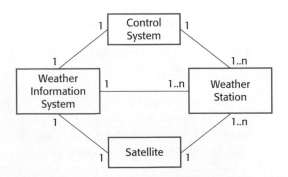

Figure 7.1 System context for the weather station

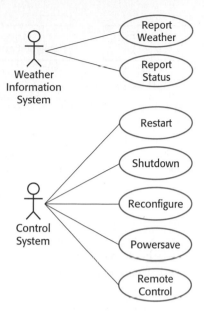

Figure 7.2 Weather station use cases

so on. This is shown in Figure 7.3, which describes the Report weather use case from Figure 7.2. Examples of some other use cases are on the Web.

7.1.2 Architectural design

Figure 7.3 Use case description—Report weather

Once the interactions between the software system and the system's environment have been defined, you use this information as a basis for designing the system architecture. Of course, you need to combine this with your general knowledge of the principles of architectural design and with more detailed domain knowledge.

System	Weather station
Use case	Report weather
Actors	Weather information system, Weather station
Dat	The weather station sends a summary of the weather data that has been collected from the instruments in the collection period to the weather information system. The data sent are the maximum, minimum, and average ground and air temperatures; the maximum, minimum, and average air pressures; the maximum, minimum, and average wind speeds; the total rainfall; and the wind direction as sampled at five-minute intervals.
Stimulus	The weather information system establishes a satellite communication link with the weather station and requests transmission of the data.
Response	The summarized data are sent to the weather information system.
Comments	Weather stations are usually asked to report once per hour but this frequency may differ from one station to another and may be modified in the future.

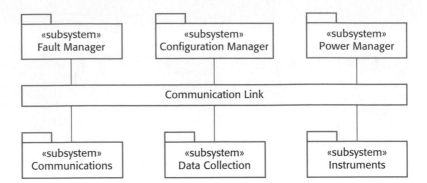

You identify the major components that make up the system and their interactions, and then may organize the components using an architectural pattern such as a layered or client–server model. However, this is not essential at this stage.

The high-level architectural design for the weather station software is shown in Figure 7.4. The weather station is composed of independent subsystems that communicate by broadcasting messages on a common infrastructure, shown as the Communication link in Figure 7.4. Each subsystem listens for messages on that infrastructure and picks up the messages that are intended for them. This is another commonly used architectural style in addition to those described in Chapter 6.

For example, when the communications subsystem receives a control command, such as shutdown, the command is picked up by each of the other subsystems, which then shut themselves down in the correct way. The key benefit of this architecture is that it is easy to support different configurations of subsystems because the sender of a message does not need to address the message to a particular subsystem.

Figure 7.5 shows the architecture of the data collection subsystem, which is included in Figure 7.4. The Transmitter and Receiver objects are concerned with managing communications and the WeatherData object encapsulates the information that is collected from the instruments and transmitted to the weather information system. This arrangement follows the producer-consumer pattern, discussed in Chapter 20.

7.1.3 Object class identification

By this stage in the design process, you should have some ideas about the essential objects in the system that you are designing. As your understanding of the design develops, you refine these ideas about the system objects. The use case description helps to identify objects and operations in the system. From the description of the Report weather use case, it is obvious that objects representing the instruments that collect weather data will be required, as will an object representing the summary of the weather data. You also usually need a high-level

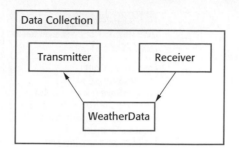

Figure 7.5 Architecture of data collection system

system object or objects that encapsulate the system interactions defined in the use cases. With these objects in mind, you can start to identify the object classes in the system.

There have been various proposals made about how to identify object classes in object-oriented systems:

1. Use a grammatical analysis of a natural language description of the system to be constructed. Objects and attributes are nouns; operations or services are verbs (Abbott, 1983).

2. Use tangible entities (things) in the application domain such as aircraft, roles such as manager or doctor, events such as requests, interactions such as meetings, locations such as offices, organizational units such as companies, and so on (Coad and Yourdon, 1990; Shlaer and Mellor, 1988; Wirfs-Brock et al., 1990).

3. Use a scenario-based analysis where various scenarios of system use are identified and analyzed in turn. As each scenario is analyzed, the team responsible for the analysis must identify the required objects, attributes, and operations (Beck and Cunningham, 1989).

In practice, you have to use several knowledge sources to discover object classes. Object classes, attributes, and operations that are initially identified from the informal system description can be a starting point for the design. Further information from application domain knowledge or scenario analysis may then be used to refine and extend the initial objects. This information can be collected from requirements documents, discussions with users, or from analyses of existing systems.

In the wilderness weather station, object identification is based on the tangible hardware in the system. I don't have space to include all the system objects here, but I have shown five object classes in Figure 7.6. The Ground thermometer, Anemometer, and Barometer objects are application domain objects, and the WeatherStation and WeatherData objects have been identified from the system description and the scenario (use case) description:

1. The WeatherStation object class provides the basic interface of the weather station with its environment. Its operations reflect the interactions shown in

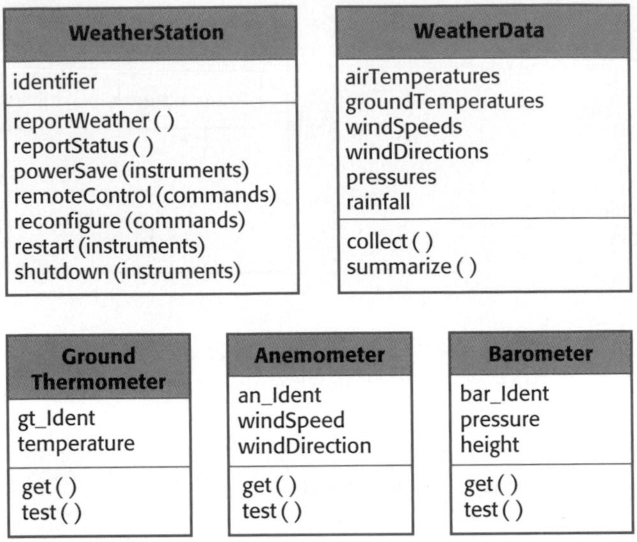

Figure 7.6 Weather station objects

Figure 7.3. In this case, I use a single object class to encapsulate all of these interactions, but in other designs you could design the system interface as several different classes.

2. The WeatherData object class is responsible for processing the report weather command. It sends the summarized data from the weather station instruments to the weather information system.

3. The Ground thermometer, Anemometer, and Barometer object classes are directly related to instruments in the system. They reflect tangible hardware entities in the system and the operations are concerned with controlling that hardware. These objects operate autonomously to collect data at the specified frequency and store the collected data locally. This data is delivered to the WeatherData object on request.

You use knowledge of the application domain to identify other objects, attributes, and services. We know that weather stations are often located in remote places and include various instruments that sometimes go wrong. Instrument failures should be reported automatically. This implies that you need attributes and operations to check the correct functioning of the instruments. There are many remote weather stations so each weather station should have its own identifier.

At this stage in the design process, you should focus on the objects themselves, without thinking about how these might be implemented. Once you have identified the objects, you then refine the object design. You look for common features and then design the inheritance hierarchy for the system. For example, you may identify an Instrument superclass, which defines the common features of all instruments, such as an identifier, and get and test operations. You may also add new attributes and operations to the superclass, such as an attribute that maintains the frequency of data collection.

7.1.4 Design models

Design or system models, as I discussed in Chapter 5, show the objects or object classes in a system. They also show the associations and relationships between these entities. These models are the bridge between the system requirements and the implementation of a system. They have to be abstract so that unnecessary detail doesn't hide the relationships between them and the system requirements. However, they also have to include enough detail for programmers to make implementation decisions.

Generally, you get around this type of conflict by developing models at different levels of detail. Where there are close links between requirements engineers, designers, and programmers, then abstract models may be all that are required. Specific design decisions may be made as the system is implemented, with problems resolved through informal discussions. When the links between system specifiers, designers, and programmers are indirect (e.g., where a system is being designed in one part of an organization but implemented elsewhere), then more detailed models are likely to be needed.

An important step in the design process, therefore, is to decide on the design models that you need and the level of detail required in these models. This depends on the type of system that is being developed. You design a sequential data-processing system in a different way from an embedded real-time system, so you will need different design models. The UML supports 13 different types of models but, as I discussed in Chapter 5, you rarely use all of these. Minimizing the number of models that are produced reduces the costs of the design and the time required to complete the design process.

When you use the UML to develop a design, you will normally develop two kinds of design model:

1. Structural models, which describe the static structure of the system using object classes and their relationships. Important relationships that may be documented at this stage are generalization (inheritance) relationships, uses/used-by relationships, and composition relationships.

2. Dynamic models, which describe the dynamic structure of the system and show the interactions between the system objects. Interactions that may be documented include the sequence of service requests made by objects and the state changes that are triggered by these object interactions.

In the early stages of the design process, I think there are three models that are particularly useful for adding detail to use case and architectural models:

1. Subsystem models, which that show logical groupings of objects into coherent subsystems. These are represented using a form of class diagram with each subsystem shown as a package with enclosed objects. Subsystem models are static (structural) models.

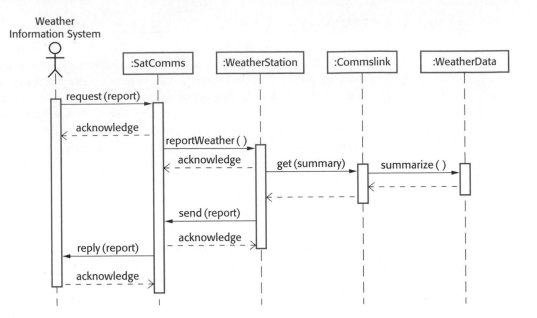

Figure 7.7 Sequence
diagram describing
data collection

2. Sequence models, which show the sequence of object interactions. These are represented using a UML sequence or a collaboration diagram. Sequence models are dynamic models.

3. State machine model, which show how individual objects change their state in response to events. These are represented in the UML using state diagrams. State machine models are dynamic models.

A subsystem model is a useful static model as it shows how a design is organized into logically related groups of objects. I have already shown this type of model in Figure 7.4 to show the subsystems in the weather mapping system. As well as subsystem models, you may also design detailed object models, showing all of the objects in the systems and their associations (inheritance, generalization, aggregation, etc.). However, there is a danger in doing too much modeling. You should not make detailed decisions about the implementation that really should be left to the system programmers.

Sequence models are dynamic models that describe, for each mode of interaction, the sequence of object interactions that take place. When documenting a design, you should produce a sequence model for each significant interaction. If you have developed a use case model then there should be a sequence model for each use case that you have identified.

Figure 7.7 is an example of a sequence model, shown as a UML sequence diagram. This diagram shows the sequence of interactions that take place when an external system requests the summarized data from the weather station. You read sequence diagrams from top to bottom:

1. The SatComms object receives a request from the weather information system to collect a weather report from a weather station. It acknowledges receipt of

this request. The stick arrowhead on the sent message indicates that the external system does not wait for a reply but can carry on with other processing.

2. SatComms sends a message to WeatherStation, via a satellite link, to create a summary of the collected weather data. Again, the stick arrowhead indicates that SatComms does not suspend itself waiting for a reply.

3. WeatherStation sends a message to a Commslink object to summarize the weather data. In this case, the squared-off style of arrowhead indicates that the instance of the WeatherStation object class waits for a reply.

4. Commslink calls the summarize method in the object WeatherData and waits for a reply.

5. The weather data summary is computed and returned to WeatherStation via the Commslink object.

6. WeatherStation then calls the SatComms object to transmit the summarized data to the weather information system, through the satellite communications system.

The SatComms and WeatherStation objects may be implemented as concurrent processes, whose execution can be suspended and resumed. The SatComms object instance listens for messages from the external system, decodes these messages and initiates weather station operations.

Sequence diagrams are used to model the combined behavior of a group of objects but you may also want to summarize the behavior of an object or a subsystem in response to messages and events. To do this, you can use a state machine model that shows how the object instance changes state depending on the messages that it receives. The UML includes state diagrams, initially invented by Harel (1987) to describe state machine models.

Figure 7.8 is a state diagram for the weather station system that shows how it responds to requests for various services.

You can read this diagram as follows:

1. If the system state is Shutdown then it can respond to a restart(), a reconfigure(), or a powerSave() message. The unlabeled arrow with the black blob indicates that the Shutdown state is the initial state. A restart() message causes a transition to normal operation. Both the powerSave() and reconfigure() messages cause a transition to a state in which the system reconfigures itself. The state diagram shows that reconfiguration is only allowed if the system has been shut down.

2. In the Running state, the system expects further messages. If a shutdown() message is received, the object returns to the shutdown state.

3. If a reportWeather() message is received, the system moves to the Summarizing state. When the summary is complete, the system moves to a Transmitting state where the information is transmitted to the remote system. It then returns to the Running state.

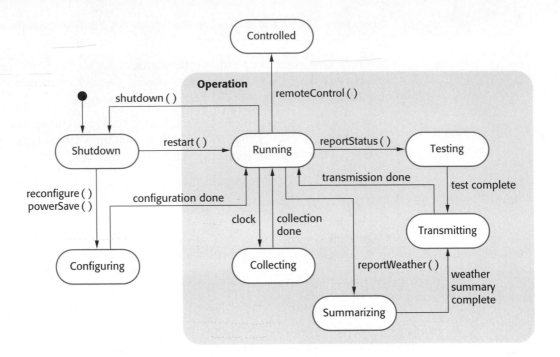

Figure 7.8 Weather
station state diagram

4. If a reportStatus() message is received, the system moves to the Testing state, then the Transmitting state, before returning to the Running state.

5. If a signal from the clock is received, the system moves to the Collecting state, where it collects data from the instruments. Each instrument is instructed in turn to collect its data from the associated sensors.

6. If a remoteControl() message is received, the system moves to a controlled state in which it responds to a different set of messages from the remote control room. These are not shown on this diagram.

State diagrams are useful high-level models of a system or an object's operation. You don't usually need a state diagram for all of the objects in the system. Many of the objects in a system are relatively simple and a state model adds unnecessary detail to the design.

7.1.5 Interface specification

An important part of any design process is the specification of the interfaces between the components in the design. You need to specify interfaces so that objects and sub-systems can be designed in parallel. Once an interface has been specified, the developers of other objects may assume that interface will be implemented.

Interface design is concerned with specifying the detail of the interface to an object or to a group of objects. This means defining the signatures and semantics of

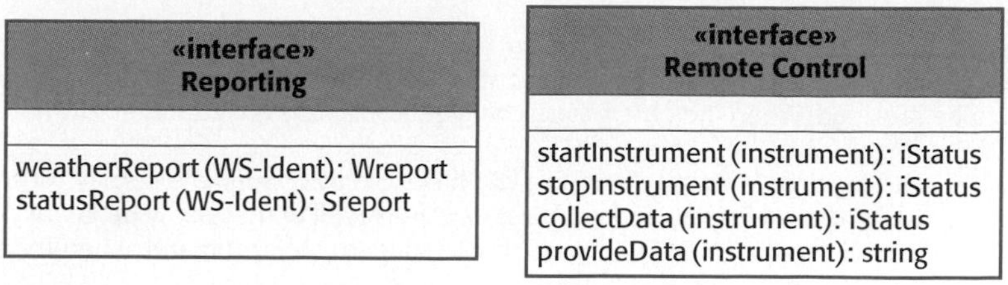

«interface» **Reporting**
weatherReport (WS-Ident): Wreport statusReport (WS-Ident): Sreport

«interface» **Remote Control**
startInstrument (instrument): iStatus stopInstrument (instrument): iStatus collectData (instrument): iStatus provideData (instrument): string

Figure 7.9 Weather station interfaces

the services that are provided by the object or by a group of objects. Interfaces can be specified in the UML using the same notation as a class diagram. However, there is no attribute section and the UML stereotype «interface» should be included in the name part. The semantics of the interface may be defined using the object constraint language (OCL). I explain this in Chapter 17, where I cover component-based software engineering. I also show an alternative way to represent interfaces in the UML.

You should not include details of the data representation in an interface design, as attributes are not defined in an interface specification. However, you should include operations to access and update data. As the data representation is hidden, it can be easily changed without affecting the objects that use that data. This leads to a design that is inherently more maintainable. For example, an array representation of a stack may be changed to a list representation without affecting other objects that use the stack. By contrast, it often makes sense to expose the attributes in a static design model, as this is the most compact way of illustrating essential characteristics of the objects.

There is not a simple 1:1 relationship between objects and interfaces. The same object may have several interfaces, each of which is a viewpoint on the methods that it provides. This is supported directly in Java, where interfaces are declared separately from objects and objects 'implement' interfaces. Equally, a group of objects may all be accessed through a single interface.

Figure 7.9 shows two interfaces that may be defined for the weather station. The left-hand interface is a reporting interface that defines the operation names that are used to generate weather and status reports. These map directly to operations in the WeatherStation object. The remote control interface provides four operations, which map onto a single method in the WeatherStation object. In this case, the individual operations are encoded in the command string associated with the remoteControl method, shown in Figure 7.6.

7.2 Design patterns

Design patterns were derived from ideas put forward by Christopher Alexander (Alexander et al., 1977), who suggested that there were certain common patterns of building design that were inherently pleasing and effective. The pattern is a description of the problem and the essence of its solution, so that the solution may be reused in

Pattern name: Observer

Description: Separates the display of the state of an object from the object itself and allows alternative displays to be provided. When the object state changes, all displays are automatically notified and updated to reflect the change.

Problem description: In many situations, you have to provide multiple displays of state information, such as a graphical display and a tabular display. Not all of these may be known when the information is specified. All alternative presentations should support interaction and, when the state is changed, all displays must be updated.

This pattern may be used in all situations where more than one display format for state information is required and where it is not necessary for the object that maintains the state information to know about the specific display formats used.

Solution description: This involves two abstract objects, Subject and Observer, and two concrete objects, ConcreteSubject and ConcreteObject, which inherit the attributes of the related abstract objects. The abstract objects include general operations that are applicable in all situations. The state to be displayed is maintained in ConcreteSubject, which inherits operations from Subject allowing it to add and remove Observers (each observer corresponds to a display) and to issue a notification when the state has changed.

The ConcreteObserver maintains a copy of the state of ConcreteSubject and implements the Update() interface of Observer that allows these copies to be kept in step. The ConcreteObserver automatically displays the state and reflects changes whenever the state is updated.

The UML model of the pattern is shown in Figure 7.12.

Consequences: The subject only knows the abstract Observer and does not know details of the concrete class. Therefore there is minimal coupling between these objects. Because of this lack of knowledge, optimizations that enhance display performance are impractical. Changes to the subject may cause a set of linked updates to observers to be generated, some of which may not be necessary.

Figure 7.10 The Observer pattern

different settings. The pattern is not a detailed specification. Rather, you can think of it as a description of accumulated wisdom and experience, a well-tried solution to a common problem.

A quote from the Hillside Group web site (http://hillside.net), which is dedicated to maintaining information about patterns, encapsulates their role in reuse:

> *Patterns and Pattern Languages are ways to describe best practices, good designs, and capture experience in a way that it is possible for others to reuse this experience.*

Patterns have made a huge impact on object-oriented software design. As well as being tested solutions to common problems, they have become a vocabulary for talking about a design. You can therefore explain your design by describing the patterns that you have used. This is particularly true for the best-known design patterns that were originally described by the 'Gang of Four' in their patterns book, (Gamma et al., 1995). Other particularly important pattern descriptions are those published in a series of books by authors from Siemens, a large European technology company (Buschmann et al., 1996; Buschmann et al., 2007a; Buschmann et al., 2007b; Kircher and Jain, 2004; Schmidt et al., 2000).

Design patterns are usually associated with object-oriented design. Published patterns often rely on object characteristics such as inheritance and polymorphism to provide generality. However, the general principle of encapsulating experience in a

abstract object   *Subject*   *observer*

concrete objects   *concrete Subject*   *concrete observer*

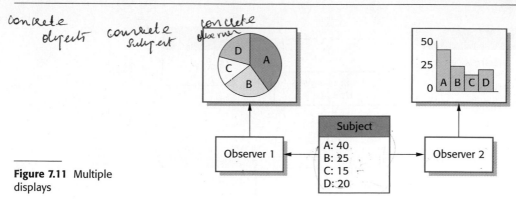

Figure 7.11 Multiple displays

pattern is one that is equally applicable to any kind of software design. So, you could have configuration patterns for COTS systems. Patterns are a way of reusing the knowledge and experience of other designers.

The four essential elements of design patterns were defined by the 'Gang of Four' in their patterns book:

1. A name that is a meaningful reference to the pattern.

2. A description of the problem area that explains when the pattern may be applied.

3. A solution description of the parts of the design solution, their relationships, and their responsibilities. This is not a concrete design description. It is a template for a design solution that can be instantiated in different ways. This is often expressed graphically and shows the relationships between the objects and object classes in the solution.

4. A statement of the consequences—the results and trade-offs—of applying the pattern. This can help designers understand whether or not a pattern can be used in a particular situation.

Gamma and his co-authors break down the problem description into motivation (a description of why the pattern is useful) and applicability (a description of situations in which the pattern may be used). Under the description of the solution, they describe the pattern structure, participants, collaborations, and implementation.

To illustrate pattern description, I use the Observer pattern, taken from the book by Gamma et al. (Gamma et al., 1995). This is shown in Figure 7.10. In my description, I use the four essential description elements and also include a brief statement of what the pattern can do. This pattern can be used in situations where different presentations of an object's state are required. It separates the object that must be displayed from the different forms of presentation. This is illustrated in Figure 7.11, which shows two graphical presentations of the same data set.

Graphical representations are normally used to illustrate the object classes in patterns and their relationships. These supplement the pattern description and add

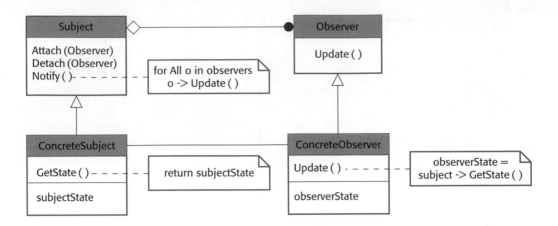

Figure 7.12 A UML
model of the Observer
pattern

detail to the solution description. Figure 7.12 is the representation in UML of the Observer pattern.

To use patterns in your design, you need to recognize that any design problem you are facing may have an associated pattern that can be applied. Examples of such problems, documented in the 'Gang of Four's original patterns book, include:

1. Tell several objects that the state of some other object has changed (Observer pattern).

2. Tidy up the interfaces to a number of related objects that have often been developed incrementally (Façade pattern).

3. Provide a standard way of accessing the elements in a collection, irrespective of how that collection is implemented (Iterator pattern).

4. Allow for the possibility of extending the functionality of an existing class at run-time (Decorator pattern).

Patterns support high-level, concept reuse. When you try to reuse executable components you are inevitably constrained by detailed design decisions that have been made by the implementers of these components. These range from the particular algorithms that have been used to implement the components to the objects and types in the component interfaces. When these design decisions conflict with your particular requirements, reusing the component is either impossible or introduces inefficiencies into your system. Using patterns means that you reuse the ideas but can adapt the implementation to suit the system that you are developing.

When you start designing a system, it can be difficult to know, in advance, if you will need a particular pattern. Therefore, using patterns in a design process often involves developing a design, experiencing a problem, and then recognizing that a pattern can be used. This is certainly possible if you focus on the 23 general-purpose patterns documented in the original patterns book. However, if your problem is a different one, you may find it difficult to find an appropriate pattern amongst the hundreds of different patterns that have been proposed.

Patterns are a great idea but you need experience of software design to use them effectively. You have to recognize situations where a pattern can be applied. Inexperienced programmers, even if they have read the pattern books, will always find it hard to decide whether they can reuse a pattern or need to develop a special-purpose solution.

7.3 Implementation issues

Software engineering includes all of the activities involved in software development from the initial requirements of the system through to maintenance and management of the deployed system. A critical stage of this process is, of course, system implementation, where you create an executable version of the software. Implementation may involve developing programs in high- or low-level programming languages or tailoring and adapting generic, off-the-shelf systems to meet the specific requirements of an organization.

I assume that most readers of this book will understand programming principles and will have some programming experience. As this chapter is intended to offer a language-independent approach, I haven't focused on issues of good programming practice as this has to use language-specific examples. Instead, I introduce some aspects of implementation that are particularly important to software engineering that are often not covered in programming texts. These are:

1. *Reuse* Most modern software is constructed by reusing existing components or systems. When you are developing software, you should make as much use as possible of existing code.

2. *Configuration management* During the development process, many different versions of each software component are created. If you don't keep track of these versions in a configuration management system, you are liable to include the wrong versions of these components in your system.

3. *Host-target development* Production software does not usually execute on the same computer as the software development environment. Rather, you develop it on one computer (the host system) and execute it on a separate computer (the target system). The host and target systems are sometimes of the same type but, often they are completely different.

7.3.1 Reuse

From the 1960s to the 1990s, most new software was developed from scratch, by writing all code in a high-level programming language. The only significant reuse or software was the reuse of functions and objects in programming language libraries. However, costs and schedule pressure meant that this approach became increasingly unviable, especially for commercial and Internet-based systems. Consequently, an approach to development based around the reuse of existing software emerged and is now generally used for business systems, scientific software, and, increasingly, in embedded systems engineering.

Software reuse is possible at a number of different levels:

1. *The abstraction level* At this level, you don't reuse software directly but rather use knowledge of successful abstractions in the design of your software. Design patterns and architectural patterns (covered in Chapter 6) are ways of representing abstract knowledge for reuse.

2. *The object level* At this level, you directly reuse objects from a library rather than writing the code yourself. To implement this type of reuse, you have to find appropriate libraries and discover if the objects and methods offer the functionality that you need. For example, if you need to process mail messages in a Java program, you may use objects and methods from a JavaMail library.

3. *The component level* Components are collections of objects and object classes that operate together to provide related functions and services. You often have to adapt and extend the component by adding some code of your own. An example of component-level reuse is where you build your user interface using a framework. This is a set of general object classes that implement event handling, display management, etc. You add connections to the data to be displayed and write code to define specific display details such as screen layout and colors.

4. *The system level* At this level, you reuse entire application systems. This usually involves some kind of configuration of these systems. This may be done by adding and modifying code (if you are reusing a software product line) or by using the system's own configuration interface. Most commercial systems are now built in this way where generic COTS (commercial off-the-shelf) systems are adapted and reused. Sometimes this approach may involve reusing several different systems and integrating these to create a new system.

By reusing existing software, you can develop new systems more quickly, with fewer development risks and also lower costs. As the reused software has been tested in other applications, it should be more reliable than new software. However, there are costs associated with reuse:

1. The costs of the time spent in looking for software to reuse and assessing whether or not it meets your needs. You may have to test the software to make sure that it will work in your environment, especially if this is different from its development environment.

2. Where applicable, the costs of buying the reusable software. For large off-the-shelf systems, these costs can be very high.

3. The costs of adapting and configuring the reusable software components or systems to reflect the requirements of the system that you are developing.

4. The costs of integrating reusable software elements with each other (if you are using software from different sources) and with the new code that you have developed. Integrating reusable software from different providers can be difficult and expensive because the providers may make conflicting assumptions about how their respective software will be reused.

How to reuse existing knowledge and software should be the first thing you should think about when starting a software development project. You should consider the possibilities of reuse before designing the software in detail, as you may wish to adapt your design to reuse existing software assets. As I discussed in Chapter 2, in a reuse-oriented development process, you search for reusable elements then modify your requirements and design to make best use of these.

For a large number of application systems, software engineering really means software reuse. I therefore devote several chapters in the software technologies section of the book to this topic (Chapters 16, 17, and 19).

7.3.2 Configuration management

In software development, change happens all the time, so change management is absolutely essential. When a team of people are developing software, you have to make sure that team members don't interfere with each others' work. That is, if two people are working on a component, their changes have to be coordinated. Otherwise, one programmer may make changes and overwrite the other's work. You also have to ensure that everyone can access the most up-to-date versions of software components, otherwise developers may redo work that has already been done. When something goes wrong with a new version of a system, you have to be able to go back to a working version of the system or component.

Configuration management is the name given to the general process of managing a changing software system. The aim of configuration management is to support the system integration process so that all developers can access the project code and documents in a controlled way, find out what changes have been made, and compile and link components to create a system. There are, therefore, three fundamental configuration management activities:

1. Version management, where support is provided to keep track of the different versions of software components. Version management systems include facilities to coordinate development by several programmers. They stop one developer overwriting code that has been submitted to the system by someone else.

2. System integration, where support is provided to help developers define what versions of components are used to create each version of a system. This description is then used to build a system automatically by compiling and linking the required components.

3.   Problem tracking, where support is provided to allow users to report bugs and other problems, and to allow all developers to see who is working on these problems and when they are fixed.

Software configuration management tools support each of the above activities. These tools may be designed to work together in a comprehensive change management system, such as ClearCase (Bellagio and Milligan, 2005). In integrated configuration management systems, version management, system integration, and problem-tracking tools are designed together. They share a user interface style and are integrated through a common code repository.

Alternatively, separate tools, installed in an integrated development environment, may be used. Version management may be supported using a version management system such as Subversion (Pilato et al., 2008), which can support multi-site, multi-team development. System integration support may be built into the language or rely on a separate toolset such as the GNU build system. This includes what is perhaps the best-known integration tool, Unix make. Bug tracking or issue tracking systems, such as Bugzilla, are used to report bugs and other issues and to keep track of whether or not these have been fixed.

Because of its importance in professional software engineering, I discuss change and configuration management in more detail in Chapter 25.

7.3.3   Host-target development

Most software development is based on a host-target model. Software is developed on one computer (the host), but runs on a separate machine (the target). More generally, we can talk about a development platform and an execution platform. A platform is more than just hardware. It includes the installed operating system plus other supporting software such as a database management system or, for development platforms, an interactive development environment.

Sometimes, the development and execution platforms are the same, making it possible to develop the software and test it on the same machine. More commonly, however, they are different so that you need to either move your developed software to the execution platform for testing or run a simulator on your development machine.

Simulators are often used when developing embedded systems. You simulate hardware devices, such as sensors, and the events in the environment in which the system will be deployed. Simulators speed up the development process for embedded systems as each developer can have their own execution platform with no need to download the software to the target hardware. However, simulators are expensive to develop and so are only usually available for the most popular hardware architectures.

If the target system has installed middleware or other software that you need to use, then you need to be able to test the system using that software. It may be impractical to install that software on your development machine, even if it is the same as the target platform, because of license restrictions. In those circumstances, you need to transfer your developed code to the execution platform to test the system.

UML deployment diagrams

UML deployment diagrams show how software components are physically deployed on processors; that is, the deployment diagram shows the hardware and software in the system and the middleware used to connect the different components in the system. Essentially, you can think of deployment diagrams as a way of defining and documenting the target environment.

http://www.SoftwareEngineering-9.com/Web/Deployment/

A software development platform should provide a range of tools to support software engineering processes. These may include:

1. An integrated compiler and syntax-directed editing system that allows you to create, edit, and compile code.

2. A language debugging system.

3. Graphical editing tools, such as tools to edit UML models.

4. Testing tools, such as JUnit (Massol, 2003) that can automatically run a set of tests on a new version of a program.

5. Project support tools that help you organize the code for different development projects.

As well as these standard tools, your development system may include more specialized tools such as static analyzers (discussed in Chapter 15). Normally, development environments for teams also include a shared server that runs a change and configuration management system and, perhaps, a system to support requirements management.

Software development tools are often grouped to create an integrated development environment (IDE). An IDE is a set of software tools that supports different aspects of software development, within some common framework and user interface. Generally, IDEs are created to support development in a specific programming language such as Java. The language IDE may be developed specially, or may be an instantiation of a general-purpose IDE, with specific language-support tools.

A general-purpose IDE is a framework for hosting software tools that provides data management facilities for the software being developed, and integration mechanisms, that allow tools to work together. The best-known general-purpose IDE is the Eclipse environment (Carlson, 2005). This environment is based on a plug-in architecture so that it can be specialized for different languages and application domains (Clayberg and Rubel, 2006). Therefore, you can install Eclipse and tailor it for your specific needs by adding plug-ins. For example, you may add a set of plug-ins to support networked systems development in Java or embedded systems engineering using C.

As part of the development process, you need to make decisions about how the developed software will be deployed on the target platform. This is straightforward for embedded systems, where the target is usually a single computer. However, for distributed systems, you need to decide on the specific platforms where the components will be deployed. Issues that you have to consider in making this decision are:

1. *The hardware and software requirements of a component* If a component is designed for a specific hardware architecture, or relies on some other software system, it must obviously be deployed on a platform that provides the required hardware and software support.

2. *The availability requirements of the system* High-availability systems may require components to be deployed on more than one platform. This means that, in the event of platform failure, an alternative implementation of the component is available.

3. *Component communications* If there is a high level of communications traffic between components, it usually makes sense to deploy them on the same platform or on platforms that are physically close to one other. This reduces communications latency, the delay between the time a message is sent by one component and received by another.

You can document your decisions on hardware and software deployment using UML deployment diagrams, which show how software components are distributed across hardware platforms.

If you are developing an embedded system, you may have to take into account target characteristics, such as its physical size, power capabilities, the need for real-time responses to sensor events, the physical characteristics of actuators, and its real-time operating system. I discuss embedded systems engineering in Chapter 20.

7.4 Open source development

Open source development is an approach to software development in which the source code of a software system is published and volunteers are invited to participate in the development process (Raymond, 2001). Its roots are in the Free Software Foundation (http://www.fsf.org), which advocates that source code should not be proprietary but rather should always be available for users to examine and modify as they wish. There was an assumption that the code would be controlled and developed by a small core group, rather than users of the code.

Open source software extended this idea by using the Internet to recruit a much larger population of volunteer developers. Many of them are also users of the code. In principle at least, any contributor to an open source project may report and fix bugs and propose new features and functionality. However, in practice, successful open source systems still rely on a core group of developers who control changes to the software.

The best-known open source product is, of course, the Linux operating system which is widely used as a server system and, increasingly, as a desktop environment. Other important open source products are Java, the Apache web server, and the mySQL database management system. Major players in the computer industry such as IBM and Sun support the open source movement and base their software on open source products. There are thousands of other, lesser known open source systems and components that may also be used.

It is usually fairly cheap or free to acquire open source software. You can normally download open source software without charge. However, if you want documentation and support, then you may have to pay for this, but costs are usually fairly low. The other key benefit of using open source products is that mature open source systems are usually very reliable. The reason for this is that they have a large population of users who are willing to fix problems themselves rather than report these problems to the developer and wait for a new release of the system. Bugs are discovered and repaired more quickly than is usually possible with proprietary software.

For a company involved in software development, there are two open source issues that have to be considered:

1.   Should the product that is being developed make use of open source components?

2.   Should an open source approach be used for the software's development?

The answers to these questions depend on the type of software that is being developed and the background and experience of the development team.

If you are developing a software product for sale, then time to market and reduced costs are critical. If you are developing in a domain in which there are high-quality open source systems available, you can save time and money by using these systems. However, if you are developing software to a specific set of organizational requirements, then using open source components may not be an option. You may have to integrate your software with existing systems that are incompatible with available open source systems. Even then, however, it could be quicker and cheaper to modify the open source system rather than redevelop the functionality that you need.

More and more product companies are using an open source approach to development. Their business model is not reliant on selling a software product but rather on selling support for that product. They believe that involving the open source community will allow software to be developed more cheaply, more quickly, and will create a community of users for the software. Again, however, this is really only applicable for general software products rather than specific organizational applications.

Many companies believe that adopting an open source approach will reveal confidential business knowledge to their competitors and so are reluctant to adopt this development model. However, if you are working in a small company and you open source your software, this may reassure customers that they will be able to support the software if your company goes out of business.

Publishing the source code of a system does not mean that people from the wider community will necessarily help with its development. Most successful open source products have been platform products rather than application systems. There are a limited number of developers who might be interested in specialized application systems. As such, making a software system open source does not guarantee community involvement.

7.4.1 Open source licensing

Although a fundamental principle of open-source development is that source code should be freely available, this does not mean that anyone can do as they wish with that code. Legally, the developer of the code (either a company or an individual) still owns the code. They can place restrictions on how it is used by including legally binding conditions in an open source software license (St. Laurent, 2004). Some open source developers believe that if an open source component is used to develop a new system, then that system should also be open source. Others are willing to allow their code to be used without this restriction. The developed systems may be proprietary and sold as closed source systems.

Most open source licenses are derived from one of three general models:

1. The GNU General Public License (GPL). This is a so-called 'reciprocal' license that, simplistically, means that if you use open source software that is licensed under the GPL license, then you must make that software open source.

2. The GNU Lesser General Public License (LGPL). This is a variant of the GPL license where you can write components that link to open source code without having to publish the source of these components. However, if you change the licensed component, then you must publish this as open source.

3. The Berkley Standard Distribution (BSD) License. This is a non-reciprocal license, which means you are not obliged to republish any changes or modifications made to open source code. You can include the code in proprietary systems that are sold. If you use open source components, you must acknowledge the original creator of the code.

Licensing issues are important because if you use open-source software as part of a software product, then you may be obliged by the terms of the license to make your own product open source. If you are trying to sell your software, you may wish to keep it secret. This means that you may wish to avoid using GPL-licensed open source software in its development.

If you are building software that runs on an open source platform, such as Linux, then licenses are not a problem. However, as soon as you start including open source components in your software you need to set up processes and databases to keep track of what's been used and their license conditions. Bayersdorfer (2007) suggests that companies managing projects that use open source should:

1. Establish a system for maintaining information about open source components that are downloaded and used. You have to keep a copy of the license for each

component that was valid at the time the component was used. Licenses may change so you need to know the conditions that you have agreed to.

2. Be aware of the different types of licenses and understand how a component is licensed before it is used. You may decide to use a component in one system but not in another because you plan to use these systems in different ways.

3. Be aware of evolution pathways for components. You need to know a bit about the open source project where components are developed to understand how they might change in future.

4. Educate people about open source. It's not enough to have procedures in place to ensure compliance with license conditions. You also need to educate developers about open source and open source licensing.

5. Have auditing systems in place. Developers, under tight deadlines, might be tempted to break the terms of a license. If possible, you should have software in place to detect and stop this.

6. Participate in the open source community. If you rely on open source products, you should participate in the community and help support their development.

The business model of software is changing. It is becoming increasingly difficult to build a business by selling specialized software systems. Many companies prefer to make their software open source and then sell support and consultancy to software users. This trend is likely to accelerate, with increasing use of open source software and with more and more software available in this form.

KEY POINTS

■ Software design and implementation are interleaved activities. The level of detail in the design depends on the type of system being developed and whether you are using a plan-driven or agile approach.

■ The process of object-oriented design includes activities to design the system architecture, identify objects in the system, describe the design using different object models, and document the component interfaces.

■ A range of different models may be produced during an object-oriented design process. These include static models (class models, generalization models, association models) and dynamic models (sequence models, state machine models).

■ Component interfaces must be defined precisely so that other objects can use them. A UML interface stereotype may be used to define interfaces.

■ When developing software, you should always consider the possibility of reusing existing software, either as components, services, or complete systems.

▪ Configuration management is the process of managing changes to an evolving software system. It is essential when a team of people are cooperating to develop software.

▪ Most software development is host-target development. You use an IDE on a host machine to develop the software, which is transferred to a target machine for execution.

▪ Open source development involves making the source code of a system publicly available. This means that many people can propose changes and improvements to the software.

FURTHER READING

Design Patterns: Elements of Reusable Object-oriented Software. This is the original software patterns handbook that introduced software patterns to a wide community. (E. Gamma, R. Helm, R. Johnson and J. Vlissides, Addison-Wesley, 1995.)

Applying UML and Patterns: An Introduction to Object-oriented Analysis and Design and Iterative Development, 3rd edition. Larman writes clearly on object-oriented design and, as well as discussing the use of the UML. This is a good introduction to using patterns in the design process. (C. Larman, Prentice Hall, 2004.)

Producing Open Source Software: How to Run a Successful Free Software Project. His book is a comprehensive guide to the background to open source software, licensing issues, and the practicalities of running an open source development project. (K. Fogel, O'Reilly Media Inc., 2008.)

Further reading on software reuse is suggested in Chapter 16 and on configuration management in Chapter 25.

EXERCISES

7.1. Using the structured notation shown in Figure 7.3, specify the weather station use cases for Report status and Reconfigure. You should make reasonable assumptions about the functionality that is required here.

7.2. Assume that the MHC-PMS is being developed using an object-oriented approach. Draw a use case diagram showing at least six possible use cases for this system.

7.3. Using the UML graphical notation for object classes, design the following object classes, identifying attributes and operations. Use your own experience to decide on the attributes and operations that should be associated with these objects.

▪ a telephone

▪ a printer for a personal computer

▪ a personal stereo system

  ■ a bank account

  ■ a library catalog

7.4. Using the weather station objects identified in Figure 7.6 as a starting point, identify further objects that may be used in this system. Design an inheritance hierarchy for the objects that you have identified.

7.5. Develop the design of the weather station to show the interaction between the data collection subsystem and the instruments that collect weather data. Use sequence diagrams to show this interaction.

7.6. Identify possible objects in the following systems and develop an object-oriented design for them. You may make any reasonable assumptions about the systems when deriving the design.

  ■ A group diary and time management system is intended to support the timetabling of meetings and appointments across a group of co-workers. When an appointment is to be made that involves a number of people, the system finds a common slot in each of their diaries and arranges the appointment for that time. If no common slots are available, it interacts with the user to rearrange his or her personal diary to make room for the appointment.

  ■ A filling station (gas station) is to be set up for fully automated operation. Drivers swipe their credit card through a reader connected to the pump; the card is verified by communication with a credit company computer, and a fuel limit is established. The driver may then take the fuel required. When fuel delivery is complete and the pump hose is returned to its holster, the driver's credit card account is debited with the cost of the fuel taken. The credit card is returned after debiting. If the card is invalid, the pump returns it before fuel is dispensed.

7.7. Draw a sequence diagram showing the interactions of objects in a group diary system when a group of people are arranging a meeting.

7.8. Draw a UML state diagram showing the possible state changes in either the group diary or the filling station system.

7.9. Using examples, explain why configuration management is important when a team of people are developing a software product.

7.10. A small company has developed a specialized product that it configures specially for each customer. New customers usually have specific requirements to be incorporated into their system, and they pay for these to be developed. The company has an opportunity to bid for a new contract, which would more than double its customer base. The new customer also wishes to have some involvement in the configuration of the system. Explain why, in these circumstances, it might be a good idea for the company owning the software to make it open source.

REFERENCES

Abbott, R. (1983). 'Program Design by Informal English Descriptions'. *Comm. ACM*, **26** (11), 882–94.

Alexander, C., Ishikawa, S. and Silverstein, M. (1977). *A Pattern Language: Towns, Building, Construction*. Oxford: Oxford University Press.

Bayersdorfer, M. (2007). 'Managing a Project with Open Source Components'. *ACM Interactions*, **14** (6), 33–4.

Beck, K. and Cunningham, W. (1989). 'A Laboratory for Teaching Object-Oriented Thinking'. *Proc. OOPSLA'89* (Conference on Object-oriented Programming, Systems, Languages and Applications), ACM Press. 1–6.

Bellagio, D. E. and Milligan, T. J. (2005). *Software Configuration Management Strategies and IBM Rational Clearcase: A Practical Introduction*. Boston: Pearson Education (IBM Press).

Buschmann, F., Henney, K. and Schmidt, D. C. (2007a). *Pattern-oriented Software Architecture Volume 4: A Pattern Language for Distributed Computing*. New York: John Wiley & Sons.

Buschmann, F., Henney, K. and Schmidt, D. C. (2007b). *Pattern-oriented Software Architecture Volume 5: On Patterns and Pattern Languages*. New York: John Wiley & Sons.

Buschmann, F., Meunier, R., Rohnert, H. and Sommerlad, P. (1996). *Pattern-oriented Software Architecture Volume 1: A System of Patterns*. New York: John Wiley & Sons.

Carlson, D. (2005). *Eclipse Distilled*. Boston: Addison-Wesley.

Clayberg, E. and Rubel, D. (2006). *Eclipse: Building Commercial-Quality Plug-Ins*. Boston: Addison Wesley.

Coad, P. and Yourdon, E. (1990). *Object-oriented Analysis*. Englewood Cliffs, NJ: Prentice Hall.

Gamma, E., Helm, R., Johnson, R. and Vlissides, J. (1995). *Design Patterns: Elements of Reusable Object-Oriented Software*. Reading, Mass.: Addison-Wesley.

Harel, D. (1987). 'Statecharts: A Visual Formalism for Complex Systems'. *Sci. Comput. Programming*, **8** (3), 231–74.

Kircher, M. and Jain, P. (2004). *Pattern-Oriented Software Architecture Volume 3: Patterns for Resource Management*. New York: John Wiley & Sons.

Massol, V. (2003). *JUnit in Action*. Greenwich, CT: Manning Publications.

Pilato, C., Collins-Sussman, B. and Fitzpatrick, B. (2008). *Version Control with Subversion*. Sebastopol, Calif.: O'Reilly Media Inc.

Raymond, E. S. (2001). *The Cathedral and the Bazaar: Musings on Linux and Open Source by an Accidental Revolutionary*. Sebastopol. Calif.: O'Reilly Media, Inc.

Schmidt, D., Stal, M., Rohnert, H. and Buschmann, F. (2000). *Pattern-Oriented Software Architecture Volume 2: Patterns for Concurrent and Networked Objects*. New York: John Wiley & Sons.

Shlaer, S. and Mellor, S. (1988). *Object-Oriented Systems Analysis: Modeling the World in Data*. Englewood Cliffs, NJ: Yourdon Press.

St. Laurent, A. (2004). *Understanding Open Source and Free Software Licensing*. Sebastopol, Calif.: O'Reilly Media Inc.

Wirfs-Brock, R., Wilkerson, B. and Weiner, L. (1990). *Designing Object-Oriented Software*. Englewood Cliffs, NJ: Prentice Hall.

8

Software testing

Objectives

The objective of this chapter is to introduce software testing and software testing processes. When you have read the chapter, you will:

- understand the stages of testing from testing, during development to acceptance testing by system customers;

- have been introduced to techniques that help you choose test cases that are geared to discovering program defects;

- understand test-first development, where you design tests before writing code and run these tests automatically;

- know the important differences between component, system, and release testing and be aware of user testing processes and techniques.

Contents

Testing is intended to show that a program does what it is intended to do and to discover program defects before it is put into use. When you test software, you execute a program using artificial data. You check the results of the test run for errors, anomalies, or information about the program's non-functional attributes.

The testing process has two distinct goals:

1. To demonstrate to the developer and the customer that the software meets its requirements. For custom software, this means that there should be at least one test for every requirement in the requirements document. For generic software products, it means that there should be tests for all of the system features, plus combinations of these features, that will be incorporated in the product release.

2. To discover situations in which the behavior of the software is incorrect, undesirable, or does not conform to its specification. These are a consequence of software defects. Defect testing is concerned with rooting out undesirable system behavior such as system crashes, unwanted interactions with other systems, incorrect computations, and data corruption.

The first goal leads to validation testing, where you expect the system to perform correctly using a given set of test cases that reflect the system's expected use. The second goal leads to defect testing, where the test cases are designed to expose defects. The test cases in defect testing can be deliberately obscure and need not reflect how the system is normally used. Of course, there is no definite boundary between these two approaches to testing. During validation testing, you will find defects in the system; during defect testing, some of the tests will show that the program meets its requirements.

The diagram shown in Figure 8.1 may help to explain the differences between validation testing and defect testing. Think of the system being tested as a black box. The system accepts inputs from some input set I and generates outputs in an output set O. Some of the outputs will be erroneous. These are the outputs in set O_e that are generated by the system in response to inputs in the set I_e. The priority in defect testing is to find those inputs in the set I_e because these reveal problems with the system. Validation testing involves testing with correct inputs that are outside I_e. These stimulate the system to generate the expected correct outputs.

Testing cannot demonstrate that the software is free of defects or that it will behave as specified in every circumstance. It is always possible that a test that you have overlooked could discover further problems with the system. As Edsger Dijkstra, an early contributor to the development of software engineering, eloquently stated (Dijkstra et al., 1972):

Testing can only show the presence of errors, not their absence

Testing is part of a broader process of software verification and validation (V & V). Verification and validation are not the same thing, although they are often confused.

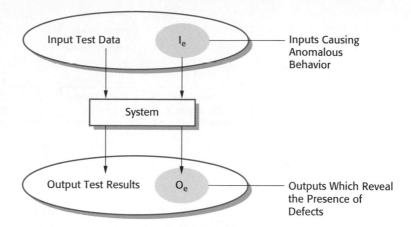

Figure 8.1 An
input-output model
of program testing

Barry Boehm, a pioneer of software engineering, succinctly expressed the difference
between them (Boehm, 1979):

■ 'Validation: Are we building the right product?'

■ 'Verification: Are we building the product right?'

Verification and validation processes are concerned with checking that software
being developed meets its specification and delivers the functionality expected by the
people paying for the software. These checking processes start as soon as requirements
become available and continue through all stages of the development process.

The aim of verification is to check that the software meets its stated functional and
non-functional requirements. Validation, however, is a more general process. The aim
of validation is to ensure that the software meets the customer's expectations. It goes
beyond simply checking conformance with the specification to demonstrating that the
software does what the customer expects it to do. Validation is essential because, as
I discussed in Chapter 4, requirements specifications do not always reflect the real
wishes or needs of system customers and users.

The ultimate goal of verification and validation processes is to establish confidence that the software system is 'fit for purpose'. This means that the system must
be good enough for its intended use. The level of required confidence depends on the
system's purpose, the expectations of the system users, and the current marketing
environment for the system:

1. *Software purpose* The more critical the software, the more important that it is
    reliable. For example, the level of confidence required for software used to con-
    trol a safety-critical system is much higher than that required for a prototype
    that has been developed to demonstrate new product ideas.

2. *User expectations* Because of their experiences with buggy, unreliable software,
    many users have low expectations of software quality. They are not surprised
    when their software fails. When a new system is installed, users may tolerate

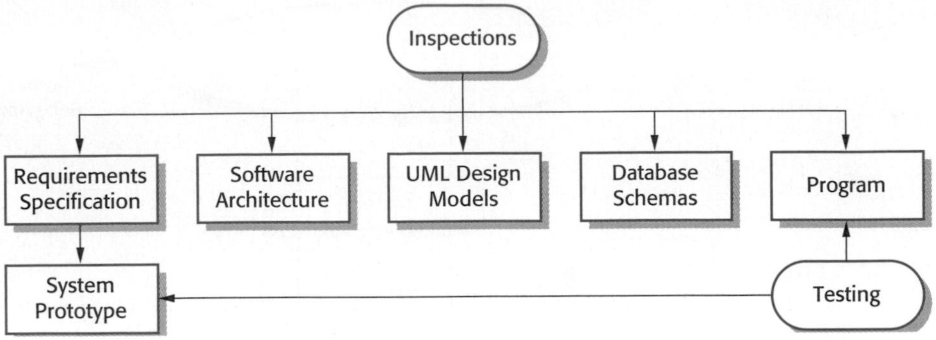

```
                              ┌──────────────┐
                              │  Inspections │
                              └──────────────┘
```

Figure 8.2 Inspections and testing

failures because the benefits of use outweigh the costs of failure recovery. In these situations, you may not need to devote as much time to testing the software. However, as software matures, users expect it to become more reliable so more thorough testing of later versions may be required.

3. *Marketing environment* When a system is marketed, the sellers of the system must take into account competing products, the price that customers are willing to pay for a system, and the required schedule for delivering that system. In a competitive environment, a software company may decide to release a program before it has been fully tested and debugged because they want to be the first into the market. If a software product is very cheap, users may be willing to tolerate a lower level of reliability.

As well as software testing, the verification and validation process may involve software inspections and reviews. Inspections and reviews analyze and check the system requirements, design models, the program source code, and even proposed system tests. These are so-called 'static' V & V techniques in which you don't need to execute the software to verify it. Figure 8.2 shows that software inspections and testing support V & V at different stages in the software process. The arrows indicate the stages in the process where the techniques may be used.

Inspections mostly focus on the source code of a system but any readable representation of the software, such as its requirements or a design model, can be inspected. When you inspect a system, you use knowledge of the system, its application domain, and the programming or modeling language to discover errors.

There are three advantages of software inspection over testing:

1. During testing, errors can mask (hide) other errors. When an error leads to unexpected outputs, you can never be sure if later output anomalies are due to a new error or are side effects of the original error. Because inspection is a static process, you don't have to be concerned with interactions between errors. Consequently, a single inspection session can discover many errors in a system.

Test planning

Test planning is concerned with scheduling and resourcing all of the activities in the testing process. It involves defining the testing process, taking into account the people and the time available. Usually, a test plan will be created, which defines what is to be tested, the predicted testing schedule, and how tests will be recorded. For critical systems, the test plan may also include details of the tests to be run on the software.

http://www.SoftwareEngineering-9.com/Web/Testing/Planning.html

2. Incomplete versions of a system can be inspected without additional costs. If a program is incomplete, then you need to develop specialized test harnesses to test the parts that are available. This obviously adds to the system development costs.

3. As well as searching for program defects, an inspection can also consider broader quality attributes of a program, such as compliance with standards, portability, and maintainability. You can look for inefficiencies, inappropriate algorithms, and poor programming style that could make the system difficult to maintain and update.

Program inspections are an old idea and there have been several studies and experiments that have demonstrated that inspections are more effective for defect discovery than program testing. Fagan (1986) reported that more than 60% of the errors in a program can be detected using informal program inspections. In the Cleanroom process (Prowell et al., 1999), it is claimed that more than 90% of defects can be discovered in program inspections.

However, inspections cannot replace software testing. Inspections are not good for discovering defects that arise because of unexpected interactions between different parts of a program, timing problems, or problems with system performance. Furthermore, especially in small companies or development groups, it can be difficult and expensive to put together a separate inspection team as all potential members of the team may also be software developers. I discuss reviews and inspections in more detail in Chapter 24 (Quality Management). Automated static analysis, where the source text of a program is automatically analyzed to discover anomalies, is explained in Chapter 15. In this chapter, I focus on testing and testing processes.

Figure 8.3 is an abstract model of the 'traditional' testing process, as used in plan-driven development. Test cases are specifications of the inputs to the test and the expected output from the system (the test results), plus a statement of what is being tested. Test data are the inputs that have been devised to test a system. Test data can sometimes be generated automatically, but automatic test case generation is impossible, as people who understand what the system is supposed to do must be involved to specify the expected test results. However, test execution can be automated. The expected results are automatically compared with the predicted results so there is no need for a person to look for errors and anomalies in the test run.

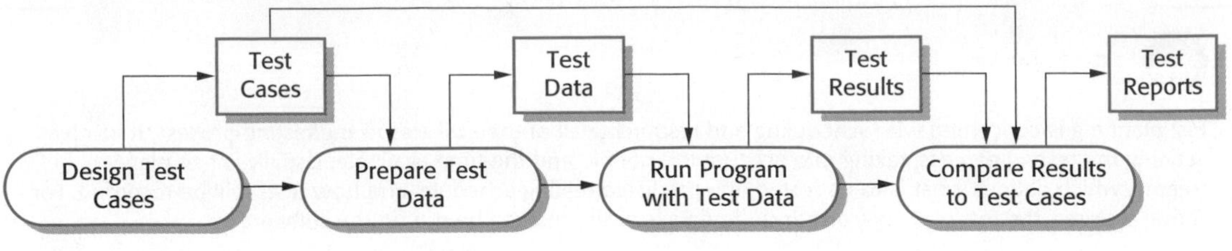

Design Test Cases → Prepare Test Data → Run Program with Test Data → Compare Results to Test Cases

Test Cases · Test Data · Test Results · Test Reports

Figure 8.3 A model of the software testing process

Typically, a commercial software system has to go through three stages of testing:

1. Development testing, where the system is tested during development to discover bugs and defects. System designers and programmers are likely to be involved in the testing process.

2. Release testing, where a separate testing team tests a complete version of the system before it is released to users. The aim of release testing is to check that the system meets the requirements of system stakeholders.

3. User testing, where users or potential users of a system test the system in their own environment. For software products, the 'user' may be an internal marketing group who decide if the software can be marketed, released, and sold. Acceptance testing is one type of user testing where the customer formally tests a system to decide if it should be accepted from the system supplier or if further development is required.

In practice, the testing process usually involves a mixture of manual and automated testing. In manual testing, a tester runs the program with some test data and compares the results to their expectations. They note and report discrepancies to the program developers. In automated testing, the tests are encoded in a program that is run each time the system under development is to be tested. This is usually faster than manual testing, especially when it involves regression testing—re-running previous tests to check that changes to the program have not introduced new bugs.

The use of automated testing has increased considerably over the past few years. However, testing can never be completely automated as automated tests can only check that a program does what it is supposed to do. It is practically impossible to use automated testing to test systems that depend on how things look (e.g., a graphical user interface), or to test that a program does not have unwanted side effects.

8.1 Development testing

Development testing includes all testing activities that are carried out by the team developing the system. The tester of the software is usually the programmer who developed that software, although this is not always the case. Some development processes use programmer/tester pairs (Cusamano and Selby, 1998) where each

Debugging

Debugging is the process of fixing errors and problems that have been discovered by testing. Using information from the program tests, debuggers use their knowledge of the programming language and the intended outcome of the test to locate and repair the program error. This process is often supported by interactive debugging tools that provide extra information about program execution.

http://www.SoftwareEngineering-9.com/Web/Testing/Debugging.html

programmer has an associated tester who develops tests and assists with the testing process. For critical systems, a more formal process may be used, with a separate testing group within the development team. They are responsible for developing tests and maintaining detailed records of test results.

During development, testing may be carried out at three levels of granularity:

1. Unit testing, where individual program units or object classes are tested. Unit testing should focus on testing the functionality of objects or methods.

2. Component testing, where several individual units are integrated to create composite components. Component testing should focus on testing component interfaces.

3. System testing, where some or all of the components in a system are integrated and the system is tested as a whole. System testing should focus on testing component interactions.

Development testing is primarily a defect testing process, where the aim of testing is to discover bugs in the software. It is therefore usually interleaved with debugging—the process of locating problems with the code and changing the program to fix these problems.

8.1.1 Unit testing

Unit testing is the process of testing program components, such as methods or object classes. Individual functions or methods are the simplest type of component. Your tests should be calls to these routines with different input parameters. You can use the approaches to test case design discussed in Section 8.1.2, to design the function or method tests.

When you are testing object classes, you should design your tests to provide coverage of all of the features of the object. This means that you should:

• test all operations associated with the object;

• set and check the value of all attributes associated with the object;

• put the object into all possible states. This means that you should simulate all events that cause a state change.

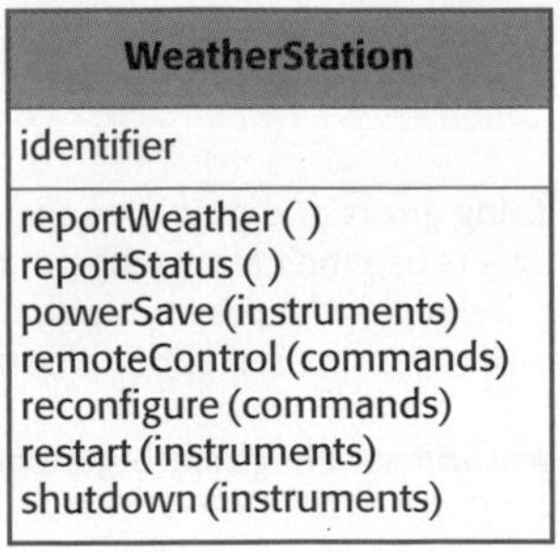

WeatherStation
identifier
reportWeather ( )   reportStatus ( )   powerSave (instruments)   remoteControl (commands)   reconfigure (commands)   restart (instruments)   shutdown (instruments)

Figure 8.4 The weather station object interface

Consider, for example, the weather station object from the example that I discussed in Chapter 7. The interface of this object is shown in Figure 8.4. It has a single attribute, which is its identifier. This is a constant that is set when the weather station is installed. You therefore only need a test that checks if it has been properly set up. You need to define test cases for all of the methods associated with the object such as reportWeather, reportStatus, etc. Ideally, you should test methods in isolation but, in some cases, some test sequences are necessary. For example, to test the method that shuts down the weather station instruments (shutdown), you need to have executed the restart method.

Generalization or inheritance makes object class testing more complicated. You can't simply test an operation in the class where it is defined and assume that it will work as expected in the subclasses that inherit the operation. The operation that is inherited may make assumptions about other operations and attributes. These may not be valid in some subclasses that inherit the operation. You therefore have to test the inherited operation in all of the contexts where it is used.

To test the states of the weather station, you use a state model, such as the one shown in Figure 7.8 in the previous chapter. Using this model, you can identify sequences of state transitions that have to be tested and define event sequences to force these transitions. In principle, you should test every possible state transition sequence, although in practice this may be too expensive. Examples of state sequences that should be tested in the weather station include:

Shutdown → Running → Shutdown
Configuring → Running → Testing → Transmitting → Running
Running → Collecting → Running → Summarizing → Transmitting → Running

Whenever possible, you should automate unit testing. In automated unit testing, you make use of a test automation framework (such as JUnit) to write and run your program tests. Unit testing frameworks provide generic test classes that you extend to create specific test cases. They can then run all of the tests that you have implemented and report, often through some GUI, on the success or failure of the tests. An entire test suite can often be run in a few seconds so it is possible to execute all the tests every time you make a change to the program.

An automated test has three parts:

1. A setup part, where you initialize the system with the test case, namely the inputs and expected outputs.

2. A call part, where you call the object or method to be tested.

3. An assertion part where you compare the result of the call with the expected result. If the assertion evaluates to true, the test has been successful; if false, then it has failed.

Sometimes the object that you are testing has dependencies on other objects that may not have been written or which slow down the testing process if they are used. For example, if your object calls a database, this may involve a slow setup process before it can be used. In these cases, you may decide to use mock objects. Mock objects are objects with the same interface as the external objects being used that simulate its functionality. Therefore, a mock object simulating a database may have only a few data items that are organized in an array. They can therefore be accessed quickly, without the overheads of calling a database and accessing disks. Similarly, mock objects can be used to simulate abnormal operation or rare events. For example, if your system is intended to take action at certain times of day, your mock object can simply return those times, irrespective of the actual clock time.

8.1.2 Choosing unit test cases

Testing is expensive and time consuming, so it is important that you choose effective unit test cases. Effectiveness, in this case, means two things:

1. The test cases should show that, when used as expected, the component that you are testing does what it is supposed to do.

2. If there are defects in the component, these should be revealed by test cases.

You should therefore write two kinds of test case. The first of these should reflect normal operation of a program and should show that the component works. For example, if you are testing a component that creates and initializes a new patient record, then your test case should show that the record exists in a database and that its fields have been set as specified. The other kind of test case should be based on testing experience of where common problems arise. It should use abnormal inputs to check that these are properly processed and do not crash the component.

I discuss two possible strategies here that can be effective in helping you choose test cases. These are:

1. Partition testing, where you identify groups of inputs that have common characteristics and should be processed in the same way. You should choose tests from within each of these groups.

2. Guideline-based testing, where you use testing guidelines to choose test cases. These guidelines reflect previous experience of the kinds of errors that programmers often make when developing components.

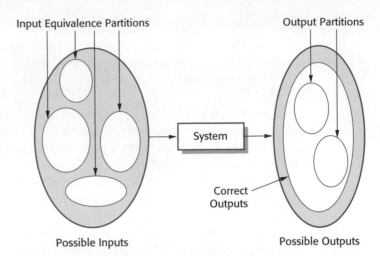

Input Equivalence Partitions

Output Partitions

System

Correct
Outputs

Figure 8.5 Equivalence
partitioning

Possible Inputs

Possible Outputs

The input data and output results of a program often fall into a number of different classes with common characteristics. Examples of these classes are positive numbers, negative numbers, and menu selections. Programs normally behave in a comparable way for all members of a class. That is, if you test a program that does a computation and requires two positive numbers, then you would expect the program to behave in the same way for all positive numbers.

Because of this equivalent behavior, these classes are sometimes called equivalence partitions or domains (Bezier, 1990). One systematic approach to test case design is based on identifying all input and output partitions for a system or component. Test cases are designed so that the inputs or outputs lie within these partitions. Partition testing can be used to design test cases for both systems and components.

In Figure 8.5, the large shaded ellipse on the left represents the set of all possible inputs to the program that is being tested. The smaller unshaded ellipses represent equivalence partitions. A program being tested should process all of the members of an input equivalence partitions in the same way. Output equivalence partitions are partitions within which all of the outputs have something in common. Sometimes there is a 1:1 mapping between input and output equivalence partitions. However, this is not always the case; you may need to define a separate input equivalence partition, where the only common characteristic of the inputs is that they generate outputs within the same output partition. The shaded area in the left ellipse represents inputs that are invalid. The shaded area in the right ellipse represents exceptions that may occur (i.e., responses to invalid inputs).

Once you have identified a set of partitions, you choose test cases from each of these partitions. A good rule of thumb for test case selection is to choose test cases on the boundaries of the partitions, plus cases close to the midpoint of the partition. The reason for this is that designers and programmers tend to consider typical values of inputs when developing a system. You test these by choosing the midpoint of the partition. Boundary values are often atypical (e.g., zero may behave differently from other non-negative numbers) so are sometimes overlooked by developers. Program failures often occur when processing these atypical values.

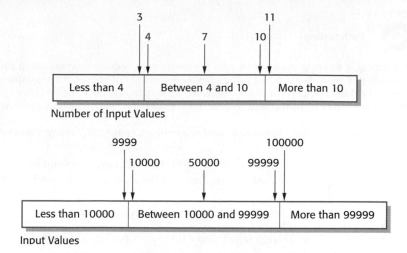

Figure 8.6 Equivalence partitions

You identify partitions by using the program specification or user documentation and from experience where you predict the classes of input value that are likely to detect errors. For example, say a program specification states that the program accepts 4 to 8 inputs which are five-digit integers greater than 10,000. You use this information to identify the input partitions and possible test input values. These are shown in Figure 8.6.

When you use the specification of a system to identify equivalence partitions, this is called 'black-box testing'. Here, you don't need any knowledge of how the system works. However, it may be helpful to supplement the black-box tests with 'white-box testing', where you look at the code of the program to find other possible tests. For example, your code may include exceptions to handle incorrect inputs. You can use this knowledge to identify 'exception partitions'—different ranges where the same exception handling should be applied.

Equivalence partitioning is an effective approach to testing because it helps account for errors that programmers often make when processing inputs at the edges of partitions. You can also use testing guidelines to help choose test cases. Guidelines encapsulate knowledge of what kinds of test cases are effective for discovering errors. For example, when you are testing programs with sequences, arrays, or lists, guidelines that could help reveal defects include:

1. Test software with sequences that have only a single value. Programmers naturally think of sequences as made up of several values and sometimes they embed this assumption in their programs. Consequently, if presented with a single-value sequence, a program may not work properly.

2. Use different sequences of different sizes in different tests. This decreases the chances that a program with defects will accidentally produce a correct output because of some accidental characteristics of the input.

3. Derive tests so that the first, middle, and last elements of the sequence are accessed. This approach is reveals problems at partition boundaries.

Path testing

Path testing is a testing strategy that aims to exercise every independent execution path through a component or program. If every independent path is executed, then all statements in the component must have been executed at least once. All conditional statements are tested for both true and false cases. In an object-oriented development process, path testing may be used when testing the methods associated with objects.

http://www.SoftwareEngineering-9.com/Web/Testing/PathTest.html

Whittaker's book (2002) includes many examples of guidelines that can be used in test case design. Some of the most general guidelines that he suggests are:

■ Choose inputs that force the system to generate all error messages;

■ Design inputs that cause input buffers to overflow;

■ Repeat the same input or series of inputs numerous times;

■ Force invalid outputs to be generated;

■ Force computation results to be too large or too small.

As you gain experience with testing, you can develop your own guidelines about how to choose effective test cases. I give more examples of testing guidelines in the next section of this chapter.

8.1.3 Component testing

Software components are often composite components that are made up of several interacting objects. For example, in the weather station system, the reconfiguration component includes objects that deal with each aspect of the reconfiguration. You access the functionality of these objects through the defined component interface. Testing composite components should therefore focus on showing that the component interface behaves according to its specification. You can assume that unit tests on the individual objects within the component have been completed.

Figure 8.7 illustrates the idea of component interface testing. Assume that components A, B, and C have been integrated to create a larger component or subsystem. The test cases are not applied to the individual components but rather to the interface of the composite component created by combining these components. Interface errors in the composite component may not be detectable by testing the individual objects because these errors result from interactions between the objects in the component.

There are different types of interface between program components and, consequently, different types of interface error that can occur:

1. *Parameter interfaces* These are interfaces in which data or sometimes function references are passed from one component to another. Methods in an object have a parameter interface.

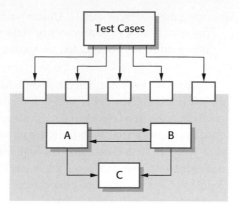

Figure 8.7 Interface testing

2. *Shared memory interfaces* These are interfaces in which a block of memory is shared between components. Data is placed in the memory by one subsystem and retrieved from there by other sub-systems. This type of interface is often used in embedded systems, where sensors create data that is retrieved and processed by other system components.

3. *Procedural interfaces* These are interfaces in which one component encapsulates a set of procedures that can be called by other components. Objects and reusable components have this form of interface.

4. *Message passing interfaces* These are interfaces in which one component requests a service from another component by passing a message to it. A return message includes the results of executing the service. Some object-oriented systems have this form of interface, as do client–server systems.

Interface errors are one of the most common forms of error in complex systems (Lutz, 1993). These errors fall into three classes:

■ *Interface misuse* A calling component calls some other component and makes an error in the use of its interface. This type of error is common with parameter interfaces, where parameters may be of the wrong type or be passed in the wrong order, or the wrong number of parameters may be passed.

■ *Interface misunderstanding* A calling component misunderstands the specification of the interface of the called component and makes assumptions about its behavior. The called component does not behave as expected which then causes unexpected behavior in the calling component. For example, a binary search method may be called with a parameter that is an unordered array. The search would then fail.

■ *Timing errors* These occur in real-time systems that use a shared memory or a message-passing interface. The producer of data and the consumer of data may operate at different speeds. Unless particular care is taken in the interface design, the consumer can access out-of-date information because the producer of the information has not updated the shared interface information.

Testing for interface defects is difficult because some interface faults may only manifest themselves under unusual conditions. For example, say an object implements a queue as a fixed-length data structure. A calling object may assume that the queue is implemented as an infinite data structure and may not check for queue overflow when an item is entered. This condition can only be detected during testing by designing test cases that force the queue to overflow and cause that overflow to corrupt the object behavior in some detectable way.

A further problem may arise because of interactions between faults in different modules or objects. Faults in one object may only be detected when some other object behaves in an unexpected way. For example, an object may call another object to receive some service and assume that the response is correct. If the called service is faulty in some way, the returned value may be valid but incorrect. This is not immediately detected but only becomes obvious when some later computation goes wrong.

Some general guidelines for interface testing are:

1. Examine the code to be tested and explicitly list each call to an external component. Design a set of tests in which the values of the parameters to the external components are at the extreme ends of their ranges. These extreme values are most likely to reveal interface inconsistencies.

2. Where pointers are passed across an interface, always test the interface with null pointer parameters.

3. Where a component is called through a procedural interface, design tests that deliberately cause the component to fail. Differing failure assumptions are one of the most common specification misunderstandings.

4. Use stress testing in message passing systems. This means that you should design tests that generate many more messages than are likely to occur in practice. This is an effective way of revealing timing problems.

5. Where several components interact through shared memory, design tests that vary the order in which these components are activated. These tests may reveal implicit assumptions made by the programmer about the order in which the shared data is produced and consumed.

Inspections and reviews can sometimes be more cost effective than testing for discovering interface errors. Inspections can concentrate on component interfaces and questions about the assumed interface behavior asked during the inspection process. A strongly typed language such as Java allows many interface errors to be trapped by the compiler. Static analyzers (see Chapter 15) can detect a wide range of interface errors.

Incremental integration and testing

System testing involves integrating different components then testing the integrated system that you have created. You should always use an incremental approach to integration and testing (i.e., you should integrate a component, test the system, integrate another component, test again, and so on). This means that if problems occur, it is probably due to interactions with the most recently integrated component.

Incremental integration and testing is fundamental to agile methods such as XP, where regression tests (see Section 8.2) are run every time a new increment is integrated.

http://www.SoftwareEngineering-9.com/Web/Testing/Integration.html

8.1.4 System testing

System testing during development involves integrating components to create a version of the system and then testing the integrated system. System testing checks that components are compatible, interact correctly and transfer the right data at the right time across their interfaces. It obviously overlaps with component testing but there are two important differences:

1. During system testing, reusable components that have been separately developed and off-the-shelf systems may be integrated with newly developed components. The complete system is then tested.

2. Components developed by different team members or groups may be integrated at this stage. System testing is a collective rather than an individual process. In some companies, system testing may involve a separate testing team with no involvement from designers and programmers.

When you integrate components to create a system, you get emergent behavior. This means that some elements of system functionality only become obvious when you put the components together. This may be planned emergent behavior, which has to be tested. For example, you may integrate an authentication component with a component that updates information. You then have a system feature that restricts information updating to authorized users. Sometimes, however, the emergent behavior is unplanned and unwanted. You have to develop tests that check that the system is only doing what it is supposed to do.

Therefore system testing should focus on testing the interactions between the components and objects that make up a system. You may also test reusable components or systems to check that they work as expected when they are integrated with new components. This interaction testing should discover those component bugs that are only revealed when a component is used by other components in the system. Interaction testing also helps find misunderstandings, made by component developers, about other components in the system.

Because of its focus on interactions, use case–based testing is an effective approach to system testing. Typically, each use case is implemented by several components or objects in the system. Testing the use case forces these interactions to

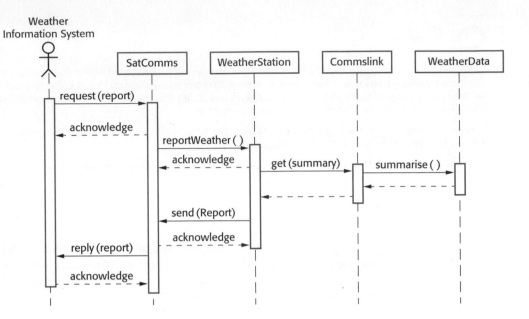

Figure 8.8 Collect weather data sequence chart

occur. If you have developed a sequence diagram to model the use case implementation, you can see the objects or components that are involved in the interaction.

To illustrate this, I use an example from the wilderness weather station system where the weather station is asked to report summarized weather data to a remote computer. The use case for this is described in Figure 7.3 (see previous chapter). Figure 8.8 (which is a copy of Figure 7.7) shows the sequence of operations in the weather station when it responds to a request to collect data for the mapping system. You can use this diagram to identify operations that will be tested and to help design the test cases to execute the tests. Therefore, issuing a request for a report will result in the execution of the following thread of methods:

SatComms:request → WeatherStation:reportWeather → Commslink:Get(summary)
→ WeatherData:summarize

The sequence diagram helps you design the specific test cases that you need as it shows what inputs are required and what outputs are created:

1.   An input of a request for a report should have an associated acknowledgment. A report should ultimately be returned from the request. During testing, you should create summarized data that can be used to check that the report is correctly organized.

2.   An input request for a report to WeatherStation results in a summarized report being generated. You can test this in isolation by creating raw data corresponding to the summary that you have prepared for the test of SatComms and checking that the WeatherStation object correctly produces this summary. This raw data is also used to test the WeatherData object.

Of course, I have simplified the sequence diagram in Figure 8.8 so that it does not show exceptions. A complete use case/scenario test must also take these into account and ensure that objects correctly handle exceptions.

For most systems, it is difficult to know how much system testing is essential and when you should to stop testing. Exhaustive testing, where every possible program execution sequence is tested, is impossible. Testing, therefore, has to be based on a subset of possible test cases. Ideally, software companies should have policies for choosing this subset. These policies might be based on general testing policies, such as a policy that all program statements should be executed at least once. Alternatively, they may be based on experience of system usage and focus on testing the features of the operational system. For example:

1. All system functions that are accessed through menus should be tested.

2. Combinations of functions (e.g., text formatting) that are accessed through the same menu must be tested.

3. Where user input is provided, all functions must be tested with both correct and incorrect input.

It is clear from experience with major software products such as word processors or spreadsheets that similar guidelines are normally used during product testing. When features of the software are used in isolation, they normally work. Problems arise, as Whittaker (2002) explains, when combinations of less commonly used features have not been tested together. He gives the example of how, in a commonly used word processor, using footnotes with a multicolumn layout causes incorrect layout of the text.

Automated system testing is usually more difficult than automated unit or component testing. Automated unit testing relies on predicting the outputs then encoding these predictions in a program. The prediction is then compared with the result. However, the point of implementing a system may be to generate outputs that are large or cannot be easily predicted. You may be able to examine an output and check its credibility without necessarily being able to create it in advance.

8.2 Test-driven development

Test-driven development (TDD) is an approach to program development in which you interleave testing and code development (Beck, 2002; Jeffries and Melnik, 2007). Essentially, you develop the code incrementally, along with a test for that increment. You don't move on to the next increment until the code that you have developed passes its test. Test-driven development was introduced as part of agile methods such as Extreme Programming. However, it can also be used in plan-driven development processes.

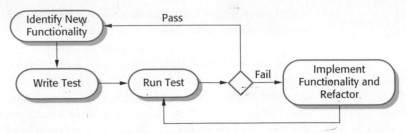

Figure 8.9 Test-driven development

The fundamental TDD process is shown in Figure 8.9. The steps in the process are as follows:

1. You start by identifying the increment of functionality that is required. This should normally be small and implementable in a few lines of code.

2. You write a test for this functionality and implement this as an automated test. This means that the test can be executed and will report whether or not it has passed or failed.

3. You then run the test, along with all other tests that have been implemented. Initially, you have not implemented the functionality so the new test will fail. This is deliberate as it shows that the test adds something to the test set.

4. You then implement the functionality and re-run the test. This may involve refactoring existing code to improve it and add new code to what's already there.

5. Once all tests run successfully, you move on to implementing the next chunk of functionality.

An automated testing environment, such as the JUnit environment that supports Java program testing (Massol and Husted, 2003), is essential for TDD. As the code is developed in very small increments, you have to be able to run every test each time that you add functionality or refactor the program. Therefore, the tests are embedded in a separate program that runs the tests and invokes the system that is being tested. Using this approach, it is possible to run hundreds of separate tests in a few seconds.

A strong argument for test-driven development is that it helps programmers clarify their ideas of what a code segment is actually supposed to do. To write a test, you need to understand what is intended, as this understanding makes it easier to write the required code. Of course, if you have incomplete knowledge or understanding, then test-driven development won't help. If you don't know enough to write the tests, you won't develop the required code. For example, if your computation involves division, you should check that you are not dividing the numbers by zero. If you forget to write a test for this, then the code to check will never be included in the program.

As well as better problem understanding, other benefits of test-driven development are:

1. *Code coverage* In principle, every code segment that you write should have at least one associated test. Therefore, you can be confident that all of the code in

the system has actually been executed. Code is tested as it is written so defects are discovered early in the development process.

2. *Regression testing* A test suite is developed incrementally as a program is developed. You can always run regression tests to check that changes to the program have not introduced new bugs.

3. *Simplified debugging* When a test fails, it should be obvious where the problem lies. The newly written code needs to be checked and modified. You do not need to use debugging tools to locate the problem. Reports of the use of test-driven development suggest that it is hardly ever necessary to use an automated debugger in test-driven development (Martin, 2007).

4. *System documentation* The tests themselves act as a form of documentation that describe what the code should be doing. Reading the tests can make it easier to understand the code.

One of the most important benefits of test-driven development is that it reduces the costs of regression testing. Regression testing involves running test sets that have successfully executed after changes have been made to a system. The regression test checks that these changes have not introduced new bugs into the system and that the new code interacts as expected with the existing code. Regression testing is very expensive and often impractical when a system is manually tested, as the costs in time and effort are very high. In such situations, you have to try and choose the most relevant tests to re-run and it is easy to miss important tests.

However, automated testing, which is fundamental to test-first development, dramatically reduces the costs of regression testing. Existing tests may be re-run quickly and cheaply. After making a change to a system in test-first development, all existing tests must run successfully before any further functionality is added. As a programmer, you can be confident that the new functionality that you have added has not caused or revealed problems with existing code.

Test-driven development is of most use in new software development where the functionality is either implemented in new code or by using well-tested standard libraries. If you are reusing large code components or legacy systems then you need to write tests for these systems as a whole. Test-driven development may also be ineffective with multi-threaded systems. The different threads may be interleaved at different times in different test runs, and so may produce different results.

If you use test-driven development, you still need a system testing process to validate the system; that is, to check that it meets the requirements of all of the system stakeholders. System testing also tests performance, reliability, and checks that the system does not do things that it shouldn't do, such as produce unwanted outputs, etc. Andrea (2007) suggests how testing tools can be extended to integrate some aspects of system testing with TDD.

Test-driven development has proved to be a successful approach for small and medium-sized projects. Generally, programmers who have adopted this approach are happy with it and find it a more productive way to develop software (Jeffries and

Melnik, 2007). In some trials, it has been shown to lead to improved code quality; in others, the results have been inconclusive. However, there is no evidence that TDD leads to poorer quality code.

8.3 Release testing

Release testing is the process of testing a particular release of a system that is intended for use outside of the development team. Normally, the system release is for customers and users. In a complex project, however, the release could be for other teams that are developing related systems. For software products, the release could be for product management who then prepare it for sale.

There are two important distinctions between release testing and system testing during the development process:

1. A separate team that has not been involved in the system development should be responsible for release testing.

2. System testing by the development team should focus on discovering bugs in the system (defect testing). The objective of release testing is to check that the system meets its requirements and is good enough for external use (validation testing).

The primary goal of the release testing process is to convince the supplier of the system that it is good enough for use. If so, it can be released as a product or delivered to the customer. Release testing, therefore, has to show that the system delivers its specified functionality, performance, and dependability, and that it does not fail during normal use. It should take into account all of the system requirements, not just the requirements of the end-users of the system.

Release testing is usually a black-box testing process where tests are derived from the system specification. The system is treated as a black box whose behavior can only be determined by studying its inputs and the related outputs. Another name for this is 'functional testing', so-called because the tester is only concerned with functionality and not the implementation of the software.

8.3.1 Requirements-based testing

A general principle of good requirements engineering practice is that requirements should be testable; that is, the requirement should be written so that a test can be designed for that requirement. A tester can then check that the requirement has been satisfied. Requirements-based testing, therefore, is a systematic approach to test case design where you consider each requirement and derive a set of tests for it. Requirements-based testing is validation rather than defect testing—you are trying to demonstrate that the system has properly implemented its requirements.

For example, consider related requirements for the MHC-PMS (introduced in Chapter 1), which are concerned with checking for drug allergies:

If a patient is known to be allergic to any particular medication, then prescription of that medication shall result in a warning message being issued to the system user.

If a prescriber chooses to ignore an allergy warning, they shall provide a reason why this has been ignored.

To check if these requirements have been satisfied, you may need to develop several related tests:

1. Set up a patient record with no known allergies. Prescribe medication for allergies that are known to exist. Check that a warning message is not issued by the system.

2. Set up a patient record with a known allergy. Prescribe the medication to that the patient is allergic to, and check that the warning is issued by the system.

3. Set up a patient record in which allergies to two or more drugs are recorded. Prescribe both of these drugs separately and check that the correct warning for each drug is issued.

4. Prescribe two drugs that the patient is allergic to. Check that two warnings are correctly issued.

5. Prescribe a drug that issues a warning and overrule that warning. Check that the system requires the user to provide information explaining why the warning was overruled.

You can see from this that testing a requirement does not mean just writing a single test. You normally have to write several tests to ensure that you have coverage of the requirement. You should also maintain traceability records of your requirements-based testing, which link the tests to the specific requirements that are being tested.

8.3.2 Scenario testing

Scenario testing is an approach to release testing where you devise typical scenarios of use and use these to develop test cases for the system. A scenario is a story that describes one way in which the system might be used. Scenarios should be realistic and real system users should be able to relate to them. If you have used scenarios as part of the requirements engineering process (described in Chapter 4), then you may be able to reuse these as testing scenarios.

In a short paper on scenario testing, Kaner (2003) suggests that a scenario test should be a narrative story that is credible and fairly complex. It should motivate stakeholders; that is, they should relate to the scenario and believe that it is important

Kate is a nurse who specializes in mental health care. One of her responsibilities is to visit patients at home to check that their treatment is effective and that they are not suffering from medication side effects.

On a day for home visits, Kate logs into the MHC-PMS and uses it to print her schedule of home visits for that day, along with summary information about the patients to be visited. She requests that the records for these patients be downloaded to her laptop. She is prompted for her key phrase to encrypt the records on the laptop.

One of the patients that she visits is Jim, who is being treated with medication for depression. Jim feels that the medication is helping him but believes that it has the side effect of keeping him awake at night. Kate looks up Jim's record and is prompted for her key phrase to decrypt the record. She checks the drug prescribed and queries its side effects. Sleeplessness is a known side effect so she notes the problem in Jim's record and suggests that he visits the clinic to have his medication changed. He agrees so Kate enters a prompt to call him when she gets back to the clinic to make an appointment with a physician. She ends the consultation and the system re-encrypts Jim's record.

After, finishing her consultations, Kate returns to the clinic and uploads the records of patients visited to the database. The system generates a call list for Kate of those patients who she has to contact for follow-up information and make clinic appointments.

Figure 8.10 A usage scenario for the MHC-PMS

that the system passes the test. He also suggests that it should be easy to evaluate. If there are problems with the system, then the release testing team should recognize them. As an example of a possible scenario from the MHC-PMS, Figure 8.10 describes one way that the system may be used on a home visit.

It tests a number of features of the MHC-PMS:

1. Authentication by logging on to the system.

2. Downloading and uploading of specified patient records to a laptop.

3. Home visit scheduling.

4. Encryption and decryption of patient records on a mobile device.

5. Record retrieval and modification.

6. Links with the drugs database that maintains side-effect information.

7. The system for call prompting.

If you are a release tester, you run through this scenario, playing the role of Kate and observing how the system behaves in response to different inputs. As 'Kate', you may make deliberate mistakes, such as inputting the wrong key phrase to decode records. This checks the response of the system to errors. You should carefully note any problems that arise, including performance problems. If a system is too slow, this will change the way that it is used. For example, if it takes too long to encrypt a record, then users who are short of time may skip this stage. If they then lose their laptop, an unauthorized person could then view the patient records.

When you use a scenario-based approach, you are normally testing several requirements within the same scenario. Therefore, as well as checking individual requirements, you are also checking that combinations of requirements do not cause problems.

8.3.3 Performance testing

Once a system has been completely integrated, it is possible to test for emergent properties, such as performance and reliability. Performance tests have to be designed to ensure that the system can process its intended load. This usually involves running a series of tests where you increase the load until the system performance becomes unacceptable.

As with other types of testing, performance testing is concerned both with demonstrating that the system meets its requirements and discovering problems and defects in the system. To test whether performance requirements are being achieved, you may have to construct an operational profile. An operational profile (see Chapter 15) is a set of tests that reflect the actual mix of work that will be handled by the system. Therefore, if 90% of the transactions in a system are of type A; 5% of type B; and the remainder of types C, D, and E, then you have to design the operational profile so that the vast majority of tests are of type A. Otherwise, you will not get an accurate test of the operational performance of the system.

This approach, of course, is not necessarily the best approach for defect testing. Experience has shown that an effective way to discover defects is to design tests around the limits of the system. In performance testing, this means stressing the system by making demands that are outside the design limits of the software. This is known as 'stress testing'. For example, say you are testing a transaction processing system that is designed to process up to 300 transactions per second. You start by testing this system with fewer than 300 transactions per second. You then gradually increase the load on the system beyond 300 transactions per second until it is well beyond the maximum design load of the system and the system fails. This type of testing has two functions:

1. It tests the failure behavior of the system. Circumstances may arise through an unexpected combination of events where the load placed on the system exceeds the maximum anticipated load. In these circumstances, it is important that system failure should not cause data corruption or unexpected loss of user services. Stress testing checks that overloading the system causes it to 'fail-soft' rather than collapse under its load.

2. It stresses the system and may cause defects to come to light that would not normally be discovered. Although it can be argued that these defects are unlikely to cause system failures in normal usage, there may be unusual combinations of normal circumstances that the stress testing replicates.

Stress testing is particularly relevant to distributed systems based on a network of processors. These systems often exhibit severe degradation when they are heavily loaded. The network becomes swamped with coordination data that the different processes must exchange. The processes become slower and slower as they wait for the required data from other processes. Stress testing helps you discover when the degradation begins so that you can add checks to the system to reject transactions beyond this point.

8.4 User testing

User or customer testing is a stage in the testing process in which users or customers provide input and advice on system testing. This may involve formally testing a system that has been commissioned from an external supplier, or could be an informal process where users experiment with a new software product to see if they like it and that it does what they need. User testing is essential, even when comprehensive system and release testing have been carried out. The reason for this is that influences from the user's working environment have a major effect on the reliability, performance, usability, and robustness of a system.

It is practically impossible for a system developer to replicate the system's working environment, as tests in the developer's environment are inevitably artificial. For example, a system that is intended for use in a hospital is used in a clinical environment where other things are going on, such as patient emergencies, conversations with relatives, etc. These all affect the use of a system, but developers cannot include them in their testing environment.

In practice, there are three different types of user testing:

1. Alpha testing, where users of the software work with the development team to test the software at the developer's site.

2. Beta testing, where a release of the software is made available to users to allow them to experiment and to raise problems that they discover with the system developers.

3. Acceptance testing, where customers test a system to decide whether or not it is ready to be accepted from the system developers and deployed in the customer environment.

In alpha testing, users and developers work together to test a system as it is being developed. This means that the users can identify problems and issues that are not readily apparent to the development testing team. Developers can only really work from the requirements but these often do not reflect other factors that affect the practical use of the software. Users can therefore provide information about practice that helps with the design of more realistic tests.

Alpha testing is often used when developing software products that are sold as shrink-wrapped systems. Users of these products may be willing to get involved in the alpha testing process because this gives them early information about new system features that they can exploit. It also reduces the risk that unanticipated changes to the software will have disruptive effects on their business. However, alpha testing may also be used when custom software is being developed. Agile methods, such as XP, advocate user involvement in the development process and that users should play a key role in designing tests for the system.

Beta testing takes place when an early, sometimes unfinished, release of a software system is made available to customers and users for evaluation. Beta testers

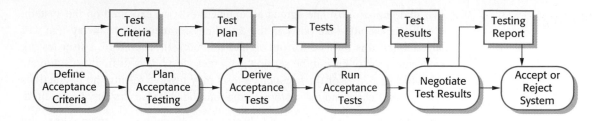

Figure 8.11 The acceptance testing process

may be a selected group of customers who are early adopters of the system. Alternatively, the software may be made publicly available for use by anyone who is interested in it. Beta testing is mostly used for software products that are used in many different environments (as opposed to custom systems which are generally used in a defined environment). It is impossible for product developers to know and replicate all the environments in which the software will be used. Beta testing is therefore essential to discover interaction problems between the software and features of the environment where it is used. Beta testing is also a form of marketing—customers learn about their system and what it can do for them.

Acceptance testing is an inherent part of custom systems development. It takes place after release testing. It involves a customer formally testing a system to decide whether or not it should be accepted from the system developer. Acceptance implies that payment should be made for the system.

There are six stages in the acceptance testing process, as shown in Figure 8.11. They are:

1. *Define acceptance criteria* This stage should, ideally, take place early in the process before the contract for the system is signed. The acceptance criteria should be part of the system contract and be agreed between the customer and the developer. In practice, however, it can be difficult to define criteria so early in the process. Detailed requirements may not be available and there may be significant requirements change during the development process.

2. *Plan acceptance testing* This involves deciding on the resources, time, and budget for acceptance testing and establishing a testing schedule. The acceptance test plan should also discuss the required coverage of the requirements and the order in which system features are tested. It should define risks to the testing process, such as system crashes and inadequate performance, and discuss how these risks can be mitigated.

3. *Derive acceptance tests* Once acceptance criteria have been established, tests have to be designed to check whether or not a system is acceptable. Acceptance tests should aim to test both the functional and non-functional characteristics (e.g., performance) of the system. They should, ideally, provide complete coverage of the system requirements. In practice, it is difficult to establish completely objective acceptance criteria. There is often scope for argument about whether or not a test shows that a criterion has definitely been met.

4. *Run acceptance tests* The agreed acceptance tests are executed on the system. Ideally, this should take place in the actual environment where the system will be used, but this may be disruptive and impractical. Therefore, a user testing environment may have to be set up to run these tests. It is difficult to automate this process as part of the acceptance tests may involve testing the interactions between end-users and the system. Some training of end-users may be required.

5. *Negotiate test results* It is very unlikely that all of the defined acceptance tests will pass and that there will be no problems with the system. If this is the case, then acceptance testing is complete and the system can be handed over. More commonly, some problems will be discovered. In such cases, the developer and the customer have to negotiate to decide if the system is good enough to be put into use. They must also agree on the developer's response to identified problems.

6. *Reject/accept system* This stage involves a meeting between the developers and the customer to decide on whether or not the system should be accepted. If the system is not good enough for use, then further development is required to fix the identified problems. Once complete, the acceptance testing phase is repeated.

In agile methods, such as XP, acceptance testing has a rather different meaning. In principle, it shares the notion that users should decide whether or not the system is acceptable. However, in XP, the user is part of the development team (i.e., he or she is an alpha tester) and provides the system requirements in terms of user stories. He or she is also responsible for defining the tests, which decide whether or not the developed software supports the user story. The tests are automated and development does not proceed until the story acceptance tests have passed. There is, therefore, no separate acceptance testing activity.

As I have discussed in Chapter 3, one problem with user involvement is ensuring that the user who is embedded in the development team is a 'typical' user with general knowledge of how the system will be used. It can be difficult to find such a user, and so the acceptance tests may actually not be a true reflection of practice. Furthermore, the requirement for automated testing severely limits the flexibility of testing interactive systems. For such systems, acceptance testing may require groups of end-users to use the system as if it was part of their everyday work.

You might think that acceptance testing is a clear-cut contractual issue. If a system does not pass its acceptance tests, then it should not be accepted and payment should not be made. However, the reality is more complex. Customers want to use the software as soon as they can because of the benefits of its immediate deployment. They may have bought new hardware, trained staff, and changed their processes. They may be willing to accept the software, irrespective of problems, because the costs of not using the software are greater than the costs of working around the problems. Therefore, the outcome of negotiations may be conditional acceptance of the system. The customer may accept the system so that deployment can begin. The system provider agrees to repair urgent problems and deliver a new version to the customer as quickly as possible.

KEY POINTS

■ Testing can only show the presence of errors in a program. It cannot demonstrate that there are no remaining faults.

■ Development testing is the responsibility of the software development team. A separate team should be responsible for testing a system before it is released to customers. In the user testing process, customers or system users provide test data and check that tests are successful.

■ Development testing includes unit testing, in which you test individual objects and methods; component testing, in which you test related groups of objects; and system testing, in which you test partial or complete systems.

■ When testing software, you should try to 'break' the software by using experience and guidelines to choose types of test cases that have been effective in discovering defects in other systems.

■ Wherever possible, you should write automated tests. The tests are embedded in a program that can be run every time a change is made to a system.

■ Test-first development is an approach to development where tests are written before the code to be tested. Small code changes are made and the code is refactored until all tests execute successfully.

■ Scenario testing is useful because it replicates the practical use of the system. It involves inventing a typical usage scenario and using this to derive test cases.

■ Acceptance testing is a user testing process where the aim is to decide if the software is good enough to be deployed and used in its operational environment.

FURTHER READING

'How to design practical test cases'. A how-to article on test case design by an author from a Japanese company that has a very good reputation for delivering software with very few faults. (T. Yamaura, *IEEE Software*, **15**(6), November 1998.) http://dx.doi.org/10.1109/52.730835.

How to Break Software: A Practical Guide to Testing. This is a practical, rather than theoretical, book on software testing in which the author presents a set of experience-based guidelines on designing tests that are likely to be effective in discovering system faults. (J. A. Whittaker, Addison-Wesley, 2002.)

'Software Testing and Verification'. This special issue of the *IBM Systems Journal* includes a number of papers on testing, including a good general overview, papers on test metrics, and test automation. (*IBM Systems Journal*, **41**(1), January 2002.)

'Test-driven development'. This special issue on test-driven development includes a good general overview of TDD as well as experience papers on how TDD has been used for different types of software. (*IEEE Software*, **24** (3) May/June 2007.)

EXERCISES

8.1. Explain why it is not necessary for a program to be completely free of defects before it is delivered to its customers.

8.2. Explain why testing can only detect the presence of errors, not their absence.

8.3. Some people argue that developers should not be involved in testing their own code but that all testing should be the responsibility of a separate team. Give arguments for and against testing by the developers themselves.

8.4. You have been asked to test a method called 'catWhiteSpace' in a 'Paragraph' object that, within the paragraph, replaces sequences of blank characters with a single blank character. Identify testing partitions for this example and derive a set of tests for the 'catWhiteSpace' method.

8.5. What is regression testing? Explain how the use of automated tests and a testing framework such as JUnit simplifies regression testing.

8.6. The MHC-PMS is constructed by adapting an off-the-shelf information system. What do you think are the differences between testing such a system and testing software that is developed using an object-oriented language such as Java?

8.7. Write a scenario that could be used to help design tests for the wilderness weather station system.

8.8. What do you understand by the term 'stress testing'? Suggest how you might stress test the MHC-PMS.

8.9. What are the benefits of involving users in release testing at an early stage in the testing process? Are there disadvantages in user involvement?

8.10. A common approach to system testing is to test the system until the testing budget is exhausted and then deliver the system to customers. Discuss the ethics of this approach for systems that are delivered to external customers.

REFERENCES

Andrea, J. (2007). 'Envisioning the Next Generation of Functional Testing Tools'. *IEEE Software*, 24 (3), 58–65.

Beck, K. (2002). *Test Driven Development: By Example*. Boston: Addison-Wesley.

Bezier, B. (1990). *Software Testing Techniques, 2nd edition*. New York: Van Nostrand Rheinhold.

Boehm, B. W. (1979). 'Software engineering; R & D Trends and defense needs.' In *Research Directions in Software Technology*. Wegner, P. (ed.). Cambridge, Mass.: MIT Press. 1–9.

Cusamano, M. and Selby, R. W. (1998). *Microsoft Secrets*. New York: Simon and Shuster.

Dijkstra, E. W., Dahl, O. J. and Hoare, C. A. R. (1972). *Structured Programming*. London: Academic Press.

Fagan, M. E. (1986). 'Advances in Software Inspections'. *IEEE Trans. on Software Eng.*, **SE-12** (7), 744–51.

Jeffries, R. and Melnik, G. (2007). 'TDD: The Art of Fearless Programming'. *IEEE Software*, **24**, 24–30.

Kaner, C. (2003). 'The power of 'What If . . .' and nine ways to fuel your imagination: Cem Kaner on scenario testing'. *Software Testing and Quality Engineering*, **5** (5), 16–22.

Lutz, R. R. (1993). 'Analyzing Software Requirements Errors in Safety-Critical Embedded Systems'. RE'93, San Diego, Calif.: IEEE.

Martin, R. C. (2007). 'Professionalism and Test-Driven Development'. *IEEE Software*, **24** (3), 32–6.

Massol, V. and Husted, T. (2003). *JUnit in Action*. Greenwich, Conn.: Manning Publications Co.

Prowell, S. J., Trammell, C. J., Linger, R. C. and Poore, J. H. (1999). *Cleanroom Software Engineering: Technology and Process*. Reading, Mass.: Addison-Wesley.

Whittaker, J. W. (2002). *How to Break Software: A Practical Guide to Testing*. Boston: Addison-Wesley.

9

Software evolution

Objectives

The objectives of this chapter are to explain why software evolution is an important part of software engineering and to describe software evolution processes. When you have read this chapter, you will:

■ understand that change is inevitable if software systems are to remain useful and that software development and evolution may be integrated in a spiral model;

■ understand software evolution processes and influences on these processes;

■ have learned about different types of software maintenance and the factors that affect maintenance costs; and

■ understand how legacy systems can be assessed to decide whether they should be scrapped, maintained, reengineered, or replaced.

Contents

Software development does not stop when a system is delivered but continues throughout the lifetime of the system. After a system has been deployed, it inevitably has to change if it is to remain useful. Business changes and changes to user expectations generate new requirements for the existing software. Parts of the software may have to be modified to correct errors that are found in operation, to adapt it for changes to its hardware and software platform, and to improve its performance or other non-functional characteristics.

Software evolution is important because organizations have invested large amounts of money in their software and are now completely dependent on these systems. Their systems are critical business assets and they have to invest in system change to maintain the value of these assets. Consequently, most large companies spend more on maintaining existing systems than on new systems development. Based on an informal industry poll, Erlikh (2000) suggests that 85–90% of organizational software costs are evolution costs. Other surveys suggest that about two-thirds of software costs are evolution costs. For sure, the costs of software change are a large part of the IT budget for all companies.

Software evolution may be triggered by changing business requirements, by reports of software defects, or by changes to other systems in a software system's environment. Hopkins and Jenkins (2008) have coined the term 'brownfield software development' to describe situations in which software systems have to be developed and managed in an environment where they are dependent on many other software systems.

Therefore, the evolution of a system can rarely be considered in isolation. Changes to the environment lead to system change that may then trigger further environmental changes. Of course, the fact that systems have to evolve in a 'systems-rich' environment often increases the difficulties and costs of evolution. As well as understanding and analyzing an impact of a proposed change on the system itself, you may also have to assess how this may affect other systems in the operational environment.

Useful software systems often have a very long lifetime. For example, large military or infrastructure systems, such as air traffic control systems, may have a lifetime of 30 years or more. Business systems are often more than 10 years old. Software cost a lot of money so a company has to use a software system for many years to get a return on its investment. Obviously, the requirements of the installed systems change as the business and its environment change. Therefore, new releases of the systems, incorporating changes, and updates, are usually created at regular intervals.

You should, therefore, think of software engineering as a spiral process with requirements, design, implementation, and testing going on throughout the lifetime of the system (Figure 9.1). You start by creating release 1 of the system. Once delivered, changes are proposed and the development of release 2 starts almost immediately. In fact, the need for evolution may become obvious even before the system is deployed so that later releases of the software may be under development before the current version has been released.

This model of software evolution implies that a single organization is responsible for both the initial software development and the evolution of the software. Most

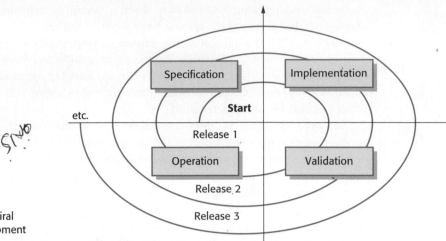

Figure 9.1 A spiral model of development and evolution

packaged software products are developed using this approach. For custom software, a different approach is commonly used. A software company develops software for a customer and the customer's own development staff then take over the system. They are responsible for software evolution. Alternatively, the software customer might issue a separate contract to a different company for system support and evolution.

In this case, there are likely to be discontinuities in the spiral process. Requirements and design documents may not be passed from one company to another. Companies may merge or reorganize and inherit software from other companies, and then find that this has to be changed. When the transition from development to evolution is not seamless, the process of changing the software after delivery is often called 'software maintenance'. As I discuss later in this chapter, maintenance involves extra process activities, such as program understanding, in addition to the normal activities of software development.

Rajlich and Bennett (2000) proposed an alternative view of the software evolution life cycle, as shown in Figure 9.2. In this model, they distinguish between evolution and servicing. Evolution is the phase in which significant changes to the software architecture and functionality may be made. During servicing, the only changes that are made are relatively small, essential changes.

During evolution, the software is used successfully and there is a constant stream of proposed requirements changes. However, as the software is modified, its structure tends to degrade and changes become more and more expensive. This often happens after a few years of use when other environmental changes, such as hardware and operating systems, are also often required. At some stage in the life cycle, the software reaches a transition point where significant changes, implementing new requirements, become less and less cost effective.

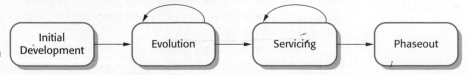

Figure 9.2 Evolution and servicing

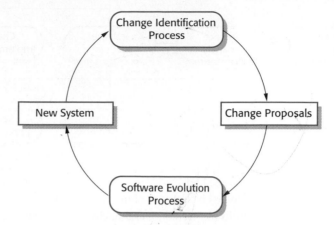

Figure 9.3 Change identification and evolution processes

At that stage, the software moves from evolution to servicing. During the servicing phase, the software is still useful and used but only small tactical changes are made to it. During this stage, the company is usually considering how the software can be replaced. In the final stage, phase-out, the software may still be used but no further changes are being implemented. Users have to work around any problems that they discover.

9.1 Evolution processes

Software evolution processes vary depending on the type of software being maintained, the development processes used in an organization and the skills of the people involved. In some organizations, evolution may be an informal process where change requests mostly come from conversations between the system users and developers. In other companies, it is a formalized process with structured documentation produced at each stage in the process.

System change proposals are the driver for system evolution in all organizations. Change proposals may come from existing requirements that have not been implemented in the released system, requests for new requirements, bug reports from system stakeholders, and new ideas for software improvement from the system development team. The processes of change identification and system evolution are cyclic and continue throughout the lifetime of a system (Figure 9.3).

Change proposals should be linked to the components of the system that have to be modified to implement these proposals. This allows the cost and the impact of the change to be assessed. This is part of the general process of change management, which also should ensure that the correct versions of components are included in each system release. I cover change and configuration management in Chapter 25.

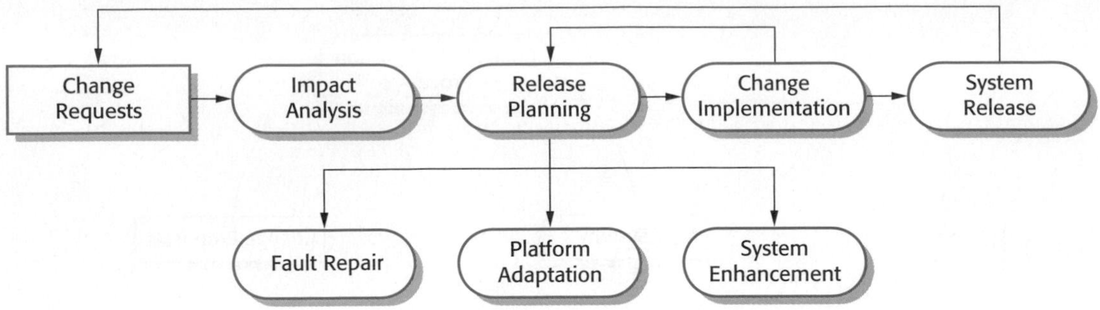

Figure 9.4 The
software evolution
process

Figure 9.4, adapted from Arthur (1988), shows an overview of the evolution process. The process includes the fundamental activities of change analysis, release planning, system implementation, and releasing a system to customers. The cost and impact of these changes are assessed to see how much of the system is affected by the change and how much it might cost to implement the change. If the proposed changes are accepted, a new release of the system is planned. During release planning, all proposed changes (fault repair, adaptation, and new functionality) are considered. A decision is then made on which changes to implement in the next version of the system. The changes are implemented and validated, and a new version of the system is released. The process then iterates with a new set of changes proposed for the next release.

You can think of change implementation as an iteration of the development process, where the revisions to the system are designed, implemented, and tested. However, a critical difference is that the first stage of change implementation may involve program understanding, especially if the original system developers are not responsible for change implementation. During this program understanding phase, you have to understand how the program is structured, how it delivers functionality, and how the proposed change might affect the program. You need this understanding to make sure that the implemented change does not cause new problems when it is introduced into the existing system.

Ideally, the change implementation stage of this process should modify the system specification, design, and implementation to reflect the changes to the system (Figure 9.5). New requirements that reflect the system changes are proposed, analyzed, and validated. System components are redesigned and implemented and the system is retested. If appropriate, prototyping of the proposed changes may be carried out as part of the change analysis process.

During the evolution process, the requirements are analyzed in detail and implications of the changes emerge that were not apparent in the earlier change analysis process. This means that the proposed changes may be modified and further customer discussions may be required before they are implemented.

Change requests sometimes relate to system problems that have to be tackled urgently. These urgent changes can arise for three reasons:

1. If a serious system fault occurs that has to be repaired to allow normal operation to continue.

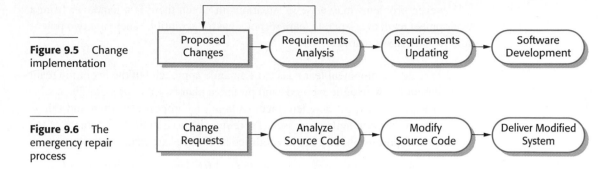

Figure 9.5 Change implementation

Figure 9.6 The emergency repair process

2. If changes to the systems operating environment have unexpected effects that disrupt normal operation.

3. If there are unanticipated changes to the business running the system, such as the emergence of new competitors or the introduction of new legislation that affects the system.

In these cases, the need to make the change quickly means that you may not be able to follow the formal change analysis process. Rather than modify the requirements and design, you make an emergency fix to the program to solve the immediate problem (Figure 9.6). However, the danger is that the requirements, the software design, and the code become inconsistent. Although you may intend to document the change in the requirements and design, additional emergency fixes to the software may then be needed. These take priority over documentation. Eventually, the original change is forgotten and the system documentation and code are never realigned.

Emergency system repairs usually have to be completed as quickly as possible. You chose a quick and workable solution rather than the best solution as far as system structure is concerned. This accelerates the process of software ageing so that future changes become progressively more difficult and maintenance costs increase.

Ideally, when emergency code repairs are made the change request should remain outstanding after the code faults have been fixed. It can then be reimplemented more carefully after further analysis. Of course, the code of the repair may be reused. An alternative, better solution to the problem may be discovered when more time is available for analysis. In practice, however, it is almost inevitable that these improvements will have a low priority. They are often forgotten and, if further system changes are made, it then becomes unrealistic to redo the emergency repairs.

Agile methods and processes, discussed in Chapter 3, may be used for program evolution as well as program development. In fact, because these methods are based on incremental development, making the transition from agile development to post-delivery evolution should be seamless. Techniques such as automated regression testing are useful when system changes are made. Changes may be expressed as user stories and customer involvement can prioritize changes that are required in an operational system. In short, evolution simply involves continuing the agile development process.

However, problems may arise in situations in which there is a handover from a development team to a separate team responsible for evolution. There are two potentially problematic situations:

1. Where the development team has used an agile approach but the evolution team is unfamiliar with agile methods and prefers a plan-based approach. The evolution team may expect detailed documentation to support evolution and this is rarely produced in agile processes. There may be no definitive statement of the system requirements that can be modified as changes are made to the system.

2. Where a plan-based approach has been used for development but the evolution team prefers to use agile methods. In this case, the evolution team may have to start from scratch developing automated tests and the code in the system may not have been refactored and simplified as is expected in agile development. In this case, some reengineering may be required to improve the code before it can be used in an agile development process.

Poole and Huisman (2001) report on their experiences in using Extreme Programming for maintaining a large system that was originally developed using a plan-based approach. After reengineering the system to improve its structure, XP was used very successfully in the maintenance process.

9.2 Program evolution dynamics

Program evolution dynamics is the study of system change. In the 1970s and 1980s, Lehman and Belady (1985) carried out several empirical studies of system change with a view to understanding more about characteristics of software evolution. The work continued in the 1990s as Lehman and others investigated the significance of feedback in evolution processes (Lehman, 1996; Lehman et al., 1998; Lehman et al., 2001). From these studies, they proposed 'Lehman's laws' concerning system change (Figure 9.7).

Lehman and Belady claim these laws are likely to be true for all types of large organizational software systems (what they call E-type systems). These are systems in which the requirements are changing to reflect changing business needs. New releases of the system are essential for the system to provide business value.

The first law states that system maintenance is an inevitable process. As the system's environment changes, new requirements emerge and the system must be modified. When the modified system is reintroduced to the environment, this promotes more environmental changes, so the evolution process starts again.

The second law states that, as a system is changed, its structure is degraded. The only way to avoid this happening is to invest in preventative maintenance. You spend time improving the software structure without adding to its functionality. Obviously, this means additional costs, over and above those of implementing required system changes.

Law	Description
Continuing change	A program that is used in a real-world environment must necessarily change, or else become progressively less useful in that environment.
Increasing complexity	As an evolving program changes, its structure tends to become more complex. Extra resources must be devoted to preserving and simplifying the structure.
Large program evolution	Program evolution is a self-regulating process. System attributes such as size, time between releases, and the number of reported errors is approximately invariant for each system release.
Organizational stability	Over a program's lifetime, its rate of development is approximately constant and independent of the resources devoted to system development.
Conservation of familiarity	Over the lifetime of a system, the incremental change in each release is approximately constant.
Continuing growth	The functionality offered by systems has to continually increase to maintain user satisfaction.
Declining quality	The quality of systems will decline unless they are modified to reflect changes in their operational environment.
Feedback system	Evolution processes incorporate multiagent, multiloop feedback systems and you have to treat them as feedback systems to achieve significant product improvement.

Figure 9.7 Lehman's laws

The third law is, perhaps, the most interesting and the most contentious of Lehman's laws. It suggests that large systems have a dynamic of their own that is established at an early stage in the development process. This determines the gross trends of the system maintenance process and limits the number of possible system changes. Lehman and Belady suggest that this law is a consequence of structural factors that influence and constrain system change, and organizational factors that affect the evolution process.

The structural factors that affect the third law come from the complexity of large systems. As you change and extend a program, its structure tends to degrade. This is true of all types of system (not just software) and it occurs because you are adapting a structure intended for one purpose for a different purpose. This degradation, if unchecked, makes it more and more difficult to make further changes to the program. Making small changes reduces the extent of structural degradation and so lessens the risks of causing serious system dependability problems. If you try and make large changes, there is a high probability that these will introduce new faults. These then inhibit further program changes.

The organizational factors that affect the third law reflect the fact that large systems are usually produced by large organizations. These companies have internal bureaucracies that set the change budget for each system and control the decision-making process. Companies have to make decisions on the risks and value of the changes and the costs involved. Such decisions take time to make and, sometimes, it takes longer to decide on the changes to be made than change implementation. The speed of the organization's decision-making processes therefore governs the rate of change of the system.

Lehman's fourth law suggests that most large programming projects work in a 'saturated' state. That is, a change to resources or staffing has imperceptible effects on the long-term evolution of the system. This is consistent with the third law, which suggests that program evolution is largely independent of management decisions. This law confirms that large software development teams are often unproductive because communication overheads dominate the work of the team.

Lehman's fifth law is concerned with the change increments in each system release. Adding new functionality to a system inevitably introduces new system faults. The more functionality added in each release, the more faults there will be. Therefore, a large increment in functionality in one system release means that this will have to be followed by a further release in which the new system faults are repaired. Relatively little new functionality should be included in this release. This law suggests that you should not budget for large functionality increments in each release without taking into account the need for fault repair.

The first five laws were in Lehman's initial proposals; the remaining laws were added after further work. The sixth and seventh laws are similar and essentially say that users of software will become increasingly unhappy with it unless it is maintained and new functionality is added to it. The final law reflects the most recent work on feedback processes, although it is not yet clear how this can be applied in practical software development.

Lehman's observations seem generally sensible. They should be taken into account when planning the maintenance process. It may be that business considerations require them to be ignored at any one time. For example, for marketing reasons, it may be necessary to make several major system changes in a single release. The likely consequences of this are that one or more releases devoted to error repair are likely to be required. You often see this in personal computer software when a major new release of an application is often quickly followed by a bug repair update.

9.3 Software maintenance

Software maintenance is the general process of changing a system after it has been delivered. The term is usually applied to custom software in which separate development groups are involved before and after delivery. The changes made to the software may be simple changes to correct coding errors, more extensive changes to correct design errors, or significant enhancements to correct specification errors or accommodate new requirements. Changes are implemented by modifying existing system components and, where necessary, by adding new components to the system.

There are three different types of software maintenance:

1. *Fault repairs* Coding errors are usually relatively cheap to correct; design errors are more expensive as they may involve rewriting several program components. Requirements errors are the most expensive to repair because of the extensive system redesign which may be necessary.

2. *Environmental adaptation* This type of maintenance is required when some aspect of the system's environment such as the hardware, the platform operating system, or other support software changes. The application system must be modified to adapt it to cope with these environmental changes.

3. *Functionality addition* This type of maintenance is necessary when the system requirements change in response to organizational or business change. The scale of the changes required to the software is often much greater than for the other types of maintenance.

In practice, there is not a clear-cut distinction between these types of maintenance. When you adapt the system to a new environment, you may add functionality to take advantage of new environmental features. Software faults are often exposed because users use the system in unanticipated ways. Changing the system to accommodate their way of working is the best way to fix these faults.

These types of maintenance are generally recognized but different people sometimes give them different names. 'Corrective maintenance' is universally used to refer to maintenance for fault repair. However, 'adaptive maintenance' sometimes means adapting to a new environment and sometimes means adapting the software to new requirements. 'Perfective maintenance' sometimes means perfecting the software by implementing new requirements; in other cases it means maintaining the functionality of the system but improving its structure and its performance. Because of this naming uncertainty, I have avoided the use of all of these terms in this chapter.

There have been several studies of software maintenance which have looked at the relationships between maintenance and development and between different maintenance activities (Krogstie et al., 2005; Lientz and Swanson, 1980; Nosek and Palvia, 1990; Sousa, 1998). Because of differences in terminology, the details of these studies cannot be compared. In spite of changes in technology and different application domains, it seems that there has been remarkably little change in the distribution of evolution effort since the 1980s.

The surveys broadly agree that software maintenance takes up a higher proportion of IT budgets than new development (roughly two-thirds maintenance, one-third development). They also agree that more of the maintenance budget is spent on implementing new requirements than on fixing bugs. Figure 9.8 shows an approximate distribution of maintenance costs. The specific percentages will obviously vary from one organization to another but, universally, repairing system faults is not the most expensive maintenance activity. Evolving the system to cope with new environments and new or changed requirements consumes most maintenance effort.

The relative costs of maintenance and new development vary from one application domain to another. Guimaraes (1983) found that the maintenance costs for business application systems are broadly comparable with system development costs.

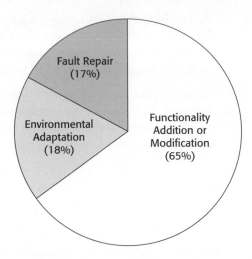

Figure 9.8
Maintenance effort
distribution

For embedded real-time systems, maintenance costs were up to four times more than development costs. The high reliability and performance requirements of these systems mean that modules have to be tightly linked and hence difficult to change. Although these estimates are more than 25 years old, it is unlikely that the cost distributions for different types of system have significantly changed.

It is usually cost effective to invest effort in designing and implementing a system to reduce the costs of future changes. Adding new functionality after delivery is expensive because you have to spend time learning the system and analyzing the impact of the proposed changes. Therefore, work done during development to make the software easier to understand and change is likely to reduce evolution costs. Good software engineering techniques, such as precise specification, the use of object-oriented development, and configuration management, contribute to maintenance cost reduction.

Figure 9.9 shows how overall lifetime costs may decrease as more effort is expended during system development to produce a maintainable system. Because of the potential reduction in costs of understanding, analysis, and testing, there is a significant multiplier effect when the system is developed for maintainability. For System 1, extra development costs of $25,000 are invested in making the system more maintainable. This results in a savings of $100,000 in maintenance costs over

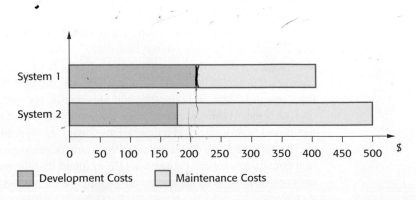

Figure 9.9
Development and
maintenance costs

Legacy systems

Legacy systems are old systems that are still useful and are sometimes critical to business operation. They may be implemented using outdated languages and technology or may use other systems that are expensive to maintain. Often their structure has been degraded by change and documentation is missing or out of date. Nevertheless, it may not be cost effective to replace these systems. They may only be used at certain times of the year or it may be too risky to replace them because the specification has been lost.

http://www.SoftwareEngineering-9.com/Web/LegacySys/

the lifetime of the system. This assumes that a percentage increase in development costs results in a comparable percentage decrease in overall system costs.

These estimates are hypothetical but there is no doubt that developing software to make it more maintainable is cost effective, when the whole life costs of the software are taken into account. This is the rationale for refactoring in agile development. Without refactoring, the code becomes more and more difficult and expensive to change. However, in plan-based development, the reality is that additional investment in code improvement is rarely made during development. This is mostly due to the ways most organizations run their budgets. Investing in maintainability leads to short-term cost increases, which are measurable. Unfortunately, the long-term gains can't be measured at the same time so companies are reluctant to spend money for an unknown future return.

It is usually more expensive to add functionality after a system is in operation than it is to implement the same functionality during development. The reasons for this are:

1. *Team stability* After a system has been delivered, it is normal for the development team to be broken up and for people to work on new projects. The new team or the individuals responsible for system maintenance do not understand the system or the background to system design decisions. They need to spend time understanding the existing system before implementing changes to it.

2. *Poor development practice* The contract to maintain a system is usually separate from the system development contract. The maintenance contract may be given to a different company rather than the original system developer. This factor, along with the lack of team stability, means that there is no incentive for a development team to write maintainable software. If a development team can cut corners to save effort during development it is worthwhile for them to do so, even if this means that the software is more difficult to change in the future.

3. *Staff skills* Maintenance staff are often relatively inexperienced and unfamiliar with the application domain. Maintenance has a poor image among software engineers. It is seen as a less-skilled process than system development and is often allocated to the most junior staff. Furthermore, old systems may be written in obsolete programming languages. The maintenance staff may not have much experience of development in these languages and must learn these languages to maintain the system.

Documentation

System documentation can help the maintenance process by providing maintainers with information about the structure and organization of the system and the features that it offers to system users. Although proponents of agile approaches such as XP suggest that the code should be the principal documentation, higher-level design models and information about dependencies and constraints can make it easier to understand and make changes to the code.

I have written a separate chapter on documentation that you can download.

http://www.SoftwareEngineering-9.com/Web/ExtraChaps/Documentation.pdf

4. *Program age and structure* As changes are made to programs, their structure tends to degrade. Consequently, as programs age, they become harder to understand and change. Some systems have been developed without modern software engineering techniques. They may never have been well structured and were perhaps optimized for efficiency rather than understandability. System documentation may be lost or inconsistent. Old systems may not have been subject to stringent configuration management so time is often wasted finding the right versions of system components to change.

The first three of these problems stem from the fact that many organizations still consider development and maintenance to be separate activities. Maintenance is seen as a second-class activity and there is no incentive to spend money during development to reduce the costs of system change. The only long-term solution to this problem is to accept that systems rarely have a defined lifetime but continue in use, in some form, for an indefinite period. As I suggested in the introduction, you should think of systems as evolving throughout their lifetime through a continual development process.

The fourth issue, the problem of degraded system structure, is the easiest problem to address. Software reengineering techniques (described later in this chapter) may be applied to improve the system structure and understandability. Architectural transformations can adapt the system to new hardware. Refactoring can improve the quality of the system code and make it easier to change.

9.3.1 Maintenance prediction

Managers hate surprises, especially if these result in unexpectedly high costs. You should therefore try to predict what system changes might be proposed and what parts of the system are likely to be the most difficult to maintain. You should also try to estimate the overall maintenance costs for a system in a given time period. Figure 9.10 shows these predictions and associated questions.

Predicting the number of change requests for a system requires an understanding of the relationship between the system and its external environment. Some systems have a very complex relationship with their external environment and changes to that

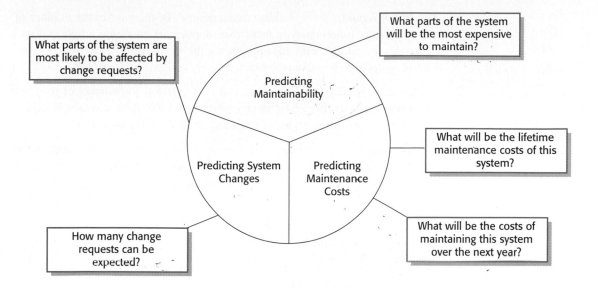

Figure 9.10
Maintenance prediction

environment inevitably result in changes to the system. To evaluate the relationships between a system and its environment, you should assess:

1. *The number and complexity of system interfaces* The larger the number of interfaces and the more complex these interfaces, the more likely it is that interface changes will be required as new requirements are proposed.

2. *The number of inherently volatile system requirements* As I discussed in Chapter 4, requirements that reflect organizational policies and procedures are likely to be more volatile than requirements that are based on stable domain characteristics.

3. *The business processes in which the system is used* As business processes evolve, they generate system change requests. The more business processes that use a system, the more the demands for system change.

For many years, researchers have looked at the relationships between program complexity, as measured by metrics such as cyclomatic complexity (McCabe, 1976), and maintainability (Banker et al., 1993; Coleman et al., 1994; Kafura and Reddy, 1987; Kozlov et al., 2008). It is not surprising that these studies have found that the more complex a system or component, the more expensive it is to maintain. Complexity measurements are particularly useful in identifying program components that are likely to be expensive to maintain. Kafura and Reddy (1987) examined a number of system components and found that maintenance effort tended to be focused on a small number of complex components. To reduce maintenance costs, therefore, you should try to replace complex system components with simpler alternatives.

After a system has been put into service, you may be able to use process data to help predict maintainability. Examples of process metrics that can be used for assessing maintainability are as follows:

1. *Number of requests for corrective maintenance* An increase in the number of bug and failure reports may indicate that more errors are being introduced into the program than are being repaired during the maintenance process. This may indicate a decline in maintainability.

2. *Average time required for impact analysis* This reflects the number of program components that are affected by the change request. If this time increases, it implies more and more components are affected and maintainability is decreasing.

3. *Average time taken to implement a change request* This is not the same as the time for impact analysis although it may correlate with it. This is the amount of time that you need to modify the system and its documentation, after you have assessed which components are affected. An increase in the time needed to implement a change may indicate a decline in maintainability.

4. *Number of outstanding change requests* An increase in this number over time may imply a decline in maintainability.

You use predicted information about change requests and predictions about system maintainability to predict maintenance costs. Most managers combine this information with intuition and experience to estimate costs. The COCOMO 2 model of cost estimation (Boehm et al., 2000), discussed in Chapter 24, suggests that an estimate for software maintenance effort can be based on the effort to understand existing code and the effort to develop the new code.

9.3.2 Software reengineering

As I discussed in the previous section, the process of system evolution involves understanding the program that has to be changed and then implementing these changes. However, many systems, especially older legacy systems, are difficult to understand and change. The programs may have been optimized for performance or space utilization at the expense of understandability, or, over time, the initial program structure may have been corrupted by a series of changes.

To make legacy software systems easier to maintain, you can reengineer these systems to improve their structure and understandability. Reengineering may involve redocumenting the system, refactoring the system architecture, translating programs to a modern programming language, and modifying and updating the structure and values of the system's data. The functionality of the software is not changed and, normally, you should try to avoid making major changes to the system architecture.

There are two important benefits from reengineering rather than replacement:

1. *Reduced risk* There is a high risk in redeveloping business-critical software. Errors may be made in the system specification or there may be development problems. Delays in introducing the new software may mean that business is lost and extra costs are incurred.

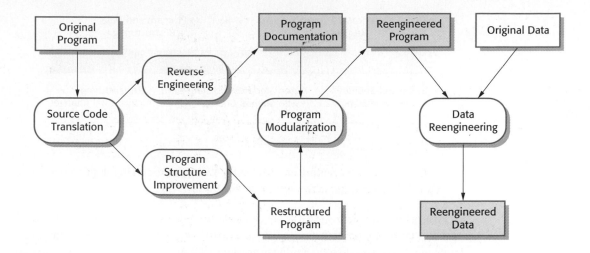

Figure 9.11 The reengineering process

2. *Reduced cost* The cost of reengineering may be significantly less than the cost of developing new software. Ulrich (1990) quotes an example of a commercial system for which the reimplementation costs were estimated at $50 million. The system was successfully reengineered for $12 million. I suspect that, with modern software technology, the relative cost of reimplementation is probably less than this but will still considerably exceed the costs of reengineering.

Figure 9.11 is a general model of the reengineering process. The input to the process is a legacy program and the output is an improved and restructured version of the same program. The activities in this reengineering process are as follows:

1. *Source code translation* Using a translation tool, the program is converted from an old programming language to a more modern version of the same language or to a different language.

2. *Reverse engineering* The program is analyzed and information extracted from it. This helps to document its organization and functionality. Again, this process is usually completely automated.

3. *Program structure improvement* The control structure of the program is analyzed and modified to make it easier to read and understand. This can be partially automated but some manual intervention is usually required.

4. *Program modularization* Related parts of the program are grouped together and, where appropriate, redundancy is removed. In some cases, this stage may involve architectural refactoring (e.g., a system that uses several different data stores may be refactored to use a single repository). This is a manual process.

5. *Data reengineering* The data processed by the program is changed to reflect program changes. This may mean redefining database schemas and converting existing databases to the new structure. You should usually also clean up the

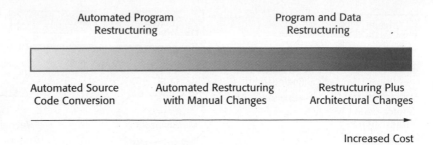

Figure 9.12
Reengineering
approaches

data. This involves finding and correcting mistakes, removing duplicate records, etc. Tools are available to support data reengineering.

Program reengineering may not necessarily require all of the steps in Figure 9.11. You don't need source code translation if you still use the application's programming language. If you can do all reengineering automatically, then recovering documentation through reverse engineering may be unnecessary. Data reengineering is only required if the data structures in the program change during system reengineering.

To make the reengineered system interoperate with the new software, you may have to develop adaptor services, as discussed in Chapter 19. These hide the original interfaces of the software system and present new, better-structured interfaces that can be used by other components. This process of legacy system wrapping is an important technique for developing large-scale reusable services.

The costs of reengineering obviously depend on the extent of the work that is carried out. There is a spectrum of possible approaches to reengineering, as shown in Figure 9.12. Costs increase from left to right so that source code translation is the cheapest option. Reengineering as part of architectural migration is the most expensive.

The problem with software reengineering is that there are practical limits to how much you can improve a system by reengineering. It isn't possible, for example, to convert a system written using a functional approach to an object-oriented system. Major architectural changes or radical reorganizing of the system data management cannot be carried out automatically, so they are very expensive. Although reengineering can improve maintainability, the reengineered system will probably not be as maintainable as a new system developed using modern software engineering methods.

9.3.3   Preventative maintenance by refactoring

Refactoring is the process of making improvements to a program to slow down degradation through change (Opdyke and Johnson, 1990). It means modifying a program to improve its structure, to reduce its complexity, or to make it easier to understand. Refactoring is sometimes considered to be limited to object-oriented development but the principles can be applied to any development approach. When you refactor a program, you should not add functionality but should concentrate on program improvement. You can therefore think of refactoring as 'preventative maintenance' that reduces the problems of future change.

Although reengineering and refactoring are both intended to make software easier to understand and change, they are not the same thing. Reengineering takes place after a system has been maintained for some time and maintenance costs are increasing. You use automated tools to process and reengineer a legacy system to create a new system that is more maintainable. Refactoring is a continuous process of improvement throughout the development and evolution process. It is intended to avoid the structure and code degradation that increases the costs and difficulties of maintaining a system.

Refactoring is an inherent part of agile methods such as extreme programming because these methods are based around change. Program quality is therefore liable to degrade quickly so agile developers frequently refactor their programs to avoid this degradation. The emphasis on regression testing in agile methods lowers the risk of introducing new errors through refactoring. Any errors that are introduced should be detectable as previously successful tests should then fail. However, refactoring is not dependent on other 'agile activities' and can be used with any approach to development.

Fowler et al. (1999) suggest that there are stereotypical situations (he calls them 'bad smells') in which the code of a program can be improved. Examples of bad smells that can be improved through refactoring include:

1. *Duplicate code* The same of very similar code may be included at different places in a program. This can be removed and implemented as a single method or function that is called as required.

2. *Long methods* If a method is too long, it should be redesigned as a number of shorter methods.

3. *Switch (case) statements* These often involve duplication, where the switch depends on the type of some value. The switch statements may be scattered around a program. In object-oriented languages, you can often use polymorphism to achieve the same thing.

4. *Data clumping* Data clumps occur when the same group of data items (fields in classes, parameters in methods) reoccur in several places in a program. These can often be replaced with an object encapsulating all of the data.

5. *Speculative generality* This occurs when developers include generality in a program in case it is required in future. This can often simply be removed.

Fowler, in his book and website, also suggests some primitive refactoring transformations that can be used singly or together to deal with the bad smells. Examples of these transformations include Extract method, where you remove duplication and create a new method; Consolidate conditional expression, where you replace a sequence of tests with a single test; and Pull up method, where you replace similar methods in subclasses with a single method in a super class. Interactive development environments, such as Eclipse, include refactoring support in their editors. This makes it easier to find dependent parts of a program that have to be changed to implement the refactoring.

Refactoring, carried out during program development, is an effective way to reduce the long-term maintenance costs of a program. However, if you take over a program for maintenance whose structure has been significantly degraded, then it may be practically impossible to refactor the code alone. You may also have to think about design refactoring, which is likely to be a more expensive and difficult problem. Design refactoring involves identifying relevant design patterns (discussed in Chapter 7) and replacing existing code with code that implements these design patterns (Kerievsky, 2004). I don't have space to discuss this here.

9.4 Legacy system management

For new software systems developed using modern software engineering processes, such as incremental development and CBSE, it is possible to plan how to integrate system development and evolution. More and more companies are starting to understand that the system development process is a whole life-cycle process and that an artificial separation between software development and software maintenance is unhelpful. However, there are still many legacy systems that are critical business systems. These have to be extended and adapted to changing e-business practices.

Most organizations usually have a portfolio of legacy systems that they use, with a limited budget for maintaining and upgrading these systems. They have to decide how to get the best return on their investment. This involves making a realistic assessment of their legacy systems and then deciding on the most appropriate strategy for evolving these systems. There are four strategic options:

1. *Scrap the system completely* This option should be chosen when the system is not making an effective contribution to business processes. This commonly occurs when business processes have changed since the system was installed and are no longer reliant on the legacy system.

2. *Leave the system unchanged and continue with regular maintenance* This option should be chosen when the system is still required but is fairly stable and the system users make relatively few change requests.

3. *Reengineer the system to improve its maintainability* This option should be chosen when the system quality has been degraded by change and where a new change to the system is still being proposed. This process may include developing new interface components so that the original system can work with other, newer systems.

4. *Replace all or part of the system with a new system* This option should be chosen when factors, such as new hardware, mean that the old system cannot continue in operation or where off-the-shelf systems would allow the new system to be developed at a reasonable cost. In many cases, an evolutionary replacement strategy can be adopted in which major system components are replaced by off-the-shelf systems with other components reused wherever possible.

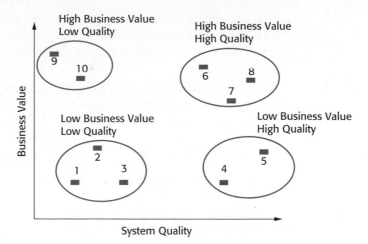

Figure 9.13 An example of a legacy system assessment

Naturally, these options are not exclusive. When a system is composed of several programs, different options may be applied to each program.

When you are assessing a legacy system, you have to look at it from a business perspective and a technical perspective (Warren, 1998). From a business perspective, you have to decide whether or not the business really needs the system. From a technical perspective, you have to assess the quality of the application software and the system's support software and hardware. You then use a combination of the business value and the system quality to inform your decision on what to do with the legacy system.

For example, assume that an organization has 10 legacy systems. You should assess the quality and the business value of each of these systems. You may then create a chart showing relative business value and system quality. This is shown in Figure 9.13.

From Figure 9.13, you can see that there are four clusters of systems:

1. *Low quality, low business value* Keeping these systems in operation will be expensive and the rate of the return to the business will be fairly small. These systems should be scrapped.

2. *Low quality, high business value* These systems are making an important business contribution so they cannot be scrapped. However, their low quality means that it is expensive to maintain them. These systems should be reengineered to improve their quality. They may be replaced, if a suitable off-the-shelf system is available.

3. *High quality, low business value* These are systems that don't contribute much to the business but which may not be very expensive to maintain. It is not worth replacing these systems so normal system maintenance may be continued if expensive changes are not required and the system hardware remains in use. If expensive changes become necessary, the software should be scrapped.

4.   *High quality, high business value* These systems have to be kept in operation. However, their high quality means that you don't have to invest in transformation or system replacement. Normal system maintenance should be continued.

To assess the business value of a system, you have to identify system stakeholders, such as end-users of the system and their managers, and ask a series of questions about the system. There are four basic issues that you have to discuss:

1.   *The use of the system* If systems are only used occasionally or by a small number of people, they may have a low business value. A legacy system may have been developed to meet a business need that has either changed or that can now be met more effectively in other ways. You have to be careful, however, about occasional but important use of systems. For example, in a university, a student registration system may only be used at the beginning of each academic year. However, it is an essential system with a high business value.

2.   *The business processes that are supported* When a system is introduced, business processes are designed to exploit the system's capabilities. If the system is inflexible, changing these business processes may be impossible. However, as the environment changes, the original business processes may become obsolete. Therefore, a system may have a low business value because it forces the use of inefficient business processes.

3.   *The system dependability* System dependability is not only a technical problem but also a business problem. If a system is not dependable and the problems directly affect the business customers or mean that people in the business are diverted from other tasks to solve these problems, the system has a low business value.

4.   *The system outputs* The key issue here is the importance of the system outputs to the successful functioning of the business. If the business depends on these outputs, then the system has a high business value. Conversely, if these outputs can be easily generated in some other way or if the system produces outputs that are rarely used, then its business value may be low.

For example, let's assume that a company provides a travel ordering system that is used by staff responsible for arranging travel. They can place orders with an approved travel agent. Tickets are then delivered and the company is invoiced for these. However, a business value assessment may reveal that this system is only used for a fairly small percentage of travel orders placed. People making travel arrangements find it cheaper and more convenient to deal directly with travel suppliers through their websites. This system may still be used, but there is no real point in keeping it. The same functionality is available from external systems.

Conversely, say a company has developed a system that keeps track of all previous customer orders and automatically generates reminders for customers to reorder goods. This results in a large number of repeat orders and keeps customers satisfied

Factor	Questions
Supplier stability	Is the supplier still in existence? Is the supplier financially stable and likely to continue in existence? If the supplier is no longer in business, does someone else maintain the systems?
Failure rate	Does the hardware have a high rate of reported failures? Does the support software crash and force system restarts?
Age	How old is the hardware and software? The older the hardware and support software, the more obsolete it will be. It may still function correctly but there could be significant economic and business benefits to moving to a more modern system.
Performance	Is the performance of the system adequate? Do performance problems have a significant effect on system users?
Support requirements	What local support is required by the hardware and software? If there are high costs associated with this support, it may be worth considering system replacement.
Maintenance costs	What are the costs of hardware maintenance and support software licences? Older hardware may have higher maintenance costs than modern systems. Support software may have high annual licensing costs.
Interoperability	Are there problems interfacing the system to other systems? Can compilers, for example, be used with current versions of the operating system? Is hardware emulation required?

Figure 9.14 Factors used in environment assessment

because they feel that their supplier is aware of their needs. The outputs from such a system are very important to the business and this system therefore has a high business value.

To assess a software system from a technical perspective, you need to consider both the application system itself and the environment in which the system operates. The environment includes the hardware and all associated support software (compilers, development environments, etc.) that are required to maintain the system. The environment is important because many system changes result from changes to the environment, such as upgrades to the hardware or operating system.

If possible, in the process of environmental assessment, you should make measurements of the system and its maintenance processes. Examples of data that may be useful include the costs of maintaining the system hardware and support software, the number of hardware faults that occur over some time period and the frequency of patches and fixes applied to the system support software.

Factors that you should consider during the environment assessment are shown in Figure 9.14. Notice that these are not all technical characteristics of the environment. You also have to consider the reliability of the suppliers of the hardware and support software. If these suppliers are no longer in business, there may not be support for their systems.

To assess the technical quality of an application system, you have to assess a range of factors (Figure 9.15) that are primarily related to the system dependability,

Factor	Questions
Understandability	How difficult is it to understand the source code of the current system? How complex are the control structures that are used? Do variables have meaningful names that reflect their function?
Documentation	What system documentation is available? Is the documentation complete, consistent, and current?
Data	Is there an explicit data model for the system? To what extent is data duplicated across files? Is the data used by the system up-to-date and consistent?
Performance	Is the performance of the application adequate? Do performance problems have a significant effect on system users?
Programming language	Are modern compilers available for the programming language used to develop the system? Is the programming language still used for new system development?
Configuration management	Are all versions of all parts of the system managed by a configuration management system? Is there an explicit description of the versions of components that are used in the current system?
Test data	Does test data for the system exist? Is there a record of regression tests carried out when new features have been added to the system?
Personnel skills	Are there people available who have the skills to maintain the application? Are there people available who have experience with the system?

Figure 9.15 Factors used in application assessment

the difficulties of maintaining the system and the system documentation. You may also collect data that will help you judge the quality of the system. Data that may be useful in quality assessment are:

1. *The number of system change requests* System changes usually corrupt the system structure and make further changes more difficult. The higher this accumulated value, the lower the quality of the system.

2. *The number of user interfaces* This is an important factor in forms-based systems where each form can be considered as a separate user interface. The more interfaces, the more likely that there will be inconsistencies and redundancies in these interfaces.

3. *The volume of data used by the system* The higher the volume of data (number of files, size of database, etc.), the more likely that it is that there will be data inconsistencies that reduce the system quality.

Ideally, objective assessment should be used to inform decisions about what to do with a legacy system. However, in many cases, decisions are not really objective but are based on organizational or political considerations. For example, if two businesses merge, the most politically powerful partner will usually keep its systems and scrap the other systems. If senior management in an organization decide to move to a new hardware platform, then this may require applications to be replaced. If there is no budget available for system transformation in a particular year, then system maintenance may be continued, even though this will result in higher long-term costs.

KEY POINTS

- Software development and evolution can be thought of as an integrated, iterative process that can be represented using a spiral model.

- For custom systems, the costs of software maintenance usually exceed the software development costs.

- The process of software evolution is driven by requests for changes and includes change impact analysis, release planning, and change implementation.

- Lehman's laws, such as the notion that change is continuous, describe a number of insights derived from long-term studies of system evolution.

- There are three types of software maintenance, namely bug fixing, modifying the software to work in a new environment, and implementing new or changed requirements.

- Software reengineering is concerned with restructuring and redocumenting software to make it easier to understand and change.

- Refactoring, making small program changes that preserve functionality, can be thought of as preventative maintenance.

- The business value of a legacy system and the quality of the application software and its environment should be assessed to determine whether the system should be replaced, transformed, or maintained.

FURTHER READING

'Software Maintenance and Evolution: A Roadmap'. As well as discussing research challenges, this paper is a good, short overview of software maintenance and evolution by leading researchers in this area. The research problems that they identify have not yet been solved. (V. Rajlich and K.H. Bennett, *Proc. 20th Int. Conf. on Software Engineering*, IEEE Press, 2000.) http://doi.acm.org/10.1145/336512.336534.

Modernizing Legacy Systems: Software Technologies, Engineering Processes, and Business Practices. This excellent book covers general issues of software maintenance and evolution as well as legacy system migration. The book is based on a large case study of the transformation of a COBOL system to a Java-based client-server system. (R. C. Seacord, D. Plakosh and G. A. Lewis, Addison-Wesley, 2003.)

Working Effectively with Legacy Code. Solid practical advice on the problems and difficulties of dealing with legacy systems. (M. Feathers, John Wiley & Sons, 2004.)

EXERCISES

9.1. Explain why a software system that is used in a real-world environment must change or become progressively less useful.

9.2. Explain the rationale underlying Lehman's laws. Under what circumstances might the laws break down?

9.3. From Figure 9.4, you can see that impact analysis is an important subprocess in the software evolution process. Using a diagram, suggest what activities might be involved in change impact analysis.

9.4. As a software project manager in a company that specializes in the development of software for the offshore oil industry, you have been given the task of discovering the factors that affect the maintainability of the systems developed by your company. Suggest how you might set up a program to analyze the maintenance process and discover appropriate maintainability metrics for your company.

9.5. Briefly describe the three main types of software maintenance. Why is it sometimes difficult to distinguish between them?

9.6. What are the principal factors that affect the costs of system reengineering?

9.7. Under what circumstances might an organization decide to scrap a system when the system assessment suggests that it is of high quality and of high business value.

9.8. What are the strategic options for legacy system evolution? When would you normally replace all or part of a system rather than continue maintenance of the software?

9.9. Explain why problems with support software might mean that an organization has to replace its legacy systems.

9.10. Do software engineers have a professional responsibility to produce code that can be maintained and changed even if this is not explicitly requested by their employer?

REFERENCES

Arthur, L. J. (1988). *Software Evolution*. New York: John Wiley & Sons.

Banker, R. D., Datar, S. M., Kemerer, C. F. and Zweig, D. (1993). 'Software Complexity and Maintenance Costs'. *Comm. ACM*, **36** (11), 81–94.

Boehm, B. W., Abts, C., Brown, A. W., Chulani, S., Clark, B. K., Horowitz, E., Madachy, R., Reifer, D. and Steece, B. (2000). *Software Cost Estimation with COCOMO II*. Upper Saddle River, NJ: Prentice Hall.

Coleman, D., Ash, D., Lowther, B. and Oman, P. (1994). 'Using Metrics to Evaluate Software System Maintainability'. *IEEE Computer*, **27** (8), 44–49.

Erlikh, L. (2000). 'Leveraging legacy system dollars for E-business'. *IT Professional*, **2** (3), May/June 2000, 17–23.

Fowler, M., Beck, K., Brant, J., Opdyke, W. and Roberts, D. (1999). *Refactoring: Improving the Design of Existing Code*. Boston: Addison-Wesley.

Guimaraes, T. (1983). 'Managing Application Program Maintenance Expenditures'. *Comm. ACM*, **26** (10), 739–46.

Hopkins, R. and Jenkins, K. (2008). *Eating the IT Elephant: Moving from Greenfield Development to Brownfield*. Boston: IBM Press.

Kafura, D. and Reddy, G. R. (1987). 'The use of software complexity metrics in software maintenance'. *IEEE Trans. on Software Engineering*, **SE-13** (3), 335–43.

Kerievsky, J. (2004). *Refactoring to Patterns*. Boston: Addison Wesley.

Kozlov, D., Koskinen, J., Sakkinen, M. and Markkula, J. (2008). 'Assessing maintainability change over multiple software releases'. *J. of Software Maintenance and Evolution*, **20** (1), 31–58.

Krogstie, J., Jahr, A. and Sjoberg, D. I. K. (2005). 'A longitudinal study of development and maintenance in Norway: Report from the 2003 investigation'. *Information and Software Technology*, **48** (11), 993–1005.

Lehman, M. M. (1996). 'Laws of Software Evolution Revisited'. Proc. European Workshop on Software Process Technology (EWSPT'96), Springer-Verlag. 108–24.

Lehman, M. M. and Belady, L. (1985). *Program Evolution: Processes of Software Change*. London: Academic Press.

Lehman, M. M., Perry, D. E. and Ramil, J. F. (1998). 'On Evidence Supporting the FEAST Hypothesis and the Laws of Software Evolution'. Proc. Metrics '98, Bethesda. Maryland: IEEE Computer Society Press. 84–8.

Lehman, M. M., Ramil, J. F. and Sandler, U. (2001). 'An Approach to Modelling Long-term Growth Trends in Software Systems'. Proc. Int. Conf. on Software Maintenance, Florence, Italy: 219–28.

Lientz, B. P. and Swanson, E. B. (1980). *Software Maintenance Management*. Reading, Mass.: Addison-Wesley.

McCabe, T. J. (1976). 'A complexity measure'. *IEEE Trans. on Software Engineering.*, **SE-2** (4), 308–20.

Nosek, J. T. and Palvia, P. (1990). 'Software maintenance management: changes in the last decade'. *Software Maintenance: Research and Practice*, **2** (3), 157–74.

Opdyke, W. F. and Johnson, R. E. (1990). 'Refactoring: An Aid in Designing Application Frameworks and Evolving Object-Oriented Systems'. 1990 Symposium on Object-Oriented Programming Emphasizing Practical Applications (SOOPPA '90), Poughkeepsie, New York.

Poole, C. and Huisman, J. W. (2001). 'Using Extreme Programming in a Maintenance Environment'. *IEEE Software*, **18** (6), 42–50.

Rajlich, V. T. and Bennett, K. H. (2000). 'A Staged Model for the Software Life Cycle'. *IEEE Computer*, **33** (7), 66–71.

Sousa, M. J. (1998). 'A Survey on the Software Maintenance Process'. 14th IEEE International Conference on Software Maintenance (ICSM '98), Washington, D.C.: 265–74.

Ulrich, W. M. (1990). 'The Evolutionary Growth of Software Reengineering and the Decade Ahead'. *American Programmer*, **3** (10), 14–20.

Warren, I. E. (1998). *The Renaissance of Legacy Systems*. London: Springer.

PART 2

Dependability and Security

As software systems increase in size and complexity, I strongly believe that the most significant challenge that we face in software engineering is ensuring that we can trust these systems. To trust a system, we must have confidence that it will be available when required and perform as expected. It must be secure so that our computers or data are not threatened by it. This means that issues of system dependability and security are often more important than the details of system functionality. This part of the book has therefore been designed to introduce students and practising software engineers to the important topics of dependability and security.

The first chapter in this section, Chapter 10, covers sociotechnical systems, which at first sight, may not appear to have much to do with software dependability. However, many security and dependability failures stem from human and organizational causes and we cannot ignore these when considering system dependability and security. Software engineers must be aware of this and should not imagine that better techniques and technology can ensure that our systems are completely dependable and secure.

Chapter 11 introduces the basic concepts of dependability and security and explains the fundamental principles of avoidance, detection, and recovery that are used to build dependable systems. Chapter 12 supplements Chapter 4, which covers requirements engineering, with a discussion of specific approaches that are used for deriving and specifying system requirements for security and dependability. I briefly introduce the use of formal specification in Chapter 12, and an additional chapter on this topic is available on the Web.

Chapters 13 and 14 are concerned with software engineering techniques for the development of dependable and secure systems. I cover dependability engineering and security engineering separately, but they have much in common. I discuss the importance of software architectures and present design guidelines and programming techniques that help achieve dependability and security. I also explain why it is important to use redundancy and diversity to ensure that systems can cope with failures and external attacks. I introduce the increasingly important topic of software survivability or resilience, which allows systems to continue to deliver essential services while their security is being threatened.

Finally, in this section, Chapter 15 is concerned with dependability and security assurance. I explain the use of static analysis and model checking for system verification and fault detection. These techniques have been successfully used in critical systems engineering. I also cover specific approaches to testing the dependability and security of systems and explain why a dependability case may be necessary to convince an external regulator that a system is safe and secure.

10

Sociotechnical systems

Objectives

The objectives of this chapter are to introduce the concept of a sociotechnical system—a system that includes people, software, and hardware—and to show that you need to take a systems perspective on security and dependability. When you have read this chapter, you will:

- know what is meant by a sociotechnical system and understand the difference between a technical, computer-based system and a sociotechnical system;

- have been introduced to the concept of emergent system properties, such as reliability, performance, safety, and security;

- know about the procurement, development, and operational activities that are involved in the systems engineering process;

- understand why software dependability and security should not be considered in isolation and how they are affected by systems issues, such as operator errors.

Contents

In a computer system, the software and the hardware are interdependent. Without hardware, a software system is an abstraction, which is simply a representation of some human knowledge and ideas. Without software, hardware is a set of inert electronic devices. However, if you put them together to form a system, you create a machine that can carry out complex computations and deliver the results of these computations to its environment.

This illustrates one of the fundamental characteristics of a system—it is more than the sum of its parts. Systems have properties that only become apparent when their components are integrated and operate together. Therefore software engineering is not an isolated activity, but is an intrinsic part of more general systems engineering processes. Software systems are not isolated systems but rather essential components of more extensive systems that have some human, social, or organizational purpose.

For example, the wilderness weather system software controls the instruments in a weather station. It communicates with other software systems and is a part of wider national and international weather forecasting systems. As well as hardware and software, these systems include processes for forecasting the weather, people who operate the system and analyze its outputs. The system also includes the organizations that depend on the system to help them provide weather forecasts to individuals, government, industry, etc. These broader systems are sometimes called sociotechnical systems. They include nontechnical elements such as people, processes, regulations, etc., as well as technical components such as computers, software, and other equipment.

Sociotechnical systems are so complex that it is practically impossible to understand them as a whole. Rather, you have to view them as layers, as shown in Figure 10.1. These layers make up the sociotechnical systems stack:

1. *The equipment layer* This layer is composed of hardware devices, some of which may be computers.

2. *The operating system layer* This layer interacts with the hardware and provides a set of common facilities for higher software layers in the system.

3. *The communications and data management layer* This layer extends the operating system facilities and provides an interface that allows interaction with more extensive functionality, such as access to remote systems, access to a system database, etc. This is sometimes called middleware, as it is in between the application and the operating system.

4. *The application layer* This layer delivers the application-specific functionality that is required. There may be many different application programs in this layer.

5. *The business process layer* At this level, the organizational business processes, which make use of the software system, are defined and enacted.

6. *The organizational layer* This layer includes higher-level strategic processes as well as business rules, policies, and norms that should be followed when using the system.

7. *The social layer* At this layer, the laws and regulations of society that govern the operation of the system are defined.

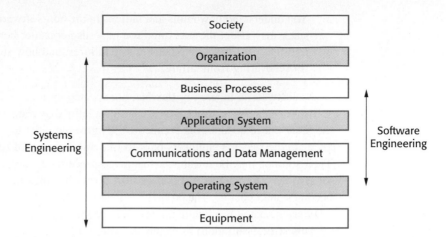

Figure 10.1 The sociotechnical systems stack

In principle, most interactions are between neighboring layers, with each layer hiding the detail of the layer below from the layer above. In practice, this is not always the case. There can be unexpected interactions between layers, which result in problems for the system as a whole. For example, say there is a change in the law governing access to personal information. This comes from the social layer. It leads to new organizational procedures and changes to the business processes. However, the application system may not be able to provide the required level of privacy so changes have to be implemented in the communications and data management layer.

Thinking holistically about systems, rather than simply considering software in isolation, it is essential when considering software security and dependability. Software failure, in itself, rarely has serious consequences because software is intangible and, even when damaged, is easily and cheaply restored. However, when these software failures ripple through other parts of the system, they affect the software's physical and human environment. Here, the consequences of failure are more significant. People may have to do extra work to contain or recover from the failure; for example, there may be physical damage to equipment, data may be lost or corrupted, or confidentiality may be breached with unknown consequences.

You must, therefore, take a system-level view when you are designing software that has to be secure and dependable. You need to understand the consequences of software failures for other elements in the system. You also need to understand how these other system elements may be the cause of software failures and how they can help to protect against and recover from software failures.

Therefore, it is a system rather than a software failure that is the real problem. This means that you need to examine how the software interacts with its immediate environment to ensure that:

1. Software failures are, as far as possible, contained within the enclosing layers of the system stack and do not seriously affect the operation of adjoining layers. In particular, software failures should not lead to system failures.

2. You understand how faults and failures in the non-software layers of the systems stack may affect the software. You may also consider how checks may be built into the software to help detect these failures, and how support can be provided for recovering from failure.

As software is inherently flexible, unexpected system problems are often left to software engineers to solve. Say a radar installation has been sited so that ghosting of the radar image occurs. It is impractical to move the radar to a site with less interference, so the systems engineers have to find another way of removing this ghosting. Their solution may be to enhance the image-processing capabilities of the software to remove the ghost images. This may slow down the software so that its performance becomes unacceptable. The problem may then be characterized as a 'software failure', whereas, in fact, it is a failure in the design process for the system as a whole.

This sort of situation, in which software engineers are left with the problem of enhancing software capabilities without increasing hardware costs, is very common. Many so-called software failures are not a consequence of inherent software problems but rather are the result of trying to change the software to accommodate modified system engineering requirements. A good example of this was the failure of the Denver airport baggage system (Swartz, 1996), where the controlling software was expected to deal with limitations of the equipment used.

Systems engineering (Stevens et al., 1998; Thayer, 2002; Thomé, 1993; White et al., 1993) is the process of designing entire systems—not just the software in these systems. Software is the controlling and integrating element in these systems and software engineering costs are often the main cost component in the overall system costs. As a software engineer, it helps if you have a broader awareness of how software interacts with other hardware and software systems, and how it is supposed to be used. This knowledge helps you understand the limits of software, to design better software, and to participate in a systems engineering group.

10.1 Complex systems

The term 'system' is one that is universally used. We talk about computer systems, operating systems, payment systems, the education system, the system of government, and so on. These are all obviously quite different uses of the word 'system', although they share the characteristic that, somehow, the system is more than simply the sum of its parts.

Abstract systems, such as the system of government, are outside the scope of this book. Rather, I focus on systems that include computers and that have some specific purpose such as to enable communication, support navigation, or compute salaries. A useful working definition of these types of systems is as follows:

A system is a purposeful collection of interrelated components, of different kinds, which work together to achieve some objective.

This general definition embraces a vast range of systems. For example, a simple system, such as laser pointer, may include a few hardware components plus a small amount of control software. By contrast, an air traffic control system includes thousands of hardware and software components plus human users who make decisions based on information from that computer system.

A characteristic of all complex systems is that the properties and behavior of the system components are inextricably intermingled. The successful functioning of each system component depends on the functioning of other components. Thus, software can only operate if the processor is operational. The processor can only carry out computations if the software system defining these computations has been successfully installed.

Complex systems are usually hierarchical and so include other systems. For example, a police command and control system may include a geographical information system to provide details of the location of incidents. These included systems are called 'subsystems'. Subsystems can operate as independent systems in their own right. For example, the same geographical information system may be used in systems for transport logistics and emergency command and control.

Systems that include software fall into two categories:

1. *Technical computer-based systems* These are systems that include hardware and software components but not procedures and processes. Examples of technical systems include televisions, mobile phones, and other equipment with embedded software. Most software for PCs, computer games, etc., also falls into this category. Individuals and organizations use technical systems for a particular purpose but knowledge of this purpose is not part of the system. For example, the word processor I am using is not aware that is it being used to write a book.

2. *Sociotechnical systems* These include one or more technical systems but, crucially, also include people who understand the purpose of the system within the system itself. Sociotechnical systems have defined operational processes and people (the operators) are inherent parts of the system. They are governed by organizational policies and rules and may be affected by external constraints such as national laws and regulatory policies. For example, this book was created through a sociotechnical publishing system that includes various processes and technical systems.

Sociotechnical systems are enterprise systems that are intended to help deliver a business goal. This might be to increase sales, reduce material used in manufacturing, collect taxes, maintain a safe airspace, etc. Because they are embedded in an organizational environment, the procurement, development, and use of these systems are influenced by the organization's policies and procedures, and by its working culture. The users of the system are people who are influenced by the way the organization is managed and by their interactions with other people inside and outside of the organization.

When you are trying to develop sociotechnical systems, you need to understand the organizational environment in which they are used. If you don't, the systems may not meet business needs and users and their managers may reject the system.

Organizational factors from the system's environment that may affect the requirements, design, and operation of a sociotechnical system include:

1. *Process changes* The system may require changes to the work processes in the environment. If so, training will certainly be required. If changes are significant, or if they involve people losing their jobs, there is a danger that the users will resist the introduction of the system.

2. *Job changes* New systems may de-skill the users in an environment or cause them to change the way they work. If so, users may actively resist the introduction of the system into the organization. Designs that involve managers having to change their way of working to fit a new computer system are often resented. The managers may feel that their status in the organization is being reduced by the system.

3. *Organizational changes* The system may change the political power structure in an organization. For example, if an organization is dependent on a complex system, those who control access to that system have a great deal of political power.

Sociotechnical systems have three characteristics that are particularly important when considering security and dependability:

1. They have emergent properties that are properties of the system as a whole, rather than associated with individual parts of the system. Emergent properties depend on both the system components and the relationships between them. Given this complexity, the emergent properties can only be evaluated once the system has been assembled. Security and dependability are emergent system properties.

2. They are often nondeterministic. This means that when presented with a specific input, they may not always produce the same output. The system's behavior depends on the human operators and people do not always react in the same way. Furthermore, use of the system may create new relationships between the system components and hence change its emergent behavior. System faults and failures may therefore be transient, and people may disagree about whether or not a failure has actually occurred.

3. The extent to which the system supports organizational objectives does not just depend on the system itself. It also depends on the stability of these objectives, the relationships, and conflicts between organizational objectives and how people in the organization interpret these objectives. New management may reinterpret the organizational objectives that a system was designed to support so that a 'successful' system may then be seen as a 'failure'.

Sociotechnical considerations are often critical in determining whether or not a system has successfully met its objectives. Unfortunately, taking these into account is very difficult for engineers who have little experience of social or cultural studies.

Property	Description
Volume	The volume of a system (the total space occupied) varies depending on how the component assemblies are arranged and connected.
Reliability	System reliability depends on component reliability but unexpected interactions can cause new types of failures and therefore affect the reliability of the system.
Security	The security of the system (its ability to resist attack) is a complex property that cannot be easily measured. Attacks may be devised that were not anticipated by the system designers and so may defeat built-in safeguards.
Repairability	This property reflects how easy it is to fix a problem with the system once it has been discovered. It depends on being able to diagnose the problem, access the components that are faulty, and modify or replace these components.
Usability	This property reflects how easy it is to use the system. It depends on the technical system components, its operators, and its operating environment.

Figure 10.2
Examples of
emergent properties

To help understand the effects of systems on organizations, various methodologies have been developed, such as Mumford's sociotechnics (1989) and Checkland's Soft Systems Methodology (1981; Checkland and Scholes, 1990). There have also been sociological studies of the effects of computer-based systems on work (Ackroyd et al., 1992; Anderson et al., 1989; Suchman, 1987).

10.1.1 Emergent system properties

The complex relationships between the components in a system mean that a system is more than simply the sum of its parts. It has properties that are properties of the system as a whole. These 'emergent properties' (Checkland, 1981) cannot be attributed to any specific part of the system. Rather, they only emerge once the system components have been integrated. Some of these properties, such as weight, can be derived directly from the comparable properties of subsystems. More often, however, they result from complex subsystem interrelationships. The system property cannot be calculated directly from the properties of the individual system components. Examples of some emergent properties are shown in Figure 10.2.

There are two types of emergent properties:

1. Functional emergent properties when the purpose of a system only emerges after its components are integrated. For example, a bicycle has the functional property of being a transportation device once it has been assembled from its components.

2. Non-functional emergent properties, which relate to the behavior of the system in its operational environment. Reliability, performance, safety, and security are examples of emergent properties. These are critical for computer-based systems, as failure to achieve a minimum defined level in these properties usually makes

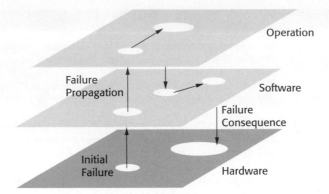

Figure 10.3 Failure propagation

the system unusable. Some users may not need some of the system functions, so the system may be acceptable without them. However, a system that is unreliable or too slow is likely to be rejected by all its users.

Emergent dependability properties, such as reliability, depend on both the properties of individual components and their interactions. The components in a system are interdependent. Failures in one component can be propagated through the system and affect the operation of other components. However, it is often difficult to anticipate how these component failures will affect other components. It is, therefore, practically impossible to estimate overall system reliability from data about the reliability of system components.

In a sociotechnical system, you need to consider reliability from three perspectives:

1. *Hardware reliability* What is the probability of hardware components failing and how long does it take to repair a failed component?

2. *Software reliability* How likely is it that a software component will produce an incorrect output? Software failure is distinct from hardware failure in that software does not wear out. Failures are often transient. The system carries on working after an incorrect result has been produced.

3. *Operator reliability* How likely is it that the operator of a system will make an error and provide an incorrect input? How likely is it that the software will fail to detect this error and propagate the mistake?

Hardware, software, and operator reliability are not independent. Figure 10.3 shows how failures at one level can be propagated to other levels in the system. Hardware failure can generate spurious signals that are outside the range of inputs expected by the software. The software can then behave unpredictably and produce unexpected outputs. These may confuse and consequently stress the system operator.

Operator error is most likely when the operator is feeling stressed. So a hardware failure may then mean that the system operator makes mistakes which, in turn, could lead to further software problems or additional processing. This could overload the hardware, causing more failures and so on. Thus, the initial failure, which might be recoverable, can rapidly develop into a serious problem that may result in a complete shutdown of the system.

The reliability of a system depends on the context in which that system is used. However, the system's environment cannot be completely specified, nor can the system designers place restrictions on that environment for operational systems. Different systems operating within an environment may react to problems in unpredictable ways, thus affecting the reliability of all of these systems.

For example, say a system is designed to operate at normal room temperature. To allow for variations and exceptional conditions, the electronic components of a system are designed to operate within a certain range of temperatures, say from 0 degrees to 45 degrees. Outside this temperature range, the components will behave in an unpredictable way. Now assume that this system is installed close to an air conditioner. If this air conditioner fails and vents hot gas over the electronics, then the system may overheat. The components, and hence the whole system, may then fail.

If this system had been installed elsewhere in that environment, this problem would not have occurred. When the air conditioner worked properly there were no problems. However, because of the physical closeness of these machines, an unanticipated relationship existed between them that led to system failure.

Like reliability, emergent properties such as performance or usability are hard to assess but can be measured after the system is operational. Properties, such as safety and security, however, are not measurable. Here, you are not simply concerned with attributes that relate to the behavior of the system but also with unwanted or unacceptable behavior. A secure system is one that does not allow unauthorized access to its data. However, it is clearly impossible to predict all possible modes of access and explicitly forbid them. Therefore, it may only be possible to assess these 'shall not' properties by default. That is, you only know that a system is not secure when someone manages to penetrate the system.

10.1.2 Non-determinism

A deterministic system is one that is completely predictable. If we ignore timing issues, software systems that run on completely reliable hardware and that are presented with a sequence of inputs will always produce the same sequence of outputs. Of course, there is no such thing as completely reliable hardware, but hardware is usually reliable enough to think of hardware systems as deterministic.

People, on the other hand, are nondeterministic. When presented with exactly the same input (say a request to complete a task), their responses will depend on their emotional and physical state, the person making the request, other people in the environment, and whatever else they are doing. Sometimes they will be happy to do the work and, at other times, they will refuse.

Sociotechnical systems are non-deterministic partly because they include people and partly because changes to the hardware, software, and data in these systems are so frequent. The interactions between these changes are complex and so the behavior of the system is unpredictable. This is not a problem in itself but, from a dependability perspective, it can make it difficult to decide whether or not a system failure has occurred, and to estimate the frequency of system failures.

For example, say a system is presented with a set of 20 test inputs. It processes these inputs and the results are recorded. At some later time, the same 20 test inputs are processed and the results compared to the previous stored results. Five of them are different. Does this mean that there have been five failures? Or are the differences simply reasonable variations in the system's behavior? You can only find this out by looking at the results in more depth and making judgments about the way the system has handled each input.

10.1.3 Success criteria

Generally, complex sociotechnical systems are developed to tackle what are sometimes called 'wicked problems' (Rittel and Webber, 1973). A wicked problem is a problem that is so complex and which involves so many related entities that there is no definitive problem specification. Different stakeholders see the problem in different ways and no one has a full understanding of the problem as a whole. The true nature of the problem may only emerge as a solution is developed. An extreme example of a wicked problem is earthquake planning. No one can accurately predict where the epicenter of an earthquake will be, what time it will occur, or what effect it will have on the local environment. It is impossible to specify in detail how to deal with a major earthquake.

This makes it difficult to define the success criteria for a system. How do you decide if a new system contributes, as planned, to the business goals of the company that paid for the system? The judgment of success is not usually made against the original reasons for procuring and developing the system. Rather, it is based on whether or not the system is effective at the time it is deployed. As the business environment can change very quickly, the business goals may have changed significantly during the development of the system.

The situation is even more complex when there are multiple conflicting goals that are interpreted differently by different stakeholders. For instance, the system on which the MHC-PMS (discussed in Chapter 1) is based was designed to support two distinct business goals:

1. Improve the quality of care for sufferers from mental illness.

2. Increase income by providing detailed reports of care provided and the costs of that care.

Unfortunately, these proved to be conflicting goals because the information required to satisfy the reporting goal meant that doctors and nurses had to provide additional information, over and above the health records that are normally maintained. This reduced the quality of care for patients as it meant that clinical staff had less time to talk with them. From a doctor's perspective, this system was not an improvement on the previous manual system; from a manager's perspective, it was.

The nature of security and dependability attributes sometimes makes it even more difficult to decide if a system is successful. The intention of a new system may be to improve security by replacing an existing system with a more secure data environment. Say, after installation, the system is attacked, a security breach occurs, and some data is corrupted. Does this mean that the system is a failure? We cannot tell, because we don't know the extent of the losses that would have occurred with the old system, given the same attacks.

10.2 Systems engineering

Systems engineering encompasses all of the activities involved in procuring, specifying, designing, implementing, validating, deploying, operating, and maintaining sociotechnical systems. Systems engineers are not just concerned with software but also with hardware and the system's interactions with users and its environment. They must think about the services that the system provides, the constraints under which the system must be built and operated, and the ways in which the system is used to fulfill its purpose or purposes.

There are three overlapping stages (Figure 10.4) in the lifetime of large and complex sociotechnical systems:

1. *Procurement or acquisition* During this stage, the purpose of a system is decided; high-level system requirements are established; decisions are made on how functionality will be distributed across hardware, software, and people; and the components that will make up the system are purchased.

2. *Development* During this stage, the system is developed. Development processes include all of the activities involved in system development such as requirements definition, system design, hardware and software engineering, system integration, and testing. Operational processes are defined and the training courses for system users are designed.

3. *Operation* At this stage, the system is deployed, users are trained, and the system is brought into use. The planned operational processes usually then have to change to reflect the real working environment where the system is used. Over time, the system evolves as new requirements are identified. Eventually, the system declines in value and it is decommissioned and replaced.

These stages are not independent. Once the system is operational, new equipment and software may have to be procured to replace obsolete system components, to provide new functionality, or to cope with increased demand. Similarly, requests for changes during operation require further system development.

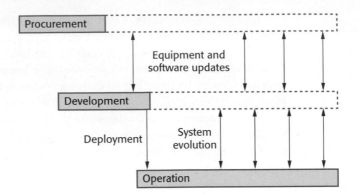

Figure 10.4 Stages of systems engineering

The overall security and dependability of a system is influenced by activities at all of these stages. Design options may be restricted by procurement decisions on the scope of the system and on its hardware and software. It may be impossible to implement some kinds of system safeguards. They may introduce vulnerabilities that could lead to future system failures. Human errors made during the specification, design, and development stages may mean that faults are introduced into the system. Inadequate testing may mean that faults are not discovered before a system is deployed. During operation, errors in configuring the system for deployment may lead to further vulnerabilities. System operators may make mistakes in using the system. Assumptions made during the original procurement may be forgotten when system changes are made and, again, vulnerabilities can be introduced into the system.

An important difference between systems and software engineering is the involvement of a range of professional disciplines throughout the lifetime of the system. For example, the technical disciplines that may be involved in the procurement and development of a new system for air traffic management are shown in Figure 10.5. Architects and civil engineers are involved because new air traffic management systems usually have to be installed in a new building. Electrical and mechanical engineers are involved to specify and maintain the power and air conditioning. Electronic engineers are concerned with computers, radars, and other equipment. Ergonomists design the controller workstations and software engineers and user interface designers are responsible for the software in the system.

The involvement of a range of professional disciplines is essential because there are so many different aspects of complex sociotechnical systems. However, differences between disciplines can introduce vulnerabilities into systems and so compromise the security and dependability of the system being developed:

1. Different disciplines use the same words to mean different things. Misunderstandings are common in discussions between engineers from different backgrounds. If these are not discovered and resolved during system development, they can lead to errors in delivered systems. For example, an electronic engineer who may know a little bit about C# programming may not understand that a method in Java is comparable to a function in C.

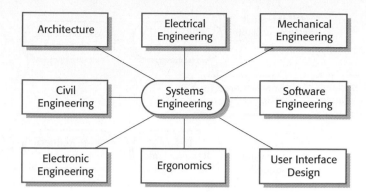

Figure 10.5
Professional disciplines involved in systems engineering

2. Each discipline makes assumptions about what can or can't be done by other disciplines. These are often based on an inadequate understanding of what is actually possible. For example, a user interface designer may propose a graphical UI for an embedded system that requires a great deal of processing and so overloads the processor in the system.

3. Disciplines try to protect their professional boundaries and may argue for certain design decisions because these decisions will call for their professional expertise. Therefore, a software engineer may argue for a software-based door locking system in a building, although a mechanical, key-based system may be more reliable.

10.3 System procurement

The initial phase of systems engineering is system procurement (sometimes called system acquisition). At this stage, decisions are made on the scope of a system that is to be purchased, system budgets and timescales, and the high-level system requirements. Using this information, further decisions are then made on whether to procure a system, the type of system required, and the supplier or suppliers of the system. The drivers for these decisions are:

1. *The state of other organizational systems* If the organization has a mixture of systems that cannot easily communicate or that are expensive to maintain, then procuring a replacement system may lead to significant business benefits.

2. *The need to comply with external regulations* Increasingly, businesses are regulated and have to demonstrate compliance with externally defined regulations (e.g., Sarbanes-Oxley accounting regulations in the United States). This may require the replacement of noncompliant systems or the provision of new systems specifically to monitor compliance.

3. *External competition* If a business needs to compete more effectively or maintain a competitive position, investment in new systems that improve the efficiency of

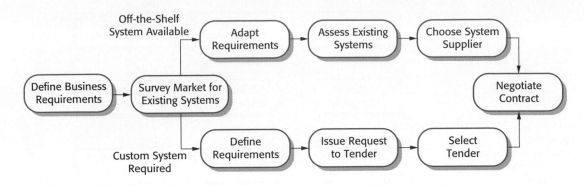

Figure 10.6 System
procurement processes

business processes may be advisable. For military systems, the need to improve capability in the face of new threats is an important reason for procuring new systems.

4. *Business reorganization* Businesses and other organizations frequently restructure with the intention of improving efficiency and/or customer service. Reorganizations lead to changes in business processes that require new systems support.

5. *Available budget* The budget available is an obvious factor in determining the scope of new systems that can be procured.

In addition, new government systems are often procured to reflect political changes and political policies. For example, politicians may decide to buy new surveillance systems, which they claim will counter terrorism. Buying such systems shows voters that they are taking action. However, such systems are often procured without a cost-benefit analysis, where the benefits that result from different spending options are compared.

Large, complex systems usually consist of a mixture of off-the-shelf and specially built components. One reason why more and more software is included in systems is that it allows more use of existing hardware components, with the software acting as 'glue' to make these hardware components work together effectively. The need to develop this 'glueware' is one reason why the savings from using off-the-shelf components are sometimes not as great as anticipated.

Figure 10.6 shows a simplified model of the procurement process for both COTS system components and system components that have to be specially designed and developed. Important points about the process shown in this diagram are:

1. Off-the-shelf components do not usually match requirements exactly, unless the requirements have been written with these components in mind. Therefore, choosing a system means that you have to find the closest match between the system requirements and the facilities offered by off-the-shelf systems. You may then have to modify the requirements. This can have knock-on effects on other subsystems.

2. When a system is to be built specially, the specification of requirements is part of the contract for the system being acquired. It is therefore a legal as well as a technical document.

3. After a contractor has been selected, to build a system, there is a contract negotiation period where you may have to negotiate further changes to the requirements and discuss issues such as the cost of changes to the system. Similarly, once a COTS system has been selected, you may negotiate with the supplier on costs, licence conditions, possible changes to the system, etc.

The software and hardware in sociotechnical systems are usually developed by a different organization (the supplier) from the organization that is procuring the overall sociotechnical system. The reason for this is that the customer's business is rarely software development so its employees do not have the skills needed to develop the systems themselves. In fact, very few companies have the capabilities to design, manufacture, and test all the components of a large, complex sociotechnical system.

Consequently, the system supplier, who is usually called the principal contractor, often contracts out the development of different subsystems to a number of subcontractors. For large systems, such as air traffic control systems, a group of suppliers may form a consortium to bid for the contract. The consortium should include all of the capabilities required for this type of system. This includes computer hardware suppliers, software developers, peripheral suppliers, and suppliers of specialist equipment such as radar systems.

The procurer deals with the contractor rather than the subcontractors so that there is a single procurer/supplier interface. The subcontractors design and build parts of the system to a specification that is produced by the principal contractor. Once completed, the principal contractor integrates these different components and delivers them to the customer. Depending on the contract, the procurer may allow the principal contractor a free choice of subcontractors or may require the principal contractor to choose subcontractors from an approved list.

Decisions and choices made during system procurement have a profound effect on the security and dependability of a system. For example, if a decision is made to procure an off-the-shelf system, then the organization has to accept that they have very limited influence over the security and dependability requirements of this system. These largely depend on decisions made by system vendors. In addition, off-the-shelf systems may have known security weaknesses or require complex configuration. Configuration errors, where entry points to the system are not properly secured, are a major source of security problems.

On the other hand, a decision to procure a custom system means that significant effort must be devoted to understanding and defining security and dependability requirements. If a company has limited experience in this area, this is quite a difficult thing to do. If the required level of dependability as well as acceptable system performance is to be achieved, then the development time may have to be extended and the budget increased.

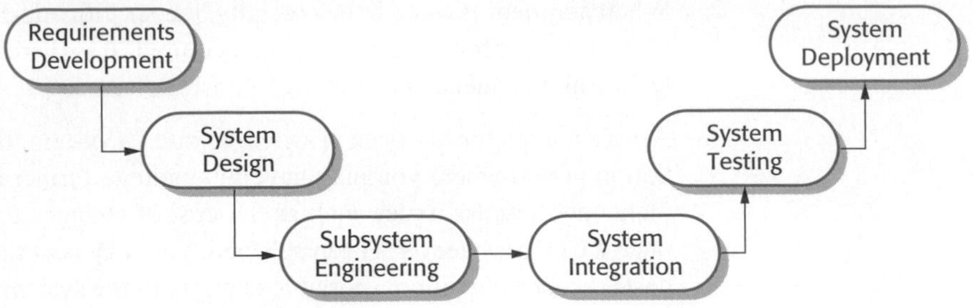

Figure 10.7 Systems
development

10.4 System development

The goals of the system development process are to develop or acquire all of the components of a system and then to integrate these components to create the final system. The requirements are the bridge between the procurement and the development processes. During procurement, business and high-level functional and non-functional system requirements are defined. You can think of this as the start of development, hence the overlapping processes shown in Figure 10.4. Once contracts for the system components have been agreed, more detailed requirements engineering then takes place.

Figure 10.7 is a model of the systems development process. This systems engineering process was an important influence on the 'waterfall' model of the software process that I discussed in Chapter 2. Although it is now accepted that the 'waterfall' model is not usually appropriate for software development, most systems development processes are plan-driven processes that still follow this model.

Plan-driven processes are used in systems engineering because different parts of the system are being developed at the same time. For systems that include hardware and other equipment, changes during development can be very expensive or, sometimes, practically impossible. It is essential therefore, that the system requirements are fully understood before hardware development or building work begins. Reworking the system design to solve hardware problems is rarely possible. For this reason, more and more system functionality is being assigned to the system software. This allows some changes to be made during system development, in response to new system requirements that inevitably arise.

One of the most confusing aspects of systems engineering is that companies use different terminology for each stage of the process. The process structure also varies. Sometimes, requirements engineering is part of the development process and sometimes it is a separate activity. However, there are essentially six fundamental activities in systems development:

1. *Requirements development* The high-level and business requirements identified during the procurement process have to be developed in more detail. Requirements may have to be allocated to hardware, software, or processes and prioritized for implementation.

2. *System design* This process overlaps significantly with the requirements development process. It involves establishing the overall architecture of the system, identifying the different system components and understanding the relationships between them.

3. *Subsystem engineering* This stage involves developing the software components of the system; configuring off-the-shelf hardware and software, designing, if necessary, special-purpose hardware; defining the operational processes for the system; and redesigning essential business processes.

4. *System integration* During this stage, the components are put together to create a new system. Only then do the emergent system properties become apparent.

5. *System testing* This is usually an extensive, prolonged activity where problems are discovered. The subsystem engineering and system integration phases are reentered to repair these problems, tune the performance of the system, and implement new requirements. System testing may involve both testing by the system developer and acceptance/user testing by the organization that has procured the system.

6. *System deployment* This is the process of making the system available to its users, transferring data from existing systems, and establishing communications with other systems in the environment. The process culminates with a 'go live' after which users start to use the system to support their work.

Although the overall process is plan driven, the processes of requirements development and system design are inextricably linked. The requirements and the high-level design are developed concurrently. Constraints posed by existing systems may limit design choices and these choices may be specified in the requirements. You may have to do some initial design to structure and organize the requirements engineering process. As the design process continues, you may discover problems with existing requirements and new requirements may emerge. Consequently, you can think of these linked processes as a spiral, as shown in Figure 10.8.

The spiral reflects the reality that requirements affect design decisions and vice versa, and so it makes sense to interleave these processes. Starting in the center, each round of the spiral may add detail to the requirements and the design. Some rounds may focus on requirements, and some on design. Sometimes new knowledge collected during the requirements and design process means that the problem statement itself has to be changed.

For almost all systems, there are many possible designs that meet the requirements. These cover a range of solutions that combine hardware, software, and human operations. The solution that you choose for further development may be the most appropriate technical solution that meets the requirements. However, wider organizational and political considerations may influence the choice of solution. For example, a government client may prefer to use national rather than foreign suppliers for its system, even if national products are technically inferior. These influences usually take effect in the review and assessment phase of the spiral model where

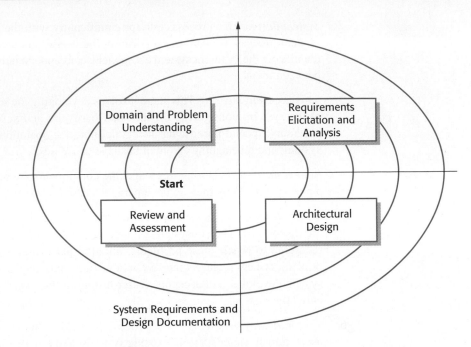

Figure 10.8
Requirements and
design spiral

designs and requirements may be accepted or rejected. The process ends when a review decides that the requirements and high-level design are sufficiently detailed for subsystems to be specified and designed.

In the subsystem engineering phase, the hardware and software components of the system are implemented. For some types of system, such as spacecraft, all hardware and software components may be designed and built during the development process. However, in most systems, some components are commercial off-the-shelf (COTS) systems. It is usually much cheaper to buy existing products than to develop special-purpose components.

Subsystems are usually developed in parallel. When problems that cut across subsystem boundaries are encountered, a system modification request must be made. Where systems involve extensive hardware engineering, making modifications after manufacturing has started is usually very expensive. Often 'work-arounds' that compensate for the problem must be found. These 'work-arounds' usually involve software changes because of the software's inherent flexibility.

During systems integration, you take the independently developed subsystems and put them together to make up a complete system. This integration can be done using a 'big-bang' approach, where all the subsystems are integrated at the same time. However, for technical and managerial reasons, an incremental integration process where subsystems are integrated one at a time is the best approach:

1. It is usually impossible to schedule the development of the subsystems so that they are all finished at the same time.

2. Incremental integration reduces the cost of error location. If many subsystems are simultaneously integrated, an error that arises during testing may be in any of

these subsystems. When a single subsystem is integrated with an already working system, errors that occur are probably in the newly integrated subsystem or in the interactions between the existing subsystems and the new subsystem.

As more and more systems are built by integrating COTS hardware and software components, the distinction between implementation and integration is increasingly blurred. In some cases, there is no need to develop new hardware or software and the integration is, essentially, the implementation phase of the system.

During and after the integration process, the system is tested. This testing should focus on testing the interfaces between components and the behavior of the system as a whole. Inevitably, this will also reveal problems with individual subsystems that have to be repaired.

Subsystem faults that are a consequence of invalid assumptions about other subsystems are often revealed during system integration. This may lead to disputes between the contractors responsible for implementing different subsystems. When problems are discovered in subsystem interaction, the contractors may argue about which subsystem is faulty. Negotiations on how to solve the problems can take weeks or months.

The final stage of the system development process is system delivery and deployment. The software is installed on the hardware and is readied for operation. This may involve more system configuration to reflect the local environment where it is used, the transfer of data from existing systems, and the preparation of user documentation and training. At this stage, you may also have to reconfigure other systems in the environment to ensure that the new system interoperates with them.

Although straightforward in principle, many difficulties can arise during deployment. The user environment may be different from that anticipated by the system developers and adapting the system to cope with diverse user environments can be difficult. The existing data may require extensive cleanup and parts of it may be missing. The interfaces to other systems may not be properly documented.

The influence of system development processes on dependability and security is obvious. It is during these processes that decisions are made on dependability and security requirements and on trade-offs between costs, schedule, performance, and dependability. Human errors at all stages of the development process may lead to the introduction of faults into the system which, in operation, can lead to system failure. Testing and validation processes are inevitably constrained by the costs and time available. As a result, the system may not be properly tested. Users are left to test the system as it is being used. Finally, problems in system deployment may mean that there is a mismatch between the system and its operational environment. These can lead to human errors when using the system.

10.5 System operation

Operational processes are the processes that are involved in using the system for its defined purpose. For example, operators of an air traffic control system follow specific processes when aircraft enter and leave airspace, when they have to change height or speed, when an emergency occurs, and so on. For new systems, these operational processes have to be defined and documented during the system development process. Operators may have to be trained and other work processes adapted to make effective use of the new system. Undetected problems may arise at this stage because the system specification may contain errors or omissions. Although the system may perform to specification, its functions may not meet the real operational needs. Consequently, the operators may not use the system as its designers intended.

The key benefit of having system operators is that people have a unique capability of being able to respond effectively to unexpected situations, even when they have never had direct experience of these situations. Therefore, when things go wrong, the operators can often recover the situation although this may sometimes mean that the defined process is violated. Operators also use their local knowledge to adapt and improve processes. Normally, the actual operational processes are different from those anticipated by the system designers.

Consequently, you should design operational processes to be flexible and adaptable. The operational processes should not be too constraining, they should not require operations to be done in a particular order, and the system software should not rely on a specific process being followed. Operators usually improve the process because they know what does and does not work in a real situation.

A problem that may only emerge after the system goes into operation is the operation of the new system alongside existing systems. There may be physical problems of incompatibility or it may be difficult to transfer data from one system to another. More subtle problems might arise because different systems have different user interfaces. Introducing a new system may increase the operator error rate, as the operators use user interface commands for the wrong system.

10.5.1 Human error

I suggested earlier in the chapter that non-determinism was an important issue in sociotechnical systems and that one reason for this is that the people in the system do not always behave in the same way. Sometimes they make mistakes in using the system and this has the potential to cause system failure. For example, an operator may forget to record that some action has been taken so that another operator (erroneously) repeats that action. If the action is to debit or credit a bank account, say, then a system failure occurs as the amount in the account is then incorrect.

As Reason discusses (2000) human errors will always occur and there are two ways to view the problem of human error:

1. *The person approach.* Errors are considered to be the responsibility of the individual and 'unsafe acts' (such as an operator failing to engage a safety barrier) are a consequence of individual carelessness or reckless behavior. People who adopt this approach believe that human errors can be reduced by threats of disciplinary action, more stringent procedures, retraining, etc. Their view is that the error is the fault of the individual responsible for making the mistake.

2. *The systems approach.* The basic assumption is that people are fallible and will make mistakes. The errors that people make are often a consequence of system design decisions that lead to erroneous ways of working, or of organizational factors, which affect the system operators. Good systems should recognize the possibility of human error and include barriers and safeguards that detect human errors and allow the system to recover before failure occurs. When a failure does occur, the issue is not finding an individual to blame but to understand how and why the system defences did not trap the error.

I believe that the systems approach is the right one and that systems engineers should assume that human errors will occur during system operation. Therefore, to improve the security and dependability of a system, designers have to think about the defenses and barriers to human error that should be included in a system. They should also think about whether these barriers should be built into the technical components of the system. If not, they could be part of the processes and procedures for using the system or could be operator guidelines that are reliant on human checking and judgment.

Examples of defenses that may be included in a system are:

1. An air traffic control system may include an automated conflict alert system. When a controller instructs an aircraft to change its speed or altitude, the system extrapolates its trajectory to see if it could intersect with any other aircraft. If so, it sounds an alarm.

2. The same system may have a clearly defined procedure to record the control instructions that have been issued. These procedures help the controller check if they have issued the instruction correctly and make the information available to others for checking.

3. Air traffic control usually involves a team of controllers who constantly monitor each other's work. Therefore, when a mistake is made, it is likely that it will be detected and corrected before an incident occurs.

Inevitably, all barriers have weaknesses of some kind. Reason calls these 'latent conditions' as they usually only contribute to system failure when some other problem occurs. For example, in the above defenses, a weakness of a conflict alert system is that it may lead to many false alarms. Controllers may therefore ignore warnings from the system. A weakness of a procedural system may be that unusual but essential information can't be easily recorded. Human checking may fail when all of the people involved are under stress and make the same mistake.

Latent conditions lead to system failure when the defenses built into the system do not trap an active failure by a system operator. The human error is a trigger for the failure but should not be considered to be the sole cause of the failure. Reason explains this using his well-known 'Swiss cheese' model of system failure (Figure 10.9).

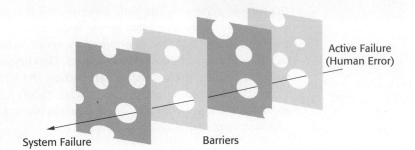

Active Failure
(Human Error)

Figure 10.9
Reason's Swiss cheese
model of system failure

System Failure

Barriers

In this model, the defenses built into a system are compared to slices of Swiss cheese. Some types of Swiss cheese, such as Emmental, have holes and so the analogy is that the latent conditions are comparable to the holes in cheese slices. The position of these holes is not static but changes depending on the state of the overall sociotechnical system. If each slice represents a barrier, failures can occur when the holes line up at the same time as a human operational error. An active failure of system operation gets through the holes and leads to an overall system failure.

Normally, of course, the holes should not be aligned so operational failures are trapped by the system. To reduce the probability that system failure will result from human error, designers should:

1. Design a system so that different types of barriers are included. This means that the 'holes' will probably be in different places and so there is less chance of the holes lining up and failing to trap an error.

2. Minimize the number of latent conditions in a system. Effectively, this means reducing the number and size of system 'holes'.

Of course, the design of the system as a whole should also attempt to avoid the active failures that can trigger a system failure. This may involve designing the operational processes and the system to ensure that operators are not overworked, distracted, or presented with excessive amounts of information.

10.5.2 System evolution

Large, complex systems have a very long lifetime. During their life, they are changed to correct errors in the original system requirements and to implement new requirements that have emerged. The system's computers are likely to be replaced with new, faster machines. The organization that uses the system may reorganize itself and hence use the system in a different way. The external environment of the system may change, forcing changes to the system. Hence evolution, where the system changes to accommodate environmental change, is a process that runs alongside normal system operational processes. System evolution involves reentering the development process to make changes and extensions to the system's hardware, software, and operational processes.

Legacy systems

Legacy systems are sociotechnical computer-based systems that have been developed in the past, often using older or obsolete technology. These systems include not only hardware and software but also legacy processes and procedures—old ways of doing things that are difficult to change because they rely on legacy software. Changes to one part of the system inevitably involve changes to other components. Legacy systems are often business-critical systems. They are maintained because it is too risky to replace them.

http://www.SoftwareEngineering-9.com/LegacySys/

System evolution, like software evolution (discussed in Chapter 9), is inherently costly for several reasons:

1. Proposed changes have to be analyzed very carefully from a business and a technical perspective. Changes have to contribute to the goals of the system and should not simply be technically motivated.

2. Because subsystems are never completely independent, changes to one subsystem may adversely affect the performance or behavior of other subsystems. Consequent changes to these subsystems may therefore be needed.

3. The reasons for original design decisions are often unrecorded. Those responsible for the system evolution have to work out why particular design decisions were made.

4. As systems age, their structure typically becomes corrupted by change so the costs of making further changes increases.

Systems that have evolved over time are often reliant on obsolete hardware and software technology. If they have a critical role in an organization, they are known as 'legacy systems'. These are usually systems that the organization would like to replace but don't do so as the risks or costs of replacement cannot be justified.

From a dependability and security perspective, changes to a system are often a source of problems and vulnerabilities. If the people implementing the change are different from those who developed the system, they may be unaware that a design decision was made for dependability and security reasons. Therefore, they may change the system and lose some safeguards that were deliberately implemented when the system was built. Furthermore, as testing is so expensive, complete retesting may be impossible after every system change. Adverse side effects of changes that introduce or expose faults in other system components may not then be discovered.

KEY POINTS

■ Sociotechnical systems include computer hardware, software, and people, and are situated within an organization. They are designed to support organizational or business goals and objectives.

■ Human and organizational factors such as organizational structure and politics have a significant effect on the operation of sociotechnical systems.

■ The emergent properties of a system are characteristics of the system as a whole rather than of its component parts. They include properties such as performance, reliability, usability, safety, and security. The success or failure of a system is often dependent on these emergent properties.

■ The fundamental systems engineering processes are system procurement, system development, and system operation.

■ System procurement covers all of the activities involved in deciding what system to buy and who should supply that system. High-level requirements are developed as part of the procurement process.

■ System development includes requirements specification, design, construction, integration, and testing. System integration, where subsystems from more than one supplier must be made to work together, is particularly critical.

■ When a system is put into use, the operational processes and the system itself have to change to reflect changing business requirements.

■ Human errors are inevitable and systems should include barriers to detect these errors before they lead to system failure. Reason's Swiss cheese model explains how human error plus latent defects in the barriers can lead to system failure.

FURTHER READING

'Airport 95: Automated baggage system'. An excellent, readable case study of what can go wrong with a systems engineering project and how software tends to get the blame for wider systems failures. (*ACM Software Engineering Notes*, 21, March 1996.)
http://doi.acm.org/10.1145/227531.227544.

'Software system engineering: A tutorial'. A good general overview of systems engineering, although Thayer focuses exclusively on computer-based systems and does not discuss sociotechnical issues. (R. H. Thayer. *IEEE Computer*, April 2002.)
http://dx.doi.org/10.1109/MC.2002.993773.

Trust in Technology: A Socio-technical Perspective. This book is a set of papers that are all concerned, in some way, with the dependability of sociotechnical systems. (K. Clarke, G. Hardstone, M. Rouncefield and I. Sommerville (eds.), Springer, 2006.)

'Fundamentals of Systems Engineering'. This is the introductory chapter in NASA's systems engineering handbook. It presents an overview of the systems engineering process for space systems. Although these are mostly technical systems, there are sociotechnical issues to be considered. Dependability is obviously critically important. (In *NASA Systems Engineering Handbook*, NASA-SP2007-6105, 2007.) http://education.ksc.nasa.gov/esmdspacegrant/Documents/NASA%20SP-2007-6105%20Rev%201%20Final%2031Dec2007.pdf.

EXERCISES

10.1. Give two examples of government functions that are supported by complex sociotechnical systems and explain why, in the foreseeable future, these functions cannot be completely automated.

10.2. Explain why the environment in which a computer-based system is installed may have unanticipated effects on the system that lead to system failure. Illustrate your answer with a different example from that used in this chapter.

10.3. Why is it impossible to infer the emergent properties of a complex system from the properties of the system components?

10.4. Why is it sometimes difficult to decide whether or not there has been a failure in a sociotechnical system? Illustrate your answer by using examples from the MHC-PMS that has been discussed in earlier chapters.

10.5. What is a 'wicked problem'? Explain why the development of a national medical records system should be considered a 'wicked problem'.

10.6. A multimedia virtual museum system offering virtual experiences of ancient Greece is to be developed for a consortium of European museums. The system should provide users with the facility to view 3-D models of ancient Greece through a standard web browser and should also support an immersive virtual reality experience. What political and organizational difficulties might arise when the system is installed in the museums that make up the consortium?

10.7. Why is system integration a particularly critical part of the systems development process? Suggest three sociotechnical issues that may cause difficulties in the system integration process.

10.8. Explain why legacy systems may be critical to the operation of a business.

10.9. What are the arguments for and against considering system engineering as a profession in its own right, like electrical engineering or software engineering?

10.10. You are an engineer involved in the development of a financial system. During installation, you discover that this system will make a significant number of people redundant. The people in the environment deny you access to essential information to complete the system installation. To what extent should you, as a systems engineer, become involved in this situation? Is it your professional responsibility to complete the installation as contracted? Should you simply abandon the work until the procuring organization has sorted out the problem?

REFERENCES

Ackroyd, S., Harper, R., Hughes, J. A. and Shapiro, D. (1992). *Information Technology and Practical Police Work*. Milton Keynes: Open University Press.

Anderson, R. J., Hughes, J. A. and Sharrock, W. W. (1989). *Working for Profit: The Social Organization of Calculability in an Entrepreneurial Firm*. Aldershot: Avebury.

Checkland, P. (1981). *Systems Thinking, Systems Practice*. Chichester: John Wiley & Sons.

Checkland, P. and Scholes, J. (1990). *Soft Systems Methodology in Action*. Chichester: John Wiley & Sons.

Mumford, E. (1989). 'User Participation in a Changing Environment—Why we need it'. In *Participation in Systems Development*. Knight, K. (ed.). London: Kogan Page.

Reason, J. (2000). 'Human error: Models and management'. *British Medical J.*, **320** 768–70.

Rittel, H. and Webber, M. (1973). 'Dilemmas in a General Theory of Planning'. *Policy Sciences*, **4**, 155–69.

Stevens, R., Brook, P., Jackson, K. and Arnold, S. (1998). *Systems Engineering: Coping with Complexity*. London: Prentice Hall.

Suchman, L. (1987). *Plans and situated actions: the problem of human-machine communication*. New York: Cambridge University Press.

Swartz, A. J. (1996). 'Airport 95: Automated Baggage System?' *ACM Software Engineering Notes*, **21** (2), 79–83.

Thayer, R. H. (2002). 'Software System Engineering: A Tutorial.' *IEEE Computer*, **35** (4), 68–73.

Thomé, B. (1993). 'Systems Engineering: Principles and Practice of Computer-based Systems Engineering'. Chichester: John Wiley & Sons.

White, S., Alford, M., Holtzman, J., Kuehl, S., McCay, B., Oliver, D., Owens, D., Tully, C. and Willey, A. (1993). 'Systems Engineering of Computer-Based Systems'. *IEEE Computer*, **26** (11), 54–65.

11

Dependability and security

Objectives

The objective of this chapter is to introduce software dependability and security. When you have read this chapter, you will:

- understand why dependability and security are usually more important than the functional characteristics of a software system;

- understand the four principal dimensions of dependability, namely availability, reliability, safety, and security;

- be aware of the specialized terminology that is used when discussing security and dependability;

- understand that to achieve secure, dependable software, you need to avoid mistakes during the development of a system, to detect and remove errors when the system is in use, and to limit the damage caused by operational failures.

Contents

As computer systems have become deeply embedded in our business and personal lives, the problems that result from system and software failure are increasing. A failure of server software in an e-commerce company could lead to a major loss of revenue, and possibly also customers for that company. A software error in an embedded control system in a car could lead to expensive recalls of that model for repair and, in the worst case, could be a contributory factor in accidents. The infection of company PCs with malware requires expensive cleanup operations to sort out the problem and could result in the loss or damage to sensitive information.

Because software-intensive systems are so important to governments, companies, and individuals, it is essential that widely used software is trustworthy. The software should be available when required and should operate correctly and without undesirable side effects, such as unauthorized information disclosure. The term 'dependability' was proposed by Laprie (1995) to cover the related systems attributes of availability, reliability, safety, and security. As I discuss in Section 11.1, these properties are inextricably linked, so having a single term to cover them all makes sense.

The dependability of systems is now usually more important than their detailed functionality for the following reasons:

1. *System failures affect a large number of people.* Many systems include functionality that is rarely used. If this functionality were left out of the system, only a small number of users would be affected. System failures, which affect the availability of a system, potentially affect all users of the system. Failure may mean that normal business is impossible.

2. *Users often reject systems that are unreliable, unsafe, or insecure.* If users find that a system is unreliable or insecure, they will refuse to use it. Furthermore, they may also refuse to buy or use other products from the same company that produced the unreliable system, because they believe that these products are also likely to be unreliable or insecure.

3. *System failure costs may be enormous.* For some applications, such as a reactor control system or an aircraft navigation system, the cost of system failure is orders of magnitude greater than the cost of the control system.

4. *Undependable systems may cause information loss.* Data is very expensive to collect and maintain; it is usually worth much more than the computer system on which it is processed. The cost of recovering lost or corrupt data is usually very high.

As I discussed in Chapter 10, software is always part of a broader system. It executes in an operational environment that includes the hardware on which the software executes, the human users of that software, and the organizational or business processes where the software is used. When designing a dependable system, you therefore have to consider:

1. *Hardware failure* System hardware may fail because of mistakes in its design, because components fail as a result of manufacturing errors, or because the components have reached the end of their natural life.

Critical systems

Some classes of system are 'critical systems' where system failure may result in injury to people, damage to the environment, or extensive economic losses. Examples of critical systems include embedded systems in medical devices, such as an insulin pump (safety-critical), spacecraft navigation systems (mission-critical), and online money transfer systems (business critical).

Critical systems are very expensive to develop. Not only must they be developed so that failures are very rare but they must also include recovery mechanisms that are used if and when failures occur.

http://www.SoftwareEngineering-9.com/Web/Dependability/CritSys.html

2. *Software failure* System software may fail because of mistakes in its specification, design, or implementation.

3. *Operational failure* Human users may fail to use or operate the system correctly. As hardware and software have become more reliable, failures in operation are now, perhaps, the largest single cause of system failures.

These failures are often interrelated. A failed hardware component may mean system operators have to cope with an unexpected situation and additional workload. This puts them under stress and people under stress often make mistakes. This can cause the software to fail, which means more work for the operators, even more stress, and so on.

As a result, it is particularly important that designers of dependable, software-intensive systems take a holistic systems perspective, rather than focus on a single aspect of the system such as its software or hardware. If hardware, software, and operational processes are designed separately, without taking into account the potential weaknesses of other parts of the system, then it is more likely that errors will occur at the interfaces between the different parts of the system.

11.1 Dependability properties

All of us are familiar with the problem of computer system failure. For no obvious reason, our computers sometimes crash or go wrong in some way. Programs running on these computers may not operate as expected and occasionally may corrupt the data that is managed by the system. We have learned to live with these failures but few of us completely trust the personal computers that we normally use.

The dependability of a computer system is a property of the system that reflects its trustworthiness. Trustworthiness here essentially means the degree of confidence a user has that the system will operate as they expect, and that the system will not 'fail' in normal use. It is not meaningful to express dependability numerically.

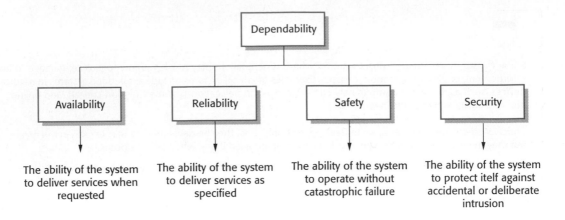

Figure 11.1
Principal
dependability
properties

Rather, we use relative terms such as 'not dependable,' 'very dependable,' and 'ultra-dependable' to reflect the degrees of trust that we might have in a system.

Trustworthiness and usefulness are not, of course, the same thing. I don't think that the word processor that I used to write this book is a very dependable system. It sometimes freezes and has to be restarted. Nevertheless, because it is very useful, I am prepared to tolerate occasional failure. However, to reflect my lack of trust in the system I save my work frequently and keep multiple backup copies of it. I compensate for the lack of system dependability by actions that limit the damage that could result from system failure.

There are four principal dimensions to dependability, as shown in Figure 11.1.

1. *Availability* Informally, the availability of a system is the probability that it will be up and running and able to deliver useful services to users at any given time.

2. *Reliability* Informally, the reliability of a system is the probability, over a given period of time, that the system will correctly deliver services as expected by the user.

3. *Safety* Informally, the safety of a system is a judgment of how likely it is that the system will cause damage to people or its environment.

4. *Security* Informally, the security of a system is a judgment of how likely it is that the system can resist accidental or deliberate intrusions.

The dependability properties shown in Figure 11.1 are complex properties that can be broken down into a number of other, simpler properties. For example, security includes 'integrity' (ensuring that the systems program and data are not damaged) and 'confidentiality' (ensuring that information can only be accessed by people who are authorized). Reliability includes 'correctness' (ensuring the system services are as specified), 'precision' (ensuring information is delivered at an appropriate level of detail), and 'timeliness' (ensuring that information is delivered when it is required).

Of course, these dependability properties are not all applicable to all systems. For the insulin pump system, introduced in Chapter 1, the most important properties are availability (it must work when required), reliability (it must deliver the correct dose of insulin), and safety (it must never deliver a dangerous dose of insulin). Security is not an issue as the pump will not maintain confidential information. It is not networked and so cannot be maliciously attacked. For the wilderness weather system, availability and reliability are the most important properties because the costs of repair may be very high. For the patient information system, security is particularly important because of the sensitive private data that is maintained.

As well as these four main dependability properties, you may also think of other system properties as dependability properties:

1. *Repairability* System failures are inevitable, but the disruption caused by failure can be minimized if the system can be repaired quickly. For that to happen, it must be possible to diagnose the problem, access the component that has failed, and make changes to fix that component. Repairability in software is enhanced when the organization using the system has access to the source code and has the skills to make changes to it. Open source software makes this easier but the reuse of components can make it more difficult.

2. *Maintainability* As systems are used, new requirements emerge and it is important to maintain the usefulness of a system by changing it to accommodate these new requirements. Maintainable software is software that can be adapted economically to cope with new requirements, and where there is a low probability that making changes will introduce new errors into the system.

3. *Survivability* A very important attribute for Internet-based systems is survivability (Ellison et al., 1999b). Survivability is the ability of a system to continue to deliver service whilst under attack and, potentially, whilst part of the system is disabled. Work on survivability focuses on identifying key system components and ensuring that they can deliver a minimal service. Three strategies are used to enhance survivability—resistance to attack, attack recognition, and recovery from the damage caused by an attack (Ellison et al., 1999a; Ellison et al., 2002). I discuss this in more detail in Chapter 14.

4. *Error tolerance* This property can be considered as part of usability and reflects the extent to which the system has been designed so that user input errors are avoided and tolerated. When user errors occur, the system should, as far as possible, detect these errors and either fix them automatically or request the user to reinput their data.

The notion of system dependability as an encompassing property was introduced because the dependability properties of availability, security, reliability, and safety are closely related. Safe system operation usually depends on the system being available and operating reliably. A system may become unreliable because an intruder has corrupted its data. Denial of service attacks on a system are intended to compromise the system's availability. If a system is infected with a virus, you cannot then be confident in its reliability or safety because the virus may change its behavior.

To develop dependable software, you therefore need to ensure that:

1. You avoid the introduction of accidental errors into the system during software specification and development.

2. You design verification and validation processes that are effective in discovering residual errors that affect the dependability of the system.

3. You design protection mechanisms that guard against external attacks that can compromise the availability or security of the system.

4. You configure the deployed system and its supporting software correctly for its operating environment.

In addition, you should usually assume that your software is not perfect and that software failures may occur. Your system should therefore include recovery mechanisms that make it possible to restore normal system service as quickly as possible.

The need for fault tolerance means that dependable systems have to include redundant code to help them monitor themselves, detect erroneous states, and recover from faults before failures occur. This affects the performance of systems, as additional checking is required each time the system executes. Therefore, designers usually have to trade off performance and dependability. You may need to leave checks out of the system because these slow the system down. However, the consequential risk here is that some failures occur because a fault has not been detected.

Because of extra design, implementation, and validation costs, increasing the dependability of a system significantly increases development costs. In particular, validation costs are high for systems that must be ultra-dependable such as safety-critical control systems. As well as validating that the system meets its requirements, the validation process may have to prove to an external regulator that the system is safe. For example, aircraft systems have to demonstrate to regulators, such as the Federal Aviation Authority, that the probability of a catastrophic system failure that affects aircraft safety is extremely low.

Figure 11.2 shows that the relationship between costs and incremental improvements in dependability. If your software is not very dependable, you can get significant improvements at relatively low costs by using better software engineering. However, if you are already using good practice, the costs of improvement are much greater and the benefits from that improvement are less. There is also the problem of testing your software to demonstrate that it is dependable. This relies on running many tests and looking at the number of failures that occur. As your software becomes more dependable, you see fewer and fewer failures. Consequently, more and more tests are needed to try and assess how many problems remain in the software. As testing is very expensive, this dramatically increases the cost of high-dependability systems.

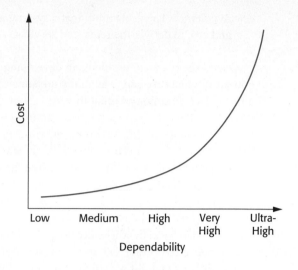

Figure 11.2
Cost/dependability
curve

11.2 Availability and reliability

System availability and reliability are closely related properties that can both be expressed as numerical probabilities. The availability of a system is the probability that the system will be up and running to deliver these services to users on request. The reliability of a system is the probability that the system's services will be delivered as defined in the system specification. If, on average, 2 inputs in every 1,000 cause failures, then the reliability, expressed as a rate of occurrence of failure, is 0.002. If the availability is 0.999, this means that, over some time period, the system is available for 99.9% of that time.

Reliability and availability are closely related but sometimes one is more important than the other. If users expect continuous service from a system then the system has a high availability requirement. It must be available whenever a demand is made. However, if the losses that result from a system failure are low and the system can recover quickly then failures don't seriously affect system users. In such systems, the reliability requirements may be relatively low.

A telephone exchange switch that routes phone calls is an example of a system where availability is more important than reliability. Users expect a dial tone when they pick up a phone, so the system has high availability requirements. If a system fault occurs while a connection is being set up, this is often quickly recoverable. Exchange switches can usually reset the system and retry the connection attempt. This can be done very quickly and phone users may not even notice that a failure has occurred. Furthermore, even if a call is interrupted, the consequences are usually not serious. Therefore, availability rather than reliability is the key dependability requirement for this type of system.

System reliability and availability may be defined more precisely as follows:

1. *Reliability* The probability of failure-free operation over a specified time, in a given environment, for a specific purpose.

2. *Availability* The probability that a system, at a point in time, will be operational and able to deliver the requested services.

One of the practical problems in developing reliable systems is that our intuitive notions of reliability and availability are sometimes broader than these limited definitions. The definition of reliability states that the environment in which the system is used and the purpose that it is used for must be taken into account. If you measure system reliability in one environment, you can't assume that the reliability will be the same if the system is used in a different way.

For example, let's say that you measure the reliability of a word processor in an office environment where most users are uninterested in the operation of the software. They follow the instructions for its use and do not try to experiment with the system. If you then measure the reliability of the same system in a university environment, then the reliability may be quite different. Here, students may explore the boundaries of the system and use the system in unexpected ways. This may result in system failures that did not occur in the more constrained office environment.

These standard definitions of availability and reliability do not take into account the severity of failure or the consequences of unavailability. People often accept minor system failures but are very concerned about serious failures that have high consequential costs. For example, computer failures that corrupt stored data are less acceptable than failures that freeze the machine and that can be resolved by restarting the computer.

A strict definition of reliability relates the system implementation to its specification. That is, the system is behaving reliably if its behavior is consistent with that defined in the specification. However, a common cause of perceived unreliability is that the system specification does not match the expectations of the system users. Unfortunately, many specifications are incomplete or incorrect and it is left to software engineers to interpret how the system should behave. As they are not domain experts, they may not, therefore, implement the behavior that users expect. It is also true, of course, that users don't read system specifications. They may therefore have unrealistic expectations of the system.

Availability and reliability are obviously linked as system failures may crash the system. However, availability does not just depend on the number of system crashes, but also on the time needed to repair the faults that have caused the failure. Therefore, if system A fails once a year and system B fails once a month then A is clearly more reliable then B. However, assume that system A takes three days to restart after a failure, whereas system B takes 10 minutes to restart. The availability of system B over the year (120 minutes of down time) is much better than that of system A (4,320 minutes of down time).

The disruption caused by unavailable systems is not reflected in the simple availability metric that specifies the percentage of time that the system is available. The time when the system fails is also significant. If a system is unavailable for an hour each day between 3 am and 4 am, this may not affect many users. However, if the same system is unavailable for 10 minutes during the working day, system unavailability will probably have a much greater effect.

Term	Description
Human error or mistake	Human behavior that results in the introduction of faults into a system. For example, in the wilderness weather system, a programmer might decide that the way to compute the time for the next transmission is to add 1 hour to the current time. This works except when the transmission time is between 23.00 and midnight (midnight is 00.00 in the 24-hour clock).
System fault	A characteristic of a software system that can lead to a system error. The fault is the inclusion of the code to add 1 hour to the time of the last transmission, without a check if the time is greater than or equal to 23.00.
System error	An erroneous system state that can lead to system behavior that is unexpected by system users. The value of transmission time is set incorrectly (to 24.XX rather than 00.XX) when the faulty code is executed.
System failure	An event that occurs at some point in time when the system does not deliver a service as expected by its users. No weather data is transmitted because the time is invalid.

Figure 11.3
Reliability terminology

System reliability and availability problems are mostly caused by system failures. Some of these failures are a consequence of specification errors or failures in other related systems such as a communications system. However, many failures are a consequence of erroneous system behavior that derives from faults in the system. When discussing reliability, it is helpful to use precise terminology and distinguish between the terms 'fault,' 'error,' and 'failure.' I have defined these terms in Figure 11.3 and have illustrated each definition with an example from the wilderness weather system.

When an input or a sequence of inputs causes faulty code in a system to be executed, an erroneous state is created that may lead to a software failure. Figure 11.4, derived from Littlewood (1990), shows a software system as a mapping of a set of inputs to a set of outputs. Given an input or input sequence, the program responds by producing a corresponding output. For example, given an input of a URL, a web browser produces an output that is the display of the requested web page.

Most inputs do not lead to system failure. However, some inputs or input combinations, shown in the shaded ellipse I_e in Figure 11.4, cause system failures or erroneous outputs to be generated. The program's reliability depends on the number of system inputs that are members of the set of inputs that lead to an erroneous output. If inputs in the set I_e are executed by frequently used parts of the system, then failures will be frequent. However, if the inputs in I_e are executed by code that is rarely used, then users will hardly ever see failures.

Because each user of a system uses it in different ways, they have different perceptions of its reliability. Faults that affect the reliability of the system for one user may never be revealed under someone else's mode of working (Figure 11.5). In Figure 11.5, the set of erroneous inputs correspond to the ellipse labeled I_e in Figure 11.4. The set of inputs produced by User 2 intersects with this erroneous input set. User 2 will

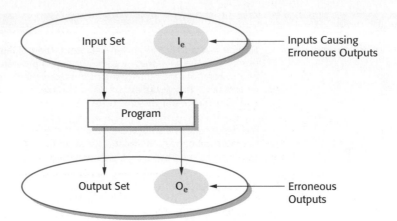

Figure 11.4
A system as an
input/output
mapping

therefore experience some system failures. User 1 and User 3, however, never use inputs from the erroneous set. For them, the software will always be reliable.

The practical reliability of a program depends on the number of inputs causing erroneous outputs (failures) during normal use of the system by most users. Software faults that only occur in exceptional situations have little practical effect on the system's reliability. Consequently, removing software faults may not significantly improve the overall reliability of the system. Mills et al. (1987) found that removing 60% of known errors in their software led to a 3% reliability improvement. Adams (1984), in a study of IBM software products, noted that many defects in the products were only likely to cause failures after hundreds or thousands of months of product usage.

System faults do not always result in system errors and system errors do not necessarily result in system failures. The reasons for this are as follows:

1. Not all code in a program is executed. The code that includes a fault (e.g., the failure to initialize a variable) may never be executed because of the way that the software is used.

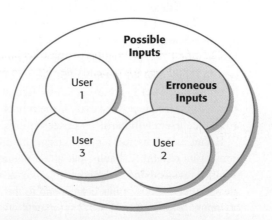

Figure 11.5 Software
usage patterns

2. Errors are transient. A state variable may have an incorrect value caused by the execution of faulty code. However, before this is accessed and causes a system failure, some other system input may be processed that resets the state to a valid value.

3. The system may include fault detection and protection mechanisms. These ensure that the erroneous behavior is discovered and corrected before the system services are affected.

Another reason why the faults in a system may not lead to system failures is that, in practice, users adapt their behavior to avoid using inputs that they know cause program failures. Experienced users 'work around' software features that they have found to be unreliable. For example, I avoid certain features, such as automatic numbering in the word processing system that I used to write this book. When I used auto-numbering, it often went wrong. Repairing the faults in unused features makes no practical difference to the system reliability. As users share information on problems and work-arounds, the effects of software problems are reduced.

The distinction between faults, errors, and failures, explained in Figure 11.3, helps identify three complementary approaches that are used to improve the reliability of a system:

1. *Fault avoidance* Development techniques are used that either minimize the possibility of human errors and/or that trap mistakes before they result in the introduction of system faults. Examples of such techniques include avoiding error-prone programming language constructs such as pointers and the use of static analysis to detect program anomalies.

2. *Fault detection and removal* The use of verification and validation techniques that increase the chances that faults will be detected and removed before the system is used. Systematic testing and debugging is an example of a fault-detection technique.

3. *Fault tolerance* These are techniques that ensure that faults in a system do not result in system errors or that system errors do not result in system failures. The incorporation of self-checking facilities in a system and the use of redundant system modules are examples of fault tolerance techniques.

The practical application of these techniques is discussed in Chapter 13, which covers techniques for dependable software engineering.

11.3 Safety

Safety-critical systems are systems where it is essential that system operation is always safe; that is, the system should never damage people or the system's environment even if the system fails. Examples of safety-critical systems include control and monitoring systems in aircraft, process control systems in chemical and pharmaceutical plants, and automobile control systems.

Hardware control of safety-critical systems is simpler to implement and analyze than software control. However, we now build systems of such complexity that they cannot be controlled by hardware alone. Software control is essential because of the need to manage large numbers of sensors and actuators with complex control laws. For example, advanced, aerodynamically unstable, military aircraft require continual software-controlled adjustment of their flight surfaces to ensure that they do not crash.

Safety-critical software falls into two classes:

1. *Primary safety-critical software* This is software that is embedded as a controller in a system. Malfunctioning of such software can cause a hardware malfunction, which results in human injury or environmental damage. The insulin pump software, introduced in Chapter 1, is an example of a primary safety-critical system. System failure may lead to user injury.

2. *Secondary safety-critical software* This is software that can indirectly result in an injury. An example of such software is a computer-aided engineering design system whose malfunctioning might result in a design fault in the object being designed. This fault may cause injury to people if the designed system malfunctions. Another example of a secondary safety-critical system is the mental health care management system, MHC-PMS. Failure of this system, whereby an unstable patient may not be treated properly, could lead to that patient injuring themselves or others.

System reliability and system safety are related but a reliable system can be unsafe and vice versa. The software may still behave in such a way that the resultant system behavior leads to an accident. There are four reasons why software systems that are reliable are not necessarily safe:

1. We can never be 100% certain that a software system is fault-free and fault-tolerant. Undetected faults can be dormant for a long time and software failures can occur after many years of reliable operation.

2. The specification may be incomplete in that it does not describe the required behavior of the system in some critical situations. A high percentage of system malfunctions (Boehm et al., 1975; Endres, 1975; Lutz, 1993; Nakajo and Kume, 1991) are the result of specification rather than design errors. In a study of errors in embedded systems, Lutz concludes:

    > . . . difficulties with requirements are the key root cause of the safety-related software errors, which have persisted until integration and system testing.

3. Hardware malfunctions may cause the system to behave in an unpredictable way, and present the software with an unanticipated environment. When components are close to physical failure, they may behave erratically and generate signals that are outside the ranges that can be handled by the software.

Term	Definition
Accident (or mishap)	An unplanned event or sequence of events which results in human death or injury, damage to property, or to the environment. An overdose of insulin is an example of an accident.
Hazard	A condition with the potential for causing or contributing to an accident. A failure of the sensor that measures blood glucose is an example of a hazard.
Damage	A measure of the loss resulting from a mishap. Damage can range from many people being killed as a result of an accident to minor injury or property damage. Damage resulting from an overdose of insulin could be serious injury or the death of the user of the insulin pump.
Hazard severity	An assessment of the worst possible damage that could result from a particular hazard. Hazard severity can range from catastrophic, where many people are killed, to minor, where only minor damage results. When an individual death is a possibility, a reasonable assessment of hazard severity is 'very high.'
Hazard probability	The probability of the events occurring which create a hazard. Probability values tend to be arbitrary but range from 'probable' (say 1/100 chance of a hazard occurring) to 'implausible' (no conceivable situations are likely in which the hazard could occur). The probability of a sensor failure in the insulin pump that results in an overdose is probably low.
Risk	This is a measure of the probability that the system will cause an accident. The risk is assessed by considering the hazard probability, the hazard severity, and the probability that the hazard will lead to an accident. The risk of an insulin overdose is probably medium to low.

Figure 11.6
Safety terminology

4. The system operators may generate inputs that are not individually incorrect but which, in some situations, can lead to a system malfunction. An anecdotal example of this occurred when an aircraft undercarriage collapsed whilst the aircraft was on the ground. Apparently, a technician pressed a button that instructed the utility management software to raise the undercarriage. The software carried out the mechanic's instruction perfectly. However, the system should have disallowed the command unless the plane was in the air.

A specialized vocabulary has evolved to discuss safety-critical systems and it is important to understand the specific terms used. Figure 11.6 summarizes some definitions of important terms, with examples taken from the insulin pump system.

The key to assuring safety is to ensure either that accidents do not occur or that the consequences of an accident are minimal. This can be achieved in three complementary ways:

1. *Hazard avoidance* The system is designed so that hazards are avoided. For example, a cutting system that requires an operator to use two hands to press

separate buttons simultaneously avoids the hazard of the operator's hands being in the blade pathway.

2. *Hazard detection and removal* The system is designed so that hazards are detected and removed before they result in an accident. For example, a chemical plant system may detect excessive pressure and open a relief valve to reduce these pressures before an explosion occurs.

3. *Damage limitation* The system may include protection features that minimize the damage that may result from an accident. For example, an aircraft engine normally includes automatic fire extinguishers. If a fire occurs, it can often be controlled before it poses a threat to the aircraft.

Accidents most often occur when several things go wrong at the same time. An analysis of serious accidents (Perrow, 1984) suggests that they were almost all due to a combination of failures in different parts of a system. Unanticipated combinations of subsystem failures led to interactions that resulted in overall system failure. For example, failure of an air-conditioning system could lead to overheating, which then causes the system hardware to generate incorrect signals. Perrow also suggests that it is impossible to anticipate all possible combinations of failures. Accidents are therefore an inevitable part of using complex systems.

Some people have used this as an argument against software control. Because of the complexity of software, there are more interactions between the different parts of a system. This means that there will probably be more combinations of faults that could lead to system failure.

However, software-controlled systems can monitor a wider range of conditions than electro-mechanical systems. They can be adapted relatively easily. They use computer hardware, which has very high inherent reliability and which is physically small and lightweight. Software-controlled systems can provide sophisticated safety interlocks. They can support control strategies that reduce the amount of time people need to spend in hazardous environments. Although software control may introduce more ways in which a system can go wrong, it also allows better monitoring and protection and hence can contribute to improvements in system safety.

In all cases, it is important to maintain a sense of proportion about system safety. It is impossible to make a system 100% safe and society has to decide whether or not the consequences of an occasional accident are worth the benefits that come from the use of advanced technologies. It is also a social and political decision about how to deploy limited national resources to reduce risk to the population as a whole.

11.4 Security

Security is a system attribute that reflects the ability of the system to protect itself from external attacks, which may be accidental or deliberate. These external attacks are possible because most general-purpose computers are now networked and are

Term	Definition
Asset	Something of value which has to be protected. The asset may be the software system itself or data used by that system.
Exposure	Possible loss or harm to a computing system. This can be loss or damage to data, or can be a loss of time and effort if recovery is necessary after a security breach.
Vulnerability	A weakness in a computer-based system that may be exploited to cause loss or harm.
Attack	An exploitation of a system's vulnerability. Generally, this is from outside the system and is a deliberate attempt to cause some damage.
Threats	Circumstances that have potential to cause loss or harm. You can think of these as a system vulnerability that is subjected to an attack.
Control	A protective measure that reduces a system's vulnerability. Encryption is an example of a control that reduces a vulnerability of a weak access control system.

Figure 11.7
Security terminology

therefore accessible by outsiders. Examples of attacks might be the installation of viruses and Trojan horses, unauthorized use of system services or unauthorized modification of a system or its data. If you really want a secure system, it is best not to connect it to the Internet. Then, your security problems are limited to ensuring that authorized users do not abuse the system. In practice, however, there are huge benefits from networked access for most large systems so disconnecting from the Internet is not cost effective.

For some systems, security is the most important dimension of system dependability. Military systems, systems for electronic commerce, and systems that involve the processing and interchange of confidential information must be designed so that they achieve a high level of security. If an airline reservation system is unavailable, for example, this causes inconvenience and some delays in issuing tickets. However, if the system is insecure then an attacker could delete all bookings and it would be practically impossible for normal airline operations to continue.

As with other aspects of dependability, there is a specialized terminology associated with security. Some important terms, as discussed by Pfleeger (Pfleeger and Pfleeger, 2007), are defined in Figure 11.7. Figure 11.8 takes the security concepts described in Figure 11.7 and shows how they relate to the following scenario taken from the MHC-PMS:

> *Clinic staff log on to the MHC-PMS with a username and password. The system requires passwords to be at least eight letters long but allows any password to be set without further checking. A criminal finds out that a well-paid sports star is receiving treatment for mental health problems. He would like to gain illegal access to information in this system so that he can blackmail the star.*

Term	Example
Asset	The records of each patient that is receiving or has received treatment.
Exposure	Potential financial loss from future patients who do not seek treatment because they do not trust the clinic to maintain their data. Financial loss from legal action by the sports star. Loss of reputation.
Vulnerability	A weak password system which makes it easy for users to set guessable passwords. User ids that are the same as names.
Attack	An impersonation of an authorized user.
Threat	An unauthorized user will gain access to the system by guessing the credentials (login name and password) of an authorized user.
Control	A password checking system that disallows user passwords that are proper names or words that are normally included in a dictionary.

Figure 11.8
Examples of security
terminology

*By posing as a concerned relative and talking with the nurses in the mental
health clinic, he discovers how to access the system and personal information
about the nurses. By checking name badges, he discovers the names of some of
the people allowed access. He then attempts to log on to the system by using
these names and systematically guessing possible passwords (such as children's names).*

In any networked system, there are three main types of security threats:

1. *Threats to the confidentiality of the system and its data* These can disclose information to people or programs that are not authorized to have access to that
   information.

2. *Threats to the integrity of the system and its data* These threats can damage or
   corrupt the software or its data.

3. *Threats to the availability of the system and its data* These threats can restrict
   access to the software or its data for authorized users.

These threats are, of course, interdependent. If an attack makes the system
unavailable, then you will not be able to update information that changes with
time. This means that the integrity of the system may be compromised. If an
attack succeeds and the integrity of the system is compromised, then it may have
to be taken down to repair the problem. Therefore, the availability of the system
is reduced.

In practice, most vulnerabilities in sociotechnical systems result from human failings rather than technical problems. People choose easy-to-guess passwords or write

down their passwords in places where they can be found. System administrators make errors in setting up access control or configuration files and users don't install or use protection software. However, as I discussed in Section 10.5, we have to be very careful when classifying a problem as a user error. Human problems often reflect poor systems design decisions that require, for example, frequent password changes (so that users write down their passwords) or complex configuration mechanisms.

The controls that you might put in place to enhance system security are comparable to those for reliability and safety:

Prevention

1. *Vulnerability avoidance* Controls that are intended to ensure that attacks are unsuccessful. The strategy here is to design the system so that security problems are avoided. For example, sensitive military systems are not connected to public networks so that external access is impossible. You should also think of encryption as a control based on avoidance. Any unauthorized access to encrypted data means that it cannot be read by the attacker. In practice, it is very expensive and time consuming to crack strong encryption.

   Detection

2. *Attack detection and neutralization* Controls that are intended to detect and repel attacks. These controls involve including functionality in a system that monitors its operation and checks for unusual patterns of activity. If these are detected, then action may be taken, such as shutting down parts of the system, restricting access to certain users, etc.

   Correction

3. *Exposure limitation and recovery* Controls that support recovery from problems. These can range from automated backup strategies and information 'mirroring' to insurance policies that cover the costs associated with a successful attack on the system.

Without a reasonable level of security, we cannot be confident in a system's availability, reliability, and safety. Methods for certifying availability, reliability, and security assume that the operational software is the same as the software that was originally installed. If the system has been attacked and the software has been compromised in some way (for example, if the software has been modified to include a worm), then the reliability and safety arguments no longer hold.

Errors in the development of a system can lead to security loopholes. If a system does not respond to unexpected inputs or if array bounds are not checked, then attackers can exploit these weaknesses to gain access to the system. Major security incidents such as the original Internet worm (Spafford, 1989) and the Code Red worm more than 10 years later (Berghel, 2001) took advantage of the same vulnerability. Programs in C# do not include array bound checking, so it is possible to overwrite part of memory with code that allows unauthorized access to the system.

KEY POINTS

■ Failure of critical computer systems can lead to large economic losses, serious information loss, physical damage, or threats to human life.

■ The dependability of a computer system is a system property that reflects the user's degree of trust in the system. The most important dimensions of dependability are availability, reliability, safety, and security.

■ The availability of a system is the probability that the system will be able to deliver services to its users when requested to do so. Reliability is the probability that system services will be delivered as specified.

■ Perceived reliability is related to the probability of an error occurring in operational use. A program may contain known faults but may still be experienced as reliable by its users. They may never use features of the system that are affected by the faults.

■ The safety of a system is a system attribute that reflects the system's ability to operate, normally or abnormally, without injury to people or damage to the environment.

■ Security reflects the ability of a system to protect itself against external attacks. Security failures may lead to loss of availability, damage to the system or its data, or the leakage of information to unauthorized people.

■ Without a reasonable level of security, the availability, reliability, and safety of the system may be compromised if external attacks damage the system. If a system is unreliable, it is difficult to ensure system safety or security, as they may be compromised by system failures.

FURTHER READING

'The evolution of information assurance'. An excellent article discussing the need to protect critical information in an organization from accidents and attacks. (R. Cummings, *IEEE Computer*, **35** (12), December 2002.) http://dx.doi.org/10.1109/MC.2002.1106181.

'Designing Safety Critical Computer Systems'. This is a good introduction to the field of safety-critical systems, which discusses the fundamental concepts of hazards and risks. More accessible than Dunn's book on safety-critical systems. (W. R. Dunn, *IEEE Computer,* **36** (11), November 2003.) http://dx.doi.org/10.1109/MC.2003.1244533.

Secrets and Lies: Digital Security in a Networked World. An excellent, very readable book on computer security which approaches the subject from a sociotechnical perspective. Schneier's columns on security issues in general (URL below) are also very good. (B. Schneier, John Wiley & Sons, 2004.) http://www.schneier.com/essays.html.

EXERCISES

11.1. Suggest six reasons why software dependability is important in most sociotechnical systems.

11.2. What are the most important dimensions of system dependability?

11.3. Why do the costs of assuring dependability increase exponentially as the reliability requirement increases?

11.4. Giving reasons for your answer, suggest which dependability attributes are likely to be most critical for the following systems:

An Internet server provided by an ISP with thousands of customers

A computer-controlled scalpel used in keyhole surgery

A directional control system used in a satellite launch vehicle

An Internet-based personal finance management system

11.5. Identify six consumer products that are likely to be controlled by safety-critical software systems.

11.6. Reliability and safety are related but distinct dependability attributes. Describe the most important distinction between these attributes and explain why it is possible for a reliable system to be unsafe and vice versa.

11.7. In a medical system that is designed to deliver radiation to treat tumors, suggest one hazard that may arise and propose one software feature that may be used to ensure that the identified hazard does not result in an accident.

11.8. In computer security terms, explain the differences between an attack and a threat.

11.9. Using the MHC-PMS as an example, identify three threats to this system (in addition to the threat shown in Figure 11.8). Suggest controls that might be put in place to reduce the chances of a successful attack based on these threats.

11.10. As an expert in computer security, you have been approached by an organization that campaigns for the rights of torture victims and have been asked to help the organization gain unauthorized access to the computer systems of an American company. This will help them confirm or deny that this company is selling equipment that is used directly in the torture of political prisoners. Discuss the ethical dilemmas that this request raises and how you would react to this request.

REFERENCES

Adams, E. N. (1984). 'Optimizing preventative service of software products'. *IBM J. Res & Dev.,* **28** (1), 2–14.

Berghel, H. (2001). 'The Code Red Worm'. *Comm. ACM,* **44** (12), 15–19.

Boehm, B. W., McClean, R. L. and Urfig, D. B. (1975). 'Some experience with automated aids to the design of large-scale reliable software'. *IEEE Trans. on Software Engineering.,* **SE-1** (1), 125–33.

Ellison, R., Linger, R., Lipson, H., Mead, N. and Moore, A. (2002). 'Foundations of Survivable Systems Engineering'. *Crosstalk: The Journal of Defense Software Engineering,* **12**, 10–15.

Ellison, R. J., Fisher, D. A., Linger, R. C., Lipson, H. F., Longstaff, T. A. and Mead, N. R. (1999a). 'Survivability: Protecting Your Critical Systems'. *IEEE Internet Computing,* **3** (6), 55–63.

Ellison, R. J., Linger, R. C., Longstaff, T. and Mead, N. R. (1999b). 'Survivable Network System Analysis: A Case Study'. *IEEE Software,* **16** (4), 70–7.

Endres, A. (1975). 'An analysis of errors and their causes in system programs'. *IEEE Trans. on Software Engineering.,* **SE-1** (2), 140–9.

Laprie, J.-C. (1995). 'Dependable Computing: Concepts, Limits, Challenges'. FTCS- 25: 25th IEEE Symposium on Fault-Tolerant Computing, Pasadena, Calif.: IEEE Press.

Littlewood, B. (1990). 'Software Reliability Growth Models'. In *Software Reliability Handbook.* Rook, P. (ed.). Amsterdam: Elsevier. 401–412.

Lutz, R. R. (1993). 'Analysing Software Requirements Errors in Safety-Critical Embedded Systems'. RE'93, San Diego, Calif: IEEE.

Mills, H. D., Dyer, M. and Linger, R. (1987). 'Cleanroom Software Engineering'. *IEEE Software,* **4** (5), 19–25.

Nakajo, T. and Kume, H. (1991). 'A Case History Analysis of Software Error-Cause Relationships'. *IEEE Trans. on Software Eng.,* **18** (8), 830–8.

Perrow, C. (1984). *Normal Accidents: Living with High-Risk Technology.* New York: Basic Books.

Pfleeger, C. P. and Pfleeger, S. L. (2007). *Security in Computing, 4th edition.* Boston: Addison-Wesley.

Spafford, E. (1989). 'The Internet Worm: Crisis and Aftermath'. *Comm. ACM,* **32** (6), 678–87.

12

Dependability and security specification

Objectives

The objective of this chapter is to explain how to specify functional and non-functional dependability and security requirements. When you have read this chapter, you will:

- understand how a risk-driven approach can be used for identifying and analyzing safety, reliability, and security requirements;

- understand how fault trees can be used to help analyze risks and derive safety requirements;

- have been introduced to metrics for reliability specification and how these are used to specify measurable reliability requirements;

- know the different types of security requirements that may be required in a complex system;

- be aware of the advantages and disadvantages of using formal, mathematical specifications of a system.

Contents

In September 1993, a plane landed at Warsaw airport in Poland during a thunderstorm. For nine seconds after landing, the brakes on the computer-controlled braking system did not work. The braking system had not recognized that the plane had landed and assumed that the aircraft was still airborne. A safety feature on the aircraft had stopped the deployment of the reverse thrust system, which slows down the aircraft, because this can be dangerous if the plane is in the air. The plane ran off the end of the runway, hit an earth bank, and caught fire.

The inquiry into the accident showed that the braking system software had operated according to its specification. There were no errors in the program. However, the software specification was incomplete and had not taken into account a rare situation, which arose in this case. The software worked but the system failed.

This illustrates that system dependability does not just depend on good engineering. It also requires attention to detail when the system requirements are derived and the inclusion of special software requirements that are geared to ensuring the dependability and security of a system. Those dependability and security requirements are of two types:

1. Functional requirements, which define checking and recovery facilities that should be included in the system and features that provide protection against system failures and external attacks.

2. Non-functional requirements, which define the required reliability and availability of the system.

The starting point for generating functional dependability and security requirements is often high-level business or domain rules, policies, or regulations. These are high-level requirements that are perhaps best described as 'shall not' requirements. By contrast, with normal functional requirements that define what the system shall do, 'shall not' requirements define system behavior that is unacceptable. Examples of 'shall not' requirements are:

"The system shall not allow users to modify access permissions on any files that they have not created." (security)

"The system shall not allow reverse thrust mode to be selected when the aircraft is in flight." (safety)

"The system shall not allow the simultaneous activation of more than three alarm signals." (safety)

These 'shall not' requirements cannot be implemented directly but have to be decomposed into more specific software functional requirements. Alternatively, they may be implemented through system design decisions such as a decision to use particular types of equipment in the system.

Figure 12.1 Risk-driven specification

12.1 Risk-driven requirements specification

Dependability and security requirements can be thought of as protection requirements. These specify how a system should protect itself from internal faults, stop system failures causing damage to its environment, stop accidents or attacks from the system's environment damaging the system, and facilitate recovery in the event of failure. To discover these protection requirements, you need to understand the risks to the system and its environment. A risk-driven approach to requirements specification takes into account the dangerous events that may occur, the probability that these will actually occur, the probability that damage will result from such an event, and the extent of the damage caused. Security and dependability requirements can then be established, based on an analysis of possible causes of dangerous events.

Risk-driven specification is an approach that has been widely used by safety- and security-critical systems developers. It focuses on those events that could cause the most damage or that are likely to occur frequently. Events that have only minor consequences or that are extremely rare may be ignored. In safety-critical systems, the risks are associated with hazards that can result in accidents; in security-critical systems, the risks come from insider and outsider attacks on a system that are intended to exploit possible vulnerabilities.

A general risk-driven specification process (Figure 12.1) involves understanding the risks faced by the system, discovering their root causes, and generating requirements to manage these risks. The stages in this process are:

1. *Risk identification* Potential risks to the system are identified. These are dependent on the environment in which the system is to be used. Risks may arise from interactions between the system and rare conditions in its operating environment. The Warsaw accident that I discussed earlier happened when crosswinds generated during a thunderstorm caused the plane to tilt so that (unusually) it landed on one wheel rather than two wheels.

2. *Risk analysis and classification* Each risk is considered separately. Those that are potentially serious and not implausible are selected for further analysis.

At this stage, risks may be eliminated because they are unlikely to arise or because they cannot be detected by the software (e.g., an allergic reaction to the sensor in the insulin pump system).

3. *Risk decomposition* Each risk is analyzed to discover potential root causes of that risk. Root causes are the reasons why a system may fail. They may be software or hardware errors or inherent vulnerabilities that result from system design decisions.

4. *Risk reduction* Proposals for ways in which the identified risks may be reduced or eliminated are made. These contribute to the system dependability requirements that define the defenses against the risk and how the risk will be managed.

For large systems, risk analysis may be structured into phases (Leveson, 1995), where each phase considers different types of risks:

1. Preliminary risk analysis, where major risks from the system's environment are identified. These are independent from the technology used for system development. The aim of preliminary risk analysis is to develop an initial set of security and dependability requirements for the system.

2. Life-cycle risk analysis, which takes place during system development and which is mostly concerned with risks that arise from system design decisions. Different technologies and system architectures have their own associated risks. At this stage, you should extend the requirements to protect against these risks.

3. Operational risk analysis, which is concerned with the system user interface and risks from operator errors. Again, once decisions have been made on the user interface design, further protection requirements may have to be added.

These phases are necessary because it is impossible to make all dependability and security decisions without complete information about the system implementation. Security and dependability requirements are particularly affected by technology choices and design decisions. System checks may have to be included to ensure that third-party components have operated correctly. Security requirements may have to be modified because they conflict with the security features that are provided by an off-the-shelf system.

For example, a security requirement may be that users should identify themselves to a system using a pass phrase rather than a password. Pass phrases are considered to be more secure than passwords. They are harder for an attacker to guess or to discover using an automated password cracking system. However, if a decision is made to use an existing system that only supports password-based authentication, then this security requirement cannot be supported. It may then be necessary to include additional functionality in the system to compensate for the increased risks of using passwords rather than pass phrases.

The IEC standard for safety management

The IEC (International Electrotechnical Commission) has defined a standard for safety management for protection systems (i.e., systems that are intended to trigger safeguards when some dangerous situation arises). An example of a protection system is a system that automatically stops a train if it goes through a red signal. This standard includes extensive guidance on the process of safety specification.

http://www.SoftwareEngineering-9.com/Web/SafetyLifeCycle/

12.2 Safety specification

Safety-critical systems are systems in which failures may affect the environment of the system and cause injury or death to the people in that environment. The principal concern of safety specification is to identify requirements that will minimize the probability that such system failures will occur. Safety requirements are primarily protection requirements and are not concerned with normal system operation. They may specify that the system should be shut down so that safety is maintained. In deriving safety requirements, you therefore need to find an acceptable balance between safety and functionality and avoid overprotection. There is no point in building a very safe system if it does not operate in a cost-effective way.

Recall from the discussion in Chapter 10 that safety-critical systems use a specialized terminology where a hazard is something that could (but need not) result in death or injury to a person, and a risk is the probability that the system will enter a hazardous state. Therefore safety specification is usually focused on the hazards that may arise in a given situation, and the events that can lead to these hazards.

The activities in the general risk-based specification process, shown in Figure 12.1, map onto the safety specification process as follows:

1. *Risk identification* In safety specification, this is the hazard identification process that identifies hazards that may threaten the system.

2. *Risk analysis* This is a process of hazard assessment to decide which hazards are the most dangerous and/or the most likely to occur. These should be prioritized when deriving safety requirements.

3. *Risk decomposition* This process is concerned with discovering the events that can lead to the occurrence of a hazard. In safety specification, the process is known as hazard analysis.

4. *Risk reduction* This process is based on the outcome of hazard analysis and leads to identification of safety requirements. These may be concerned with ensuring that a hazard does not arise or lead to an accident or that if an accident does occur, the associated damage is minimized.

12.2.1 Hazard identification

In safety-critical systems, the principal risks come from hazards that can lead to an accident. You can tackle the hazard identification problem by considering different types of hazards, such as physical hazards, electrical hazards, biological hazards, radiation hazards, service failure hazards, and so on. Each of these classes can then be analyzed to discover specific hazards that could occur. Possible combinations of hazards that are potentially dangerous must also be identified.

The insulin pump system that I have used as an example in earlier chapters is a safety-critical system, because failure can cause injury or even death to the system user. Accidents that may occur when using this machine include the user suffering from long-term consequences of poor blood sugar control (eye, heart, and kidney problems); cognitive dysfunction as a result of low blood sugar levels; or the occurrence of some other medical conditions, such as an allergic reaction.

Some of the hazards in the insulin pump system are:

- insulin overdose computation (service failure);

- insulin underdose computation (service failure);

- failure of the hardware monitoring system (service failure);

- power failure due to exhausted battery (electrical);

- electrical interference with other medical equipment such as a heart pacemaker (electrical);

- poor sensor and actuator contact caused by incorrect fitting (physical);

- parts of machine breaking off in patient's body (physical);

- infection caused by introduction of machine (biological);

- allergic reaction to the materials or insulin used in the machine (biological).

Experienced engineers, working with domain experts and professional safety advisers, identify hazards from previous experience and from an analysis of the application domain. Group working techniques such as brainstorming may be used, where a group of people exchange ideas. For the insulin pump system, people who may be involved include doctors, medical physicists, and engineers and software designers.

Software-related hazards are normally concerned with failure to deliver a system service, or with the failure of monitoring and protection systems. Monitoring and protection systems are included in a device to detect conditions, such as low battery levels, which could lead to device failure.

12.2.2 Hazard assessment

The hazard assessment process focuses on understanding the probability that a hazard will occur and the consequences if an accident or incident associated with that hazard should occur. You need to make this analysis to understand whether a hazard

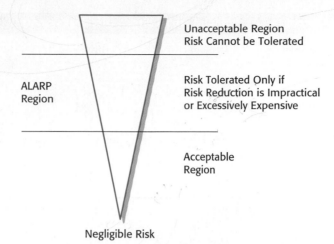

Unacceptable Region
Risk Cannot be Tolerated

ALARP
Region

Risk Tolerated Only if
Risk Reduction is Impractical
or Excessively Expensive

Acceptable
Region

Negligible Risk

Figure 12.2
The risk triangle

is a serious threat to the system or environment. The analysis also provides a basis for deciding on how to manage the risk associated with the hazard.

For each hazard, the outcome of the analysis and classification process is a statement of acceptability. This is expressed in terms of risk, where the risk takes into account the likelihood of an accident and its consequences. There are three risk categories that you can use in hazard assessment:

1. Intolerable risks in safety-critical systems are those that threaten human life. The system must be designed so that such hazards either cannot arise or, that if they do, features in the system will ensure that they are detected before they cause an accident. In the case of the insulin pump, an intolerable risk is that an overdose of insulin should be delivered.

2. As low as reasonably practical (ALARP) risks are those that have less serious consequences or that are serious but have a very low probability of occurrence. The system should be designed so that the probability of an accident arising because of a hazard is minimized, subject to other considerations such as cost and delivery. An ALARP risk for an insulin pump might be the failure of the hardware monitoring system. The consequences of this are, at worst, a short-term insulin underdose. This is a situation that would not lead to a serious accident.

3. Acceptable risks are those where the associated accidents normally result in minor damage. System designers should take all possible steps to reduce 'acceptable' risks, so long as these do not increase costs, delivery time, or other non-functional system attributes. An acceptable risk in the case of the insulin pump might be the risk of an allergic reaction arising in the user. This usually causes only minor skin irritation. It would not be worth using special, more expensive materials in the device to reduce this risk.

Figure 12.2 (Brazendale and Bell, 1994), developed for safety-critical systems, shows these three regions. The shape of the diagram reflects the costs of ensuring risks do not result in incidents or accidents. The cost of system design to cope with

Identified hazard	Hazard probability	Accident severity	Estimated risk	Acceptability
1. Insulin overdose computation	Medium	High	High	Intolerable
2. Insulin underdose computation	Medium	Low	Low	Acceptable
3. Failure of hardware monitoring system	Medium	Medium	Low	ALARP
4. Power failure	High	Low	Low	Acceptable
5. Machine incorrectly fitted	High	High	High	Intolerable
6. Machine breaks in patient	Low	High	Medium	ALARP
7. Machine causes infection	Medium	Medium	Medium	ALARP
8. Electrical interference	Low	High	Medium	ALARP
9. Allergic reaction	Low	Low	Low	Acceptable

Figure 12.3 Risk classification for the insulin pump

the risk is indicated by the width of the triangle. The highest costs are incurred by risks at the top of the diagram, the lowest costs by risks at the apex of the triangle.

The boundaries between the regions in Figure 12.2 are not technical but rather depend on social and political factors. Over time, society has become more risk-averse so the boundaries have moved downwards. Although the financial costs of accepting risks and paying for any resulting accidents may be less than the costs of accident prevention, public opinion may demand that money be spent to reduce the likelihood of a system accident, thus incurring additional costs.

For example, it may be cheaper for a company to clean up pollution on the rare occasion it occurs, rather than to install systems for pollution prevention. However, because the public and the press will not tolerate such accidents, clearing up the damage rather than preventing the accident is no longer acceptable. Such events may also lead to a reclassification of risk. For example, risks that were thought to be improbable (and hence in the ALARP region) may be reclassified as intolerable because of events, such as terrorist attacks, or accidents that have occurred.

Hazard assessment involves estimating hazard probability and risk severity. This is usually difficult as hazards and accidents are uncommon so the engineers involved may not have direct experience of previous incidents or accidents. Probabilities and severities are assigned using relative terms such as 'probable,' 'unlikely,' and 'rare' and 'high,' 'medium,' and 'low'. It is only possible to quantify these terms if enough accident and incident data is available for statistical analysis.

Figure 12.3 shows a risk classification for the hazards identified in the previous section for the insulin delivery system. I have separated the hazards that relate to the incorrect computation of insulin into an insulin overdose and an insulin underdose. An insulin overdose is potentially more serious than an insulin underdose in the short term. Insulin overdose can result in cognitive dysfunction, coma, and ultimately death. Insulin underdoses lead to high levels of blood sugar. In the short term, these cause tiredness but are not very serious; in the longer term, however, they can lead to serious heart, kidney, and eye problems.

Hazards 4–9 in Figure 12.3 are not software related, but software nevertheless has a role to play in hazard detection. The hardware monitoring software should monitor the system state and warn of potential problems. The warning will often allow the hazard to be detected before it causes an accident. Examples of hazards that might be detected are power failure, which is detected by monitoring the battery, and incorrect placement of machine, which may be detected by monitoring signals from the blood sugar sensor.

The monitoring software in the system is, of course, safety related. Failure to detect a hazard could result in an accident. If the monitoring system fails but the hardware is working correctly then this is not a serious failure. However, if the monitoring system fails and hardware failure cannot then be detected, then this could have more serious consequences.

12.2.3 Hazard analysis

Hazard analysis is the process of discovering the root causes of hazards in a safety-critical system. Your aim is to find out what events or combination of events could cause a system failure that results in a hazard. To do this, you can use either a top-down or a bottom-up approach. Deductive, top-down techniques, which tend to be easier to use, start with the hazard and work up from that to the possible system failure. Inductive, bottom-up techniques start with a proposed system failure and identify what hazards might result from that failure.

Various techniques have been proposed as possible approaches to hazard decomposition or analysis. These are summarized by Storey (1996). They include reviews and checklists, formal techniques such as Petri net analysis (Peterson, 1981), formal logic (Jahanian and Mok, 1986), and fault tree analysis (Leveson and Stolzy, 1987; Storey, 1996). As I don't have space to cover all of these techniques here, I focus on a widely used approach to hazard analysis based on fault trees. This technique is fairly easy to understand without specialist domain knowledge.

To do a fault tree analysis, you start with the hazards that have been identified. For each hazard, you then work backwards to discover the possible causes of that hazard. You put the hazard at the root of the tree and identify the system states that can lead to that hazard. For each of these states, you then identify further system states that can lead to them. You continue this decomposition until you reach the root cause(s) of the risk. Hazards that can only arise from a combination of root causes are usually less likely to lead to an accident than hazards with a single root cause.

Figure 12.4 is a fault tree for the software-related hazards in the insulin delivery system that could lead to an incorrect dose of insulin being delivered. In this case, I have

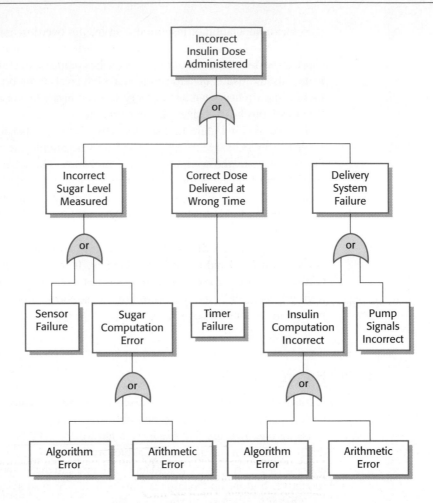

Figure 12.4 An example of a fault tree

merged insulin underdose and insulin overdose into a single hazard, namely 'incorrect insulin dose administered.' This reduces the number of fault trees that are required. Of course, when you specify how the software should react to this hazard, you have to distinguish between an insulin underdose and an insulin overdose. As I have said, they are not equally serious—in the short term, an overdose is the more serious hazard.

From Figure 12.4, you can see that:

1. There are three conditions that could lead to the administration of an incorrect dose of insulin. The level of blood sugar may have been incorrectly measured so the insulin requirement has been computed with an incorrect input. The delivery system may not respond correctly to commands specifying the amount of insulin to be injected. Alternatively, the dose may be correctly computed but it is delivered too early or too late.

2. The left branch of the fault tree, concerned with incorrect measurement of the blood sugar level, looks at how this might happen. This could occur either

because the sensor that provides an input to calculate the sugar level has failed or because the calculation of the blood sugar level has been carried out incorrectly. The sugar level is calculated from some measured parameter, such as the conductivity of the skin. Incorrect computation can result from either an incorrect algorithm or an arithmetic error that results from the use of floating point numbers.

3. The central branch of the tree is concerned with timing problems and concludes that these can only result from system timer failure.

4. The right branch of the tree, concerned with delivery system failure, examines possible causes of this failure. These could result from an incorrect computation of the insulin requirement, or from a failure to send the correct signals to the pump that delivers the insulin. Again, an incorrect computation can result from algorithm failure or arithmetic errors.

Fault trees are also used to identify potential hardware problems. Hardware fault trees may provide insights into requirements for software to detect and, perhaps, correct these problems. For example, insulin doses are not administered at a very high frequency, no more than two or three times per hour and sometimes less often than this. Therefore, processor capacity is available to run diagnostic and self-checking programs. Hardware errors such as sensor, pump, or timer errors can be discovered and warnings issued before they have a serious effect on the patient.

12.2.4 Risk reduction

Once potential risks and their root causes have been identified, you are then able to derive safety requirements that manage the risks and ensure that incidents or accidents do not occur. There are three possible strategies that you can use:

1. *Hazard avoidance* The system is designed so that the hazard cannot occur.

2. *Hazard detection and removal* The system is designed so that hazards are detected and neutralized before they result in an accident.

3. *Damage limitation* The system is designed so that the consequences of an accident are minimized.

Normally, designers of critical systems use a combination of these approaches. In a safety-critical system, intolerable hazards may be handled by minimizing their probability and adding a protection system that provides a safety backup. For example, in a chemical plant control system, the system will attempt to detect and avoid excess pressure in the reactor. However, there may also be an independent protection system that monitors the pressure and opens a relief valve if high pressure is detected.

In the insulin delivery system, a 'safe state' is a shutdown state where no insulin is injected. Over a short period this is not a threat to the diabetic's health. For the

SR1: The system shall not deliver a single dose of insulin that is greater than a specified maximum dose for a system user.

SR2: The system shall not deliver a daily cumulative dose of insulin that is greater than a specified maximum daily dose for a system user.

SR3: The system shall include a hardware diagnostic facility that shall be executed at least four times per hour.

SR4: The system shall include an exception handler for all of the exceptions that are identified in Table 3.

SR5: The audible alarm shall be sounded when any hardware or software anomaly is discovered and a diagnostic message, as defined in Table 4, shall be displayed.

SR6: In the event of an alarm, insulin delivery shall be suspended until the user has reset the system and cleared the alarm.

Figure 12.5
Examples of safety
requirements

software failures that could lead to an incorrect dose of insulin are considered, the following 'solutions' might be developed:

1. *Arithmetic error* This may occur when an arithmetic computation causes a representation failure. The specification should identify all possible arithmetic errors that may occur and state that an exception handler must be included for each possible error. The specification should set out the action to be taken for each of these errors. The default safe action is to shut down the delivery system and activate a warning alarm.

2. *Algorithmic error* This is a more difficult situation as there is no clear program exception that must be handled. This type of error could be detected by comparing the required insulin dose computed with the previously delivered dose. If it is much higher, this may mean that the amount has been computed incorrectly. The system may also keep track of the dose sequence. After a number of above-average doses have been delivered, a warning may be issued and further dosage limited.

Some of the resulting safety requirements for the insulin pump software are shown in Figure 12.5. These are user requirements and, naturally, they would be expressed in more detail in the system requirements specification. In Figure 12.5, the references to Tables 3 and 4 relate to tables that are included in the requirements document—they are not shown here.

12.3 Reliability specification

As I discussed in Chapter 10, the overall reliability of a system depends on the hardware reliability, the software reliability, and the reliability of the system operators. The system software has to take this into account. As well as including requirements that compensate for software failure, there may also be related reliability requirements to help detect and recover from hardware failures and operator errors.

Reliability is different from safety and security in that it is a measurable system attribute. That is, it is possible to specify the level of reliability that is required, monitor the system's operation over time, and check if the required reliability has been achieved. For example, a reliability requirement might be that system failures that require a reboot should not occur more than once per week. Every time such a failure occurs, it can be logged and you can check if the required level of reliability has been achieved. If not, you either modify your reliability requirement or submit a change request to address the underlying system problems. You may decide to accept a lower level of reliability because of the costs of changing the system to improve reliability or because fixing the problem may have adverse side effects, such as lower performance or throughput.

By contrast, both safety and security are about avoiding undesirable situations, rather than specifying a desired 'level' of safety or security. Even one such situation in the lifetime of a system may be unacceptable and, if it occurs, system changes have to be made. It makes no sense to make statements like 'system faults should result in fewer than 10 injuries per year.' As soon as one injury occurs, the system problem must be rectified.

Reliability requirements are, therefore, of two kinds:

1. Non-functional requirements, which define the number of failures that are acceptable during normal use of the system, or the time in which the system is unavailable for use. These are quantitative reliability requirements.

2. Functional requirements, which define system and software functions that avoid, detect, or tolerate faults in the software and so ensure that these faults do not lead to system failure.

Quantitative reliability requirements lead to related functional system requirements. To achieve some required level of reliability, the functional and design requirements of the system should specify the faults to be detected and the actions that should be taken to ensure that these faults do not lead to system failures.

The process of reliability specification can be based on the general risk-driven specification process shown in Figure 12.1:

1. *Risk identification* At this stage, you identify the types of system failures that may lead to economic losses of some kind. For example, an e-commerce system may be unavailable so that customers cannot place orders, or a failure that corrupts data may require time to restore the system database from a backup and rerun transactions that have been processed. The list of possible failure types, shown in Figure 12.6, can be used as a starting point for risk identification.

2. *Risk analysis* This involves estimating the costs and consequences of different types of software failure and selecting high-consequence failures for further analysis.

Failure type	Description
Loss of service	The system is unavailable and cannot deliver its services to users. You may separate this into loss of critical services and loss of non-critical services, where the consequences of a failure in non-critical services are less than the consequences of critical service failure.
Incorrect service delivery	The system does not deliver a service correctly to users. Again, this may be specified in terms of minor and major errors or errors in the delivery of critical and non-critical services.
System/data corruption	The failure of the system causes damage to the system itself or its data. This will usually but not necessarily be in conjunction with other types of failures.

Figure 12.6   Types
of system failure

3. *Risk decomposition* At this stage, you do a root cause analysis of serious and probable system failures. However, this may be impossible at the requirements stage as the root causes may depend on system design decisions. You may have to return to this activity during design and development.

4. *Risk reduction* At this stage, you should generate quantitative reliability specifications that set out the acceptable probabilities of the different types of failures. These should, of course, take into account the costs of failures. You may use different probabilities for different system services. You may also generate functional reliability requirements. Again, this may have to wait until system design decisions have been made. However, as I discuss in Section 12.3.2, it is sometimes difficult to create quantitative specifications. You may only be able to identify functional reliability requirements.

12.3.1   Reliability metrics

In general terms, reliability can be specified as a probability that a system failure will occur when a system is in use within a specified operating environment. If you are willing to accept, for example, that 1 in any 1,000 transactions may fail, then you can specify the failure probability as 0.001. This doesn't mean, of course, that you will see 1 failure in every 1,000 transactions. It means that if you observe N thousand transactions, the number of failures that you observe should be around N. You can refine this for different kinds of failure or for different parts of the system. You may decide that critical components must have a lower probability of failure than noncritical components.

There are two important metrics that are used to specify reliability plus an additional metric that is used to specify the related system attribute of availability. The choice of metric depends on the type of system that is being specified and the requirements of the application domain. The metrics are:

1. *Probability of failure on demand (POFOD)* If you use this metric, you define the probability that a demand for service from a system will result in a system

Availability	Explanation
0.9	The system is available for 90% of the time. This means that, in a 24-hour period (1,440 minutes), the system will be unavailable for 144 minutes.
0.99	In a 24-hour period, the system is unavailable for 14.4 minutes.
0.999	The system is unavailable for 84 seconds in a 24-hour period.
0.9999	The system is unavailable for 8.4 seconds in a 24-hour period. Roughly, one minute per week.

Figure 12.7
Availability
specification

failure. So, POFOD = 0.001 means that there is a 1/1,000 chance that a failure will occur when a demand is made.

2. *Rate of occurrence of failures (ROCOF)* This metric sets out the probable number of system failures that are likely to be observed relative to a certain time period (e.g., an hour), or to the number of system executions. In the example above, the ROCOF is 1/1,000. The reciprocal of ROCOF is the mean time to failure (MTTF), which is sometimes used as a reliability metric. MTTF is the average number of time units between observed system failures. Therefore, a ROCOF of two failures per hour implies that the mean time to failure is 30 minutes.

3. *Availability (AVAIL)* The availability of a system reflects its ability to deliver services when requested. AVAIL is the probability that a system will be operational when a demand is made for service. Therefore, an availability of 0.9999, means that, on average, the system will be available for 99.99% of the operating time. Figure 12.7 shows what different levels of availability mean in practice.

POFOD should be used as a reliability metric in situations where a failure on demand can lead to a serious system failure. This applies irrespective of the frequency of the demands. For example, a protection system that monitors a chemical reactor and shuts down the reaction if it is overheating should have its reliability specified using POFOD. Generally, demands on a protection system are infrequent as the system is a last line of defense, after all other recovery strategies have failed. Therefore a POFOD of 0.001 (1 failure in 1,000 demands) might seem to be risky, but if there are only two or three demands on the system in its lifetime, then you will probably never see a system failure.

ROCOF is the most appropriate metric to use in situations where demands on systems are made regularly rather than intermittently. For example, in a system that handles a large number of transactions, you may specify a ROCOF of 10 failures per day. This means that you are willing to accept that an average of 10 transactions per day will not complete successfully and will have to be canceled. Alternatively, you may specify ROCOF as the number of failures per 1,000 transactions.

If the absolute time between failures is important, you may specify the reliability as the mean time between failures. For example, if you are specifying the required reliability for a system with long transactions (such as a computer-aided design system), you should specify the reliability with a long mean time to failure. The MTTF should be much longer than the average time that a user works on his or her models without saving their results. This would mean that users would be unlikely to lose work through a system failure in any one session.

To assess the reliability of a system, you have to capture data about its operation. The data required may include:

1. The number of system failures given a number of requests for system services. This is used to measure the POFOD.

2. The time or the number of transactions between system failures plus the total elapsed time or total number of transactions. This is used to measure ROCOF and MTTF.

3. The repair or restart time after a system failure that leads to loss of service. This is used in the measurement of availability. Availability does not just depend on the time between failures but also on the time required to get the system back into operation.

The time units that may be used are calendar time or processor time or a discrete unit such as number of transactions. In systems that spend much of their time waiting to respond to a service request, such as telephone switching systems, the time unit that should be used is processor time. If you use calendar time, then this will include the time when the system was doing nothing.

You should use calendar time for systems that are in continuous operation. Monitoring systems, such as alarm systems, and other types of process control systems fall into this category. Systems that process transactions such as bank ATMs or airline reservation systems have variable loads placed on them depending on the time of day. In these cases, the unit of 'time' used could be the number of transactions (i.e., the ROCOF would be number of failed transactions per N thousand transactions).

12.3.2 Non-functional reliability requirements

Non-functional reliability requirements are quantitative specifications of the required reliability and availability of a system, calculated using one of the metrics described in the previous section. Quantitative reliability and availability specification has been used for many years in safety-critical systems but is only rarely used in business critical systems. However, as more and more companies demand 24/7 service from their systems, it is likely that such techniques will be increasingly used.

There are several advantages in deriving quantitative reliability specifications:

1. The process of deciding what required level of the reliability helps to clarify what stakeholders really need. It helps stakeholders understand that there are different types of system failure, and it makes clear to them that high levels of reliability are very expensive to achieve.

2. It provides a basis for assessing when to stop testing a system. You stop when the system has achieved its required reliability level.

3. It is a means of assessing different design strategies intended to improve the reliability of a system. You can make a judgment about how each strategy might lead to the required levels of reliability.

4. If a regulator has to approve a system before it goes into service (e.g., all systems that are critical to flight safety on an aircraft are regulated), then evidence that a required reliability target has been met is important for system certification.

To establish the required level of system reliability, you have to consider the associated losses that could result from a system failure. These are not simply financial losses, but also loss of reputation for a business. Loss of reputation means that customers will go elsewhere. Although the short-term losses from a system failure may be relatively small, the longer-term losses may be much more significant. For example, if you try to access an e-commerce site and find that it is unavailable, you may try to find what you want elsewhere rather than wait for the system to become available. If this happens more than once, you will probably not shop at that site again.

The problem with specifying reliability using metrics such as POFOD, ROCOF, and AVAIL is that it is possible to overspecify reliability and thus incur high development and validation costs. The reason for this is that system stakeholders find it difficult to translate their practical experience into quantitative specifications. They may think that a POFOD of 0.001 (1 failure in 1,000 demands) represents a relatively unreliable system. However, as I have explained, if demands for a service are uncommon, it actually represents a very high level of reliability.

If you specify reliability as a metric, it is obviously important to assess that the required level of reliability has been achieved. You do this assessment as part of system testing. To assess the reliability of a system statistically, you have to observe a number of failures. If you have, for example, a POFOD of 0.0001 (1 failure in 10,000 demands), then you may have to design tests that make 50 or 60 thousand demands on a system and where several failures are observed. It may be practically impossible to design and implement this number of tests. Therefore, overspecification of reliability leads to very high testing costs.

When you specify the availability of a system, you may have similar problems. Although a very high level of availability may seem to be desirable, most systems have very intermittent demand patterns (e.g., a business system will mostly be used during normal business hours) and a single availability figure does not really reflect user needs. You need high availability when the system is being used but not at other times. Depending, of course, on the type of system, there may be no real practical difference between an availability of 0.999 and an availability of 0.9999.

A fundamental problem with overspecification is that it may be practically impossible to show that a very high level of reliability or availability has been achieved. For example, say a system was intended for use in a safety-critical application and was therefore required to never fail over its total lifetime. Assume that 1,000 copies of the system are to be installed and the system is executed 1,000 times per second. The projected lifetime of the system is 10 years. The total number of system executions is therefore approximately $3*10^{14}$. There is no point in specifying that the rate of occurrence of failure should be $1/10^{15}$ executions (this allows for some safety factor) as you cannot test the system for long enough to validate this level of reliability.

Organizations must therefore be realistic about whether it is worth specifying and validating a very high level of reliability. High reliability levels are clearly justified in systems where reliable operation is critical, such as telephone switching systems, or where system failure may result in large economic losses. They are probably not justified for many types of business or scientific systems. Such systems have modest reliability requirements, as the costs of failure are simply processing delays and it is straightforward and relatively inexpensive to recover from these.

There are a number of steps that you can take to avoid the overspecification of system reliability:

1. Specify the availability and reliability requirements for different types of failures. There should be a lower probability of serious failures occurring than minor failures.

2. Specify the availability and reliability requirements for different services separately. Failures that affect the most critical services should be specified as less probable than those with only local effects. You may decide to limit the quantitative reliability specification to the most critical system services.

3. Decide whether you really need high reliability in a software system or whether the overall system dependability goals can be achieved in other ways. For example, you may use error detection mechanisms to check the outputs of a system and have processes in place to correct errors. There may then be no need for a high level of reliability in the system that generates the outputs.

To illustrate this latter point, consider the reliability requirements for a bank ATM system that dispenses cash and provides other services to customers. If there are hardware or software ATM problems, then these lead to incorrect entries in the customer account database. These could be avoided by specifying a very high level of hardware and software reliability in the ATM.

However, banks have many years of experience of how to identify and correct incorrect account transactions. They use accounting methods to detect when things have gone wrong. Most transactions that fail can simply be canceled, resulting in no loss to the bank and minor customer inconvenience. Banks that run ATM networks therefore accept that ATM failures may mean that a small number of transactions are incorrect but they think it more cost effective to fix these later rather than to incur very high costs in avoiding faulty transactions.

For a bank (and for the bank's customers), the availability of the ATM network is more important than whether or not individual ATM transactions fail. Lack of availability means more demand on counter services, customer dissatisfaction, engineering costs to repair the network, etc. Therefore, for transaction-based systems, such as banking and e-commerce systems, the focus of reliability specification is usually on specifying the availability of the system.

To specify the availability of an ATM network, you should identify the system services and specify the required availability for each of these. These are:

- the customer account database service;

- the individual services provided by an ATM such as 'withdraw cash,' 'provide account information,' etc.

Here, the database service is most critical as failure of this service means that all of the ATMs in the network are out of action. Therefore, you should specify this to have a high level of availability. In this case, an acceptable figure for database availability (ignoring issues such as scheduled maintenance and upgrades) would probably be around 0.9999, between 7 am and 11 pm. This means a down time of less than one minute per week. In practice, this would mean that very few customers would be affected and would only lead to minor customer inconvenience.

For an individual ATM, the overall availability depends on mechanical reliability and the fact that it can run out of cash. Software issues are likely to have less effect than factors such as these. Therefore, a lower level of availability for the ATM software is acceptable. The overall availability of the ATM software might therefore be specified as 0.999, which means that a machine might be unavailable for between one and two minutes each day.

To illustrate failure-based reliability specification, consider the reliability requirements for the control software in the insulin pump. This system delivers insulin a number of times per day and monitors the user's blood glucose several times per hour. Because the use of the system is intermittent and failure consequences are serious, the most appropriate reliability metric is POFOD (probability of failure on demand).

There are two possible types of failure in the insulin pump:

1. Transient software failures that can be repaired by user actions such as resetting or recalibrating the machine. For these types of failures, a relatively low value of POFOD (say 0.002) may be acceptable. This means that one failure may occur in every 500 demands made on the machine. This is approximately once every 3.5 days, because the blood sugar is checked about five times per hour.

2. Permanent software failures that require the software to be reinstalled by the manufacturer. The probability of this type of failure should be much lower. Roughly once a year is the minimum figure, so POFOD should be no more than 0.00002.

However, failure to deliver insulin does not have immediate safety implications, so commercial factors rather than the safety factors govern the level of reliability required. Service costs are high because users need fast repair and replacement. It is in the manufacturer's interest to limit the number of permanent failures that require repair.

RR1: A pre-defined range for all operator inputs shall be defined and the system shall check that all operator inputs fall within this pre-defined range. (Checking)

RR2: Copies of the patient database shall be maintained on two separate servers that are not housed in the same building. (Recovery, redundancy)

RR3: N-version programming shall be used to implement the braking control system. (Redundancy)

RR4: The system must be implemented in a safe subset of Ada and checked using static analysis. (Process)

Figure 12.8
Examples of
functional
reliability
requirements

12.3.3 Functional reliability specification

Functional reliability specification involves identifying requirements that define constraints and features that contribute to system reliability. For systems where the reliability has been quantitatively specified, these functional requirements may be necessary to ensure that a required level of reliability is achieved.

There are three types of functional reliability requirements for a system:

1. *Checking requirements* These requirements identify checks on inputs to the system to ensure that incorrect or out-of-range inputs are detected before they are processed by the system.

2. *Recovery requirements* These requirements are geared to helping the system recover after a failure has occurred. Typically, these requirements are concerned with maintaining copies of the system and its data and specifying how to restore system services after a failure.

3. *Redundancy requirements* These specify redundant features of the system that ensure that a single component failure does not lead to a complete loss of service. I discuss this in more detail in the next chapter.

In addition, the reliability requirements may include process requirements for reliability. These are requirements to ensure that good practice, known to reduce the number of faults in a system, is used in the development process. Some examples of functional reliability and process requirements are shown in Figure 12.8.

There are no simple rules for deriving functional reliability requirements. In organizations that develop critical systems, there is usually organizational knowledge about possible reliability requirements and how these impact the actual reliability of a system. These organizations may specialize in specific types of system such as railway control systems, so the reliability requirements can be reused across a range of systems

12.4 Security specification

The specification of security requirements for systems has something in common with safety requirements. It is impractical to specify them quantitatively, and security requirements are often 'shall not' requirements that define unacceptable system behavior rather than required system functionality. However, security is a more challenging problem than safety, for a number of reasons:

1. When considering safety, you can assume that the environment in which the system is installed is not hostile. No one is trying to cause a safety-related incident. When considering security, you have to assume that attacks on the system are deliberate and that the attacker may have knowledge of system weaknesses.

2. When system failures occur that pose a risk to safety, you look for the errors or omissions that have caused the failure. When deliberate attacks cause system failures, finding the root cause may be more difficult as the attacker may try to conceal the cause of the failure.

3. It is usually acceptable to shut down a system or to degrade system services to avoid a safety-related failure. However, attacks on a system may be so-called denial of service attacks, which are intended to shut down the system. Shutting down the system means that the attack has been successful.

4. Safety-related events are not generated by an intelligent adversary. An attacker can probe a system's defenses in a series of attacks, modifying the attacks as he or she learns more about the system and its responses.

These distinctions mean that security requirements usually have to be more extensive than safety requirements. Safety requirements lead to the generation of functional system requirements that provide protection against events and faults that could cause safety-related failures. They are mostly concerned with checking for problems and taking actions if these problems occur. By contrast, there are many types of security requirements that cover the different threats faced by a system. Firesmith (2003) has identified 10 types of security requirements that may be included in a system specification:

1. Identification requirements specify whether or not a system should identify its users before interacting with them.

2. Authentication requirements specify how users are identified.

3. Authorization requirements specify the privileges and access permissions of identified users.

4. Immunity requirements specify how a system should protect itself against viruses, worms, and similar threats.

5. Integrity requirements specify how data corruption can be avoided.

Security risk management

Safety is a legal issue and businesses cannot decide to opt out of producing safe systems. However, some aspects of security are business issues—a business can decide not to implement some security measures and to cover the losses that may result from this decision. Risk management is the process of deciding what assets must be protected and how much can be spent on protecting them.

http://www.SoftwareEngineering-9.com/Web/Security/RiskMan.html

6. Intrusion detection requirements specify what mechanisms should be used to detect attacks on the system.

7. Non-repudiation requirements specify that a party in a transaction cannot deny its involvement in that transaction.

8. Privacy requirements specify how data privacy is to be maintained.

9. Security auditing requirements specify how system use can be audited and checked.

10. System maintenance security requirements specify how an application can prevent authorized changes from accidentally defeating its security mechanisms.

Of course, you will not see all of these types of security requirements in every system. The particular requirements depend on the type of system, the situation of use, and the expected users.

The risk analysis and assessment process discussed in Section 12.1 may be used to identify system security requirements. As I discussed, there are three stages to this process:

1. *Preliminary risk analysis* At this stage, decisions on the detailed system requirements, the system design, or the implementation technology have not been made. The aim of this assessment process is to derive security requirements for the system as a whole.

2. *Life-cycle risk analysis* This risk assessment takes place during the system development life cycle after design choices have been made. The additional security requirements take account of the technologies used in building the system and system design and implementation decisions.

3. *Operational risk analysis* This risk assessment considers the risks posed by malicious attacks on the operational system by users, with or without insider knowledge of the system.

The risk assessment and analysis processes used in security requirements specification are variants of the generic risk-driven specification process discussed in

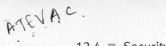

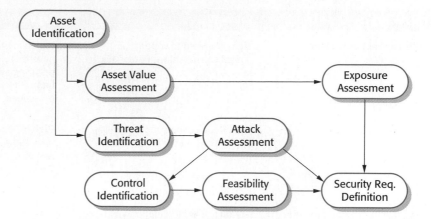

Figure 12.9 The preliminary risk assessment process for security requirements

Section 12.1. A risk-driven security requirements process is shown in Figure 12.9. This may appear to be different from the risk-driven process in Figure 12.1, but I indicate how each stage corresponds to stages in the generic process by including the generic process activity in brackets. The process stages are:

1. Asset identification, where the system assets that may require protection are identified. The system itself or particular system functions may be identified as assets as well as the data associated with the system (risk identification).

2. Asset value assessment, where you estimate the value of the identified assets (risk analysis).

3. Exposure assessment, where you assess the potential losses associated with each asset. This should take into account direct losses such as the theft of information, the costs of recovery, and the possible loss of reputation (risk analysis).

4. Threat identification, where you identify the threats to system assets (risk analysis).

5. Attack assessment, where you decompose each threat into attacks that might be made on the system and the possible ways in which these attacks may occur. You may use attack trees (Schneier, 1999) to analyze the possible attacks. These are similar to fault trees as you start with a threat at the root of the tree and identify possible causal attacks and how these might be made (risk decomposition).

6. Control identification, where you propose the controls that might be put in place to protect an asset. The controls are the technical mechanisms, such as encryption, that you can use to protect assets (risk reduction).

7. Feasibility assessment, where you assess the technical feasibility and the costs of the proposed controls. It is not worth having expensive controls to protect assets that don't have a high value (risk reduction).

8. Security requirements definition, where knowledge of the exposure, threats, and control assessments is used to derive system security requirements. These may

Asset	Value	Exposure
The information system	High. Required to support all clinical consultations. Potentially safety-critical.	High. Financial loss as clinics may have to be canceled. Costs of restoring system. Possible patient harm if treatment cannot be prescribed.
The patient database	High. Required to support all clinical consultations. Potentially safety-critical.	High. Financial loss as clinics may have to be canceled. Costs of restoring system. Possible patient harm if treatment cannot be prescribed.
An individual patient record	Normally low although may be high for specific high-profile patients.	Low direct losses but possible loss of reputation.

Figure 12.10 Asset analysis in a preliminary risk assessment report for the MHC-PMS

be requirements for the system infrastructure or the application system (risk reduction).

An important input to the risk assessment and management process is the organizational security policy. An organizational security policy applies to all systems and should set out what should and what should not be allowed. For example, one aspect of a military security policy may state 'Readers may only examine documents whose classification is the same as or below the reader's vetting level.' This means that if a reader has been vetted to a 'secret' level, they may access documents that are classed as 'secret,' 'confidential,' or 'open' but not documents classed as 'top secret.'

The security policy sets out conditions that should always be maintained by a security system and so helps identify threats that might arise. Threats are anything that could threaten business security. In practice, security policies are usually informal documents that define what is and what isn't allowed. However, Bishop (2005) discusses the possibility of expressing security policies in a formal language and generating automated checks to ensure that the policy is being followed.

To illustrate this process of security risk analysis, consider the hospital information system for mental health care, MHC-PMS. I don't have space to discuss a complete risk assessment here but rather draw on this system as a source of examples. I have shown these as a fragment of a report (Figures 12.10 and 12.11) that might be generated from the preliminary risk assessment process. This preliminary risk analysis report is used in defining the security requirements.

From the risk analysis for the hospital information system, you can derive security requirements. Some examples of these requirements are:

1. Patient information shall be downloaded, at the start of a clinic session, from the database to a secure area on the system client.

Threat	Probability	Control	Feasibility
Unauthorized user gains access as system manager and makes system unavailable	Low	Only allow system management from specific locations that are physically secure.	Low cost of implementation but care must be taken with key distribution and to ensure that keys are available in the event of an emergency.
Unauthorized user gains access as system user and accesses confidential information	High	Require all users to authenticate themselves using a biometric mechanism. Log all changes to patient information to track system usage.	Technically feasible but high-cost solution. Possible user resistance. Simple and transparent to implement and also supports recovery.

Figure 12.11
Threat and control analysis in a preliminary risk assessment report

2. All patient information on the system client shall be encrypted.

3. Patient information shall be uploaded to the database when a clinic session is over and deleted from the client computer.

4. A log of all changes made to the system database and the initiator of these changes shall be maintained on a separate computer from the database server.

The first two requirements are related—patient information is downloaded to a local machine so that consultations may continue if the patient database server is attacked or becomes unavailable. However, this information must be deleted so that later users of the client computer cannot access the information. The fourth requirement is a recovery and auditing requirement. It means that changes can be recovered by replaying the change log and that it is possible to discover who has made the changes. This accountability discourages misuse of the system by authorized staff.

12.5 Formal specification

For more than 30 years, many researchers have advocated the use of formal methods of software development. Formal methods are mathematically-based approaches to software development where you define a formal model of the software. You may then formally analyze this model and use it as a basis for a formal system specification. In principle, it is possible to start with a formal model for the software and prove that a developed program is consistent with that model, thus eliminating software failures resulting from programming errors.

Formal specification techniques

Formal system specifications may be expressed using two fundamental approaches, either as models of the system interfaces (algebraic specifications) or as models of the system state. You can download an extra web chapter on this topic, where I show examples of both of these approaches. The chapter includes a formal specification of part of the insulin pump system.

http://www.SoftwareEngineering-9.com/Web/ExtraChaps/FormalSpec.pdf

The starting point for all formal development processes is a formal system model, which serves as a system specification. To create this model, you translate the system's user requirements, which are expressed in natural language, diagrams, and tables, into a mathematical language which has formally defined semantics. The formal specification is an unambiguous description of what the system should do. Using manual or tool-supported methods, you can check that a program's behavior is consistent with the specification.

Formal specifications are not just essential for a verification of the design and implementation of software. They are the most precise way of specifying systems, and so reduce the scope for misunderstanding. Furthermore, constructing a formal specification forces a detailed analysis of the requirements and this is an effective way of discovering requirements problems. In a natural language specification, errors can be concealed by the imprecision of the language. This is not the case if the system is formally specified.

Formal specifications are usually developed as part of a plan-based software process, where the system is completely specified before development. The system requirements and design are defined in detail and are carefully analyzed and checked before implementation begins. If a formal specification of the software is developed, this usually comes after the system requirements have been specified but before the detailed system design. There is a tight feedback loop between the detailed requirements specification and the formal specification.

Figure 12.12 shows the stages of software specification and its interface with software design in a plan-based software process. As it is expensive to develop formal specifications, you may decide to limit the use of this approach to those components that are critical to the system's operation. You identify these in the architectural design of the system.

Over the past few years, automated support for analyzing a formal specification has been developed. Model checkers (Clarke et al., 2000) are software tools that take a state-based formal specification (a system model) as an input, along with the specification of some formally expressed desirable property, such as 'there are no unreachable states.' The model checking program exhaustively analyzes the specification and either reports that the system property is satisfied by the model or presents an example that shows it is not satisfied. Model checking is closely related to the notion of static analysis and I discuss these general approaches to system verification in Chapter 15.

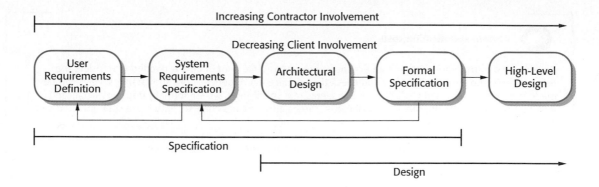

Figure 12.12 Formal specification in a plan-based software process

The advantages of developing a formal specification and using this in a formal development process are:

1. As you develop a formal specification in detail, you develop a deep and detailed understanding of the system requirements. Even if you do not use the specification in a formal development process, requirements error detection is a potent argument for developing a formal specification (Hall, 1990). Requirements problems that are discovered early are usually much cheaper to correct than if they are found at later stages in the development process.

2. As the specification is expressed in a language with formally defined semantics, you can analyze it automatically to discover inconsistencies and incompleteness.

3. If you use a method such as the B method, you can transform the formal specification into a program through a sequence of correctness-preserving transformations. The resulting program is therefore guaranteed to meet its specification.

4. Program testing costs may be reduced because you have verified the program against its specification.

In spite of these advantages, formal methods have had limited impact on practical software development, even for critical systems. Consequently, there is very little experience in the community of developing and using formal system specifications. The arguments that are put forward against developing a formal system specification are:

1. Problem owners and domain experts cannot understand a formal specification so they cannot check that it accurately represents their requirements. Software engineers, who understand the formal specification, may not understand the application domain so they too cannot be sure that the formal specification is an accurate reflection of the system requirements.

2. It is fairly easy to quantify the costs of creating a formal specification, but more difficult to estimate the possible cost savings that will result from its use. As a result, managers are unwilling to take the risk of adopting this approach.

Formal specification costs

Developing a formal specification is an expensive process as quite a lot of time is needed to translate the requirements into a formal language and check the specification. Experience has shown that savings can be made in system testing and verification and it seems that specifying a system formally does not significantly increase the overall development costs. However, the balance of costs changes, with more costs incurred early in the development process.

http://www.SoftwareEngineering-9.com/Web/FormalSpecCosts/

3. Most software engineers have not been trained to use formal specification languages. Hence, they are reluctant to propose their use in development processes.

4. It is difficult to scale current approaches to formal specification up to very large systems. When formal specification is used, it is mostly for specifying critical kernel software rather than complete systems.

5. Formal specification is not compatible with agile methods of development.

Nevertheless, at the time of writing, formal methods have been used in the development of a number of safety- and security-critical applications. They may also be used cost effectively in the development and validation of critical parts of a larger, more complex software system (Badeau and Amelot, 2005; Hall, 1996; Hall and Chapman, 2002; Miller et al., 2005; Wordworth, 1996). They are the basis of tools used in static verification such as the driver verification system used by Microsoft (Ball et al., 2004; Ball et al., 2006) and the SPARK/Ada language (Barnes, 2003) for critical systems engineering.

KEY POINTS

■ Risk analysis is an important activity in the specification of security and dependability requirements. It involves identifying risks that can result in accidents or incidents. System requirements are then generated to ensure that these risks do not occur and, if they do, that they do not lead to an incident or accident.

■ A hazard-driven approach may be used to understand the safety requirements for a system. You identify potential hazards and decompose these (using methods such as fault tree analysis) to discover their root causes. You then specify requirements to avoid or recover from these problems.

■ Reliability requirements can be defined quantitatively in the system requirements specification. Reliability metrics include probability of failure on demand (POFOD), rate of occurrence of failure (ROCOF), and availability (AVAIL).

■ It is important not to overspecify the required system reliability as this leads to unnecessary additional costs in the development and validation processes.

■ Security requirements are more difficult to identify than safety requirements because a system attacker can use knowledge of system vulnerabilities to plan a system attack, and can learn about vulnerabilities from unsuccessful attacks.

■ To specify security requirements, you should identify the assets that are to be protected and define how security techniques and technology should be used to protect these assets.

■ Formal methods of software development rely on a system specification that is expressed as a mathematical model. Developing a formal specification has the key benefit of stimulating a detailed examination and analysis of the system requirements.

FURTHER READING

Safeware: System Safety and Computers. This is a thorough discussion of all aspects of safety-critical systems. It is particularly strong in its description of hazard analysis and the derivation of requirements from this. (N. Leveson, Addison-Wesley, 1995.)

'Security Use Cases.' A good article, available on the Web, that focuses on how use cases can be used in security specification. The author also has a number of good articles on security specification that are referenced in this article. (D. G. Firesmith, *Journal of Object Technology*, **2** (3), May–June 2003.) http://www.jot.fm/issues/issue_2003_05/column6/.

'Ten Commandments of Formal Methods . . .Ten Years Later.' This is a set of guidelines for the use of formal methods that was first proposed in 1996 and which are revisited in this paper. It is a good summary of the practical issues around the use of formal methods. (J. P. Bowen and M. G. Hinchey, *IEEE Computer*, **39** (1), January 2006.) http://dx.doi.org/10.1109/MC.2006.35.

'Security Requirements for the Rest of Us: A Survey.' A good starting point for reading about security requirements specification. The authors focus on lightweight rather than formal approaches. (I. A. Tøndel, M. G. Jaatun, and P. H. Meland, *IEEE Software*, **25** (1), January/February 2008.) http://dx.doi.org/10.1109/MS.2008.19.

EXERCISES

12.1. Explain why the boundaries in the risk triangle shown in Figure 12.12 are liable to change with time and changing social attitudes.

12.2. Explain why the risk-based approach is interpreted in different ways when specifying safety and security.

12.3. In the insulin pump system, the user has to change the needle and insulin supply at regular intervals and may also change the maximum single dose and the maximum daily dose that may be administered. Suggest three user errors that might occur and propose safety requirements that would avoid these errors resulting in an accident.

12.4. A safety-critical software system for treating cancer patients has two principal components:

■ A radiation therapy machine that delivers controlled doses of radiation to tumor sites. This machine is controlled by an embedded software system.

■ A treatment database that includes details of the treatment given to each patient. Treatment requirements are entered in this database and are automatically downloaded to the radiation therapy machine.

Identify three hazards that may arise in this system. For each hazard, suggest a defensive requirement that will reduce the probability that these hazards will result in an accident. Explain why your suggested defense is likely to reduce the risk associated with the hazard.

12.5. Suggest appropriate reliability metrics for the classes of software systems below. Give reasons for your choice of metric. Predict the usage of these systems and suggest appropriate values for the reliability metrics.

■ a system that monitors patients in a hospital intensive care unit

■ a word processor

■ an automated vending machine control system

■ a system to control braking in a car

■ a system to control a refrigeration unit

■ a management report generator

12.6. A train protection system automatically applies the brakes of a train if the speed limit for a segment of track is exceeded, or if the train enters a track segment that is currently signaled with a red light (i.e., the segment should not be entered). Giving reasons for your answer, choose a reliability metric that might be used to specify the required reliability for such a system.

12.7. There are two essential safety requirements for the train protection system:

■ The train shall not enter a segment of track that is signaled with a red light.

■ The train shall not exceed the specified speed limit for a section of track.

Assuming that the signal status and the speed limit for the track segment are transmitted to onboard software on the train before it enters the track segment, propose five possible functional system requirements for the onboard software that may be generated from the system safety requirements.

12.8. Explain why there is a need for both preliminary security risk assessment and life-cycle security risk assessment during the development of a system.

12.9. Extend the table in Figure 12.11 to identify two further threats to the MHC-PMS, along with associated controls. Use these as a basis for generating further software security requirements that implement the proposed controls.

12.10. Should software engineers working on the specification and development of safety-related systems be professionally certified in some way? Explain your reasoning.

REFERENCES

Badeau, F. and Amelot, A. (2005). 'Using B as a High Level Programming Language in an Industrial Project: Roissy VAL'. Proc. ZB 2005: Formal Specification and Development in Z and B, Guildford, UK: Springer.

Ball, T., Bounimova, E., Cook, B., Levin, V., Lichtenberg, J., McGarvey, C., Ondrusek, B., Rajamani, S. K. and Ustuner, A. (2006). 'Thorough Static Analysis of Device Drivers'. Proc. EuroSys 2006, Leuven, Belgium.

Ball, T., Cook, B., Levin, V. and Rajamani, S. K. (2004). 'SLAM and Static Driver Verifier: Technology Transfer of Formal Methods Inside Microsoft'. Proc. Integrated Formal Methods 2004, Canterbury, UK: Springer.

Barnes, J. P. (2003). *High-integrity Software: The SPARK Approach to Safety and Security*. Harlow, UK: Addison-Wesley.

Bishop, M. (2005). *Introduction to Computer Security*. Boston: Addison-Wesley.

Brazendale, J. and Bell, R. (1994). 'Safety-related control and protection systems: standards update'. *IEE Computing and Control Engineering J.*, **5** (1), 6–12.

Clarke, E. M., Grumberg, O. and Peled, D. A. (2000). *Model Checking*. Cambridge, Mass.: MIT Press.

Firesmith, D. G. (2003). 'Engineering Security Requirements'. *Journal of Object Technology*, **2** (1), 53–68.

Hall, A. (1990). 'Seven Myths of Formal Methods'. *IEEE Software*, **7** (5), 11–20.

Hall, A. (1996). 'Using Formal methods to Develop an ATC Information System'. *IEEE Software*, **13** (2), 66–76.

Hall, A. and Chapman, R. (2002). 'Correctness by Construction: Developing a Commercially Secure System'. *IEEE Software*, **19** (1), 18–25.

Jahanian, F. and Mok, A. K. (1986). 'Safety analysis of timing properties in real-time systems'. *IEEE Trans.on Software Engineering.*, **SE-12** (9), 890–904.

Leveson, N. and Stolzy, J. (1987). 'Safety analysis using Petri nets'. *IEEE Transactions on Software Engineering*, **13** (3), 386–397.

Leveson, N. G. (1995). *Safeware: System Safety and Computers*. Reading, Mass.: Addison-Wesley.

Miller, S. P., Anderson, E. A., Wagner, L. G., Whalen, M. W. and Heimdahl, M. P. E. (2005). 'Formal Verification of Flight Control Software'. *Proc. AIAA Guidance*, Navigation and Control Conference, San Francisco.

Peterson, J. L. (1981). *Petri Net Theory and the Modeling of Systems*. New York: McGraw-Hill.

Schneier, B. (1999). 'Attack Trees'. *Dr Dobbs Journal*, **24** (12), 1–9.

Storey, N. (1996). *Safety-Critical Computer Systems*. Harlow, UK: Addison-Wesley.

Wordsworth, J. (1996). *Software Engineering with B*. Wokingham: Addison-Wesley.

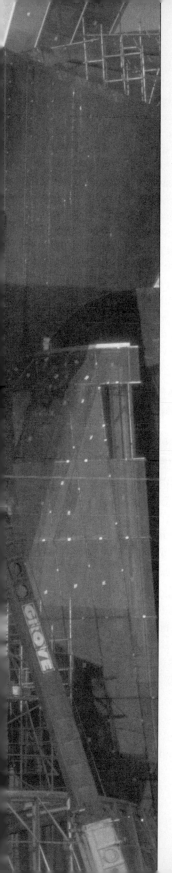

13

Dependability engineering

Objectives

The objective of this chapter is to discuss processes and techniques for developing highly dependable systems. When you have read this chapter you will:

- understand how system dependability can be achieved by using redundant and diverse components;

- know how dependable software processes contribute to the development of dependable software;

- understand how different architectural styles may be used to implement software redundancy and diversity;

- be aware of good programming practice that should be used in dependable systems engineering.

Contents

The use of software engineering techniques, better programming languages, and better quality management has led to significant improvements in dependability for most software. Nevertheless, system failures may still occur that affect the system's availability or lead to incorrect results being produced. In some cases, these failures simply cause minor inconvenience. System vendors may simply decide to live with these failures, without correcting the errors in their systems. However, in some systems, failure can lead to loss of life or significant economic or reputational losses. These are known as 'critical systems', for which a high level of dependability is essential.

Examples of critical systems include process control systems, protection systems that shut down other systems in the event of failure, medical systems, telecommunications switches, and flight control systems. Special development tools and techniques may be used to enhance the dependability of the software in a critical system. These tools and techniques usually increase the costs of system development but they reduce the risk of system failure and the losses that may result from such a failure.

Dependability engineering is concerned with the techniques that are used to enhance the dependability of both critical and non-critical systems. These techniques support three complementary approaches that are used in developing dependable software:

1. *Fault avoidance* The software design and implementation process should use approaches to software development that help avoid design and programming errors and so minimize the number of faults that are likely to arise when the system is executing. Fewer faults mean less chance of run-time failures.

2. *Fault detection and correction* The verification and validation processes are designed to discover and remove faults in a program, before it is deployed for operational use. Critical systems require very extensive verification and validation to discover as many faults as possible before deployment and to convince the system stakeholders that the system is dependable. I cover this topic in Chapter 15.

3. *Fault tolerance* The system is designed so that faults or unexpected system behavior during execution are detected at run-time and are managed in such a way that system failure does not occur. Simple approaches to fault tolerance based on built-in run-time checking may be included in all systems. However, more specialized fault-tolerance techniques (such as the use of fault-tolerant system architectures) are generally only used when a very high level of system availability and reliability is required.

Unfortunately, applying fault-avoidance, fault-detection, and fault-tolerance techniques leads to a situation of diminishing returns. The cost of finding and removing the remaining faults in a software system rises exponentially as program faults are discovered and removed (Figure 13.1). As the software becomes more reliable, you need to spend more and more time and effort to find fewer and fewer faults. At some stage, even for critical systems, the costs of this additional effort become unjustifiable.

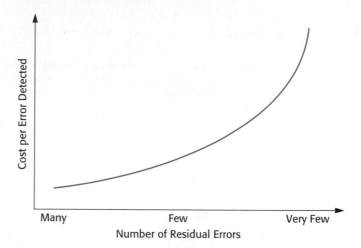

Figure 13.1 The increasing costs of residual fault removal

As a result, software development companies accept that their software will always contain some residual faults. The level of faults depends on the type of system. Shrink-wrapped products have a relatively high level of faults, whereas critical systems usually have a much lower fault density.

The rationale for accepting faults is that, if and when the system fails, it is cheaper to pay for the consequences of failure than it would be to discover and remove the faults before system delivery. However, as discussed in Chapter 11, the decision to release faulty software is not simply an economic decision. The social and political acceptability of system failure must also be taken into account.

Many critical systems, such as aircraft systems, medical systems, and accounting systems, are used in regulated domains such as air transport, medicine, and finance. National governments define regulations that apply in these domains and appoint a regulatory body to ensure that companies follow these regulations. In practice, this means that the regulator often has to be convinced that critical software systems can be trusted and this requires clear evidence that shows that these systems are dependable.

Therefore, the development process for critical systems is not just concerned with producing a dependable system; it must also produce the evidence that can convince a regulator that the system is dependable. Producing such evidence consumes a high proportion of the development costs for critical systems and so is an important contributory factor to the high costs of critical systems. I discuss the issues of producing safety and dependability cases in Chapter 15.

13.1 Redundancy and diversity

Redundancy and diversity are fundamental strategies for enhancing the dependability of any type of system. Redundancy means that spare capacity is included in a system that can be used if part of that system fails. Diversity means that redundant

The Ariane 5 explosion

In 1996, the European Space Agency's Ariane 5 rocket exploded 37 seconds after liftoff on its maiden flight. The fault was caused by a software systems failure. There was a backup system but this was not diverse and so the software in the backup computer failed in exactly the same way. The rocket and its satellite payload were destroyed.

http://www.SoftwareEngineering-9.com/Web/DependabilityEng/Ariane/

components of the system are of different types, thus increasing the chances that they will not fail in exactly the same way.

We use redundancy and diversity to enhance dependability in our everyday lives. As an example of redundancy, most people keep spare light bulbs in their homes so that they can quickly recover from the failure of a light bulb that is in use. Commonly, to secure our homes we use more than one lock (redundancy) and, usually, the locks used are of different types (diversity). This means that if an intruder finds a way to defeat one of the locks, they have to find a different way of defeating the other lock before they can gain entry. As a matter of routine, we should all back up our computers and so maintain redundant copies of our data. To avoid problems with disk failure, backups should be kept on a separate, diverse, external device.

Software systems that are designed for dependability may include redundant components that provide the same functionality as other system components. These are switched into the system if the primary component fails. If these redundant components are diverse (i.e., not the same as other components), a common fault in replicated components will not result in a system failure. Redundancy may also be provided by including additional checking code, which is not strictly necessary for the system to function. This code can detect some kinds of faults before they cause failures. It can invoke recovery mechanisms to ensure that the system continues to operate.

In systems for which availability is a critical requirement, redundant servers are normally used. These automatically come into operation if a designated server fails. Sometimes, to ensure that attacks on the system cannot exploit a common vulnerability, these servers may be of different types and may run different operating systems. Using different operating systems is one example of software diversity and redundancy, where comparable functionality is provided in different ways. I discuss software diversity in more detail in Section 13.3.4.

Diversity and redundancy may also be also used to achieve dependable processes by ensuring that process activities, such as software validation, do not rely on a single process or method. This improves software dependability because it reduces the chances of process failure, where human errors made during the software development process lead to software errors. For example, validation activities may include program testing, manual program inspections, and static analysis as fault-finding techniques. These are complementary techniques in that any one technique might find faults that are missed by the other methods. Furthermore, different team members may be responsible for the same process activity (e.g., a program inspection).

Dependable operational processes

This chapter discusses dependable development processes but an equally important contributor to system dependability is a system's operational processes. In designing these operational processes, you have to take into account human factors and always bear in mind that people are liable to make mistakes when using a system. A dependable process should be designed to avoid human errors and, when mistakes are made, the software should detect the mistakes and allow them to be corrected.

http://www.SoftwareEngineering-9.com/Web/DependabilityEng/HumanFactors/

People tackle tasks in different ways depending on their personality, experience, and education, so this kind of redundancy provides a diverse perspective on the system.

As I discuss in Section 13.3.4, achieving software diversity is not straightforward. Diversity and redundancy make systems more complex and usually harder to understand. Not only is there more code to write and check, additional functionality must also be added to the system to detect component failure and to switch control to alternative components. This additional complexity means that it is more likely that programmers will make errors and less likely that people checking the system will find these errors.

As a consequence, some people think that it is best to avoid software redundancy and diversity. Their view is that the best approach is to design the software to be as simple as possible, with extremely rigorous software verification and validation procedures (Parnas et al., 1990). More can be spent on verification and validation because of the savings that result from not having to develop redundant software components.

Both approaches are used in commercial, safety-critical systems. For example, the Airbus 340 flight control hardware and software is both diverse and redundant (Storey, 1996). The flight control software on the Boeing 777 is based on a redundant hardware but each computer runs the same software, which has been extensively validated. The Boeing 777 flight control system designers have focused on simplicity rather than redundancy. Both of these aircraft are very reliable, so both the diverse and the simple approach to dependability can clearly be successful.

13.2 Dependable processes

Dependable software processes are software processes that are designed to produce dependable software. A company using a dependable process can be sure that the process has been properly enacted and documented and that appropriate development techniques have been used for critical systems development. The rationale for investing in dependable processes is that a good software process is likely to lead to delivered software that contains fewer errors and is therefore less likely to fail in execution. Figure 13.2 shows some of the attributes of dependable software processes.

The evidence that a dependable process has been used is often important in convincing a regulator that the most effective software engineering practice has been applied in developing the software. System developers will normally present a model of the process to a regulator, along with evidence that the process has been

Process Characteristic	Description
Documentable	The process should have a defined process model that sets out the activities in the process and the documentation that is to be produced during these activities.
Standardized	A comprehensive set of software development standards covering software production and documentation should be available.
Auditable	The process should be understandable by people apart from process participants, who can check that process standards are being followed and make suggestions for process improvement.
Diverse	The process should include redundant and diverse verification and validation activities.
Robust	The process should be able to recover from failures of individual process activities.

Figure 13.2
Attributes of dependable processes

followed. The regulator also has to be convinced that the process is used consistently by all of the process participants and that it can be used in different development projects. This means that the process must be explicitly defined and repeatable:

1. An explicitly defined process is one that has a defined process model that is used to drive the software production process. There must be data collected during the process that demonstrates that all of the necessary steps in the process model have been enacted.

2. A repeatable process is one that does not rely on individual interpretation and judgment. Rather, the process can be repeated across projects and with different team members, irrespective of who is involved in the development. This is particularly important for critical systems, which often have a long development cycle during which there are often significant changes in the development team.

Dependable processes make use of redundancy and diversity to achieve reliability. They often include different activities that have the same aim. For example, program inspections and testing aim to discover errors in a program. The approaches are complementary so that together they are likely to discover a higher proportion of errors than would be found using one technique on its own.

The activities that are used in dependable processes obviously depend on the type of software that is being developed. In general, however, these activities should be geared to avoiding the introduction of errors into a system, detecting and removing errors, and maintaining information about the process itself. Examples of activities that might be included in a dependable process include:

1. Requirements reviews to check that the requirements are, as far as possible, complete and consistent.

The safety life cycle

The International Electrotechnical Commission has devised a process standard (IEC 61508) for protection systems engineering. This is based around the notion of a safety life cycle, which makes a clear distinction between safety engineering and system engineering. The first stages of the IEC 61508 safety life cycle define the scope of the system, assess the potential system hazards, and estimate the risks they pose. This is followed by the specification of the safety requirements and the allocation of these safety requirements to different subsystems. The idea is to limit the extent of safety-critical functionality to allow specific techniques for critical systems engineering to be applied to the development of the safety-critical system.

http://www.SoftwareEngineering-9.com/Web/SafetyLifeCycle/

2. Requirements management to ensure that changes to the requirements are controlled and that the impact of proposed requirements changes is understood by all developers affected by the change.

3. Formal specification, where a mathematical model of the software is created and analyzed. I discussed the benefits of formal specification in Chapter 12. Perhaps its most important benefit is that it forces a very detailed analysis of the system requirements. This analysis itself is likely to discover requirements problems that may have been missed in requirements reviews.

4. System modeling, where the software design is explicitly documented as a set of graphical models, and the links between the requirements and these models are explicitly documented.

5. Design and program inspections, where the different descriptions of the system are inspected and checked by different people. Inspections are often driven by checklists of common design and programming errors.

6. Static analysis, where automated checks are carried out on the source code of the program. These look for anomalies that could indicate programming errors or omissions. I discuss static analysis in Chapter 15.

7. Test planning and management, where a comprehensive set of system tests is designed. The testing process has to be carefully managed to demonstrate that these tests provide coverage of the system requirements and have been correctly applied in the testing process.

As well as process activities that focus on system development and testing, there must also be well-defined quality management and change management processes. Although the specific activities in a dependable process may vary from one company to another, the need for effective quality and change management is universal.

Quality management processes (discussed in Chapter 24) establish a set of process and product standards. They also include activities that capture process information to demonstrate that these standards have been followed. For example, there may be a standard defined for carrying out program inspections. The inspection team leader is responsible for documenting the process to show that the inspection standard has been followed.

Change management, discussed in Chapter 25, is concerned with managing changes to a system, ensuring that accepted changes are actually implemented and confirming that planned releases of the software include the planned changes. One common problem with software is that the wrong components are included in a system build. This can lead to a situation where an executing system includes components that have not been checked during the development process. Configuration management procedures must be defined as part of the change management process to ensure that this does not happen.

There is a widely held view that agile approaches, as discussed in Chapter 3, are not really suitable for dependable processes (Boehm, 2002). Agile approaches focus on developing the software rather than on documenting what has been done. They often have a fairly informal approach to change and quality management. Plan-based approaches to dependable systems development, which create documentation that regulators and other external system stakeholders can understand, are generally preferred. Nevertheless, the benefits of agile approaches are equally applicable to critical systems. There have been reports of successes in applying agile methods in this area (Lindvall, et al., 2004) and it is likely that variants of agile methods that are suitable for critical systems engineering will be developed.

13.3 Dependable system architectures

As I have discussed, dependable systems development should be based around a dependable process. However, although you probably need a dependable process to create dependable systems, this is not enough in itself to ensure dependability. You also need to design a system architecture for dependability, especially when fault tolerance is required. This means that the architecture has to be designed to include redundant components and mechanisms that allow control to be switched from one component to another.

Examples of systems that may need fault-tolerant architectures are systems in aircraft that must be in operation throughout the duration of the flight, telecommunication systems, and critical command and control systems. Pullum (2001) describes different types of fault-tolerant architecture that have been proposed and Torres-Pomales surveys software fault-tolerance techniques (2000).

The simplest realization of a dependable architecture is in replicated servers, where two or more servers carry out the same task. Requests for processing are channeled through a server management component that routes each request to a particular server. This component also keeps track of server responses. In the event of server failure, which is usually detected by a lack of response, the faulty server is switched out of the system. Unprocessed requests are resubmitted to other servers for processing.

This replicated server approach is widely used for transaction processing systems where it is easy to maintain copies of transactions to be processed. Transaction processing systems are designed so that data is only updated once a transaction has finished correctly so delays in processing do not affect the integrity of the system.

It can be an efficient way of using hardware if the backup server is one that is normally used for low-priority tasks. If a problem occurs with a primary server, its processing is transferred to the backup server, which gives that work the highest priority.

Replicated servers provide redundancy but not usually diversity. The hardware is usually identical and they run the same version of the software. Therefore, they can cope with hardware failures and software failures that are localized to a single machine. They cannot cope with software design problems that cause all versions of the software to fail at the same time. To handle software design failures, a system has to include diverse software and hardware, as I have discussed in Section 13.1.

Software diversity and redundancy can be implemented in a number of different architectural styles. I describe some of these in the remainder of this section.

13.3.1 Protection systems

A protection system is a specialized system that is associated with some other system. This is usually a control system for some process, such as a chemical manufacturing process or an equipment control system, such as the system on a driverless train. An example of a protection system might be a system on a train that detects if the train has gone through a red signal. If so, and there is no indication that the train control system is decelerating the train, then the protection system automatically applies the train brakes to bring it to a halt. Protection systems independently monitor their environment and, if the sensors indicate a problem that the controlled system is not dealing with, then the protection system is activated to shut down the process or equipment.

Figure 13.3 illustrates the relationship between a protection system and a controlled system. The protection system monitors both the controlled equipment and the environment. If a problem is detected, it issues commands to the actuators to shut down the system or invoke other protection mechanisms such as opening a pressure-release valve. Notice that there are two sets of sensors. One set is used for normal system monitoring and the other specifically for the protection system. In the event of sensor failure, there are backups that will allow the protection system to continue in operation. There may also be redundant actuators in the system.

A protection system only includes the critical functionality that is required to move the system from a potentially unsafe state to a safe state (system shutdown). It is an instance of a more general fault-tolerant architecture in which a principal system is supported by a smaller and simpler backup system that only includes essential functionality. For example, the U.S. space shuttle control software has a backup system that includes 'get you home' functionality; that is, the backup system can land the vehicle if the principal control system fails.

The advantage of this kind of architecture is that protection system software can be much simpler than the software that is controlling the protected process. The only function of the protection system is to monitor operation and to ensure that the system is brought to a safe state in the event of an emergency. Therefore, it is possible to invest more effort in fault avoidance and fault detection. You can check that the software

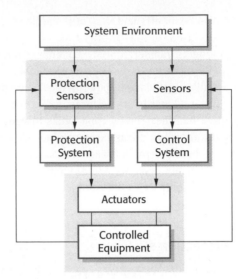

Figure 13.3 Protection system architecture

specification is correct and consistent and that the software is correct with respect to its specification. The aim is to ensure that the reliability of the protection system is such that it has a very low probability of failure on demand (say, 0.001). Given that demands on the protection system should be rare, a probability of failure on demand of 1/1,000 means that protection system failures should be very rare indeed.

13.3.2 Self-monitoring architectures

A self-monitoring architecture is a system architecture in which the system is designed to monitor its own operation and to take some action if a problem is detected. This is achieved by carrying out computations on separate channels and comparing the outputs of these computations. If the outputs are identical and are available at the same time, then it is judged that the system is operating correctly. If the outputs are different, then a failure is assumed. When this occurs, the system will normally raise a failure exception on the status output line, which will lead to control being transferred to another system. This is illustrated in Figure 13.4.

To be effective in detecting both hardware and software faults, self-monitoring systems have to be designed so that:

1. The hardware used in each channel is diverse. In practice, this might mean that each channel uses a different processor type to carry out the required computations, or the chipset making up the system may be sourced from different manufacturers. This reduces the probability of common processor design faults affecting the computation.

2. The software used in each channel is diverse. Otherwise, the same software error could arise at the same time on each channel. I discuss the difficulties of achieving truly diverse software in Section 13.3.4.

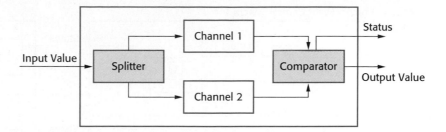

Figure 13.4 Self-monitoring architecture

On its own, this architecture may be used in situations where it is important for computations to be correct, but where availability is not essential. If the answers from each channel differ, the system simply shuts down. For many medical treatment and diagnostic systems, reliability is more important than availability as an incorrect system response could lead to the patient receiving incorrect treatment. However, if the system simply shuts down in the event of an error, this is an inconvenience but the patient will not usually be harmed by the system.

In situations where high availability is required, you have to use several self-checking systems in parallel. You need a switching unit that detects faults and selects a result from one of the systems, where both channels are producing a consistent response. Such an approach is used in the flight control system for the Airbus 340 series of aircraft, in which five self-checking computers are used. Figure 13.5 is a simplified diagram illustrating this organization.

In the Airbus flight control system, each of the flight control computers carry out the computations in parallel, using the same inputs. The outputs are connected to hardware filters that detect if the status indicates a fault and, if so, that the output from that computer is switched off. The output is then taken from an alternative system. Therefore, it is possible for four computers to fail and for the aircraft operation to continue. In more than 15 years of operation, there have been no reports of situations where control of the aircraft has been lost due to total flight control system failure.

The designers of the Airbus system have tried to achieve diversity in a number of different ways:

1. The primary flight control computers use a different processor from the secondary flight control systems.

2. The chipset that is used in each channel in the primary and secondary systems is supplied by a different manufacturer.

3. The software in the secondary flight control systems provides critical functionality only—it is less complex than the primary software.

4. The software for each channel in both the primary and the secondary systems is developed using different programming languages and by different teams.

5. Different programming languages are used in the secondary and primary systems.

As I discuss in the following section, these do not guarantee diversity but they reduce the probability of common failures in different channels.

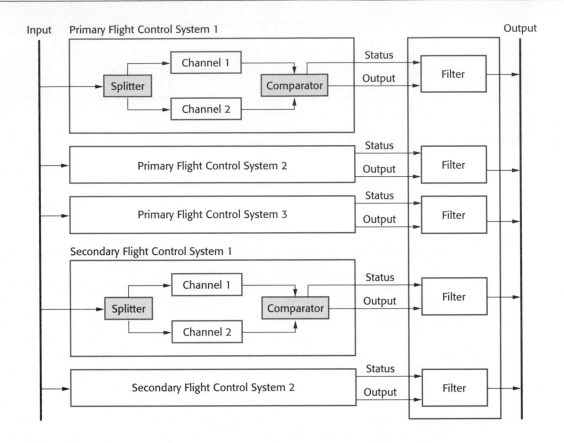

13.3.3 N-version programming

Self-monitoring architectures are examples of systems in which multiversion programming is used to provide software redundancy and diversity. This notion of multiversion programming has been derived from hardware systems where the notion of triple modular redundancy (TMR) has been used for many years to build systems that are tolerant of hardware failures (Figure 13.6).

In a TMR system, the hardware unit is replicated three (or sometimes more) times. The output from each unit is passed to an output comparator that is usually implemented as a voting system. This system compares all of its inputs and, if two or more are the same, then that value is output. If one of the units fails and does not produce the same output as the other units, its output is ignored. A fault manager may try to repair the faulty unit automatically but if this is impossible, the system is automatically reconfigured to take the unit out of service. The system then continues to function with two working units.

This approach to fault tolerance relies on most hardware failures being the result of component failure rather than design faults. The components are therefore likely to fail independently. It assumes that, when fully operational, all hardware units perform to specification. There is therefore a low probability of simultaneous component failure in all hardware units.

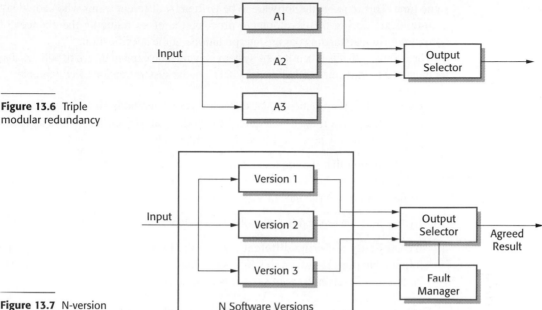

Figure 13.6 Triple modular redundancy

Figure 13.7 N-version programming

Of course, the components could all have a common design fault and thus all produce the same (wrong) answer. Using hardware units that have a common specification but which are designed and built by different manufacturers reduces the chances of such a common mode failure. It is assumed that the probability of different teams making the same design or manufacturing error is small.

A similar approach can be used for fault-tolerant software where N diverse versions of a software system execute in parallel (Avizienis, 1985; Avizienis,1995). This approach to software fault tolerance, illustrated in Figure 13.7, has been used in railway signaling systems, aircraft systems, and reactor protection systems.

Using a common specification, the same software system is implemented by a number of teams. These versions are executed on separate computers. Their outputs are compared using a voting system, and inconsistent outputs or outputs that are not produced in time are rejected. At least three versions of the system should be available so that two versions should be consistent in the event of a single failure.

N-version programming may be less expensive that self-checking architectures in systems for which a high level of availability is required. However, it still requires several different teams to develop different versions of the software. This leads to very high software development costs. As a result, this approach is only used in systems where it is impractical to provide a protection system that can guard against safety-critical failures.

13.3.4 Software diversity

All of the above fault-tolerant architectures rely on software diversity to achieve fault tolerance. This is based on the assumption that diverse implementations of the same specification (or a part of the specification, for protection systems) are independent. They should not include common errors and so will not fail in the same way, at the same time. This requires the software to be written by different teams who should not communicate during the development process, therefore reducing the chances of common misunderstandings or misinterpretations of the specification.

The company that is procuring the system may include explicit diversity policies that are intended to maximize the differences between the system versions. For example:

1. By including requirements that different design methods should be used. For example, one team may be required to produce an object-oriented design and another team may produce a function-oriented design.

2. By stipulating that the implementations are to be written in different programming languages. For example, in a three-version system, Ada, C++, and Java could be used to write the software versions.

3. By requiring the use of different tools and development environments for the system.

4. By explicitly requiring different algorithms to be used in some parts of the implementation. However, this limits the freedom of the design team and may be difficult to reconcile with system performance requirements.

Each development team should work with a detailed system specification (sometimes called the *V-spec*) that has been derived from the system requirements specification (Avizienis, 1995). This should be sufficiently detailed to ensure that there are no ambiguities in the specification. As well as specifying the functionality of the system, the detailed specification should define where system outputs for comparison should be generated.

Ideally, the diverse versions of the system should have no dependencies and so should fail in completely different ways. If this is the case, then the overall reliability of a diverse system is obtained by multiplying the reliabilities of each channel. So, if each channel has a probability of failure on demand of 0.001, then the overall POFOD of a three-channel system (with all channels independent) is a million times greater than the reliability of a single-channel system.

In practice, however, achieving complete channel independence is impossible. It has been shown experimentally that independent design teams often make the same mistakes or misunderstand the same parts of the specification (Brilliant, et., 1990; Knight and Leveson, 1986; Leveson, 1995). There are several reasons for this:

1. Members of different teams are often from the same cultural background and may have been educated using the same approach and textbooks. This means that they may find the same things difficult to understand and have common difficulties in communicating with domain experts. It is quite possible that they will, independently, make the same mistakes and design the same algorithms to solve a problem.

2. If the requirements are incorrect or they are based on misunderstandings about the environment of the system, then these mistakes will be reflected in each implementation of the system.

3. In a critical system, the V-spec is a detailed document based on the system's requirements, which provides full details to the teams on how the system should

behave. There cannot be scope for interpretation by the software developers. If there are errors in this document, then these will be presented to all of the development teams and implemented in all versions of the system.

One way to reduce the possibility of common specification errors is to develop detailed specifications for the system independently, and to define the specifications in different languages. One development team might work from a formal specification, another from a state-based system model, and a third from a natural language specification. This helps avoid some errors of specification interpretation, but does not get around the problem of specification errors. It also introduces the possibility of errors in the translation of the requirements, leading to inconsistent specifications.

In an analysis of the experiments, Hatton (1997), concluded that a three-channel system was somewhere between five to nine times more reliable than a single-channel system. He concluded that improvements in reliability that could be obtained by devoting more resources to a single version could not match this and so N-version approaches were likely to lead to more reliable systems than single version approaches.

What is unclear, however, is whether the improvements in reliability from a multiversion system are worth the extra development costs. For many systems, the extra costs may not be justifiable as a well-engineered single version system may be good enough. It is only in safety and mission critical systems, where the costs of failure are very high, that multiversion software may be required. Even in such situations (e.g., a spacecraft system), it may be enough to provide a simple backup with limited functionality until the principal system can be repaired and restarted.

13.4 Dependable programming

Generally, I have avoided discussions of programming in this book because it is almost impossible to discuss programming without getting into the details of a specific programming language. There are now so many different approaches and languages used for software development that I have avoided using a single language for examples in this book. However, when considering dependability engineering, there is a set of accepted good programming practices that are fairly universal and which help reduce faults in delivered systems.

A list of good practice guidelines is shown in Figure 13.8. They can be applied in whatever programming language is used for systems development, although the way they are used depends on the specific languages and notations that are used for system development.

Guideline 1: Control the visibility of information in a program

A security principle that is adopted by military organizations is the 'need to know' principle. Only those individuals who need to know a particular piece of information in order to carry out their duties are given that information. Information that is not directly relevant to their work is withheld.

> Dependable programming guidelines
> 1. Limit the visibility of information in a program
> 2. Check all inputs for validity
> 3. Provide a handler for all exceptions
> 4. Minimize the use of error-prone constructs
> 5. Provide restart capabilities
> 6. Check array bounds
> 7. Include timeouts when calling external components
> 8. Name all constants that represent real-world values

Figure 13.8 Good practice guidelines for dependable programming

When programming, you should adopt an analogous principle to control access to the variables and data structures that you use. Program components should only be allowed access to data that they need for their implementation. Other program data should be inaccessible, and hidden from them. If you hide information, it cannot be corrupted by program components that are not supposed to use it. If the interface remains the same, the data representation may be changed without affecting other components in the system.

You can achieve this by implementing data structures in your program as abstract data types. An abstract data type is a data type in which the internal structure and representation of a variable of that type is hidden. The structure and attributes of the type are not externally visible and all access to the data is through operations. For example, you might have an abstract data type that represents a queue of requests for service. Operations should include get and put, which add and remove items from the queue, and an operation that returns the number of items in the queue. You might initially implement the queue as an array but subsequently decide to change the implementation to a linked list. This can be achieved without any changes to code using the queue, because the queue representation is never directly accessed.

You can also use abstract data types to implement checks that an assigned value is within range. For example, say you wish to represent the temperature of a chemical process, where allowed temperatures are within the range 20–200 degrees Celsius. By including a check on the value being assigned within the abstract data type operation, you can ensure that the value of the temperature is never outside the required range.

In some object-oriented languages, you can implement abstract data types using interface definitions, where you declare the interface to an object without reference to its implementation. For example, you can define an interface Queue, which supports methods to place objects onto the queue, remove them from the queue, and query the size of the queue. In the object class that implements this interface, the attributes and methods should be private to that class.

Guideline 2: Check all inputs for validity

All programs take inputs from their environment and process them. The specification makes assumptions about these inputs that reflect their real-world use. For example, it may be assumed that a bank account number is always an eight digit positive integer. In many cases, however, the system specification does not define what actions should be taken if the input is incorrect. Inevitably, users will make mistakes and will sometimes enter the wrong data. Sometimes, as I discuss in Chapter 14, malicious attacks on a system rely on deliberately entering incorrect input. Even when the input comes from sensors or other systems, these systems can go wrong and provide incorrect values.

You should therefore always check the validity of inputs as soon as these are read from the program's operating environment. The checks involved obviously depend on the inputs themselves but possible checks that may be used are as follows:

1. *Range checks* You may expect inputs to be within a particular range. For example, an input that represents a probability should be within the range 0.0 to 1.0; an input that represents the temperature of a liquid water should be between 0 degrees Celsius and 100 degrees Celsius, and so on.

2. *Size checks* You may expect inputs to be a given number of characters (e.g., eight characters to represent a bank account). In other cases, the size may not be fixed but there may be a realistic upper limit. For example, it is unlikely that a person's name will have more than 40 characters.

3. *Representation checks* You may expect an input to be of a particular type, which is represented in a standard way. For example, people's names do not include numeric characters, e-mail addresses are made up of two parts, separated by a @ sign, etc.

4 *Reasonableness checks* Where an input is one of a series and you know something about the relationships between the members of the series, then you can check that an input value is reasonable. For example, if the input value represents the readings of a household electricity meter, then you would expect the amount of electricity used to be approximately the same as in the corresponding period in the previous year. Of course, there will be variations but order of magnitude differences suggest that a problem has arisen.

The actions that you take if an input validation check fails depend on the type of system being implemented. In some cases, you report the problem to the user and request that the value be reinput. Where a value comes from a sensor, you might use the most recent valid value. In embedded real-time systems, you might have to estimate the value based on history, so that the system can continue in operation.

Guideline 3: Provide a handler for all exceptions

During program execution, errors or unexpected events inevitably occur. These may arise because of a program fault or may be a result of unpredictable external circumstances. An error or an unexpected event that occurs during the execution of a program is called an 'exception'. Examples of exceptions might be a system power failure, an attempt to access non-existent data, or numeric overflow or underflow.

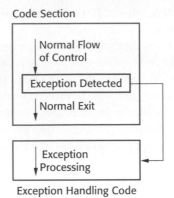

Code Section

Figure 13.9 Exception handling

Exception Handling Code

Exceptions may be caused by hardware or software conditions. When an exception occurs, it must be managed by the system. This can be done within the program itself or may involve transferring control to a system exception handling mechanism. Typically, the system's exception management mechanism reports the error and shuts down execution. Therefore, to ensure that program exceptions do not cause system failure, you should define an exception handler for all possible exceptions that may arise, and make sure that all exceptions are detected and explicitly handled.

In programming languages such as C, if-statements must be used to detect exceptions and to transfer control to the exception handling code. This means that you have to explicitly check for exceptions wherever in the program they may occur. However, this approach adds significant complexity to the task of exception handling, increasing the chances that you will make mistakes and therefore mishandle the exception.

Some programming languages, such as Java, C++, and Ada, include constructs that support exception handling so that you do not need extra conditional statements to check for exceptions. These programming languages include a special built-in type (often called Exception) and different exceptions may be declared to be of this type. When an exceptional situation occurs, the exception is signaled and the language runtime system transfers control to an exception handler. This is a code section that states exception names and appropriate actions to handle each exception (Figure 13.9). Notice that the exception handler is outside the normal flow of control and that this normal control flow does not resume after the exception has been handled.

Exception handlers usually do one or more of three things:

1. Signal to a higher-level component that an exception has occurred, and provide information to that component about the type of exception. You use this approach when one component calls another and the calling component needs to know if the called component has executed successfully. If not, it is up to the calling component to take action to recover from the problem.

2. Carry out some alternative processing to that which was originally intended. Therefore, the exception handler takes some actions to recover from the problem. Processing may then continue as normal or the exception handler

may indicate that an exception has occurred so that a calling component is aware of the problem.

3. Pass control to a run-time support system that handles the exception. This is often the default when faults occur in a program (e.g., when a numeric value overflows). The usual action of the run-time system is to halt processing. You should only use this approach when it is possible to move the system to a safe and quiescent state, before handing control to the run-time system.

Handling exceptions within a program makes it possible to detect and recover from some input errors and unexpected external events. As such, it provides a degree of fault tolerance—the program detects faults and can take action to recover from these. As most input errors and unexpected external events are usually transient, it is often possible to continue normal operation after the exception has been processed.

Guideline 4: Minimize the use of error-prone constructs

Faults in programs, and therefore many program failures, are usually a consequence of human error. Programmers make mistakes because they lose track of the numerous relationships between the state variables. They write program statements that result in unexpected behavior and system state changes. People will always make mistakes, but in the late 1960s it became clear that some approaches to programming were more likely to introduce errors into a program than others.

Some programming language constructs and programming techniques are inherently error prone and so should be avoided or, at least, used as little as possible. Potentially error-prone constructs include:

1. *Unconditional branch (go-to) statements* The dangers of go-to statements were recognized as long ago as 1968 (Dijkstra, 1968) and, as a consequence, these have been excluded from modern programming languages. However, they are still allowed in languages such as C. The use of go-to statements leads to 'spaghetti code' that is tangled and difficult to understand and debug.

2. *Floating-point numbers* The representation of floating-point numbers in a fixed-length memory word is inherently imprecise. This is a particular problem when numbers are compared because representation imprecision may lead to invalid comparisons. For example, 3.00000000 may sometimes be represented as 2.99999999 and sometimes as 3.00000001. A comparison would show these to be unequal. Fixed-point numbers, where a number is represented to a given number of decimal places, are generally safer because exact comparisons are possible.

3. *Pointers* Programming languages such as C and C++ support low-level constructs called pointers, which hold addresses that refer directly to areas of the machine memory (they point to a memory location). Errors in the use of pointers can be devastating if they are set incorrectly and therefore point to the wrong

area of memory. They also make bound checking of arrays and other structures harder to implement.

4. *Dynamic memory allocation* Program memory may be allocated at run-time rather than at compile-time. The danger with this is that the memory may not be properly deallocated, so eventually the system runs out of available memory. This can be a very difficult error to detect because the system may run successfully for a long time before the problem occurs.

5. *Parallelism* When processes are executing concurrently, there can be subtle timing dependencies between them. Timing problems cannot usually be detected by program inspection, and the peculiar combination of circumstances that cause a timing problem may not occur during system testing. Parallelism may be unavoidable, but its use should be carefully controlled to minimize interprocess dependencies.

6. *Recursion* When a procedure or method calls itself or calls another procedure, which then calls the original calling procedure, this is 'recursion'. The use of recursion can result in concise programs; however it can be difficult to follow the logic of recursive programs. Programming errors are therefore more difficult to detect. Recursion errors may result in the allocation of all the system's memory as temporary stack variables are created.

7. *Interrupts* These are a means of forcing control to transfer to a section of code irrespective of the code currently executing. The dangers of this are obvious; the interrupt may cause a critical operation to be terminated.

8. *Inheritance* The problem with inheritance in object-oriented programming is that the code associated with an object is not all in one place. This makes it more difficult to understand the behavior of the object. Hence, it is more likely that programming errors will be missed. Furthermore, inheritance, when combined with dynamic binding, can cause timing problems at run-time. Different instances of a method may be bound to a call, depending on the parameter types. Consequently, different amounts of time will be spent searching for the correct method instance.

9. *Aliasing* This occurs when more than one name is used to refer to the same entity in a program; for example, if two pointers with different names point to the same memory location. It is easy for program readers to miss statements that change the entity when they have several names to consider.

10. *Unbounded arrays* In languages like C, arrays are simply ways of accessing memory and you can make assignments beyond the end of an array. The run-time system does not check that assignments actually refer to elements in the array. Buffer overflow, where an attacker deliberately constructs a program to write memory beyond the end of a buffer that is implemented as an array, is a known security vulnerability.

11. *Default input processing* Some systems provide a default for input processing, irrespective of the input that is presented to the system. This is a security loophole

that an attacker may exploit by presenting the program with unexpected inputs that are not rejected by the system.

Some standards for safety-critical systems development completely prohibit the use of these constructs. However, such an extreme position is not normally practical. All of these constructs and techniques are useful, though they must be used with care. Wherever possible, their potentially dangerous effects should be controlled by using them within abstract data types or objects. These act as natural 'firewalls' limiting the damage caused if errors occur.

Guideline 5: Provide restart capabilities

Many organizational information systems are based around short transactions where processing user inputs takes a relatively short time. These systems are designed so that changes to the system's database are only finalized after all other processing has been successfully completed. If something goes wrong during processing, the database is not updated and so does not become inconsistent. Virtually all e-commerce systems, where you only commit to your purchase on the final screen, work in this way.

User interactions with e-commerce systems usually last a few minutes and involve minimal processing. Database transactions are short, and are usually completed in less than a second. However, other types of systems such as CAD systems and word processing systems involve long transactions. In a long transaction system, the time between starting to use the system and finishing work may be several minutes or hours. If the system fails during a long transaction, then all of the work may be lost. Similarly, in computationally intensive systems such as some e-science systems, minutes or hours of processing may be required to complete the computation. All of this time is lost in the event of a system failure.

In all of these types of systems, you should provide a restart capability that is based on keeping copies of data that is collected or generated during processing. The restart facility should allow the system to restart using these copies, rather than having to start all over from the beginning. These copies are sometimes called checkpoints. For example:

1. In an e-commerce system, you can keep copies of forms filled in by a user and allow them to access and submit these forms without having to fill them in again.

2. In a long transaction or computationally intensive system, you can automatically save data every few minutes and, in the event of a system failure, restart with the most recently saved data. You should also allow for user error and provide a way for users to go back to the most recent checkpoint and start again from there.

If an exception occurs and it is impossible to continue normal operation, you can handle the exception using backward error recovery. This means that you reset the state of the system to the saved state in the checkpoint and restart operation from that point.

Guideline 6: Check array bounds

All programming languages allow the specification of arrays—sequential data structures that are accessed using a numeric index. These arrays are usually laid out in contiguous areas within the working memory of a program. Arrays are specified to be of a particular size, which reflects how they are used. For example, if you wish to represent the ages of up to 10,000 people, then you might declare an array with 10,000 locations to hold the age data.

Some programming languages, such as Java, always check that when a value is entered into an array, the index is within that array. So, if an array A is indexed from 0 to 10,000, an attempt to enter values into elements A [-5] or A [12345] will lead to an exception being raised. However, programming languages such as C and C++ do not automatically include array bound checks and simply calculate an offset from the beginning of the array. Therefore, A [12345] would access the word that was 12345 locations from the beginning of the array, irrespective of whether or not this was part of the array.

The reason why these languages do not include automatic array-bound checking is that this introduces an overhead every time the array is accessed. The majority of array accesses are correct so the bound check is mostly unnecessary and increases the execution time of the program. However, the lack of bound checking leads to security vulnerabilities, such as buffer overflow, which I discuss in Chapter 14. More generally, it introduces a vulnerability into the system that can result in system failure. If you are using a language that does not include array-bound checking, you should always include extra code that ensures the array index is within bounds. This is easily accomplished by implementing the array as an abstract data type, as I have discussed in Guideline 1.

Guideline 7: Include timeouts when calling external components

In distributed systems, components of the system execute on different computers and calls are made across the network from component to component. To receive some service, component A may call component B. A waits for B to respond before continuing execution. However, if component B fails to respond for some reason, then component A cannot continue. It simply waits indefinitely for a response. A person who is waiting for a response from the system sees a silent system failure, with no response from the system. They have no alternative but to kill the waiting process and restart the system.

To avoid this, you should always include timeouts when calling external components. A timeout is an automatic assumption that a called component has failed and will not produce a response. You define a time period during which you expect to receive a response from a called component. If you have not received a response in that time, you assume failure and take back control from the called component. You can then attempt to recover from the failure or tell the system user what has happened and allow them to decide what to do.

Guideline 8: Name all constants that represent real-world values

All non-trivial programs include a number of constant values that represent the values of real-world entities. These values are not modified as the program executes. Sometimes, these are absolute constants and never change (e.g., the speed of light) but more often they are values that change relatively slowly over time. For example, a program to calculate personal tax will include constants that are the current tax rates. These change from year to year and so the program must be updated with the new constant values.

You should always include a section in your program in which you name all real-world constant values that are used. When using the constants, you should refer to them by name rather than by their value. This has two advantages as far as dependability is concerned:

1. You are less likely to make mistakes and use the wrong value. It is easy to mistype a number and the system will often be unable to detect a mistake. For example, say a tax rate is 34%. A simple transposition error might lead to this being mistyped as 43%. However, if you mistype a name (such as Standard-tax-rate), this is usually detected by the compiler as an undeclared variable.

2. When a value changes, you do not have to look through the whole program to discover where you have used that value. All you need do is to change the value associated with the constant declaration. The new value is then automatically included everywhere that it is needed.

KEY POINTS

■ Dependability in a program can be achieved by avoiding the introduction of faults, by detecting and removing faults before system deployment, and by including fault-tolerance facilities that allow the system to remain operational after a fault has caused a system failure.

■ The use of redundancy and diversity in hardware, software processes, and software systems is essential to the development of dependable systems.

■ The use of a well-defined, repeatable process is essential if faults in a system are to be minimized. The process should include verification and validation activities at all stages, from requirements definition through to system implementation.

■ Dependable system architectures are system architectures that are designed for fault tolerance. There are a number of architectural styles that support fault tolerance including protection systems, self-monitoring architectures, and N-version programming.

■ Software diversity is difficult to achieve because it is practically impossible to ensure that each version of the software is truly independent.

■ Dependable programming relies on the inclusion of redundancy in a program to check the validity of inputs and the values of program variables.

■ Some programming constructs and techniques, such as go-to statements, pointers, recursion, inheritance, and floating-point numbers, are inherently error prone. You should try to avoid these constructs when developing dependable systems.

FURTHER READING

Software Fault Tolerance Techniques and Implementation. A comprehensive discussion of techniques to achieve software fault tolerance and fault-tolerant architectures. The book also covers general issues of software dependability. (L. L. Pullum, Artech House, 2001.)

'Software Reliability Engineering: A Roadmap'. This survey paper by a leading researcher in software reliability summarizes the state of the art in software reliability engineering as well as discussing future research challenges. (M. R. Lyu, *Proc. Future of Software Engineering*, IEEE Computer Society, 2007.) http://dx.doi.org/10.1109/FOSE.2007.24.

EXERCISES

13.1. Give four reasons why it is hardly ever cost effective for companies to ensure that their software is free of faults.

13.2. Explain why it is reasonable to assume that the use of dependable processes will lead to the creation of dependable software.

13.3. Give two examples of diverse, redundant activities that might be incorporated into dependable processes.

13.4. What is the common characteristic of all architectural styles that are geared to supporting software fault tolerance?

13.5. Imagine you are implementing a software-based control system. Suggest circumstances in which it would be appropriate to use a fault-tolerant architecture, and explain why this approach would be required.

13.6. You are responsible for the design of a communications switch that has to provide 24/7 availability, but which is not safety-critical. Giving reasons for your answer, suggest an architectural style that might be used for this system.

13.7. It has been suggested that the control software for a radiation therapy machine, used to treat patients with cancer, should be implemented using N-version programming. Comment on whether or not you think this is a good suggestion.

13.8. Give two reasons why different versions of a system based around software diversity may fail in a similar way.

13.9. Explain why you should explicitly handle all exceptions in a system that is intended to have a high level of availability.

13.10. The use of techniques for the production of safe software, as discussed in this chapter, obviously includes considerable extra costs. What extra costs can be justified if 100 lives would be saved over the 15-year lifetime of a system? Would the same costs be justified if 10 lives were saved? How much is a life worth? Do the earning capabilities of the people affected make a difference to this judgment?

REFERENCES

Avizienis, A. (1985). 'The N-Version Approach to Fault-Tolerant Software'. *IEEE Trans. on Software Eng.,* **SE-11** (12), 1491–501.

Avizienis, A. A. (1995). 'A Methodology of N-Version Programming'. In *Software Fault Tolerance.* Lyu, M. R. (ed.). Chichester: John Wiley & Sons. 23–46.

Boehm, B. (2002). 'Get Ready for Agile Methods, With Care'. *IEEE Computer,* **35** (1), 64–9.

Brilliant, S. S., Knight, J. C. and Leveson, N. G. (1990). 'Analysis of Faults in an N-Version Software Experiment'. *IEEE Trans. On Software Engineering,* **16** (2), 238–47.

Dijkstra, E. W. (1968). 'Goto statement considered harmful'. *Comm. ACM.,* **11** (3), 147–8.

Hatton, L. (1997). 'N-version design versus one good version'. *IEEE Software,* **14** (6), 71–6.

Knight, J. C. and Leveson, N. G. (1986). 'An experimental evaluation of the assumption of independence in multi-version programming'. *IEEE Trans. on Software Engineering.,* **SE-12** (1), 96–109.

Leveson, N. G. (1995). Safeware: *System Safety and Computers. Reading,* Mass.: Addison-Wesley.

Lindvall, M., Muthig, D., Dagnino, A., Wallin, C., Stupperich, M., Kiefer, D., May, J. and Kahkonen, T. (2004). 'Agile Software Development in Large Organizations'. *IEEE Computer,* **37** (12), 26–34.

Parnas, D. L., Van Schouwen, J. and Shu, P. K. (1990). 'Evaluation of Safety-Critical Software'. *Comm. ACM,* **33** (6), 636–51.

Pullum, L. L. (2001). *Software Fault Tolerance Techniques and Implementation.* Norwood, Mass.: Artech House.

Storey, N. (1996). *Safety-Critical Computer Systems.* Harlow, UK: Addison-Wesley.

Torres-Pomales, W. (2000). 'Software Fault Tolerance: A Tutorial.'
http://ntrs.nasa.gov/archive/nasa/casi./20000120144_2000175863.pdf.

14

Security engineering

Objectives

The objective of this chapter is to introduce issues that should be considered when you are designing secure application systems. When you have read this chapter, you will:

- understand the difference between application security and infrastructure security;

- know how life-cycle risk assessment and operational risk assessment are used to understand security issues that affect a system design;

- be aware of software architectures and design guidelines for secure systems development;

- understand the notion of system survivability and why survivability analysis is important for complex software systems.

Contents

The widespread use of the Internet in the 1990s introduced a new challenge for software engineers—designing and implementing systems that were secure. As more and more systems were connected to the Internet, a variety of different external attacks were devised to threaten these systems. The problems of producing dependable systems were hugely increased. Systems engineers had to consider threats from malicious and technically skilled attackers as well as problems resulting from accidental mistakes in the development process.

It is now essential to design systems to withstand external attacks and to recover from such attacks. Without security precautions, it is almost inevitable that attackers will compromise a networked system. They may misuse the system hardware, steal confidential data, or disrupt the services offered by the system. System security engineering is therefore an increasingly important aspect of the systems engineering process.

Security engineering is concerned with the development and evolution of systems that can resist malicious attacks, which are intended to damage the system or its data. Software security engineering is part of the more general field of computer security. This has become a priority for businesses and individuals as more and more criminals try to exploit networked systems for illegal purposes. Software engineers should be aware of the security threats faced by systems and ways in which these threats can be neutralized.

My intention in this chapter is to introduce security engineering to software engineers, with a focus on design issues that affect application security. The chapter is not about computer security as a whole and so doesn't cover topics such as encryption, access control, authorization mechanisms, viruses and Trojan horses, etc. These are described in detail in general texts on computer security (Anderson, 2008; Bishop, 2005; Pfleeger and Pfleeger, 2007).

This chapter adds to the discussion of security elsewhere in the book. You should read the material here along with:

- Section 10.1, where I explain how security and dependability are closely related;

- Section 10.4, where I introduce security terminology;

- Section 12.1, where I introduce the general notion of risk-driven specification;

- Section 12.4, where I discuss general issues of security requirements specification;

- Section 15.3, where I explain a number of approaches to security testing.

When you consider security issues, you have to consider both the application software (the control system, the information system, etc.) and the infrastructure on which this system is built (Figure 14.1). The infrastructure for complex applications may include:

- an operating system platform, such as Linux or Windows;

- other generic applications that run on that system, such as web browsers and e-mail clients;

- a database management system;

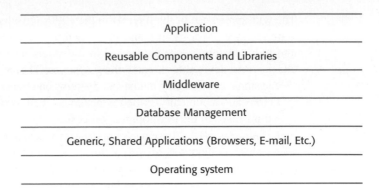

| Application |
| Reusable Components and Libraries |
| Middleware |
| Database Management |
| Generic, Shared Applications (Browsers, E-mail, Etc.) |
| Operating system |

Figure 14.1 System layers where security may be compromised

- middleware that supports distributed computing and database access;

- libraries of reusable components that are used by the application software.

The majority of external attacks focus on system infrastructures because infrastructure components (e.g., web browsers) are well known and widely available. Attackers can probe these systems for weaknesses and share information about vulnerabilities that they have discovered. As many people use the same software, attacks have wide applicability. Infrastructure vulnerabilities may lead to attackers gaining unauthorized access to an application system and its data.

In practice, there is an important distinction between application security and infrastructure security:

1. Application security is a software engineering problem where software engineers should ensure that the system is designed to resist attacks.

2. Infrastructure security is a management problem where system managers configure the infrastructure to resist attacks. System managers have to set up the infrastructure to make the most effective use of whatever infrastructure security features are available. They also have to repair infrastructure security vulnerabilities that come to light as the software is used.

System security management is not a single task but includes a range of activities such as user and permission management, system software deployment and maintenance, and attack monitoring, detection and recovery:

1. User and permission management includes adding and removing users from the system, ensuring that appropriate user authentication mechanisms are in place and setting up the permissions in the system so that users only have access to the resources that they need.

2. System software deployment and maintenance includes installing system software and middleware and configuring these properly so that security vulnerabilities are avoided. It also involves updating this software regularly with new versions or patches, which repair security problems that have been discovered.

Insider attacks and social engineering

Insider attacks are attacks on a system carried out by a trusted individual (an insider) who abuses that trust. For example, a nurse, working in a hospital may access confidential medical records of patients that he or she is not caring for. Insider attacks are difficult to counter because the extra security techniques that may be used would disrupt trustworthy system users.

Social engineering is a way of fooling accredited users into disclosing their credentials. An attacker can therefore behave as an insider when accessing the system.

http://www.SoftwareEngineering-9.com/Web/SecurityEng/insiders.html

3. Attack monitoring, detection and recovery includes activities which monitor the system for unauthorized access, detect, and put in place strategies for resisting attacks, and backup activities so that normal operation can be resumed after an external attack.

Security management is vitally important, but it is not usually considered to be part of application security engineering. Rather, application security engineering is concerned with designing a system so that it is as secure as possible, given budget and usability constraints. Part of this process is 'design for management', where you design systems to minimize the chance of security management errors leading to successful attacks on the system.

For critical control systems and embedded systems, it is normal practice to select an appropriate infrastructure to support the application system. For example, embedded system developers usually choose a real-time operating system that provides the embedded application with the facilities that it needs. Known vulnerabilities and security requirements can be taken into account. This means that an holistic approach can be taken to security engineering. Application security requirements may be implemented through the infrastructure or the application itself.

However, application systems in an organization are usually implemented using the existing infrastructure (operating system, database, etc.). Therefore, the risks of using that infrastructure and its security features must be taken into account as part of the system design process.

14.1 Security risk management

Security risk assessment and management is essential for effective security engineering. Risk management is concerned with assessing the possible losses that might ensue from attacks on assets in the system, and balancing these losses against the costs of security procedures that may reduce these losses. Credit card companies do this all the time. It is relatively easy to introduce new technology to reduce credit card fraud. However, it is often cheaper for them to compensate users for their losses due to fraud than to buy and deploy fraud-reduction technology. As costs drop and attacks increase, this balance may change. For example, credit card companies are now encoding information on an on-card chip instead of a magnetic strip. This makes card copying much more difficult.

Risk management is a business issue rather than a technical issue so software engineers should not decide what controls should be included in a system. It is up to senior management to decide whether or not to accept the cost of security or the exposure that results from a lack of security procedures. Rather, the role of software engineers is to provide informed technical guidance and judgment on security issues. They are, therefore, essential participants in the risk management process.

As I explained in Chapter 12, a critical input to the risk assessment and management process is the organizational security policy. The organizational security policy applies to all systems and should set out what should and should not be allowed. The security policy sets out conditions that should always be maintained by a security system and so helps to identify risks and threats that might arise. The security policy therefore defines what is and what is not allowed. In the security engineering process, you design the mechanisms to implement this policy.

Risk assessment starts before the decision to acquire the system has been made and should continue throughout the system development process and after the system has gone into use (Alberts and Dorofee, 2002). I also introduced, in Chapter 12, the idea that this risk assessment is a staged process:

1. *Preliminary risk assessment* At this stage, decisions on the detailed system requirements, the system design, or the implementation technology have not been made. The aim of this assessment process is to decide if an adequate level of security can be achieved at a reasonable cost. If this is the case, you can then derive specific security requirements for the system. You do not have information about potential vulnerabilities in the system or the controls that are included in reused system components or middleware.

2. *Life-cycle risk assessment* This risk assessment takes place during the system development life cycle and is informed by the technical system design and implementation decisions. The results of the assessment may lead to changes to the security requirements and the addition of new requirements. Known and potential vulnerabilities are identified and this knowledge is used to inform decision making about the system functionality and how it is to be implemented, tested, and deployed.

3. *Operational risk assessment* After a system has been deployed and put into use, risk assessment should continue to take account of how the system is

used and proposals for new and changed requirements. Assumptions about the operating requirement made when the system was specified may be incorrect. Organizational changes may mean that the system is used in different ways from those originally planned. Operational risk assessment therefore leads to new security requirements that have to be implemented as the system evolves.

Preliminary risk assessment focuses on deriving security requirements. In Chapter 12, I show how an initial set of security requirements may be derived from a preliminary risk assessment. In this section, I concentrate on life cycle and operational risk assessment to illustrate how the specification and design of a system are influenced by technology and the way that the system is used.

To carry out a risk assessment, you need to identify the possible threats to a system. One way to do this, is to develop a set of 'misuse cases' (Alexander, 2003; Sindre and Opdahl, 2005). I have already discussed how use cases—typical interactions with a system—may be used to derive system requirements. Misuse cases are scenarios that represent malicious interactions with a system. You can use these to discuss and identify possible threats and, therefore also determine the system's security requirements. They can be used alongside use cases when deriving the system requirements.

Pfleeger and Pfleeger (2007) characterize threats under four headings, which may be used as a starting point for identifying possible misuse cases. These headings are as follows:

1. Interception threats that allow an attacker to gain access to an asset. So, a possible misuse case for the MHC-PMS might be a situation where an attacker gains access to the records of an individual celebrity patient.

2. Interruption threats that allow an attacker to make part of the system unavailable. Therefore, a possible misuse case might be a denial of service attack on a system database server.

3. Modification threats that allow an attacker to tamper with a system asset. In the MHC-PMS, this could be represented by a misuse case where an attacker changes the information in a patient record.

4. Fabrication threats that allow an attacker to insert false information into a system. This is perhaps not a credible threat in the MHC-PMS but would certainly be a threat in a banking system, where false transactions might be added to the system that transfer money to the perpetrator's bank account.

Misuse cases are not just useful in preliminary risk assessment but may be used for security analysis in life-cycle risk analysis and operational risk analysis. They provide a useful basis for playing out hypothetical attacks on the system and assessing the security implications of design decisions that have been made.

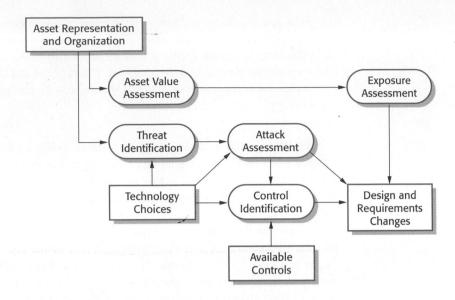

Figure 14.2 Life-cycle risk analysis

14.1.1 Life-cycle risk assessment

Based on organizational security policies, preliminary risk assessment should identify the most important security requirements for a system. These reflect how the security policy should be implemented in that application, identify the assets to be protected, and decide what approach should be used to provide that protection. However, maintaining security is about paying attention to detail. It is impossible for the initial security requirements to take all details that affect security into account.

Life-cycle risk assessment identifies the design and implementation details that affect security. This is the important distinction between life-cycle risk assessment and preliminary risk assessment. Life-cycle risk assessment affects the interpretation of existing security requirements, generates new requirements, and influences the overall design of the system.

When assessing risks at this stage, you should have much more detailed information about what needs to be protected, and you also will know something about the vulnerabilities in the system. Some of these vulnerabilities will be inherent in the design choices made. For example, a vulnerability in all password-based systems is that an authorized user reveals their password to an unauthorized user. Alternatively, if an organization has a policy of developing software in C, you will know that the application may have vulnerabilities because the language does not include array bound checking.

Security risk assessment should be part of all life-cycle activities from requirements engineering to system deployment. The process followed is similar to the preliminary risk assessment process with the addition of activities concerned with design vulnerability identification and assessment. The outcome of the risk assessment is a set of engineering decisions that affect the system design or implementation, or limit the way in which it is used.

A model of the life-cycle risk analysis process, based on the preliminary risk analysis process that I described in Figure 12.9, is shown in Figure 14.2. The most important difference between these processes is that you now have information about information representation and distribution and the database organization for the high-level assets that have to be protected. You are also aware of important design decisions such as the software to be reused, infrastructure controls and protection, etc. Based on this information, your analysis identifies changes to the security requirements and the system design to provide additional protection for the important system assets.

Two examples illustrate how protection requirements are influenced by decisions on information representation and distribution:

1. You may make a design decision to separate personal patient information and information about treatments received, with a key linking these records. The treatment information is much less sensitive than the personal patient information so may not need as extensive protection. If the key is protected, then an attacker will only be able to access routine information, without being able to link this to an individual patient.

2. Assume that, at the beginning of a session, a design decision is made to copy patient records to a local client system. This allows work to continue if the server is unavailable. It makes it possible for a health-care worker to access patient records from a laptop, even if no network connection is available. However, you now have two sets of records to protect and the client copies are subject to additional risks, such as theft of the laptop computer. You, therefore, have to think about what controls should be used to reduce risk. For example, client records on the laptop may have to be encrypted.

To illustrate how decisions on development technologies influence security, assume that the health-care provider has decided to build a MHC-PMS using an off-the-shelf information system for maintaining patient records. This system has to be configured for each type of clinic in which it is used. This decision has been made because it appears to offer the most extensive functionality for the lowest development cost and fastest deployment time.

When you develop an application by reusing an existing system, you have to accept the design decisions made by the developers of that system. Let us assume that some of these design decisions are as follows:

1. System users are authenticated using a login name/password combination. No other authentication method is supported.

2. The system architecture is client-server, with clients accessing data through a standard web browser on a client PC.

3. Information is presented to users as an editable web form. They can change information in place and upload the revised information to the server.

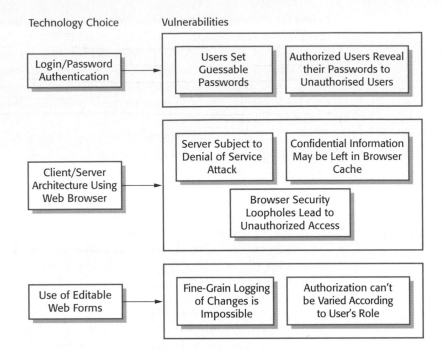

Technology Choice   Vulnerabilities

Login/Password Authentication → Users Set Guessable Passwords | Authorized Users Reveal their Passwords to Unauthorised Users

Client/Server Architecture Using Web Browser → Server Subject to Denial of Service Attack | Confidential Information May be Left in Browser Cache | Browser Security Loopholes Lead to Unauthorized Access

Use of Editable Web Forms → Fine-Grain Logging of Changes is Impossible | Authorization can't be Varied According to User's Role

Figure 14.3
Vulnerabilities associated with technology choices

For a generic system, these design decisions are perfectly acceptable, but a lifecycle risk analysis reveals that they have associated vulnerabilities. Examples of possible vulnerabilities are shown in Figure 14.3.

Once vulnerabilities have been identified, you then have to make a decision on what steps that you can take to reduce the associated risks. This will often involve making decisions about additional system security requirements or the operational process of using the system. I don't have space here to discuss all the requirements that might be proposed to address the inherent vulnerabilities, but some examples of requirements might be the following:

1. A password checker program shall be made available and shall be run daily. User passwords that appear in the system dictionary shall be identified and users with weak passwords reported to system administrators.

2. Access to the system shall only be allowed to client computers that have been approved and registered with the system administrators.

3. All client computers shall have a single web browser installed as approved by system administrators.

As an off-the-shelf system is used, it isn't possible to include a password checker in the application system itself, so a separate system must be used. Password checkers analyze the strength of user passwords when they are set up, and notify users if they have chosen weak passwords. Therefore, vulnerable passwords can be identified reasonably quickly after they have been set up, and action can then be taken to ensure that users change their password.

The second and third requirements mean that all users will always access the system through the same browser. You can decide what is the most secure browser when the system is deployed and install that on all client computers. Security updates are simplified because there is no need to update different browsers when security vulnerabilities are discovered and fixed.

14.1.2 Operational risk assessment

Security risk assessment should continue throughout the lifetime of the system to identify emerging risks and system changes that may be required to cope with these risks. This process is called operational risk assessment. New risks may emerge because of changing system requirements, changes in the system infrastructure, or changes in the environment in which the system is used.

The process of operational risk assessment is similar to the life-cycle risk assessment process, but with the addition of further information about the environment in which the system is used. The environment is important because characteristics of the environment can lead to new risks to the system. For example, say a system is being used in an environment in which users are frequently interrupted. A risk is that the interruption will mean that the user has to leave their computer unattended. It may then be possible for an unauthorized person to gain access to the information in the system. This could then generate a requirement for a password-protected screen saver to be run after a short period of inactivity.

14.2 Design for security

It is generally true that it is very difficult to add security to a system after it has been implemented. Therefore, you need to take security issues into account during the systems design process. In this section, I focus primarily on issues of system design, because this topic isn't given the attention it deserves in computer security books. Implementation issues and mistakes also have a major impact on security but these are often dependent on the specific technology used. I recommend Viega and McGraw's book (2002) as a good introduction to programming for security.

Here, I focus on a number of general, application-independent issues relevant to secure systems design:

1. Architectural design—how do architectural design decisions affect the security of a system?

2. Good practice—what is accepted good practice when designing secure systems?

3. Design for deployment—what support should be designed into systems to avoid the introduction of vulnerabilities when a system is deployed for use?

⬤ **Denial of service attacks**

Denial of service attacks attempt to bring down a networked system by bombarding it with a huge number of service requests. These place a load on the system for which it was not designed and they exclude legitimate requests for system service. Consequently, the system may become unavailable either because it crashes with the heavy load or has to be taken offline by system managers to stop the flow of requests.

http://www.SoftwareEngineering-9.com/Web/Security/DoS.html

Of course, these are not the only design issues that are important for security. Every application is different and security design also has to take into account the purpose, criticality, and operational environment of the application. For example, if you are designing a military system, you need to adopt their security classification model (secret, top secret, etc.). If you are designing a system that maintains personal information, you may have to take into account data protection legislation that places restrictions on how data is managed.

There is a close relationship between dependability and security. The use of redundancy and diversity, which is fundamental for achieving dependability, may mean that a system can resist and recover from attacks that target specific design or implementation characteristics. Mechanisms to support a high level of availability may help the system to recover from so-called denial of service attacks, where the aim of an attacker is to bring down the system and stop it working properly.

Designing a system to be secure inevitably involves compromises. It is certainly possible to design multiple security measures into a system that will reduce the chances of a successful attack. However, security measures often require a lot of additional computation and so affect the overall performance of a system. For example, you can reduce the chances of confidential information being disclosed by encrypting that information. However, this means that users of the information have to wait for it to be decrypted and this may slow down their work.

There are also tensions between security and usability. Security measures sometimes require the user to remember and provide additional information (e.g., multiple passwords). However, sometimes users forget this information, so the additional security means that they can't use the system. Designers therefore have to find a balance between security, performance, and usability. This will depend on the type of system and where it is being used. For example, in a military system, users are familiar with high-security systems and so are willing to accept and follow processes that require frequent checks. In a system for stock trading, however, interruptions of operation for security checks would be completely unacceptable.

14.2.1 Architectural design

As I have discussed in Chapter 11, the choice of software architecture can have profound effects on the emergent properties of a system. If an inappropriate architecture is used, it may be very difficult to maintain the confidentiality and integrity of information in the system or to guarantee a required level of system availability.

In designing a system architecture that maintains security, you need to consider two fundamental issues:

1. Protection—how should the system be organized so that critical assets can be protected against external attack?

2. Distribution—how should system assets be distributed so that the effects of a successful attack are minimized?

These issues are potentially conflicting. If you put all your assets in one place, then you can build layers of protection around them. As you only have to build a single protection system, you may be able to afford a strong system with several protection layers. However, if that protection fails, then all your assets are compromised. Adding several layers of protection also affects the usability of a system so it may mean that it is more difficult to meet system usability and performance requirements.

On the other hand, if you distribute assets, they are more expensive to protect because protection systems have to be implemented for each copy. Typically, then, you cannot afford as many protection layers. The chances are greater that the protection will be breached. However, if this happens, you don't suffer a total loss. It may be possible to duplicate and distribute information assets so that if one copy is corrupted or inaccessible, then the other copy can be used. However, if the information is confidential, keeping additional copies increases the risk that an intruder will gain access to this information.

For the patient record system, it is appropriate to use a centralized database architecture. To provide protection, you use a layered architecture with the critical protected assets at the lowest level in the system, with various layers of protection around them. Figure 14.4 illustrates this for the patient record system in which the critical assets to be protected are the records of individual patients.

In order to access and modify patient records, an attacker has to penetrate three system layers:

1. *Platform-level protection* The top level controls access to the platform on which the patient record system runs. This usually involves a user signing on to a particular computer. The platform will also normally include support for maintaining the integrity of files on the system, backups, etc.

2. *Application-level protection* The next protection level is built into the application itself. It involves a user accessing the application, being authenticated, and getting authorization to take actions such as viewing or modifying data. Application-specific integrity management support may be available.

3. *Record-level protection* This level is invoked when access to specific records is required, and involves checking that a user is authorized to carry out the requested operations on that record. Protection at this level might also involve

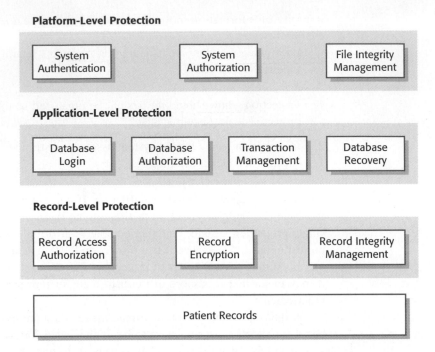

Figure 14.4 A layered protection architecture

encryption to ensure that records cannot be browsed using a file browser. Integrity checking using, for example, cryptographic checksums, can detect changes that have been made outside the normal record update mechanisms.

The number of protection layers that you need in any particular application depends on the criticality of the data. Not all applications need protection at the record level and, therefore, coarser-grain access control is more commonly used. To achieve security, you should not allow the same user credentials to be used at each level. Ideally, if you have a password-based system, then the application password should be different from both the system password and the record-level password. However, multiple passwords are difficult for users to remember and they find repeated requests to authenticate themselves irritating. You often, therefore, have to compromise on security in favor of system usability.

If protection of data is a critical requirement, then a client–server architecture should be used, with the protection mechanisms built into the server. However, if the protection is compromised, then the losses associated with an attack are likely to be high, as are the costs of recovery (e.g., all user credentials may have to be reissued). The system is vulnerable to denial of service attacks, which overload the server and make it impossible for anyone to access the system database.

If you think that denial of service attacks are a major risk, you may decide to use a distributed object architecture for the application. In this situation, illustrated in Figure 14.5, the system's assets are distributed across a number of different platforms, with separate protection mechanisms used for each of these. An attack on one node might mean that some assets are unavailable but it would still be possible to

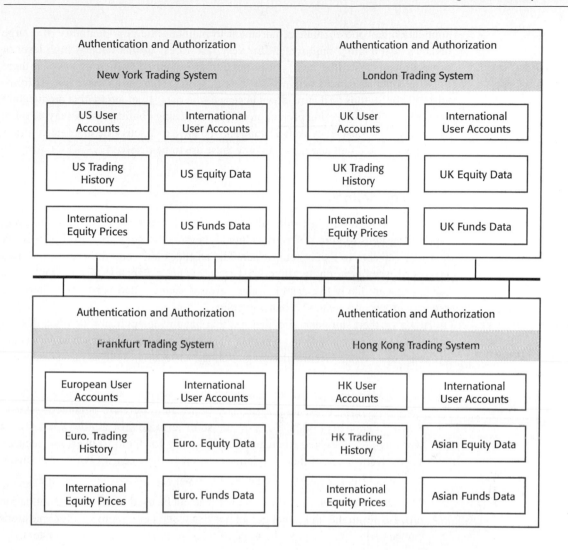

Figure 14.5
Distributed assets
in an equity trading
system

provide some system services. Data can be replicated across the nodes in the system so that recovery from attacks is simplified.

Figure 14.5 shows the architecture of a banking system for trading in stocks and funds on the New York, London, Frankfurt, and Hong Kong markets. The system is distributed so that data about each market is maintained separately. Assets required to support the critical activity of equity trading (user accounts and prices) are replicated and available on all nodes. If a node of the system is attacked and becomes unavailable, the critical activity of equity trading can be transferred to another country and so can still be available to users.

I have already discussed the problem of finding a balance between security and system performance. A problem of secure system design is that in many cases, the architectural style that is most suitable for meeting the security requirements may not be the best one for meeting the performance requirements. For example, say an application has one absolute requirement to maintain the confidentiality of a large database and another requirement for very fast access to that data. A high level of protection suggests that layers of protection are required, which means that there must be communications between the system layers. This has an inevitable performance overhead, thus will slow down access to the data. If an alternative architecture is used, then implementing protection and guaranteeing confidentiality may be more difficult and expensive. In such a situation, you have to discuss the inherent conflicts with the system client and agree on how these are to be resolved.

14.2.2 Design guidelines

There are no hard and fast rules about how to achieve system security. Different types of systems require different technical measures to achieve a level of security that is acceptable to the system owner. The attitudes and requirements of different groups of users profoundly affect what is and is not acceptable. For example, in a bank, users are likely to accept a higher level of security, and hence more intrusive security procedures than, say, in a university.

However, there are general guidelines that have wide applicability when designing system security solutions, which encapsulate good design practice for secure systems engineering. General design guidelines for security, such as those discussed, below, have two principal uses:

1. They help raise awareness of security issues in a software engineering team. Software engineers often focus on the short-term goal of getting the software working and delivered to customers. It is easy for them to overlook security issues. Knowledge of these guidelines can mean that security issues are considered when software design decisions are made.

2. They can be used as a review checklist that can be used in the system validation process. From the high-level guidelines discussed here, more specific questions can be derived that explore how security has been engineered into a system.

The 10 design guidelines, summarized in Figure 14.6, have been derived from a range of different sources (Schneier, 2000; Viega and McGraw, 2002; Wheeler, 2003). I have focused here on guidelines that are particularly applicable to the software specification and design processes. More general principles, such as 'Secure the weakest link in a system', 'Keep it simple', and 'Avoid security through obscurity' are also important but are less directly relevant to engineering decision making.

Guideline 1: Base security decisions on an explicit security policy

A security policy is a high-level statement that sets out fundamental security conditions for an organization. It defines the 'what' of security rather than the 'how', so the policy should not define the mechanisms to be used to provide and enforce security. In principle, all aspects of the security policy should be reflected in the system

Security guidelines
1 Base security decisions on an explicit security policy
2 Avoid a single point of failure
3 Fail securely
4 Balance security and usability
5 Log user actions
6 Use redundancy and diversity to reduce risk
7 Validate all inputs
8 Compartmentalize your assets
9 Design for deployment
10 Design for recoverability

Figure 14.6 Design guidelines for secure systems engineering

requirements. In practice, especially if a rapid application development process is used, this is unlikely to happen. Designers, therefore, should consult the security policy as it provides a framework for making and evaluating design decisions.

For example, say you are designing an access control system for the MHC-PMS. The hospital security policy may state that only accredited clinical staff may modify electronic patient records. Your system therefore has to include mechanisms that check the accreditation of anyone attempting to modify the system and that reject modifications from people who are not accredited.

The problem that you may face is that many organizations do not have an explicit systems security policy. Over time, changes may have been made to systems in response to identified problems, but with no overarching policy document to guide the evolution of a system. In such situations, you need to work out and document the policy from examples, and confirm it with managers in the company.

Guideline 2: Avoid a single point of failure

In any critical system, it is good design practice to try to avoid a single point of failure. This means that a single failure in part of the system should not result in an overall systems failure. In security terms, this means that you should not rely on a single mechanism to ensure security, rather you should employ several different techniques. This is sometimes called 'defense in depth'.

For example, if you use a password to authenticate users to a system, you might also include a challenge/response authentication mechanism where users have to pre-register questions and answers with the system. After password authentication, they must then answer questions correctly before being allowed access. To protect the integrity of data in a system, you might keep an executable log of all changes made to the data (see Guideline 5). In the event of a failure, you can replay the log to re-create the data set. You might also make a copy of all data that is modified before the change is made.

Guideline 3: Fail securely

System failures are inevitable in all systems and, in the same way that safety-critical systems should always fail-safe, security critical systems should always 'fail-secure'. When the system fails, you should not use fallback procedures that are less secure than the system itself. Nor should system failure mean that an attacker can access data that would not normally be allowed.

For example, in the patient information system, I suggested a requirement that patient data should be downloaded to a system client at the beginning of a clinic session. This speeds up access and means that access is possible if the server is unavailable. Normally, the server deletes this data at the end of the clinic session. However, if the server has failed, then there is the possibility that the information will be maintained on the client. A fail-secure approach in those circumstances is to encrypt all patient data stored on the client. This means that an unauthorized user cannot read the data.

Guideline 4: Balance security and usability

The demands of security and usability are often contradictory. To make a system secure, you have to introduce checks that users are authorized to use the system and that they are acting in accordance with security policies. All of these inevitably make demands on users—they may have to remember login names and passwords, only use the system from certain computers, and so on. These mean that it takes users more time to get started with the system and use it effectively. As you add security features to a system, it is inevitable that it will become less usable. I recommend Cranor and Garfinkel's book (2005) that discusses a wide range of issues in the general area of security and usability.

There comes a point where it is counterproductive to keep adding on new security features at the expense of usability. For example, if you require users to input multiple passwords or to change their passwords to impossible-to-remember character strings at frequent intervals, they will simply write down these passwords. An attacker (especially an insider) may then be able to find the passwords that have been written down and gain access to the system.

Guideline 5: Log user actions

If it is practically possible to do so, you should always maintain a log of user actions. This log should, at least, record who did what, the assets used, and the time and date of the action. As I discuss in Guideline 2, if you maintain this as a list of executable commands, you have the option of replaying the log to recover from failures. Of course, you also need tools that allow you to analyze the log and detect potentially anomalous actions. These tools can scan the log and find anomalous actions, and thus help detect attacks and trace how the attacker gained access to the system.

Apart from helping recover from failure, a log of user actions is useful because it acts as a deterrent to insider attacks. If people know that their actions are being logged, then they are less likely to do unauthorized things. This is most effective for casual attacks, such as a nurse looking up patient records, or for detecting attacks where legitimate user credentials have been stolen through social engineering. Of course, this is not foolproof, as technically skilled insiders can also access and change the log.

Guideline 6: Use redundancy and diversity to reduce risk

Redundancy means that you maintain more than one version of software or data in a system. Diversity, when applied to software, means that the different versions should not rely on the same platform or be implemented using the same technologies. Therefore, a platform or technology vulnerability will not affect all versions and so lead to a common failure. I explained in Chapter 13 how redundancy and diversity are the fundamental mechanisms used in dependability engineering.

I have already discussed examples of redundancy—maintaining patient information on both the server and the client, firstly in the mental health-care system, and then in the distributed equity trading system shown in Figure 14.5. In the patient records system, you could use diverse operating systems on the client and the server (e.g., Linux on the server, Windows on the client). This ensures that an attack based on an operating system vulnerability will not affect both the server and the client. Of course, you have to trade off such benefits against the increased management cost of maintaining different operating systems in an organization.

Guideline 7: Validate all inputs

A common attack on a system involves providing the system with unexpected inputs that cause it to behave in an unanticipated way. These may simply cause a system crash, resulting in a loss of service, or the inputs could be made up of malicious code that is executed by the system. Buffer overflow vulnerabilities, first demonstrated in the Internet worm (Spafford, 1989) and commonly used by attackers (Berghel, 2001), may be triggered using long input strings. So-called 'SQL poisoning', where a malicious user inputs an SQL fragment that is interpreted by a server, is another fairly common attack.

As I explained in Chapter 13, you can avoid many of these problems if you design input validation into your system. Essentially, you should never accept any input without applying some checks to it. As part of the requirements, you should define the checks that should be applied. You should use knowledge of the input to define these checks. For example, if a surname is to be input, you might check that there are no embedded spaces and that the only punctuation used is a hyphen. You might also check the number of characters input and reject inputs that are obviously too long. For example, no one has a family name with more than 40 characters and no addresses are more than 100 characters long. If you use menus to present allowed inputs, you avoid some of the problems of input validation.

Guideline 8: Compartmentalize your assets

Compartmentalizing means that you should not provide all-or-nothing access to information in a system. Rather, you should organize the information in a system into compartments. Users should only have access to the information that they need, rather than to all of the information in a system. This means that the effects of an attack may be contained. Some information may be lost or damaged but it is unlikely that all of the information in the system will be affected.

For example, in the patient information system, you should design the system so that at any one clinic, the clinic staff normally only have access to the records of patients that have an appointment at that clinic. They should not normally have access to all patient records in the system. Not only does this limit the potential loss from insider attacks, it also means that if an intruder steals their credentials, then the amount of damage that they can cause is limited.

Having said this, you also may have to have mechanisms in the system to grant unexpected access—say to a patient who is seriously ill and requires urgent treatment without an appointment. In those circumstances, you might use some alternative secure mechanism to override the compartmentalization in the system. In such situations, where security is relaxed to maintain system availability, it is essential that you use a logging mechanism to record system usage. You can then check the logs to trace any unauthorized use.

Guideline 9: Design for deployment

Many security problems arise because the system is not configured correctly when it is deployed in its operational environment. You should therefore always design your system so that facilities are included to simplify deployment in the customer's environment and to check for potential configuration errors and omissions in the deployed system. This is an important topic, which I cover in detail later in Section 14.2.3.

Guideline 10: Design for recoverability

Irrespective of how much effort you put into maintaining systems security, you should always design your system with the assumption that a security failure could occur. Therefore, you should think about how to recover from possible failures and restore the system to a secure operational state. For example, you may include a backup authentication system in case your password authentication is compromised.

For example, say an unauthorized person from outside the clinic gains access to the patient records system and you don't know how they obtained a valid login/password combination. You need to reinitialize the authentication system and not just change the credentials used by the intruder. This is essential because the intruder may also have gained access to other user passwords. You need, therefore, to ensure that all authorized users change their passwords. You also must ensure that the unauthorized person does not have access to the password changing mechanism.

You therefore have to design your system to deny access to everyone until they have changed their password and to authenticate real users for password change,

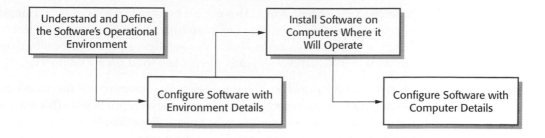

Figure 14.7 Software deployment

assuming that their chosen passwords may not be secure. One way of doing this is to use a challenge/response mechanism, where users have to answer questions for which they have pre-registered answers. This is only invoked when passwords are changed, allowing for recovery from the attack with relatively little user disruption.

14.2.3 Design for deployment

The deployment of a system involves configuring the software to operate in an operational environment, installing the system on the computers in that environment, and then configuring the installed system for these computers (Figure 14.7). Configuration may be a simple process that involves setting some built-in parameters in the software to reflect user preferences. Sometimes, however, configuration is complex and requires the specific definition of business models and rules that affect the execution of the software.

It is at this stage of the software process that vulnerabilities in the software are often accidentally introduced. For example, during installation, software often has to be configured with a list of allowed users. When delivered, this list simply consists of a generic administrator login such as 'admin' and a default password, such as 'password'. This makes it easy for an administrator to set up the system. Their first action should be to introduce a new login name and password, and to delete the generic login name. However, it's easy to forget to do this. An attacker who knows of the default login may then be able to gain privileged access to the system.

Configuration and deployment are often seen as system administration issues and so are considered to be outside the scope of software engineering processes. Certainly, good management practice can avoid many security problems that arise from configuration and deployment mistakes. However, software designers have the responsibility to 'design for deployment'. You should always provide built-in support for deployment that will reduce the probability that system administrators (or users) will make mistakes when configuring the software.

I recommend four ways to incorporate deployment support in a system:

1. *Include support for viewing and analyzing configurations* You should always include facilities in a system that allow administrators or permitted users to examine the current configuration of the system. This facility is, surprisingly, lacking from most software systems and users are frustrated by the difficulties of finding configuration settings. For example, in the version of the word processor that I used to write this chapter, it is impossible to see or print the settings of all system

preferences on a single screen. However, if an administrator can get a complete picture of a configuration, they are more likely to spot errors and omissions. Ideally, a configuration display should also highlight aspects of the configuration that are potentially unsafe—for example, if a password has not been set up.

2. *Minimize default privileges* You should design software so that the default configuration of a system provides minimum essential privileges. This way, the damage that any attacker can do can be limited. For example, the default system administrator authentication should only allow access to a program that enables an administrator to set up new credentials. It should not allow access to any other system facilities. Once the new credentials have been set up, the default login and password should be deleted automatically.

3. *Localize configuration settings* When designing system configuration support, you should ensure that everything in a configuration that affects the same part of a system is set up in the same place. To use the word processor example again, in the version that I use, I can set up some security information, such as a password to control access to the document, using the Preferences/Security menu. Other information is set up in the Tools/Protect Document menu. If configuration information is not localized, it is easy to forget to set it up or, in some cases, not even be aware that some security facilities are included in the system.

4. *Provide easy ways to fix security vulnerabilities* You should include straightforward mechanisms for updating the system to repair security vulnerabilities that have been discovered. These could include automatic checking for security updates, or downloading of these updates as soon as they are available. It is important that users cannot bypass these mechanisms as, inevitably, they will consider other work to be more important. There are several recorded examples of major security problems that arose (e.g., complete failure of a hospital network) because users did not update their software when asked to do so.

14.3 System survivability

So far, I have discussed security engineering from the perspective of an application that is under development. The system procurer and developer have control over all aspects of the system that might be attacked. In reality, as I suggested in Figure 14.1, modern distributed systems inevitably rely on an infrastructure that includes off-the-shelf systems and reusable components that have been developed by different organizations. The security of these systems does not just depend on local design decisions. It is also affected by the security of external applications, web services, and the network infrastructure.

This means that, irrespective of how much attention is paid to security, it cannot be guaranteed that a system will be able to resist external attacks. Consequently, for complex networked systems, you should assume that penetration is possible and that the integrity of the system cannot be guaranteed. You should therefore think about how to make the system resilient so that it survives to deliver essential services to users.

Survivability or resilience (Westmark, 2004) is an emergent property of a system as a whole, rather than a property of individual components, which may not themselves be survivable. The survivability of a system reflects its ability to continue to deliver essential business or mission-critical services to legitimate users while it is under attack or after part of the system has been damaged. The damage could be caused by an attack or by a system failure.

Work on system survivability was prompted by the fact that our economic and social lives are dependent on a computer-controlled critical infrastructure. This includes the infrastructure for delivering utilities (power, water, gas, etc.) and, equally critically, the infrastructure for delivering and managing information (telephones, Internet, postal service, etc.). However, survivability is not simply a critical infrastructure issue. Any organization that relies on critical networked computer systems should be concerned with how its business would be affected if their systems did not survive a malicious attack or catastrophic system failure. Therefore, for business critical systems, survivability analysis and design should be part of the security engineering process.

Maintaining the availability of critical services is the essence of survivability. This means that you have to know:

- the system services that are the most critical for a business;

- the minimal quality of service that must be maintained;

- how these services might be compromised;

- how these services can be protected;

- how you can recover quickly if the services become unavailable.

For example, in a system that handles ambulance dispatch in response to emergency calls, the critical services are those concerned with taking calls and dispatching ambulances to the medical emergency. Other services, such as call logging and ambulance location management, are less critical, either because they do not require real-time processing or because alternative mechanisms may be used. For example, to find an ambulance's location you can call the ambulance crew and ask them where they are.

Ellison and colleagues (1999a; 1999b; 2002) have designed a method of analysis called Survivable Systems Analysis. This is used to assess vulnerabilities in systems and to support the design of system architectures and features that promote system survivability. They argue that achieving survivability depends on three complementary strategies:

1. *Resistance* Avoiding problems by building capabilities into the system to repel attacks. For example, a system may use digital certificates to authenticate users, thus making it more difficult for unauthorized users to gain access.

2. *Recognition* Detecting problems by building capabilities into the system to detect attacks and failures and assess the resultant damage. For example, checksums may be associated with critical data so that corruptions to that data can be detected.

3. *Recovery* Tolerating problems by building capabilities into the system to deliver essential services while under attack, and to recover full functionality after an

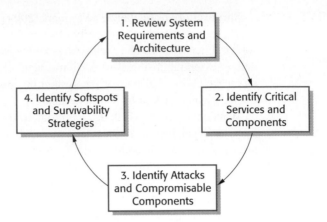

Figure 14.8 Stages in survivability analysis

attack. For example, fault tolerance mechanisms using diverse implementations of the same functionality may be included to cope with a loss of service from one part of the system.

Survivable systems analysis is a four-stage process (Figure 14.8) that analyzes the current or proposed system requirements and architecture; identifies critical services, attack scenarios, and system 'softspots'; and proposes changes to improve the survivability of a system. The key activities in each of these stages are as follows:

1. *System understanding* For an existing or proposed system, review the goals of the system (sometimes called the mission objectives), the system requirements, and the system architecture.

2. *Critical service identification* The services that must always be maintained and the components that are required to maintain these services are identified.

3. *Attack simulation* Scenarios or use cases for possible attacks are identified along with the system components that would be affected by these attacks.

4. *Survivability analysis* Components that are both essential and compromisable by an attack are identified and survivability strategies based on resistance, recognition, and recovery are identified.

Ellison and his colleagues present an excellent case study of the method based on a system to support mental health treatment (1999b). This system is similar to the MHC-PMS that I have used as an example in this book. Rather than repeat their analysis, I use the equity trading system, as shown in Figure 14.5, to illustrate some of the features of survivability analysis.

As you can see from Figure 14.5, this system already has already made some provision for survivability. User accounts and equity prices are replicated across servers so that orders can be placed even if the local server is unavailable. Let's assume that the capability for authorized users to place orders for stock is the key service that must be maintained. To ensure that users trust the system, it is essential that integrity be maintained. Orders must be accurate and reflect the actual sales or purchases made by a system user.

Attack	Resistance	Recognition	Recovery
Unauthorized user places malicious orders	Require a dealing password that is different from the login password to place orders.	Send copy of order by e-mail to authorized user with contact phone number (so that they can detect malicious orders). Maintain user's order history and check for unusual trading patterns.	Provide mechanism to automatically 'undo' trades and restore user accounts. Refund users for losses that are due to malicious trading. Insure against consequential losses.
Corruption of transactions database	Require privileged users to be authorized using a stronger authentication mechanism, such as digital certificates.	Maintain read-only copies of transactions for an office on an international server. Periodically compare transactions to check for corruption. Maintain cryptographic checksum with all transaction records to detect corruption.	Recover database from backup copies. Provide a mechanism to replay trades from a specified time to re-create the transactions database.

Figure 14.9
Survivability analysis in an equity trading system

To maintain this ordering service, there are three components of the system that are used:

1. *User authentication* This allows authorized users to log on to the system.

2. *Price quotation* This allows the buying and selling price of a stock to be quoted.

3. *Order placement* This allows buy and sell orders at a given price to be made.

These components obviously make use of essential data assets such as a user account database, a price database, and an order transaction database. These must survive attacks if service is to be maintained.

There are several different types of attack on this system that might be made. Let's consider two possibilities here:

1. A malicious user has a grudge against an accredited system user. He gains access to the system using their credentials. Malicious orders are placed and stock is bought and sold, with the intention of causing problems for the authorized user.

2. An unauthorized user corrupts the database of transactions by gaining permission to issue SQL commands directly. Reconciliation of sales and purchases is therefore impossible.

Figure 14.9 shows examples of resistance, recognition, and recovery strategies that might be used to help counter these attacks.

Increasing the survivability or resilience of a system of course costs money. Companies may be reluctant to invest in survivability if they have never suffered a serious attack or associated loss. However, just as it is best to buy good locks and an alarm before rather than after your house is burgled, it is best to invest in survivability before, rather than after, a successful attack. Survivability analysis is not yet part of most software engineering processes but, as more and more systems become business critical, such analyzes are likely to become more widely used.

KEY POINTS

■ Security engineering focuses on how to develop and maintain software systems that can resist malicious attacks intended to damage a computer-based system or its data.

■ Security threats can be threats to the confidentiality, integrity, or availability of a system or its data.

■ Security risk management involves assessing the losses that might ensue from attacks on a system, and deriving security requirements that are aimed at eliminating or reducing these losses.

■ Design for security involves designing a secure system architecture, following good practice for secure systems design, and including functionality to minimize the possibility of introducing vulnerabilities when the system is deployed.

■ Key issues when designing a secure systems architecture include organizing the system structure to protect key assets and distributing the system assets to minimize the losses from a successful attack.

■ Security design guidelines sensitize system designers to security issues that they may not have considered. They provide a basis for creating security review checklists.

■ To support secure deployment you should provide a way of displaying and analyzing system configurations, localize configuration settings so that important configurations are not forgotten, minimize default privileges assigned to system users, and provide ways to repair security vulnerabilities.

■ System survivability reflects the ability of a system to continue to deliver essential business or mission-critical services to legitimate users while it is under attack, or after part of the system has been damaged.

FURTHER READING

'Survivable Network System Analysis: A Case Study.' An excellent paper that introduces the notion of system survivability and uses a case study of a mental health record treatment system to illustrate the application of a survivability method. (R. J. Ellison, R. C. Linger, T. Longstaff and N. R. Mead, *IEEE Software*, **16** (4), July/August 1999.)

Building Secure Software: How to Avoid Security Problems the Right Way. A good practical book covering security from a programming perspective. (J. Viega and G. McGraw, Addison-Wesley, 2002.)

Security Engineering: A Guide to Building Dependable Distributed Systems, 2nd edition. This is a thorough and comprehensive discussion of the problems of building secure systems. The focus is on systems rather than software engineering with extensive coverage of hardware and networking, with excellent examples drawn from real system failures. (R. Anderson, John Wiley & Sons, 2008.)

EXERCISES

14.1. Explain the important differences between application security engineering and infrastructure security engineering.

14.2. For the MHC-PMS, suggest an example of an asset, exposure, vulnerability, attack, threat, and control.

14.3. Explain why there is a need for risk assessment to be a continuing process from the early stages of requirements engineering through to the operational use of a system.

14.4. Using your answers to question 2 about the MHC-PMS, assess the risks associated with that system and propose two system requirements that might reduce these risks.

14.5. Explain, using an analogy drawn from a non-software engineering context, why a layered approach to asset protection should be used.

14.6. Explain why it is important to use diverse technologies to support distributed systems in situations where system availability is critical.

14.7. What is social engineering? Why is it difficult to protect against it in large organizations?

14.8. For any off-the-shelf software system that you use (e.g., Microsoft Word), analyze the configuration facilities included and discuss any problems that you find.

14.9. Explain how the complementary strategies of resistance, recognition, and recovery may be used to enhance the survivability of a system.

14.10. For the equity trading system discussed in Section 14.2.1, whose architecture is shown in Figure 14.5, suggest two further plausible attacks on the system and propose possible strategies that could counter these attacks.

REFERENCES

Alberts, C. and Dorofee, A. (2002). *Managing Information Security Risks: The OCTAVE Approach*. Boston: Addison-Wesley.

Alexander, I. (2003). 'Misuse Cases: Use Cases with Hostile Intent'. *IEEE Software*, **20** (1), 58–66.

Anderson, R. (2008). *Security Engineering, 2nd edition*. Chichester: John Wiley & Sons.

Berghel, H. (2001). 'The Code Red Worm'. *Comm. ACM*, **44** (12), 15–19.

Bishop, M. (2005). *Introduction to Computer Security*. Boston: Addison-Wesley.

Cranor, L. and Garfinkel, S. (2005). *Security and Usability: Designing secure systems that people can use*. Sebastopol, Calif.: O'Reilly Media Inc.

Ellison, R., Linger, R., Lipson, H., Mead, N. and Moore, A. (2002). 'Foundations of Survivable Systems Engineering'. *Crosstalk: The Journal of Defense Software Engineering*, **12**, 10–15.

Ellison, R. J., Fisher, D. A., Linger, R. C., Lipson, H. F., Longstaff, T. A. and Mead, N. R. (1999a). 'Survivability: Protecting Your Critical Systems'. *IEEE Internet Computing*, **3** (6), 55–63.

Ellison, R. J., Linger, R. C., Longstaff, T. and Mead, N. R. (1999b). 'Survivable Network System Analysis: A Case Study'. *IEEE Software*, 16 (4), 70–7.

Pfleeger, C. P. and Pfleeger, S. L. (2007). *Security in Computing, 4th edition*. Boston: Addison-Wesley.

Schneier, B. (2000). Secrets and Lies: *Digital Security in a Networked World*. New York: John Wiley & Sons.

Sindre, G. and Opdahl, A. L. (2005). 'Eliciting Security Requirements through Misuse Cases'. *Requirements Engineering*, **10** (1), 34–44.

Spafford, E. (1989). 'The Internet Worm: Crisis and Aftermath'. *Comm ACM*, **32** (6), 678–87.

Viega, J. and McGraw, G. (2002). *Building Secure Software*. Boston: Addison-Wesley.

Westmark, V. R. (2004). 'A Definition for Information System Survivability'. 37th Hawaii Int. Conf. on System Sciences, Hawaii: 903–1003.

Wheeler, D. A. (2003). *Secure Programming for Linux and UNix HOWTO*. Web published: http://www.dwheeler.com/secure-programs/Secure-Programs-HOWTO/index.html.

15

Dependability and security assurance

Objectives

The objective of this chapter is to describe the verification and validation techniques that are used in the development of critical systems. When you have read this chapter, you will:

- understand how different approaches to static analysis may be used in the verification of critical software systems;

- understand the basics of reliability and security testing and the inherent problems of testing critical systems;

- know why process assurance is important, especially for software that has to be certified by a regulator;

- have been introduced to safety and dependability cases that present arguments and evidence of system safety and dependability.

Contents

Dependability and security assurance is concerned with checking that a critical system meets its dependability requirements. This requires verification and validation (V & V) processes that look for specification, design, and program errors that may affect the availability, safety, reliability, or security of a system.

The verification and validation of a critical system has much in common with the validation of any other software system. The V & V processes should demonstrate that the system meets its specification and that the system services and behavior support the customer's requirements. In doing so, they usually uncover requirements and design errors and program bugs that have to be repaired. However, critical systems require particularly stringent testing and analysis for two reasons:

1. *Costs of failure* The costs and consequences of critical systems failure are potentially much greater than for non-critical systems. You lower the risks of system failure by spending more on system verification and validation. It is usually cheaper to find and remove defects before the system is delivered than to pay for the consequent costs of accidents or disruptions to system service.

2. *Validation of dependability attributes* You may have to make a formal case to customers and a regulator that the system meets its specified dependability requirements (availability, reliability, safety, and security). In some cases, external regulators, such as national aviation authorities, may have to certify that the system is safe before it can be deployed. To obtain this certification, you have to demonstrate how the system has been validated. To do so, you may also have to design and carry out special V & V procedures that collect evidence about the system's dependability.

For these reasons, verification and validation costs for critical systems are usually much higher than for other classes of systems. Typically, more than half of a critical system's development costs are spent on V & V.

Although V & V costs are high, they are justified as they are usually significantly less than the losses that result from an accident. For example, in 1996, a mission-critical software system on the Ariane 5 rocket failed and several satellites were destroyed. No one was injured but the total losses from this accident were hundreds of millions of dollars. The subsequent enquiry discovered that deficiencies in system V & V were partly responsible for this failure. More effective reviews, which would have been relatively cheap, could have discovered the problem that caused the accident.

Although the primary focus of dependability and security assurance is on the validation of the system itself, related activities should verify that the defined system development process has been followed. As I explained in Chapter 13, system quality is affected by the quality of processes used to develop the system. In short, good processes lead to good systems.

The outcome of dependability and security assurance processes is a body of tangible evidence, such as review reports, test results, etc., about the dependability of a system. This evidence may subsequently be used to justify a decision that this system is dependable and secure enough to be deployed and used. Sometimes, the evidence of system dependability is assembled in a dependability or safety case. This is used to convince a customer or an external regulator that the developer's confidence in the system's dependability or safety is justified.

15.1 Static analysis

Static analysis techniques are system verification techniques that don't involve executing a program. Rather, they work on a source representation of the software—either a model of the specification or design, or the source code of the program. Static analysis techniques can be used to check the specification and design models of a system to pick up errors before an executable version of the system is available. They also have the advantage that the presence of errors does not disrupt system checking. When you test a program, defects can mask or hide other defects so you have to remove a detected defect then repeat the testing process.

As I discussed in Chapter 8, perhaps the most commonly used static analysis technique is peer review and inspection, where a specification, design, or program is checked by a group of people. They examine the design or code in detail, looking for possible errors or omissions. Another technique is using design modeling tools to check for anomalies in the UML, such as the same name being used for different objects. However, for critical systems, additional static analysis techniques may be used:

1. Formal verification, where you produce mathematically rigorous arguments that a program conforms to its specification.

2. Model checking, where a theorem prover is used to check a formal description of the system for inconsistencies.

3. Automated program analysis, where the source code of a program is checked for patterns that are known to be potentially erroneous.

These techniques are closely related. Model checking relies on a formal model of the system that may be created from a formal specification. Static analyzers may use formal assertions embedded in a program as comments to check that the associated code is consistent with these assertions.

15.1.1 Verification and formal methods

Formal methods of software development, as I discussed in Chapter 12, rely on a formal model of the system that serves as a system specification. These formal methods are mainly concerned with a mathematical analysis of the specification; with transforming the specification to a more detailed, semantically equivalent representation; or with formally verifying that one representation of the system is semantically equivalent to another representation.

Cleanroom development

Cleanroom software development is based on formal software verification and statistical testing. The objective of the Cleanroom process is zero-defects software to ensure that delivered systems have a high level of reliability. In the Cleanroom process each software increment is formally specified and this specification is transformed into an implementation. Software correctness is demonstrated using a formal approach. There is no unit testing for defects in the process and the system testing is focused on assessing the system's reliability.

http://www.SoftwareEngineering-9.com/Web/Cleanroom/

Formal methods may be used at different stages in the V & V process:

1. A formal specification of the system may be developed and mathematically analyzed for inconsistency. This technique is effective in discovering specification errors and omissions. Model checking, discussed in the next section, is one approach to specification analysis.

2. You can formally verify, using mathematical arguments, that the code of a software system is consistent with its specification. This requires a formal specification. It is effective in discovering programming and some design errors.

Because of the wide semantic gap between a formal system specification and program code, it is difficult to prove that a separately developed program is consistent with its specification. Work on program verification is now, therefore, based on transformational development. In a transformational development process, a formal specification is transformed through a series of representations to program code. Software tools support the development of the transformations and help verify that corresponding representations of the system are consistent. The B method is probably the most widely used formal transformational method (Abrial, 2005; Wordsworth, 1996). It has been used for the development of train control systems and avionics software.

Proponents of formal methods claim that the use of these methods leads to more reliable and safer systems. Formal verification demonstrates that the developed program meets its specification and that implementation errors will not compromise the dependability of the system. If you develop a formal model of concurrent systems using a specification written in a language such as CSP (Schneider, 1999), you can discover conditions that might result in deadlock in the final program, and be able to address these. This is very difficult to do by testing alone.

However, formal specification and proof do not guarantee that the software will be reliable in practical use. The reasons for this are as follows:

1. The specification may not reflect the real requirements of system users. As I discussed in Chapter 12, system users rarely understand formal notations so they cannot directly read the formal specification to find errors and omissions. This means that there is a significant likelihood that the formal specification contains errors and is not an accurate representation of the system requirements.

2. The proof may contain errors. Program proofs are large and complex, so, like large and complex programs, they usually contain errors.

3. The proof may make incorrect assumptions about the way that the system is used. If the system is not used as anticipated, the proof may be invalid.

Verifying a non-trivial software system takes a great deal of time and requires mathematical expertise and specialized software tools, such as theorem provers. It is therefore an expensive process and, as the system size increases, the costs of formal verification increase disproportionately. Many software engineers therefore think that formal verification is not cost effective. They believe that the same level of confidence in the system can be achieved more cheaply by using other validation techniques, such as inspections and system testing.

In spite of their disadvantages, my view is that formal methods and formal verification have an important role to play in the development of critical software systems. Formal specifications are very effective in discovering those specification problems that are the most common causes of system failure. Although formal verification is still impractical for large systems, it can be used to verify critical-safety and security-critical components.

15.1.2 Model checking

Formally verifying programs using a deductive approach is difficult and expensive but alternative approaches to formal analysis have been developed that are based on a more restricted notion of correctness. The most successful of these approaches is called model checking (Baier and Katoen, 2008). This has been widely used to check hardware systems designs and is increasingly being used in critical software systems such as the control software in NASA's Mars exploration vehicles (Regan and Hamilton, 2004) and telephone call processing software (Chandra et al., 2002).

Model checking involves creating a model of a system and checking the correctness of that model using specialized software tools. Many different model-checking tools have been developed—for software, the most widely used is probably SPIN (Holzmann, 2003). The stages involved in model checking are shown in Figure 15.1.

The model-checking process involves building a formal model of a system, usually as an extended finite state machine. Models are expressed in the language of whatever model-checking system is used—for example, the SPIN model checker uses a language called Promela. A set of desirable system properties are identified and written in a formal notation, usually based on temporal logic. An example of such a property in the wilderness weather system might be that the system will always reach the 'transmitting' state from the 'recording' state.

The model checker then explores all paths through the model (i.e., all possible state transitions), checking that the property holds for each path. If it does, then the model checker confirms that the model is correct with respect to that property. If it does not hold for a particular path, the model checker outputs a counter-example illustrating where the property is not true. Model checking is particularly useful in

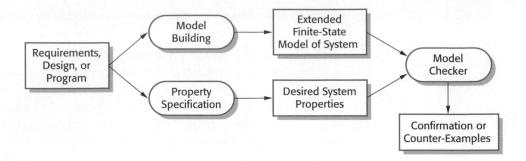

the validation of concurrent systems, which are notoriously difficult to test because of their sensitivity to time. The checker can explore interleaved, concurrent transitions and discover potential problems.

A key issue in model checking is the creation of the system model. If the model has to be created manually (from a requirements or design document), it is an expensive process as model creation takes a great deal of time. In addition, there is the possibility that the model created will not be an accurate model of the requirements or design. It is, therefore, best if the model can be created automatically from the program source code. The Java Pathfinder system (Visser et al., 2003) is an example of a model-checking system that works directly from a representation of Java code.

Model checking is computationally very expensive because it uses an exhaustive approach to check all paths through the system model. As the size of the system increases, so too does the number of states, with a consequent increase in the number of paths to be checked. This means that, for large systems, model checking may be impractical, due to the computer time required to run the checks.

However, as algorithms for identifying those parts of the state that do not have explored to check a particular property improve, it will become increasingly practical to use model-checking routinely in critical systems development. It is not really applicable to data-oriented organizational systems, but it can be used to verify embedded software systems that are modeled as state machines.

15.1.3 Automatic static analysis

As I discussed in Chapter 8, program inspections are often driven by checklists of errors and heuristics. These identify common errors in different programming languages. For some errors and heuristics, it is possible to automate the process of checking programs against these lists, which has resulted in the development of automated static analyzers that can find code fragments that may be incorrect.

Static analysis tools work on the source code of a system and, for some types of analysis at least, no further inputs are required. This means that programmers do not need to learn specialized notations to write program specifications so the benefits of analysis can be immediately clear. This makes automated static analysis easier to introduce into a development process than formal verification or model checking. It is, therefore, probably the most widely used static analysis technique.

Fault class	Static analysis check
Data faults	Variables used before initialization Variables declared but never used Variables assigned twice but never used between assignments Possible array bound violations Undeclared variables
Control faults	Unreachable code Unconditional branches into loops
Input/output faults	Variables output twice with no intervening assignment
Interface faults	Parameter-type mismatches Parameter number mismatches Non-usage of the results of functions Uncalled functions and procedures
Storage management faults	Unassigned pointers Pointer arithmetic Memory leaks

Figure 15.2
Automated static
analysis checks

Automated static analyzers are software tools that scan the source text of a program and detect possible faults and anomalies. They parse the program text and thus recognize the different types of statements in a program. They can then detect whether or not statements are well formed, make inferences about the control flow in the program, and, in many cases, compute the set of all possible values for program data. They complement the error detection facilities provided by the language compiler, and can be used as part of the inspection process or as a separate V & V process activity. Automated static analysis is faster and cheaper than detailed code reviews. However, it cannot discover some classes of errors that could be identified in program inspection meetings.

The intention of automatic static analysis is to draw a code reader's attention to anomalies in the program, such as variables that are used without initialization, variables that are unused, or data whose value could go out of range. Examples of the problems that can be detected by static analysis are shown in Figure 15.2. Of course, the specific checks made are programming-language specific and depend on what is and isn't allowed in the language. Anomalies are often a result of programming errors or omissions, so they highlight things that could go wrong when the program is executed. However, you should understand that these anomalies are not necessarily program faults; they may be deliberate constructs introduced by the programmer, or the anomaly may have no adverse consequences.

There are three levels of checking that may be implemented in static analyzers:

1. *Characteristic error checking* At this level, the static analyzer knows about common errors that are made by programmers in languages such as Java or C. The tool analyzes the code looking for patterns that are characteristic of that

problem and highlights these to the programmer. Although relatively simple, analysis based on common errors can be very cost effective. Zheng and his collaborators (2006) studied the use of static analysis against a large code base in C and C++ and discovered that 90% of the errors in the programs resulted from 10 types of characteristic error.

2. *User-defined error checking* In this approach, the users of the static analyzer may define error patterns, thus extending the types of error that may be detected. This is particularly useful in situations where ordering must be maintained (e.g., method A must always be called before method B). Over time, an organization can collect information about common bugs that occur in their programs and extend the static analysis tools to highlight these errors.

3. *Assertion checking* This is the most general and most powerful approach to static analysis. Developers include formal assertions (often written as stylized comments) in their program that state relationships that must hold at that point in a program. For example, an assertion might be included that states that the value of some variable must lie in the range x..y. The analyzer symbolically executes the code and highlights statements where the assertion may not hold. This approach is used in analyzers such as Splint (Evans and Larochelle, 2002) and the SPARK Examiner (Croxford and Sutton, 2006).

Static analysis is effective in finding errors in programs but commonly generates a large number of 'false positives'. These are code sections where there are no errors but where the static analyzer's rules have detected a potential for errors. The number of false positives can be reduced by adding more information to the program in the form of assertions but, obviously, this requires additional work by the developer of the code. Work has to be done in screening out these false positives before the code itself can be checked for errors.

Static analysis is particularly valuable for security checking (Evans and Larochelle, 2002). Static analyzers can be tailored to check for well-known problems, such as buffer overflow or unchecked inputs, which can be exploited by attackers. Checking for well-known problems is effective for improving security as most attackers base their attacks on common vulnerabilities.

As I discuss later, security testing is difficult because attackers often do unexpected things that testers find difficult to anticipate. Static analyzers can incorporate detailed security expertise that testers may not have and may be applied before a program is tested. If you use static analysis, you can make claims that are true for all possible program executions, not just those that correspond to the tests that you have designed.

Static analysis is now routinely used by many organizations in their software development processes. Microsoft introduced static analysis in the development of device drivers (Larus, et al., 2003) where program failures can have a serious effect. They have now extended the approach across a much wider range of their software to look for security problems as well as errors that affect program reliability (Ball, et al., 2006). Many critical systems, including avionics and nuclear systems, are routinely statically analyzed as part of the V & V process (Nguyen and Ourghanlian, 2003).

Figure 15.3 Reliability measurement

15.2 Reliability testing

Reliability testing is a testing process that aims to measure the reliability of a system. As I explained in Chapter 10, there are several reliability metrics such as POFOD, probability of failure on demand and ROCOF, the rate of occurrence of failure. These may be used to quantitatively specify the required software reliability. You can check in the reliability testing process if the system has achieved that required reliability level.

The process of measuring the reliability of a system is illustrated in Figure 15.3. This process involves four stages:

1. You start by studying existing systems of the same type to understand how these are used in practice. This is important as you are trying to measure the reliability as it is seen by a system uscr. Your aim is to define an operational profile. An operational profile identifies classes of system inputs and the probability that these inputs will occur in normal use.

2. You then construct a set of test data that reflects the operational profile. This means that you create test data with the same probability distribution as the test data for the systems that you have studied. Normally, you will use a test data generator to support this process.

3. You test the system using these data and count the number and type of failures that occur. The times of these failures are also logged. As I discussed in Chapter 10, the time units chosen should be appropriate for the reliability metric used.

4. After you have observed a statistically significant number of failures, you can compute the software reliability and work out the appropriate reliability metric value.

This four-step approach is sometimes called 'statistical testing'. The aim of statistical testing is to assess system reliability. This contrasts with defect testing, discussed in Chapter 8, where the aim is to discover system faults. Prowell et al. (1999) give a good description of statistical testing in their book on Cleanroom software engineering.

This conceptually attractive approach to reliability measurement is not easy to apply in practice. The principal difficulties that arise are:

1. *Operational profile uncertainty* The operational profiles based on experience with other systems may not be an accurate reflection of the real use of the system.

2. *High costs of test data generation* It can be very expensive to generate the large volume of data required in an operational profile unless the process can be totally automated.

3. *Statistical uncertainty when high reliability is specified* You have to generate a statistically significant number of failures to allow accurate reliability measurements. When the software is already reliable, relatively few failures occur and it is difficult to generate new failures.

4. *Recognizing failure* It is not always obvious whether or not a system failure has occurred. If you have a formal specification, you may be able to identify deviations from that specification but, if the specification is in natural language, there may be ambiguities that mean observers could disagree on whether the system has failed.

By far the best way to generate the large data set required for reliability measurement is to use a test data generator, which can be set up to automatically generate inputs matching the operational profile. However, it is not usually possible to automate the production of all test data for interactive systems because the inputs are often a response to system outputs. Data sets for these systems have to be generated manually, with correspondingly higher costs. Even where complete automation is possible, writing commands for the test data generator may take a significant amount of time.

Statistical testing may be used in conjunction with fault injection to gather data about how effective the process of defect testing has been. Fault injection (Voas, 1997) is the deliberate injection of errors into a program. When the program is executed, these lead to program faults and associated failures. You then analyze the failure to discover if the root cause is one the errors that you have added to the program. If you find that X% of the injected faults lead to failures, then proponents of fault injection argue that this suggests that the defect testing process will also have discovered X% of the actual faults in the program.

This, of course, assumes that the distribution and type of injected faults matches the actual faults that arise in practice. It is reasonable to think that this might be true for faults due to programming errors, but fault injection is not effective in predicting the number of faults that stem from requirements or design errors.

Statistical testing often reveals errors in the software that have not been discovered by other V & V processes. These errors may mean that a system's reliability falls short of requirements and repairs have to be made. After these repairs are complete, the system can be retested to reassess its reliability. After this repair and retest process has been repeated several times, it may be possible to extrapolate the results and predict when some required level of reliability will be achieved. This requires fitting the extrapolated data to a reliability growth model, which shows how reliability tends to improve over time. This helps with the planning of testing. Sometimes, a growth model may reveal that a required level of reliability will never be achieved, so the requirements have to be renegotiated.

15.2.1 Operational profiles

The operational profile of a software system reflects how it will be used in practice. It consists of a specification of classes of input and the probability of their occurrence. When a new software system replaces an existing automated system, it is

Reliability growth modeling

A reliability growth model is a model of how the system reliability changes over time during the testing process. As system failures are discovered, the underlying faults causing these failures are repaired so that the reliability of the system should improve during system testing and debugging. To predict reliability, the conceptual reliability growth model must then be translated into a mathematical model.

http://www.SoftwareEngineering-9.com/Web/DepSecAssur/RGM.html

reasonably easy to assess the probable pattern of usage of the new software. It should correspond to the existing usage, with some allowance made for the new functionality that is (presumably) included in the new software. For example, an operational profile can be specified for telephone switching systems because telecommunication companies know the call patterns that these systems have to handle.

Typically, the operational profile is such that the inputs that have the highest probability of being generated fall into a small number of classes, as shown on the left of Figure 15.4. There is a very large number of classes where inputs are highly improbable but not impossible. These are shown on the right of Figure 15.4. The ellipsis (. . .) means that there are many more of these unusual inputs than are shown.

Musa (1998) discusses the development of operational profiles in telecommunication systems. As there is a long history of collecting usage data in that domain, the process of operational profile development is relatively straightforward. It simply reflects the historical usage data. For a system that required about 15 person-years of development effort, an operational profile was developed in about 1 person-month. In other cases, operational profile generation took longer (2–3 person-years) but the cost was spread over a number of system releases. Musa reckons that his company had at least a 10-fold return on the investment required to develop an operational profile.

However, when a software system is new and innovative, it is difficult to anticipate how it will be used. Consequently, it is practically impossible to create an accurate operational profile. Many different users with different expectations, backgrounds, and experience may use the new system. There is no historical usage database. These users may make use of systems in ways that were not anticipated by the system developers.

Developing an accurate operational profile is certainly possible for some types of system, such as telecommunication systems, that have a standardized pattern of use. For other system types, however, there are many different users who each have their own ways of using the system. As I discussed in Chapter 10, different users can get quite different impressions of reliability because they use the system in different ways.

The problem is further compounded because operational profiles are not static but change as the system is used. As users learn about a new system and become more confident with it, they start to use it in more sophisticated ways. Because of this, it is often impossible to develop a trustworthy operational profile. Consequently, you cannot be confident about the accuracy of any reliability measurements, as they may be based on incorrect assumptions about the ways in which the system is used.

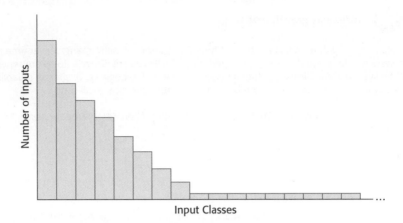

Figure 15.4 An operational profile

15.3 Security testing

The assessment of system security is increasingly important as more and more critical systems are Internet-enabled and so can be accessed by anyone with a network connection. There are daily stories of attacks on web-based systems, and viruses and worms are regularly distributed using Internet protocols.

All of this means that the verification and validation processes for web-based systems must focus on security assessment, where the ability of the system to resist different types of attack is tested. However, as Anderson explains (2001), this type of security assessment is very difficult to carry out. Consequently, systems are often deployed with security loopholes. Attackers use these to gain access to the system or to cause damage to the system or its data.

Fundamentally, there are two reasons why security testing is so difficult:

1. Security requirements, like some safety requirements, are 'shall not' requirements. That is, they specify what should not happen rather than system functionality or required behavior. It is not usually possible to define this unwanted behavior as simple constraints to be checked by the system.

   If resources are available, you can demonstrate, in principle at least, that a system meets its functional requirements. However, it is impossible to prove that a system does not do something. Irrespective of the amount of testing, security vulnerabilities may remain in a system after it has been deployed. You may, of course, generate functional requirements that are designed to guard the system against some known types of attack. However, you cannot derive requirements for unknown or unanticipated types of attack. Even in systems that have been in use for many years, an ingenious attacker can discover a new form of attack and can penetrate what was thought to be a secure system.

2. The people attacking a system are intelligent and are actively looking for vulnerabilities that they can exploit. They are willing to experiment with the system and to try things that are far outside normal activity and system use. For example, in a surname field they may enter 1,000 characters with a mixture of letters, punctuation, and numbers. Furthermore, once they find a vulnerability, they can exchange information about this and so increase the number of potential attackers.

Attackers may try to discover the assumptions made by system developers and then contradict these assumptions to see what happens. They are in a position to use and explore a system over a period of time and analyze it using software tools to discover vulnerabilities that they may be able to exploit. They may, in fact, have more time to spend on looking for vulnerabilities than system test engineers, as testers must also focus on testing the system.

For this reason, static analysis can be particularly useful as a security testing tool. A static analysis of a program can quickly guide the testing team to areas of a program that may include errors and vulnerabilities. Anomalies revealed in the static analysis can be directly fixed or can help identify tests that need to be done to reveal whether or not these anomalies actually represent a risk to the system.

To check the security of a system, you can use a combination of testing, tool-based analysis, and formal verification:

1. *Experience-based testing* In this case, the system is analyzed against types of attack that are known to the validation team. This may involve developing test cases or examining the source code of a system. For example, to check that the system is not susceptible to the well-known SQL poisoning attack, you might test the system using inputs that include SQL commands. To check that buffer overflow errors will not occur, you can examine all input buffers to see if the program is checking that assignments to buffer elements are within bounds.

   This type of validation is usually carried out in conjunction with tool-based validation, where the tool gives you information that helps focus system testing. Checklists of known security problems may be created to assist with the process. Figure 15.5 gives some examples of questions that might be used to drive experience-based testing. Checks on whether the design and programming guidelines for security (Chapter 14) have been followed might also be included in a security problem checklist.

2. *Tiger teams* This is a form of experience-based testing where it is possible to draw on experience from outside the development team to test an application system. You set up a 'tiger team' who are given the objective of breaching the system security. They simulate attacks on the system and use their ingenuity to discover new ways to compromise the system security. Tiger team members should have previous experience with security testing and finding security weaknesses in systems.

3. *Tool-based testing* For this method, various security tools such as password checkers are used to analyze the system. Password checkers detect insecure passwords such as common names or strings of consecutive letters. This

Security checklist
1. Do all files that are created in the application have appropriate access permissions? The wrong access permissions may lead to these files being accessed by unauthorized users.
2. Does the system automatically terminate user sessions after a period of inactivity? Sessions that are left active may allow unauthorized access through an unattended computer.
3. If the system is written in a programming language without array bound checking, are there situations where buffer overflow may be exploited? Buffer overflow may allow attackers to send code strings to the system and then execute them.
4. If passwords are set, does the system check that passwords are 'strong'? Strong passwords consist of mixed letters, numbers, and punctuation, and are not normal dictionary entries. They are more difficult to break than simple passwords.
5. Are inputs from the system's environment always checked against an input specification? Incorrect processing of badly formed inputs is a common cause of security vulnerabilities.

Figure 15.5 Examples of entries in a security checklist

approach is really an extension of experience-based validation, where experience of security flaws is embodied in the tools used. Static analysis is, of course, another type of tool-based testing.

4. *Formal verification* A system can be verified against a formal security specification. However, as in other areas, formal verification for security is not widely used.

Security testing is, inevitably, limited by the time and resources available to the test team. This means that you should normally adopt a risk-based approach to security testing and focus on what you think are the most significant risks faced by the system. If you have an analysis of the security risks to the system, these can be used to drive the testing process. As well as testing the system against the security requirements derived from these risks, the test team should also try to break the system by adopting alternative approaches that threaten the system assets.

It is very difficult for end-users of a system to verify its security. Consequently, government bodies in North America and in Europe have established sets of security evaluation criteria that can be checked by specialized evaluators (Pfleeger and Pfleeger, 2007). Software product suppliers can submit their products for evaluation and certification against these criteria. Therefore, if you have a requirement for a particular level of security, you can choose a product that has been validated to that level. In practice, however, these criteria have primarily been used in military systems and as of yet have not achieved much commercial acceptance.

15.4 Process assurance

As I discussed in Chapter 13, experience has shown that dependable processes lead to dependable systems. That is, if a process is based on good software engineering practices, then it is more likely that the resulting software product will be dependable.

Regulation of software

Regulators are created by governments to ensure that private industry does not profit by failing to follow national standards for safety, security, and so on. There are regulators in many different industries such as nuclear power, aviation, and banking. As software systems have become increasingly important in the critical infrastructure of countries, these regulators have become increasingly concerned with safety and dependability cases for software systems.

http://www.SoftwareEngineering-9.com/Web/DepSecAssur/Regulation.html

Of course, a good process does not guarantee dependability. However, evidence that a dependable process has been used increases overall confidence that a system is dependable. Process assurance is concerned with collecting information about processes used during system development, and the outcomes of these processes. This information provides evidence of the analyses, reviews, and tests that have been carried out during software development.

Process assurance is concerned with two things:

1. Do we have the right processes? Do the system development processes used in the organization include appropriate controls and V & V subprocesses for the type of system being developed?

2. Are we doing the processes right? Has the organization carried out the development work as defined in its software process descriptions and have the defined outcomes from the software processes been produced?

Companies that have extensive experience of critical systems engineering have evolved their processes to reflect good verification and validation practice. In some cases, this has involved discussions with the external regulator to agree on what processes should be used. Although there is a great deal of process variation between companies, activities that you would expect to see in critical systems development processes include requirements management, change management and configuration control, system modeling, reviews and inspections, test planning, and test coverage analysis. The notion of process improvement, where good practice is introduced and institutionalized in processes, is covered in Chapter 26.

The other aspect of process assurance is checking that processes have been properly enacted. This normally involves ensuring that processes are properly documented and checking this process documentation. For example, part of a dependable process may involve formal program inspections. The documentation for each inspection should include the checklists used to drive the inspection, a list of the people involved, the problems identified during the inspection, and the actions required.

Demonstrating that a dependable process has been used therefore involves producing a lot of documentary evidence about the process and the software being developed. The need for this extensive documentation means that agile processes are

Licensing of software engineers

In some areas of engineering, safety engineers must be licensed engineers. Inexperienced, poorly qualified engineers are not allowed to take responsibility for safety. This does not currently apply to software engineers, although there has been extensive discussion on the licensing of software engineers in several states in the United States (Knight and Leveson, 2002). However, future process standards for safety-critical software development may require that project safety engineers should be licensed engineers, with a defined minimum level of qualifications and experience.

http://www.SoftwareEngineering-9.com/Web/DepSecAssur/Licensing.html

rarely used in systems where safety or dependability certification is required. Agile processes focus on the software itself and (rightly) argue that a great deal of process documentation is never actually used after it has been produced. However, you have to create evidence and document process activities when process information is used as part of a system safety or dependability case.

15.4.1 Processes for safety assurance

Most work on process assurance has been done in the area of safety-critical systems development. It is important that a safety-critical systems development process include V & V processes that are geared to safety analysis and assurance for two reasons:

1. Accidents are rare events in critical systems and it may be practically impossible to simulate them during the testing of a system. You can't rely on extensive testing to replicate the conditions that can lead to an accident.

2. Safety requirements, as I discussed in Chapter 12, are sometimes 'shall not' requirements that exclude unsafe system behavior. It is impossible to demonstrate conclusively through testing and other validation activities that these requirements have been met.

Specific safety assurance activities should be included at all stages in the software development process. These safety assurance activities record the analyses that have been carried out and the person or people responsible for these analyses. Safety assurance activities that are incorporated into software processes may include the following:

1. Hazard logging and monitoring, which trace hazards from preliminary hazard analysis through to testing and system validation.

2. Safety reviews, which are used throughout the development process.

3. Safety certification, where the safety of critical components is formally certified. This involves a group external to the system development team

examining the available evidence and deciding whether or not a system or component should be considered to be safe before it is made available for use.

To support these safety assurance processes, project safety engineers should be appointed who have explicit responsibility for the safety aspects of a system. This means that these individuals will be held responsible if a safety-related system failure occurs. They must be able to demonstrate that the safety assurance activities have been properly carried out.

Safety engineers work with quality managers to ensure that a detailed configuration management system is used to track all safety-related documentation and keep it in step with the associated technical documentation. This is essential in all dependable processes. There is little point in having stringent validation procedures if a failure of configuration management means that the wrong system is delivered to the customer. Configuration and quality management are covered in Chapters 24 and 25.

The hazard analysis process that is an essential part of safety-critical systems development is an example of a safety assurance process. Hazard analysis is concerned with identifying hazards, their probability of occurrence, and the probability of each hazard leading to an accident. If there is program code that checks for and handles each hazard, then you can argue that these hazards will not result in accidents. Such arguments may be supplemented by safety arguments, as discussed later in this chapter. Where external certification is required before a system is used (e.g., in an aircraft), it is usually a condition of certification that this traceability can be demonstrated.

The central safety document that should be produced is the hazard log. This document provides evidence of how identified hazards have been taken into account during software development. This hazard log is used at each stage of the software development process to document how that development stage has taken the hazards into account. A simplified example of a hazard log entry for the insulin delivery system is shown in Figure 15.6. This form documents the process of hazard analysis and shows design requirements that have been generated during this process. These design requirements are intended to ensure that the control system can never deliver an insulin overdose to a user of the insulin pump.

As shown in Figure 15.6, individuals who have safety responsibilities should be explicitly identified. This is important for two reasons:

1. When people are identified, they can be held accountable for their actions. This means that they are likely to take more care because any problems can be traced back to their work.

2. In the event of an accident, there may be legal proceedings or an enquiry. It is important to be able to identify who was responsible for safety assurance so that they can account for their actions.

Hazard Log					Page 4: Printed 20.02.2009
System: Insulin Pump System *Safety Engineer:* James Brown			*File:* InsulinPump/Safety/HazardLog *Log version:* 1/3		
Identified Hazard	Insulin overdose delivered to patient				
Identified by	Jane Williams				
Criticality class	1				
Identified risk	High				
Fault tree identified	YES	*Date*	24.01.07	*Location*	Hazard Log, Page 5
Fault tree creators	Jane Williams and Bill Smith				
Fault tree checked	YES	*Date*	28.01.07	*Checker*	James Brown

System safety design requirements

1. The system shall include self-testing software that will test the sensor system, the clock, and the insulin delivery system.
2. The self-checking software shall be executed once per minute.
3. In the event of the self-checking software discovering a fault in any of the system components, an audible warning shall be issued and the pump display shall indicate the name of the component where the fault has been discovered. The delivery of insulin shall be suspended.
4. The system shall incorporate an override system that allows the system user to modify the computed dose of insulin that is to be delivered by the system.
5. The amount of override shall be no greater than a pre-set value (maxOverride), which is set when the system is configured by medical staff.

Figure 15.6 A simplified hazard log entry

15.5 Safety and dependability cases

Security and dependability assurance processes generate a lot of information. This may include test results, information about the development processes used, records of review meetings, etc. This information provides evidence about the security and dependability of a system, and is used to help decide whether or not the system is dependable enough for operational use.

Safety and dependability cases are structured documents setting out detailed arguments and evidence that a system is safe or that a required level of security or dependability has been achieved. They are sometimes called assurance cases. Essentially, a safety or dependability case pulls together all of the available evidence that demonstrates that a system is trustworthy. For many types of critical system, the production of a safety case is a legal requirement. The case must satisfy a regulator or certification body before the system can be deployed.

The responsibility of a regulator is to check that a completed system is as safe or dependable as practicable, so their role primarily comes into play when a development project is complete. However, regulators and developers rarely work in isolation; they communicate with the development team to establish what has to be included in the safety case. The regulator and developers jointly examine processes and procedures to make sure that these are being enacted and documented to the regulator's satisfaction.

Dependability cases are usually developed during and after the system development process. This can sometimes cause problems if the development process activities do not produce evidence for the system's dependability. Graydon et al. (2007) argue that the development of a safety and dependability case should be tightly integrated with system design and implementation. This means that system design decisions may be influenced by the requirements of the dependability case. Design choices that may add significantly to the difficulties and costs of case development can be avoided.

Dependability cases are generalizations of system safety cases. A safety case is a set of documents that includes a description of the system to be certified, information about the processes used to develop the system and, critically, logical arguments that demonstrate that the system is likely to be safe. More succinctly, Bishop and Bloomfield (1998) define a safety case as:

> *A documented body of evidence that provides a convincing and valid argument that a system is adequately safe for a given application in a given environment.*

The organization and contents of a safety or dependability case depend on the type of system that is to be certified and its context of operation. Figure 15.7 shows one possible structure for a safety case but there are no widely used industrial standards in this area for safety cases. Safety case structures vary, depending on the industry and the maturity of the domain. For example, nuclear safety cases have been required for many years. They are very comprehensive and presented in a way that is familiar to nuclear engineers. However, safety cases for medical devices have been introduced much more recently. Their structure is more flexible and the cases themselves are less detailed than nuclear cases.

Of course, software itself is not dangerous. It is only when it is embedded in a large computer-based or sociotechnical system that software failures can result in failures of other equipment or processes that can cause injury or death. Therefore, a software safety case is always part of a wider system safety case that demonstrates the safety of the overall system. When constructing a software safety case, you have to relate software failures to wider system failures and demonstrate either that these software failures will not occur or that they will not be propagated in such a way that dangerous system failures may occur.

15.5.1 Structured arguments

The decision on whether or not a system is sufficiently dependable to be used should be based on logical arguments. These should demonstrate that the evidence presented supports the claims about a system's security and dependability. These claims may be absolute (event X will or will not happen) or probabilistic (the probability of

Chapter	Description
System description	An overview of the system and a description of its critical components.
Safety requirements	The safety requirements abstracted from the system requirements specification. Details of other relevant system requirements may also be included.
Hazard and risk analysis	Documents describing the hazards and risks that have been identified and the measures taken to reduce risk. Hazard analyses and hazard logs.
Design analysis	A set of structured arguments (see Section 15.5.1) that justify why the design is safe.
Verification and validation	A description of the V & V procedures used and, where appropriate, the test plans for the system. Summaries of the test results showing defects that have been detected and corrected. If formal methods have been used, a formal system specification and any analyses of that specification. Records of static analyses of the source code.
Review reports	Records of all design and safety reviews.
Team competences	Evidence of the competence of all of the team involved in safety-related systems development and validation.
Process QA	Records of the quality assurance processes (see Chapter 24) carried out during system development.
Change management processes	Records of all changes proposed, actions taken and, where appropriate, justification of the safety of these changes. Information about configuration management procedures and configuration management logs.
Associated safety cases	References to other safety cases that may impact the safety case.

Figure 15.7 The contents of a software safety case

occurrence of event Y is 0.n). An argument links the evidence and the claim. As shown in Figure 15.8, an argument is a relationship between what is thought to be the case (the claim) and a body of evidence that has been collected. The argument, essentially, explains why the claim, which is an assertion about system security or dependability, can be inferred from the available evidence.

For example, the insulin pump is a safety-critical device whose failure could cause injury to a user. In many countries, this means that a regulatory authority (in the UK, the Medical Devices Directorate) has to be convinced of the system's safety before the device can be sold and used. To make this decision, the regulator assesses the safety case for the system, which presents structured arguments that normal operation of the system will not cause harm to a user.

Safety cases usually rely on structured, claim-based arguments. For example, the following argument might be used to justify a claim that computations carried out by the control software will not lead to an overdose of insulin being delivered to a pump user. Of course, this is a very simplified argument. In a real safety case more detailed references to the evidence would be presented.

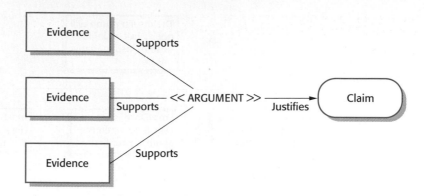

Figure 15.8 Structured arguments

Claim: The maximum single dose computed by the insulin pump will not exceed maxDose, where maxDose has been assessed as a safe single dose for a particular patient.

Evidence: Safety argument for insulin pump software control program (I discuss safety arguments later in this section).

Evidence: Test data sets for insulin pump. In 400 tests, the value of currentDose was correctly computed and never exceeded maxDose.

Evidence: Static analysis report for insulin pump control program. The static analysis of the control software revealed no anomalies that affected the value of currentDose, the program variable that holds the dose of insulin to be delivered.

Argument: The evidence presented shows that the maximum dose of insulin that can be computed is equal to maxDose.

It is therefore reasonable to assume, with a high level of confidence, that the evidence justifies the claim that the insulin pump will not compute a dose of insulin to be delivered that exceeds the maximum single dose.

Notice that the evidence presented is both redundant and diverse. The software is checked using several different mechanisms with significant overlap between them. As I discussed in Chapter 13, the use of redundant and diverse processes increases confidence. If there are omissions and mistakes that are not detected by one validation process, there is a good chance that these will be found by one of the others.

Of course, there will normally be many claims about the dependability and security of a system, with the validity of one claim often depending on whether or not other claims are valid. Therefore, claims may be organized in a hierarchy. Figure 15.9 shows part of this claim hierarchy for the insulin pump. To demonstrate that a high-level claim is valid, you first have to work through the arguments for lower-level claims. If you can show that each of these lower-level claims is justified, then you may be able to infer that the higher-level claims are justified.

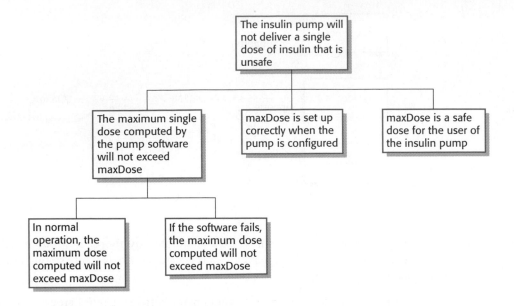

Figure 15.9
A safety claim
hierarchy for
the insulin pump

15.5.2 Structured safety arguments

Structured safety arguments are a type of structured argument, which demonstrate that a program meets its safety obligations. In a safety argument, it is not necessary to prove that the program works as intended. It is only necessary to show that program execution cannot result in an unsafe state. This means that safety arguments are cheaper to make than correctness arguments. You don't have to consider all program states—you can simply concentrate on states that could lead to an accident.

A general assumption that underlies work in system safety is that the number of system faults that can lead to safety-critical hazards is significantly less than the total number of faults that may exist in the system. Safety assurance can concentrate on these faults that have hazard potential. If it can be demonstrated that these faults cannot occur or, if they occur, the associated hazard will not result in an accident, then the system is safe. This is the basis of structured safety arguments.

Structured safety arguments are intended to demonstrate that, assuming normal execution conditions, a program should be safe. They are usually based on contradiction. The steps involved in creating a safety argument are the following:

1. You start by assuming that an unsafe state, which has been identified by the system hazard analysis, can be reached by executing the program.

2. You write a predicate (a logical expression) that defines this unsafe state.

3. You then systematically analyze a system model or the program and show that, for all program paths leading to that state, the terminating condition of these paths contradicts the unsafe state predicate. If this is the case, the initial assumption of an unsafe state is incorrect.

```
— The insulin dose to be delivered is a function of
— blood sugar level, the previous dose delivered and
— the time of delivery of the previous dose
currentDose = computeInsulin () ;

// Safety check—adjust currentDose if necessary.

// if statement 1
if (previousDose == 0)
{
    if (currentDose > maxDose/2)
        currentDose = maxDose/2 ;
}
else
    if (currentDose > (previousDose * 2) )
        currentDose = previousDose * 2 ;

// if statement 2

if ( currentDose < minimumDose )
    currentDose = 0 ;
else if ( currentDose > maxDose )
    currentDose = maxDose ;
administerInsulin (currentDose) ;
```

Figure 15.10 Insulin dose computation with safety checks

4.   When you have repeated this analysis for all identified hazards then you have strong evidence that the system is safe.

Structured safety arguments can be applied at different levels, from requirements through design models to code. At the requirements level, you are trying to demonstrate that there are no missing safety requirements and that the requirements do not make invalid assumptions about the system. At the design level, you might analyze a state model of the system to find unsafe states. At the code level, you consider all of the paths through the safety-critical code to show that the execution of all paths leads to a contradiction.

As an example, consider the code in Figure 15.10, which might be part of the implementation of the insulin delivery system. The code computes the dose of insulin to be delivered then applies some safety checks to reduce the probability than an overdose of insulin will be injected. Developing a safety argument for this code involves demonstrating that the dose of insulin administered is never greater than the maximum safe level for a single dose. This is established for each individual diabetic user in discussions with their medical advisors.

To demonstrate safety, you do not have to prove that the system delivers the 'correct' dose, merely that it never delivers an overdose to the patient. You work on the assumption that maxDose is the safe level for that system user.

To construct the safety argument, you identify the predicate that defines the unsafe state, which is that currentDose > maxDose. You then demonstrate that all program paths lead to a contradiction of this unsafe assertion. If this is the case, the

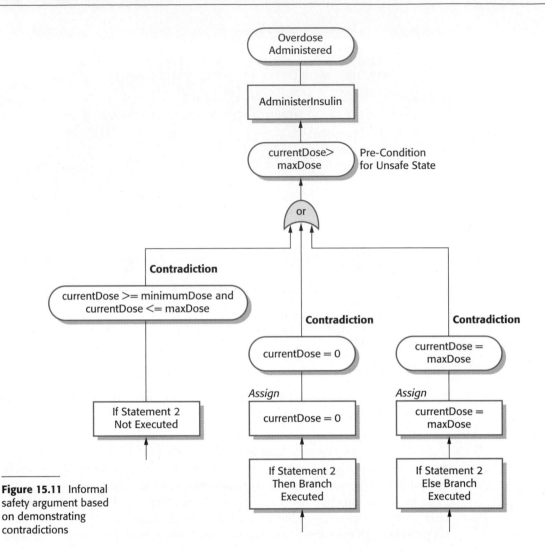

Figure 15.11 Informal safety argument based on demonstrating contradictions

unsafe condition cannot be true. If you can do this, you can be confident that the program will not compute an unsafe dose of insulin. You can structure and present the safety arguments graphically, as shown in Figure 15.11.

To construct a structured argument for a program does not make an unsafe computation, you first identify all possible paths through the code that could lead to the potentially unsafe state. You work backwards from this unsafe state and consider the last assignment to all of the state variables on each path leading to this unsafe state. If you can show that none of the values of these variables is unsafe, then you have shown that your initial assumption (that the computation is unsafe) is incorrect.

Working backwards is important because it means you can ignore all states apart from the final states that lead to the exit condition for the code. The previous values don't matter to the safety of the system. In this example, all you need to be concerned with is the set of possible values of currentDose immediately before the administerInsulin method is executed. You can ignore computations, such as if-statement 1 in Figure 15.10, in the safety argument because their results are over-written in later program statements.

In the safety argument shown in Figure 15.11, there are three possible program paths that lead to the call to the administerInsulin method. You have to show that the amount of insulin delivered never exceeds maxDose. All possible program paths to administerInsulin are considered:

1. Neither branch of if-statement 2 is executed. This can only happen if currentDose is either greater than or equal to minimumDose and less than or equal to maxDose. This is the post-condition—an assertion that is true after the statement has been executed.

2. The then-branch of if-statement 2 is executed. In this case, the assignment setting currentDose to zero is executed. Therefore, its post-condition is currentDose = 0.

3. The else-if-branch of if-statement 2 is executed. In this case, the assignment setting currentDose to maxDose is executed. Therefore, after this statement has been executed, we know that the post-condition is currentDose = maxDose.

In all three cases, the post-conditions contradict the unsafe pre-condition that the dose administered is greater than maxDose. We can therefore claim that the computation is safe.

Structured arguments can be used in the same way to demonstrate that certain security properties of a system are true. For example, if you wish to show that a computation will never lead to the permissions on a resource being changed, you may be able to use a structured security argument to show this. However, the evidence from structured arguments is less reliable for security validation. This is because there is a possibility that the attacker may corrupt the code of the system. In such a case, the code executed is not the code that you have claimed is secure.

KEY POINTS

■ Static analysis is an approach to V & V that examines the source code (or other representation) of a system, looking for errors and anomalies. It allows all parts of a program to be checked, not just those parts that are exercised by system tests.

■ Model checking is a formal approach to static analysis that exhaustively checks all states in a system for potential errors.

■ Statistical testing is used to estimate software reliability. It relies on testing the system with a test data set that reflects the operational profile of the software. Test data may be generated automatically.

■ Security validation is difficult because security requirements state what should not happen in a system, rather than what should. Furthermore, system attackers are intelligent and may have more time to probe for weaknesses than is available for security testing.

■ Security validation may be carried out using experience-based analysis, tool-based analysis, or 'tiger teams' that simulate attacks on a system.

■ It is important to have a well-defined, certified process for safety-critical systems development. The process must include the identification and monitoring of potential hazards.

■ Safety and dependability cases collect all of the evidence that demonstrates a system is safe and dependable. Safety cases are required when an external regulator must certify the system before it is used.

■ Safety cases are usually based on structured arguments. Structured safety arguments show that an identified hazardous condition can never occur by considering all program paths that lead to an unsafe condition, and showing that the condition cannot hold.

FURTHER READING

Software Reliability Engineering: More Reliable Software, Faster and Cheaper, 2nd edition. This is probably the definitive book on the use of operational profiles and reliability models for reliability assessment. It includes details of experiences with statistical testing. (J. D. Musa, McGraw-Hill, 2004.)

'NASA's Mission Reliable'. A discussion of how NASA has used static analysis and model checking for assuring the reliability of spacecraft software. (P. Regan and S. Hamilton, *IEEE Computer,* **37** (1), January 2004.) http://dx.doi.org/10.1109/MC.2004.1260727.

Dependability cases. An example-based introduction to defining a dependability case. (C. B. Weinstock, J. B. Goodenough, J. J. Hudak, Software Engineering Institute, CMU/SEI-2004-TN-016, 2004.) http://www.sei.cmu.edu/publications/documents/04.reports/04tn016.html.

How to Break Web Software: Functional and Security Testing of Web Applications and Web Services. A short book that provides good practical advice on how to run security tests on networked applications. (M. Andrews and J. A. Whittaker, Addison-Wesley, 2006.)

'Using static analysis to find bugs'. This paper describes Findbugs, a Java static analyzer that uses simple techniques to find potential security violations and runtime errors. (N. Ayewah et al., *IEEE Software,* **25** (5), Sept/Oct 2008.) http://dx.doi.org/10.1109/MS.2008.130.

EXERCISES

15.1. Explain when it may be cost effective to use formal specification and verification in the development of safety-critical software systems. Why do you think that critical systems engineers are against the use of formal methods?

15.2. Suggest a list of conditions that could be detected by a static analyzer for Java, C++, or any another programming language that you use. Comment on this list compared to the list given in Figure 15.2.

15.3. Explain why it is practically impossible to validate reliability specifications when these are expressed in terms of a very small number of failures over the total lifetime of a system.

15.4. Explain why ensuring system reliability is not a guarantee of system safety.

15.5. Using examples, explain why security testing is a very difficult process.

15.6. Suggest how you would go about validating a password protection system for an application that you have developed. Explain the function of any tools that you think may be useful.

15.7. The MHC-PMS has to be secure against attacks that might reveal confidential patient information. Some of these attacks have been discussed in Chapter 14. Using this information, extend the checklist in Figure 15.5 to guide testers of the MHC-PMS.

15.8. List four types of systems that may require software safety cases, explaining why safety cases are required.

15.9. The door lock control mechanism in a nuclear waste storage facility is designed for safe operation. It ensures that entry to the storeroom is only permitted when radiation shields are in place or when the radiation level in the room falls below some given value (dangerLevel). So:

   i. If remotely controlled radiation shields are in place within a room, an authorized operator may open the door.

   ii. If the radiation level in a room is below a specified value, an authorized operator may open the door.

   iii. An authorized operator is identified by the input of an authorized door entry code.

The code shown in Figure 15.12 (see below) controls the door-locking mechanism. Note that the safe state is that entry should not be permitted. Using the approach discussed in section 15.5.2, develop a safety argument for this code. Use the line numbers to refer to specific statements. If you find that the code is unsafe, suggest how it should be modified to make it safe.

```
1       entryCode = lock.getEntryCode () ;
2       if (entryCode == lock.authorizedCode)
3       {
4               shieldStatus = Shield.getStatus ();
5               radiationLevel = RadSensor.get ();
6               if (radiationLevel < dangerLevel)
7                       state = safe;
8               else
9                       state = unsafe;
10              if (shieldStatus == Shield.inPlace() )
11                      state = safe;
12              if (state == safe)
13                      {
14                              Door.locked = false ;
15                              Door.unlock ();
16                      }
17              else
18              {
19                      Door.lock ( );
20                      Door.locked := true ;
21              }
22      }
```

Figure 15.12 Door entry code

15.10. Assume you were part of a team that developed software for a chemical plant, which failed, causing a serious pollution incident. Your boss is interviewed on television and states that the validation process is comprehensive and that there are no faults in the software. She asserts that the problems must be due to poor operational procedures. A newspaper approaches you for your opinion. Discuss how you should handle such an interview.

REFERENCES

Abrial, J. R. (2005). *The B Book: Assigning Programs to Meanings*. Cambridge, UK: Cambridge University Press.

Anderson, R. (2001). *Security Engineering: A Guide to Building Dependable Distributed Systems*. Chichester, UK: John Wiley & Sons.

Baier, C. and Katoen, J.-P. (2008). *Principles of Model Checking*. Cambridge, Mass.: MIT Press.

Ball, T., Bounimova, E., Cook, B., Levin, V., Lichtenberg, J., McGarvey, C., Ondrusek, B., S. K., R. and Ustuner, A. (2006). 'Thorough Static Analysis of Device Drivers'. *Proc. EuroSys* 2006, Leuven, Belgium.

Bishop, P. and Bloomfield, R. E. (1998). 'A methodology for safety case development'. *Proc. Safety-critical Systems Symposium*, Birmingham, UK: Springer.

Chandra, S., Godefroid, P. and Palm, C. (2002). 'Software model checking in practice: An industrial case study'. *Proc. 24th Int. Conf. on Software Eng.* (ICSE 2002), Orland, Fla.: IEEE Computer Society, 431–41.

Croxford, M. and Sutton, J. (2006). 'Breaking Through the V and V Bottleneck'. *Proc. 2nd Int. Eurospace—Ada-Europe Symposium on Ada in Europe*, Frankfurt, Germany: Springer-LNCS, 344–54.

Evans, D. and Larochelle, D. (2002). 'Improving Security Using Extensible Lightweight Static Analysis'. *IEEE Software*, **19** (1), 42–51.

Graydon, P. J., Knight, J. C. and Strunk, E. A. (2007). 'Assurance Based Development of Critical Systems'. *Proc. 37th Annual IEEE Conf. on Dependable Systems and Networks*, Edinburgh, Scotland: 347–57.

Holzmann, G. J. (2003). *The SPIN Model Checker*. Boston: Addison-Wesley.

Knight, J. C. and Leveson, N. G. (2002). 'Should software engineers be licensed?' *Comm.* ACM, **45** (11), 87–90.

Larus, J. R., Ball, T., Das, M., Deline, R., Fahndrich, M., Pincus, J., Rajamani, S. K. and Venkatapathy, R. (2003). 'Righting Software'. *IEEE Software*, **21** (3), 92–100.

Musa, J. D. (1998). *Software Reliability Engineering: More Reliable Software, Faster Development and Testing*. New York: McGraw-Hill.

Nguyen, T. and Ourghanlian, A. (2003). 'Dependability assessment of safety-critical system software by static analysis methods'. *Proc. IEEE Conf. on Dependable Systems and Networks (DSN' 2003)*, San Francisco, Calif.: IEEE Computer Society, 75–9.

Pfleeger, C. P. and Pfleeger, S. L. (2007). *Security in Computing, 4th edition*. Boston: Addison-Wesley.

Prowell, S. J., Trammell, C. J., Linger, R. C. and Poore, J. H. (1999). *Cleanroom Software Engineering: Technology and Process*. Reading, Mass.: Addison-Wesley.

Regan, P. and Hamilton, S. (2004). 'NASA's Mission Reliable'. *IEEE Computer*, **37** (1), 59–68.

Schneider, S. (1999). *Concurrent and Real-time Systems: The CSP Approach*. Chichester, UK: John Wiley and Sons.

Visser, W., Havelund, K., Brat, G., Park, S. and Lerda, F. (2003). 'Model Checking Programs'. *Automated Software Engineering J.*, **10** (2), 203–32.

Voas, J. (1997). 'Fault Injection for the Masses'. *IEEE Computer*, **30** (12), 129–30.

Wordsworth, J. (1996). *Software Engineering with* B. Wokingham: Addison-Wesley.

Zheng, J., Williams, L., Nagappan, N., Snipes, W., Hudepohl, J. P. and Vouk, M. A. (2006). 'On the value of static analysis for fault detection in software'. *IEEE Trans. on Software Eng.*, **32** (4), 240–5.

PART 3

Advanced Software Engineering

I have entitled this part of the book 'Advanced Software Engineering' because you have to understand the basics of the discipline, covered in Chapters 1–9, to benefit from the material covered here. Many of the topics discussed here reflect industrial software engineering practice in the development of distributed and real-time systems.

Software reuse has now become the dominant development paradigm for web-based information systems and enterprise systems. The most common approach to reuse is COTS reuse where a large system is configured for the needs of an organization and little or no original software development is required. I introduce the general topic of reuse in Chapter 16 and focus in this chapter on the reuse of COTS systems.

Chapter 17 is also concerned with the reuse of software components rather than entire software systems. Component-based software engineering is a process of component composition, with new code being developed to integrate reusable components. In this chapter, I explain what is meant by a component and why standard component models are needed for effective component reuse. I also discuss the general process of component-based software engineering and the problems of component composition.

The majority of large systems are now distributed systems and Chapter 18 covers issues and problems of building distributed systems. I introduce the client–server approach as a fundamental paradigm of distributed systems engineering, and explain various ways of implementing this architectural style. The final section in this chapter explains how providing software as a distributed application service will radically change the market for software products.

Chapter 19 introduces the related topic of service-oriented architectures, which link the notions of distribution and reuse. Services are reusable software components whose functionality can be accessed over the Internet and made available to a range of clients. In this chapter, I explain what is involved in creating services (service engineering) and composing services to create new software systems.

Embedded systems are the most widely used instances of software systems and Chapter 20 covers this important topic. I introduce the idea of a real-time embedded system and describe three architectural patterns that are used in embedded systems design. I then go on to explain the process of timing analysis and conclude the chapter with a discussion of real-time operating systems.

Finally, Chapter 21 covers aspect-oriented software development (AOSD). AOSD is also related to reuse and proposes a new approach, based on aspects, to organizing and structuring software systems. Although not yet mainstream software engineering, AOSD has the potential to significantly improve our current approaches to software implementation.

16

Software reuse

Objectives

The objectives of this chapter are to introduce software reuse and to describe approaches to system development based on large-scale system reuse. When you have read this chapter, you will:

■ understand the benefits and problems of reusing software when developing new systems;

■ understand the concept of an application framework as a set of reusable objects and how frameworks can be used in application development;

■ have been introduced to software product lines, which are made up of a common core architecture and configurable, reusable components;

■ have learned how systems can be developed by configuring and composing off-the-shelf application software systems.

Contents

Reuse-based software engineering is a software engineering strategy where the development process is geared to reusing existing software. Although reuse was proposed as a development strategy more than 40 years ago (McIlroy, 1968), it is only since 2000 that 'development with reuse' has become the norm for new business systems. The move to reuse-based development has been in response to demands for lower software production and maintenance costs, faster delivery of systems, and increased software quality. More and more companies see their software as a valuable asset. They are promoting reuse to increase their return on software investments.

The availability of reusable software has increased dramatically. The open source movement has meant that there is a huge reusable code base available at low cost. This may be in the form of program libraries or entire applications. There are many domain-specific application systems available that can be tailored and adapted to the needs of a specific company. Some large companies provide a range of reusable components for their customers. Standards, such as web service standards, have made it easier to develop general services and reuse them across a range of applications.

Reuse-based software engineering is an approach to development that tries to maximize the reuse of existing software. The software units that are reused may be of radically different sizes. For example:

1. *Application system reuse* The whole of an application system may be reused by incorporating it without changing into other systems or by configuring the application for different customers. Alternatively, application families that have a common architecture, but which are tailored for specific customers, may be developed. I cover application system reuse later in this chapter.

2. *Component reuse* Components of an application, ranging in size from subsystems to single objects, may be reused. For example, a pattern-matching system developed as part of a text-processing system may be reused in a database management system. I cover component reuse in Chapters 17 and 19.

3. *Object and function reuse* Software components that implement a single function, such as a mathematical function, or an object class may be reused. This form of reuse, based around standard libraries, has been common for the past 40 years. Many libraries of functions and classes are freely available. You reuse the classes and functions in these libraries by linking them with newly developed application code. In areas such as mathematical algorithms and graphics, where specialized expertise is needed to develop efficient objects and functions, this is a particularly effective approach.

Software systems and components are potentially reusable entities, but their specific nature sometimes means that it is expensive to modify them for a new situation. A complementary form of reuse is 'concept reuse' where, rather than reuse a software component, you reuse an idea, a way, or working or an algorithm. The concept that you reuse is represented in an abstract notation (e.g., a system model), which does not include implementation detail. It can, therefore, be configured and adapted for a range of situations. Concept reuse can be embodied in approaches such as design

Benefit	Explanation
Increased dependability	Reused software, which has been tried and tested in working systems, should be more dependable than new software. Its design and implementation faults should have been found and fixed.
Reduced process risk	The cost of existing software is already known, whereas the costs of development are always a matter of judgment. This is an important factor for project management because it reduces the margin of error in project cost estimation. This is particularly true when relatively large software components such as subsystems are reused.
Effective use of specialists	Instead of doing the same work over and over again, application specialists can develop reusable software that encapsulates their knowledge.
Standards compliance	Some standards, such as user interface standards, can be implemented as a set of reusable components. For example, if menus in a user interface are implemented using reusable components, all applications present the same menu formats to users. The use of standard user interfaces improves dependability because users make fewer mistakes when presented with a familiar interface.
Accelerated development	Bringing a system to market as early as possible is often more important than overall development costs. Reusing software can speed up system production because both development and validation time may be reduced.

Figure 16.1 Benefits of software reuse

patterns (covered in Chapter 7), configurable system products, and program generators. When concepts are reused, the reuse process includes an activity where the abstract concepts are instantiated to create executable reusable components.

An obvious advantage of software reuse is that overall development costs should be reduced. Fewer software components need to be specified, designed, implemented, and validated. However, cost reduction is only one advantage of reuse. In Figure 16.1, I have listed other advantages of reusing software assets.

However, there are costs and problems associated with reuse (Figure 16.2). There is a significant cost associated with understanding whether or not a component is suitable for reuse in a particular situation, and in testing that component to ensure its dependability. These additional costs mean that the reductions in overall development costs through reuse may be less than anticipated.

As I discussed in Chapter 2, software development processes have to be adapted to take reuse into account. In particular, there has to be a requirements refinement stage where the requirements for the system are modified to reflect the reusable software that is available. The design and implementation stages of the system may also include explicit activities to look for and evaluate candidate components for reuse.

Software reuse is most effective when it is planned as part of an organization-wide reuse program. A reuse program involves the creation of reusable assets and the adaptation of development processes to incorporate these assets in new software. The importance of reuse planning has been recognized for many years in Japan (Matsumoto, 1984), where reuse is an integral part of the Japanese 'factory' approach

Problem	Explanation
Increased maintenance costs	If the source code of a reused software system or component is not available, then maintenance costs may be higher because the reused elements of the system may become increasingly incompatible with system changes.
Lack of tool support	Some software tools do not support development with reuse. It may be difficult or impossible to integrate these tools with a component library system. The software process assumed by these tools may not take reuse into account. This is particularly true for tools that support embedded systems engineering, less so for object-oriented development tools.
Not-invented-here syndrome	Some software engineers prefer to rewrite components because they believe they can improve on them. This is partly to do with trust and partly to do with the fact that writing original software is seen as more challenging than reusing other people's software.
Creating, maintaining, and using a component library	Populating a reusable component library and ensuring the software developers can use this library can be expensive. Development processes have to be adapted to ensure that the library is used.
Finding, understanding, and adapting reusable components	Software components have to be discovered in a library, understood and, sometimes, adapted to work in a new environment. Engineers must be reasonably confident of finding a component in the library before they include a component search as part of their normal development process.

Figure 16.2 Problems with reuse

to software development (Cusamano, 1989). Companies such as Hewlett-Packard have also been very successful in their reuse programs (Griss and Wosser, 1995), and their experience has been documented in a book by Jacobson et al. (1997).

16.1 The reuse landscape

Over the past 20 years, many techniques have been developed to support software reuse. These techniques exploit the facts that systems in the same application domain are similar and have potential for reuse; that reuse is possible at different levels from simple functions to complete applications; and that standards for reusable components facilitate reuse. Figure 16.3 sets out a number of possible ways of implementing software reuse, with each described briefly in Figure 16.4.

Given this array of techniques for reuse, the key question is "which is the most appropriate technique to use in a particular situation?" Obviously, this depends on the requirements for the system being developed, the technology and reusable assets available, and the expertise of the development team. Key factors that you should consider when planning reuse are:

1. *The development schedule for the software* If the software has to be developed quickly, you should try to reuse off-the-shelf systems rather than individual components. These are large-grain reusable assets. Although the fit to

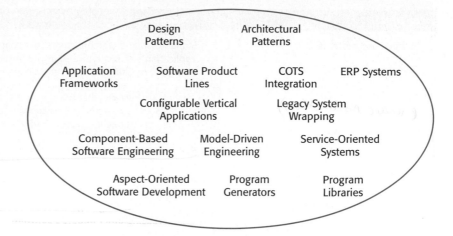

Figure 16.3 The reuse landscape

requirements may be imperfect, this approach minimizes the amount of development required.

2. *The expected software lifetime* If you are developing a long-lifetime system, you should focus on the maintainability of the system. You should not just think about the immediate benefits of reuse but also of the long-term implications.

    Over its lifetime, you will have to adapt the system to new requirements, which will mean making changes to parts of the system. If you do not have access to the source code, you may prefer to avoid off-the-shelf components and systems from external suppliers; suppliers may not be able to continue support for the reused software.

3. *The background, skills, and experience of the development team* All reuse technologies are fairly complex and you need quite a lot of time to understand and use them effectively. Therefore, if the development team has skills in a particular area, this is probably where you should focus.

4. *The criticality of the software and its non-functional requirements* For a critical system that has to be certified by an external regulator, you may have to create a dependability case for the system (discussed in Chapter 15). This is difficult if you don't have access to the source code of the software. If your software has stringent performance requirements, it may be impossible to use strategies such as generator-based reuse, where you generate the code from a reusable domain-specific representation of a system. These systems often generate relatively inefficient code.

5. *The application domain* In some application domains, such as manufacturing and medical information systems, there are several generic products that may be reused by configuring them to a local situation. If you are working in such a domain, you should always consider these as an option.

Approach	Description
Architectural patterns	Standard software architectures that support common types of application systems are used as the basis of applications. Described in Chapters 6, 13, and Chapter 20.
Design patterns *(Generic Abstractions)*	Generic abstractions that occur across applications are represented as design patterns showing abstract and concrete objects and interactions. Described in Chapter 7.
Component-based development	Systems are developed by integrating components (collections of objects) that conform to component-model standards. Described in Chapter 17.
Application frameworks	Collections of abstract and concrete classes are adapted and extended to create application systems.
Legacy system wrapping	Legacy systems (see Chapter 9) are 'wrapped' by defining a set of interfaces and providing access to these legacy systems through these interfaces.
Service-oriented systems	Systems are developed by linking shared services, which may be externally provided. Described in Chapter 19.
Software product lines	An application type is generalized around a common architecture so that it can be adapted for different customers.
COTS product reuse	Systems are developed by configuring and integrating existing application systems.
ERP systems	Large-scale systems that encapsulate generic business functionality and rules are configured for an organization.
Configurable vertical applications	Generic systems are designed so that they can be configured to the needs of specific system customers.
Program libraries	Class and function libraries that implement commonly used abstractions are available for reuse.
Model-driven engineering	Software is represented as domain models and implementation independent models and code is generated from these models. Described in Chapter 5.
Program generators	A generator system embeds knowledge of a type of application and is used to generate systems in that domain from a user-supplied system model.
Aspect-oriented software development	Shared components are woven into an application at different places when the program is compiled. Described in Chapter 21.

Figure 16.4
Approaches that
support software
reuse

6. *The platform on which the system will run* Some components models, such as .NET, are specific to Microsoft platforms. Similarly, generic application systems may be platform-specific and you may only be able to reuse these if your system is designed for the same platform.

Generator-based reuse

Generator-based reuse involves incorporating reusable concepts and knowledge into automated tools and providing an easy way for tool users to integrate specific code with this generic knowledge. This approach is usually most effective in domain-specific applications. Known solutions to problems in that domain are embedded in the generator system and selected by the user to create a new system.

http://www.SoftwareEngineering-9.com/Web/Reuse/Generator.html

The range of available reuse techniques is such that, in most situations, there is the possibility of some software reuse. Whether or not reuse is achieved is often a managerial rather than a technical issue. Managers may be unwilling to compromise their requirements to allow reusable components to be used. They may not understand the risks associated with reuse as well as they understand the risks of original development. Although the risks of new software development may be higher, some managers may prefer known to unknown risks.

16.2 Application frameworks

Early enthusiasts for object-oriented development suggested that one of the key benefits of using an object-oriented approach was that objects could be reused in different systems. However, experience has shown that objects are often too small and are specialized for a particular application. It takes longer to understand and adapt the object than to reimplement it. It has now become clear that object-oriented reuse is best supported in an object-oriented development process through larger-grain abstractions called frameworks.

As the name suggests, a framework is a generic structure that is extended to create a more specific subsystem or application. Schmidt et al. (2004) define a framework to be:

> ". . . an integrated set of software artefacts (such as classes, objects and components) that collaborate to provide a reusable architecture for a family of related applications."

Frameworks provide support for generic features that are likely to be used in all applications of a similar type. For example, a user interface framework will provide support for interface event handling and will include a set of widgets that can be used to construct displays. It is then left to the developer to specialize these by adding specific functionality for a particular application. For example, in a user interface framework, the developer defines display layouts that are appropriate to the application being implemented.

Frameworks support design reuse in that they provide a skeleton architecture for the application as well as the reuse of specific classes in the system. The architecture

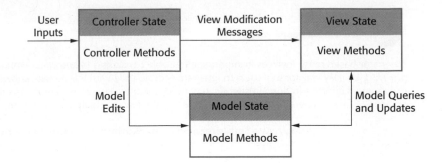

Figure 16.5 The
Model-View-Controller
pattern

is defined by the object classes and their interactions. Classes are reused directly and may be extended using features such as inheritance.

Frameworks are implemented as a collection of concrete and abstract object classes in an object-oriented programming language. Therefore, frameworks are language-specific. There are frameworks available in all of the commonly used object-oriented programming languages (e.g., Java, C#, C++, as well as dynamic languages such as Ruby and Python). In fact, a framework can incorporate several other frameworks, where each of these is designed to support the development of part of the application. You can use a framework to create a complete application or to implement part of an application, such as the graphical user interface.

Fayad and Schmidt (1997) discuss three classes of frameworks:

1. *System infrastructure frameworks* These frameworks support the development of system infrastructures such as communications, user interfaces, and compilers (Schmidt, 1997).

2. *Middleware integration frameworks* These consist of a set of standards and associated object classes that support component communication and information exchange. Examples of this type of framework include Microsoft's .NET and Enterprise Java Beans (EJB). These frameworks provide support for standardized component models, as discussed in Chapter 17.

3. *Enterprise application frameworks* These are concerned with specific application domains such as telecommunications or financial systems (Baumer, et al., 1997). These embed application domain knowledge and support the development of end-user applications.

Web application frameworks (WAFs) are a more recent and very important type of framework. WAFs that support the construction of dynamic websites are now widely available. The architecture of a WAF is usually based on the Model-View-Controller (MVC) composite pattern (Gamma et al., 1995), shown in Figure 16.5.

The MVC pattern was originally proposed in the 1980s as an approach to GUI design that allowed for multiple presentations of an object and separate styles of interaction with each of these presentations. It allows for the separation of the application state from the user interface to application. An MVC framework supports the presentation of data in different ways and allows interaction with each of these presentations. When the data is modified through one of the presentations, the system model is changed and the controllers associated with each view update their presentation.

Frameworks are often implementations of design patterns, as discussed in Chapter 7. For example, an MVC framework includes the Observer pattern, the Strategy pattern, the Composite pattern, and a number of others that are discussed by Gamma et al. (1995). The general nature of patterns and their use of abstract and concrete classes allows for extensibility. Without patterns, frameworks would, almost certainly, be impractical.

Web application frameworks usually incorporate one or more specialized frameworks that support specific application features. Although each framework includes slightly different functionality, most web application frameworks support the following features:

1. *Security* WAFs may include classes to help implement user authentication (login) and access control to ensure that users can only access permitted functionality in the system.

2. *Dynamic web pages* Classes are provided to help you define web page templates and to populate these dynamically with specific data from the system database.

3. *Database support* Frameworks don't usually include a database but rather assume that a separate database, such as MySQL, will be used. The framework may provide classes that provide an abstract interface to different databases.

4. *Session management* Classes to create and manage sessions (a number of interactions with the system by a user) are usually part of a WAF.

5. *User interaction* Most web frameworks now provide AJAX support (Holdener, 2008), which allows more interactive web pages to be created.

To extend a framework you do not change the framework code. Rather, you add concrete classes that inherit operations from abstract classes in the framework. In addition, you may have to define callbacks. Callbacks are methods that are called in response to events recognized by the framework. Schmidt et al. (2004) call this 'inversion of control'. The framework objects, rather than the application-specific objects, are responsible for control in the system. In response to events from the user interface, database, etc., these framework objects invoke 'hook methods' that are then linked to user-provided functionality. The application-specific functionality responds to the event in an appropriate way (Figure 16.6). For example, a framework will have a method that handles a mouse click from the environment. This method calls the hook method, which you must configure to call the appropriate application methods to handle the mouse click.

Applications that are constructed using frameworks can be the basis for further reuse through the concept of software product lines or application families. Because these applications are constructed using a framework, modifying family members to

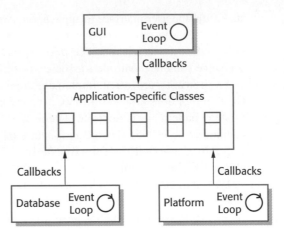

Figure 16.6 Inversion
of control in frameworks

create instances of the system is often a straightforward process. It involves rewriting concrete classes and methods that you have added to the framework.

However, frameworks are usually more general than software product lines, which focus on a specific family of application system. For example, you can use a web-based framework to build different types of web-based applications. One of these might be a software product line that supports web-based help desks. This 'help desk product line' may then be further specialized to provide particular types of help desk support.

Frameworks are an effective approach to reuse, but are expensive to introduce into software development processes. They are inherently complex and it can take several months to learn to use them. It can be difficult and expensive to evaluate available frameworks to choose the most appropriate one. Debugging framework-based applications is difficult because you may not understand how the framework methods interact. This is a general problem with reusable software. Debugging tools may provide information about the reused system components, which a developer does not understand.

16.3 Software product lines

One of the most effective approaches to reuse is to create software product lines or application families. A software product line is a set of applications with a common architecture and shared components, with each application specialized to reflect different requirements. The core system is designed to be configured and adapted to suit the needs of different system customers. This may involve the configuration of some components, implementing additional components, and modifying some of the components to reflect new requirements.

Developing applications by adapting a generic version of the application means that a high proportion of the application code is reused. Furthermore, application experience is often transferable from one system to another. Consequently, when software engineers join a development team, their learning process is shortened. Testing is simplified because tests for large parts of the application may also be reused, thus reducing the overall application development time.

Software product lines usually emerge from existing applications. That is, an organization develops an application then, when a similar system is required, informally reuses code from this in the new application. The same process is used as other similar applications are developed. However, change tends to corrupt application structure so, as more new instances are developed, it becomes increasingly difficult to create a new version. Consequently, a decision to design a generic product line may then be made. This involves identifying common functionality in product instances and including this in a base application, which is then used for future development. This base application is deliberately structured to simplify reuse and reconfiguration.

Application frameworks and software product lines obviously have much in common. They both support a common architecture and components, and require new development to create a specific version of a system. The main differences between these approaches are as follows:

1. Application frameworks rely on object-oriented features such as inheritance and polymorphism to implement extensions to the framework. Generally, the framework code is not modified and the possible modifications are limited to whatever is allowed by the framework. Software product lines are not necessarily created using an object-oriented approach. Application components are changed, deleted, or rewritten. There are no limits, in principle at least, to the changes that can be made.

2. Application frameworks are primarily focused on providing technical rather than domain-specific support. For example, there are application frameworks to create web-based applications. A software product line usually embeds detailed domain and platform information. For example, there could be a software product line concerned with web-based applications for health record management.

3. Software product lines are often control applications for equipment. For example, there may be a software product line for a family of printers. This means that the product line has to provide support for hardware interfacing. Application frameworks are usually software-oriented and they rarely provide support for hardware interfacing.

4. Software product lines are made up of a family of related applications, owned by the same organization. When you create a new application, your starting point is often the closest member of the application family, not the generic core application.

If you are developing a software product line using an object-oriented programming language, then you may use an application framework as a basis for the system. You create the core of the product line by extending the framework with domain-specific components using its built-in mechanisms. There is then a second phase of development where versions of the system for different customers are created.

Various types of specialization of a software product line may be developed:

1. *Platform specialization* Versions of the application are developed for different platforms. For example, versions of the application may exist for Windows, Mac OS, and Linux platforms. In this case, the functionality of the application is normally unchanged; only those components that interface with the hardware and operating system are modified.

2. *Environment specialization* Versions of the application are created to handle particular operating environments and peripheral devices. For example, a system for the emergency services may exist in different versions, depending on the vehicle communications system. In this case, the system components are changed to reflect the functionality of the communications equipment used.

3. *Functional specialization* Versions of the application are created for specific customers who have different requirements. For example, a library automation system may be modified depending on whether it is used in a public library, a reference library, or a university library. In this case, components that implement functionality may be modified and new components added to the system.

4. *Process specialization* The system is adapted to cope with specific business processes. For example, an ordering system may be adapted to cope with a centralized ordering process in one company and a distributed process in another.

The architecture of a software product line often reflects a general, application-specific architectural style or pattern. For example, consider a product line system that is designed to handle vehicle despatching for emergency services. Operators of this system take calls about incidents, find the appropriate vehicle to respond to the incident and dispatch the vehicle to the incident site. The developers of such a system may market versions of this for police, fire, and ambulance services.

This vehicle despatching system is an example of a resource management architecture (Figure 16.7). You can see how this four-layer structure is instantiated in Figure 16.8, which shows the modules that might be included in a vehicle despatching system product line. The components at each level in the product line system are as follows:

1. At the interaction level, there are components providing an operator display interface and an interface with the communications systems used.

2. At the I/O management level (level 2), there are components that handle operator authentication, generate reports of incidents and vehicles despatched, support map output and route planning, and provide a mechanism for operators to query the system databases.

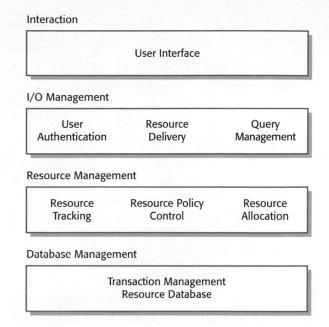

Figure 16.7 The
architecture of a
resource allocation
system

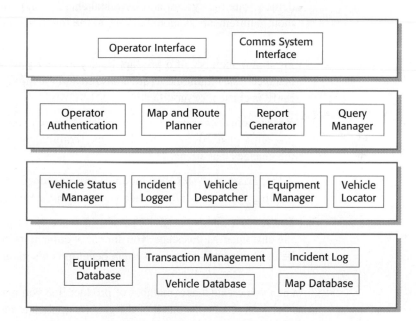

Figure 16.8 The
product line architecture
of a vehicle dispatcher
system

3. At the resource management level (level 3) there are components that allow
    vehicles to be located and despatched, components to update the status of vehi-
    cles and equipment, and a component to log details of incidents.

4. At the database level, as well as the usual transaction management support,
    there are separate databases of vehicles, equipment, and maps.

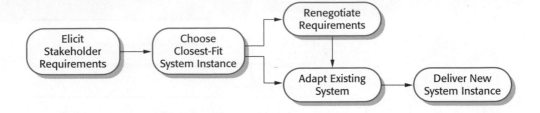

Figure 16.9 Product
instance development

To create a specific version of this system, you may have to modify individual
components. For example, the police have a large number of vehicles but a small
number of vehicle types, whereas the fire service has many types of specialized
vehicles. Therefore, you may have to define a different vehicle database structure
when implementing a system for these different services.

Figure 16.9 shows the steps involved in extending a software product line to create a new application. The steps involved in this general process are as follows:

1. *Elicit stakeholder requirements* You may start with a normal requirements engineering process. However, because a system already exists, you will need to
   demonstrate the system and have stakeholders experiment with it, expressing
   their requirements as modifications to the functions provided.

2. *Select the existing system that is the closest fit to the requirements* When creating a new member of a product line, you may start with the nearest product
   instance. The requirements are analyzed and the family member that is the closest fit is chosen for modification.

3. *Renegotiate requirements* As more details of required changes emerge and the
   project is planned, there may be some requirements renegotiation to minimize
   the changes that are needed.

4. *Adapt existing system* New modules are developed for the existing system and
   existing system modules are adapted to meet the new requirements.

5. *Deliver new family member* The new instance of the product line is delivered to
   the customer. At this stage, you should document its key features so that it may
   be used as a basis for other system developments in the future.

When you create a new member of product line you may have to find a compromise between reusing as much of the generic application as possible and satisfying
detailed stakeholder requirements. The more detailed the system requirements, the
less likely it is that the existing components will meet these requirements. However,
if stakeholders are willing to be flexible and to limit the system modifications that
are required, you can usually deliver the system more quickly and at a lower cost.

Software product lines are designed to be reconfigured and this reconfiguration
may involve adding or removing components from the system, defining parameters
and constraints for system components, and including knowledge of business

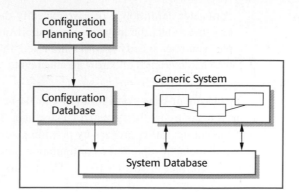

Figure 16.10
Deployment-time
configuration

processes. This configuration may occur at different stages in the development process:

1. *Design-time configuration* The organization that is developing the software modifies a common product line core by developing, selecting, or adapting components to create a new system for a customer.

2. *Deployment-time configuration* A generic system is designed for configuration by a customer or consultants working with the customer. Knowledge of the customer's specific requirements and the system's operating environment is embedded in a set of configuration files that are used by the generic system.

When a system is configured at design time, the supplier starts with either a generic system or an existing product instance. By modifying and extending modules in this system, they create a specific system that delivers the required customer functionality. This usually involves changing and extending the source code of the system so greater flexibility is possible than with deployment-time configuration.

Deployment-time configuration involves using a configuration tool to create a specific system configuration that is recorded in a configuration database or as a set of configuration files (Figure 16.10). The executing system consults this database when executing so that its functionality may be specialized to its execution context.

There are several levels of deployment-time configuration that may be provided in a system:

1. Component selection, where you select the modules in a system that provide the required functionality. For example, in a patient information system, you may select an image management component that allows you to link medical images (x-rays, CT scans, etc.) to the patient's medical record.

2. Workflow and rule definition, where you define workflows (how information is processed, stage by stage) and validation rules that should apply to information entered by users or generated by the system.

3. Parameter definition, where you specify the values of specific system parameters that reflect the instance of the application that you are creating. For example, you may specify the maximum length of fields for data input by a user or the characteristics of hardware attached to the system.

Deployment-time configuration can be very complex and it may take many months to configure the system for a customer. Large configurable systems may support the configuration process by providing software tools, such as a configuration planning tools, to support the configuration process. I discuss deployment-time configuration further in Section 16.4.1. This covers the reuse of COTS systems that have to be configured to work in different operational environments.

Design-time configuration is used when it is impossible to use the existing deployment-time configuration facilities in a system to develop a new system version. However, over time, when you have created several family members with comparable functionality, you may decide to refactor the core product line to include functionality that has been implemented in several application family members. You then make that new functionality configurable when the system is deployed.

16.4 COTS product reuse

A commercial-off-the-shelf (COTS) product is a software system that can be adapted to the needs of different customers without changing the source code of the system. Virtually all desktop software and a wide variety of server products are COTS software. Because this software is designed for general use, it usually includes many features and functions. It therefore has the potential to be reused in different environments and as part of different applications. Torchiano and Morisio (2004) also discovered that using open source products were often used as COTS products. That is, the open source systems were used without change and without looking at the source code.

COTS products are adapted by using built-in configuration mechanisms that allow the functionality of the system to be tailored to specific customer needs. For example, in a hospital patient record system, separate input forms and output reports might be defined for different types of patient. Other configuration features may allow the system to accept plug-ins that extend functionality or check user inputs to ensure that they are valid.

This approach to software reuse has been very widely adopted by large companies over the last 15 or so years, as it offers significant benefits over customized software development:

1. As with other types of reuse, more rapid deployment of a reliable system may be possible.

2.   It is possible to see what functionality is provided by the applications and so it is easier to judge whether or not they are likely to be suitable. Other companies may already use the applications so experience of the systems is available.

3.   Some development risks are avoided by using existing software. However, this approach has its own risks, as I discuss below.

4.   Businesses can focus on their core activity without having to devote a lot of resources to IT systems development.

5.   As operating platforms evolve, technology updates may be simplified as these are the responsibility of the COTS product vendor rather than the customer.

Of course, this approach to software engineering has its own problems:

1.   Requirements usually have to be adapted to reflect the functionality and mode of operation of the COTS product. This can lead to disruptive changes to existing business processes.

2.   The COTS product may be based on assumptions that are practically impossible to change. The customer must therefore adapt their business to reflect these assumptions.

3.   Choosing the right COTS system for an enterprise can be a difficult process, especially as many COTS products are not well documented. Making the wrong choice could be disastrous as it may be impossible to make the new system work as required.

4.   There may be a lack of local expertise to support systems development. Consequently, the customer has to rely on the vendor and external consultants for development advice. This advice may be biased and geared to selling products and services, rather than meeting the real needs of the customer.

5.   The COTS product vendor controls system support and evolution. They may go out of business, be taken over, or may make changes that cause difficulties for customers.

Software reuse based on COTS has become increasingly common. The vast majority of new business information processing systems are now built using COTS rather than using an object-oriented approach. Although there are often problems with this approach to system development (Tracz, 2001), success stories (Baker, 2002; Balk and Kedia, 2000; Brownsword and Morris, 2003; Pfarr and Reis, 2002) show that COTS-based reuse reduces effort and the time to deploy the system.

There are two types of COTS product reuse, namely COTS-solution systems and COTS-integrated systems. COTS-solution systems consist of a generic application from a single vendor that is configured to customer requirements. COTS-integrated systems involve integrating two or more COTS systems (perhaps from different

COTS-solution systems	COTS-integrated systems
Single product that provides the functionality required by a customer	Several heterogeneous system products are integrated to provide customized functionality
Based around a generic solution and standardized processes	Flexible solutions may be developed for customer processes
Development focus is on system configuration	Development focus is on system integration
System vendor is responsible for maintenance	System owner is responsible for maintenance
System vendor provides the platform for the system	System owner provides the platform for the system

Figure 16.11 COTS-solution and COTS-integrated systems

vendors) to create an application system. Figure 16.11 summarizes the differences between these different approaches.

16.4.1 COTS-solution systems

COTS-solution systems are generic application systems that may be designed to support a particular business type, business activity, or sometimes, a complete business enterprise. For example, a COTS-solution system may be produced for dentists that handles appointments, dental records, patient recall, etc. At a larger scale, an Enterprise Resource Planning (ERP) system may support all of the manufacturing, ordering, and customer relationship management activities in a large company.

Domain-specific COTS-solution systems, such as systems to support a business function (e.g., document management), provide functionality that is likely to be required by a range of potential users. However, they also incorporate built-in assumptions about how users work and these may cause problems in specific situations. For example, a system to support student registration in a university may assume that students will be registered for one degree at one university. However, if universities collaborate to offer joint degrees, then it may be practically impossible to represent this in the system.

ERP systems, such as those produced by SAP and BEA, are large-scale integrated systems designed to support business practices such as ordering and invoicing, inventory management, and manufacturing scheduling (O'Leary, 2000). The configuration process for these systems involves gathering detailed information about the customer's business and business processes, and embedding this in a configuration database. This often requires detailed knowledge of configuration notations and tools and is usually carried out by consultants working alongside system customers.

A generic ERP system includes a number of modules that may be composed in different ways to create a system for a customer. The configuration process

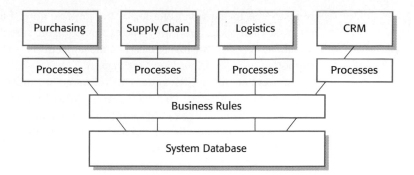

Figure 16.12 The architecture of an ERP system

involves choosing which modules are to be included, configuring these individual modules, defining business processes and business rules, and defining the structure and organization of the system database. A model of the overall architecture of an ERP system that supports a range of business functions is shown in Figure 16.12.

The key features of this architecture are:

1. A number of modules to support different business functions. These are large-grain modules that may support entire departments or divisions of the business. In the example shown in Figure 16.12, the modules that have been selected for inclusion in the system are a module to support purchasing, a module to support supply chain management, a logistics module to support the delivery of goods, and a customer relationship management (CRM) module to maintain customer information.

2. A defined set of business processes, associated with each module, which relate to activities in that module. For example, there may be a definition of the ordering process that defines how orders are created and approved. This will specify the roles and activities involved in placing an order.

3. A common database that maintains information about all related business functions. This means that it should not be necessary to replicate information, such as customer details, in different parts of the business.

4. A set of business rules that apply to all data in the database. Therefore, when data is input from one function, these rules should ensure that it is consistent with the data required by other functions. For example, there may be a business rule that all expense claims have to be approved by someone more senior than the person making the claim.

ERP systems are used in almost all large companies to support some or all of their functions. They are, therefore, a very widely used form of software reuse. However, the obvious limitation of this approach to reuse is that the functionality of the system is restricted to the functionality of the generic core. Furthermore, a company's processes and operations have to be expressed in the system configuration language, and there may be a mismatch between the concepts in the business and the concepts supported in the configuration language.

For example, in an ERP system that was sold to a university, the concept of a customer had to be defined. This caused great difficulties when configuring the system. However, universities have multiple types of customers, such as students, research funding agencies, educational charities, etc., each of which have different characteristics. None of them are really comparable to the notion of a commercial customer (i.e., a person or business that buys products or services). A serious mismatch between the business model used by the system and that of the buyer of the system makes it highly probable that the ERP system will not meet the buyer's real needs (Scott, 1999).

Both domain-specific COTS products and ERP systems usually require extensive configuration to adapt them to the requirements of each organization where they are installed. This configuration may involve:

1. Selecting the required functionality from the system (e.g., by deciding what modules should be included).

2. Establishing a data model that defines how the organization's data will be structured in the system database.

3. Defining business rules that apply to that data.

4. Defining the expected interactions with external systems.

5. Designing the input forms and the output reports generated by the system.

6. Designing new business processes that conform to the underlying process model supported by the system.

7. Setting parameters that define how the system is deployed on its underlying platform.

Once the configuration settings are completed, a COTS-solution system is then ready for testing. Testing is a major problem when systems are configured rather than programmed using a conventional language. Because these systems are built using a reliable platform, obvious system failures and crashes are relatively rare. Rather the problems are often subtle and relate to the interactions between the operational processes and the system configuration. These may only be detectable by end-users and so may not be discovered during the system testing process. Furthermore, automated unit testing, supported by testing frameworks such as JUnit, cannot be used. The underlying system is unlikely to support any kind of test automation and there may be no complete system specification that can be used to derive system tests.

16.4.2 COTS-integrated systems

COTS-integrated systems are applications that include two or more COTS products or, sometimes, legacy application systems. You may use this approach when there is no single COTS system that meets all of your needs or when you wish to integrate a new COTS product with systems that you already use. The COTS products may interact through their APIs (Application Programming Interfaces) or service interfaces if these are defined. Alternatively, they may be composed by connecting the output of one system to the input of another or by updating the databases used by the COTS applications.

To develop systems using COTS products, you have to make a number of design choices:

1. *Which COTS products offer the most appropriate functionality?* Typically, there will be several COTS products available, which can be combined in different ways. If you don't already have experience with a COTS product, it can be difficult to decide which product is the most suitable.

2. *How will data be exchanged?* Different products normally use unique data structures and formats. You have to write adaptors that convert from one representation to another. These adaptors are run-time systems that operate alongside the COTS products.

3. *What features of a product will actually be used?* COTS products may include more functionality than you need and functionality may be duplicated across different products. You have to decide which features in what product are most appropriate for your requirements. If possible, you should also deny access to unused functionality because this can interfere with normal system operation. The failure of the first flight of the Ariane 5 rocket (Nuseibeh, 1997) was a consequence of a failure in an inertial navigation system that was reused from the Ariane 4 system. However, the functionality that failed was not actually required in Ariane 5.

Consider the following scenario as an illustration of COTS integration. A large organization intends to develop a procurement system that allows staff to place orders from their desk. By introducing this system across the organization, the company estimates that it can save $5 million per year. By centralizing buying, the new procurement system can ensure that orders are always made from suppliers who offer the best prices and should reduce the paperwork costs associated with orders. As with manual systems, the system involves choosing the goods available from a supplier, creating an order, having the order approved, sending the order to a supplier, receiving the goods, and confirming that payment should be made.

The company has a legacy ordering system that is used by a central procurement office. This order processing software is integrated with an existing invoicing and delivery system. To create the new ordering system, the legacy system is integrated with a web-based e-commerce platform and an e-mail system that

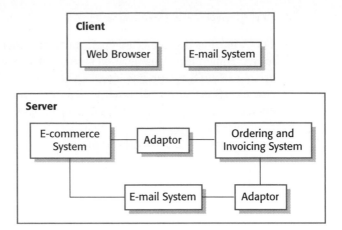

Figure 16.13 A COTS-integrated procurement system

handles communications with users. The structure of the final procurement system, constructed using COTS, is shown in Figure 16.13.

This procurement system is a client–server based and, on the client, standard web browsing and e-mail software are used. On the server, the e-commerce platform has to integrate with the existing ordering system through an adaptor. The e-commerce system has its own format for orders, confirmations of delivery, and so forth, and these have to be converted into the format used by the ordering system. The e-commerce system uses the e-mail system to send notifications to users, but the ordering system was never designed for this. Therefore, another adaptor has to be written to convert the notifications from the ordering system into e-mail messages.

Months, sometimes years, of implementation effort can be saved, and the time to develop and deploy a system can be drastically reduced using a COTS-integrated approach. The procurement system described above was implemented and deployed in a very large company in nine months, rather than the three years that they estimated would be required to develop the system in Java.

COTS integration can be simplified if a service-oriented approach is used. Essentially, a service-oriented approach means allowing access to the application system's functionality through a standard service interface, with a service for each discrete unit of functionality. Some applications may offer a service interface but, sometimes, this service interface has to be implemented by the system integrator. Essentially, you have to program a wrapper that hides the application and provides externally visible services (Figure 16.14). This approach is particularly valuable for legacy systems that have to be integrated with newer application systems.

In principle, integrating COTS products is the same as integrating any other components. You have to understand the system interfaces and use them exclusively to communicate with the software; you have to trade off specific requirements against rapid development and reuse; and you have to design a system architecture that allows the COTS systems to operate together.

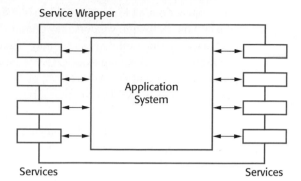

Service Wrapper

Application System

Services   Services

Figure 16.14
Application wrapping

However, the fact that these products are usually large systems in their own right, and are often sold as separate standalone systems, introduces additional problems. Boehm and Abts (1999) discuss four important COTS system integration problems:

1. *Lack of control over functionality and performance* Although the published interface of a product may appear to offer the required facilities, these may not be properly implemented or may perform poorly. The product may have hidden operations that interfere with its use in a specific situation. Fixing these problems may be a priority for the COTS product integrator but may not be of real concern for the product vendor. Users may simply have to find work-arounds to problems if they wish to reuse the COTS product.

2. *Problems with COTS system interoperability* It is sometimes difficult to get COTS products to work together because each product embeds its own assumptions about how it will be used. Garlan et al. (1995), reporting on their experience of trying to integrate four COTS products, found that three of these products were event-based but each used a different model of events. Each system assumed that it had exclusive access to the event queue. As a consequence, integration was very difficult. The project required five times as much effort as originally predicted. The schedule was extended to two years rather than the predicted six months. In a retrospective analysis of their work 10 years later, Garlan et al. (2009) concluded that the integration problems that they discovered had not been solved. Torchiano and Morisio (2004) found that lack of compliance with standards in some COTS products meant that integration was more difficult than anticipated.

3. *No control over system evolution* Vendors of COTS products make their own decisions on system changes, in response to market pressures. For PC products, in particular, new versions are often produced frequently and may not be compatible with all previous versions. New versions may have additional unwanted functionality, and previous versions may become unavailable and unsupported.

4. *Support from COTS vendors* The level of support available from COTS vendors varies widely. Vendor support is particularly important when problems arise as

developers do not have access to the source code and detailed documentation of the system. Although vendors may commit to providing support, changing market and economic circumstances may make it difficult for them to deliver this commitment. For example, a COTS system vendor may decide to discontinue a product because of limited demand, or they may be taken over by another company that does not wish to support all of the products that have been acquired.

Boehm and Abts reckon that, in many cases, the cost of system maintenance and evolution may be greater for COTS-integrated systems. All of the above difficulties are life-cycle problems; they don't just affect the initial development of the system. The further removed the people involved in the system maintenance become from the original system developers, the more likely it is that real difficulties will arise with the integrated COTS products.

KEY POINTS

■ Most new business software systems are now developed by reusing knowledge and code from previously implemented systems.

■ There are many different ways to reuse software. These range from the reuse of classes and methods in libraries to the reuse of complete application systems.

■ The advantages of software reuse are lower costs, faster software development, and lower risks. System dependability is increased. Specialists can be used more effectively by concentrating their expertise on the design of reusable components.

■ Application frameworks are collections of concrete and abstract objects that are designed for reuse through specialization and the addition of new objects. They usually incorporate good design practice through design patterns.

■ Software product lines are related applications that are developed from one or more base applications. A generic system is adapted and specialized to meet specific requirements for functionality, target platform, or operational configuration.

■ COTS product reuse is concerned with the reuse of large-scale, off-the-shelf systems. These provide a lot of functionality and their reuse can radically reduce costs and development time. Systems may be developed by configuring a single, generic COTS product or by integrating two or more COTS products.

■ Enterprise Resource Planning systems are examples of large-scale COTS reuse. You create an instance of an ERP system by configuring a generic system with information about the customer's business processes and rules.

■ Potential problems with COTS-based reuse include lack of control over functionality and performance, lack of control over system evolution, the need for support from external vendors, and difficulties in ensuring that systems can interoperate.

FURTHER READING

Reuse-based Software Engineering. A comprehensive discussion of different approaches to software reuse. The authors cover technical reuse issues and managing reuse processes. (H. Mili, A. Mili, S. Yacoub and E. Addy, John Wiley & Sons, 2002.)

'Overlooked Aspects of COTS-Based Development'. An interesting article that discusses a survey of developers using a COTS-based approach, and the problems that they encountered. (M. Torchiano and M. Morisio, *IEEE Software*, **21** (2), March–April 2004.) http://dx.doi.org/10.1109/MS.2004.1270770.

'Construction by Configuration: A New Challenge for Software Engineering'. This is an invited paper that I wrote in which I discuss the problems and difficulties of constructing a new application by configuring existing systems. (I. Sommerville, *Proc. 19th Australian Software Engineering Conference*, 2008.) http://dx.doi.org/10.1109/ASWEC.2008.75.

'Architectural Mismatch: Why Reuse Is Still So Hard'. This article looks back on an earlier paper that discussed the problems of reusing and integrating a number of COTS systems. The authors concluded that, although some progress has been made, there were still problems in conflicting assumptions made by the designers of the individual systems. (D. Garlan et al., *IEEE Software*, **26** (4), July–August 2009.) http://dx.doi.org//10.1109/MS.2009.86.

EXERCISES

16.1. What are the major technical and nontechnical factors that hinder software reuse? Do you personally reuse much software and, if not, why not?

16.2. Suggest why the savings in cost from reusing existing software are not simply proportional to the size of the components that are reused.

16.3. Give four circumstances where you might recommend against software reuse.

16.4. Explain what is meant by 'inversion of control' in application frameworks. Explain why this approach could cause problems if you integrated two separate systems that were originally created using the same application framework.

16.5. Using the example of the weather station system described in Chapters 1 and Chapter 7, suggest a product line architecture for a family of applications that are concerned with remote monitoring and data collection. You should present your architecture as a layered model, showing the components that might be included at each level.

16.6. Most desktop software, such as word processing software, can be configured in a number of different ways. Examine software that you regularly use and list the configuration options for that software. Suggest difficulties that users might have in configuring the software. If you use Microsoft Office or Open Office, these are good examples to use for this exercise.

16.7. Why have many large companies chosen ERP systems as the basis for their organizational information system? What problems may arise when deploying a large-scale ERP system in an organization?

16.8. Identify six possible risks that can arise when systems are constructed using COTS. What steps can a company take to reduce these risks?

16.9. Explain why adaptors are usually needed when systems are constructed by integrating COTS products. Suggest three practical problems that might arise in writing adaptor software to link two COTS application products.

16.10. The reuse of software raises a number of copyright and intellectual property issues. If a customer pays a software contractor to develop a system, who has the right to reuse the developed code? Does the software contractor have the right to use that code as a basis for a generic component? What payment mechanisms might be used to reimburse providers of reusable components? Discuss these issues and other ethical issues associated with the reuse of software.

REFERENCES

Baker, T. (2002). 'Lessons Learned Integrating COTS into Systems'. *Proc. ICCBSS 2002 (1st Int. Conf on COTS-based Software Systems)*, Orlando, Fla:: Springer, 21–30.

Balk, L. D. and Kedia, A. (2000). 'PPT: A COTS Integration Case Study'. *Proc. Int. Conf. on Software Eng.*, Limerick, Ireland: ACM Press, 42–9.

Baumer, D., Gryczan, G., Knoll, R., Lilienthal, C., Riehle, D. and Zullighoven, H. (1997). 'Framework Development for Large Systems'. *Comm.* ACM, **40** (10), 52–9.

Boehm, B. and Abts, C. (1999). 'COTS Integration: Plug and Pray?' *IEEE Computer*, **32** (1), 135–38.

Brownsword, L. and Morris, E. (2003). 'The Good News about COTS'. http://www.sei.cmu.edu/news-at-sei/features/2003/1q03/feature-1-1q03.htm

Cusamano, M. (1989). 'The Software Factory: A Historical Interpretation'. *IEEE Software*, **6** (2), 23–30.

Fayad, M. E. and Schmidt, D. C. (1997). 'Object-oriented Application Frameworks'. *Comm.* ACM, **40** (10), 32–38.

Gamma, E., Helm, R., Johnson, R. and Vlissides, J. (1995). *Design Patterns: Elements of Reusable Object-Oriented Software*. Reading, Mass.: Addison-Wesley.

Garlan, D., Allen, R. and Ockerbloom, J. (1995). 'Architectural Mismatch: Why Reuse is so Hard'. *IEEE Software*, **12** (6), 17–26.

Garlan, D., Allen, R. and Ockerbloom, J. (2009). 'Architectural Mismatch: Why Reuse is Still so Hard'. *IEEE Software*, **26** (4), 66–9.

Griss, M. L. and Wosser, M. (1995). 'Making reuse work at Hewlett-Packard'. *IEEE Software*, **12** (1), 105–7.

Holdener, A. T. (2008). *Ajax: The Definitive Guide*. Sebastopol, Calif.: O'Reilly and Associates.

Jacobson, I., Griss, M. and Jonsson, P. (1997). *Software Reuse*. Reading, Mass.: Addison-Wesley.

Matsumoto, Y. (1984). 'Some Experience in Promoting Reusable Software: Presentation in Higher Abstract Levels'. *IEEE. Trans. on Software Engineering*, **SE-10** (5), 502–12.

McIlroy, M. D. (1968). 'Mass-produced software components'. *Proc. NATO Conf. on Software Eng.*, Garmisch, Germany: Springer-Verlag.

Nuseibeh, B. (1997). 'Ariane 5: Who Dunnit?' *IEEE Software*, **14** (3), 15–6.

O'Leary, D. E. (2000). *Enterprise Resource Planning Systems: Systems, Life Cycle, Electronic Commerce and Risk*. Cambridge, UK: Cambridge University Press.

Pfarr, T. and Reis, J. E. (2002). 'The Integration of COTS/GOTS within NASA's HST Command and Control System'. *Proc. ICCBSS 2002 (1st Int. Conf on COTS-based Software Systems)*, Orlando, Fla.: Springer, 209–21.

Schmidt, D. C. (1997). 'Applying design patterns and frameworks to develop object-oriented communications software'. In *Handbook of Programming Languages, Vol. 1*. (ed.). New York: Macmillan Computer Publishing.

Schmidt, D. C., Gokhale, A. and Natarajan, B. (2004). 'Leveraging Application Frameworks'. *ACM Queue*, **2** (5 (July/August)), 66–75.

Scott, J. E. (1999). 'The FoxMeyer Drug's Bankruptcy: Was it a Failure of ERP'. Proc. *Association for Information Systems 5th Americas Conf. on Information Systems*, Milwaukee, WI.

Torchiano, M. and Morisio, M. (2004). 'Overlooked Aspects of COTS-Based Development'. *IEEE Software*, **21** (2), 88–93.

Tracz, W. (2001). 'COTS Myths and Other Lessons Learned in *Component-Based Software Development*'. In *Component-based Software Engineering*. Heineman, G. T. and Councill, W. T. (ed.). Boston: Addison-Wesley, 99–112.

17

Component-based software engineering

Objectives

The objective of this chapter is to describe an approach to software reuse based on the composition of reusable, standardized components. When you have read this chapter you will:

■ know that component-based software engineering is concerned with developing standardized components based on a component model, and composing these into application systems;

■ understand what is meant by a component and a component model;

■ know the principal activities in the CBSE process for reuse and the CBSE process with reuse;

■ understand some of the difficulties and problems that arise during the process of component composition.

Contents

As I explained in Chapter 16, many new business systems are now developed by configuring off-the-shelf systems. However, when a company cannot use an off-the-shelf system because it does not meet their requirements, the software they need has to be specially developed. For custom software, component-based software engineering is an effective, reuse-oriented way to develop new enterprise systems.

Component-based software engineering (CBSE) emerged in the late 1990s as an approach to software systems development based on reusing software components. Its creation was motivated by designers' frustration that object-oriented development had not led to extensive reuse, as had been originally suggested. Single object classes were too detailed and specific, and often had to be bound with an application at compile time. You had to have detailed knowledge of the classes to use them, and this usually meant that you had to have the component source code. This meant that selling or distributing objects as individual reusable components was practically impossible.

Components are higher-level abstractions than objects and are defined by their interfaces. They are usually larger than individual objects and all implementation details are hidden from other components. CBSE is the process of defining, implementing, and integrating or composing loosely coupled, independent components into systems. It has become as an important software development approach because software systems are becoming larger and more complex. Customers are demanding more dependable software that is delivered and deployed more quickly. The only way that we can cope with complexity and deliver better software more quickly is to reuse rather than reimplement software components.

The essentials of component-based software engineering are:

1. Independent components that are completely specified by their interfaces. There should be a clear separation between the component interface and its implementation. This means that one implementation of a component can be replaced by another, without changing other parts of the system.

2. Component standards that facilitate the integration of components. These standards are embodied in a component model. They define, at the very minimum, how component interfaces should be specified and how components communicate. Some models go much further and define interfaces that should be implemented by all conformant components. If components conform to standards, then their operation is independent of their programming language. Components written in different languages can be integrated into the same system.

3. Middleware that provides software support for component integration. To make independent, distributed components work together, you need middleware support that handles component communications. Middleware for component support handles low-level issues efficiently and allows you to focus on application-related problems. In addition, middleware for component support may provide support for resource allocation, transaction management, security, and concurrency.

4. A development process that is geared to component-based software engineering. You need a development process that allows requirements to evolve, depending

Problems with CBSE

CBSE is now a mainstream approach to software engineering—it is a good way to build systems. However, when used as an approach to reuse, problems include component trustworthiness, component certification, requirements compromises, and predicting the properties of components, especially when they are integrated with other components.

http://www.SoftwareEngineering-9.com/Web/CBSE/problems.html

on the functionality of available components. I discuss CBSE development processes in Section 17.2.

Component-based development embodies good software engineering practice. It makes sense to design a system using components, even if you have to develop rather than reuse these components. Underlying CBSE are sound design principles that support the construction of understandable and maintainable software:

1. Components are independent so they do not interfere with each other's operation. Implementation details are hidden. The component's implementation can be changed without affecting the rest of the system.

2. Components communicate through well-defined interfaces. If these interfaces are maintained, one component can be replaced by another, which provides additional or enhanced functionality.

3. Component infrastructures offer a range of standard services that can be used in application systems. This reduces the amount of new code that has to be developed.

The initial motivation for CBSE was the need to support both reuse and distributed software engineering. A component was seen as an element of a software system that could be accessed, using a remote procedure call mechanism, by other components running on separate computers. Each system that reused a component had to incorporate its own copy of that component. This idea of a component extended the notion of distributed objects, as defined in distributed systems models such as the CORBA specification (Pope, 1997). Several different protocols and standards have been developed to support this view of a component, such as Sun's Enterprise Java Beans (EJB), Microsoft's COM and .NET, and CORBA's CCM (Lau and Wang, 2007).

In practice, these multiple standards have hindered the uptake of CBSE. It was impossible for components developed using different approaches to work together. Components that are developed for different platforms, such as .NET or J2EE, cannot interoperate. Furthermore, the standards and protocols proposed were complex and difficult to understand. This was also a barrier to their adoption.

In response to these problems, the notion of a component as a service was developed, and standards were proposed to support service-oriented software engineering.

The most significant difference between a component as a service and the original notion of a component is that services are stand-alone entities that are external to a program using them. When you build a service-oriented system, you reference the external service rather than including a copy of that service in your system.

Service-oriented software engineering, which I discuss in Chapter 19, is therefore a type of component-based software engineering. It uses a simpler notion of a component than that originally proposed in CBSE. It has been driven, from the outset, by standards. In situations where COTS-based reuse is impractical, service-oriented CBSE is becoming the dominant approach for the development of business systems.

17.1 Components and component models

There is general agreement in the CBSE community that a component is an independent software unit that can be composed with other components to create a software system. Beyond that, however, people have proposed varying definitions of a software component. Councill and Heineman (2001) define a component as:

> *"A software element that conforms to a standard component model and can be independently deployed and composed without modification according to a composition standard."*

This definition is essentially based on standards so that a software unit that conforms to these standards is a component. Szyperski (2002), however, does not mention standards in his definition of a component but focuses instead on the key characteristics of components:

> *"A software component is a unit of composition with contractually-specified interfaces and explicit context dependencies only. A software component can be deployed independently and is subject to composition by third parties."*

Both of these definitions are based on the notion of a component as an element that is included in a system, rather than a service that is referenced by the system. However, they are also compatible with the idea of a service as a component.

Szyperski also states that a component has no externally observable state. This means that copies of components are indistinguishable. However, some component models, such as the Enterprise Java Beans model, allow stateful components, so these do not correspond with Szyperski's definition. Although stateless components are certainly simpler to use, there are some systems where stateful components are more convenient and reduce system complexity.

What the above definitions have in common is that they agree that components are independent, and that they are the fundamental unit of composition in a system. In my view, a better definition of a component can be derived by combining these

Component Characteristic	Description
Standardized	Component standardization means that a component used in a CBSE process has to conform to a standard component model. This model may define component interfaces, component metadata, documentation, composition, and deployment.
Independent	A component should be independent—it should be possible to compose and deploy it without having to use other specific components. In situations where the component needs externally provided services, these should be explicitly set out in a 'requires' interface specification.
Composable	For a component to be composable, all external interactions must take place through publicly defined interfaces. In addition, it must provide external access to information about itself, such as its methods and attributes.
Deployable	To be deployable, a component has to be self-contained. It must be able to operate as a stand-alone entity on a component platform that provides an implementation of the component model. This usually means that the component is binary and does not have to be compiled before it is deployed. If a component is implemented as a service, it does not have to be deployed by a user of a component. Rather, it is deployed by the service provider.
Documented	Components have to be fully documented so that potential users can decide whether or not the components meet their needs. The syntax and, ideally, the semantics of all component interfaces should be specified.

Figure 17.1
Component
characteristics

proposals. Figure 17.1 shows what I consider to be the essential characteristics of a component as used in CBSE.

A useful way of thinking about a component is as a provider of one or more services. When a system needs a service, it calls on a component to provide that service without caring about where that component is executing or the programming language used to develop the component. For example, a component in a library system might provide a search service that allows users to search different library catalogs. A component that converts from one graphical format to another (e.g., TIFF to JPEG) provides a data conversion service, etc.

Viewing a component as a service provider emphasizes two critical characteristics of a reusable component:

1. The component is an independent executable entity that is defined by its interfaces. You don't need any knowledge of its source code to use it. It can either be referenced as an external service or included directly in a program.

2. The services offered by a component are made available through an interface and all interactions are through that interface. The component interface is expressed in terms of parameterized operations and its internal state is never exposed.

Component and objects

Components are often implemented in object-oriented languages and, in some cases, accessing the 'provides' interface of a component is done through method calls. However, components and object classes are not the same thing. Unlike object classes, components are independently deployable, do not define types, are language-independent, and are based on a standard component model.

http://www.SoftwareEngineering-9.com/Web/CBSE/objects.html

Components have two related interfaces, as shown in Figure 17.2. These interfaces reflect the services that the component provides and the services that the component requires to operate correctly:

- The 'provides' interface defines the services provided by the component. This interface, essentially, is the component API. It defines the methods that can be called by a user of the component. In a UML component diagram, the 'provides' interface for a component is indicated by a circle at the end of a line from the component icon.

- The 'requires' interface specifies what services must be provided by other components in the system if a component is to operate correctly. If these are not available, then the component will not work. This does not compromise the independence or deployability of a component because the 'requires' interface does not define how these services should be provided. In the UML, the symbol for a 'requires' interface is a semicircle at the end of a line from the component icon. Notice that 'provides' and 'requires' interface icons can fit together like a ball and socket.

To illustrate these interfaces, Figure 17.3 shows a model of a component that has been designed to collect and collate information from an array of sensors. It runs autonomously to collect data over a period of time and, on request, provides collated data to a calling component. The 'provides' interface includes methods to add, remove, start, stop, and test sensors. The report method returns the sensor data that has been collected, and the listAll method provides information about the attached sensors. Although I have not shown this here, these methods have associated parameters specifying the sensor identifiers, locations, and so on.

The 'requires' interface is used to connect the component to the sensors. It assumes that sensors have a data interface, accessed through sensorData, and a management

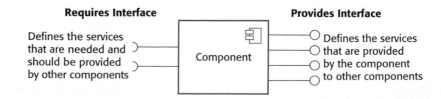

Figure 17.2
Component interfaces

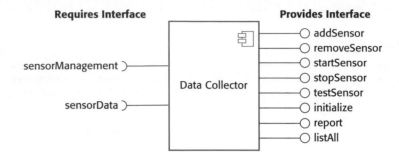

Figure 17.3 A model of a data collector component

interface, accessed through sensorManagement. This interface has been designed to connect to different types of sensor so it does not include specific sensor operations such as Test, provideReading, etc. Instead, the commands used by a specific type of sensor are embedded in a string, which is a parameter to the operations in the 'requires' interface. Adaptor components parse this string and translate the embedded commands into the specific control interface of each type of sensor. I discuss the use of adaptors later in this chapter, where I show how the data collector component is linked to a sensor (Figure 17.12).

A critical difference between a component as an external service and a component as a program element is that services are completely independent entities. They do not have a 'requires' interface. Different programs can use these services without the need to implement any additional support required by the service.

17.1.1 Component models

A component model is a definition of standards for component implementation, documentation, and deployment. These standards are for component developers to ensure that components can interoperate. They are also for providers of component execution infrastructures who provide middleware to support component operation. Many component models have been proposed, but the most important models are now the WebServices model, Sun's Enterprise Java Beans (EJB) model, and Microsoft's .NET model (Lau and Wang, 2007).

The basic elements of an ideal component model are discussed by Weinreich and Sametinger (2001). I summarize these model elements in Figure 17.4. This diagram shows that the elements of a component model define the component interfaces, the information that you need to use the component in a program, and how a component should be deployed:

1. *Interfaces* Components are defined by specifying their interfaces. The component model specifies how the interfaces should be defined and the elements, such as operation names, parameters, and exceptions, which should be included in the interface definition. The model should also specify the language used to define the component interfaces. For web services, this is WSDL, which I discuss in

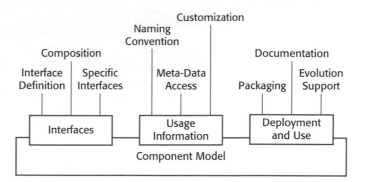

Figure 17.4 Basic elements of a component model

Chapter 19; EJB is Java-specific so Java is used as the interface definition language; in .NET, interfaces are defined using the Common Intermediate Language (CIL). Some component models require specific interfaces that must be defined by a component. These are used to compose the component with the component model infrastructure, which provides standardized services such as security and transaction management.

2. *Usage* In order for components to be distributed and accessed remotely, they need to have a unique name or handle associated with them. This has to be globally unique—for example, in EJB, a hierarchical name is generated with the root based on an Internet domain name. Services have a unique URI (Uniform Resource Identifier).

    Component meta-data is data about the component itself, such as information about its interfaces and attributes. The meta-data is important because it allows users of the component to find out what services are provided and required. Component model implementations normally include specific ways (such as the use of a reflection interface in Java) to access this component meta-data.

    Components are generic entities and, when deployed, they have to be configured to fit into an application system. For example, you could configure the Data collector component (Figure 17.2) by defining the maximum number of sensors in a sensor array. The component model may therefore specify how the binary components can be customized for a particular deployment environment.

3. *Deployment* The component model includes a specification of how components should be packaged for deployment as independent, executable entities. Because components are independent entities, they have to be packaged with all supporting software that is not provided by the component infrastructure, or is not defined in a 'requires' interface. Deployment information includes information about the contents of a package and its binary organization.

    Inevitably, as new requirements emerge, components will have to be changed or replaced. The component model may therefore include rules governing when and how component replacement is allowed. Finally, the component model may

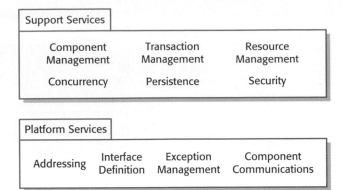

Figure 17.5
Middleware services
defined in a component
model

define the component documentation that should be produced. This is used to find the component and to decide whether it is appropriate.

For components that are implemented as program units rather than external services, the component model sets out the services to be provided by the middleware that supports the executing components. Weinreich and Sametinger (2001) use the analogy of an operating system to explain component models. An operating system provides a set of generic services that can be used by applications. A component model implementation provides comparable shared services for components. Figure 17.5 shows some of the services that may be provided by an implementation of a component model.

The services provided by a component model implementation fall into two categories:

1. Platform services, which enable components to communicate and interoperate in a distributed environment. These are the fundamental services that must be available in all component-based systems.

2. Support services, which are common services that are likely to be required by many different components. For example, many components require authentication to ensure that the user of component services is authorized. It makes sense to provide a standard set of middleware services for use by all components. This reduces the costs of component development and potential component incompatibilities can be avoided.

The middleware implements the component services and provides interfaces to these services. To make use of the services provided by a component model infrastructure, you can think of the components as being deployed in a 'container'. A container is an implementation of the support services plus a definition of the interfaces that a component must provide to integrate it with the container. Including the component in the container means that the component can access the support services and the container can access the component interfaces. When in use, the component interfaces themselves are not accessed directly by other components;

rather, they are accessed through a container interface that invokes code to access the interface of the embedded component.

Containers are large and complex and, when you deploy a component in a container, you get access to all middleware services. However, simple components may not need all of the facilities offered by the supporting middleware. The approach taken in web services to common service provision is therefore rather different. For web services, standards have been defined for common services such as transaction management and security and these standards have been implemented as program libraries. If you are implementing a service component, you only use the common services that you need.

17.2 CBSE processes

CBSE processes are software processes that support component-based software engineering. They take into account the possibilities of reuse and the different process activities involved in developing and using reusable components. Figure 17.6 (Kotonya, 2003) presents an overview of the processes in CBSE. At the highest level, there are two types of CBSE processes:

1. *Development for reuse* This process is concerned with developing components or services that will be reused in other applications. It usually involves generalizing existing components.

2. *Development with reuse* This is the process of developing new applications using existing components and services.

These processes have different objectives and therefore, include different activities. In the development for reuse process, the objective is to produce one or more reusable components. You know the components that you will be working with and you have access to their source code to generalize them. In development with reuse, you don't know what components are available, so you need to discover these components and design your system to make the most effective use of them. You may not have access to the component source code.

You can see from Figure 17.6 that the basic processes of CBSE with and for reuse have supporting processes that are concerned with component acquisition, component management, and component certification:

1. Component acquisition is the process of acquiring components for reuse or development into a reusable component. It may involve accessing locally developed components or services or finding these components from an external source.

2. Component management is concerned with managing a company's reusable components, ensuring that they are properly cataloged, stored, and made available for reuse.

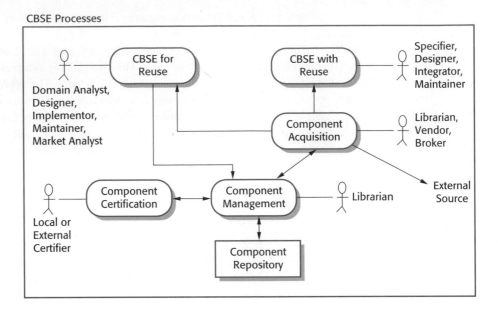

CBSE Processes

Figure 17.6 CBSE processes

3. Component certification is the process of checking a component and certifying that it meets its specification.

Components maintained by an organization may be stored in a component repository that includes both the components and information about their use.

17.2.1 CBSE for reuse

CBSE for reuse is the process of developing reusable components and making them available for reuse through a component management system. The vision of early supporters of CBSE (Szyperski, 2002) was that a thriving component marketplace would develop. There would be specialist component providers and component vendors who would organize the sale of components from different developers. Software developers would buy components to include in a system or pay for services as they were used. However, this vision has not been realized. There are relatively few component suppliers and buying components is uncommon. At the time of writing, the service market is also undeveloped although there are predictions that it will expand significantly over the next few years.

Consequently, CBSE for reuse is most likely to take place within an organization that has made a commitment to reuse-driven software engineering. They wish to exploit the software assets that have been developed in different parts of the company. However, these internally developed components are not usually reusable without change. They often include application-specific features and interfaces that are unlikely to be required in other programs where the component is reused.

To make components reusable, you have to adapt and extend the application-specific components to create more generic and therefore more reusable versions. Obviously, this adaptation has an associated cost. Thus you have to decide first, whether a component is likely to be reused and second, whether the cost savings from future reuse justify the costs of making the component reusable.

To answer the first of these questions, you have to decide whether or not the component implements one or more stable domain abstractions. Stable domain abstractions are fundamental elements of the application domain that change slowly. For example, in a banking system, domain abstractions might include accounts, account holders, and statements. In a hospital management system, domain abstractions might include patients, treatments, and nurses. These domain abstractions are sometimes called 'business objects'. If the component is an implementation of a commonly used domain abstraction or group of related business objects, it can probably be reused.

To answer the question about the cost effectiveness, you have to assess the costs of changes that are required to make the component reusable. These costs are the costs of component documentation, component validation, and making the component more generic. Changes that you may make to a component to make it more reusable include:

- removing application-specific methods;

- changing names to make them more general;

- adding methods to provide more complete functional coverage;

- making exception handling consistent for all methods;

- adding a 'configuration' interface to allow the component to be adapted to different situations of use;

- integrating required components to increase independence.

The problem of exception handling is a particularly difficult one. Components should not handle exceptions themselves, because each application will have its own requirements for exception handling. Rather, the component should define what exceptions can arise and should publish these as part of the interface. For example, a simple component implementing a stack data structure should detect and publish stack overflow and stack underflow exceptions. In practice, however, there are two problems with this:

1. Publishing all exceptions leads to bloated interfaces that are harder to understand. This may put off potential users of the component.

2. The operation of the component may depend on local exception handling, and changing this may have serious implications for the functionality of the component.

Mili et al. (2002) discuss ways of estimating the costs of making a component reusable and the returns from that investment. The benefits of reusing rather than redeveloping a component are not simply productivity gains. There are also quality gains, because a reused component should be more dependable, and time-to-market gains. These are the increased returns that accrue from deploying the software more quickly. Mili et al. present various formulas for estimating these gains, as does the COCOMO model discussed in Chapter 23 (Boehm, et al., 2000). However, the parameters of these formulas are difficult to estimate accurately, and the formulas must be adapted to local circumstances, making them difficult to use. I suspect that few software project managers use these models to estimate the return on investment from component reusability.

Obviously, whether or not a component is reusable depends on its application domain and functionality. As you add generality to a component, you increase its reusability. However, this normally means that the component has more operations and is more complex, which makes the component harder to understand and use.

There is, therefore, an inevitable trade-off between reusability and usability of a component. To make a component reusable you have to provide a set of generic interfaces with operations that cater to all of the ways in which the component could be used. Making the component usable means providing a simple, minimal interface that is easy to understand. Reusability adds complexity and hence reduces component understandability. It is therefore more difficult to decide when and how to reuse that component. When designing a reusable component, you must, therefore, find a compromise between generality and understandability.

A potential source of components is existing legacy systems. As I discussed in Chapter 9, these are systems that fulfill an important business function but are written using obsolete software technologies. Because of this, it may be difficult to use them with new systems. However, if you convert these old systems to components, their functionality can be reused in new applications.

Of course, these legacy systems do not normally have clearly defined 'requires' and 'provides' interfaces. To make these components reusable, you have to create a wrapper that defines the component interfaces. The wrapper hides the complexity of the underlying code and provides an interface for external components to access services that are provided. Although this wrapper is a fairly complex piece of software, the cost of wrapper development is often much less than the cost of reimplementing the legacy system. I discuss this approach in more detail in Chapter 19, where I explain how the features in a legacy system can be accessed through services.

Once you have developed and tested a reusable component or service, this then has to be managed for future reuse. Management involves deciding how to classify the component so that it can be discovered, making the component available either in a repository or as a service, maintaining information about the use of the component and keeping track of different component versions. If the component is open source, you may make it available in a public repository such as Sourceforge. If it is intended for use in a company, then you may use an internal repository system.

A company with a reuse program may carry out some form of component certification before the component is made available for reuse. Certification means that

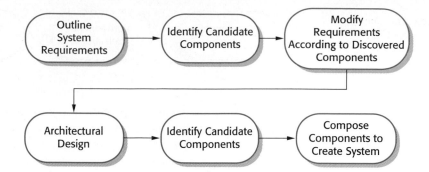

Figure 17.7 CBSE with reuse

someone apart from the developer checks the quality of the component. They test the component and certify that it has reached an acceptable quality standard, before it is made available for reuse. However, this can be an expensive process and many companies simply leave testing and quality checking to the component developers.

17.2.2 CBSE with reuse

The successful reuse of components requires a development process tailored to CBSE. The CBSE with reuse process has to include activities that find and integrate reusable components. The structure of such a process was discussed in Chapter 2 and Figure 17.7 shows the principal activities within that process. Some of the activities within this process, such as the initial discovery of user requirements, are carried out in the same way as in other software processes. However, the essential differences between CBSE with reuse and software processes for original software development are:

1. The user requirements are initially developed in outline rather than in detail, and stakeholders are encouraged to be as flexible as possible in defining their requirements. Requirements that are too specific limit the number of components that could meet these requirements. However, unlike incremental development, you need a complete set of requirements so that you can identify as many components as possible for reuse.

2. Requirements are refined and modified early in the process depending on the components available. If the user requirements cannot be satisfied from available components, you should discuss the related requirements that can be supported. Users may be willing to change their minds if this means cheaper or quicker system delivery.

3. There is a further component search and design refinement activity after the system architecture has been designed. Some apparently usable components may turn out to be unsuitable or do not work properly with other chosen components. Although not shown in Figure 17.7, this implies that further requirements changes may be necessary.

Figure 17.8 The
component
identification
process

Figure 17.8 The
component
identification
process

4.   Development is a composition process where the discovered components are
      integrated. This involves integrating the components with the component model
      infrastructure and, often, developing adaptors that reconcile the interfaces
      of incompatible components. Of course, additional functionality may also be
      required over and above that provided by reused components.

The architectural design stage is particularly important. Jacobson et al. (1997)
found that defining a robust architecture is critical for successful reuse. During the
architectural design activity, you may choose a component model and implementation platform. However, many companies have a standard development platform
(e.g., .NET) so the component model is pre-determined. As I discussed in Chapter 6,
you also establish the high-level organization of the system at this stage and make
decisions about system distribution and control.

An activity that is unique to the CBSE process is identifying candidate components or services for reuse. This involves a number of subactivities, as shown in
Figure 17.8. Initially, your focus should be on search and selection. You need to convince yourself that there are components available to meet your requirements.
Obviously, you should do some initial checking that the component is suitable but
detailed testing may not be required. In the later stage, after the system architecture
has been designed, you should spend more time on component validation. You need
to be confident that the identified components are really suited to your application; if
not, then you have to repeat the search and selection processes.

The first step in identifying components is to look for components that are available locally or from trusted suppliers. As I said in the previous section, there are relatively few component vendors so you are therefore most likely to be looking for
components that have been developed in your own company. Software development
companies can build their own database of reusable components without the risks
inherent in using components from external suppliers. Alternatively, you may decide
to search code libraries available on the Web, such as Sourceforge or Google Code,
to see if source code for the component that you need is available. If you are looking
for services, then there are a number of specialized web search engines available that
can discover public web services.

Once the component search process has identified possible components, you have
to select candidate components for assessment. In some cases, this will be a straightforward task. Components on the list will directly implement the user requirements
and there will not be competing components that match these requirements. In other
cases, however, the selection process is much more complex. There will not be a clear
mapping of requirements onto components and you may find that several components
have to be integrated to meet a specific requirement or group of requirements.

The Ariane 5 launcher Failure

While developing the Ariane 5 space launcher, the designers decided to reuse the inertial reference software that had performed successfully in the Ariane 4 launcher. The inertial reference software maintains the stability of the rocket. They decided to reuse this without change (as you would do with components), although it included additional functionality that was not required in Ariane 5.

In the first launch of Ariane 5, the inertial navigation software failed and the rocket could not be controlled. Ground controllers instructed the launcher to self-destruct and the rocket and its payload were destroyed. The cause of the problem was an unhandled exception when a conversion of a fixed-point number to an integer resulted in a numeric overflow. This caused the run-time system to shut down the inertial reference system and launcher stability could not be maintained. The fault had never occurred in Ariane 4 because it had less powerful engines and the value that was converted could not be large enough for the conversion to overflow.

The fault occurred in code that was not required for Ariane 5. The validation tests for the reused software were based on Ariane 5 requirements. Because there were no requirements for the function that failed, no tests were developed. Consequently, the problem with the software was never discovered during launch simulation tests.

Figure 17.9 An example of validation failure with reused software

You, therefore, have to decide which component compositions provide the best coverage of the requirements.

Once you have selected components for possible inclusion in a system, you should then validate them to check that they behave as advertised. The extent of the validation required depends on the source of the components. If you are using a component that has been developed by a known and trusted source, you may decide that component testing is unnecessary. You simply test the component when it is integrated with other components. On the other hand, if you are using a component from an unknown source, you should always check and test that component before including it in your system.

Component validation involves developing a set of test cases for a component (or, possibly, extending test cases supplied with that component) and developing a test harness to run component tests. The major problem with component validation is that the component specification may not be sufficiently detailed to allow you to develop a complete set of component tests. Components are usually specified informally, with the only formal documentation being their interface specification. This may not include enough information for you to develop a complete set of tests that would convince you that the component's advertised interface is what you require.

As well as testing that a component for reuse does what you require, you may also have to check that the component does not include any malicious code or functionality that you don't need. Professional developers rarely use components from untrusted sources, especially if these sources do not provide source code. Therefore, the malicious code problem does not usually arise. However, components may often contain functionality that you don't need and you have to check that this functionality will not interfere with your use of the component.

The problem with unnecessary functionality is that it may be activated by the component itself. This can slow down the component, cause it to produce surprising results or, in some cases, cause serious system failures. Figure 17.9 summarizes a situation where unnecessary functionality in a reused system caused a catastrophic software failure.

The problem in the Ariane 5 launcher arose because the assumptions made about the software for Ariane 4 were invalid for Ariane 5. This is a general problem with reusable components. They are originally implemented for an application environment and, naturally, embed assumptions about that environment. These assumptions are rarely documented so, when the component is reused, it is impossible to derive tests to check if the assumptions are still valid. If you are reusing a component in a different environment, you may not discover the embedded environmental assumptions until you use the component in an operational system.

17.3 Component composition

Component composition is the process of integrating components with each other, and with specially written 'glue code' to create a system or another component. There are several different ways in which you can compose components, as shown in Figure 17.10. From left to right these diagrams illustrate sequential composition, hierarchical composition and additive composition. In the discussion below, I assume that you are composing two components (A and B) to create a new component:

1. Sequential composition is situation (a) in Figure 17.10. You create a new component from 2 existing components by calling the existing components in sequence. You can think of the composition as a composition of the 'provides interfaces'. That is, the services offered by component A are called and the results returned by A are then used in the call to the services offered by component B. The components do not call each other in sequential composition. Some extra glue code is required to call the component services in the right order and to ensure that the results delivered by component A are compatible with the inputs expected by component B. The 'provides' interface of the composition depends on the combined functionality of A and B but will not normally be a composition of their 'provides interfaces'. This type of composition may be used with components that are program elements or components that are services.

2. Hierarchical composition is situation (b) in Figure 17.10. This type of composition occurs when one component calls directly on the services provided by another component. The called component provides the services that are required by the calling component. Therefore, the 'provides' interface of the called component must be compatible with the 'requires' interface of the calling component. Component A calls on component B directly and, if their interfaces match, there may be no need for additional code. However, if there is a mismatch between the 'requires' interface of A and the 'provides' interface of B, then some conversion code may be required. As services do not have a 'requires' interface, this mode of composition is not used when components are implemented as web services.

3. Additive composition corresponds to situation (c) in Figure 17.10. This occurs when two or more components are put together (added) to create a new component,

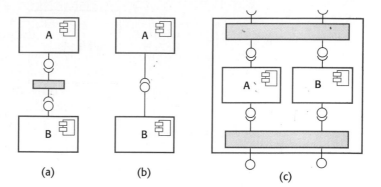

Figure 17.10 Types of component composition

(a)   (b)   (c)

which combines their functionality. The 'provides' interface and 'requires' interface of the new component is a combination of the corresponding interfaces in components A and B. The components are called separately through the external interface of the composed component. A and B are not dependent and do not call each other. This type of composition may be used with components that are program units or components that are services.

You might use all the forms of component composition when creating a system. In all cases, you may have to write 'glue code' that links the components. For example, for sequential composition, the output of component A typically becomes the input to component B. You need intermediate statements that call component A, collect the result, and then call component B with that result as a parameter. When one component calls another, you may need to introduce an intermediate component that ensures that the 'provides' interface and the 'requires' interface are compatible.

When you write new components especially for composition, you should design the interfaces of these components so that they are compatible with other components in the system. You can therefore easily compose these components into a single unit. However, when components are developed independently for reuse, you will often be faced with interface incompatibilities. This means that the interfaces of the components that you wish to compose are not the same. Three types of incompatibility can occur:

1. *Parameter incompatibility* The operations on each side of the interface have the same name but their parameter types or the number of parameters are different.

2. *Operation incompatibility* The names of the operations in the 'provides' and 'requires' interfaces are different.

3. *Operation incompleteness* The 'provides' interface of a component is a subset of the 'requires' interface of another component or vice versa.

In all cases, you tackle the problem of incompatibility by writing an adaptor that reconciles the interfaces of the two components being reused. An adaptor component converts one interface to another. The precise form of the adaptor depends on the type

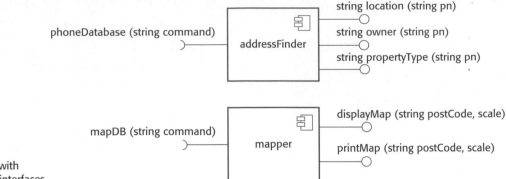

Figure 17.11
Components with
incompatible interfaces

of composition. Sometimes, as in the next example, the adaptor takes a result from one component and converts it into a form where it can be used as an input to another. In other cases, the adaptor may be called by component A as a proxy for component B. This situation occurs if A wishes to call B but the details of the 'requires' interface of A do not match the details of the 'provides' interface of B. The adaptor reconciles these differences by converting its input parameters from A into the required input parameters for B. It then calls B to deliver the services required by A.

To illustrate adaptors, consider the two components shown in Figure 17.11, whose interfaces are incompatible. These might be part of a system used by the emergency services. When the emergency operator takes a call, the phone number is input to the **addressFinder** component to locate the address. Then, using the mapper component, the operator prints a map to be sent to the vehicle dispatched to the emergency. In fact, the components would have more complex interfaces than those shown here, but the simplified version illustrates the concept of an adaptor.

The first component, **addressFinder**, finds the address that matches a phone number. It can also return the owner of the property associated with the phone number and the type of property. The **mapper** component takes a post code (in the United States, a standard ZIP code with the additional four digits identifying property location) and displays or prints a street map of the area around that code at a specified scale.

These components are composable in principle because the property location includes the post or ZIP code. However, you have to write an adaptor component called **postCodeStripper** that takes the location data from addressFinder and strips out the post code. This post code is then used as an input to mapper and the street map is displayed at a scale of 1:10,000. The following code, which is an example of sequential composition, illustrates the sequence of calls that is required to implement this:

```
address = addressFinder.location (phonenumber) ;
postCode = postCodeStripper.getPostCode (address) ;
mapper.displayMap(postCode, 10000) ;
```

"services"

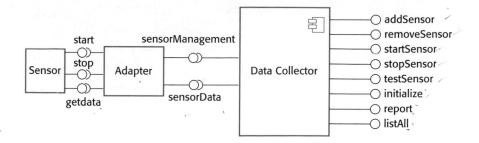

Figure 17.12 An adaptor linking a data collector and a sensor

Another case in which an adaptor component may be used is in hierarchical composition, where one component wishes to make use of another but there is an incompatibility between the 'provides' interface and 'requires' interface of the components in the composition. I have illustrated the use of an adaptor in Figure 17.12 where an adaptor is used to link a data collector and a sensor component. These could be used in the implementation of a wilderness weather station system, as discussed in Chapter 7.

The sensor and data collector components are composed using an adapter that reconciles the 'requires' interface of the data collection component with the 'provides' interface of the sensor component. The data collector component has been designed with a generic 'requires' interface that supports sensor data collection and sensor management. For each of these operations, the parameter is a text string representing the specific sensor commands. For example, to issue a collect command, you would say **sensorData**("collect"). As I have shown in Figure 17.12, the sensor itself has separate operations such as start, stop, and getdata.

The adaptor parses the input string, identifies the command (e.g., collect) and then calls **Sensor.getdata** to collect the sensor value. It then returns the result (as a character string) to the data collector component. This interface style means that the data collector can interact with different types of sensor. A separate adaptor, which converts the sensor commands from **Data collector** to the actual sensor interface, is implemented for each type of sensor.

The above discussion of component composition assumes you can tell from the component documentation whether or not interfaces are compatible. Of course, the interface definition includes the operation name and parameter types, so you can make some assessment of the compatibility from this. However, you depend on the component documentation to decide whether the interfaces are semantically compatible.

To illustrate this problem, consider the composition shown in Figure 17.13. These components are used to implement a system that downloads images from a digital camera and stores them in a photograph library. The system user can provide additional information to describe and catalog the photograph. To avoid clutter,

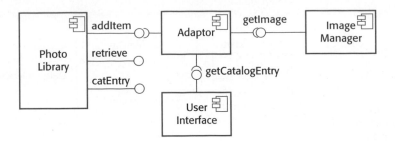

Figure 17.13 Photo library composition

I have not shown all interface methods here. Rather, I simply show the methods that are needed to illustrate the component documentation problem. The methods in the interface of Photo Library are:

```
public void addItem (Identifier pid ; Photograph p; CatalogEntry
photodesc) ;
public Photograph retrieve (Identifier pid) ;
public CatalogEntry catEntry (Identifier pid);
```

Assume that the documentation for the addItem method in Photo Library is:

This method adds a photograph to the library and associates the photograph identifier and catalogue descriptor with the photograph.

This description appears to explain what the component does, but consider the following questions:

- What happens if the photograph identifier is already associated with a photograph in the library?

- Is the photograph descriptor associated with the catalog entry as well as the photograph? That is, if you delete the photograph, do you also delete the catalog information?

There is not enough information in the informal description of addItem to answer these questions. Of course, it is possible to add more information to the natural language description of the method, but in general, the best way to resolve ambiguities is to use a formal language to describe the interface. The specification shown in Figure 17.14 is part of the description of the interface of **Photo Library** that adds information to the informal description.

The specification in Figure 17.14 uses pre- and post-conditions that are defined in a notation based on the object constraint language (OCL), which is part of the UML (Warmer and Kleppe, 2003). OCL is designed to describe constraints in UML object models; it allows you to express predicates that must always be true, that must be

```
— The context keyword names the component to which the conditions apply

context addItem

— The preconditions specify what must be true before execution of addItem
pre:      PhotoLibrary.libSize() > 0
          PhotoLibrary.retrieve(pid) = null

— The postconditions specify what is true after execution
post:     libSize () = libSize()@pre + 1
          PhotoLibrary.retrieve(pid) = p
          PhotoLibrary.catEntry(pid) = photodesc

context delete

pre:      PhotoLibrary.retrieve(pid) <>null ;

post:     PhotoLibrary.retrieve(pid) = null
          PhotoLibrary.catEntry(pid) = PhotoLibrary.catEntry(pid)@pre
          PhotoLibrary.libSize() = libSize()@pre−1
```

Figure 17.14 The
OCL description
of the Photo Library
interface

true before a method has executed; and that must be true after a method has executed. These are invariants, pre-conditions, and post-conditions. To access the value of a variable before an operation, you add @pre after its name. Therefore, using age as an example:

```
age = age@pre + 1
```

This statement means that the value of age after an operation is one more than it was before that operation.

OCL-based approaches are increasingly used to add semantic information to UML models, and OCL descriptions may be used to drive code generators in model-driven engineering. The general approach has been derived from Meyer's Design by Contract approach (Meyer, 1992), in which the interfaces and obligations of communicating objects are formally specified and enforced by the run-time system. Meyer suggests that using Design by Contract is essential if we are to develop trusted components (Meyer, 2003).

Figure 17.14 includes a specification for the addItem and delete methods in **Photo Library**. The method being specified is indicated by the keyword context and the pre- and post-conditions by the keywords pre and post. The pre-conditions for addItem state that:

1. There must not be a photograph in the library with the same identifier as the photograph to be entered.

2. The library must exist—assume that creating a library adds a single item to it so that the size of a library is always greater than zero.

3. The post-conditions for addItem state that:

    The size of the library has increased by 1 (so only a single entry has been made).

    If you retrieve using the same identifier, then you get back the photograph that you added.

    If you look up the catalogue using that identifier, you get back the catalogue entry that you made.

The specification of delete provides further information. The pre-condition states that to delete an item, it must be in the library and, after deletion, the photo can no longer be retrieved and the size of the library is reduced by 1. However, delete does not delete the catalogue entry—you can still retrieve it after the photo has been deleted. The reason for this is that you may wish to maintain information in the catalog about why a photo was deleted, its new location, and so on.

When you create a system by composing components, you may find that there are potential conflicts between functional and non-functional requirements, the need to deliver a system as quickly as possible and the need to create a system that can evolve as requirements change. The decisions where you may have to take trade-offs into account are:

1. What composition of components is most effective for delivering the functional requirements for the system?

2. What composition of the components will make it easier to adapt the composite component when its requirements change?

3. What will be the emergent properties of the composed system? These are properties such as performance and dependability. You can only assess these once the complete system is implemented.

Unfortunately, there are many situations where the solutions to the composition problems may conflict. For example, consider a situation such as that illustrated in Figure 17.15, where a system can be created through two alternative compositions. The system is a data collection and reporting system where data is collected from different sources, stored in a database and then different reports summarizing that data are produced.

Here, there is a potential conflict between adaptability and performance. Composition (a) is more adaptable but composition (b) is perhaps faster and more reliable. The advantages of composition (a) are that reporting and data management are separate, so there is more flexibility for future change. The data management system could be replaced and, if reports are required that the current reporting component cannot produce, that component can also be replaced without having to change the data management component.

In composition (b), a database component with built-in reporting facilities (e.g., Microsoft Access) is used. The key advantage of composition (b) is that there are fewer components, so this will be a faster implementation because there are no component

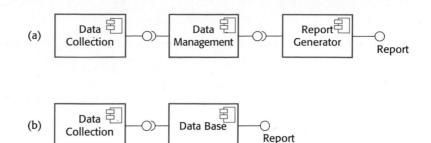

Figure 17.15 Data collection and report generation components

communication overheads. Furthermore, data integrity rules that apply to the database will also apply to reports. These reports will not be able to combine data in incorrect ways. In composition (a), there are no such constraints so errors in reports could occur.

In general, a good composition principle to follow is the principle of separation of concerns. That is, you should try to design your system in such a way that each component has a clearly defined role and that, ideally, these roles should not overlap. However, it may be cheaper to buy one multi-functional component rather than two or three separate components. Furthermore, there may be dependability or performance penalties when multiple components are used.

KEY POINTS

■ Component-based software engineering is a reuse-based approach to defining, implementing, and composing loosely coupled independent components into systems.

■ A component is a software unit whose functionality and dependencies are completely defined by a set of public interfaces. Components can be composed with other components without knowledge of their implementation and can be deployed as an executable unit.

■ Components may be implemented as program units that are included in a system or as external services that are referenced from within a system.

■ A component model defines a set of standards for components, including interface standards, usage standards, and deployment standards. The implementation of the component model provides a set of common services that may be used by all components.

■ During the CBSE process, you have to interleave the processes of requirements engineering and system design. You have to trade off desirable requirements against the services that are available from existing reusable components.

■ Component composition is the process of 'wiring' components together to create a system. Types of composition include sequential composition, hierarchical composition, and additive composition.

■ When composing reusable components that have not been written for your application, you may need to write adaptors or 'glue code' to reconcile the different component interfaces.

■ When choosing compositions, you have to consider the required functionality of the system, the non-functional requirements and the ease with which one component can be replaced when the system is changed.

FURTHER READING

Component-based Software Engineering: Putting the Pieces Together. This book is a collection of papers from various authors on different aspects of CBSE. Like all collections, it is rather mixed but it has better coverage of general issues of software engineering with components than Szyperski's book. (G. T. Heineman and W. T. Councill, Addison-Wesley, 2001.)

Component Software: Beyond Object-Oriented Programming, 2nd ed. This updated edition of the first book on CBSE covers technical and nontechnical issues in CBSE. It has more detail on specific technologies than Heineman and Councill's book and includes a thorough discussion of market issues. (C. Szyperski, Addison-Wesley, 2002.)

'Specification, Implementation and Deployment of Components'. A good introduction to the fundamentals of CBSE. The same issue of the *CACM* includes articles on components and component-based development. (I. Crnkovic, B. Hnich, T. Jonsson and Z. Kiziltan, *Comm. ACM*, **45** (10), October 2002.) http://dx.doi.org/10.1145/570907.570928.

'Software Component Models'. This is a comprehensive discussion of commercial and research component models that classifies these models and explains the differences between them. (K-K. Lau and Z. Wang, *IEEE Transactions on Software Engineering*, **33** (10), October 2007.) http://dx.doi.org/10.1109/TSE.2007.70726.

EXERCISES

17.1. Why is it important that all component interactions are defined through 'requires' and 'provides' interfaces?

17.2. The principle of component independence means that it ought to be possible to replace one component with another that is implemented in a completely different way. Using an example, explain how such component replacement could have undesired consequences and may lead to system failure.

17.3. What are the fundamental differences between components as program elements and components as services?

17.4. Why is it important that components should be based on a standard component model?

17.5. Using an example of a component that implements an abstract data type such as a stack or a list, show why it is usually necessary to extend and adapt components for reuse.

17.6. Explain why it is difficult to validate a reusable component without the component source code. In what ways would a formal component specification simplify the problems of validation?

17.7. Design the 'provides' interface and the 'requires' interface of a reusable component that may be used to represent a patient in the MHC-PMS.

17.8. Using examples, illustrate the different types of adaptor needed to support sequential composition, hierarchical composition, and additive composition.

17.9. Design the interfaces of components that might be used in a system for an emergency control room. You should design interfaces for a call-logging component that records calls made, and a vehicle discovery component that, given a post code (zip code) and an incident type, finds the nearest suitable vehicle to be despatched to the incident.

17.10. It has been suggested that an independent certification authority should be established. Vendors would submit their components to this authority, which would validate that the component was trustworthy. What would be the advantages and disadvantages of such a certification authority?

REFERENCES

Boehm, B. W., Abts, C., Brown, A. W., Chulani, S., Clark, B. K., Horowitz, E., Madachy, R., Reifer, D. and Steece, B. (2000). *Software Cost Estimation with COCOMO II*. Upper Saddle River, NJ.: Prentice Hall.

Councill, W. T. and Heineman, G. T. (2001). 'Definition of a Software Component and its Elements'. In *Component-based Software Engineering*. Heineman, G. T. and Councill, W. T. (ed.). Boston: Addison-Wesley, 5–20.

Jacobson, I., Griss, M. and Jonsson, P. (1997). *Software Reuse*. Reading, Mass.: Addison-Wesley.

Kotonya, G. (2003). 'The CBSE Process: Issues and Future Visions'. *Proc. 2nd CBSEnet workshop*, Budapest, Hungary.

Lau, K.-K. and Wang, Z. (2007). 'Software Component Models'. *IEEE Trans. on Software Eng.*, **33** (10), 709–24.

Meyer, B. (1992). 'Design by Contract'. *IEEE Computer,* **25** (10), 40–51.

Meyer, B. (2003). 'The Grand Challenge of Trusted Components'. *ICSE 25: Int. Conf. on Software Eng.*, Portland, Oregon: IEEE Press.

Mili, H., Mili, A., Yacoub, S. and Addy, E. (2002). *Reuse-based Software Engineering*. New York: John Wiley & Sons.

Pope, A. (1997). *The CORBA Reference Guide: Understanding the Common Object Request Broker Architecture*. Harlow, UK: Addison-Wesley.

Szyperski, C. (2002). *Component Software: Beyond Object-oriented Programming, 2nd ed*. Harlow, UK: Addison-Wesley.

Warmer, J. and Kleppe, A. (2003). *The Object Constraint Language: Getting your models ready for MDA*. Boston: Addison-Wesley.

Weinreich, R. and Sametinger, J. (2001). 'Component Models and Component Services: Concepts and Principles'. In *Component-Based Software Engineering*. Heineman, G. T. and Councill, W. T. (ed.). Boston: Addison-Wesley, 33–48.

18

Distributed software engineering

Objectives

The objective of this chapter is to introduce distributed systems engineering and distributed systems architectures. When you have read this chapter, you will:

- know the key issues that have to be considered when designing and implementing distributed software systems;

- understand the client–server computing model and the layered architecture of client–server systems;

- have been introduced to commonly used patterns for distributed systems architectures and know the types of system for which each architecture is most applicable;

- understand the notion of software as a service, providing web-based access to remotely deployed application systems.

Contents

Virtually all large computer-based systems are now distributed systems. A distributed system is one involving several computers, in contrast with centralized systems where all of the system components execute on a single computer. Tanenbaum and Van Steen (2007) define a distributed system to be:

". . .a collection of independent computers that appears to the user as a single coherent system."

Obviously, the engineering of distributed systems has a great deal in common with the engineering of any other software. However, there are specific issues that have to be taken into account when designing this type of system. These arise because the system components may be running on independently managed computers and they communicate across a network.

Coulouris et al. (2005) identify the following advantages of using a distributed approach to systems development:

1. *Resource sharing* A distributed system allows the sharing of hardware and software resources—such as disks, printers, files, and compilers—that are associated with computers on a network.

2. *Openness* Distributed systems are normally open systems, which means that they are designed around standard protocols that allow equipment and software from different vendors to be combined.

3. *Concurrency* In a distributed system, several processes may operate at the same time on separate computers on the network. These processes may (but need not) communicate with each other during their normal operation.

4. *Scalability* In principle at least, distributed systems are scalable in that the capabilities of the system can be increased by adding new resources to cope with new demands on the system. In practice, the network linking the individual computers in the system may limit the system scalability.

5. *Fault tolerance* The availability of several computers and the potential for replicating information means that distributed systems can be tolerant of some hardware and software failures (see Chapter 13). In most distributed systems, a degraded service can be provided when failures occur; complete loss of service only occurs when there is a network failure.

For large-scale organizational systems, these advantages mean that distributed systems have largely replaced mainframe legacy systems that were developed in the 1990s. However, there are many personal computer application systems (e.g., photo editing systems) that are not distributed and which run on a single computer system. Most embedded systems are also single processor systems.

Distributed systems are inherently more complex than centralized systems. This makes them more difficult to design, implement, and test. It is harder to understand the emergent properties of distributed systems because of the complexity of the interactions between system components and the system infrastructure. For example, rather than the performance of the system being dependent on the execution speed of one processor, it depends on the network bandwidth, the network load, and the speed of all of the computers that are part of the system. Moving resources from one part of the system to another can significantly affect the system's performance.

Furthermore, as all users of the WWW know, distributed systems are unpredictable in their response. The response time depends on the overall load on the system, its architecture and the network load. As all of these may change over a short time, the time taken to respond to a user request may vary dramatically from one request to another.

The most important development that has affected distributed software systems in the past few years is the service-oriented approach. Much of this chapter focuses on general issues of distributed systems, but I cover the notion of applications deployed as services in Section 18.4. This complements the material in Chapter 19, which focuses on services as components in a service-oriented architecture, and more general issues of service-oriented software engineering.

18.1 Distributed systems issues

As I discussed in the introduction to this chapter, distributed systems are more complex than systems that run on a single processor. This complexity arises because it is practically impossible to have a top-down model of control of these systems. The nodes in the system that deliver functionality are often independent systems with no single authority in charge of them. The network connecting these nodes is a separately managed system. It is a complex system in its own right and cannot be controlled by the owners of systems using the network. There is therefore an inherent unpredictability in the operation of distributed systems that has to be taken into account by the system designer.

Some of the most important design issues that have to be considered in distributed systems engineering are:

1. *Transparency* To what extent should the distributed system appear to the user as a single system? When it is useful for users to understand that the system is distributed?

2. *Openness* Should a system be designed using standard protocols that support interoperability or should more specialized protocols be used that restrict the freedom of the designer?

3. *Scalability* How can the system be constructed so that it is scaleable? That is, how can the overall system be designed so that its capacity can be increased in response to increasing demands made on the system?

4. *Security* How can usable security policies be defined and implemented that apply across a set of independently managed systems?

CORBA – Common Object Request Broker Architecture

CORBA is a well-known specification for a middleware system that was developed in the 1990s by the Object Management Group. It was intended as an open standard that would allow the development of middleware to support distributed component communications and execution, plus provide a set of standard services that could be used by these components.

Several implementations of CORBA were produced but the system never achieved critical mass. Users preferred proprietary systems or moved to service-oriented architectures.

http://www.SoftwareEngineering-9.com/Web/DistribSys/Corba.html

5. *Quality of service* How should the quality of service that is delivered to system users be specified and how should the system be implemented to deliver an acceptable quality of service to all users?

6. *Failure management* How can system failures be detected, contained (so that they have minimal effects on other components in the system), and repaired?

In an ideal world, the fact that a system is distributed would be transparent to users. This means that users would see the system as a single system whose behavior is not affected by the way that the system is distributed. In practice, this is impossible to achieve. Central control of a distributed system is impossible and, as a result, individual computers in a system may behave differently at different times. Furthermore, because it always takes a finite length of time for signals to travel across a network, network delays are unavoidable. The length of these delays depends on the location of resources in the system, the quality of the user's network connection, and the network load.

The design approach to achieving transparency depends on creating abstractions of the resources in a distributed system so that the physical realization of these resources can be changed without having to make changes in the application system. Middleware (discussed in Section 18.1.2) is used to map the logical resources referenced by a program onto the actual physical resources, and to manage the interactions between these resources.

In practice, it is impossible to make a system completely transparent and users, generally, are aware that they are dealing with a distributed system. You may therefore decide that it is best to expose the distribution to users. They can then be prepared for some of the consequences of distribution such as network delays, remote node failures, etc.

Open distributed systems are systems that are built according to generally accepted standards. This means that components from any supplier can be integrated into the system and can interoperate with the other system components. At the networking level, openness is now taken for granted with systems conforming to Internet protocols but at the component level, openness is still not universal. Openness implies that system components can be independently developed in any programming language and, if these conform to standards, they will work with other components.

The CORBA standard (Pope, 1997) developed in the 1990s, was intended to achieve this but this never achieved a critical mass of adopters. Rather, many companies chose to develop systems using proprietary standards for components from companies such as Sun and Microsoft. These provided better implementations and support software and better long-term support for industrial protocols.

Web service standards (discussed in Chapter 19) for service-oriented architectures were developed to be open standards. However, there is significant resistance to these standards because of their perceived inefficiency. Some developers of service-based systems have opted instead for so-called RESTful protocols as these have an inherently lower overhead than web service protocols.

The scalability of a system reflects its ability to deliver a high quality of service as demands on the system increase. Neuman (1994) identifies three dimensions of scalability:

1. *Size* It should be possible to add more resources to a system to cope with increasing numbers of users.

2. *Distribution* It should be possible to geographically disperse the components of a system without degrading its performance.

3. *Manageability* It should be possible to manage a system as it increases in size, even if parts of the system are located in independent organizations.

In terms of size, there is a distinction between scaling up and scaling out. Scaling up means replacing resources in the system with more powerful resources. For example, you may increase the memory in a server from 16 GB to 64 GB. Scaling out means adding additional resources to the system (e.g., an extra web server to work alongside an existing server). Scaling out is often more cost effective than scaling up but usually means that the system has to be designed so that concurrent processing is possible.

I have discussed general security issues and issues of security engineering in Part 2 of this book. However, when a system is distributed, the number of ways that the system may be attacked is significantly increased, compared to centralized systems. If a part of the system is successfully attacked then the attacker may be able to use this as a 'back door' into other parts of the system.

The types of attacks that a distributed system must defend itself against are the following:

1. Interception, where communications between parts of the system are intercepted by an attacker so that there is a loss of confidentiality.

2. Interruption, where system services are attacked and cannot be delivered as expected. Denial of service attacks involve bombarding a node with illegitimate service requests so that it cannot deal with valid requests.

3. Modification, where data or services in the system are changed by an attacker.

4. Fabrication, where an attacker generates information that should not exist and then uses this to gain some privileges. For example, an attacker may generate a false password entry and use this to gain access to a system.

The major difficulty in distributed systems is establishing a security policy that can be reliably applied to all of the components in a system. As I discussed in Chapter 11, a security policy sets out the level of security to be achieved by a system. Security mechanisms, such as encryption and authentication, are used to enforce the security policy. The difficulties in a distributed system arise because different organizations may own parts of the system. These organizations may have mutually incompatible security policies and security mechanisms. Security compromises may have to be made in order to allow the systems to work together.

The quality of service (QoS) offered by a distributed system reflects the system's ability to deliver its services dependably and with a response time and throughput that is acceptable to its users. Ideally, the QoS requirements should be specified in advance and the system designed and configured to deliver that QoS. Unfortunately, this is not always practicable, for two reasons:

1. It may not be cost effective to design and configure the system to deliver a high QoS under peak load. This could involve making resources available that are unused for much of the time. One of the main arguments for 'cloud computing' is that it partially addresses this problem. Using a cloud, it is easy to add resources as demand increases.

2. The QoS parameters may be mutually contradictory. For example, increased reliability may mean reduced throughput, as checking procedures are introduced to ensure that all system inputs are valid.

QoS is particularly critical when the system is dealing with time-critical data such as sound or video streams. In these circumstances, if the QoS falls below a threshold value then the sound or video may become so degraded that it is impossible to understand. Systems dealing with sound and video should include QoS negotiation and management components. These should evaluate the QoS requirements against the available resources and, if these are insufficient, negotiate for more resources or for a reduced QoS target.

In a distributed system, it is inevitable that failures will occur, so the system has to be designed to be resilient to these failures. Failure is so ubiquitous that one flippant definition of a distributed system suggested by Leslie Lamport, a prominent distributed systems researcher, is:

> *"You know that you have a distributed system when the crash of a system that you've never heard of stops you getting any work done."*

Failure management involves applying the fault tolerance techniques discussed in Chapter 13. Distributed systems should therefore include mechanisms for discovering if a component of the system has failed, should continue to deliver as many services as possible in spite of that failure and, as far as possible, should automatically recover from the failure.

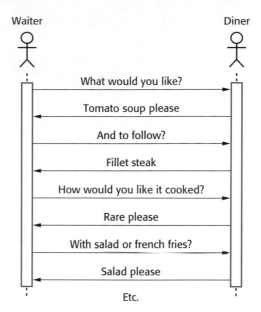

Figure 18.1 Procedural interaction between a diner and a waiter

18.1.1 Models of interaction

There are two fundamental types of interaction that may take place between the computers in a distributed computing system: procedural interaction and message-based interaction. Procedural interaction involves one computer calling on a known service offered by some other computer and (usually) waiting for that service to be delivered. Message-based interaction involves the 'sending' computer defining information about what is required in a message, which is then sent to another computer. Messages usually transmit more information in a single interaction than a procedure call to another machine.

To illustrate the difference between procedural and message-based interaction, consider a situation where you are ordering a meal in a restaurant. When you have a conversation with the waiter, you are involved in a series of synchronous, procedural interactions that define your order. You make a request; the waiter acknowledges that request; you make another request, which is acknowledged; and so on. This is comparable to components interacting in a software system where one component calls methods from other components. The waiter writes down your order along with the order of other people with you. He or she then passes this order, which includes details of everything that has been ordered, to the kitchen to prepare the food. Essentially, the waiter is passing a message to the kitchen staff defining the food to be prepared. This is message-based interaction.

I have illustrated this in Figure 18.1, which shows the synchronous ordering process as a series of calls and in Figure 18.2, which shows a hypothetical XML message that defines an order made by the table of three people. The difference between these forms of information exchange is clear. The waiter takes the order as a series of interactions, with each interaction defining part of the order. However,

```
<starter>
  <dish name = "soup" type = "tomato" />
  <dish name = "soup" type = "fish" />
  <dish name = "pigeon salad" />
</starter>
<main course>
  <dish name = "steak" type = "sirloin" cooking = "medium" />
  <dish name = "steak" type = "fillet" cooking = "rare" />
  <dish name = "sea bass">
</main>
<accompaniment>
  <dish name = "french fries" portions = "2" />
  <dish name = "salad" portions = "1" />
</accompaniment>
```

Figure 18.2
Message-based
interaction
between a
waiter and the
kitchen staff

the waiter has a single interaction with the kitchen where the message defines the complete order.

Procedural communication in a distributed system is usually implemented using remote procedure calls (RPCs). In RPC one component calls another component as if it was a local procedure or method. The middleware in the system intercepts this call and passes it to a remote component. This carries out the required computation and, via the middleware, returns the result to the calling component. In Java, remote method invocations (RMI) are comparable with, though not identical to, RPCs. The RMI framework handles the invocation of remote methods in a Java program.

RPCs require a 'stub' for the called procedure to be accessible on the computer that is initiating the call. The stub is called and it translates the procedure parameters into a standard representation for transmission to the remote procedure. Through the middleware, it then sends the request for execution to the remote procedure. The remote procedure uses library functions to convert the parameters into the required format, carries out the computation, and then communicates the results via the 'stub' that is representing the caller.

Message-based interaction normally involves one component creating a message that details the services required from another component. Through the system middleware, this is sent to the receiving component. The receiver parses the message, carries out the computations, and creates a message for the sending component with the required results. This is then passed to the middleware for transmission to the sending component.

A problem with the RPC approach to interaction is that both the caller and the callee need to be available at the time of the communication, and they must know how to refer to each other. In essence, an RPC has the same requirements as a local procedure or method call. By contrast, in a message-based approach, unavailability can be tolerated as the message simply stays in a queue until the receiver becomes available. Furthermore, it is not necessary for the sender and receiver of the message to be aware of each other. They simply communicate with the middleware, which is responsible for ensuring that messages are passed to the appropriate system.

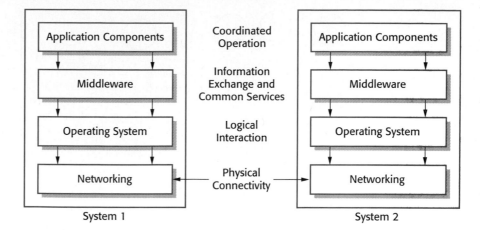

Figure 18.3
Middleware in a
distributed system

18.1.2 Middleware

The components in a distributed system may be implemented in different programming languages and may execute on completely different types of processor. Models of data, information representation, and protocols for communication may all be different. A distributed system therefore requires software that can manage these diverse parts, and ensure that they can communicate and exchange data.

The term 'middleware' is used to refer to this software—it sits in the middle between the distributed components of the system. This is illustrated in Figure 18.3, which shows that middleware is a layer between the operating system and application programs. Middleware is normally implemented as a set of libraries, which are installed on each distributed computer, plus a run-time system to manage communications.

Bernstein (1996) describes types of middleware that are available to support distributed computing. Middleware is general-purpose software that is usually bought off the shelf rather than written specially by application developers. Examples of middleware include software for managing communications with databases, transaction managers, data converters, and communication controllers.

In a distributed system, middleware normally provides two distinct types of support:

1. Interaction support, where the middleware coordinates interactions between different components in the system. The middleware provides location transparency in that it isn't necessary for components to know the physical locations of other components. It may also support parameter conversion if different programming languages are used to implement components, event detection, and communication, etc.

2. The provision of common services, where the middleware provides reusable implementations of services that may be required by several components in the distributed system. By using these common services, components can easily interoperate and provide user services in a consistent way.

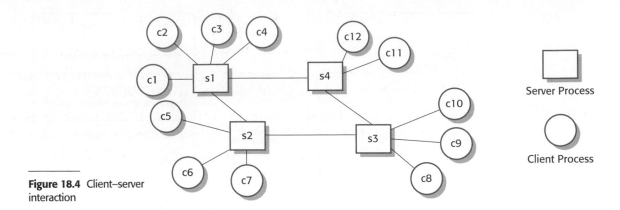

Figure 18.4 Client–server interaction

I have already given examples of the interaction support that middleware can provide in Section 18.1.1. You use middleware to support remote procedure and remote method calls, message exchange, etc.

Common services are those services that may be required by different components irrespective of the functionality of these components. As I discussed in Chapter 17, these may include security services (authentication and authorization), notification and naming services, and transaction management services, etc. You can think of these common services as being provided by a middleware container. You then deploy your component in that container and it can access and use these common services.

18.2 Client–server computing

Distributed systems that are accessed over the Internet are normally organized as client–server systems. In a client–server system, the user interacts with a program running on their local computer (e.g., a web browser or phone-based application). This interacts with another program running on a remote computer (e.g., a web server). The remote computer provides services, such as access to web pages, which are available to external clients. This client–server model, as I discussed in Chapter 6, is a very general architectural model of an application. It is not restricted to applications distributed across several machines. You can also use it as a logical interaction model where the client and the server run on the same computer.

In a client–server architecture, an application is modeled as a set of services that are provided by servers. Clients may access these services and present results to end users (Orfali and Harkey, 1998). Clients need to be aware of the servers that are available but do not know of the existence of other clients. Clients and servers are separate processes, as shown in Figure 18.4. This illustrates a situation in which there are four servers (s1–s4), that deliver different services. Each service has a set of associated clients that access these services.

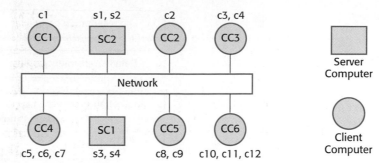

Figure 18.5 Mapping of clients and servers to networked computers

Figure 18.4 shows client and server processes rather than processors. It is normal for several client processes to run on a single processor. For example, on your PC, you may run a mail client that downloads mail from a remote mail server. You may also run a web browser that interacts with a remote web server and a print client that sends documents to a remote printer. Figure 18.5 illustrates the situation where the 12 logical clients shown in Figure 18.4 are running on six computers. The four server processes are mapped onto two physical server computers.

Several different server processes may run on the same processor but, often, servers are implemented as multiprocessor systems in which a separate instance of the server process runs on each machine. Load-balancing software distributes requests for service from clients to different servers so that each server does the same amount of work. This allows a higher volume of transactions with clients to be handled, without degrading the response to individual clients.

Client–server systems depend on there being a clear separation between the presentation of information and the computations that create and process that information. Consequently, you should design the architecture of distributed client–server systems so that they are structured into several logical layers, with clear interfaces between these layers. This allows each layer to be distributed to a different computer. Figure 18.6 illustrates this model, showing an application structured into four layers:

- A presentation layer that is concerned with presenting information to the user and managing all user interaction;

- A data management layer that manages the data that is passed to and from the client. This layer may implement checks on the data, generate web pages, etc.;

- An application processing layer that is concerned with implementing the logic of the application and so providing the required functionality to end users;

- A database layer that stores the data and provides transaction management services, etc.

The following section explains how different client–server architectures distribute these logical layers in different ways. The client–server model also underlies the notion of software as a service (SaaS), an increasingly important way of deploying software and accessing it over the Internet. I discuss this in Section 18.4.

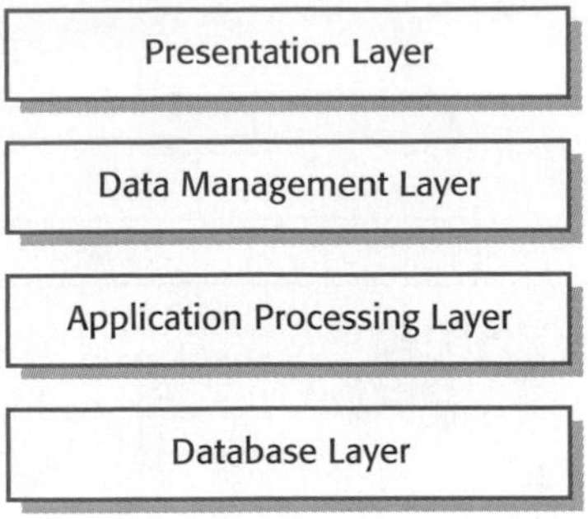

Figure 18.6 Layered architectural model for client–server application

18.3 Architectural patterns for distributed systems

As I explained in the introduction to this chapter, designers of distributed systems have to organize their system designs to find a balance between performance, dependability, security, and manageability of the system. There is no universal model of system organization that is appropriate for all circumstances so various distributed architectural styles have emerged. When designing a distributed application, you should choose an architectural style that supports the critical non-functional requirements of your system.

In this section, I discuss five architectural styles:

1. Master-slave architecture, which is used in real-time systems in which guaranteed interaction response times are required.

2. Two-tier client–server architecture, which is used for simple client–server systems, and in situations where it is important to centralize the system for security reasons. In such cases, communication between the client and server is normally encrypted.

3. Multitier client–server architecture, which is used when there is a high volume of transactions to be processed by the server.

4. Distributed component architecture, which is used when resources from different systems and databases need to be combined, or as an implementation model for multi-tier client–server systems.

5. Peer-to-peer architecture, which is used when clients exchange locally stored information and the role of the server is to introduce clients to each other. It may also be used when a large number of independent computations may have to be made.

18.3.1 Master-slave architectures

Master-slave architectures for distributed systems are commonly used in real-time systems where there may be separate processors associated with data acquisition from the system's environment, data processing, and computation and

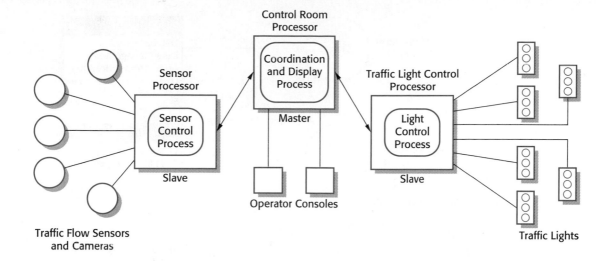

Figure 18.7 A traffic management system with a master-slave architecture

actuator management. Actuators, as I discuss in Chapter 20, are devices controlled by the software system that act to change the system's environment. For example, an actuator may control a valve and change its state from 'open' to 'closed'. The 'master' process is usually responsible for computation, coordination, and communications and it controls the 'slave' processes. 'Slave' processes are dedicated to specific actions, such as the acquisition of data from an array of sensors.

Figure 18.7 illustrates this architectural model. It is a model of a traffic control system in a city and has three logical processes that run on separate processors. The master process is the control room process, which communicates with separate slave processes that are responsible for collecting traffic data and managing the operation of traffic lights.

A set of distributed sensors collects information on the traffic flow. The sensor control process polls the sensors periodically to capture the traffic flow information and collates this information for further processing. The sensor processor is itself polled periodically for information by the master process that is concerned with displaying traffic status to operators, computing traffic light sequences and accepting operator commands to modify these sequences. The control room system sends commands to a traffic light control process that converts these into signals to control the traffic light hardware. The master control room system is itself organized as a client–server system, with the client processes running on the operator's consoles.

You use this master-slave model of a distributed system in situations where you can predict the distributed processing that is required, and where processing can be easily localized to slave processors. This situation is common in real-time systems, where it is important to meet processing deadlines. Slave processors can be used for computationally intensive operations, such as signal processing and the management of equipment controlled by the system.

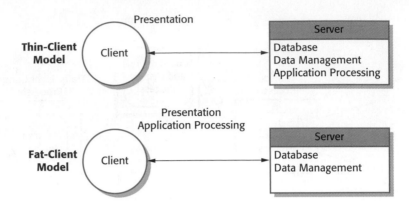

18.3.2 Two-tier client–server architectures

In Section 18.2, I discussed the general form of client–server systems in which part of the application system runs on the user's computer (the client), and part runs on a remote computer (the server). I also presented a layered application model (Figure 18.6) where the different layers in the system may execute on different computers.

A two-tier client–server architecture is the simplest form of client–server architecture. The system is implemented as a single logical server plus an indefinite number of clients that use that server. This is illustrated in Figure 18.8, which shows two forms of this architectural model:

1. A thin-client model, where the presentation layer is implemented on the client and all other layers (data management, application processing, and database) are implemented on a server. The client software may be a specially written program on the client to handle presentation. More often, however, a web browser on the client computer is used for presentation of the data.

2. A fat-client model, where some or all of the application processing is carried out on the client. Data management and database functions are implemented on the server.

The advantage of the thin-client model is that it is simple to manage the clients. This is a major issue if there are a large number of clients, as it may be difficult and expensive to install new software on all of them. If a web browser is used as the client, there is no need to install any software.

The disadvantage of the thin-client approach, however is that it may place a heavy processing load on both the server and the network. The server is responsible for all computation and this may lead to the generation of significant network traffic between the client and the server. Implementing a system using this model may therefore require additional investment in network and server capacity. However, browsers may carry out some local processing by executing scripts (e.g., Javascript) in the web page that is accessed by the browser.

The fat-client model makes use of available processing power on the computer running the client software, and distributes some or all of the application processing

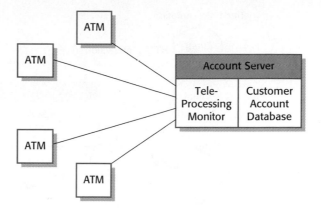

Figure 18.9 A fat-client architecture for an ATM system

and the presentation to the client. The server is essentially a transaction server that manages all database transactions. Data management is straightforward as there is no need to manage the interaction between the client and the application processing system. Of course, the problem with the fat-client model is that it requires additional system management to deploy and maintain the software on the client computer.

An example of a situation in which a fat-client architecture is used is in a bank ATM system, which delivers cash and other banking services to users. The ATM is the client computer and the server is, typically, a mainframe running the customer account database. A mainframe computer is a powerful machine that is designed for transaction processing. It can therefore handle the large volume of transactions generated by ATMs, other teller systems, and online banking. The software in the teller machine carries out a lot of the customer-related processing associated with a transaction.

Figure 18.9 shows a simplified version of the ATM system organization. Notice that the ATMs do not connect directly to the customer database, but rather to a teleprocessing monitor. A teleprocessing (TP) monitor is a middleware system that organizes communications with remote clients and serializes client transactions for processing by the database. This ensures that transactions are independent and do not interfere with one other. Using serial transactions means that the system can recover from faults without corrupting the system data.

Whereas a fat-client model distributes processing more effectively than a thin-client model, system management is more complex. Application functionality is spread across many computers. When the application software has to be changed, this involves reinstallation on every client computer. This can be a major cost if there are hundreds of clients in the system. The system may have to be designed to support remote software upgrades and it may be necessary to shut down all system services until the client software has been replaced.

18.3.3 Multi-tier client–server architectures

The fundamental problem with a two-tier client–server approach is that the logical layers in the system—presentation, application processing, data management, and database—must be mapped onto two computer systems: the client and the server.

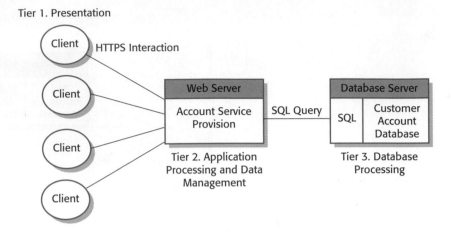

Tier 1. Presentation

Figure 18.10 Three-tier architecture for an Internet banking system

This may lead to problems with scalability and performance if the thin-client model is chosen, or problems of system management if the fat-client model is used. To avoid some of these problems, a 'multi-tier client–server' architecture can be used. In this architecture, the different layers of the system, namely presentation, data management, application processing, and database, are separate processes that may execute on different processors.

An Internet banking system (Figure 18.10) is an example of a multi-tier client–server architecture, where there are three tiers in the system. The bank's customer database (usually hosted on a mainframe computer as discussed above) provides database services. A web server provides data management services such as web page generation and some application services. Application services such as facilities to transfer cash, generate statements, pay bills, and so on are implemented in the web server and as scripts that are executed by the client. The user's own computer with an Internet browser is the client. This system is scalable because it is relatively easy to add servers (scale out) as the number of customers increase.

In this case, the use of a three-tier architecture allows the information transfer between the web server and the database server to be optimized. The communications between these systems can use fast, low-level data exchange protocols. Efficient middleware that supports database queries in SQL (Structured Query Language) is used to handle information retrieval from the database.

The three-tier client–server model can be extended to a multi-tier variant, where additional servers are added to the system. This may involve using a web server for data management and separate servers for application processing and database services. Multi-tier systems may also be used when applications need to access and use data from different databases. In this case, you may need to add an integration server to the system. The integration server collects the distributed data and presents it to the application server as if it were from a single database. As I discuss in the following section, distributed component architectures may be used to implement multi-tier client–server systems.

Multi-tier client–server systems that distribute the application processing across several servers are inherently more scalable than two-tier architectures. The

Architecture	Applications
Two-tier client–server architecture with thin clients	Legacy system applications that are used when separating application processing and data management is impractical. Clients may access these as services, as discussed in Section 18.4.
	Computationally intensive applications such as compilers with little or no data management.
	Data-intensive applications (browsing and querying) with non-intensive application processing. Browsing the Web is the most common example of a situation where this architecture is used.
Two-tier client-server architecture with fat clients	Applications where application processing is provided by off-the-shelf software (e.g., Microsoft Excel) on the client.
	Applications where computationally intensive processing of data (e.g., data visualization) is required.
	Mobile applications where internet connectivity cannot be guaranteed. Some local processing using cached information from the database is therefore possible.
Multi-tier client–server architecture	Large-scale applications with hundreds or thousands of clients.
	Applications where both the data and the application are volatile.
	Applications where data from multiple sources are integrated.

Figure 18.11 Use of client–server architectural patterns

application processing is often the most volatile part of the system and it can be easily updated because it is centrally located. Processing, in some cases, may be distributed between the application logic and the data management servers, thus leading to more rapid response to client requests.

Designers of client–server architectures must take a number of factors into account when choosing the most appropriate distribution architecture. Situations in which the client–server architectures discussed here are likely to be appropriate are described in Figure 18.11.

18.3.4 Distributed component architectures

By organizing processing into layers, as shown in Figure 18.6, each layer of a system can be implemented as a separate logical server. This model works well for many types of application. However, it limits the flexibility of system designers in that they have to decide what services should be included in each layer. In practice, however, it is not always clear whether a service is a data management service, an application service, or a database service. Designers must also plan for scalability and so provide some means for servers to be replicated as more clients are added to the system.

A more general approach to distributed system design is to design the system as a set of services, without attempting to allocate these services to layers in the system. Each service, or group of related services, is implemented using a separate component. In a distributed component architecture (Figure 18.12) the system is organized as a set of interacting components or objects. These components provide an interface

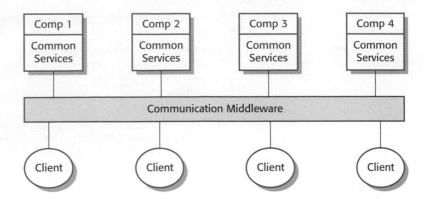

Figure 18.12
A distributed
component
architecture

to a set of services that they provide. Other components call on these services through middleware, using remote procedure or method calls.

Distributed component systems are reliant on middleware, which manages component interactions, reconciles differences between types of the parameters passed between components, and provides a set of common services that application components can use. CORBA (Orfali et al., 1997) was an early example of such middleware but is now not widely used. It has been largely supplanted by proprietary software such as Enterprise Java Beans (EJB) or .NET.

The benefits of using a distributed component model for implementing distributed systems are the following:

1. It allows the system designer to delay decisions on where and how services should be provided. Service-providing components may execute on any node of the network. There is no need to decide in advance whether a service is part of a data management layer, an application layer, etc.

2. It is a very open system architecture that allows new resources to be added as required. New system services can be added easily without major disruption to the existing system.

3. The system is flexible and scalable. New components or replicated components can be added as the load on the system increases, without disrupting other parts of the system.

4. It is possible to reconfigure the system dynamically with components migrating across the network as required. This may be important where there are fluctuating patterns of demand on services. A service-providing component can migrate to the same processor as service-requesting objects, thus improving the performance of the system.

A distributed component architecture can be used as a logical model that allows you to structure and organize the system. In this case, you think about how to provide application functionality solely in terms of services and combinations of services. You then work out how to provide these services using a set of distributed components. For

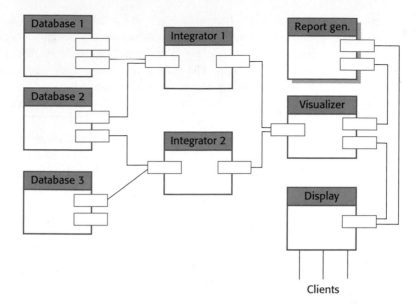

Figure 18.13
A distributed
component
architecture for
a data mining system

example, in a retail application there may be application components concerned with stock control, customer communications, goods ordering, and so on.

Data mining systems are a good example of a type of system in which a distributed component architecture is the best architectural pattern to use. A data mining system looks for relationships between the data that is stored in a number of databases (Figure 18.13). Data mining systems usually pull in information from several separate databases, carry out computationally intensive processing, and display their results graphically.

An example of such a data mining application might be a system for a retail business that sells food and books. The marketing department wants to find relationships between a customer's food and book purchases. For instance, a relatively high proportion of people who buy pizzas might also buy crime novels. With this knowledge, the business can specifically target customers who make specific food purchases with information about new novels when they are published.

In this example, each sales database can be encapsulated as a distributed component with an interface that provides read-only access to its data. Integrator components are each concerned with specific types of relationships, and they collect information from all of the databases to try to deduce the relationships. There might be an integrator component that is concerned with seasonal variations in goods sold, and another that is concerned with relationships between different types of goods.

Visualizer components interact with integrator components to produce a visualization or a report on the relationships that have been discovered. Because of the large volumes of data that are handled, visualizer components normally present their results graphically. Finally, a display component may be responsible for delivering the graphical models to clients for final presentation.

A distributed component architecture rather than a layered architecture is appropriate for this type of application because you can add new databases to the system without major disruption. Each new database is simply accessed by adding another distributed component. The database access components provide a simplified interface that controls access to the data. The databases that are accessed may reside on different machines. The architecture also makes it easy to mine new types of relationship by adding new integrator components.

Distributed component architectures suffer from two major disadvantages:

1. They are more complex to design than client–server systems. Multi-layer client–server systems appear to be a fairly intuitive way to think about systems. They reflect many human transactions where people request and receive services from other people who specialize in providing these services. By contrast, distributed component architectures are more difficult for people to visualize and understand.

2. Standardized middleware for distributed component systems has never been accepted by the community. Rather different vendors, such as Microsoft and Sun, have developed different, incompatible middleware. This middleware is complex and reliance on it increases the overall complexity of distributed component systems.

As a result of these problems, service-oriented architectures (discussed in Chapter 19) are replacing distributed component architectures in many situations. However, distributed component systems have performance benefits over service-oriented systems. RPC communications are usually faster than the message-based interaction used in service-oriented systems. Component-based architectures are therefore more appropriate for high-throughput systems in which large numbers of transactions have to be processed quickly.

18.3.5 Peer-to-peer architectures

The client–server model of computing that I have discussed in previous sections of the chapter makes a clear distinction between servers, which are providers of services and clients, which are receivers of services. This model usually leads to an uneven distribution of load on the system, where servers do more work than clients. This may lead to organizations spending a lot on server capacity while there is unused processing capacity on the hundreds or thousands of PCs that are used to access the system servers.

Peer-to-peer (p2p) systems are decentralized systems in which computations may be carried out by any node on the network. In principle at least, no distinctions are made between clients and servers. In peer-to-peer applications, the overall system is designed to take advantage of the computational power and storage available across a potentially huge network of computers. The standards and protocols that enable communications across the nodes are embedded in the application itself and each node must run a copy of that application.

Peer-to-peer technologies have mostly been used for personal rather than business systems (Oram, 2001). For example, file-sharing systems based on the Gnutella and BitTorrent protocols are used to exchange files on users' PCs. Instant messaging systems such as ICQ and Jabber provide direct communications between users without an intermediate server. SETI@home is a long-running project to process data from radio telescopes on home PCs to search for indications of extraterrestrial life. Freenet is a decentralized database that has been designed to make it easier to publish information anonymously, and to make it difficult for authorities to suppress this information. Voice over IP (VOIP) phone services, such as Skype, rely on peer-to-peer communication between the parties involved in the phone call or conference.

However, peer-to-peer systems are also being used by businesses to harness the power in their PC networks (McDougall, 2000). Intel and Boeing have both implemented p2p systems for computationally intensive applications. This takes advantage of unused processing capacity on local computers. Instead of buying expensive high-performance hardware, engineering computations can be run overnight when desktop computers are unused. Businesses also make extensive use of commercial p2p systems, such as messaging and VOIP systems.

It is appropriate to use a peer-to-peer architectural model for a system in two circumstances:

1. Where the system is computationally intensive and it is possible to separate the processing required into a large number of independent computations. For example, a peer-to-peer system that supports computational drug discovery distributes computations that look for potential cancer treatments by analyzing a huge number of molecules to see if they have the characteristics required to suppress the growth of cancers. Each molecule can be considered separately so there is no need for the peers in the system to communicate.

2. Where the system primarily involves the exchange of information between individual computers on a network and there is no need for this information to be centrally stored or managed. Examples of such applications include file-sharing systems that allow peers to exchange local files such as music and video files, and phone systems that support voice and video communications between computers.

In principle, every node in a p2p network could be aware of every other node. Nodes could connect to and exchange data directly with any other node in the network. In practice, of course, this is impossible, so nodes are organized into 'localities' with some nodes acting as bridges to other node localities. Figure 18.14 shows this decentralized p2p architecture.

In a decentralized architecture, the nodes in the network are not simply functional elements but are also communications switches that can route data and control signals from one node to another. For example, assume that Figure 18.14 represents a decentralized, document-management system. This system is used by a consortium of researchers to share documents, and each member of the consortium maintains his or her own document store. However, when a document is retrieved, the node retrieving that document also makes it available to other nodes.

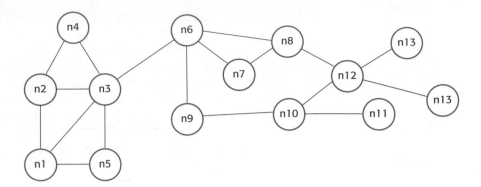

Figure 18.14
A decentralized
p2p architecture

If someone needs a document that is stored somewhere on the network, they issue a search command, which is sent to nodes in their 'locality'. These nodes check whether they have the document and, if so, return it to the requestor. If they do not have it, they route the search to other nodes. Therefore, if n1 issues a search for a document that is stored at n10, this search is routed through nodes n3, n6, and n9 to n10. When the document is finally discovered, the node holding the document then sends it to the requesting node directly by making a peer-to-peer connection.

This decentralized architecture has advantages in that it is highly redundant and hence both fault-tolerant and tolerant of nodes disconnecting from the network. However, the disadvantages here are that many different nodes may process the same search, and there is also significant overhead in replicated peer communications.

An alternative p2p architectural model, which departs from a pure p2p architecture, is a semicentralized architecture where, within the network, one or more nodes act as servers to facilitate node communications. This reduces the amount of traffic between nodes. Figure 18.15 illustrates this model.

In a semicentralized architecture, the role of the server (sometimes called a superpeer) is to help establish contact between peers in the network, or to coordinate the results of a computation. For example, if Figure 18.15 represents an instant messaging system, then network nodes communicate with the server (indicated by dashed lines) to find out what other nodes are available. Once these nodes are discovered, direct communications can be established and the connection to the server is unnecessary. Therefore nodes n2, n3, n5, and n6 are in direct communication.

In a computational p2p system, where a processor-intensive computation is distributed across a large number of nodes, it is normal for some nodes to be superpeers. Their role is to distribute work to other nodes and to collate and check the results of the computation.

Peer-to-peer architectures allow for the efficient use of capacity across a network. However, the major concerns that have inhibited their use are issues of security and trust. Peer-to-peer communications involve opening your computer to direct interactions with other peers and this means that these systems could, potentially, access any of your resources. To counter this, you need to organize your system so that these resources are protected. If this is done incorrectly, then your system may be insecure.

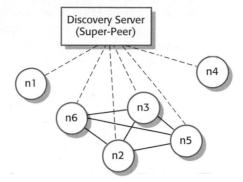

Figure 18.15
A semicentralized
p2p architecture

Problems may also occur when peers on a network deliberately behave in a malicious way. For example, there have been cases where music companies who believe that their copyright is being abused have deliberately made 'poisoned peers' available. When another peer downloads what they think is a piece of music, the actual file delivered is malware that may be a deliberately corrupted version of the music or a warning to the user of copyright infringement.

18.4 Software as a service

In the previous sections, I discussed client–server models and how functionality may be distributed between the client and the server. To implement a client–server system, you may have to install a program on the client computer, which communicates with the server, implements client-side functionality and manages the user interface. For example, a mail client, such as Outlook or Mac Mail, provides mail management features on your own computer. This avoids the problem of some thin-client systems where all of the processing is carried out at the server.

However, the problems of server overload can be significantly reduced by using a modern browser as the client software. Web technologies, such as AJAX (Holdener, 2008), support efficient management of web page presentation and local computation through scripts. This means that a browser can be configured and used as a client, with significant local processing. The application software can be thought of as a remote service, which can be accessed from any device that can run a standard browser. Well-known examples of this are web-based mail systems, such as Yahoo! and Gmail and office applications, such as Google docs.

This notion of SaaS involves hosting the software remotely and providing access to it over the Internet. The key elements of SaaS are the following:

1. Software is deployed on a server (or more commonly a number of servers) and is accessed through a web browser. It is not deployed on a local PC.

2. The software is owned and managed by a software provider, rather than the organizations using the software.

3. Users may pay for the software according to the amount of use they make of it or through an annual or monthly subscription. Sometimes, the software is free for anyone to use but users must then agree to accept advertisements, which fund the software service.

For software users, the benefit of SaaS is that the costs of management of software are transferred to the provider. The provider is responsible for fixing bugs and installing software upgrades, dealing with changes to the operating system platform, and ensuring that hardware capacity can meet demand. Software licence management costs are zero. If someone has several computers, there is no need to licence software for all of these. If a software application is only used occasionally, the pay-per-use model may be cheaper than buying an application. The software may be accessed from mobile devices, such as smart phones, from anywhere in the world.

Of course, this model of software provision has some disadvantages. The main problem, perhaps, is the costs of data transfer to the remote service. Data transfer takes place at network speeds and so transferring a large amount of data takes a lot of time. You may also have to pay the service provider according to the amount transferred. Other problems are lack of control over software evolution (the provider may change the software when they wish) and problems with laws and regulations. Many countries have laws governing the storage, management, preservation, and accessibility of data and moving data to a remote service may breach these laws.

The notion of SaaS and service-oriented architectures (SOAs), discussed in Chapter 19, are obviously related but they are not the same:

1. SaaS is a way of providing functionality on a remote server with client access through a web browser. The server maintains the user's data and state during an interaction session. Transactions are usually long transactions (e.g., editing a document).

2. SOA is an approach to structuring a software system as a set of separate, stateless services. These may be provided by multiple providers and may be distributed. Typically, transactions are short transactions where a service is called, does something, and then returns a result.

SaaS is a way of delivering application functionality to users, whereas SOA is an implementation technology for application systems. The functionality implemented using SOA need not appear to users as services. Similarly, user services do not have to be implemented using SOA. However, if SaaS is implemented using SOA, it becomes possible for applications to use service APIs to access the functionality of other applications. They can then be integrated into more complex systems. These are called mashups and represent another approach to software reuse and rapid software development.

From a software development perspective, the process of service development has much in common with other types of software development. However, service construction is not usually driven by user requirements, but by the service provider's assumptions about what users need. The software therefore needs to be able to

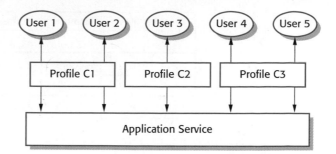

Figure 18.16
Configuration of a
software system
offered as a service

evolve quickly after the provider gets feedback from users on their requirements. Agile development with incremental delivery is therefore a commonly used approach for software that is to be deployed as a service.

When you are implementing SaaS you have to take into account that you may have users of the software from several different organizations. You have to take three factors into account:

1. *Configurability* How do you configure the software for the specific requirements of each organization?

2. *Multi-tenancy* How do you present each user of the software with the impression that they are working with their own copy of the system while, at the same time, making efficient use of system resources?

3. *Scalability* How do you design the system so that it can be scaled to accommodate an unpredictably large number of users?

The notion of product-line architectures, discussed in Chapter 16, is one way of configuring software for users who have overlapping but not identical requirements. You start with a generic system and adapt this according to the specific requirements of each user.

However, this does not work for SaaS as it would mean deploying a different copy of the service for each organization that uses the software. Rather, you need to design configurability into the system and provide a configuration interface that allows users to specify their preferences. You then use these to adjust the behavior of the software dynamically as it is used. Configuration facilities may allow for the following:

1. Branding, where users from each organization, are presented with an interface that reflects their own organization.

2. Business rules and workflows, where each organization defines its own rules that govern the use of the service and its data.

3. Database extensions, where each organization defines how the generic service data model is extended to meet its specific needs.

4. Access control, where service customers create individual accounts for their staff and define the resources and functions that are accessible to each of their users.

Tenant	Key	Name	Address
234	C100	XYZ Corp	43, Anystreet, Sometown
234	C110	BigCorp	2, Main St, Motown
435	X234	J. Bowie	56, Mill St, Starville
592	PP37	R. Burns	Alloway, Ayrshire

Figure 18.17
A multi-tenant database

Figure 18.16 illustrates this situation. This diagram shows five users of the application service, who work for three different customers of the service provider. Users interact with the service through a customer profile that defines the service configuration for their employer.

Multi-tenancy is a situation in which many different users access the same system and the system architecture is defined to allow the efficient sharing of system resources. However, it must appear to each user that they have the sole use of the system. Multi-tenancy involves designing the system so that there is an absolute separation between the system functionality and the system data. You should, therefore, design the system so that all operations are stateless. Data should either be provided by the client or should be available in a storage system or database that can be accessed from any system instance. Relational databases are not ideal for providing multi-tenancy and large service providers, such as Google, have implemented a simpler database for user data.

A particular problem in multi-tenant systems is data management. The simplest way to provide data management is for each customer to have their own database, which they may use and configure as they wish. However, this requires the service provider to maintain many different database instances (one per customer) and to make these available on demand. This is inefficient in terms of server capacity and increases the overall cost of the service.

As an alternative, the service provider can use a single database with different users being virtually isolated within that database. This is illustrated in Figure 18.17, where you can see that database entries also have a 'tenant identifier', which links these entries to specific users. By using database views, you can extract the entries for each service customer and so present users from that customer with a virtual, personal database. This can be extended to meet specific customer needs using the configuration features discussed above.

Scalability is the ability of the system to cope with increasing numbers of users without reducing the overall QoS that is delivered to any user. Generally, when considering scalability in the context of SaaS, you are considering 'scaling out', rather than 'scaling up'. Recall that 'scaling out' means adding additional servers and so also increasing the number of transactions that can be processed in parallel. Scalability is a complex topic that I cannot cover in detail here, but some general guidelines for implementing scalable software are:

1. Develop applications where each component is implemented as a simple stateless service that may be run on any server. In the course of a single transaction,

a user may therefore interact with instances of the same service that are running on several different servers.

2. Design the system using asynchronous interaction so that the application does not have to wait for the result of an interaction (such as a read request). This allows the application to carry on doing useful work while it is waiting for the interaction to finish.

3. Manage resources, such as network and database connections, as a pool so that no single server is likely to run out of resources.

4. Design your database to allow fine-grain locking. That is, do not lock out whole records in the database when only part of a record is in use.

The notion of SaaS is a major paradigm shift for distributed computing. Rather than an organization hosting multiple applications on their servers, SaaS allows these applications to be externally provided by different vendors. We are in the midst of a transition from one model to another and, in the future, this is likely to have a very significant effect on the engineering of enterprise software systems.

KEY POINTS

- The benefits of distributed systems are that they can be scaled to cope with increasing demand, can continue to provide user services (even if some parts of the system fail), and they enable resources to be shared.

- Issues to be considered in the design of distributed systems include transparency, openness, scalability, security, quality of service, and failure management.

- Client–server systems are distributed systems in which the system is structured into layers, with the presentation layer implemented on a client computer. Servers provide data management, application, and database services.

- Client–server systems may have several tiers, with different layers of the system distributed to different computers.

- Architectural patterns for distributed systems include master-slave architectures, two-tier and multi-tier client–server architectures, distributed component architectures, and peer-to-peer architectures.

- Distributed component systems require middleware to handle component communications and to allow components to be added to and removed from the system.

- Peer-to-peer architectures are decentralized architectures in which there are no distinguished clients and servers. Computations can be distributed over many systems in different organizations.

- Software as a service is a way of deploying applications as thin client–server systems, where the client is a web browser.

FURTHER READING

'Middleware: A model for distributed systems services '. Although a little dated in places, this is an excellent overview paper that summarizes the role of middleware in distributed systems and discusses the range of middleware services that may be provided. (P. A. Bernstein, *Comm. ACM*, **39** (2), February 1996.) http://dx.doi.org/10.1145/230798.230809.

Peer-to-Peer: Harnessing the Power of Disruptive Technologies. Although this book does not have a lot of information on p2p architectures, it is an excellent introduction to p2p computing and discusses the organization and approach used in a number of p2p systems. (A. Oram (ed.), O'Reilly and Associates Inc., 2001.)

'Turning software into a service '. A good overview paper that discusses the principles of service-oriented computing. Unlike many papers on this topic, it does not conceal these principles behind a discussion of the standards involved. (M. Turner, D. Budgen and P. Brereton, *IEEE Computer*, **36** (10), October 2003.) http://dx.doi.org/10.1109/MC.2003.1236470.

Distributed Systems: Principles and Paradigms, 2nd edition. A comprehensive textbook that discusses all aspects of distributed systems design and implementation. However, it does not include much discussion of the service-oriented paradigm. (A.S. Tanenbaum and M. Van Steen, Addison-Wesley, 2007.)

'Software as a Service; The Spark that will Change Software Engineering. ' A short paper that argues that the advent of SaaS will push all software development to an iterative model. (G. Goth, Distributed Systems Online, **9** (7), July 2008.) http://dx.doi.org/10.1109/MDSO.2008.21.

EXERCISES

18.1. What do you understand by 'scalability '? Discuss the differences between 'scaling up' and 'scaling out' and explain when these different approaches to scalability may be used.

18.2. Explain why distributed software systems are more complex than centralized software systems, where all of the system functionality is implemented on a single computer.

18.3. Using an example of a remote procedure call, explain how middleware coordinates the interaction of computers in a distributed system.

18.4. What is the fundamental difference between a fat-client and a thin-client approach to client–server systems architectures?

18.5. You have been asked to design a secure system that requires strong authentication and authorization. The system must be designed so that communications between parts of the system cannot be intercepted and read by an attacker. Suggest the most appropriate client–server architecture for this system and, giving reasons for your answer, propose how functionality should be distributed between the client and the server systems.

18.6. Your customer wants to develop a system for stock information where dealers can access information about companies and evaluate various investment scenarios using a simulation system. Each dealer uses this simulation in a different way, according to his or her experience and the type of stocks in question. Suggest a client–server architecture for this system that shows where functionality is located. Justify the client–server system model that you have chosen.

18.7. Using a distributed component approach, propose an architecture for a national theater booking system. Users can check seat availability and book seats at a group of theaters. The system should support ticket returns so that people may return their tickets for last-minute resale to other customers.

18.8. Give two advantages and two disadvantages of decentralized and semicentralized peer-to-peer architectures.

18.9. Explain why deploying software as a service can reduce the IT support costs for a company. What additional costs might arise if this deployment model is used?

18.10. Your company wishes to move from using desktop applications to accessing the same functionality remotely as services. Identify three risks that might arise and suggest how these risks may be reduced.

REFERENCES

Bernstein, P. A. (1996). 'Middleware: A Model for Distributed System Services'. *Comm. ACM*, **39** (2), 86–97.

Coulouris, G., Dollimore, J. and Kindberg, T. (2005). *Distributed Systems: Concepts and Design, 4th edition*. Harlow, UK.: Addison-Wesley.

Holdener, A. T. (2008). *Ajax: The Definitive Guide*. Sebastopol, Calif.: O'Reilly and Associates.

McDougall, P. (2000). 'The Power of Peer-To-Peer'. *Information Week* (August 28th, 2000).

Neuman, B. C. (1994). 'Scale in Distributed Systems'. In *Readings in Distributed Computing Systems*. Casavant, T. and Singal, M. (ed.). Los Alamitos, Calif.: IEEE Computer Society Press.

Oram, A. (2001). 'Peer-to-Peer: Harnessing the Benefits of a Disruptive Technology'.

Orfali, R. and Harkey, D. (1998). *Client/server Programming with Java and CORBA*. New York: John Wiley & Sons.

Orfali, R., Harkey, D. and Edwards, J. (1997). *Instant CORBA*. Chichester, UK: John Wiley & Sons.

Pope, A. (1997). *The CORBA Reference Guide: Understanding the Common Request Broker Architecture*. Boston: Addison-Wesley.

Tanenbaum, A. S. and Van Steen, M. (2007). *Distributed Systems: Principles and Paradigms, 2nd edition*. Upper Saddle River, NJ: Prentice Hall.

19

Service-oriented architecture

Objectives

The objective of this chapter is to introduce service-oriented software architecture as a way of building distributed applications using web services. When you have read this chapter, you will:

■ understand the basic notions of a web service, web service standards, and service-oriented architecture;

■ understand the service engineering process that is intended to produce reusable web services;

■ have been introduced to the notion of service composition as a means of service-oriented application development;

■ understand how business process models may be used as a basis for the design of service-oriented systems.

Contents

The development of the Web in the 1990s revolutionized organizational information exchange. Client computers could gain access to information on remote servers outside their own organizations. However, access was solely through a web browser and direct access to the information by other programs was not practical. This meant that opportunistic connections between servers where, for example, a program queried a number of catalogs from different suppliers, were not possible.

To get around this problem, the notion of a web service was proposed. Using a web service, organizations that wish to make their information accessible to other programs can do so by defining and publishing a web service interface. This interface defines the data available and how it can be accessed. More generally, a web service is a standard representation for some computational or information resource that can be used by other programs. These may be information resources, such as a parts catalog; computer resources, such as a specialized processor; or storage resources. For example, an archive service could be implemented that permanently and reliably stores organizational data that, by law, has to be maintained for many years.

A web service is an instance of a more general notion of a service, which is defined (Lovelock et al., 1996) as:

"an act or performance offered by one party to another. Although the process may be tied to a physical product, the performance is essentially intangible and does not normally result in ownership of any of the factors of production".

The essence of a service, therefore, is that the provision of the service is independent of the application using the service (Turner et al., 2003). Service providers can develop specialized services and offer these to a range of service users from different organizations.

Service-oriented architectures (SOAs) are a way of developing distributed systems where the system components are stand-alone services, executing on geographically distributed computers. Standard XML-based protocols, such as SOAP and WSDL, have been designed to support service communication and information exchange. Consequently, services are platform and implementation-language independent. Software systems can be constructed by composing local services and external services from different providers, with seamless interaction between the services in the system.

Figure 19.1 encapsulates the idea of a SOA. Service providers design and implement services and specify the interface to these services. They also publish information about these services in an accessible registry. Service requestors (sometimes called service clients) who wish to make use of a service discover the specification of that service and locate the service provider. They can then bind their application to that specific service and communicate with it, using standard service protocols.

From the outset, there has been an active standardization process for SOA, working alongside technical developments. All of the major hardware and software companies are committed to these standards. As a result, SOA have not

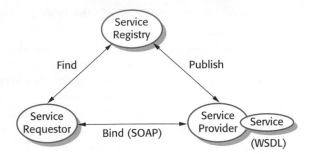

Figure 19.1 Service-oriented architecture

suffered from the incompatibilities that normally arise with technical innovations, where different suppliers maintain their proprietary version of the technology. Figure 19.2 shows the stack of key standards that have been established to support web services. Because of this early standardization, problems, such as the multiple incompatible component models in CBSE, discussed in Chapter 17, have not arisen in service-oriented system development.

Web service protocols cover all aspects of SOAs, from the basic mechanisms for service information exchange (SOAP) to programming language standards (WS-BPEL). These standards are all based on XML, a human and machine-readable notation that allows the definition of structured data where text is tagged with a meaningful identifier. XML has a range of supporting technologies, such as XSD for schema definition, which are used to extend and manipulate XML descriptions. Erl (2004) provides a good summary of XML technologies and their role in web services.

Briefly, the key standards for web SOAs are as follows:

1. *SOAP* This is a message interchange standard that supports the communication between services. It defines the essential and optional components of messages passed between services.

2. *WSDL* The Web Service Definition Language (WSDL) is a standard for service interface definition. It sets out how the service operations (operation names, parameters, and their types) and service bindings should be defined.

3. *WS-BPEL* This is a standard for a workflow language that is used to define process programs involving several different services. I discuss the notion of process programs in Section 19.3.

A service discovery standard, UDDI, was also proposed but this has not been widely adopted. The UDDI (Universal Description, Discovery and Integration) standard defines the components of a service specification, which may be used to discover the existence of a service. These include information about the service provider, the services provided, the location of the WSDL description of the service interface, and information about business relationships. The intention was that this standard would allow companies to set up registries with UDDI descriptions defining the services that they offered.

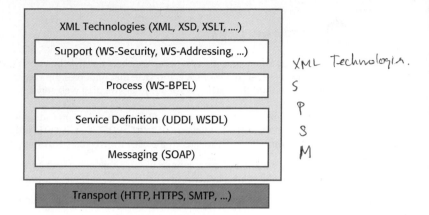

A number of companies, such as Microsoft, set up UDDI registries in the early years of the 21st century but these have now all closed. Improvements in search engine technology have made them redundant. Service discovery using a standard search engine to search for appropriately commented WSDL descriptions is now the preferred approach for discovering external services.

The principal SOA standards are supported by a range of supporting standards that focus on more specialized aspects of SOA. There are a very large number of supporting standards because they are intended to support SOA in different types of enterprise application. Some examples of these standards include the following:

1. WS-Reliable Messaging, a standard for message exchange that ensures messages will be delivered once and once only.

2. WS-Security, a set of standards supporting web service security including standards that specify the definition of security policies and standards that cover the use of digital signatures.

3. WS-Addressing, which defines how address information should be represented in a SOAP message.

4. WS-Transactions, which defines how transactions across distributed services should be coordinated.

Web service standards are a huge topic and I don't have space to discuss them in detail here. I recommend Erl's books (2004; 2005) for an overview of these standards. Their detailed descriptions are also available as public documents on the Web.

Current web services standards have been criticized as being 'heavyweight' standards that are over-general and inefficient. Implementing these standards requires a considerable amount of processing to create, transmit, and interpret the associated XML messages. For this reason, some organizations, such as Amazon, use a simpler, more efficient approach to service communication using so-called RESTful services (Richardson and Ruby, 2007). The RESTful approach supports efficient service

RESTful web services

REST (REpresentational State Transfer) is an architectural style based on transferring representations of resources from a server to a client. It is the style that underlies the web as a whole and has been used as a much simpler method than SOAP/WSDL for implementing web services.

A RESTful web service is identified by its URI (Universal Resource identifier) and communicates using the HTML protocol. It responds to HTML methods GET, PUT, POST, and DELETE and returns a resource representation to the client. Simplistically, POST means create, GET means read, PUT means update, and DELETE means delete.

RESTful services involve a lower overhead than so-called 'big web services' and are used by many organizations implementing service-based systems that do not rely on externally provided services.

http://www.SoftwareEngineering-9.com/Web/Services/REST/

interaction but it does not support enterprise-level features such as WS-Reliability and WS-Transactions. Pautasso et al. (2008) compare the RESTful approach with standardized web services.

Building applications based on services allows companies and other organizations to cooperate and make use of each other's business functions. Thus, systems that involve extensive information exchange across company boundaries, such as supply chain systems where one company orders goods from another, can easily be automated. Service-based applications may be constructed by linking services from various providers using either a standard programming language or a specialized workflow language, as discussed in Section 19.3.

SOAs are loosely coupled architectures where service bindings can change during execution. This means that a different, but equivalent version of the service may be executed at different times. Some systems will be solely built using web services and others will mix web services with locally developed components. To illustrate how applications that use a mixture of services and components may be organized, consider the following scenario:

An in-car information system provides drivers with information on weather, road traffic conditions, local information, and so forth. This is linked to the car radio so that information is delivered as a signal on a specific radio channel. The car is equipped with GPS receiver to discover its position and, based on that position, the system accesses a range of information services. Information may then be delivered in the driver's specified language.

Figure 19.3 illustrates a possible organization for such a system. The in-car software includes five modules. These handle communications with the driver, with a GPS receiver that reports the car's position and with the car radio. The Transmitter and Receiver modules handle all communications with external services.

The car communicates with an external mobile information service that aggregates information from a range of other services, providing information on weather,

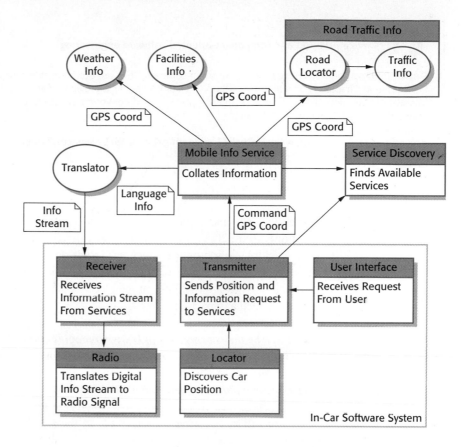

Figure 19.3 A service-based, in-car information system

traffic information, and local facilities. Different providers in different places offer these services, and the in-car system uses a discovery service to locate appropriate information services and bind to them. The discovery service is also used by the mobile information service to bind to the appropriate weather, traffic, and facilities services. Services exchange SOAP messages that include GPS position information used by the services to select the appropriate information. The aggregated information is then sent to the car through a service that translates that information into the driver's preferred language.

This example illustrates one of the key advantages of the service-oriented approach. It is not necessary to decide when the system is programmed or deployed what service provider should be used or what specific services should be accessed. As the car moves around, the in-car software uses the service discovery service to find the most appropriate information service and binds to that. Because of the use of a translation service, it can move across borders and therefore make local information available to people who don't speak the local language.

A service-oriented approach to software engineering is a new software engineering paradigm that is, in my view, as important a development as object-oriented software

Service-oriented and component-oriented software engineering

Services and components obviously have much in common. They are both reusable elements and, as I discussed in Chapter 17, it is possible to think of a component as a provider of services. However, there are important differences between services and components, and between a service-oriented and a component-oriented approach to software engineering.

http://www.SoftwareEngineering-9.com/Web/Services/Comps.html

engineering. This paradigm shift will be accelerated by the development of 'cloud computing' (Carr, 2009), where services are offered on a utility computing infrastructure hosted by major providers, such as Google and Amazon. This has had and will continue to have profound effects on systems products and business processes. Newcomer and Lomow (2005), in their book on SOA, summarize the potential of service-oriented approaches:

> *"Driven by the convergence of key technologies and the universal adoption of Web services, the service-oriented enterprise promises to significantly improve corporate agility, speed time-to-market for new products and services, reduce IT costs and improve operational efficiency."*

We are still at a relatively early stage in the development of service-oriented applications that are accessed over the Web. However, we are already seeing major changes in the ways that software is implemented and deployed, with the emergence of systems such as Google Apps and Salesforce.com. Service-oriented approaches at both the application and the implementation level means that the Web is evolving from an information store to a systems implementation platform.

19.1 Services as reusable components

In Chapter 17, I introduced component-based software engineering (CBSE), in which software systems are constructed by composing software components that are based on a standard component model. Services are a natural development of software components where the component model is, in essence, a set of standards associated with web services. A service can therefore be defined as the following:

> *A loosely-coupled, reusable software component that encapsulates discrete functionality, which may be distributed and programmatically accessed. A web service is a service that is accessed using standard Internet and XML-based protocols.*

A critical distinction between a service and a software component, as defined in CBSE, is that services should be independent and loosely coupled; that is, they should always operate in the same way, irrespective of their execution environment. Their interface is a 'provides' interface that allows access to the service functionality. Services are intended to be independent and usable in different contexts. Therefore, they do not have a 'requires' interface that, in CBSE, defines the other system components that must be present.

Services communicate by exchanging messages, expressed in XML, and these messages are distributed using standard Internet transport protocols such as HTTP and TCP/IP. I have discussed this message-based approach to component communication in Section 18.1.1. A service defines what it needs from another service by setting out its requirements in a message and sending it to that service. The receiving service parses the message, carries out the computation and, on completion, sends a reply, as a message, to the requesting service. This service then parses the reply to extract the required information. Unlike software components, services do not use remote procedure or method calls to access functionality associated with other services.

When you intend to use a web service, you need to know where the service is located (its URI) and the details of its interface. These are described in a service description expressed in an XML-based language called WSDL. The WSDL specification defines three things about a web service: what the service does, how it communicates, and where to find it:

1. The 'what' part of a WSDL document, called an interface, specifies what operations the service supports, and defines the format of the messages that are sent and received by the service.

2. The 'how' part of a WSDL document, called a binding, maps the abstract interface to a concrete set of protocols. The binding specifies the technical details of how to communicate with a web service.

3. The 'where' part of a WSDL document describes the location of a specific web service implementation (its endpoint).

The WSDL conceptual model (Figure 19.4) shows the elements of a service description. Each of these is expressed in XML and may be provided in separate files. These parts are:

1. An introductory part that usually defines the XML namespaces used and which may include a documentation section providing additional information about the service.

2. An optional description of the types used in the messages exchanged by the service.

3. A description of the service interface; that is, the operations that the service provides for other services or users.

4. A description of the input and output messages processed by the service.

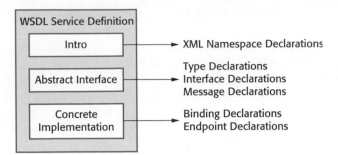

Figure 19.4 Organization of a WSDL specification

5.   A description of the binding used by the service (i.e., the messaging protocol that will be used to send and receive messages). The default is SOAP but other bindings may also be specified. The binding sets out how the input and output messages associated with the service should be packaged into a message, and specifies the communication protocols used. The binding may also specify how supporting information, such as security credentials or transaction identifiers, is included.

6.   An endpoint specification which is the physical location of the service, expressed as a Uniform Resource Identifier (URI)—the address of a resource that can be accessed over the Internet.

Complete service descriptions, written in XML, are long, detailed, and tedious to read. They usually include definitions of XML namespaces, which are qualifiers for names. A namespace identifier may precede any identifier used in the XML description, making it possible to distinguish between identifiers with the same name that have been defined in different parts of an XML description. You don't have to understand the details of namespaces to understand the examples here. You only need to know that names may be prefixed with a namespace identifier and that the namespace:name pair should be unique.

WSDL specifications are now rarely written by hand and most of the information in a specification can be automatically generated. You don't need to know the details of a specification to understand the principles of WSDL so I focus here on the description of the abstract interface. This is the part of a WSDL specification that equates to the 'provides' interface of a software component. Figure 19.5 shows part of the interface for a simple service that, given a date and a place, specified as a town within a country, returns the maximum and minimum temperature recorded in that place on that date. The input message also specifies whether these temperatures are to be returned in degrees Celsius or degrees Fahrenheit.

In Figure 19.5, the first part of the description shows part of the element and type definition that is used in the service specification. This defines the elements PlaceAndDate, MaxMinTemp, and InDataFault. I have only included the specification of PlaceAndDate, which you can think of as a record with three fields—town, country, and date. A similar approach would be used to define MaxMinTemp and InDataFault.

Define some of the types used. Assume that the namespace prefix 'ws' refers to the namespace URI for XML schemas and the namespace prefix associated with this definition is weathns.

```
<types>
    <xs: schema targetNameSpace = "http://.../weathns"
        xmlns: weathns = "http://.../weathns" >
    <xs:element name = "PlaceAndDate" type = "pdrec" />
    <xs:element name = "MaxMinTemp" type = "mmtrec" />
    <xs:element name = "InDataFault" type = "errmess" />

    <xs:complexType name = "pdrec"
    <xs:sequence>
        <xs:element name = "town" type = "xs:string"/>
        <xs:element name = "country" type = "xs:string"/>
        <xs:element name = "day" type = "xs:date" />
    </xs:complexType>
```
        Definitions of MaxMinType and InDataFault here
```
    </schema>

</types>
```
Now define the interface and its operations. In this case, there is only a single operation to return maximum and minimum temperatures.

```
<interface name = "weatherInfo" >
    <operation name = "getMaxMinTemps" pattern = "wsdlns: in-out">
    <input messageLabel = "In" element = "weathns: PlaceAndDate" />
    <output messageLabel = "Out" element = "weathns:MaxMinTemp" />
    <outfault messageLabel = "Out" element = "weathns:InDataFault" />
</operation>
</interface>
```

Figure 19.5 Part of a WSDL description for a web service

The second part of the description shows how the service interface is defined. In this example, the service weatherInfo has a single operation, although there are no restrictions on the number of operations that may be defined. The weatherInfo operation has an associated in-out pattern meaning that it takes one input message and generates one output message. The WSDL 2.0 specification allows for a number of different message exchange patterns such as in-only, in-out, out-only, in-optional-out, out-in, etc. The input and output messages, which refer to the definitions made earlier in the types section, are then defined.

The major problem with WSDL is that the definition of the service interface does not include any information about the semantics of the service or its non-functional characteristics, such as performance and dependability. It is simply a description of the service signature (i.e., the operations and their parameters). The programmer who plans to use the service has to work out what the service actually does and what the different fields in the input and output messages mean. The performance and dependability have to be discovered by experimenting with the service. Meaningful names and documentation help with understanding the functionality that is offered but it is still possible for readers to misunderstand the service.

19.2 Service engineering

Service engineering is the process of developing services for reuse in service-oriented applications. It has much in common with component engineering. Service engineers have to ensure that the service represents a reusable abstraction that could be useful in different systems. They must design and develop generally useful functionality associated with that abstraction and ensure that the service is robust and reliable. They have to document the service so that it can be discovered and understood by potential users.

There are three logical stages in the service engineering process, as shown in Figure 19.6. These are as follows:

1. Service candidate identification, where you identify possible services that might be implemented and define the service requirements.

2. Service design, where you design the logical and WSDL service interfaces.

3. Service implementation and deployment, where you implement and test the service and make it available for use.

As I discussed in Chapter 16, the development of a reusable component may start with an existing component that has already been implemented and used in an application. The same is true for services—the starting point for this process will often be an existing service or a component that is to be converted to a service. In this situation, the design process involves generalizing the existing component so that application-specific features are removed. Implementation means adapting the component by adding service interfaces and implementing the required generalizations.

19.2.1 Service candidate identification

The basic notion of service-oriented computing is that services should support business processes. As every organization has a wide range of processes, there are therefore many possible services that may be implemented. Service candidate identification therefore involves understanding and analyzing the organization's business processes to decide which reusable services could be implemented to support these processes.

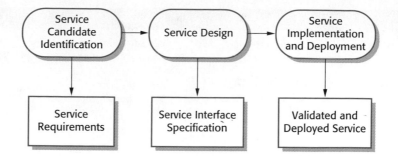

Figure 19.6 The service engineering process

Erl suggests that there are three fundamental types of service that may be identified:

1. *Utility services* These are services that implement some general functionality that may be used by different business processes. An example of a utility service is a currency conversion service that can be accessed to compute the conversion of one currency (e.g., dollars) to another (e.g., euros).

2. *Business services* These are services that are associated with a specific business function. An example of a business function in a university would be the registration of students for a course.

3. *Coordination or process services* These are services that support a more general business process which usually involves different actors and activities. An example of a coordination service in a company is an ordering service that allows orders to be placed with suppliers, goods accepted, and payments made.

Erl also suggests that services can be thought of as task-oriented or entity-oriented. Task-oriented services are those associated with some activity, whereas entity-oriented services are like objects. They are associated with a business entity such as, for example, a job application form. Figure 19.7 shows some examples of services that are task- or entity-oriented. Utility or business services may be entity- or task-oriented but coordination services are always task-oriented.

Your goal in service candidate identification should be to identify services that are logically coherent, independent, and reusable. Erl's classification is helpful in this respect as it suggests how to discover reusable services by looking at business entities and business activities. However, identifying service candidates is sometimes difficult because you have to envisage how the services will be used. You have to think of possible candidates then ask a series of questions about them to see if they are likely to be useful services. Possible questions that you might ask to identify potentially reusable services are:

1. For an entity-oriented service, is the service associated with a single logical entity that is used in different business processes? What operations are normally performed on that entity that must be supported?

	Utility	Business	Coordination
Task	Currency converter Employee locator	Validate claim form Check credit rating	Process expense claim Pay external supplier
Entity	Document style checker Web form to XML converter	Expenses form Student application form	

Figure 19.7 Service classification

2. For a task-oriented service, is the task one that is carried out by different people in the organization? Will they be willing to accept the inevitable standardization that occurs when a single support service is provided?

3. Is the service independent (i.e., to what extent does it rely on the availability of other services)?

4. For its operation, does the service have to maintain state? Services are stateless, which means that they do not maintain internal state. If state information is required, a database has to be used and this can limit service reusability. In general, services where the state is passed to the service are easier to reuse, as no database binding is required.

5. Could the service be used by clients outside of the organization? For example, an entity-oriented service associated with a catalog could be accessed by both internal and external users.

6. Are different users of the service likely to have different nonfunctional requirements? If they do, then this suggests that more than one version of a service should perhaps be implemented.

The answers to these questions help you select and refine abstractions that can be implemented as services. However, there is no formulaic way of deciding which are the best services and so service identification is a skill- and experience-based process.

The output of the service selection process is a set of identified services and associated requirements for these services. The functional service requirements should define what the service should do. The non-functional requirements should define the security, performance, and availability requirements of the service.

To help you understand the process of service candidate identification and implementation, consider the following example:

A large company, which sells computer equipment, has arranged special prices for approved configurations for some customers. To facilitate automated ordering, the company wishes to produce a catalog service that will allow customers to select the equipment that they need. Unlike a consumer catalog, orders are not placed directly through a catalog interface. Instead, goods are ordered through the web-based procurement system of each company that accesses the catalog as a web service. Most companies have their own budgeting and approval procedures for orders and their own ordering process must be followed when an order is placed.

The catalog service is an example of an entity-oriented service that supports business operations. The functional catalog service requirements are as follows:

1. A specific version of the catalog shall be provided for each user company. This shall include the configurations and equipment that may be ordered by employees of the customer company and the agreed prices for catalog items.

2. The catalog shall allow a customer employee to download a version of the catalog for offline browsing.

3. The catalog shall allow users to compare the specifications and prices of up to six catalog items.

4. The catalog shall provide browsing and search facilities for users.

5. Users of the catalog shall be able to discover the predicted delivery date for a given number of specific catalog items.

6. Users of the catalog shall be able to place 'virtual orders' where the items required will be reserved for them for 48 hours. Virtual orders must be confirmed by a real order placed by a procurement system. This must be received within 48 hours of the virtual order.

In addition to these functional requirements, the catalog has a number of non-functional requirements:

1. Access to the catalog service shall be restricted to employees of accredited organizations.

2. The prices and configurations offered to one customer shall be confidential and shall not be available to employees of any other customer.

3. The catalog shall be available without disruption of service from 0700 GMT to 1100 GMT.

4. The catalog service shall be able to process up to 10 requests per second peak load.

Notice that there is no non-functional requirement related to the response time of the catalog service. This depends on the size of the catalog and the expected number of simultaneous users. As this is not a time-critical service, there is no need to specify it at this stage.

19.2.2 Service interface design

Once you have selected candidate services, the next stage in the service engineering process is to design the service interfaces. This involves defining the operations associated with the service and their parameters. You also have to think carefully

Operation	Description
MakeCatalog	Creates a version of the catalog tailored for a specific customer. Includes an optional parameter to create a downloadable PDF version of the catalog.
Compare	Provides a comparison of up to six characteristics (e.g., price, dimensions, processor speed, etc.) of up to four catalog items.
Lookup	Displays all of the data associated with a specified catalog item.
Search	This operation takes a logical expression and searches the catalog according to that expression. It displays a list of all items that match the search expression.
CheckDelivery	Returns the predicted delivery date for an item if ordered that day.
MakeVirtualOrder	Reserves the number of items to be ordered by a customer and provides item information for the customer's own procurement system.

Figure 19.8 Functional descriptions of catalog service operations

about the design of the service operations and messages. Your aim should be to minimize the number of message exchanges that must take place to complete the service request. You have to ensure that as much information as possible is passed to the service in a message rather than using synchronous service interactions.

You should also remember that services are stateless and managing service-specific application state is the responsibility of the service user rather than the service itself. You may, therefore, have to pass this state information to and from services in input and output messages.

There are three stages to service interface design:

1. Logical interface design, where you identify the operations associated with the service, their inputs and outputs and the exceptions associated with these operations.

2. Message design, where you design the structure of the messages that are sent and received by the service.

3. WSDL development, where you translate your logical and message design to an abstract interface description written in WSDL.

The first stage, logical interface design, starts with the service requirements and defines the operation names and parameters. At this stage, you should also define the exceptions that may arise when a service operation is invoked. Figure 19.8 and Figure 19.9 show the operations that implement the requirements and the inputs, outputs, and exceptions for each of the catalog operations. At this stage, there is no need for these to be specified in detail—you add detail at the next stage of the design process.

Defining exceptions and how these can be communicated to service users is particularly important. Service engineers do not know how their services will be used.

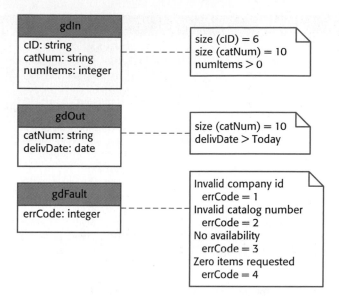

Figure 19.9 Catalog
interface design

It is usually unwise to make assumptions that service users will have completely understood the service specification. Input messages may be incorrect so you should define exceptions that report incorrect inputs to the service client. It is generally good practice in reusable component development to leave all exception handling to the user of the component. The service developer should not impose their views on how exceptions should be handled.

Once you have established an informal logical description of what the service should do, the next stage is to define the structure of the input and output messages and the types used in these messages. XML is an awkward notation to use at this stage. I think it is better to represent the messages as objects and either define them using the UML or in a programming language, such as Java. They can then be manually or automatically converted to XML. Figure 19.10 shows the structure of the input and output messages for the getDelivery operation in the catalog service.

Notice how I have added detail to the description by annotating the UML diagram with constraints. These define the length of the strings representing the company and the catalog item, and specify that the number of items must be greater than zero and that delivery must be after the current date. The annotations also show which error codes are associated with each possible fault.

The final stage of the service design process is to translate the service interface design into WSDL. As I discussed in the previous section, a WSDL representation is long and detailed and hence it is easy to make mistakes at this stage if you do this manually. However, most programming environments that support service-oriented development (e.g., the ECLIPSE environment) include tools that can translate a logical interface description into its corresponding WSDL representation.

Operation	Inputs	Outputs	Exceptions
MakeCatalog	*mcIn* Company id PDF-flag	*mcOut* URL of the catalog for that company	*mcFault* Invalid company id
Compare	*compIn* Company id Entry attribute (up to 6) Catalog number (up to 4)	*compOut* URL of page showing comparison table	*compFault* Invalid company id Invalid catalog number Unknown attribute
Lookup	*lookIn* Company id Catalog number	*lookOut* URL of page with the item information	*lookFault* Invalid company id Invalid catalog number
Search	*searchIn* Company id Search string	*searchOut* URL of web page with search results	*searchFault* Invalid company id Badly formed search string
CheckDelivery	*gdIn* Company id Catalog number Number of items required	*gdOut* Catalog number Expected delivery date	*gdFault* Invalid company id Invalid catalog number No availability Zero items requested
PlaceOrder	*poIn* Company id Number of items required Catalog number	*poOut* Catalog number Number of items required Predicted delivery date Unit price estimate Total price estimate	*poFault* Invalid company id Invalid catalog number Zero items requested

Figure 19.10 UML
definition of input and
output messages

19.2.3 Service implementation and deployment

Once you have identified candidate services and designed their interfaces, the final stage of the service engineering process is service implementation. This implementation may involve programming the service using a standard programming language such as Java or C#. Both of these languages include libraries with extensive support for service development.

Alternatively, services may be developed by implementing service interfaces to existing components or, as I discuss below, to legacy systems. This means that software assets that have already proved to be useful can be made more widely available. In the case of legacy systems, it may mean that the system functionality can be accessed by new applications. You can also develop new services by defining compositions of existing services. I cover this approach to service development in Section 19.3.

Once a service has been implemented, it then has to be tested before it is deployed. This involves examining and partitioning the service inputs (as explained in Chapter 8), creating input messages that reflect these input combinations, then checking that the outputs are expected. You should always try to generate exceptions during the test to check that the service can cope with invalid inputs. Testing tools are available that allow services to be examined and tested, and that generate tests from a WSDL specification. However, these can only test the conformity of the service interface to the WSDL. They cannot test that the service's functional behavior.

Service deployment, the final stage of the process, involves making the service available for use on a web server. Most server software makes this very simple. You only have to install the file containing the executable service in a specific directory. It then automatically becomes available for use. If the service is intended to be publicly available, you then have to provide information for external users of the service. This information helps potential external users to decide if the service is likely to meet their needs and if they can trust you, as a service provider, to deliver the service reliably and securely. Information that you may include in a service description might be the following:

1. Information about your business, contact details, etc. This is important for trust reasons. Users of a service have to be confident that it will not behave maliciously. Information about the service provider allows them to check their credentials with business information agencies.

2. An informal description of the functionality provided by the service. This helps potential users to decide if the service is what they want. However, the functional description is in natural language, so it is not an unambiguous semantic description of what the service does.

3. A detailed description of the interface types and semantics.

4. Subscription information that allows users to register for information about updates to the service.

As I have discussed, a general problem with service specifications is that the functional behavior of the service is usually specified informally, as a natural language description. Natural language descriptions are easy to read, but they are subject to misinterpretation. To address this problem, there is an active research community concerned with investigating how the semantics of services may be specified. The most promising approach to semantic specification is based on an ontology-based description, where the specific meaning of terms in a description is defined in an ontology. Ontologies are a way of standardizing the ways that terminology is used and they define the relationships between different terms. They are becoming increasingly used to help assign semantics to natural language descriptions. A language called OWL-S has been developed for describing web service ontologies (OWL_Services_Coalition, 2003).

19.2.4 Legacy system services

Legacy systems are old software systems that are used by an organization. Usually, they rely on obsolete technology but are still essential to the business. It may not be cost effective to rewrite or replace these systems and many organizations would like

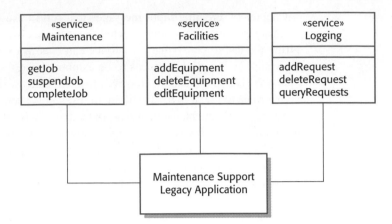

Figure 19.11 Services
providing access to a
legacy system

to use them in conjunction with more modern systems. One of the most important uses of services is to implement 'wrappers' for legacy systems that provide access to a system's functions and data. These systems can then be accessed over the Web and integrated with other applications.

To illustrate this, imagine that a large company maintains an inventory of its equipment and an associated database that keeps track of equipment maintenance and repairs. This keeps track of what maintenance requests have been made for different pieces of equipment, what regular maintenance is scheduled, when maintenance was carried out, how much time was spent on maintenance, etc. This legacy system was originally used to generate daily job lists for maintenance staff but, over time, new facilities have been added. These provide data about how much has been spent on maintenance for each piece of equipment and information to help to cost maintenance work to be carried out by external contractors. The system runs as a client–server system with special-purpose client software running on a PC.

The company now wishes to provide real-time access to this system from portable terminals used by maintenance staff. They will update the system directly with the time and resources spent on maintenance and will query the system to find their next maintenance job. In addition, call center staff require access to the system to log maintenance requests and to check their status.

It is practically impossible to enhance the system to support these requirements so the company decides to provide new applications for maintenance and call center staff. These applications rely on the legacy system, which is to be used as a basis for implementing a number of services. This is illustrated in Figure 19.11, where I have used a UML stereotype to indicate a service. New applications exchange messages with these services to access the legacy system functionality.

Some of the services provided are the following:

1. *A maintenance service* This includes operations to retrieve a maintenance job according to its job number, priority, and geographical location, and to upload details of maintenance that has been carried out to the maintenance database.

The service also provides operations that allow a maintenance job that has started but is incomplete to be suspended and restarted.

2. *A facilities service* This includes operations to add and delete new equipment and to modify the information associated with equipment in the database.

3. *A logging service* This includes operations to add a new request for service, delete maintenance requests, and query the status of outstanding requests.

Notice that the existing legacy system is not simply represented as a single service. Rather, the services that are developed to access the legacy system are coherent and support a single area of functionality. This reduces their complexity and makes them easier to understand and reuse in other applications.

19.3 Software development with services

The development of software using services is based around the idea that you compose and configure services to create new, composite services. These may be integrated with a user interface implemented in a browser to create a web application, or may be used as components in some other service composition. The services involved in the composition may be specially developed for the application, may be business services developed within a company, or may be services from an external provider.

Many companies are now converting their enterprise applications into service-oriented systems, where the basic application building block is a service rather than a component. This opens up the possibility of more widespread reuse within the company. The next stage will be the development of interorganizational applications between trusted suppliers, who will use each other's services. The final realization of the long-term vision of SOAs will rely on the development of a 'services market', where services are bought from external suppliers.

Service composition may be used to integrate separate business processes to provide an integrated process offering more extensive functionality. Say an airline wishes to provide a complete vacation package for travelers. As well as booking their flights, travelers can also book hotels in their preferred location, arrange car rentals or book a taxi from the airport, browse a travel guide, and make reservations to visit local attractions. To create this application, the airline composes its own booking service with services offered by a hotel booking agency, car rental and taxi companies, and reservation services offered by owners of local attractions. The end result is a single service that integrates the services from different providers.

You can think of this process as a sequence of separate steps as shown in Figure 19.12. Information is passed from one step to the next—for example, the car rental company is informed of the time that the flight is scheduled to arrive. The sequence of steps is called a workflow—a set of activities ordered in time, with each activity carrying out some part of the work. A workflow is a model of a business

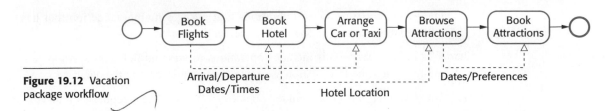

Figure 19.12 Vacation package workflow

process (i.e., sets out the steps involved in reaching a particular goal that is important for a business). In this case, the business process is the vacation booking service, offered by the airline.

Workflow is a simple idea and the above scenario of booking a vacation seems to be straightforward. In practice, service composition is much more complex than this simple model implies. For example, you have to consider the possibility of service failure and incorporate mechanisms to handle these failures. You also have to take into account exceptional demands made by users of the application. For example, say a traveler was disabled and required a wheelchair to be rented and delivered to the airport. This would require extra services to be implemented and composed, and additional steps to be added to the workflow.

You must be able to cope with situations where the workflow has to be changed because the normal execution of one of the services usually results in an incompatibility with some other service execution. For example, say a flight is booked to leave on June 1st and return on June 7th. The workflow then proceeds to the hotel booking stage. However, the resort is hosting a major convention until June 2nd, so no hotel rooms are available. The hotel booking service reports this lack of availability. This is not a failure; lack of availability is a common situation. You, therefore, then have to 'undo' the flight booking and pass the information about lack of availability back to the user. He or she then has to decide whether to change their dates or their resort. In workflow terminology, this is called a 'compensation action'. Compensation actions are used to undo actions that have already been completed but which must be changed as a result of later workflow activities.

The process of designing new services by reusing existing services is essentially a process of software design with reuse (Figure 19.13). Design with reuse inevitably involves requirements compromises. The 'ideal' requirements for the system have to be modified to reflect the services that are actually available, whose costs fall within budget and whose quality of service is acceptable.

In Figure 19.13, I have shown six key stages in the process of service construction by composition:

1. *Formulate outline workflow* In this initial stage of service design, you use the requirements for the composite service as a basis for creating an 'ideal' service design. You should create a fairly abstract design at this stage with the intention of adding details once you know more about available services.

2. *Discover services* During this stage of the process, you search service registries or catalogs to discover what services exist, who provides these services, and the details of the service provision.

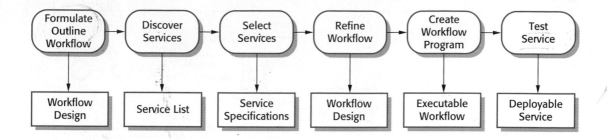

Figure 19.13 Service construction by composition

3. *Select possible services* From the set of possible service candidates that you have discovered, you then select possible services that can implement workflow activities. Your selection criteria will obviously include the functionality of the services offered. They may also include the cost of the services and the quality of service (responsiveness, availability, etc.) offered. You may decide to choose a number of functionally equivalent services, which could be bound to a workflow activity depending on details of cost and quality of service.

4. *Refine workflow* On the basis of information about the services that you have selected, you then refine the workflow. This involves adding detail to the abstract description and perhaps adding or removing workflow activities. You may then repeat the service discovery and selection stages. Once a stable set of services has been chosen and the final workflow design established, you move on to the next stage in the process.

5. *Create workflow program* During this stage, the abstract workflow design is transformed to an executable program and the service interface is defined. You can use a conventional programming language, such as Java or C#, for service implementation or a workflow language, such as WS-BPEL. As I discussed in the previous section, the service interface specification should be written in WSDL. This stage may also involve the creation of web-based user interfaces to allow the new service to be accessed from a web browser.

6. *Test completed service or application* The process of testing the completed, composite service is more complex than component testing in situations where external services are used. I discuss testing issues in Section 19.3.2.

In the remainder of this chapter, I focus on workflow design and testing. In practice, service discovery does not appear to be a major problem. It is still the case that most service reuse is within organizations, where services can be discovered using internal registries and informal communications between software engineers. Standard search engines may be used to discover publicly available services.

19.3.1 Workflow design and implementation

Workflow design involves analyzing existing or planned business processes to understand the different activities that go on and how these exchange information.

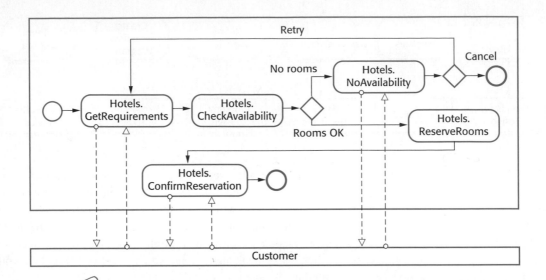

Figure 19.14 A
fragment of a hotel
booking workflow

You then define the new business process in a workflow design notation. This sets
out the stages involved in enacting the process and the information that is passed
between the different process stages. However, existing processes may be informal
and dependent on the skills and ability of the people involved—there may be no
'normal' way of working or process definition. In such cases, you have to use your
knowledge of the current process to design a workflow that achieves the same goals.

Workflows represent business process models and are usually represented using a
graphical notation such as UML activity diagrams or BPMN, the Business Process
Modeling Notation (White, 2004a; White and Miers, 2008). These offer similar features (White, 2004b). I think it is probable that BPMN and UML activity diagrams
will be integrated in the future and a standard for workflow modeling defined will be
based on this integrated language. I use BPMN for the examples in this chapter.

BPMN is a graphical language that is reasonably easy to understand. Mappings
have been defined to translate the language to lower-level, XML-based descriptions
in WS-BPEL. BPMN is therefore conformant with the stack of web service standards that I showed in Figure 19.2.

Figure 19.14 is an example of a simple BPMN model of part of the above vacation package scenario. The model shows a simplified workflow for hotel booking
and assumes the existence of a Hotels service with associated operations called
GetRequirements, CheckAvailability, ReserveRooms, NoAvailability, Confirm-
Reservation, and CancelReservation. The process involves getting requirements
from the customer, checking room availability, and then, if rooms are available, making a booking for the required dates.

This model introduces some of the core concepts of BPMN that are used to create
workflow models:

1. Activities are represented by a rectangle with rounded corners. An activity can
   be executed by a human or by an automated service.

2. Events are represented by circles. An event is something that happens during a business process. A simple circle is used to represent a starting event and a darker circle to represent an end event. A double circle (not shown) is used to represent an intermediate event. Events can be clock events, thus allowing workflows to be executed periodically or timed out.

3. A diamond is used to represent a gateway. A gateway is a stage in the process where some choice is made. For example, in Figure 19.14, there is a choice made on the basis of whether rooms are available or not.

4. A solid arrow is used to show the sequence of activities; a dashed arrow represents message flow between activities. In Figure 19.14, these messages are passed between the hotel booking service and the customer.

These key features are enough to describe the essence of most workflows. However, BPMN includes many additional features that I don't have space to describe here. These add information to a business process description that allows it to be automatically translated into an executable service. Therefore, web services, based on service compositions described in BPMN, can be generated directly from a business process model.

Figure 19.14 shows the process that is enacted in one organization, the company that provides a booking service. However, the key benefit of a service-oriented approach is that it supports interorganizational computing. This means that a computation involves services in different companies. This is represented in BPMN by developing separate workflows for each of the organizations involved with interactions between them.

To illustrate this, I use a different example, drawn from high-performance computing. A service-oriented approach has been proposed to allow resources such as high-performance computers to be shared. In this example, assume that a vector processing computer (a machine that can carry out parallel computations on arrays of values) is offered as a service (**VectorProcService**) by a research laboratory. This is accessed through another service called **SetupComputation.** These services and their interactions are shown in Figure 19.15.

In this example, the workflow for the SetupComputation service requests access to a vector processor and, if a processor is available, establishes the computation required and downloads data to the processing service. Once the computation is complete, the results are stored on the local computer. The workflow for **VectorProcService** checks if a processor is available, allocates resources for the computation, initializes the system, carries out the computation, and returns the results to the client service.

In BPMN terms, the workflow for each organization is represented in a separate pool. It is shown graphically by enclosing the workflow for each participant in the process in a rectangle, with the name written vertically on the left edge. The workflows defined in each pool are coordinated by exchanging messages; sequence flow between the activities in different pools is not allowed. In situations where different parts of an organization are involved in a workflow, this can be shown by

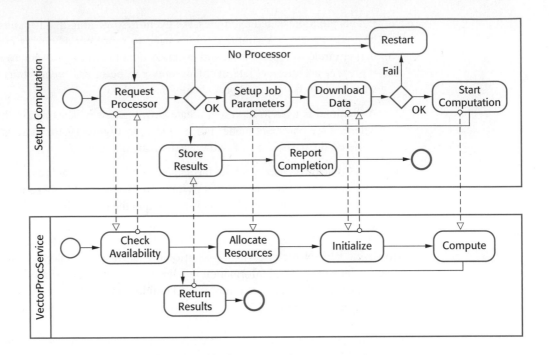

Figure 19.15
Interacting workflows

separating pools into named 'lanes'. Each lane shows the activities in that part of the organization.

Once a business process model has been designed, this has to be refined depending on the services that have been discovered. As I suggested in the discussion of Figure 19.13, the model may go through a number of iterations until a design that allows the maximum possible reuse of available services has been created.

Once the final design is available, it must then be converted to an executable program. This may involve two activities:

1. Implementing the services that are not available for reuse. As services are implementation-language independent, these services can be written in any language. Both Java and C# development environments provide support for web service composition.

2. Generating an executable version of the workflow model. This normally involves translating the model into WS-BPEL, either automatically or by hand. Although there are several tools available to automate the BPMN-WS-BPEL process, there are some circumstances where it is difficult to generate readable WS-BPEL code from a workflow model.

To provide direct support for the implementation of web service compositions, several web service standards have been developed. As I explained in the chapter introduction, the standard XML-based language is WS-BPEL (Business Process Execution Language) which is a 'programming language' to control interactions between services. This is supported by additional standards such as WS-Coordination (Cabrera et al., 2005), which is used to specify how services are coordinated, and WS-CDL (Choreography Description Language) (Kavantzas et al., 2004), which is a means of defining the message exchanges between participants (Andrews et al., 2003).

19.3.2 Service testing

Testing is important in all system development processes as it demonstrates that a system meets its functional and non-functional requirements and to detect defects that have been introduced during the development process. Many testing techniques, such as program inspections and coverage testing, rely on analysis of the software source code. However, when services are offered by an external provider, source code of the service implementation is not available. Service-based system testing cannot therefore use proven source code–based techniques.

As well as problems of understanding the implementation of the service, testers may also face further difficulties when testing services and service compositions:

1. External services are under the control of the service provider rather than the user of the service. The service provider may withdraw these services at any time or may make changes to them, which invalidates any previous application testing. These problems are handled in software components by maintaining different versions of the component. Currently, however, there are no standards proposed to deal with service versions.

2. The long-term vision of SOAs is for services to be bound dynamically to service-oriented applications. This means that an application may not always use the same service each time that it is executed. Therefore, tests may be successful when an application is bound to a particular service, but it cannot be guaranteed that that service will be used during an actual execution of the system.

3. The non-functional behavior of a service is not simply dependent on how it is used by the application that is being tested. A service may perform well during testing because it is not operating under a heavy load. In practice, the observed service behavior may be different because of the demands made by other service users.

4. The payment model for services could make service testing very expensive. There are different possible payment models—some services may be freely available, some paid for by subscription, and others paid for on a per-use basis. If services are free, then the service provider will not wish them to be loaded by applications being tested; if a subscription is required, then a service user may be reluctant to enter into a subscription agreement before testing the service. Similarly, if the usage is based on payment for each use, service users may find the cost of testing to be prohibitive.

5. I have discussed the notion of compensation actions that are invoked when an exception occurs and previous commitments that have been made (such as a flight reservation) have to be revoked. There is a problem in testing such actions as they may depend on the failure of other services. Ensuring that these services actually fail during the testing process may be very difficult.

These problems are particularly acute when external services are used. They are less serious when services are used within the same company or where cooperating companies trust services offered by their partners. In such cases, source code may be available to guide the testing process and payment for services is unlikely to be a problem. Resolving these testing problems and producing guidelines, tools, and techniques for testing service-oriented applications remains an important research issue.

KEY POINTS

- Service-oriented architecture is an approach to software engineering where reusable, standardized services are the basic building blocks for application systems.

- Service interfaces may be defined in an XML-based language called WSDL. A WSDL specification includes a definition of the interface types and operations, the binding protocol used by the service and the service location.

- Services may be classified as utility services that provide a general-purpose functionality, business services that implement part of a business process, or coordination services that coordinate the execution of other services.

- The service engineering process involves identifying candidate services for implementation, defining the service interface and implementing, and testing and deploying the service.

- Service interfaces may be defined for legacy software systems that continue to be useful for an organization. The functionality of the legacy system may then be reused in other applications.

- The development of software using services is based around the idea that programs are created by composing and configuring services to create new composite services.

- Business process models define the activities and information exchange that takes place in a business process. Activities in the business process may be implemented by services so that the business process model represents a service composition.

FURTHER READING

There is an immense amount of tutorial material on the Web covering all aspects of web services. However, I found the following two books by Thomas Erl to be the best overview and description of services and service standards. Unlike most books, Erl includes some discussion of software engineering issues in service-oriented computing. He has also written more specialized books on the design of services and SOA design patterns, although these are generally aimed at readers with experience of implementing SOA.

Service-Oriented Architecture: A Field Guide to Integrating XML and Web Services. The primary focus of this book is the underlying XML-based technologies (SOAP, WSDL, BPEL, etc.) that are a framework for SOA. (T. Erl, Prentice Hall, 2004.)

Service-Oriented Architecture: Concepts, Technology and Design. This is a more general book on the engineering of service-oriented systems. There is a little bit of overlap with the text above but Erl mostly concentrates on discussing how a service-oriented approach may be used at all stages of the software process. (T. Erl, Prentice Hall, 2005.)

'SOA realization: Service design principles'. This short web article is an excellent overview of the issues to be considered in designing services. (D. J. N. Artus, IBM, 2006.)
http://www.ibm.com/developerworks/webservices/library/ws-soa-design/.

EXERCISES

19.1. What are the most important distinctions between services and software components?

19.2. Explain why SOAs should be based on standards.

19.3. Using the same notation, extend Figure 19.5 to include definitions for MaxMinType and InDataFault. The temperatures should be represented as integers with an additional field indicating whether the temperature is in degrees Fahrenheit or degrees Celsius. InDataFault should be a simple type consisting of an error code.

19.4. Define an interface specification for the Currency Converter and Check credit rating services shown in Figure 19.7.

19.5. Design possible input and output messages for the services shown in Figure 19.11. You may specify these in the UML or in XML.

19.6. Giving reasons for your answer, suggest two important types of applications where you would *not* recommend the use of service-oriented architecture.

19.7. In Section 19.2.1, I introduced an example of a company that has developed a catalog service that is used by customers' web-based procurement systems. Using BPMN, design a workflow that uses this catalog service to look up and place orders for computer equipment.

19.8. Explain what is meant by a 'compensation action' and, using an example, show why these actions may have to be included in workflows.

19.9. For the example of the vacation package reservation service, design a workflow that will book ground transportation for a group of passengers arriving at an airport. They should be given the option of booking either a taxi or renting a car. You may assume that the taxi and car rental companies offer web services to make a reservation.

19.10. Using an example, explain in detail why the thorough testing of services that include compensation actions is difficult.

REFERENCES

Andrews, T., Curbera, F., Goland, Y., Klein, J. and Al., E. (2003). 'Business Process Execution Language for Web Services'. http://www-128.ibm.com/developerworks/library/ws-bpel/.

Cabrera, L. F., Copeland, G. and Al., E. 2005. 'Web Services Coordination (WS-Coordination)'. ftp://www6.software.ibm.com/software/developer/library/WS-Coordination.pdf.

Carr, N. (2009). *The Big Switch: Rewiring the World from Edison to Google, Reprint edition*. New York: W.W. Norton & Co.

Erl, T. (2004). *Service-Oriented Architecture: A Field Guide to Integrating XML and Web Services*. Upper Saddle River, NJ: Prentice Hall.

Erl, T. (2005). *Service-Oriented Architecture: Concepts, Technology and Design*. Upper Saddle River, NJ: Prentice Hall.

Kavantzas, N., Burdett, D. and Ritzinger, G. 2004. 'Web Services Choreography Description Language Version 1.0'. http://www.w3.org/TR/2004/WD-ws-cdl-10-20040427/.

Lovelock, C., Vandermerwe, S. and Lewis, B. (1996). *Services Marketing*. Englewood Cliffs, NJ: Prentice Hall.

Newcomer, E. and Lomow, G. (2005). *Understanding SOA with Web Services*. Boston: Addison-Wesley.

Owl_Services_Coalition. 2003. 'OWL-S: Semantic Markup for Web Services'. http://www.daml.org/services/owl-s/1.0/owl-s.pdf.

Pautasso, C., Zimmermann, O. and Leymann, F. (2008). 'RESTful Web Services vs "Big" Web Services: Making the Right Architectural Decision'. Proc. *WWW 2008*, Beijing, China: 805–14.

Richardson, L. and Ruby, S. (2007). *RESTful Web Services*. Sebastopol, Calif.: O'Reilly Media Inc.

Turner, M., Budgen, D. and Brereton, P. (2003). 'Turning Software into a Service'. *IEEE Computer*, **36** (10), 38–45.

White, S. A. (2004a). 'An Introduction to BPMN'. http://www.bpmn.org/Documents/Introduction%20to%20BPMN.

White, S. A. (2004b). 'Process Modelling Notations and Workflow Patterns'. In *Workflow Handbook 2004*. Fischer, L. (ed.). Lighthouse Point, Fla.: Future Strategies Inc. 265–294.

White, S. A. and Miers, D. (2008). *BPMN Modeling and Reference Guide: Understanding and Using BPMN*. Lighthouse Point, Fla.: Future Strategies Inc.

20

Embedded software

Objectives

The objective of this chapter is to introduce some of the characteristic features of embedded real-time systems and real-time software engineering. When you have read this chapter, you will:

■ understand the concept of embedded software, which is used to control systems that must react to external events in their environment;

■ have been introduced to a design process for real-time systems, where the software systems are organized as a set of cooperating processes;

■ understand three architectural patterns that are commonly used in embedded real-time systems design;

■ understand the organization of real-time operating systems and the role that they play in an embedded, real-time system.

Contents

Computers are used to control a wide range of systems from simple domestic machines, through games controllers, to entire manufacturing plants. These computers interact directly with hardware devices. Their software must react to events generated by the hardware and, often, issue control signals in response to these events. These signals result in an action, such as the initiation of a phone call, the movement of a character on the screen, the opening of a valve, or the display of the system status. The software in these systems is embedded in system hardware, often in read-only memory, and usually responds, in real time, to events from the system's environment. By real time, I mean that the software system has a deadline for responding to external events. If this deadline is missed, then the overall hardware–software system will not operate correctly.

Embedded software is very important economically because almost every electrical device now includes software. There are therefore many more embedded software systems than other types of software system. If you look around your house you may have three or four personal computers. But you probably have 20 or 30 embedded systems, such as systems in phones, cookers, microwaves, etc.

Responsiveness in real time is the critical difference between embedded systems and other software systems, such as information systems, web-based systems, or personal software systems, whose main purpose is data processing. For non-real-time systems, the correctness of a system can be defined by specifying how system inputs map to corresponding outputs that should be produced by the system. In response to an input, a corresponding output should be generated by the system and, often, some data should be stored. For example, if you choose a create command in a patient information system, then the correct system response is to create a new patient record in a database, and to confirm that this has been done. Within reasonable limits, it does not matter how long this takes.

However, in a real-time system, the correctness depends both on the response to an input and the time taken to generate that response. If the system takes too long to respond, then the required response may be ineffective. For example, if embedded software controlling a car braking system is too slow, then an accident may occur because it is impossible to stop the car in time.

Therefore, time is inherent in the definition of a real-time software system:

A real-time software system is a system whose correct operation depends on both the results produced by the system and the time at which these results are produced. A 'soft real-time system' is a system whose operation is degraded if results are not produced according to the specified timing requirements. If results are not produced according to the timing specification in a 'hard real-time system', this is considered to be a system failure.

Timely response is an important factor in all embedded systems but not all embedded systems require a very fast response. For example, the insulin pump software that I have used as an example in several chapters of this book is an embedded system. However, although it needs to check the glucose level at periodic intervals, it does not need to respond very quickly to external events. The wilderness weather station software is also an embedded system but, again, it does not require a fast response to external events.

As well as the need for real-time response, there are other important differences between embedded systems and other types of software system:

1. Embedded systems generally run continuously and do not terminate. They start when the hardware is switched on and must execute until the hardware is switched off. This means that techniques for reliable software engineering, as discussed in Chapter 13, may have to be used to ensure continuous operation. The real-time system may include update mechanisms that support dynamic reconfiguration so that the system can be updated while it is in service.

2. Interactions with the system's environment are uncontrollable and unpredictable. In interactive systems, the pace of the interaction is controlled by the system and, by limiting user options, the events to be processed are known in advance. By contrast, real-time embedded systems must be able to respond to unexpected events at any time. This leads to a design for real-time systems based on concurrency, with several processes executing in parallel.

3. There may be physical limitations that affect the design of a system. Examples of these include limitations on the power available to the system and on the physical space taken up by the hardware. These limitations may generate requirements for the embedded software, such as the need to conserve power and so prolong battery life. Size and weight limitations may mean that the software has to take over some hardware functions because of the need to limit the number of chips used in the system.

4. Direct hardware interaction may be necessary. In interactive systems and information systems, there is a layer of software (the device drivers) that hides the hardware from the operating system. This is possible because you can only connect a few types of device to these systems, such as keyboards, mice, displays, etc. By contrast, embedded systems may have to interact with a wide range of hardware devices that do not have separate device drivers.

5. Issues of safety and reliability may dominate the system design. Many embedded systems control devices whose failure may have high human or economic costs. Therefore, dependability is critical and the system design has to ensure safety-critical behavior at all times. This often leads to a conservative approach to design where tried and tested techniques are used instead of newer techniques that may introduce new failure modes.

Embedded systems can be thought of as reactive systems; that is, they must react to events in their environment at the speed of that environment (Berry, 1989; Lee, 2002). Response times are often governed by the laws of physics rather than chosen for human convenience. This is in contrast to other types of software where the system controls the speed of the interaction. For example, the word processor that I am using to write this book can check spelling and grammar and there are no practical limits on the time taken to do this.

20.1 Embedded systems design

The design process for embedded systems is a systems engineering process in which the software designers have to consider in detail the design and performance of the system hardware. Part of the system design process may involve deciding which system capabilities are to be implemented in software and which in hardware. For many real-time systems embedded in consumer products, such as the systems in cell phones, the costs, and power consumption of the hardware are critical. Specific processors designed to support embedded systems may be used and, for some systems, special-purpose hardware may have to be designed and built.

This means that a top-down software design process, in which the design starts with an abstract model that is decomposed and developed in a series of stages, is impractical for most real-time systems. Low-level decisions on hardware, support software, and system timing must be considered early in the process. These limit the flexibility of system designers and may mean that additional software functionality, such as battery and power management, has to be included in the system.

Given that embedded systems are reactive systems that react to events in their environment, the most general approach to embedded, real-time software design is based on a stimulus-response model. A stimulus is an event occurring in the software system's environment that causes the system to react in some way; a response is a signal or message that is sent by the software to its environment.

You can define the behavior of a real-time system by listing the stimuli received by the system, the associated responses, and the time at which the response must be produced. For example, Figure 20.1 shows possible stimuli and system responses for a burglar alarm system. I give more information about this system in Section 20.2.1.

Stimuli fall into two classes:

1. *Periodic stimuli* These occur at predictable time intervals. For example, the system may examine a sensor every 50 milliseconds and take action (respond) depending on that sensor value (the stimulus).

2. *Aperiodic stimuli* These occur irregularly and unpredictably and are usually signaled using the computer's interrupt mechanism. An example of such a stimulus would be an interrupt indicating that an I/O transfer was complete and that data was available in a buffer.

Stimuli come from sensors in the system's environment and responses are sent to actuators, as shown in Figure 20.2. A general design guideline for real-time systems

Stimulus	Response
Single sensor positive	Initiate alarm; turn on lights around site of positive sensor.
Two or more sensors positive	Initiate alarm; turn on lights around sites of positive sensors; call police with location of suspected break-in.
Voltage drop of between 10% and 20%	Switch to battery backup; run power supply test.
Voltage drop of more than 20%	Switch to battery backup; initiate alarm; call police; run power supply test.
Power supply failure	Call service technician.
Sensor failure	Call service technician.
Console panic button positive	Initiate alarm; turn on lights around console; call police.
Clear alarms	Switch off all active alarms; switch off all lights that have been switched on.

Figure 20.1 Stimuli and responses for a burglar alarm system

is to have separate processes for each type of sensor and actuator (Figure 20.3). These actuators control equipment, such as a pump, which then makes changes to the system's environment. The actuators themselves may also generate stimuli. The stimuli from actuators often indicate that some problem has occurred, which must be handled by the system.

For each type of sensor, there may be a sensor management process that handles data collection from the sensors. Data processing processes compute the required responses for the stimuli received by the system. Actuator control processes are associated with

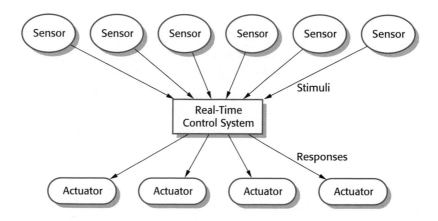

Figure 20.2 A general model of an embedded real-time system

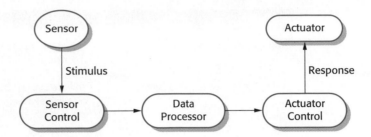

Figure 20.3 Sensor and actuator processes

each actuator and manage the operation of that actuator. This model allows data to be collected quickly from the sensor (before it is overwritten by the next input) and allows processing and the associated actuator response to be carried out later.

A real-time system has to respond to stimuli that occur at different times. You therefore have to organize the system architecture so that, as soon as a stimulus is received, control is transferred to the correct handler. This is impractical in sequential programs. Consequently, real-time software systems are normally designed as a set of concurrent, cooperating processes. To support the management of these processes, the execution platform on which the real-time system executes may include a real-time operating system (discussed in Section 20.4). The functions provided by this operating system are accessed through the run-time support system for the real-time programming language that is used.

There is no standard embedded system design process. Rather, different processes are used that depend on the type of system, available hardware, and the organization that is developing the system. The following activities may be included in a real-time software design process:

1. *Platform selection* In this activity, you choose an execution platform for the system (i.e., the hardware and the real-time operating system to be used). Factors that influence these choices include the timing constraints on the system, limitations on power available, the experience of the development team, and the price target for the delivered system.

2. *Stimuli/response identification* This involves identifying the stimuli that the system must process and the associated response or responses for each stimulus.

3. *Timing analysis* For each stimulus and associated response, you identify the timing constraints that apply to both stimulus and response processing. These are used to establish the deadlines for the processes in the system.

4. *Process design* At this stage, you aggregate the stimulus and response processing into a number of concurrent processes. A good starting point for designing the process architecture is the architectural patterns that I describe in Section 20.2. You then optimize the process architecture to reflect the specific requirements that you have to implement.

5. *Algorithm design* For each stimulus and response, you design algorithms to carry out the required computations. Algorithm designs may have to be

developed relatively early in the design process to give an indication of the amount of processing required and the time needed to complete that processing. This is especially important for computationally intensive tasks, such as signal processing.

6. *Data design* You specify the information that is exchanged by processes and the events that coordinate information exchange, and design data structures to manage this information exchange. Several concurrent processes may share these data structures.

7. *Process scheduling* You design a scheduling system that will ensure that processes are started in time to meet their deadlines.

The order of these activities in the real-time software design process depends on the type of system being developed, as well as its process and platform requirements. In some cases, you may be able to follow a fairly abstract approach where you start with the stimuli and associated processing, and decide on the hardware and execution platforms late in the process. In other cases, the choice of hardware and operating system is made before the software design starts. In such a situation, you have to design the software to take account of the constraints imposed by the hardware capabilities.

Processes in a real-time system have to be coordinated and share information. Process coordination mechanisms ensure mutual exclusion to shared resources. When one process is modifying a shared resource, other processes should not be able to change that resource. Mechanisms for ensuring mutual exclusion include semaphores (Dijkstra, 1968), monitors (Hoare, 1974), and critical regions (Brinch-Hansen, 1973). These process synchronization mechanisms are described in most operating system texts (Silberschatz et al., 2008; Tanenbaum, 2007).

When designing the information exchange between processes, you have to take into account the fact that these processes may be running at different speeds. One process is producing information; the other process is consuming that information. If the producer is running faster than the consumer, new information could overwrite a previously read information item before the consumer process has read the original information. If the consumer process is running faster than the producer process, the same item could be read twice.

To get around this problem, you should implement information exchange using a shared buffer and use mutual exclusion mechanisms to control access to that buffer. This means that information can't be overwritten before it has been read and that information cannot be read twice. Figure 20.4 illustrates the notion of a shared buffer. This is usually implemented as a circular queue, so that mismatches in speed between the producer and consumer processes can be accommodated without having to delay process execution.

The producer process always enters data in the buffer location at the tail of the queue (represented as v10 in Figure 20.4). The consumer process always retrieves information from the head of the queue (represented as v1 in Figure 20.4). After the consumer process has retrieved the information, the head of the list is adjusted to point at the next item (v2). After the producer process has added information, the tail of the list is adjusted to point at the next free slot in the list.

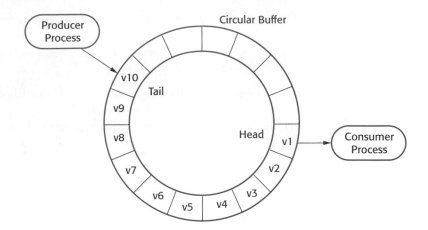

Figure 20.4 Producer/consumer processes sharing a circular buffer

Obviously, it is important to ensure that the producer and consumer process do not attempt to access the same item at the same time (i.e., when Head = Tail). You also have to ensure that the producer process does not add items to a full buffer and that the consumer process does not take items from an empty buffer. To do this, you implement the circular buffer as a process with Get and Put operations to access the buffer. The Put operation is called by the producer process and the Get operation by the consumer process. Synchronization primitives, such as semaphores or critical regions, are used to ensure that the operation of Get and Put are synchronized, so that they don't access the same location at the same time. If the buffer is full, the Put process has to wait until a slot is free; if the buffer is empty, the Get process has to wait until an entry has been made.

Once you have chosen the execution platform for the system, designed a process architecture, and decided on a scheduling policy, you may need to check that the system will meet its timing requirements. You can do this through static analysis of the system using knowledge of the timing behavior of components, or through simulation. This analysis may reveal that the system will not perform adequately. The process architecture, the scheduling policy, the execution platform, or all of these may then have to be redesigned to improve the performance of the system.

Timing constraints or other requirements may sometimes mean that it is best to implement some system functions, such as signal processing, in hardware. Modern hardware components, such as FPGAs, are flexible and can be adapted to different functions. Hardware components deliver much better performance than the equivalent software. System processing bottlenecks can be identified and replaced by hardware, thus avoiding expensive software optimization.

20.1.1 Real-time system modeling

The events that a real-time system must react to often cause the system to move from one state to another. For this reason, state models, which I introduced in Chapter 5, are often used to describe real-time systems. A state model of a system assumes that,

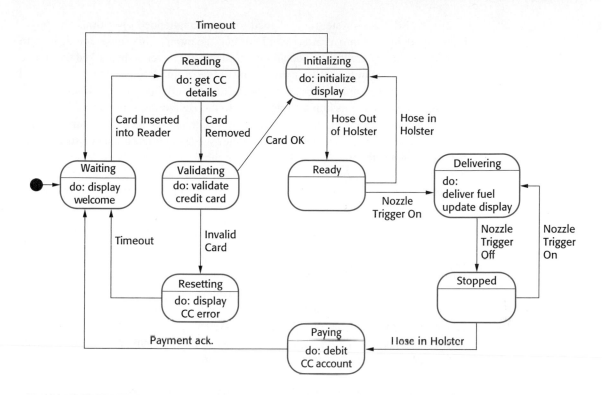

Figure 20.5 State machine model of a petrol (gas) pump

at any time, the system is in one of a number of possible states. When a stimulus is received, this may cause a transition to a different state. For example, a system controlling a valve may move from a state 'Valve open' to a state 'Valve closed' when an operator command (the stimulus) is received.

State models are a language-independent way of representing the design of a real-time system and are therefore an integral part of real-time system design methods (Gomaa, 1993). The UML supports the development of state models based on Statecharts (Harel, 1987; Harel, 1988). Statecharts are formal state machine models that support hierarchical states, so that groups of states can be considered as a single entity. Douglass discusses the use of the UML in real-time systems development (Douglass, 1999). State models are used in model-driven engineering, which I discussed in Chapter 5, to define the operation of a system. They can be transformed automatically to an executable program.

I have already illustrated this approach to system modeling in Chapter 5 where I used an example of a model of a simple microwave oven. Figure 20.5 is another example of a state machine model that shows the operation of a fuel delivery software system embedded in a petrol (gas) pump. The rounded rectangles represent system states and the arrows represent stimuli that force a transition from one state to another. The names chosen in the state machine diagram are descriptive. The associated information indicates actions taken by the system actuators or information that is displayed. Notice that this system never terminates but idles in a waiting state when the pump is not operating.

The fuel delivery system is designed to allow unattended operation. The buyer inserts a credit card into a card reader built into the pump. This causes a transition to a Reading state where the card details are read and the buyer is then asked to remove the card. Removal of the card triggers a transition to a Validating state where the card is validated. If the card is valid, the system initializes the pump and, when the fuel hose is removed from its holster, transitions to the Delivering state, where it is ready to deliver fuel. Activating the trigger on the nozzle causes fuel to be pumped; this stops when the trigger is released (for simplicity, I have ignored the pressure switch that is designed to stop fuel spillage). After the fuel delivery is complete and the buyer has replaced the hose in its holster, the system moves to a Paying state where the user's account is debited. After payment, the pump software returns to the Waiting state.

20.1.2 Real-time programming

Programming languages for real-time systems development have to include facilities to access system hardware, and it should be possible to predict the timing of particular operations in these languages. Hard real-time systems are still sometimes programmed in assembly language so that tight deadlines can be met. Systems-level languages, such as C, which allow efficient code to be generated are also widely used.

The advantage of using a systems programming language like C is that it allows the development of very efficient programs. However, these languages do not include constructs to support concurrency or the management of shared resources. Concurrency and resource management are implemented through calls to primitives provided by the real-time operating system, such as semaphores for mutual exclusion. These calls cannot be checked by the compiler, so programming errors are more likely. Programs are also often more difficult to understand because the language does not include real-time features. As well as understanding the program, the reader also has to know how real-time support is provided using system calls.

Because real-time systems must meet their timing constraints, you may not be able to use object-oriented development for hard real-time systems. Object-oriented development involves hiding data representations and accessing attribute values through operations defined with the object. This means that there is a significant performance overhead in object-oriented systems because extra code is required to mediate access to attributes and handle calls to operations. The consequent loss of performance may make it impossible to meet real-time deadlines.

A version of Java has been designed for embedded systems development (Dibble, 2008), with implementations from different companies such as IBM and Sun. This language includes a modified thread mechanism, which allows threads to be specified that will not be interrupted by the language garbage collection mechanism. Asynchronous event handling and timing specification has also been included. However, at the time of writing, this has mostly been used on platforms that have significant processor and memory capacity (e.g., a cell phone) rather than simpler embedded systems, with more limited resources. These systems are still usually implemented in C.

Real-time Java

The Java programming language has been modified in a number of ways to make it suitable for real-time systems development. These modifications include asynchronous communications; the addition of time, including absolute and relative time; a new thread model where threads cannot be interrupted by garbage collection; and a new memory management model that avoids the unpredictable delays that can result from garbage collection.

http://www.SoftwareEngineering-9.com/Web/RTS/Java.html

20.2 Architectural patterns

Architectural patterns, which I introduced in Chapter 6, are abstract, stylized descriptions of good design practice. They encapsulate knowledge about the organization of system architectures, when these architectures should be used and their advantages and disadvantages. You should not, however, think of an architectural pattern as a generic design to be instantiated. Rather, you use the pattern to understand an architecture and as starting point for creating your own specific architectural design.

As you might expect, the differences between embedded and interactive software means that different architectural patterns are used for embedded systems, rather than the architectural patterns discussed in Chapter 6. Embedded systems' patterns are process-oriented rather than object- or component-oriented. In this section, I discuss three real-time architectural patterns that are commonly used:

1. *Observe and React* This pattern is used when a set of sensors are routinely monitored and displayed. When the sensors show that some event has occurred (e.g., an incoming call on a cell phone), the system reacts by initiating a process to handle that event.

2. *Environmental Control* This pattern is used when a system includes sensors, which provide information about the environment and actuators that can change the environment. In response to environmental changes detected by the sensor, control signals are sent to the system actuators.

3. *Process Pipeline* This pattern is used when data has to be transformed from one representation to another before it can be processed. The transformation is implemented as a sequence of processing steps, which may be carried out concurrently. This allows for very fast data processing, because a separate core or processor can execute each transformation.

These patterns can of course be combined and you will often see more than one of them in a single system. For example, when the Environmental Control pattern is used, it is very common for the actuators to be monitored using the Observe and React pattern. In the event of an actuator failure, the system may

Name	Observe and React
Description	The input values of a set of sensors of the same types are collected and analyzed. These values are displayed in some way. If the sensor values indicate that some exceptional condition has arisen, then actions are initiated to draw the operator's attention to that value and, in certain cases, to take actions in response to the exceptional value.
Stimuli	Values from sensors attached to the system.
Responses	Outputs to display, alarm triggers, signals to reacting systems.
Processes	Observer, Analysis, Display, Alarm, Reactor.
Used in	Monitoring systems, alarm systems.

Figure 20.6 The Observe and React pattern

react by displaying a warning message, shutting down the actuator, switching in a backup system, etc.

The patterns that I discuss here are architectural patterns that describe the overall structure of an embedded system. Douglass (2002) describes lower-level, real-time design patterns that are used to help you make more detailed design decisions. These patterns include design patterns for execution control, communications, resource allocation, and safety and reliability.

These architectural patterns should be the starting point for an embedded systems design; however they are not design templates. If you use them as such, you will probably end up with an inefficient process architecture. You therefore have to optimize the process structure to ensure that you do not have too many processes. You also should ensure that there is a clear correspondence between the processes and the sensors and actuators in the system.

20.2.1   Observe and React

Monitoring systems are an important class of embedded real-time systems. A monitoring system examines its environment through a set of sensors and, usually, displays the state of the environment in some way. This could be on a built-in screen, on special-purpose instrument displays or on a remote display. If some exceptional event or sensor state is detected by the system, the monitoring system takes some action. Often, this involves raising an alarm to draw an operator's attention to the event. Sometimes the system may initiate some other preventative action, such as shutting down the system to preserve it from damage.

The Observe and React pattern (Figure 20.6 and Figure 20.7) is a pattern that is commonly used in monitoring systems. The values of sensors are observed and when

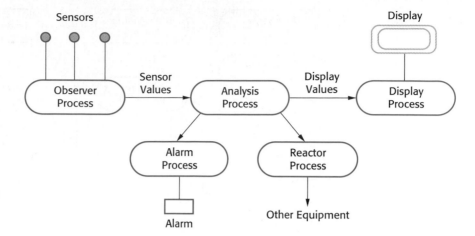

Figure 20.7 Observe and React process structure

particular values are detected, the system reacts in some way. Monitoring systems may be composed of several instantiations of the Observe and React pattern, one for each type of sensor in the system. Depending on the system requirements, you may then optimize the design by combining processes (e.g., you may use a single display process to display the information from all of the different types of sensors).

As an example of the use of this pattern, consider the design of a burglar alarm system that might be installed in an office building:

A software system is to be implemented as part of a burglar alarm system for commercial buildings. This uses several different types of sensors. These include movement detectors in individual rooms, door sensors that detect corridor doors opening, and window sensors on ground-floor windows that can detect when a window has been opened.

When a sensor detects the presence of an intruder, the system automatically calls the local police and, using a voice synthesizer, reports the location of the alarm. It switches on lights in the rooms around the active sensor and sets off an audible alarm. The sensor system is normally powered by mains power but is equipped with a battery backup. Power loss is detected using a separate power circuit monitor that monitors the mains voltage. If a voltage drop is detected, the system assumes that intruders have interrupted the power supply so an alarm is raised.

A possible process architecture for the alarm system is shown in Figure 20.8. In this diagram, the arrows represent signals sent from one process to another. This system is a 'soft' real-time system that does not have stringent timing requirements. The sensors do not need to detect high-speed events, so they need only be polled relatively infrequently. The timing requirements for this system are covered in Section 20.3.

I have already introduced the stimuli and responses in this alarm system in Figure 20.1. These are used as a starting point for the system design. The Observe

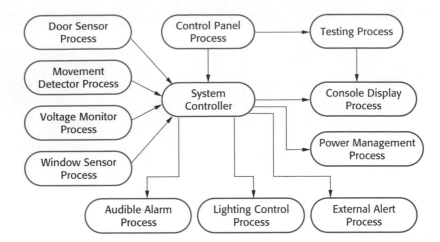

Figure 20.8 Process structure for a burglar alarm system

and React pattern is used in this design. There are observer processes associated with each type of sensor and reactor processes for each type of reaction. There is a single analysis process that checks the data from all of the sensors. The display processes in the pattern are combined into a single display process.

20.2.2 Environmental Control

Perhaps the most widespread use of embedded software is in control systems. In these systems, the software controls the operation of equipment, based on stimuli from the equipment's environment. For example, an anti-skid braking system in a car monitors the car's wheels and brake system (the system's environment). It looks for signs that the wheels are skidding when brake pressure is applied. If this is the case, the system adjusts the brake pressure to stop the wheels locking and reduce the likelihood of a skid.

Control systems may make use of the Environmental Control pattern, which is a general control pattern that includes sensor and actuator processes. This pattern is described in Figure 20.9, with the process architecture shown in Figure 20.10. A variant of this pattern leaves out the display process. This variant is used in situations where there is no requirement for user intervention or where the rate of control is so high that a display would not be meaningful.

This pattern can be the basis for a control system design with an instantiation of the Environmental Control pattern for each actuator (or actuator type) that is being controlled. You then optimize the design to reduce the number of processes. For example, you may combine actuator monitoring and actuator control processes, or may have a single monitoring and control process for several actuators. The optimizations that you choose depend on the timing requirements. You may need to monitor sensors more frequently than you send control signals, in which case it may be impractical to combine control and monitoring processes. There may also be

Name	Environmental Control
Description	The system analyzes information from a set of sensors that collect data from the system's environment. Further information may also be collected on the state of the actuators that are connected to the system. Based on the data from the sensors and actuators, control signals are sent to the actuators that then cause changes to the system's environment. Information about the sensor values and the state of the actuators may be displayed.
Stimuli	Values from sensors attached to the system and the state of the system actuators.
Responses	Control signals to actuators, display information.
Processes	Monitor, Control, Display, Actuator Driver, Actuator monitor.
Used in	Control systems.

Figure 20.9 The Environmental Control pattern

direct feedback between the actuator control and the actuator monitoring process. This allows fine-grain control decisions to be made by the actuator control process.

You can see how this pattern is used in Figure 20.11, which shows an example of a controller for a car braking system. The starting point for the design is associating an instance of the pattern with each actuator type in the system. In this case, there are four actuators, with each controlling the brake on one wheel. The individual sensor processes are combined into a single wheel-monitoring process that monitors the sensors on all wheels. This monitors the state of each wheel to check if the wheel is

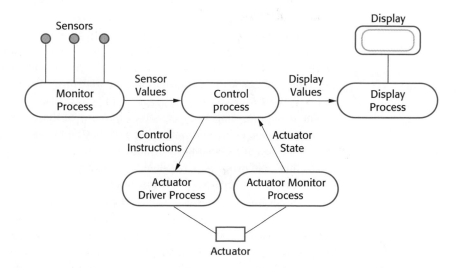

Figure 20.10 Environmental Control process structure

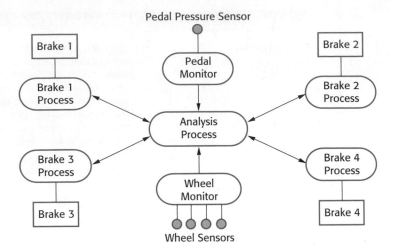

Figure 20.11 Control
system architecture for
an anti-skid braking
system

turning or locked. A separate process monitors the pressure on the brake pedal exerted by the car driver.

The system includes an anti-skid feature, which is triggered if the sensors indicate that a wheel is locked when the brake has been applied. This means that there is insufficient friction between the road and the tyre; in other words, the car is skidding. If the wheel is locked, the driver cannot steer that wheel. To counteract this, the system sends a rapid sequence of on/off signals to the brake on that wheel, which allows the wheel to turn and control to be regained.

20.2.3 Process Pipeline

Many real-time systems are concerned with collecting data from the system's environment, then transforming that data from its original representation into some other digital representation that can be more readily analyzed and processed by the system. The system may also convert digital data to analog data, which it then sends to its environment. For example, a software radio accepts incoming packets of digital data representing the radio transmission and transforms these into a sound signal that people can listen to.

The data processing that is involved in many of these systems has to be carried out very quickly. Otherwise, incoming data may be lost and outgoing signals may be broken up because essential information is missing. The Process Pipeline pattern makes this rapid processing possible by breaking down the required data processing into a sequence of separate transformations, with each transformation carried out by an independent process. This is a very efficient architecture for systems that use multiple processors or multicore processors. Each process in the pipeline can be associated with a separate processor or core, so that the processing steps can be carried out in parallel.

Name	Process Pipeline
Description	A pipeline of processes is set up with data moving in sequence from one end of the pipeline to another. The processes are often linked by synchronized buffers to allow the producer and consumer processes to run at different speeds. The culmination of a pipeline may be display or data storage or the pipeline may terminate in an actuator.
Stimuli	Input values from the environment or some other process
Responses	Output values to the environment or a shared buffer
Processes	Producer, Buffer, Consumer
Used in	Data acquisition systems, multimedia systems

Figure 20.12 The Process Pipeline pattern

Figure 20.12 is a brief description of the data pipeline pattern, and Figure 20.13 shows the process architecture for this pattern. Notice that the processes involved may produce and consume information. They are linked by synchronized buffers, as discussed in Section 20.1. This allows producer and consumer processes to operate at different speeds without data losses.

An example of a system that may use a process pipeline is a high-speed data acquisition system. Data acquisition systems collect data from sensors for subsequent processing and analysis. These systems are used in situations where the sensors are collecting a lot of data from the system's environment and it isn't possible or necessary to process that data in real time. Rather, it is collected and stored for later analysis. Data acquisition systems are often used in scientific experiments and process control systems where physical processes, such as chemical reactions, are very rapid. In these systems, the sensors may be generating data very quickly and the data acquisition system has to ensure that a sensor reading is collected before the sensor value changes.

Figure 20.14 is a simplified model of a data acquisition system than might be part of the control software in a nuclear reactor. This is a system that collects data from sensors monitoring the neutron flux (the density of neutrons) in the reactor. The sensor data is placed in a buffer from which it is extracted and processed. The average flux level is displayed on an operator's display and stored for future processing.

Figure 20.13 Process Pipeline process structure

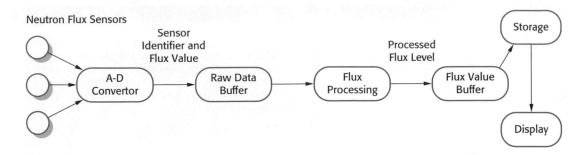

Figure 20.14 Neutron flux data acquisition

20.3 Timing analysis

As I discussed in the introduction, the correctness of a real-time system depends not just on the correctness of its outputs but also on the time at which these outputs were produced. This means that an important activity in the embedded, real-time software development process is timing analysis. In such an analysis, you calculate how often each process in the system must be executed to ensure that all inputs are processed and all system responses are produced in a timely way. The results of the timing analysis are used to decide how frequently each process should execute and how these processes should be scheduled by the real-time operating system.

Timing analysis for real-time systems is particularly difficult when the systems must deal with a mixture of periodic and aperiodic stimuli and responses. Because aperiodic stimuli are unpredictable, you have to make assumptions about the probability of these stimuli occurring and therefore requiring service at any particular time. These assumptions may be incorrect and system performance after delivery may not be adequate. Cooling's book (2003) discusses techniques for real-time system performance analysis that takes aperiodic events into account.

However, as computers have become faster it has become possible, in many systems, to design using only periodic stimuli. When processors were slow, aperiodic stimuli had to be used to ensure that critical events were processed before their deadline, as delays in processing usually involved some loss to the system. For example, the failure of a power supply in an embedded system may mean that the system has to shut down attached equipment in a controlled way, within a very short time (say 50 milliseconds). This could be implemented as a 'power fail' interrupt. However, it can also be implemented using a periodic process that runs very frequently and checks the power. So long as the time between process invocations is short, there is still time to perform a controlled shutdown of the system before the lack of power causes damage. For this reason, I focus on timing issues for periodic processes.

When you are analyzing the timing requirements of embedded real-time systems and designing systems to meet these requirements, there are three key factors that you have to consider:

1. *Deadlines* The times by which stimuli must be processed and some response produced by the system. If the system does not meet a deadline then, if it is a

hard-real time system, this is a system failure; in a soft real-time system, it results in degraded system service.

2. *Frequency* The number of times per second that a process must execute so that you are confident that it can always meet its deadlines.

3. *Execution time* The time required to process a stimulus and produce a response. Often, you have to take two execution times into account—the average execution time of a process and the worst-case execution time for that process. Execution time is not always the same because of the conditional execution of code, delays waiting for other processes, etc. In a hard real-time system, you may have to make assumptions based on the worst-case execution time to ensure that deadlines are not missed. In soft real-time systems, you may be able to base your calculations on the average execution time.

To continue the example of a power supply failure, let's assume that, after a failure event, it takes 50 ms for the supplied voltage to drop to a level where the equipment may be damaged. Therefore, the equipment shutdown process must begin within 50 ms of a power failure event. In such cases, it would be prudent to set a shorter deadline of 40 ms, because of physical variations in the equipment. This means that shutdown instructions for all attached equipment that is at risk must be issued and processed within 40 ms, assuming that the equipment is also dependent on the failing power supply.

If you detect power failure by monitoring a voltage level, you have to make more than one observation to detect that the voltage is dropping. If you run the process 250 times per second, this means that it runs every 4 ms and you may require up to two periods to detect the voltage drop. Therefore, it takes up to 8 ms to detect the problem. Consequently, the worst-case execution time of the shutdown process should not exceed 16 ms, to ensure that the deadline of 40 ms is met. This figure is calculated by subtracting the process periods (8 ms) from the deadline (40 ms) and dividing the result by two, as two process executions are necessary.

In reality, you would normally aim for something considerably less than 16 ms to give you a safety margin in case your calculations were wrong. In fact, the time required to examine a sensor and check that there has been no significant voltage loss should be much less than 16 ms. It only involves a simple comparison of two values. The average execution time of the power monitor process should be less than 1 ms.

The starting point for timing analysis in a real-time system is the timing requirements, which should set out the deadlines for each required response in the system. Figure 20.15 shows possible timing requirements for the office building burglar alarm system discussed in Section 20.2.1. To simplify this example, let us ignore stimuli generated by system testing procedures and external signals to reset the system in the event of a false alarm. This means there are only two types of stimulus to be processed by the system:

1. *Power failure* This is detected by observing a voltage drop of more than 20%. The required response is to switch the circuit to backup power by signaling an electronic power-switching device, which switches the mains power to battery backup.

Stimulus/Response	Timing Requirements
Power failure	The switch to backup power must be completed within a deadline of 50 ms.
Door alarm	Each door alarm should be polled twice per second.
Window alarm	Each window alarm should be polled twice per second.
Movement detector	Each movement detector should be polled twice per second.
Audible alarm	The audible alarm should be switched on within half a second of an alarm being raised by a sensor.
Lights switch	The lights should be switched on within half a second of an alarm being raised by a sensor.
Communications	The call to the police should be started within 2 seconds of an alarm being raised by a sensor.
Voice synthesizer	A synthesized message should be available within 2 seconds of an alarm being raised by a sensor.

Figure 20.15 Timing requirements for the burglar alarm system

2. *Intruder alarm* This is a stimulus generated by one of the system sensors. The response to this stimulus is to compute the room number of the active sensor, set up a call to the police, initiate the voice synthesizer to manage the call, and switch on the audible intruder alarm and building lights in the area.

As shown in Figure 20.15, you should list the timing constraints for each class of sensor separately, even when (as in this case) they are the same. By considering them separately, you leave scope for future change and make it easier to compute the number of times the controlling process has to be executed each second.

Allocating the system functions to concurrent processes is the next design stage. There are four types of sensors that must be polled periodically, each with an associated process. These are the voltage sensor, door sensors, window sensors, and movement detectors. Normally, the processes associated with the sensor will execute very quickly as all they are doing is checking whether or not a sensor has changed its status (e.g., from off to on). It is reasonable to assume that the execution time to check and assess the state of one sensor is no more than 1 ms.

To ensure that you meet the deadlines defined by the timing requirements, you then have to decide how frequently the related processes have to run and how many sensors should be examined during each execution of the process. There are obvious trade-offs here between frequency and execution time:

1. If you examine one sensor during each process execution, then if there are N sensors of a particular type, you must schedule the process 4N times per second to ensure that you meet the deadline of detecting a change of state within 0.25 seconds.

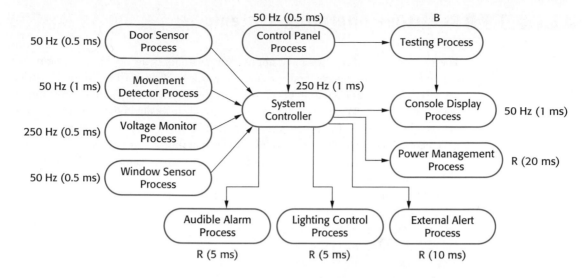

Figure 20.16 Alarm process timing

2. If you examine four sensors, say, during each process execution, then the execution time is increased to 4 ms, but you need only run the process N times/second to meet the timing requirement.

In this case, because the system requirements define actions when two or more sensors are positive, it may be sensible to examine sensors in groups, with groups based on the physical proximity of the sensors. If an intruder has entered the building then it will probably be adjacent sensors that are positive.

When you have completed the timing analysis, you may then annotate the process model with information about frequency of execution and their expected execution time (see Figure 20.16 as an example). Here, periodic processes are annotated with their frequency, processes that are started in response to a stimulus are annotated with **R**, and the testing process is a background process, annotated with **B**. This means that it only runs when processor time is available. In general, it is simpler to design a system so that there are a small number of process frequencies. The execution times represent the required worst-case execution times of the processes.

The final step in the design process is to design a scheduling system that will ensure that a process will always be scheduled to meet its deadlines. You can only do this if you know the scheduling approaches that are supported by the real-time operating system used (Burns and Wellings, 2009). The scheduler in the real-time OS allocates a process to a processor for a given amount of time. The time can be fixed, or may vary depending on the priority of the process.

In allocating process priorities, you have to consider the deadlines of each process so that processes with short deadlines receive processor time to meet these deadlines. For example, the voltage monitor process in the burglar alarm needs to be scheduled so that voltage drops can be detected and a switch made to backup power before the system fails. This should therefore have a higher priority than the processes that check sensor values, as these have fairly relaxed deadlines compared to their expected execution time.

Real-time operating systems

The execution platform for most application systems is an operating system that manages shared resources and provides features such as a file system, run-time process management, etc. However, the extensive functionality in a conventional operating system takes up a great deal of space and slows down the operation of programs. Furthermore, the process management features in the system may not be designed to allow fine-grain control over the scheduling of processes.

For these reasons, standard operating systems, such as Linux and Windows, are not normally used as the execution platform for real-time systems. Very simple embedded systems may be implemented as 'bare metal' systems. The systems themselves include system startup and shutdown, process and resource management, and process scheduling. More commonly, however, embedded applications are built on top of a real-time operating system (RTOS), which is an efficient operating system that offers the features needed by real-time systems. Examples of RTOS are Windows/CE, Vxworks, and RTLinux.

A real-time operating system manages processes and resource allocation for a real-time system. It starts and stops processes so that stimuli can be handled and allocates memory and processor resources. The components of an RTOS (Figure 20.17) depend on the size and complexity of the real-time system being developed. For all except the simplest systems, they usually include:

1. A real-time clock, which provides the information required to schedule processes periodically.

2. An interrupt handler, which manages aperiodic requests for service.

3. A scheduler, which is responsible for examining the processes that can be executed and choosing one of these for execution.

4. A resource manager, which allocates appropriate memory and processor resources to processes that have been scheduled for execution.

5. A dispatcher, which is responsible for starting the execution of processes.

Real-time operating systems for large systems, such as process control or telecommunication systems, may have additional facilities, namely disk storage management, fault management facilities that detect and report system faults, and a configuration manager that supports the dynamic reconfiguration of real-time applications.

20.4.1 Process management

Real-time systems have to handle external events quickly and, in some cases, meet deadlines for processing these events. This means that the event-handling processes must be scheduled for execution in time to detect the event. They must also be allocated

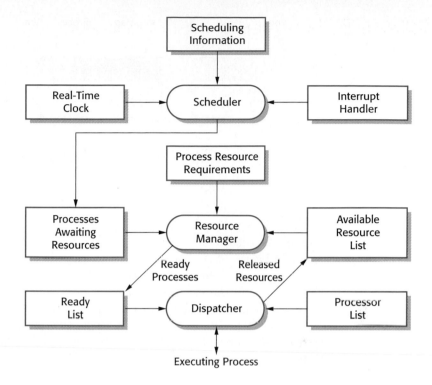

Figure 20.17
Components
of a real-time
operating system

sufficient processor resources to meet their deadline. The process manager in an RTOS is responsible for choosing processes for execution, allocating processor and memory resources, and starting and stopping process execution on a processor.

The process manager has to manage processes with different priorities. For some stimuli, such as those associated with certain exceptional events, it is essential that their processing should be completed within the specified time limits. Other processes may be safely delayed if a more critical process requires service. Consequently, the RTOS has to be able to manage at least two priority levels for system processes:

1. *Interrupt level* This is the highest priority level. It is allocated to processes that need a very fast response. One of these processes will be the real-time clock process.

2. *Clock level* This level of priority is allocated to periodic processes.

There may be a further priority level allocated to background processes (such as a self-checking process) that do not need to meet real-time deadlines. These processes are scheduled for execution when processor capacity is available.

Within each of these priority levels, different classes of process may be allocated different priorities. For example, there may be several interrupt lines. An interrupt from a very fast device may have to pre-empt processing of an interrupt from a slower device to avoid information loss. The allocation of process priorities so that all processes are serviced in time usually requires extensive analysis and simulation.

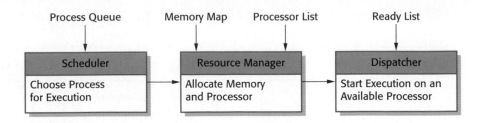

Process Queue	Memory Map	Processor List	Ready List

Scheduler	Resource Manager	Dispatcher
Choose Process for Execution	Allocate Memory and Processor	Start Execution on an Available Processor

Figure 20.18 RTOS actions required to start a process

Periodic processes are processes that must be executed at specified time intervals for data acquisition and actuator control. In most real-time systems, there will be several types of periodic process. Using the timing requirements specified in the application program, the RTOS arranges the execution of periodic processes so that they can all meet their deadlines.

The actions taken by the operating system for periodic process management are shown in Figure 20.18. The scheduler examines the list of periodic processes and selects a process to be executed. The choice depends on the process priority, the process periods, the expected execution times, and the deadlines of the ready processes. Sometimes, two processes with different deadlines should be executed at the same clock tick. In such a situation, one process must be delayed. Normally, the system will choose to delay the process with the longest deadline.

Processes that have to respond quickly to asynchronous events may be interrupt-driven. The computer's interrupt mechanism causes control to transfer to a predetermined memory location. This location contains an instruction to jump to a simple and fast interrupt service routine. The service routine disables further interrupts to avoid being interrupted itself. It then discovers the cause of the interrupt and initiates, with a high priority, a process to handle the stimulus causing the interrupt. In some high-speed data acquisition systems, the interrupt handler saves the data that the interrupt signaled was available in a buffer for later processing. Interrupts are then enabled again and control is returned to the operating system.

At any one time, there may be several processes, all with different priorities, that could be executed. The process scheduler implements system-scheduling policies that determine the order of process execution. There are two commonly used scheduling strategies:

1. *Non-pre-emptive scheduling* Once a process has been scheduled for execution it runs to completion or until it is blocked for some reason, such as waiting for input. This can cause problems, however, when there are processes with different priorities and a high-priority process has to wait for a low-priority process to finish.

2. *Pre-emptive scheduling* The execution of an executing process may be stopped if a higher-priority process requires service. The higher-priority process pre-empts the execution of the lower-priority process and is allocated to a processor.

Within these strategies, different scheduling algorithms have been developed. These include round-robin scheduling, where each process is executed in turn;

rate monotonic scheduling, where the process with the shortest period (highest frequency) is given priority; and shortest deadline first scheduling, where the process in the queue with the shortest deadline is scheduled (Burns and Wellings, 2009).

Information about the process to be executed is passed to the resource manager. The resource manager allocates memory and, in a multiprocessor system, also adds a processor to this process. The process is then placed on the 'ready list', a list of processes that are ready for execution. When a processor finishes executing a process and becomes available, the dispatcher is invoked. It scans the ready list to find a process that can be executed on the available processor and starts its execution.

KEY POINTS

■ An embedded software system is part of a hardware/software system that reacts to events in its environment. The software is 'embedded' in the hardware. Embedded systems are normally real-time systems.

■ A real-time system is a software system that must respond to events in real time. System correctness does not just depend on the results it produces, but also on the time when these results are produced.

■ Real-time systems are usually implemented as a set of communicating processes that react to stimuli to produce responses.

■ State models are an important design representation for embedded real-time systems. They are used to show how the system reacts to its environment as events trigger changes of state in the system.

■ There are several standard patterns that can be observed in different types of embedded systems. These include a pattern for monitoring the system's environment for adverse events, a pattern for actuator control and a data-processing pattern.

■ Designers of real-time systems have to do a timing analysis, which is driven by the deadlines for processing and responding to stimuli. They have to decide how often each process in the system should run and the expected and worst-case execution time for processes.

■ A real-time operating system is responsible for process and resource management. It always includes a scheduler, which is the component responsible for deciding which process should be scheduled for execution.

FURTHER READING

Software Engineering for Real-Time Systems. Written from an engineering rather than a computer science perspective, this book is a good practical guide to real-time systems engineering. It has good coverage of hardware issues, so is an excellent complement to Burns and Wellings' book (see below). (J. Cooling, Addison-Wesley, 2003.)

Real-time Systems and Programming Language: Ada, Real-time Java and C/Real-time POSIX, 4th edition. An excellent and comprehensive text that provides broad coverage of all aspects of real-time systems. (A. Burns and A. Wellings, Addison-Wesley, 2009.)

'Trends in Embedded Software Engineering'. This article suggests that model-driven development (as discussed in Chapter 5 of this book), will become an important approach to embedded systems development. This is part of a special issue on embedded systems and you may find that other articles are also useful reading. (*IEEE Software*, **26** (3), May–June 2009.) http://dx.doi.org/10.1109/MS.2009.80.

EXERCISES

20.1. Using examples, explain why real-time systems usually have to be implemented using concurrent processes.

20.2. Identify possible stimuli and the expected responses for an embedded system that controls a home refrigerator or a domestic washing machine.

20.3. Using the state-based approach to modeling, as discussed in Section 20.1.1, model the operation of an embedded software system for a voice mail system included in a landline phone. This should display the number of recorded messages on an LED display and should allow the user to dial in and listen to the recorded messages.

20.4. Explain why an object-oriented approach to software development may not be suitable for real-time systems.

20.5. Show how the Environmental Control pattern could be used as the basis of the design of a system to control the temperature in a greenhouse. The temperature should be between 10 and 30 degrees Celsius. If it falls below 10 degrees, the heating system should be switched on; if it goes above 30, the windows should be automatically opened.

20.6. Design a process architecture for an environmental monitoring system that collects data from a set of air quality sensors situated around a city. There are 5,000 sensors organized into 100 neighborhoods. Each sensor must be interrogated four times per second. When more than 30% of the sensors in a particular neighborhood indicate that the air quality is below an acceptable level, local warning lights are activated. All sensors return the readings to a central computer, which generates reports every 15 minutes on the air quality in the city.

Train protection system

- The system acquires information on the speed limit of a segment from a trackside transmitter, which continually broadcasts the segment identifier and its speed limit. The same transmitter also broadcasts information on the status of the signal controlling that track segment. The time required to broadcast track segment and signal information is 50 ms.
- The train can receive information from the trackside transmitter when it is within 10 m of a transmitter.
- The maximum train speed is 180 kph.
- Sensors on the train provide information about the current train speed (updated every 250 ms) and the train brake status (updated every 100 ms).
- If the train speed exceeds the current segment speed limit by more than 5 kph, a warning is sounded in the driver's cabin. If the train speed exceeds the current segment speed limit by more than 10 kph, the train's brakes are automatically applied until the speed falls to the segment speed limit. Train brakes should be applied within 100 ms of the time when the excessive train speed has been detected.
- If the train enters a track signaled that is signaled with a red light, the train protection system applies the train brakes and reduces the speed to zero. Train brakes should be applied within 100 ms of the time when the red light signal is received.
- The system continually updates a status display in the driver's cabin.

Figure 20.19
Requirements for a train
protection system

20.7. A train protection system automatically applies the brakes of a train if the speed limit for a segment of track is exceeded or if the train enters a track segment that is currently signaled with a red light (i.e., the segment should not be entered). Details are shown in Figure 20.19. Identify the stimuli that must be processed by the onboard train control system and the associated responses to these stimuli.

20.8. Suggest a possible process architecture for this system.

20.9. If a periodic process in the onboard train protection system is used to collect data from the trackside transmitter, how often must it be scheduled to ensure that the system is guaranteed to collect information from the transmitter? Explain how you arrived at your answer.

20.10. Why are general-purpose operating systems, such as Linux or Windows, not suitable as real-time system platforms? Use your experience of using a general-purpose system to help answer this question.

REFERENCES

Berry, G. (1989). 'Real-time programming: Special-purpose or general-purpose languages'. In *Information Processing*. Ritter, G. (ed.). Amsterdam: Elsevier Science Publishers, 11–17.

Brinch-Hansen, P. (1973). *Operating System Principles*. Englewood Cliffs, NJ: Prentice-Hall.

Burns, A. and Wellings, A. (2009). *Real-Time Systems and Programming Languages: Ada, Real-Time Java and C/Real-Time POSIX*. Boston: Addison-Wesley.

Cooling, J. (2003). *Software Engineering for Real-Time Systems*. Harlow, UK: Addison-Wesley.

Dibble, P. C. (2008). *Real-time Java Platform Programming, 2nd edition*. Charleston, SC: Booksurge Publishing.

Dijkstra, E. W. (1968). 'Cooperating Sequential Processes'. In *Programming Languages*. Genuys, F. (ed.). London: Academic Press, 43–112.

Douglass, B. P. (1999). *Real-Time UML: Developing Efficient Objects for Embedded Systems, 2nd edition*. Boston: Addison-Wesley.

Douglass, B. P. (2002). *Real-Time Design Patterns: Robust Scalable Architecture for Real-Time Systems*. Boston: Addison-Wesley.

Gomaa, H. (1993). *Software Design Methods for Concurrent and Real-Time Systems*. Reading, Mass.: Addison-Wesley.

Harel, D. (1987). 'Statecharts: A Visual Formalism for Complex Systems'. *Sci. Comput. Programming,* **8** (3), 231–74.

Harel, D. (1988). 'On Visual Formalisms'. *Comm. ACM*, **31** (5), 514–30.

Hoare, C. A. R. (1974). 'Monitors: an operating system structuring concept'. *Comm. ACM*, **21** (8), 666–77.

Lee, E. A. (2002). 'Embedded Software'. In *Advances in Computers*. Zelkowitz, M. (ed.). London: Academic Press.

Silberschatz, A., Galvin, P. B. and Gagne, G. (2008). *Operating System Concepts, 8th edition*. New York: John Wiley & Sons.

Tanenbaum, A. S. (2007). *Modern Operating Systems, 3rd edition*. Englewood Cliffs, NJ: Prentice Hall.

21

Aspect-oriented software engineering

Objectives

The objective of this chapter is to introduce you to aspect-oriented software development, which is based on the separation of concerns. When you have read this chapter, you will:

■ understand why the separation of concerns is a good guiding principle for software development;

■ have been introduced to the fundamental ideas underlying aspects and aspect-oriented software development;

■ understand how an aspect-oriented approach may be used for requirements engineering, software design, and programming;

■ be aware of the difficulties of testing aspect-oriented systems.

Contents

In most large systems, the relationships between the requirements and the program components are complex. A single requirement may be implemented by a number of components and each component may include elements of several requirements. In practice, this means that implementing a change to the requirements may involve understanding and changing several components. Alternatively, a component may provide some core functionality but also include code that implements several system requirements. Even when there appears to be significant reuse potential, it may be expensive to reuse such components. Reuse may involve modifying them to remove extra code that is not associated with the core functionality of the component.

Aspect-oriented software engineering (AOSE) is an approach to software development that is intended to address this problem and so make programs easier to maintain and reuse. AOSE is based around abstractions called aspects, which implement system functionality that may be required at several different places in a program. Aspects encapsulate functionality that cross-cuts and coexists with other functionality that is included in a system. They are used alongside other abstractions such as objects and methods. An executable aspect-oriented program is created by automatically combining (weaving) objects, methods, and aspects, according to specifications that are included in the program source code.

An important characteristic of aspects is that they include a definition of where they should be included in a program, as well as the code implementing the cross-cutting concern. You can specify that the cross-cutting code should be included before or after a specific method call or when an attribute is accessed. Essentially, the aspect is woven into the core program to create a new augmented system.

The key benefit of an aspect-oriented approach is that it supports the separation of concerns. As I explain in Section 21.1, separating concerns into independent elements rather than including different concerns in the same logical abstraction is good software engineering practice. By representing cross-cutting concerns as aspects, these concerns can be understood, reused, and modified independently, without regard for where the code is used. For example, user authentication may be represented as an aspect that requests a login name and password. This can be automatically woven into the program wherever authentication is required.

Say you have a requirement that user authentication is required before any change to personal details is made in a database. You can describe this in an aspect by stating that the authentication code should be included before each call to methods that update personal details. Subsequently, you may extend the requirement for authentication to all database updates. This can easily be implemented by modifying the aspect. You simply change the definition of where the authentication code is to be woven into the system. You do not have to search through the system looking for all occurrences of these methods. You are therefore less likely to make mistakes and introduce accidental security vulnerabilities into your program.

Research and development in aspect-orientation has primarily focused on aspect-oriented programming. Aspect-oriented programming languages such as AspectJ (Colyer and Clement, 2005; Colyer et al., 2005; Kiczales, et al., 2001; Laddad, 2003a; Laddad, 2003b) have been developed that extend object-oriented programming to include aspects. Major companies have used aspect-oriented programming in their software production processes (Colyer and Clement, 2005). However, cross-cutting concerns are equally problematic at other stages of the software development process. Researchers are now investigating how to utilize aspect-orientation in system requirements engineering and system design, and how to test and verify aspect-oriented programs.

I have included a discussion of AOSE here because its focus on separating concerns is an important way of thinking about and structuring a software system. Although some large-scale systems have been implemented using an aspect-oriented approach, the use of aspects is still not part of mainstream software engineering. As with all new technologies, advocates focus on the benefits rather than the problems and costs. Although it will be some time before AOSE is routinely used alongside other approaches to software engineering, the idea of separating concerns that underlies AOSE are important. Thinking about the separation of concerns is a good general approach to software engineering.

In the remaining sections of the chapter, I therefore focus on the concepts that are part of AOSE and discuss the advantages and disadvantages of using an aspect-oriented approach at different stages of the software development process. As my aim is to help you understand the concepts underlying AOSE, I do not go into detail of any specific approach or aspect-oriented programming language.

21.1 The separation of concerns

The separation of concerns is a key principle of software design and implementation. It means that you should organize your software so that each element in the program (class, method, procedure, etc.) does one thing and one thing only. You can then focus on that element without regard for the other elements in the program. You can understand each part of the program by knowing its concern, without the need to understand other elements. When changes are required, they are localized to a small number of elements.

The importance of separating concerns was recognized at an early stage in the history of computer science. Subroutines, which encapsulate a unit of functionality, were invented in the early 1950s and subsequent program structuring mechanisms such as procedures and object classes have been designed to provide better mechanisms for realizing the separation of concerns. However, all of these mechanisms have problems in dealing with certain types of concern that cut across other concerns. These cross-cutting concerns cannot be localized using structuring mechanisms such as objects or functions. Aspects have been invented to help manage these cross-cutting concerns.

Although it is generally agreed that separating concerns is good software engineering practice, it is harder to pin down what is actually meant by a concern. Sometimes it is defined as a functional notion (i.e., a concern is some element of functionality in a system). Alternatively, it may be defined very broadly as 'any piece of interest or focus in a program'. Neither of these definitions is particularly useful in practice. Concerns certainly are more than simply functional elements but the more general definition is so vague that it is practically useless.

In my view, most attempts to define concerns are problematic because they attempt to relate concerns to programs. In fact, as discussed by Jacobson and Ng (2004), concerns are really reflections of the system requirements and priorities of stakeholders in the system. System performance may be a concern because users want to have a rapid response from a system; some stakeholders may be concerned that the system should include particular functionality; companies who are supporting a system may be concerned that it is easy to maintain. A concern can therefore be defined as something that is of interest or significance to a stakeholder or a group of stakeholders.

If you think of concerns as a way of organizing requirements, you can see why an approach to implementation that separates concerns into different program elements is good practice. It is easier to trace concerns, expressed as a requirement or a related set of requirements, to the program components that implement these concerns. If the requirements change, then the part of the program that has to be changed is obvious.

There are several different types of stakeholder concern:

1. Functional concerns, which are related to the specific functionality to be included in a system. For example, in a train control system, a specific functional concern is train braking.

2. Quality of service concerns, which are related to the non-functional behavior of a system. These include characteristics such as performance, reliability, and availability.

3. Policy concerns, which are related to the overall policies that govern the use of a system. Policy concerns include security and safety concerns and concerns related to business rules.

4. System concerns, which are related to attributes of the system as a whole, such as its maintainability or its configurability.

5. Organizational concerns, which are related to organizational goals and priorities. These include producing a system within budget, making use of existing software assets, and maintaining the reputation of the organization.

The core concerns of a system are those functional concerns that relate to its primary purpose. Therefore, for a hospital patient information system, the core functional concerns are the creation, editing, retrieval, and management of patient records. In addition to core concerns, large systems also have secondary functional concerns. These may involve functionality that shares information with the core concerns, or which is required so that the system can satisfy its non-functional requirements.

For example, consider a system that has a requirement to provide concurrent access to a shared buffer. One process adds data to the buffer and another process

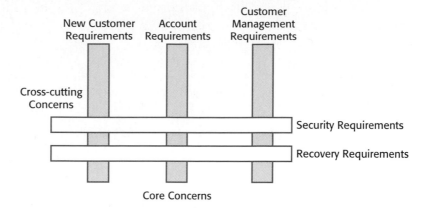

Figure 21.1 Cross-cutting concerns

takes data from the same buffer. This shared buffer is part of a data acquisition system where a producer process puts data in the buffer and a consumer process takes data from the buffer. The core concern here is to maintain a shared buffer so the core functionality is associated with adding and removing elements from the buffer. However, to ensure that the producer and consumer processes do not interfere with each other, there is an essential secondary concern of synchronization. The system must be designed so that the producer process cannot overwrite data that has not been consumed and the consumer process cannot take data from an empty buffer.

In addition to these secondary concerns, other concerns such as quality of service and organizational policies reflect essential system requirements. In general, these are system concerns—they apply to the system as a whole rather than to individual requirements or to the realization of these requirements in a program. These are called cross-cutting concerns to distinguish them from core concerns. Secondary functional concerns may also be cross-cutting although they do not always cross-cut the entire system; rather, they are associated with groupings of core concerns that provide related functionality.

Cross-cutting concerns are shown in Figure 21.1, which is based on an example of an Internet banking system. This system has requirements relating to new customers such as credit checking and address verification. It also has requirements related to the management of existing customers and the management of customer accounts. All of these are core concerns that are associated with the system's primary purpose—the provision of an Internet banking service. However, the system also has security requirements based on the bank's security policy, and recovery requirements to ensure that data is not lost in the event of a system failure. These are cross-cutting concerns as they may influence the implementation of all of the other system requirements.

Programming language abstractions, such as procedures and classes, are the mechanism that you normally use to organize and structure the core concerns of a system. However, the implementation of the core concerns in conventional programming languages usually includes additional code to implement the cross-cutting, functional, quality of service, and policy concerns. This leads to two undesirable phenomena: tangling and scattering.

```
synchronized void put (SensorRecord rec )
{
   // Check that there is space in the buffer; wait if not
   if ( numberOfEntries == bufsize)
      wait () ;
   // Add record at end of buffer
   store [back] = new SensorRecord (rec.sensorId, rec.sensorVal) ;
   back = back + 1 ;
   // If at end of buffer, next entry is at the beginning
   if (back == bufsize)
      back = 0 ;
   numberOfEntries = numberOfEntries + 1 ;
   // indicate that buffer is available
   notify () ;
} // put
```

Figure 21.2 Tangling of buffer management and synchronization code

Tangling occurs when a module in a system includes code that implements different system requirements. The example in Figure 21.2, which is a simplified implementation of part of the code for a bounded buffer system, illustrates this phenomenon. Figure 21.2 is an implementation of the put operation that adds an item for the buffer. However, if the buffer is full, it has to wait until a corresponding get operation removes an item from the buffer. The details are unimportant; essentially the wait () and notify () calls are used to synchronize the put and get operations. The code supporting the primary concern (in this case, putting a record into the buffer), is tangled with code implementing synchronization. Synchronization code, which is associated with the secondary concern of ensuring mutual exclusion, has to be included in all methods that access the shared buffer. Code associated with the synchronization concern is shown as shaded code in Figure 21.2.

The related phenomenon of scattering occurs when the implementation of a single concern (a logical requirement or set of requirements) is scattered across several components in a program. This is likely to occur when requirements related to secondary functional concerns or policy concerns are implemented.

For example, say a medical record management system, such as the MHC-PMS, has a number of components concerned with managing personal information, medication, consultations, medical images, diagnoses, and treatments. These implement the core concern of the system: maintaining records of patients. The system can be configured for different types of clinic by selecting the components that provide the functionality needed for the clinic.

However, assume there is also an important secondary concern which is the maintenance of statistical information; the health code provider wishes to record details of how many patients were admitted and discharged each month, how many patients died, what medications were issued, the reasons for consultations, and so on. These requirements have to be implemented by adding code that anonymizes the data (to maintain patient privacy) and writes it to a statistical database. A statistics component processes the statistical data and generates the statistic reports that are required.

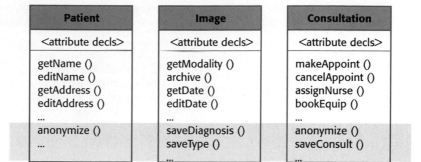

Patient	Image	Consultation
<attribute decls>	<attribute decls>	<attribute decls>
getName () editName () getAddress () editAddress () ... anonymize () ...	getModality () archive () getDate () editDate () ... saveDiagnosis () saveType () ...	makeAppoint () cancelAppoint () assignNurse () bookEquip () ... anonymize () saveConsult () ...

Figure 21.3 Scattering of methods implementing secondary concerns

This is illustrated in Figure 21.3. This diagram shows examples of three classes that might be included in the patient record system along with some of the core methods for managing patient information. The shaded area shows the methods that are required to implement the secondary statistics concern. You can see that this statistics concern is scattered throughout the other core concerns.

Problems with scattering and tangling occur when the initial system requirements change. For example, say new statistical data had to be collected in the patient record system. The changes to the system are not all located in one place and so you have to spend time looking for the components in the system that have to be changed. You then have to change each of these components to incorporate the required changes. This may be expensive because of the time required to analyze the components and then make and test the changes. There is always the possibility that you will miss some code that should be changed and so the statistics will be incorrect. Furthermore, as several changes have to be made, this increases the chances that you will make a mistake and introduce errors into the software.

21.2 Aspects, join points, and pointcuts

In this section, I introduce the most important new concepts associated with aspect-oriented software development and illustrate these using examples from the MHC-PMS. The terminology that I use was introduced by the developers of AspectJ in the late 1990s. However, the concepts are generally applicable and not specific to the AspectJ programming language. Figure 21.4 summarizes the key terms that you need to understand.

A medical records system such as the MHC-PMS includes components that handle logically related patient information. The patient component maintains personal information about a patient, the medication component holds information about medications that may be prescribed, and so on. By designing the system using a component-based approach, different instantiations of the system can be configured. For example, a version could be configured for each type of clinic with doctors only allowed to prescribe

Term	Definition
advice	The code implementing a concern.
aspect	A program abstraction that defines a cross-cutting concern. It includes the definition of a pointcut and the advice associated with that concern.
join point	An event in an executing program where the advice associated with an aspect may be executed.
join point model	The set of events that may be referenced in a pointcut.
pointcut	A statement, included in an aspect, that defines the join points where the associated aspect advice should be executed.
weaving	The incorporation of advice code at the specified join points by an aspect weaver.

Figure 21.4
Terminology used in aspect-oriented software engineering

medication relevant to that clinic. This simplifies the job of clinical staff and reduces the chances that a doctor will mistakenly prescribe the wrong medication.

However, this organization means that information in the database has to be updated from a number of different places in the system. For example, patient information may be modified when their personal details change, when their assigned medication changes, when they are assigned to a new specialist, etc. For simplicity, assume that all components in the system use a consistent naming strategy and that all database updates are implemented by methods starting with 'update'. There are therefore methods in the system such as:

```
updatePersonalInformation (patientId, infoupdate)

updateMedication (patientId, medicationupdate)
```

The patient is identified by patientId and the changes to be made are encoded in the second parameter; the details of this encoding are not important for this example. Updates are made by hospital staff, who are logged into the system.

Imagine that a security breach occurs in which patient information is maliciously changed. Perhaps someone has accidentally left his or her computer logged on and an unauthorized person has gained access to the system. Alternatively, an authorized insider may have gained access and maliciously changed the patient information. To reduce the probability of this happening again, a new security policy is introduced. Before any change to the patient database is made, the person requesting the change must reauthenticate himself or herself to the system. Details of who made the change are also logged in a separate file. This helps trace problems if they reoccur.

One way of implementing this new policy is to modify the update method in each component to call other methods to do the authentication and logging. Alternatively,

```
aspect authentication
{
    before: call (public void update* (..)) // this is a pointcut
    {
        // this is the advice that should be executed when woven into // the
        executing system
        int tries = 0 ;
        string userPassword = Password.Get ( tries ) ;
        while (tries < 3 && userPassword != thisUser.password ( ) )
        {
            // allow 3 tries to get the password right
            tries = tries + 1 ;
            userPassword = Password.Get ( tries ) ;
        }
        if (userPassword != thisUser.password ( )) then
            //if password wrong, assume user has forgotten to logout
            System.Logout (thisUser.uid) ;
    }
} // authentication
```

Figure 21.5 An
authentication aspect

the system could be modified so that each time an update method is called, method calls are added before the call to do the authentication, and then after to log the changes made. However, neither of these is a very good solution to this problem:

1. The first approach leads to a tangled implementation. Logically, updating a database, authenticating the originator of an update, and logging details of the update are separate, unrelated concerns. You may wish to include authentication elsewhere in the system without logging or may wish to log actions apart from the update action. The same authentication and logging code has to be included within several different methods.

2. The alternative approach leads to a scattered implementation. If you explicitly include method calls to do authentication and logging before and after every call to the update methods, then this code is included at several different places in the system.

Authentication and logging cut across the core concerns of the system and may have to be included in several different places. In an aspect-oriented system, you can represent these cross-cutting concerns as separate aspects. An aspect includes a specification of where the cross-cutting concern is to be woven into the program, and code to implement that concern. This is illustrated in Figure 21.5, which defines an authentication aspect. The notation that I use in this example follows the style of AspectJ but uses a simplified syntax, which should be understandable without knowledge of either Java or AspectJ.

Aspects are completely different from other program abstractions in that the aspect itself includes a specification of where it should be executed. With other abstractions, such as methods, there is a clear separation between the definition of the abstraction and its use. You cannot tell by examining the method where it will be called from; calls can be from anywhere that the method is in scope. Aspects, by contrast, include a 'pointcut'—a statement that defines where the aspect will be woven into the program.

In this example, the pointcut is a simple statement:

```
before: call (public void update* (..))
```

The meaning of this is that before the execution of any method whose name starts with the string update, followed by any other sequence of characters, the code in the aspect after the pointcut definition should be executed. The character * is called a wildcard and matches any string characters that are allowed in identifiers. The code to be executed is known as the 'advice' and is the implementation of the cross-cutting concern. In this case, the advice gets a password from the person requesting the change and checks that it matches the password of the currently logged-in user. If not, the user is logged out and the update does not proceed.

The ability to specify, using pointcuts, where code should be executed is the distinguishing characteristic of aspects. However, to understand what pointcuts mean, you need to understand another concept—the idea of a join point. A join point is an event that occurs during the execution of a program; so, it could be a method call, the initialization of a variable, the updating of a field, etc.

There are many possible types of event that may occur during program execution. A join point model defines the set of events that can be referenced in an aspect-oriented program. Join point models are not standardized and each aspect-oriented programming language has its own join point model. For example, in AspectJ events that are part of the join point model include:

■ call events—calls to a method or a constructor;

■ execution events—the execution of a method or a constructor;

■ initialization events—class or object initialization;

■ data events—accessing or updating of a field;

■ exception events—the handling of an exception.

A pointcut identifies the specific event(s) (e.g., a call to a named procedure) with which advice should be associated. This means that you can weave advice into a program in many different contexts, depending on the join point model that is supported:

1. Advice can be included before the execution of a specific method, a list of named methods, or a list of methods whose names match a pattern specification (such as update*).

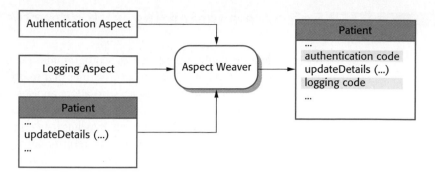

Figure 21.6 Aspect weaving

2. Advice can be included after the normal or exceptional return from a method. In the example shown in Figure 21.5, you could define a pointcut that would execute the logging code after all calls to update methods.

3. Advice can be included when a field in an object is modified; you can include advice to monitor or change that field.

The inclusion of advice at the join points specified in the pointcuts is the responsibility of an aspect weaver. Aspect weavers are extensions to compilers that process the definition of aspects and the object classes and methods that define the system. The weaver then generates a new program with the aspects included at the specified join points. The aspects are integrated so that the cross-cutting concerns are executed at the right places in the final system.

Figure 21.6 illustrates this aspect weaving for the authentication and logging aspects that should be included in the MHC-PMS. There are three different approaches to aspect weaving:

1. Source code pre-processing, where a weaver takes source code input and generates new source code in a language such as Java or C++, which can then be compiled using the standard language compiler. This approach has been adopted for the AspectX language with its associated XWeaver (Birrer et al., 2005).

2. Link time weaving, where the compiler is modified to include an aspect weaver. An aspect-oriented language such as AspectJ is processed and standard Java bytecode is generated. This can then be executed directly by a Java interpreter or further processed to generate native machine code.

3. Dynamic weaving at execution time. In this case, join points are monitored and when an event that is referenced in a pointcut occurs, the corresponding advice is integrated with the executing program.

The most commonly used approach to aspect weaving is link time weaving, as this allows for the efficient implementation of aspects without a large run-time overhead. Dynamic weaving is the most flexible approach but can incur significant performance penalties during program execution. Source code pre-processing is now rarely used.

21.3 Software engineering with aspects

Aspects were originally introduced as a programming language construct but, as I have discussed, the notion of concerns is one that really comes from the system requirements. Therefore, it makes sense to adopt an aspect-oriented approach at all stages of the system development process. In the early stages of software engineering, adopting an aspect-oriented approach means using the notion of separating concerns as a basis for thinking about the requirements and the system design. Identifying and modeling concerns should be part of the requirements engineering and design processes. Aspect-oriented programming languages then provide the technological support to maintain the separation of concerns in your implementation of the system.

When designing a system, Jacobson and Ng (2004) suggest that you should think of a system that supports different stakeholder concerns as a core system plus extensions. I have illustrated this in Figure 21.7, where I have used UML packages to represent both the core and the extensions. The core system is a set of system features that implements the essential purpose of a system. Therefore, if the purpose of a particular system is to maintain information on patients in a hospital, then the core system provides a means of creating, editing, managing, and accessing a database of patient records. The extensions to the core system reflect additional stakeholder concerns, which must be integrated with the core system. For example, it is important that a medical information system maintains the confidentiality of patient information, so one extension might be concerned with access control, another with encryption, etc.

There are several different types of extension that are derived from the different types of concern that I discussed in Section 21.1.

1. *Secondary functional extensions* These add additional capabilities to the functionality provided in the core system. For instance, using the example of the MHC-PMS, the production of reports on the drugs prescribed in the previous month would be a secondary functional extension to a patient information system.

2. *Policy extensions* These add functional capabilities to support organizational policies. Extensions that add security features are examples of policy extensions.

3. *QoS extensions* These add functional capabilities to help attain the quality of service requirements that have been specified for the system. For example, an extension might implement a cache to reduce the number of database accesses or automated backups for recovery in the event of a system failure.

4. *Infrastructure extensions* These extensions add functional capabilities to support the implementation of a system on some specific implementation platform. For example, in a patient information system, infrastructure extensions might be used to implement the interface to the underlying database management system. Changes to this interface can be made by modifying the associated infrastructure extensions.

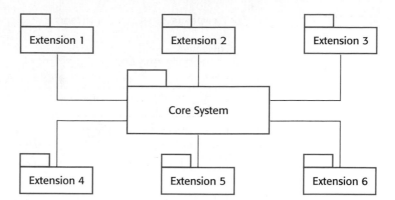

Figure 21.7 Core
system with extensions

Extensions always add some kind of functionality or additional features to the core system. Aspects are a way to implement these extensions and they can be composed with the core system functionality using the weaving facilities in the aspect-oriented programming environment.

21.3.1 Concern-oriented requirements engineering

As I suggested in Section 21.1, concerns reflect the requirements of stakeholders. These concerns may reflect the functionality required by a stakeholder, the quality of system service, organizational policies or issues that are related to the attributes of the system as a whole. It therefore makes sense to adopt an approach to requirements engineering that identifies and specifies the different stakeholder concerns. The term 'early aspects' is sometimes used to refer to the use of aspects at early stages in the software lifecycle where the separation of concerns is emphasized.

The importance of separating concerns during requirements engineering has been recognized for many years. Viewpoints that represent different system perspectives have been incorporated into a number of requirements engineering methods (Easterbrook and Nuseibeh, 1996; Finkelstein et al., 1992; Kotonya and Sommerville, 1996). These methods separate the concerns of different stakeholders. Viewpoints reflect the distinct functionality that is required by different stakeholder groups.

However, there are also requirements which cross-cut all viewpoints, as shown in Figure 21.8. This diagram shows that viewpoints may be of different types but cross-cutting concerns (such as regulation, dependability, and security) generate requirements that may impact on all of the system viewpoints. This was the major consideration in the work which I did in the development of the PreView method (Sommerville and Sawyer, 1997; Sommerville et al., 1998), which included steps to identify cross-cutting, non-functional concerns.

To develop a system that is organized in the style shown in Figure 21.7, you should identify requirements for the core system plus the requirements for the system extensions. A viewpoint-oriented approach to requirements engineering, where each viewpoint represents the requirements of related groups of stakeholders, is one

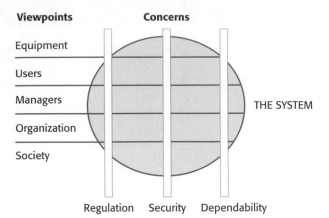

Figure 21.8 Viewpoints
and Concerns

way to separate core and secondary concerns. If you organize the requirements according to stakeholder viewpoint, you can then analyze them to discover related requirements that appear in all or most viewpoints. These represent the core functionality of the system. Other viewpoint requirements may be requirements that are specific to that viewpoint. These can be implemented as extensions to the core functionality.

For example, imagine that you are developing a software system to keep track of specialized equipment used by the emergency services. Equipment is located at different places across a region or state and, in the event of an emergency such as a flood or earthquake, the emergency services use the system to discover what equipment is available close to the site of the problem. Figure 21.9 shows outline requirements from three possible viewpoints for such a system.

You can see from this example that stakeholders from all of the different viewpoints need to be able to find specific items of equipment, browse the equipment available at each location, and check in/check out equipment from the store. These are therefore requirements for the core system. The secondary requirements support the more specific needs of each viewpoint. There are secondary requirements for system extensions supporting equipment use, management, and maintenance.

The secondary functional requirements that are identified from any one viewpoint do not, necessarily, cross-cut the requirements from other viewpoints. For example, only the maintenance viewpoint is interested in completing maintenance records. These requirements reflect the needs of that viewpoint and those concerns may not be shared with other viewpoints. In addition to the secondary functional requirements, however, there are cross-cutting concerns that generate requirements of importance to some or all viewpoints. These often reflect policy and quality of service requirements that apply to the system as a whole. As I discussed in Chapter 4, these are non-functional requirements such as requirements for security, performance, and cost.

In the equipment inventory system, an example of a cross-cutting concern is system availability. Emergencies may happen with little or no warning. Saving lives may require essential equipment to be deployed as quickly as possible. Therefore, the

1. Emergency service users

1.1 Find a specified type of equipment (e.g., heavy lifting gear)
1.2 View equipment available in a specified store
1.3 Check-out equipment
1.4 Check-in equipment
1.5 Arrange equipment to be transported to emergency
1.6 Submit damage report
1.7 Find store close to emergency

2. Emergency planners

2.1 Find a specified type of equipment
2.2 View equipment available in a specified location
2.3 Check in/check out equipment from a store
2.4 Move equipment from one store to another
2.6 Order new equipment

3. Maintenance staff

3.1 Check in/check out equipment for maintenance
3.2 View equipment available at each store
3.3 Find a specified type of equipment
3.4 View maintenance schedule for an equipment item
3.5 Complete maintenance record for an equipment item
3.6 Show all items in a store requiring maintenance

Figure 21.9
Viewpoints on an
equipment inventory
system

dependability requirements for the equipment inventory system include requirements for a high level of system availability. Some examples of these dependability requirements, with associated rationale, are shown in Figure 21.10. Using these requirements, you can then identify extensions to the core functionality for transaction logging and status reporting. These make it easier to identify problems and switch to a backup system.

The outcome of the requirements engineering process should be a set of requirements that are structured around the notion of a core system plus extensions. For example, in the inventory system, examples of core requirements might be:

Figure 21.10
Availability-related
requirements for the
equipment inventory
system

C.1 The system shall allow authorized users to view the description of any item of equipment in the emergency services inventory.

AV.1   There shall be a 'hot standby' system available in a location that is geographically well-separated from the principal system.
Rationale: The emergency may affect the principal location of the system.

AV.1.1   All transactions shall be logged at the site of the principal system and at the remote standby site.
Rationale: This allows these transactions to be replayed and the system databases made consistent.

AV.1.2   The system shall send status information to the emergency control room system every five minutes.
Rationale: The operators of the control room system can switch to the hot standby if the principal system is unavailable.

Viewpoints

I introduced the notion of viewpoints in Chapter 4, where I explained how viewpoints could be used as a way of structuring the requirements from different stakeholders. Using viewpoints, you can identify the requirements for the core system from each stakeholder grouping.

http://www.SoftwareEngineering-9.com/Web/Requirements/Viewpoints.html

C.2 The system shall include a search facility to allow authorized users to search either individual inventories or the complete inventory for a specific item of equipment or a specific type of equipment.

The system may also include an extension that is intended to support equipment procurement and replacement. Requirements for this extension might be:

E1.1 It shall be possible for authorized users to place orders with accredited suppliers for replacement items of equipment.

E1.1.1 When an item of equipment is ordered, it should be allocated to a specific inventory and flagged in that inventory as 'on order'.

As a general rule, you should avoid having too many concerns or extensions to the system. These simply confuse the reader and may lead to premature design. This limits the freedom of designers and may result in a system design that cannot meet its quality of service requirements.

21.3.2 Aspect-oriented design and programming

Aspect-oriented design is the process of designing a system that makes use of aspects to implement the cross-cutting concerns and extensions that are identified during the requirements engineering process. At this stage, you need to translate the concerns that relate to the problem to be solved to corresponding aspects in the program that is implementing the solution. You also need to understand how these aspects will be composed with other system components and ensure that composition ambiguities do not arise.

The high-level statement of requirements provides a basis for identifying some system extensions that may be implemented as aspects. You then need to develop these in more detail to identify further extensions and to understand the functionality that is required. One way to do this is to identify a set of use cases, (discussed in Chapters 4 and 5) associated with each viewpoint. Use case models are interaction-focused and more detailed than the user requirements. You can think of them as a bridge between the requirements and the design. In a use case model, you describe

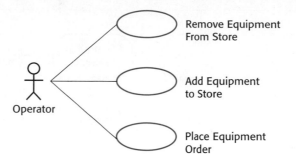

Figure 21.11 Use cases from the inventory management system

the steps of each user interaction and so start to identify and define the classes in the system.

Jacobson and Ng (2004) have written a book that discusses how use cases can be used in aspect-oriented software engineering. They suggest that each use case represents an aspect and propose extensions to the use case approach to support join points and pointcuts. They also introduce the notion of use case slices and use case modules. These include fragments of classes that implement an aspect. They can be composed to create the complete system.

Figure 21.11 shows examples of three use cases that might be part of the inventory management system. These reflect the concerns of adding equipment to an inventory and ordering equipment. Equipment ordering and adding equipment to a store are related concerns. Once ordered items have been delivered, they must be added to the inventory and delivered to one of the equipment stores.

The UML already includes the notion of extension use cases. An extension use case extends the functionality of another use case. Figure 21.12 shows how the placing of an equipment order extends the core use case for adding equipment to a specific store. If the equipment to be added does not exist, it can be ordered and added to the store when the equipment is delivered. During the development of use case models, you should look for common features and, where possible, structure the use cases as core cases plus extensions. Cross-cutting features, such as the logging of all transactions, can also be represented as extension use cases. Jacobsen and Ng discuss how extensions of this type can be implemented as aspects.

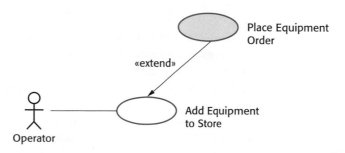

Figure 21.12 Extension use cases

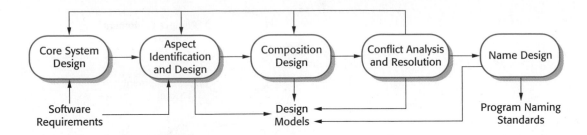

Figure 21.13 A generic
aspect-oriented design
process

Developing an effective process for aspect-oriented design is essential if aspect-oriented design is to be accepted and used. I suggest that an aspect-oriented design process should include the activities shown in Figure 21.13. These activities are:

1. *Core system design* At this stage, you design the system architecture to support the core functionality of the system. The architecture must also take into account quality of service requirements such as performance and dependability requirements.

2. *Aspect identification and design* Starting with the extensions identified in the system requirements, you should analyze these to see if they are aspects in themselves or if they should be broken down into several aspects. Once aspects have been identified, these can then be separately designed, taking into account the design of the core system features.

3. *Composition design* At this stage, you analyze the core system and aspect designs to discover where the aspects should be composed with the core system. Essentially, you are identifying the join points in a program at which aspects will be woven.

4. *Conflict analysis and resolution* A problem with aspects is that they may interfere with each other when they are composed with the core system. Conflicts occur when there is a pointcut clash with different aspects specifying that they should be composed at the same point in the program. However, there may be more subtle conflicts. When aspects are designed independently, they may make assumptions about the core system functionality that has to be modified. However, when several aspects are composed, one aspect may affect the functionality of the system in a way that was not anticipated by other aspects. The overall system behavior may then not be as expected.

5. *Name design* This is an important design activity that defines standards for naming entities in the program. This is essential to avoid the problem of accidental pointcuts. These occur when, at some program join point, the name accidentally matches that in a pointcut pattern. The advice is therefore unintentionally applied at that point. Obviously this is undesirable and can lead to unexpected program behavior. Therefore, you should design a naming scheme that minimizes the likelihood of this happening.

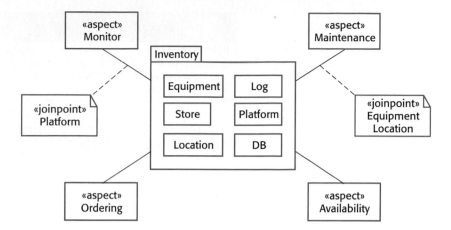

Figure 21.14 An aspect-oriented design model

This process is, naturally, an iterative process in which you make initial design proposals then refine them as you analyze and understand the design issues. Normally, you would expect to refine the extensions identified in the requirements to a larger number of aspects.

The outcome of the aspect-oriented design process is an aspect-oriented design model. This may be expressed in an extended version of the UML which includes new, aspect-specific constructs such as those proposed by Clarke and Baniassad (2005) and Jacobson and Ng (2004). The essential elements of 'aspect UML' are a means of modeling aspects and of specifying the join points at which the aspect advice should be composed with the core system.

Figure 21.14 is an example of an aspect-oriented design model. I have used the UML stereotype for an aspect proposed by Jacobson and Ng. Figure 21.14 shows the core system for an emergency services inventory plus some aspects that might be composed with that core. I have shown some core system classes and some aspects. This is a simplified picture; a complete model would include more classes and aspects. Notice how I have used UML notes to provide additional information about the classes that are cross-cut by some aspects.

Figure 21.15 is a more detailed model of an aspect. Obviously, before you design aspects, you have to have a core system design. As I don't have space to show this here, I have made a number of assumptions about classes and methods in the core system.

The first section of the aspect sets out the pointcuts that specify where it will be composed with the core system. For example, the first pointcut specifies that the aspect may be composed at the call getItemInfo (..) join point. The following section defines the extensions that are implemented by the aspect. In the example here, the extension statement can be read as:

"In the method viewItem, after the call to the method getItemInfo, a call to the method displayHistory should be included to display the maintenance record."

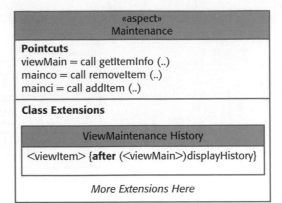

Figure 21.15 Part of a model of an aspect

Aspect-oriented programming (AOP) started at Xerox's PARC laboratories in 1997, with the development of the AspectJ programming language. This remains the most widely used aspect-oriented language, although aspect-oriented extensions of other languages, such as C# and C++, have also been implemented. Other experimental languages have also been developed to support the explicit separation of concerns and concern composition and there are experimental implementation of AOP in the .NET framework. Aspect-oriented programming is covered extensively in other books (Colyer et al., 2005; Gradecki and Lezeiki, 2003; Laddad, 2003b).

If you have followed an aspect-oriented approach to designing your system, you will already have identified the core functionality and the extensions to that functionality to be implemented as cross-cutting aspects. The focus of the programming process should then be to write code implementing the core and extension functionality and, critically, to specify the pointcuts in the aspects so that the aspect advice is woven into the base code at the correct places.

Correctly specifying pointcuts is very important as these define where the aspect advice will be composed with the core functionality. If you make a mistake in pointcut specification, then the aspect advice will be woven into the program in the wrong place. This could lead to unexpected and unpredictable program behavior. Adherence to the naming standards established during system design is essential. You also have to review all of the aspects to ensure that aspect interference will not occur if two or more aspects are woven into the core system at the same join point. In general, it is best to avoid this completely but, occasionally, it might be the best way to implement a concern. In those circumstances, you have to ensure that the aspects are completely independent. The program's behavior should not depend on the order that the aspects are woven into the program.

21.3.3 Verification and validation

As I discussed in Chapter 8, verification and validation is the process of demonstrating that a program meets its specification (verification) and meets the real needs of its stakeholders (validation). Static verification techniques focus on manual or automated analysis of the source code of the program. Dynamic validation or testing is used to discover defects in the program or to demonstrate that the program meets its requirements. When defect detection is the objective, the testing process may be guided by knowledge of the program's source code. Test coverage metrics show the effectiveness of tests in causing source code statements to be executed.

For aspect-oriented systems, the processes of validation testing are no different than for any other system. The final executable program is treated as a black box and tests are devised to show whether or not the system meets its requirements. However, the use of aspects causes real problems with program inspections and white-box testing, where the program source code is used to identify potential defect tests.

Program inspections, which I describe in Chapter 24, involve a team of readers looking at the source code of a program to discover defects that have been introduced by the programmer. It is a very effective technique of defect discovery. However, aspect-oriented programs cannot be read sequentially (i.e., from top to bottom). They are therefore more difficult for people to understand.

A general guideline for program understandability is that a reader should be able to read a program from left to right, top to bottom without having to switch attention to other parts of the code. This makes it easier for readers and also makes it less likely that programmers will make mistakes as their attention is focused on a single section of code. Improving program readability was a key reason for the introduction of structured programming (Dijkstra et al., 1972) and the elimination of unconditional branch (go-to) statements from high-level programming languages.

In an aspect-oriented system, sequential code reading is impossible. The reader has to examine each aspect, understand its pointcuts (which may be patterns), and the join point model of the aspect-oriented language. When reading the program, he or she then has to identify every potential join point and switch attention to the aspect code to see if it may be woven at that point. Their attention then returns to the main flow of control of the base code. In reality, this is cognitively impossible and the only possible way to inspect an aspect-oriented program is through the use of code-reading tools.

Code-reading tools can be written that 'flatten' an aspect-oriented program and present a program to the reader with the aspects 'woven' into the program at the specified join points. However, this is not a complete solution to the code-reading problem. The join point model in an aspect-oriented programming language may be dynamic rather than static and it may be impossible to demonstrate that the flattened program will behave in exactly the same way as the program that will execute. Furthermore, because it is possible for different aspects to have the same pointcut specification, the program-reading tool must know how the aspect weaver handles these 'competing' aspects and how the composition will be ordered.

White-box or structural testing is a systematic approach to testing where knowledge of the program source code is used to design defect tests. The aim is to design tests that provide some level of program coverage. That is, the set of tests should ensure that every logical path through the program is executed, with the consequence that each program statement is executed at least once. Program execution analyzers may be used to demonstrate that this level of test coverage has been achieved.

In an aspect-oriented system, there are two problems with this approach:

1. How can knowledge of the program code be used to systematically derive program tests?

2. What exactly does test coverage mean?

To design tests in a structured program (e.g., tests of the code of a method) without unconditional branches, you can derive a program flow graph, which reveals every logical execution path through that program. You then examine the code and, for each path through the flow graph, choose input values that will cause that path to be executed.

However, an aspect-oriented program is not a structured program. The flow of control is interrupted by 'come from' statements (Constantinos et al., 2004). At some join point in the execution of the base code, an aspect may be executed. I am not sure that it is possible to construct a structured flow diagram in such a situation. It is therefore difficult to systematically design program tests that ensure that all combinations of base code and aspects are executed.

In an aspect-oriented program, there is also the problem of deciding what 'test coverage' means. Does it mean that the code of each aspect is executed at least once? This is a very weak condition because of the interaction between aspects and the base code at the join points where the aspects are woven. Should the idea of test coverage be extended so that the code of the aspect is executed at least once at every join point specified in the aspect pointcut? In such situations, what happens if different aspects define the same pointcut? These are both theoretical and practical problems. We need tools to support aspect-oriented program testing which will help assess the extent of test coverage of a system.

As I discuss in Chapter 24, large projects normally have a separate quality assurance team who set testing standards and who require a formal assurance that program reviews and testing have been completed to these standards. The problems of inspecting and deriving tests for aspect-oriented programs are a significant barrier to the adoption of aspect-oriented software development in such large software projects.

As well as problems with inspections and white-box testing, Katz (2005) identified additional problems in testing aspect-oriented programs:

1. How should aspects be specified so that tests for these aspects may be derived?

2. How can aspects be tested independently of the base system with which they should be woven?

3. How can aspect interference be tested? As I have discussed, aspect interference occurs when two or more aspects use the same pointcut specification.

4. How can tests be designed so that all program join points are executed and appropriate aspect tests applied?

Fundamentally, these testing problems occur because aspects are tightly rather than loosely integrated with the base code of a system. They are therefore difficult to test in isolation. Because they may be woven into a program in many different places, you can't be sure that an aspect that works successfully at one join point will necessarily work at all join points. All of these remain research problems for aspect-oriented software development.

KEY POINTS

■ The main benefit of an aspect-oriented approach to software development is that it supports the separation of concerns. By representing cross-cutting concerns as aspects, individual concerns can be understood, reused, and modified without changing other parts of the program.

■ Tangling occurs when a module in a system includes code that implements different system requirements. The related phenomenon of scattering occurs when the implementation of a single concern is scattered across several components in a program.

■ Aspects include a pointcut—a statement that defines where the aspect will be woven into the program, and advice—the code to implement the cross-cutting concern. Join points are the events that can be referenced in a pointcut.

■ To ensure the separation of concerns, systems can be designed as a core system that implements the primary concerns of stakeholders, and a set of extensions that implement secondary concerns.

■ To identify concerns, you may use a viewpoint-oriented approach to requirements engineering to elicit stakeholder requirements and to identify cross-cutting quality of service and policy concerns.

■ The transition from requirements to design can be made by identifying use cases, where each use case represents a stakeholder concern. The design may be modeled using an extended version of the UML with aspect stereotypes.

■ The problems of inspecting and deriving tests for aspect-oriented programs are a significant barrier to the adoption of aspect-oriented software development in large software projects.

FURTHER READING

'Aspect-oriented programming'. This special issue of the CACM has a number of articles for a general audience, which are a good starting point for reading about aspect-oriented programming (*Comm. ACM*, **44** (10), October 2001.) http://dx.doi.org/10.1145/383845.383846.

Aspect-oriented Software Development. A multiauthor book with a wide range of papers on aspect-oriented software development, written by many of the leading researchers in the field. (R. E. Filman, T. Elrad, S. Clarke and M. Aksit, Addison-Wesley, 2005.)

Aspect-oriented Software Development with Use cases. This is a practical book for software designers. The authors discuss how to use use cases to manage the separation of concerns, and to use these as the basis of an aspect-oriented design. (I. Jacobson and P. Ng, Addison-Wesley, 2005.)

EXERCISES

21.1. What are the different types of stakeholder concern that may arise in a large system? How can aspects support the implementation of each of these types of concern?

21.2. Summarize what is meant by tangling and scattering. Using examples, explain why tangling and scattering can cause problems when system requirements change.

21.3. What is the difference between a join point and a pointcut? Explain how these facilitate the weaving of code into a program to handle cross-cutting concerns.

21.4. What assumptions underlie the idea that a system should be organized as a core system that implements the essential requirements, plus extensions that implement additional functionality? Can you think of systems where this model would not be appropriate?

21.5. What viewpoints should be considered when developing a requirements specification for the MHC-PMS? What are likely to be the most important cross-cutting concerns?

21.6. Using the outline functionality for each viewpoint shown in Figure 21.9, identify six further use cases for the equipment inventory system, in addition to those shown in Figure 21.11. Where appropriate, show how some of these might be organized as extension use cases.

21.7. Using the aspect stereotype notation illustrated in Figure 21.15, develop in more detail the Ordering and Monitor aspects, shown in Figure 21.14.

21.8. Explain how aspect interference can arise and suggest what should be done during the system design process to reduce the problems of aspect interference.

21.9. Explain why expressing pointcut specifications as patterns increases the problems of testing aspect-oriented programs. To answer this, think about how program testing normally involves comparing the expected output to the actual output produced by a program.

21.10. Suggest how you could use aspects to simplify the debugging of programs.

REFERENCES

Birrer, I., Pasetti, A. and Rohlik, O. (2005). 'The XWeaver Project: Aspect-oriented Programming for On-Board Applications'. http://control.ee.ethz.ch/index.cgi?page=publications;action=details;id=2361

Clark, S. and Baniassad, E. (2005). *Aspect-Oriented Analysis and Design: The Theme Approach.* Harlow, UK: Addison-Wesley.

Colyer, A. and Clement, A. (2005). 'Aspect-oriented programming with AspectJ'. *IBM Systems J.*, **44** (2), 301–8.

Colyer, A., Clement, A., Harley, G. and Webster, M. (2005). *eclipse AspectJ.* Upper Saddle River, NJ: Addison-Wesley.

Constantinos, C., Skotiniotis, T. and Stoerzer, T. (2004). 'AOP considered harmful'. *European Interactive Workshop on Aspects in Software (EIWAS' 04)*, Berlin, Germany.

Dijkstra, E. W., Dahl, O. J. and Hoare, C. A. R. (1972). *Structured Programming.* London: Academic Press.

Easterbrook, S. and Nuseibeh, B. (1996). 'Using ViewPoints for inconsistency management'. *BCS/IEE Software Eng. J.*, **11** (1), 31–43.

Finkelstein, A., Kramer, J., Nuseibeh, B. and Goedicke, M. (1992). 'Viewpoints: A Framework for Integrating Multiple Perspectives in System Development'. *Int. J. of Software Engineering and Knowledge Engineering*, **2** (1), 31–58.

Gradecki, J. D. and Lezeiki, N. (2003). *Mastering AspectJ: Aspect-Oriented Programming in Java.* New York: John Wiley & Sons.

Jacobson, I. and Ng, P-W. (2004). *Aspect-oriented Software Development with Use Cases.* Boston: Addison-Wesley.

Katz, S. (2005). 'A Survey of Verification and Static Analysis for Aspects'. http://www.aosd-europe.net/documents/verificM81.pdf

Kiczales, G., Hilsdale, E., Hugunin, J., Kersten, M., Palm, J. and Griswold, W. G. (2001). 'Getting Started with AspectJ'. *Comm. ACM*, **44** (10), 59–65.

Kotonya, G. and Sommerville, I. (1996). 'Requirements engineering with viewpoints'. *BCS/IEE Software Eng. J.*, **11** (1), 5–18.

Laddad, R. (2003a). *AspectJ in Action.* Greenwich, Conn.: Manning Publications Co.

Laddad, R. (2003b). *AspectJ in Action: Practical Aspect-Oriented Programming.* Greenwich, Conn.: Manning Publications.

Sommerville, I. and Sawyer, P. (1997). 'Viewpoints: principles, problems and a practical approach to requirements engineering'. *Annals of Software Engineering*, **3** 101–30.

Sommerville, I., Sawyer, P. and Viller, S. (1998). 'Viewpoints for requirements elicitation: a practical approach'. *3rd Int. Conf. on Requirements Engineering.* Colorado: IEEE Computer Society Press, 74–81.

PART 4

Software Management

It is sometimes suggested that the key difference between software engineering and other types of programming is that software engineering is a managed process. By this, I mean that the software development takes place within an organization and is subject to a range of schedule, budget, and organizational constraints. Management is therefore very important to software engineering. I introduce a range of management topics in this part of the book with a focus on technical management issues rather than 'softer' management issues such as people management, or the more strategic management of enterprise systems.

Chapter 22 introduces software project management and its first major section is concerned with risk management. Along with project planning, risk management, where managers identify what might go wrong and plan what they might do about it, is a key project management responsibility. This chapter also includes sections on people management and team working.

Chapter 23 covers project planning and estimation. I introduce bar charts as fundamental planning tools and explain why plan-driven development will remain an important development approach, in spite of the success of agile methods. I also discuss issues that influence the price charged for a system and techniques of software cost estimation. I use the COCOMO family of cost models to describe algorithmic cost modeling and explain the benefits and disadvantages of this approach.

Chapters 24 to 26 are concerned with issues of quality management. Quality management is concerned with processes and techniques for ensuring and improving the quality of software and I introduce this topic in Chapter 24. I discuss the importance of standards in quality management, the use of reviews and inspections in the quality assurance process, and the role of software measurement in quality management.

Chapter 25 discusses configuration management. This is an issue that is important for all large systems, which are developed by teams. However, the need for configuration management is not always obvious to students who have only been concerned with personal software development, so I describe the various aspects of this topic here, including configuration planning, version management, system building, and change management.

Finally, Chapter 26 covers software process improvement—how can processes be modified so that both product and process attributes are improved? I discuss the stages of a generic process improvement process, namely, process measurement, process analysis, and process change. I then go on to cover the SEI's capability-based approach to process improvement and briefly explain capability maturity models.

22

Project management

Objectives

The objective of this chapter is to introduce software project management and two important management activities, namely risk management and people management. When you have read the chapter you will:

■ know the principal tasks of software project managers;

■ have been introduced to the notion of risk management and some of the risks that can arise in software projects;

■ understand factors that influence personal motivation and what these might mean for software project managers;

■ understand key issues that influence team working, such as team composition, organization, and communication.

Contents

Software project management is an essential part of software engineering. Projects need to be managed because professional software engineering is always subject to organizational budget and schedule constraints. The project manager's job is to ensure that the software project meets and overcomes these constraints as well as delivering high-quality software. Good management cannot guarantee project success. However, bad management usually results in project failure: the software may be delivered late, cost more than originally estimated, or fail to meet the expectations of customers.

The success criteria for project management obviously vary from project to project but, for most projects, important goals are:

1. Deliver the software to the customer at the agreed time.

2. Keep overall costs within budget.

3. Deliver software that meets the customer's expectations.

4. Maintain a happy and well-functioning development team.

These goals are not unique to software engineering but are the goals of all engineering projects. However, software engineering is different from other types of engineering in a number of ways that make software management particularly challenging. Some of these differences are:

1. *The product is intangible* A manager of a shipbuilding or a civil engineering project can see the product being developed. If a schedule slips, the effect on the product is visible—parts of the structure are obviously unfinished. Software is intangible. It cannot be seen or touched. Software project managers cannot see progress by simply looking at the artifact that is being constructed. Rather, they rely on others to produce evidence that they can use to review the progress of the work.

2. *Large software projects are often 'one-off' projects* Large software projects are usually different in some ways from previous projects. Therefore, even managers who have a large body of previous experience may find it difficult to anticipate problems. Furthermore, rapid technological changes in computers and communications can make a manager's experience obsolete. Lessons learned from previous projects may not be transferable to new projects.

3. *Software processes are variable and organization-specific* The engineering process for some types of system, such as bridges and buildings, is well understood. However, software processes vary quite significantly from one organization to another. Although there has been significant progress in process standardization and improvement, we still cannot reliably predict when a particular software process is likely to lead to development problems. This is especially true when the software project is part of a wider systems engineering project.

Because of these issues, it is not surprising that some software projects are late, over budget, and behind schedule. Software systems are often new and technically innovative. Engineering projects (such as new transport systems) that are innovative often also have schedule problems. Given the difficulties involved, it is perhaps remarkable that so many software projects are delivered on time and to budget!

It is impossible to write a standard job description for a software project manager. The job varies tremendously depending on the organization and the software product being developed. However, most managers take responsibility at some stage for some or all of the following activities:

1. *Project planning* Project managers are responsible for planning, estimating and scheduling project development, and assigning people to tasks. They supervise the work to ensure that it is carried out to the required standards and monitor progress to check that the development is on time and within budget.

2. *Reporting* Project managers are usually responsible for reporting on the progress of a project to customers and to the managers of the company developing the software. They have to be able to communicate at a range of levels, from detailed technical information to management summaries. They have to write concise, coherent documents that abstract critical information from detailed project reports. They must be able to present this information during progress reviews.

3. *Risk management* Project managers have to assess the risks that may affect a project, monitor these risks, and take action when problems arise.

4. *People management* Project managers are responsible for managing a team of people. They have to choose people for their team and establish ways of working that lead to effective team performance.

5. *Proposal writing* The first stage in a software project may involve writing a proposal to win a contract to carry out an item of work. The proposal describes the objectives of the project and how it will be carried out. It usually includes cost and schedule estimates and justifies why the project contract should be awarded to a particular organization or team. Proposal writing is a critical task as the survival of many software companies depends on having enough proposals accepted and contracts awarded. There can be no set guidelines for this task; proposal writing is a skill that you acquire through practice and experience.

In this chapter, I focus on risk management and people management. Project planning is an important topic in its own right, which I discuss in Chapter 23.

22.1 Risk management

Risk management is one of the most important jobs for a project manager. Risk management involves anticipating risks that might affect the project schedule or the quality of the software being developed, and then taking action to avoid these risks

(Hall, 1998; Ould, 1999). You can think of a risk as something that you'd prefer not to have happen. Risks may threaten the project, the software that is being developed, or the organization. There are, therefore, three related categories of risk:

1. *Project risks* Risks that affect the project schedule or resources. An example of a project risk is the loss of an experienced designer. Finding a replacement designer with appropriate skills and experience may take a long time and, consequently, the software design will take longer to complete.

2. *Product risks* Risks that affect the quality or performance of the software being developed. An example of a product risk is the failure of a purchased component to perform as expected. This may affect the overall performance of the system so that it is slower than expected.

3. *Business risks* Risks that affect the organization developing or procuring the software. For example, a competitor introducing a new product is a business risk. The introduction of a competitive product may mean that the assumptions made about sales of existing software products may be unduly optimistic.

Of course, these risk types overlap. If an experienced programmer leaves a project this can be a project risk because, even if they are immediately replaced, the schedule will be affected. It inevitably takes time for a new project member to understand the work that has been done, so they cannot be immediately productive. Consequently, the delivery of the system may be delayed. The loss of a team member can also be a product risk because a replacement may not be as experienced and so could make programming errors. Finally, it can be a business risk because that programmer's experience may be crucial in winning new contracts.

You should record the results of the risk analysis in the project plan along with a consequence analysis, which sets out the consequences of the risk for the project, product, and business. Effective risk management makes it easier to cope with problems and to ensure that these do not lead to unacceptable budget or schedule slippage.

The specific risks that may affect a project depend on the project and the organizational environment in which the software is being developed. However, there are also common risks that are not related to the type of software being developed and these can occur in any project. Some of these common risks are shown in Figure 22.1.

Risk management is particularly important for software projects because of the inherent uncertainties that most projects face. These stem from loosely defined requirements, requirements changes due to changes in customer needs, difficulties in estimating the time and resources required for software development, and differences in individual skills. You have to anticipate risks; understand the impact of these risks on the project, the product, and the business; and take steps to avoid these risks. You may need to draw up contingency plans so that, if the risks do occur, you can take immediate recovery action.

Risk	Affects	Description
Staff turnover	Project	Experienced staff will leave the project before it is finished.
Management change	Project	There will be a change of organizational management with different priorities.
Hardware unavailability	Project	Hardware that is essential for the project will not be delivered on schedule.
Requirements change	Project and product	There will be a larger number of changes to the requirements than anticipated.
Specification delays	Project and product	Specifications of essential interfaces are not available on schedule.
Size underestimate	Project and product	The size of the system has been underestimated.
CASE tool underperformance	Product	CASE tools, which support the project, do not perform as anticipated.
Technology change	Business	The underlying technology on which the system is built is superseded by new technology.
Product competition	Business	A competitive product is marketed before the system is completed.

Figure 22.1
Examples of common project, product, and business risks

I AP M

An outline of the process of risk management is illustrated in Figure 22.2. It involves several stages:

1. *Risk identification* You should identify possible project, product, and business risks.

2. *Risk analysis* You should assess the likelihood and consequences of these risks.

3. *Risk planning* You should make plans to address the risk, either by avoiding it or minimizing its effects on the project.

4. *Risk monitoring* You should regularly assess the risk and your plans for risk mitigation and revise these when you learn more about the risk.

You should document the outcomes of the risk management process in a risk management plan. This should include a discussion of the risks faced by the project, an analysis of these risks, and information on how you propose to manage the risk if it seems likely to be a problem.

The risk management process is an iterative process that continues throughout the project. Once you have drawn up an initial risk management plan, you monitor the situation to detect emerging risks. As more information about the risks becomes available, you have to reanalyze the risks and decide if the risk priority has changed. You may then have to change your plans for risk avoidance and contingency management.

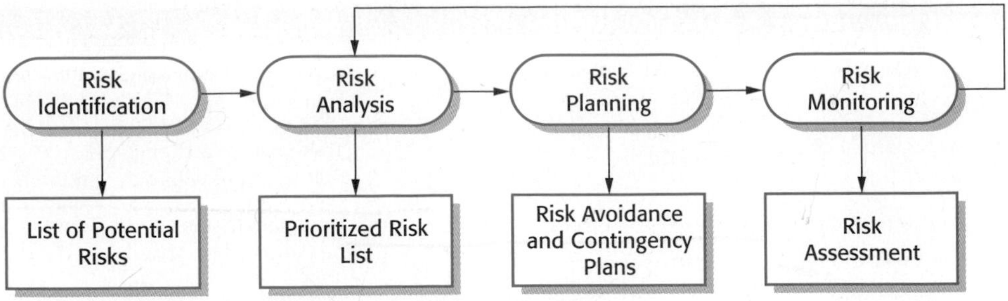

Figure 22.2
The risk
management
process

22.1.1 Risk identification

Risk identification is the first stage of the risk management process. It is concerned with identifying the risks that could pose a major threat to the software engineering process, the software being developed, or the development organization. Risk identification may be a team process where a team get together to brainstorm possible risks. Alternatively, the project manager may simply use his or her experience to identify the most probable or critical risks.

As a starting point for risk identification, a checklist of different types of risk may be used. There are at least six types of risk that may be included in a risk checklist:

1. *Technology risks* Risks that derive from the software or hardware technologies that are used to develop the system.

2. *People risks* Risks that are associated with the people in the development team.

3. *Organizational risks* Risks that derive from the organizational environment where the software is being developed.

4. *Tools risks* Risks that derive from the software tools and other support software used to develop the system.

5. *Requirements risks* Risks that derive from changes to the customer requirements and the process of managing the requirements change.

6. *Estimation risks* Risks that derive from the management estimates of the resources required to build the system.

Figure 22.3 gives some examples of possible risks in each of these categories. When you have finished the risk identification process, you should have a long list of risks that could occur and which could affect the product, the process, and the business. You then need to prune this list to a manageable size. If you have too many risks, it is practically impossible to keep track of all of them.

22.1.2 Risk analysis

During the risk analysis process, you have to consider each identified risk and make a judgment about the probability and seriousness of that risk. There is no easy way to do this. You have to rely on your own judgment and experience of previous projects

Risk type	Possible risks
Technology	The database used in the system cannot process as many transactions per second as expected. (1) Reusable software components contain defects that mean they cannot be reused as planned. (2)
People	It is impossible to recruit staff with the skills required. (3) Key staff are ill and unavailable at critical times. (4) Required training for staff is not available. (5)
Organizational	The organization is restructured so that different management are responsible for the project. (6) Organizational financial problems force reductions in the project budget. (7)
Tools	The code generated by software code generation tools is inefficient. (8) Software tools cannot work together in an integrated way. (9)
Requirements	Changes to requirements that require major design rework are proposed. (10) Customers fail to understand the impact of requirements changes. (11)
Estimation	The time required to develop the software is underestimated. (12) The rate of defect repair is underestimated. (13) The size of the software is underestimated. (14)

Figure 22.3
Examples of different types of risks

and the problems that arose in them. It is not possible to make precise, numeric assessment of the probability and seriousness of each risk. Rather, you should assign the risk to one of a number of bands:

1. The probability of the risk might be assessed as very low ($< 10\%$), low ($10\text{--}25\%$), moderate ($25\text{--}50\%$), high ($50\text{--}75\%$), or very high ($> 75\%$).

2. The effects of the risk might be assessed as catastrophic (threaten the survival of the project), serious (would cause major delays), tolerable (delays are within allowed contingency), or insignificant.

You should then tabulate the results of this analysis process using a table ordered according to the seriousness of the risk. Figure 22.4 illustrates this for the risks that I have identified in Figure 22.3. Obviously, the assessment of probability and seriousness is arbitrary here. To make this assessment, you need detailed information about the project, the process, the development team, and the organization.

Of course, both the probability and the assessment of the effects of a risk may change as more information about the risk becomes available and as risk management plans are implemented. Therefore, you should update this table during each iteration of the risk process.

Once the risks have been analyzed and ranked, you should assess which of these risks are most significant. Your judgment must depend on a combination of the probability of the risk arising and the effects of that risk. In general, catastrophic risks should always be considered, as should all serious risks that have more than a moderate probability of occurrence.

Risk	Probability	Effects
Organizational financial problems force reductions in the project budget (7).	Low	Catastrophic
It is impossible to recruit staff with the skills required for the project (3).	High	Catastrophic
Key staff are ill at critical times in the project (4).	Moderate	Serious
Faults in reusable software components have to be repaired before these components are reused. (2).	Moderate	Serious
Changes to requirements that require major design rework are proposed (10).	Moderate	Serious
The organization is restructured so that different management are responsible for the project (6).	High	Serious
The database used in the system cannot process as many transactions per second as expected (1).	Moderate	Serious
The time required to develop the software is underestimated (12).	High	Serious
Software tools cannot be integrated (9).	High	Tolerable
Customers fail to understand the impact of requirements changes (11).	Moderate	Tolerable
Required training for staff is not available (5).	Moderate	Tolerable
The rate of defect repair is underestimated (13).	Moderate	Tolerable
The size of the software is underestimated (14).	High	Tolerable
Code generated by code generation tools is inefficient (8).	Moderate	Insignificant

Figure 22.4 Risk types and examples

Boehm (1988) recommends identifying and monitoring the top 10 risks, but I think that this figure is rather arbitrary. The right number of risks to monitor must depend on the project. It might be 5 or it might be 15. However, the number of risks chosen for monitoring should be manageable. A very large number of risks would simply require too much information to be collected. From the risks identified in Figure 22.4, it is appropriate to consider the 8 risks that have catastrophic or serious consequences (Figure 22.5).

22.1.3 Risk planning

The risk planning process considers each of the key risks that have been identified, and develops strategies to manage these risks. For each of the risks, you have to think of actions that you might take to minimize the disruption to the project if the problem identified in the risk occurs. You also should think about information that you might need to collect while monitoring the project so that problems can be anticipated.

Risk	Strategy
Organizational financial problems	Prepare a briefing document for senior management showing how the project is making a very important contribution to the goals of the business and presenting reasons why cuts to the project budget would not be cost-effective.
Recruitment problems	Alert customer to potential difficulties and the possibility of delays; investigate buying-in components.
Staff illness	Reorganize team so that there is more overlap of work and people therefore understand each other's jobs.
Defective components	Replace potentially defective components with bought-in components of known reliability.
Requirements changes	Derive traceability information to assess requirements change impact; maximize information hiding in the design.
Organizational restructuring	Prepare a briefing document for senior management showing how the project is making a very important contribution to the goals of the business.
Database performance	Investigate the possibility of buying a higher-performance database.
Underestimated development time	Investigate buying-in components; investigate use of a program generator.

Figure 22.5 Strategies to help manage risk

Again, there is no simple process that can be followed for contingency planning. It relies on the judgment and experience of the project manager.

Figure 22.5 shows possible risk management strategies that have been identified for the key risks (i.e., those that are serious or intolerable) shown in Figure 22.4. These strategies fall into three categories:

1. *Avoidance strategies* Following these strategies means that the probability that the risk will arise will be reduced. An example of a risk avoidance strategy is the strategy for dealing with defective components shown in Figure 22.5.

2. *Minimization strategies* Following these strategies means that the impact of the risk will be reduced. An example of a risk minimization strategy is the strategy for staff illness shown in Figure 22.5.

3. *Contingency plans* Following these strategies means that you are prepared for the worst and have a strategy in place to deal with it. An example of a contingency strategy is the strategy for organizational financial problems that I have shown in Figure 22.5.

You can see a clear analogy here with the strategies used in critical systems to ensure reliability, security, and safety, where you must avoid, tolerate, or recover from failures. Obviously, it is best to use a strategy that avoids the risk. If this is not possible, you should use a strategy that reduces the chances that the risk will have serious effects. Finally, you should have strategies in place to cope with the risk if it arises. These should reduce the overall impact of a risk on the project or product.

Risk type	Potential indicators
Technology	Late delivery of hardware or support software; many reported technology problems.
People	Poor staff morale; poor relationships amongst team members; high staff turnover.
Organizational	Organizational gossip; lack of action by senior management.
Tools	Reluctance by team members to use tools; complaints about CASE tools; demands for higher-powered workstations.
Requirements	Many requirements change requests; customer complaints.
Estimation	Failure to meet agreed schedule; failure to clear reported defects.

Figure 22.6 Risk indicators

22.1.4 Risk monitoring

Risk monitoring is the process of checking that your assumptions about the product, process, and business risks have not changed. You should regularly assess each of the identified risks to decide whether or not that risk is becoming more or less probable. You should also think about whether or not the effects of the risk have changed. To do this, you have to look at other factors, such as the number of requirements change requests, which give you clues about the risk probability and its effects. These factors are obviously dependent on the types of risk. Figure 22.6 gives some examples of factors that may be helpful in assessing these risk types.

You should monitor risks regularly at all stages in a project. At every management review, you should consider and discuss each of the key risks separately. You should decide if the risk is more or less likely to arise and if the seriousness and consequences of the risk have changed.

22.2 Managing people

The people working in a software organization are its greatest assets. It costs a lot to recruit and retain good people and it is up to software managers to ensure that the organization gets the best possible return on its investment. In successful companies and economies, this is achieved when people are respected by the organization and are assigned responsibilities that reflect their skills and experience.

It is important that software project managers understand the technical issues that influence the work of software development. Unfortunately, however, good software engineers are not necessarily good people managers. Software engineers often have strong technical skills but may lack the softer skills that enable them to motivate and lead a project development team. As a project manager, you should be aware of the potential problems of people management and should try to develop people management skills.

In my view, there are four critical factors in people management:

1. *Consistency* People in a project team should all be treated in a comparable way. No one expects all rewards to be identical but people should not feel that their contribution to the organization is undervalued.

2. *Respect* Different people have different skills and managers should respect these differences. All members of the team should be given an opportunity to make a contribution. In some cases, of course, you will find that people simply don't fit into a team and they cannot continue, but it is important not to jump to conclusions about this at an early stage in the project.

3. *Inclusion* People contribute effectively when they feel that others listen to them and take account of their proposals. It is important to develop a working environment where all views, even those of the most junior staff, are considered.

4. *Honesty* As a manager, you should always be honest about what is going well and what is going badly in the team. You should also be honest about your level of technical knowledge and willing to defer to staff with more knowledge when necessary. If you try to cover up ignorance or problems you will eventually be found out and will lose the respect of the group.

People management, in my view, is something that has to be based on experience, rather than learned from a book. My aim in this section and the following section on teamwork is simply to introduce some of the most important people and team management problems that affect software project management. I hope the material here will sensitize you to some of the problems that managers may encounter when dealing with teams of technically talented individuals.

22.2.1 Motivating people

As a project manager, you need to motivate the people that work with you so that they contribute to the best of their abilities. Motivation means organizing the work and the working environment to encourage people to work as effectively as possible. If people are not motivated, they will not be interested in the work they are doing. They will work slowly, be more likely to make mistakes, and will not contribute to the broader goals of the team or the organization.

To provide this encouragement, you should understand a little about what motivates people. Maslow (1954) suggests that people are motivated by satisfying their needs. These needs are arranged in a series of levels, as shown in Figure 22.7. The lower levels of this hierarchy represent fundamental needs for food, sleep, and so on, and the need to feel secure in an environment. Social needs are concerned with the need to feel part of a social grouping. Esteem needs represent the need to feel

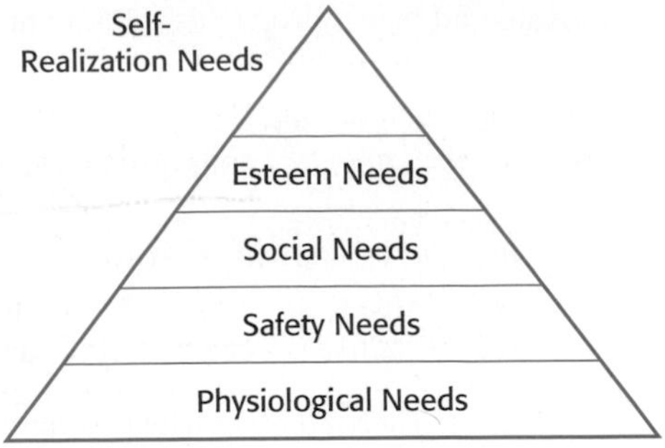

Figure 22.7 Human needs hierarchy

respected by others, and self-realization needs are concerned with personal development. People need to satisfy lower-level needs like hunger before the more abstract, higher-level needs.

People working in software development organizations are not usually hungry or thirsty or physically threatened by their environment. Therefore, making sure that people's social, esteem, and self-realization needs are satisfied is most important from a management point of view.

1. To satisfy social needs, you need to give people time to meet their co-workers and provide places for them to meet. This is relatively easy when all of the members of a development team work in the same place but, increasingly, team members are not located in the same building or even the same town or state. They may work for different organizations or from home most of the time.

   Social networking systems and teleconferencing can be used to facilitate communications but my experience with electronic systems is that they are most effective once people know each other. You therefore need to arrange some face-to-face meetings early in the project so that people can directly interact with other members of the team. Through this direct interaction, people become part of a social group and accept the goals and priorities of that group.

2. To satisfy esteem needs, you need to show people that they are valued by the organization. Public recognition of achievements is a simple yet effective way of doing this. Obviously, people must also feel that they are paid at a level that reflects their skills and experience.

3. Finally, to satisfy self-realization needs, you need to give people responsibility for their work, assign them demanding (but not impossible) tasks, and provide a training programme where people can develop their skills. Training is an important motivating influence as people like to gain new knowledge and learn new skills.

In Figure 22.8, I illustrate a problem of motivation that managers often have to face. In this example, a competent group member loses interest in the work and in

Case study: Motivation

Alice is a software project manager working in a company that develops alarm systems. This company wishes to enter the growing market of assistive technology to help elderly and disabled people live independently. Alice has been asked to lead a team of 6 developers than can develop new products based around the company's alarm technology.

Alice's assistive technology project starts well. Good working relationships develop within the team and creative new ideas are developed. The team decides to develop a peer-to-peer messaging system using digital televisions linked to the alarm network for communications. However, some months into the project, Alice notices that Dorothy, a hardware design expert, starts coming into work late, the quality of her work deteriorates and, increasingly, that she does not appear to be communicating with other members of the team.

Alice talks about the problem informally with other team members to try to find out if Dorothy's personal circumstances have changed, and if this might be affecting her work. They don't know of anything, so Alice decides to talk with Dorothy to try to understand the problem.

After some initial denials that there is a problem, Dorothy admits that she has l ost interest in the job. She expected that she would be able to develop and use her hardware interfacing skills. However, because of the product direction that has been chosen, she has little opportunity for this. Basically, she is working as a C programmer with other team members.

Although she admits that the work is challenging, she is concerned that she is not developing her interfacing skills. She is worried that finding a job that involves hardware interfacing will be difficult after this project. Because she does not want to upset the team by revealing that she is thinking about the next project, she has decided that it is best to minimize conversation with them.

Figure 22.8 Individual motivation

the group as a whole. The quality of her work falls and becomes unacceptable. This situation has to be dealt with quickly. If you don't sort out the problem, the other group members will become dissatisfied and feel that they are doing an unfair share of the work.

In this example, Alice tries to find out if Dorothy's personal circumstances could be the problem. Personal difficulties commonly affect motivation because people cannot concentrate on their work. You may have to give them time and support to resolve these issues, although you also have to make it clear that they still have a responsibility to their employer.

Dorothy's motivation problem is one that is quite common when projects develop in an unexpected direction. People who expect to do one type of work may end up doing something completely different. This becomes a problem when team members want to develop their skills in a way that is different from that taken by the project. In those circumstances, you may decide that the team member should leave the team and find opportunities elsewhere. In this example, however, Alice decides to try to convince Dorothy that broadening her experience is a positive career step. She gives Dorothy more design autonomy and organizes training courses in software engineering that will give her more opportunities after her current project has finished.

The People Capability Maturity Model

The People Capability Maturity Model (P-CMM) is a framework for assessing how well organizations manage the development of their staff. It highlights best practice in people management and provides a basis for organizations to improve their people management processes.

http://www.SoftwareEngineering-9.com/Web/Management/P-CMM.html

Maslow's model of motivation is helpful up to a point but I think that a problem with it is that it takes an exclusively personal viewpoint on motivation. It does not take adequate account of the fact that people feel themselves to be part of an organization, a professional group, and one or more cultures. This is not simply a question of satisfying social needs—people can be motivated through helping a group achieve shared goals.

Being a member of a cohesive group is highly motivating for most people. People with fulfilling jobs often like to go to work because they are motivated by the people they work with and the work that they do. Therefore, as well as thinking about individual motivation you also have to think about how a group as a whole can be motivated to achieve the organization's goals. I discuss group management issues in the next section.

Personality type also influences motivation. Bass and Dunteman (1963) classify professionals into three types:

1. Task-oriented people, who are motivated by the work they do. In software engineering, these are people who are motivated by the intellectual challenge of software development.

2. Self-oriented people, who are principally motivated by personal success and recognition. They are interested in software development as a means of achieving their own goals. This does not mean that these people are selfish and think only of their own concerns. Rather, they often have longer-term goals, such as career progression, that motivate them and they wish to be successful in their work to help realize these goals.

3. Interaction-oriented people, who are motivated by the presence and actions of co-workers. As software development becomes more user-centered, interaction-oriented individuals are becoming more involved in software engineering.

Interaction-oriented personalities usually like to work as part of a group, whereas task-oriented and self-oriented people usually prefer to act as individuals. Women are more likely to be interaction-oriented than men. They are often more effective communicators. I discuss the mix of these different personality types in groups in the case study in Figure 22.10.

Each individual's motivation is made up of elements of each class but one type of motivation is usually dominant at any one time. However, individuals can change. For example, technical people who feel they are not being properly rewarded can become self-oriented and put personal interests before technical concerns. If a group works particularly well, self-oriented people can become more interaction-oriented.

22.3 Teamwork

Most professional software is developed by project teams that range in size from two to several hundred people. However, as it is clearly impossible for everyone in a large group to work together on a single problem, large teams are usually split into a number of groups. Each group is responsible for developing part of the overall system. As a general rule, software engineering project groups should not have more than 10 members. When small groups are used, communication problems are reduced. Everyone knows everyone else and the whole group can get around a table for a meeting to discuss the project and the software that they are developing.

Putting together a group that has the right balance of technical skills, experience, and personalities is a critical management task. However, successful groups are more than simply a collection of individuals with the right balance of skills. A good group is cohesive and has a team spirit. The people involved are motivated by the success of the group as well as by their own personal goals.

In a cohesive group, members think of the group as more important than the individuals who are group members. Members of a well-led, cohesive group are loyal to the group. They identify with group goals and other group members. They attempt to protect the group, as an entity, from outside interference. This makes the group robust and able to cope with problems and unexpected situations.

The benefits of creating a cohesive group are:

1. *The group can establish its own quality standards* Because these standards are established by consensus, they are more likely to be observed than external standards imposed on the group.

2. *Individuals learn from and support each other* People in the group learn from each other. Inhibitions caused by ignorance are minimized as mutual learning is encouraged.

3. *Knowledge is shared* Continuity can be maintained if a group member leaves. Others in the group can take over critical tasks and ensure that the project is not unduly disrupted.

4. *Refactoring and continual improvement is encouraged* Group members work collectively to deliver high-quality results and fix problems, irrespective of the individuals who originally created the design or program.

Case study: Team spirit

Alice, an experienced project manager, understands the importance of creating a cohesive group. As they are developing a new product, she takes the opportunity of involving all group members in the product specification and design by getting them to discuss possible technology with elderly members of their families. She also encourages them to bring these family members to meet other members of the development group.

Alice also arranges monthly lunches for everyone in the group. These lunches are an opportunity for all team members to meet informally, talk around issues of concern, and get to know each other. At the lunch, Alice tells the group what she knows about organizational news, policies, strategies, and so forth. Each team member then briefly summarizes what they have been doing and the group discusses a general topic, such as new product ideas from elderly relatives.

Every few months, Alice organizes an 'away day' for the group where the team spends two days on 'technology updating'. Each team member prepares an update on a relevant technology and presents it to the group. This is an off-site meeting in a good hotel and plenty of time is scheduled for discussion and social interaction.

Figure 22.9 Group cohesion

Good project managers should always try to encourage group cohesiveness. They may organize social events for group members and their families, try to establish a sense of group identity by naming the group and establishing a group identity and territory, or they may get involved in explicit group-building activities such as sports and games.

One of the most effective ways of promoting cohesion is to be inclusive. This means that you should treat group members as responsible and trustworthy, and make information freely available. Sometimes, managers feel that they cannot reveal certain information to everyone in the group. This invariably creates a climate of mistrust. Simple information exchange is an effective way of making people feel valued and that they are part of a group.

You can see an example of this in the case study in Figure 22.9. Alice arranges regular informal meetings where she tells the other group members what is going on. She makes a point of involving people in the product development by asking them to come up with new ideas derived from their own family experiences. The 'away days' are also good ways of promoting cohesion—people relax together while they help each other learn about new technologies.

Whether or not a group is effective depends, to some extent, on the nature of the project and the organization doing the work. If an organization is in a state of turmoil with constant reorganizations and job insecurity, it is very difficult for team members to focus on software development. However, apart from project and organizational issues, there are three generic factors that affect team working:

1. *The people in the group* You need a mix of people in a project group as software development involves diverse activities such as negotiating with clients, programming, testing, and documentation.

2. *The group organization* A group should be organized so that individuals can contribute to the best of their abilities and tasks can be completed as expected.

3. *Technical and managerial communications* Good communications between group members, and between the software engineering team and other project stakeholders, is essential.

As with all management issues, getting the right team cannot guarantee project success. Too many other things can go wrong, including changes to the business and the business environment. However, if you don't pay attention to group composition, organization, and communications, you increase the likelihood that your project will run into difficulties.

22.3.1 Selecting group members

A manager or team leader's job is to create a cohesive group and organize their group so that they can work together effectively. This involves creating a group with the right balance of technical skills and personalities, and organizing that group so that the members work together effectively. Sometimes, people are hired from outside the organization; more often, however, software engineering groups are put together from current employees who have experience on other projects. However, managers rarely have a completely free hand in team selection. They often have to use the people who are available in the company, even when they may not be the ideal people for the job.

As I discussed in Section 22.2.1, many software engineers are motivated primarily by their work. Software development groups, therefore, are often composed of people who have their own ideas about how technical problems should be solved. This is reflected in regularly reported problems of interface standards being ignored, systems being redesigned as they are coded, unnecessary system embellishments, and so on.

A group that has complementary personalities may work better than a group that is selected solely on technical ability. People who are motivated by the work are likely to be the strongest technically. People who are self-oriented will probably be best at pushing the work forward to finish the job. People who are interaction-oriented help facilitate communications within the group. I think that it is particularly important to have interaction-oriented people in a group. They like to talk to people and can detect tensions and disagreements at an early stage, before these have a serious impact on the group.

In the case study in Figure 22.10, I have suggested how Alice, the project manager, has tried to create a group with complementary personalities. This particular group has a good mix of interaction- and task-oriented people but I have already discussed, in Figure 22.8, how Dorothy's self-oriented personality has caused problems because she has not been doing the work that she expected. Fred's part-time role in the group as a domain expert might also be a problem. He is mostly interested in

Case study: Group composition

In creating a group for assistive technology development, Alice is aware of the importance of selecting members with complementary personalities. When interviewing potential group members, she tried to assess whether they were task-oriented, self-oriented, or interaction-oriented. She felt that she was primarily a self-oriented type because she considered the project to be a way of getting noticed by senior management and possibly promoted. She therefore looked for one or perhaps two interaction-oriented personalities, with task-oriented individuals to complete the team. The final assessment that she arrived at was:

Alice—self-oriented
Brian—task-oriented
Bob—task-oriented
Carol—interaction-oriented
Dorothy—self-oriented
Ed—interaction-oriented
Fred—task-oriented

Figure 22.10 Group composition

technical challenges, so he may not interact well with other group members. The fact that he is not always part of the team means that he may not relate well to the team's goals.

It is sometimes impossible to choose a group with complementary personalities. If this is the case, the project manager has to control the group so that individual goals do not take precedence over organizational and group objectives. This control is easier to achieve if all group members participate in each stage of the project. Individual initiative is most likely when group members are given instructions without being aware of the part that their task plays in the overall project.

For example, say a software engineer is given a program design for coding and notices what appears to be possible improvements that could be made to the design. If he or she implements these improvements without understanding the rationale for the original design, any changes, though well intentioned, might have adverse implications for other parts of the system. If all the members of the group are involved in the design from the start, they will understand why design decisions have been made. They may then identify with these decisions rather than oppose them.

22.3.2 Group organization

The way that a group is organized affects the decisions that are made by that group, the ways that information is exchanged, and the interactions between the development group and external project stakeholders. Important organizational questions for project managers include:

1. Should the project manager be the technical leader of the group? The technical leader or system architect is responsible for the critical technical decisions made

Hiring the right people

Project managers are often responsible for selecting the people in the organization who will join their software engineering team. Getting the best possible people in this process is very important as poor selection decisions may be a serious risk to the project.

Key factors that should influence the selection of staff are education and training, application domain and technology experience, communication ability, adaptability, and problem-solving ability.

http://www.SoftwareEngineering-9.com/Web/Management/Selection.html

during software development. Sometimes, the project manager has the skill and experience to take on this role. However, for large projects, it is best to appoint a senior engineer to be the project architect, who will take responsibility for technical leadership.

2. Who will be involved in making critical technical decisions, and how will these be made? Will decisions be made by the system architect, the project manager, or by reaching consensus amongst a wider range of team members?

3. How will interactions with external stakeholders and senior company management be handled? In many cases, the project manager will be responsible for these interactions, assisted by the system architect if there is one. However, an alternative organizational model is to create a dedicated role concerned with external liaison, and appoint someone with appropriate interaction skills to that role.

4. How can groups integrate people who are not colocated? It is now common for groups to include members from different organizations and people to work from home as well as in a shared office. This has to be taken into account in group decision-making processes.

5. How can knowledge be shared across the group? Group organization affects information sharing as certain methods of organization are better for sharing than others. However, you should avoid too much information sharing as people become overloaded and excessive information distracts them from their work.

Small programming groups are usually organized in a fairly informal way. The group leader gets involved in the software development with the other group members. In an informal group, the work to be carried out is discussed by the group as a whole, and tasks are allocated according to ability and experience. More senior group members may be responsible for the architectural design. However, detailed design and implementation is the responsibility of the team member who is allocated to a particular task.

Extreme programming groups (Beck, 2000) are always informal groups. XP enthusiasts claim that formal structure inhibits information exchange. In XP, many decisions that are usually seen as management decisions (such as decisions on schedule) are devolved to group members. Programmers work together in pairs to develop code and take joint responsibility for the programs that are developed.

Informal groups can be very successful, particularly when most group members are experienced and competent. Such a group makes decisions by consensus, which improves cohesiveness and performance. However, if a group is composed mostly of inexperienced or incompetent members, informality can be a hindrance because no definite authority exists to direct the work, causing a lack of coordination between group members and, possibly, eventual project failure.

Hierarchical groups are groups that have a hierarchical structure with the group leader at the top of the hierarchy. He or she has more formal authority than the group members and so can direct their work. There is a clear organizational structure and decisions are made towards the top of the hierarchy and implemented by people lower down the hierarchy. Communications are primarily instructions from senior staff and there is relatively little 'upward' communication from the lower levels to the upper levels in the hierarchy.

This approach can work well when a well-understood problem can be easily broken into subproblems with subproblem solutions developed in different parts of the hierarchy. In those situations, relatively little communication across the hierarchy is required. However, such situations are relatively rare in software engineering for the following reasons:

1. Changes to the software often require changes to several parts of the system and this requires discussion and negotiation at all levels in the hierarchy.

2. Software technologies change so fast that more junior staff often know more about the technology than experienced staff. Top-down communications may mean that the project manager does not find out about the opportunities of using new technologies. More junior staff may become frustrated because of what they see as old-fashioned technologies being used for development.

Democratic and hierarchic group organizations do not formally recognize that there may be very large differences in technical ability between group members. The best programmers may be up to 25 times more productive as the worst programmers. It makes sense to use the best people in the most effective way and to provide them with as much support as possible. An early organizational model that was intended to provide this support was the chief programmer team.

To make the most effective use of highly skilled programmers, Baker (1972) and others (Aron, 1974; Brooks, 1975) suggested that teams should be built around an individual, highly skilled chief programmer. The underlying principle of the chief programmer team is that skilled and experienced staff should be responsible for all software development. They should not be concerned with routine matters and should have good technical and administrative support for their work. They should focus on the software to be developed and not spend a lot of time in external meetings.

The physical work environment

The environment in which people work affects both group communications and individual productivity. Individual workspaces are better for concentration on detailed technical work as people are less likely to be distracted by interruptions. However, shared workspaces are better for communications. A well-designed work environment takes both of these needs into account.

http://www.SoftwareEngineering-9.com/Web/Management/workspace.html

However, the chief programmer team organization is, in my view, overdependent on the chief programmer and their assistant. Other team members who are not given sufficient responsibility may become demotivated because they feel their skills are underused. They do not have the information to cope if things go wrong and are not given the opportunity to participate in decision making. There are significant project risks associated with this group organization and these may outweigh any benefits that this kind of organization might bring.

22.3.3 Group communications

It is absolutely essential that group members communicate effectively and efficiently with each other and with other project stakeholders. Group members must exchange information on the status of their work, the design decisions that have been made, and changes to previous design decisions. They have to resolve problems that arise with other stakeholders and inform these stakeholders of changes to the system, the group, and delivery plans. Good communication also helps strengthen group cohesiveness. Group members come to understand the motivations, strengths, and weaknesses of other people in the group.

The effectiveness and efficiency of communications is influenced by:

1. *Group size* As a group gets bigger, it gets harder for members to communicate effectively. The number of one-way communication links is $n * (n - 1)$, where n is the group size, so, with a group of eight members, there are 56 possible communication pathways. This means that it is quite possible that some people will rarely communicate with each other. Status differences between group members mean that communications are often one-way. Managers and experienced engineers tend to dominate communications with less experienced staff, who may be reluctant to start a conversation or make critical remarks.

2. *Group structure* People in informally structured groups communicate more effectively than people in groups with a formal, hierarchical structure. In hierarchical groups, communications tend to flow up and down the hierarchy. People at the same level may not talk to each other. This is a particular problem in a

large project with several development groups. If people working on different subsystems only communicate through their managers, then there are more likely to be delays and misunderstandings.

3. *Group composition* People with the same personality types (discussed in Section 22.2) may clash and, as a result, communications can be inhibited. Communication is also usually better in mixed-sex groups (Marshall and Heslin, 1975) than in single-sex groups. Women are often more interaction-oriented than men and may act as interaction controllers and facilitators for the group.

4. *The physical work environment* The organization of the workplace is a major factor in facilitating or inhibiting communications. See the book's webpage for more information.

5. *The available communication channels* There are many different forms of communication—face-to-face, e-mail messages, formal documents, telephone, and Web 2.0 technologies such as social networking and wikis. As project teams become increasingly distributed, with team members working remotely, you need to make use of a range of technologies to facilitate communications.

Project managers usually work to tight deadlines and, consequently, they may try to use communication channels that don't take up too much of their time. They may therefore rely on meetings and formal documents to pass on information to project staff and stakeholders. Although this may be an efficient approach to communication from a project manager's perspective, it is not usually very effective. There are often good reasons why people can't attend meetings and so they don't hear the presentation. Long documents are often never read because readers don't know if the documents are relevant. When several versions of the same document are produced, readers find it difficult to keep track of the changes.

Effective communication is achieved when communications are two way, and the people involved can discuss issues and information and establish a common understanding of proposals and problems. This can be done through meetings, although these are often dominated by powerful personalities. It is sometimes impractical to arrange meetings at short notice. More and more project teams include remote members, which also makes meetings more difficult.

To counter these problems, you may make use of web technologies such as wikis and blogs to support information exchange. Wikis support the collaborative creation and editing of documents, and blogs support threaded discussions about questions and comments made by group members. Wikis and blogs allow project members and external stakeholders to exchange information, irrespective of their location. They help manage information and keep track of discussion threads, which often become confusing when conducted by e-mail. You can also use instant messaging and teleconferences, which can be easily arranged, to resolve issues that need discussion.

KEY POINTS

■ Good software project management is essential if software engineering projects are to be developed on schedule and within budget.

■ Software management is distinct from other engineering management. Software is intangible. Projects may be novel or innovative so there is no body of experience to guide their management. Software processes are not as mature as traditional engineering processes.

■ Risk management is now recognized as one of the most important project management tasks.

■ Risk management involves identifying and assessing major project risks to establish the probability that they will occur and the consequences for the project if that risk does arise. You should make plans to avoid, manage, or deal with likely risks if or when they arise.

■ People are motivated by interaction with other people, the recognition of management and their peers, and by being given opportunities for personal development.

■ Software development groups should be fairly small and cohesive. The key factors that influence the effectiveness of a group are the people in that group, the way that it is organized, and the communication between group members.

■ Communications within a group are influenced by factors such as the status of group members, the size of the group, the gender composition of the group, personalities, and available communication channels.

FURTHER READING

The Mythical Man Month (Anniversary Edition). The problems of software management remain largely unchanged since the 1960s and this is one of the best books on the topic. An interesting and readable account of the management of one of the first very large software projects, the IBM OS/360 operating system. The anniversary edition (published 20 years after the original edition in 1975) includes other classic papers by Brooks. (F. P. Brooks, 1995, Addison-Wesley.)

Software Project Survival Guide. This is a very pragmatic account of software management that contains good practical advice for project managers with a software engineering background. It is easy to read and understand. (S. McConnell, 1998, Microsoft Press.)

Peopleware: Productive Projects and Teams, 2nd edition. This is a new edition of the classic book on the importance of treating people properly when managing software projects. It is one of the few books that recognizes the importance of the place where people work. Strongly recommended. (T. DeMarco and T. Lister, 1999, Dorset House.)

Waltzing with Bears: Managing Risk on Software Projects. A very practical and easy-to-read introduction to risks and risk management. (T. DeMarco and T. Lister, 2003, Dorset House.)

EXERCISES

22.1. Explain why the intangibility of software systems poses special problems for software project management.

22.2. Explain why the best programmers do not always make the best software managers. You may find it helpful to base your answer on the list of management activities in Section 22.1.

22.3. Using reported instances of project problems in the literature, list management difficulties and errors that occurred in these failed programming projects. (I suggest that you start with *The Mythical Man Month*, by Fred Brooks)

22.4. In addition to the risks shown in Figure 22.1, identify at least six other possible risks that could arise in software projects.

22.5. Fixed-price contracts, where the contractor bids a fixed price to complete a system development, may be used to move project risk from client to contractor. If anything goes wrong, the contractor has to pay. Suggest how the use of such contracts may increase the likelihood that product risks will arise.

22.6. Explain why keeping all members of a group informed about progress and technical decisions in a project can improve group cohesiveness.

22.7. What problems do you think might arise in extreme programming teams where many management decisions are devolved to the team members?

22.8. Write a case study in the style used here to illustrate the importance of communications in a project team. Assume that some team members work remotely and it is not possible to get the whole team together at short notice.

22.9. You are asked by your manager to deliver software to a schedule that you know can only be met by asking your project team to work unpaid overtime. All team members have young children. Discuss whether you should accept this demand from your manager or whether you should persuade your team to give their time to the organization rather than to their families. What factors might be significant in your decision?

22.10. As a programmer, you are offered promotion to a project management position but you feel that you can make a more effective contribution in a technical rather than a managerial role. Discuss whether you should accept the promotion.

REFERENCES

Aron, J. D. (1974). *The Program Development Process*. Reading, Mass.: Addison-Wesley.

Baker, F. T. (1972). 'Chief Programmer Team Management of Production Programming'. *IBM Systems J.*, 11 (1), 56–73.

Bass, B. M. and Dunteman, G. (1963). 'Behaviour in groups as a function of self, interaction and task orientation'. *J. Abnorm. Soc. Psychology.,* **66** (4), 19–28.

Beck, K. (2000). *extreme Programming Explained*. Reading, Mass.: Addison-Wesley.

Boehm, B. W. (1988). 'A Spiral Model of Software Development and Enhancement'. *IEEE Computer,* **21** (5), 61–72.

Brooks, F. P. (1975). *The Mythical Man Month*. Reading, Mass.: Addison-Wesley.

Hall, E. (1998). *Managing Risk: Methods for Software Systems Development*. Reading, Mass.: Addison-Wesley.

Marshall, J. E. and Heslin, R. (1975). 'Boys and Girls Together. Sexual composition and the effect of density on group size and cohesiveness'. *J. of Personality and Social Psychology,* **35** (5), 952–61.

Maslow, A. A. (1954). *Motivation and Personality*. New York: Harper and Row.

Ould, M. (1999). *Managing Software Quality and Business Risk*. Chichester: John Wiley & Sons.

23

Project planning

Objectives

The objective of this chapter is to introduce project planning, scheduling, and cost estimation. When you have read the chapter, you will:

■ understand the fundamentals of software costing and reasons why the price of the software may not be directly related to its development cost;

■ know what sections should be included in a project plan that is created within a plan-driven development process;

■ understand what is involved in project scheduling and the use of bar charts to present a project schedule;

■ have been introduced to the 'planning game', which is used to support project planning in extreme programming;

■ understand how the COCOMO II model can be used for algorithmic cost estimation.

Contents

Project planning is one of the most important jobs of a software project manager. As a manager, you have to break down the work into parts and assign these to project team members, anticipate problems that might arise, and prepare tentative solutions to those problems. The project plan, which is created at the start of a project, is used to communicate how the work will be done to the project team and customers, and to help assess progress on the project.

Project planning takes place at three stages in a project life cycle:

1. At the proposal stage, when you are bidding for a contract to develop or provide a software system. You need a plan at this stage to help you decide if you have the resources to complete the work and to work out the price that you should quote to a customer.

2. During the project startup phase, when you have to plan who will work on the project, how the project will be broken down into increments, how resources will be allocated across your company, etc. Here, you have more information than at the proposal stage, and can therefore refine the initial effort estimates that you have prepared.

3. Periodically throughout the project, when you modify your plan in light of experience gained and information from monitoring the progress of the work. You learn more about the system being implemented and capabilities of your development team. This information allows you to make more accurate estimates of how long the work will take. Furthermore, the software requirements are likely to change and this usually means that the work breakdown has to be altered and the schedule extended. For traditional development projects, this means that the plan created during the startup phase has to be modified. However, when an agile approach is used, plans are shorter term and continually change as the software evolves. I discuss agile planning in Section 23.4.

Planning at the proposal stage is inevitably speculative, as you do not usually have a complete set of requirements for the software to be developed. Rather, you have to respond to a call for proposals based on a high-level description of the software functionality that is required. A plan is often a required part of a proposal, so you have to produce a credible plan for carrying out the work. If you win the contract, you then usually have to replan the project, taking into account changes since the proposal was made.

When you are bidding for a contract, you have to work out the price that you will propose to the customer for developing the software. As a starting point for calculating this price, you need to draw up an estimate of your costs for completing the project work. Estimation involves working out how much effort is required to complete each activity and, from this, calculating the total cost of activities. You should always calculate software costs objectively, with the aim of accurately predicting the cost of developing the software. Once you have a reasonable estimate of the likely costs, you are then in a position to calculate the price that you will quote to

Overhead costs

When you estimate the costs of effort on a software project, you don't simply multiply the salaries of the people involved by the time spent on the project. You have to take into account all of the organizational overheads (office space, administration, etc.) that must be covered by the income from a project. You calculate the costs by computing these overheads and adding a proportion to the costs of each engineer working on a project.

http://www.SoftwareEngineering-9.com/Web/Planning/overheadcosts.html

the customer. As I discuss in the next section, many factors influence the pricing of a software project—it is not simply cost + profit.

There are three main parameters that you should use when computing the costs of a software development project:

- effort costs (the costs of paying software engineers and managers);

- hardware and software costs, including maintenance;

- travel and training costs.

For most projects, the biggest cost is the effort cost. You have to estimate the total effort (in person-months) that is likely to be required to complete the work of a project. Obviously, you have limited information to make such an estimate, so you have to make the best possible estimate and then add significant contingency (extra time and effort) in case your initial estimate is optimistic.

For commercial systems, you normally use commodity hardware, which is relatively cheap. However, software costs can be significant if you have to license middleware and platform software. Extensive travel may be needed when a project is developed at different sites. Although travel costs themselves are usually a small fraction of the effort costs, the time spent traveling is often wasted and adds significantly to the effort costs of the project. Electronic meeting systems and other software that supports remote collaboration can reduce the amount of travel required. The time saved can be devoted to more productive project work.

Once a contract to develop a system has been awarded, the outline project plan for the project has to be refined to create a project startup plan. At this stage, you should know more about the requirements for this system. However, you may not have a complete requirements specification, especially if you are using an agile approach to development. Your aim at this stage should be to create a project plan that can be used to support decision making about project staffing and budgeting. You use the plan as a basis for allocating resources to the project from within the organization and to help decide if you need to hire new staff.

The plan should also define project monitoring mechanisms. You must keep track of the progress of the project and compare actual and planned progress and costs. Although most organizations have formal procedures for monitoring, a good manager should be able to form a clear picture of what is going on through informal discussions with project staff. Informal monitoring can predict potential project problems by revealing difficulties as they occur. For example, daily discussions with project staff might reveal a particular problem in finding a software fault. Rather than waiting for a schedule slippage to be reported, the project manager could then immediately assign an expert to the problem, or decide to program around it.

The project plan always evolves during the development process. Development planning is intended to ensure that the project plan remains a useful document for staff to understand what is to be achieved and when it is to be delivered. Therefore, the schedule, cost estimate, and risks all have to be revised as the software is developed.

If an agile method is used, there is still a need for a project startup plan, as regardless of the approach used, the company still needs to plan how resources will be allocated to a project. However, this is not a detailed plan and should include only limited information about the work breakdown and project schedule. During development, an informal project plan and effort estimates are drawn up for each release of the software, with the whole team involved in the planning process.

23.1 Software pricing

In principle, the price of a software product to a customer is simply the cost of development plus profit for the developer. In practice, however, the relationship between the project cost and the price quoted to the customer is not usually so simple. When calculating a price, you should take broader organizational, economic, political, and business considerations into account, such as those shown in Figure 23.1. You need to think about organizational concerns, the risks associated with the project, and the type of contract that will be used. These may cause the price to be adjusted upwards or downwards. Because of the organizational considerations involved, deciding on a project price should be a group activity involving marketing and sales staff, senior management, and project managers.

To illustrate some of the project pricing issues, consider the following scenario:

A small software company, PharmaSoft, employs 10 software engineers. It has just finished a large project but only has contracts in place that require five development staff. However, it is bidding for a very large contract with a major pharmaceutical company that requires 30 person-years of effort over two years. The project will not start for at least 12 months but, if granted, it will transform the finances of the company.

PharmaSoft gets an opportunity to bid on a project that requires six people and has to be completed in 10 months. The costs (including overheads of this project) are estimated at $1.2 million. However, to improve its competitive position, PharmaSoft decides to bid a price to the customer of $0.8 million.

Factor	Description
Market opportunity	A development organization may quote a low price because it wishes to move into a new segment of the software market. Accepting a low profit on one project may give the organization the opportunity to make a greater profit later. The experience gained may also help it develop new products.
Cost estimate uncertainty	If an organization is unsure of its cost estimate, it may increase its price by a contingency over and above its normal profit.
Contractual terms	A customer may be willing to allow the developer to retain ownership of the source code and reuse it in other projects. The price charged may then be less than if the software source code is handed over to the customer.
Requirements volatility	If the requirements are likely to change, an organization may lower its price to win a contract. After the contract is awarded, high prices can be charged for changes to the requirements.
Financial health	Developers in financial difficulty may lower their price to gain a contract. It is better to make a smaller than normal profit or break even than to go out of business. Cash flow is more important than profit in difficult economic times.

Figure 23.1 Factors affecting software pricing

This means that, although it loses money on this contract, it can retain specialist staff for the more profitable future projects that are likely to come on stream in a year's time.

As the cost of a project is only loosely related to the price quoted to a customer, 'pricing to win' is a commonly used strategy. Pricing to win means that a company has some idea of the price that the customer expects to pay and makes a bid for the contract based on the customer's expected price. This may seem unethical and unbusinesslike, but it does have advantages for both the customer and the system provider.

A project cost is agreed on the basis of an outline proposal. Negotiations then take place between client and customer to establish the detailed project specification. This specification is constrained by the agreed cost. The buyer and seller must agree on what is acceptable system functionality. The fixed factor in many projects is not the project requirements but the cost. The requirements may be changed so that the cost is not exceeded.

For example, say a company (OilSoft) is bidding for a contract to develop a fuel delivery system for an oil company that schedules deliveries of fuel to its service stations. There is no detailed requirements document for this system, so OilSoft estimates that a price of $900,000 is likely to be competitive and within the oil company's budget. After they are granted the contract, OilSoft then negotiates the detailed requirements of the system so that basic functionality is delivered. They then estimate the additional costs for other requirements. The oil company does not necessarily lose here because it has awarded the contract to a company that it can trust. The additional requirements may be funded from a future budget, so that the oil company's budgeting is not disrupted by a high initial software cost.

23.2 Plan-driven development

Plan-driven or plan-based development is an approach to software engineering where the development process is planned in detail. A project plan is created that records the work to be done, who will do it, the development schedule, and the work products. Managers use the plan to support project decision making and as a way of measuring progress. Plan-driven development is based on engineering project management techniques and can be thought of as the 'traditional' way of managing large software development projects. This contrasts with agile development, where many decisions affecting the development are delayed and made later, as required, during the development process.

The principal argument against plan-driven development is that many early decisions have to be revised because of changes to the environment in which the software is to be developed and used. Delaying such decisions is sensible because it avoids unnecessary rework. The arguments in favor of a plan-driven approach are that early planning allows organizational issues (availability of staff, other projects, etc.) to be closely taken into account, and that potential problems and dependencies are discovered before the project starts, rather than once the project is under way.

In my view, the best approach to project planning involves a judicious mixture of plan-based and agile development. The balance depends on the type of project and skills of the people who are available. At one extreme, large security and safety-critical systems require extensive up-front analysis and may have to be certified before they are put into use. These should be mostly plan-driven. At the other extreme, small to medium-size information systems, to be used in a rapidly changing competitive environment, should be mostly agile. Where several companies are involved in a development project, a plan-driven approach is normally used to coordinate the work across each development site.

23.2.1 Project plans

In a plan-driven development project, a project plan sets out the resources available to the project, the work breakdown, and a schedule for carrying out the work. The plan should identify risks to the project and the software under development, and the approach that is taken to risk management. Although the specific details of project plans vary depending on the type of project and organization, plans normally include the following sections:

1. *Introduction* This briefly describes the objectives of the project and sets out the constraints (e.g., budget, time, etc.) that affect the management of the project.

Plan	Description
Quality plan	Describes the quality procedures and standards that will be used in a project.
Validation plan	Describes the approach, resources, and schedule used for system validation.
Configuration management plan	Describes the configuration management procedures and structures to be used.
Maintenance plan	Predicts the maintenance requirements, costs, and effort.
Staff development plan	Describes how the skills and experience of the project team members will be developed.

Figure 23.2 Project plan supplements

2. *Project organization* This describes the way in which the development team is organized, the people involved, and their roles in the team.

3. *Risk analysis* This describes possible project risks, the likelihood of these risks arising, and the risk reduction strategies that are proposed. I have covered risk management in Chapter 22.

4. *Hardware and software resource requirements* This specifies the hardware and support software required to carry out the development. If hardware has to be bought, estimates of the prices and the delivery schedule may be included.

5. *Work breakdown* This sets out the breakdown of the project into activities and identifies the milestones and deliverables associated with each activity. Milestones are key stages in the project where progress can be assessed; deliverables are work products that are delivered to the customer.

6. *Project schedule* This shows the dependencies between activities, the estimated time required to reach each milestone, and the allocation of people to activities. The ways in which the schedule may be presented are discussed in the next section of the chapter.

7. *Monitoring and reporting mechanisms* This defines the management reports that should be produced, when these should be produced, and the project monitoring mechanisms to be used.

As well as the principal project plan, which should focus on the risks to the projects and the project schedule, you may develop a number of supplementary plans to support other process activities such as testing and configuration management. Examples of possible supplementary plans are shown in Figure 23.2.

23.2.2 The planning process

Project planning is an iterative process that starts when you create an initial project plan during the project startup phase. Figure 23.3 is a UML activity diagram that

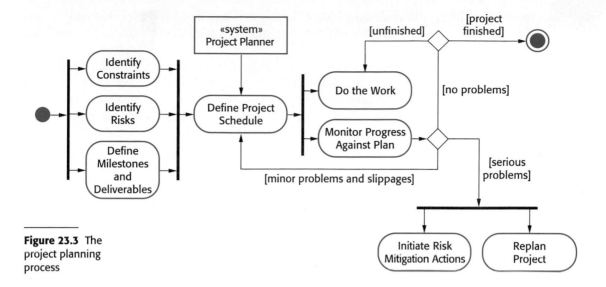

Figure 23.3 The project planning process

shows a typical workflow for a project planning process. Plan changes are inevitable. As more information about the system and the project team becomes available during the project, you should regularly revise the plan to reflect requirements, schedule, and risk changes. Changing business goals also leads to changes in project plans. As business goals change, this could affect all projects, which may then have to be replanned.

At the beginning of a planning process, you should assess the constraints affecting the project. These constraints are the required delivery date, staff available, overall budget, available tools, and so on. In conjunction with this, you should also identify the project milestones and deliverables. Milestones are points in the schedule against which you can assess progress, for example, the handover of the system for testing. Deliverables are work products that are delivered to the customer (e.g., a requirements document for the system).

The process then enters a loop. You draw up an estimated schedule for the project and the activities defined in the schedule are initiated or given permission to continue. After some time (usually about two to three weeks), you should review progress and note discrepancies from the planned schedule. Because initial estimates of project parameters are inevitably approximate, minor slippages are normal and you will have to make modifications to the original plan.

It is important to be realistic when you are creating a project plan. Problems of some description nearly always arise during a project, and these can lead to project delays. Your initial assumptions and scheduling should therefore be pessimistic rather than optimistic. There should be sufficient contingency built into your plan so that the project constraints and milestones don't need to be renegotiated every time you go around the planning loop.

If there are serious problems with the development work that are likely to lead to significant delays, you need to initiate risk mitigation actions to reduce the risks of project failure. In conjunction with these actions, you also have to replan the project.

This may involve renegotiating the project constraints and deliverables with the customer. A new schedule of when work should be completed also has to be established and agreed with the customer.

If this renegotiation is unsuccessful or the risk mitigation actions are ineffective, then you should arrange for a formal project technical review. The objectives of this review are to find an alternative approach that will allow the project to continue, and to check whether the project and the goals of the customer and software developer are still aligned.

The outcome of a review may be a decision to cancel a project. This may be a result of technical or managerial failings but, more often, is a consequence of external changes that affect the project. The development time for a large software project is often several years. During that time, the business objectives and priorities inevitably change. These changes may mean that the software is no longer required or that the original project requirements are inappropriate. Management may then decide to stop software development or to make major changes to the project to reflect the changes in the organizational objectives.

23.3 Project scheduling

Project scheduling is the process of deciding how the work in a project will be organized as separate tasks, and when and how these tasks will be executed. You estimate the calendar time needed to complete each task, the effort required, and who will work on the tasks that have been identified. You also have to estimate the resources needed to complete each task, such as the disk space required on a server, the time required on specialized hardware, such as a simulator, and what the travel budget will be. In terms of the planning stages that I discussed in the introduction of this chapter, an initial project schedule is usually created during the project startup phase. This schedule is then refined and modified during development planning.

Both plan-based and agile processes need an initial project schedule, although the level of detail may be less in an agile project plan. This initial schedule is used to plan how people will be allocated to projects and to check the progress of the project against its contractual commitments. In traditional development processes, the complete schedule is initially developed and then modified as the project progresses. In agile processes, there has to be an overall schedule that identifies when the major phases of the project will be completed. An iterative approach to scheduling is then used to plan each phase.

Scheduling in plan-driven projects (Figure 23.4) involves breaking down the total work involved in a project into separate tasks and estimating the time required to complete each task. Tasks should normally last at least a week, and no longer than 2 months. Finer subdivision means that a disproportionate amount of time must be spent on replanning and updating the project plan. The maximum amount of time for

Activity charts

An activity chart is a project schedule representation that shows which tasks can be carried out in parallel and those that must be executed in sequence, due to their dependencies on earlier activities. If a task is dependent on several other tasks then all of these must finish before it can start. The 'critical path' through the activity chart is the longest sequence of dependent tasks. This defines the project duration.

http://www.SoftwareEngineering-9.com/Web/Planning/activities.html

any task should be around 8 to 10 weeks. If it takes longer than this, the task should be subdivided for project planning and scheduling.

Some of these tasks are carried out in parallel, with different people working on different components of the system. You have to coordinate these parallel tasks and organize the work so that the workforce is used optimally and you don't introduce unnecessary dependencies between the tasks. It is important to avoid a situation where the whole project is delayed because a critical task is unfinished.

If a project is technically advanced, initial estimates will almost certainly be optimistic even when you try to consider all eventualities. In this respect, software scheduling is no different from scheduling any other type of large advanced project. New aircraft, bridges, and even new models of cars are frequently late because of unanticipated problems. Schedules, therefore, must be continually updated as better progress information becomes available. If the project being scheduled is similar to a previous project, previous estimates may be reused. However, projects may use different design methods and implementation languages, so experience from previous projects may not be applicable in the planning of a new project.

As I have already suggested, when you are estimating schedules, you must take into account the possibility that things will go wrong. People working on a project may fall ill or leave, hardware may fail, and essential support software or hardware may be delivered late. If the project is new and technically advanced, parts of it may turn out to be more difficult and take longer than originally anticipated.

A good rule of thumb is to estimate as if nothing will go wrong, then increase your estimate to cover anticipated problems. A further contingency factor to cover unanticipated problems may also be added to the estimate. This extra contingency factor depends on the type of project, the process parameters (deadline, standards, etc.), and the quality and experience of the software engineers working on the project. Contingency estimates may add 30% to 50% to the effort and time required for the project.

23.3.1 Schedule representation

Project schedules may simply be represented in a table or spreadsheet showing the tasks, effort, expected duration, and task dependencies (Figure 23.5). However, this style of representation makes it difficult to see the relationships and dependencies

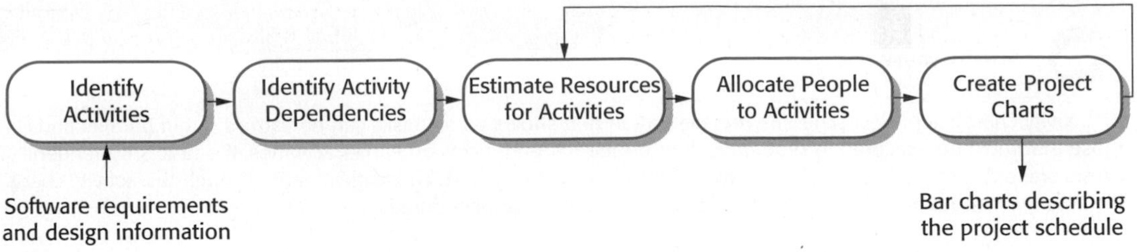

Identify Activities → Identify Activity Dependencies → Estimate Resources for Activities → Allocate People to Activities → Create Project Charts

Software requirements and design information

Bar charts describing the project schedule

Figure 23.4 The
project scheduling
process

between the different activities. For this reason, alternative graphical representations of project schedules have been developed that are often easier to read and understand. There are two types of representation that are commonly used:

1. Bar charts, which are calendar-based, show who is responsible for each activity, the expected elapsed time, and when the activity is scheduled to begin and end. Bar charts are sometimes called 'Gantt charts', after their inventor, Henry Gantt.

2. Activity networks, which are network diagrams, show the dependencies between the different activities making up a project.

Normally, a project planning tool is used to manage project schedule information. These tools usually expect you to input project information into a table and will then create a database of project information. Bar charts and activity charts can then be generated automatically from this database.

Project activities are the basic planning element. Each activity has:

1. A duration in calendar days or months.

2. An effort estimate, which reflects the number of person-days or person-months to complete the work.

3. A deadline by which the activity should be completed.

4. A defined endpoint. This represents the tangible result of completing the activity. This could be a document, the holding of a review meeting, the successful execution of all tests, etc.

When planning a project, you should also define milestones; that is, each stage in the project where a progress assessment can be made. Each milestone should be documented by a short report that summarizes the progress made and the work done. Milestones may be associated with a single task or with groups of related activities. For example, in Figure 23.5, milestone M1 is associated with task T1 and milestone M3 is associated with a pair of tasks, T2 and T4.

A special kind of milestone is the production of a project deliverable. A deliverable is a work product that is delivered to the customer. It is the outcome of a significant project phase such as specification or design. Usually, the deliverables that are

Task	Effort (person-days)	Duration (days)	Dependencies
T1	15	10	
T2	8	15	
T3	20	15	T1 (M1)
T4	5	10	
T5	5	10	T2, T4 (M3)
T6	10	5	T1, T2 (M4)
T7	25	20	T1 (M1)
T8	75	25	T4 (M2)
T9	10	15	T3, T6 (M5)
T10	20	15	T7, T8 (M6)
T11	10	10	T9 (M7)
T12	20	10	T10, T11 (M8)

Figure 23.5 Tasks, durations, and dependencies

required are specified in the project contract and the customer's view of the project's progress depends on these deliverables.

To illustrate how bar charts are used, I have created a hypothetical set of tasks as shown in Figure 23.5. This table shows tasks, estimated effort, duration, and task interdependencies. From Figure 23.5, you can see that task T3 is dependent on task T1. Task T1 must, therefore, be completed before T3 starts. For example, T1 might be the preparation of a component design and T3, the implementation of that design. Before implementation starts, the design should be complete. Notice that the estimated duration for some tasks is more than the effort required and vice versa. If the effort is less than the duration, this means that the people allocated to that task are not working full-time on it. If the effort exceeds the duration, this means that several team members are working on the task at the same time.

Figure 23.6 takes the information in Figure 23.5 and presents the project schedule in a graphical format. It is a bar chart showing a project calendar and the start and finish dates of tasks. Reading from left to right, the bar chart clearly shows when tasks start and end. The milestones (M1, M2, etc.) are also shown on the bar chart. Notice that tasks that are independent are carried out in parallel (e.g., tasks T1, T2, and T4 all start at the beginning of the project).

As well as planning the delivery schedule for the software, project managers have to allocate resources to tasks. The key resource is, of course, the software engineers who will do the work, and they have to be assigned to project activities. The resource allocation can also be input to project management tools and a bar chart generated, which shows when staff are working on the project (Figure 23.7). People may be

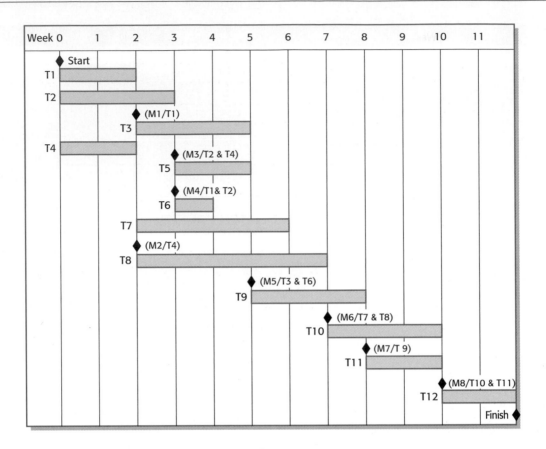

Figure 23.6
Activity bar chart

working on more than one task at the same time and, sometimes, they are not working on the project. They may be on holiday, working on other projects, attending training courses, or engaging in some other activity. I show part-time assignments using a diagonal line crossing the bar.

Large organizations usually employ a number of specialists who work on a project when needed. In Figure 23.7, you can see that Mary is a specialist, who works on only a single task in the project. This can cause scheduling problems. If one project is delayed while a specialist is working on it, this may have a knock-on effect on other projects where the specialist is also required. These may then be delayed because the specialist is not available.

If a task is delayed, this can obviously affect later tasks that are dependent on it. They cannot start until the delayed task is completed. Delays can cause serious problems with staff allocation, especially when people are working on several projects at the same time. If a task (T) is delayed, the people allocated may be assigned to other work (W). To complete this may take longer than the delay but, once assigned, they cannot simply be reassigned back to the original task, T. This may then lead to further delays in T as they complete W.

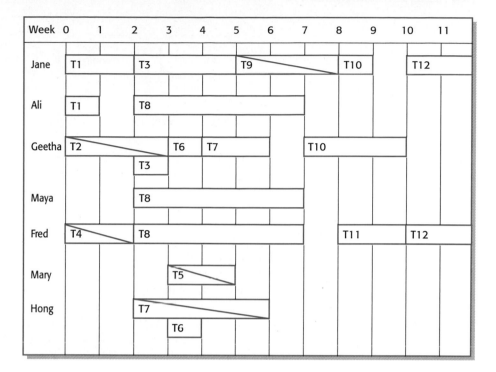

Figure 23.7 Staff allocation chart

23.4 Agile planning

Agile methods of software development are iterative approaches where the software is developed and delivered to customers in increments. Unlike plan-driven approaches, the functionality of these increments is not planned in advance but is decided during the development. The decision on what to include in an increment depends on progress and on the customer's priorities. The argument for this approach is that the customer's priorities and requirements change so it makes sense to have a flexible plan that can accommodate these changes. Cohn's book {Cohn, 2005 ##1735} is a comprehensive discussion of planning issues in agile projects.

The most commonly used agile approaches such as Scrum (Schwaber, 2004) and extreme programming (Beck, 2000) have a two-stage approach to planning, corresponding to the startup phase in plan-driven development and development planning:

1. Release planning, which looks ahead for several months and decides on the features that should be included in a release of a system.

2. Iteration planning, which has a shorter-term outlook, and focuses on planning the next increment of a system. This is typically 2 to 4 weeks of work for the team.

Figure 23.8
Planning in XP

I have already discussed the Scrum approach to planning in Chapter 3, so I concentrate here on planning in extreme programming (XP). This is called the 'planning game' and it usually involves the whole development team, including customer representatives. Figure 23.8 shows the stages in the planning game.

The system specification in XP is based on user stories that reflect the features that should be included in the system. At the start of the project, the team and the customer try to identify a set of stories, which covers all of the functionality that will be included in the final system. Some functionality will inevitably be missing, but this is not important at this stage.

The next stage is an estimation stage. The project team reads and discusses the stories and ranks them in order of the amount of time they think it will take to implement the story. This may involve breaking large stories into smaller stories. Relative estimation is often easier than absolute estimation. People often find it difficult to estimate how much effort or time is needed to do something. However, when they are presented with several things to do, they can make judgments about which stories will take the longest time and most effort. Once the ranking has been completed, the team then allocates notional effort points to the stories. A complex story may have 8 points and a simple story 2 points. You do this for all of the stories in the ranked list.

Once the stories have been estimated, the relative effort is translated into the first estimate of the total effort required by using the notion of 'velocity'. In XP, velocity is the number of effort points implemented by the team, per day. This can be estimated either from previous experience or by developing one or two stories to see how much time is required. The velocity estimate is approximate, but is refined during the development process. Once you have a velocity estimate, you can calculate the total effort in person-days to implement the system.

Release planning involves selecting and refining the stories that will reflect the features to be implemented in a release of a system and the order in which the stories should be implemented. The customer has to be involved in this process. A release date is then chosen and the stories are examined to see if the effort estimate is consistent with that date. If not, stories are added or removed from the list.

Iteration planning is the first stage into the iteration development process. Stories to be implemented for that iteration are chosen, with the number of stories reflecting the time to deliver an iteration (usually 2 or 3 weeks) and the team's velocity. When the iteration delivery date is reached, that iteration is complete, even if all of the stories have not been implemented. The team considers the stories that have been implemented and adds up their effort points. The velocity can then be recalculated and this is used in planning the next release of the system.

At the start of each iteration, there is a more detailed planning stage where the developers break stories down into development tasks. A development task should take 4–16 hours. All of the tasks that must be completed to implement all of the stories in that iteration are listed. The individual developers then sign up for the specific tasks that they will implement. Each developer knows their individual velocity so should not sign up for more tasks than they can implement in the time.

There are two important benefits from this approach to task allocation:

1. The whole team gets an overview of the tasks to be completed in an iteration. They therefore have an understanding of what other team members are doing and who to talk to if task dependencies are identified.

2. Individual developers choose the tasks to implement; they are not simply allocated tasks by a project manager. They therefore have a sense of ownership in these tasks and this is likely to motivate them to complete the task.

Halfway though an iteration, progress is reviewed. At this stage, half of the story effort points should have been completed. So, if an iteration involves 24 story points and 36 tasks, 12 story points and 18 tasks should have been completed. If this is not the case, then the customer has to be consulted and some stories removed from the iteration.

This approach to planning has the advantage that the software is always released as planned and there is no schedule slippage. If the work cannot be completed in the time allowed, the XP philosophy is to reduce the scope of the work rather than extend the schedule. However, in some cases, the increment may not be enough to be useful. Reducing the scope may create extra work for customers if they have to use an incomplete system or change their work practices between one release of the system and another.

A major difficulty in agile planning is that it is reliant on customer involvement and availability. In practice, this can be difficult to arrange, as the customer representative must sometimes give priority to other work. Customers may be more familiar with traditional project plans and may find it difficult to engage in an agile planning project.

Agile planning works well with small, stable development teams that can get together and discuss the stories to be implemented. However, where teams are large and/or geographically distributed, or when team membership changes frequently, it is practically impossible for everyone to be involved in the collaborative planning that is essential for agile project management. Consequently, large projects are usually planned using traditional approaches to project management.

23.5 Estimation techniques

Project schedule estimation is difficult. You may have to make initial estimates on the basis of a high-level user requirements definition. The software may have to run on unfamiliar computers or use new development technology. The people involved in the project and their skills will probably not be known. There are so many uncertainties that it is impossible to estimate system development costs accurately during the early stages of a project.

There is even a fundamental difficulty in assessing the accuracy of different approaches to cost and effort estimation. Project estimates are often self-fulfilling. The estimate is used to define the project budget and the product is adjusted so that the budget figure is realized. A project that is within budget may have achieved this at the expense of features in the software being developed.

I do not know of any controlled experiments with project costing where the estimated costs were not used to bias the experiment. A controlled experiment would not reveal the cost estimate to the project manager. The actual costs would then be compared with the estimated project costs. Nevertheless, organizations need to make software effort and cost estimates. There are two types of technique that can be used to do this:

1. *Experience-based techniques* The estimate of future effort requirements is based on the manager's experience of past projects and the application domain. Essentially, the manager makes an informed judgment of what the effort requirements are likely to be.

2. *Algorithmic cost modeling* In this approach, a formulaic approach is used to compute the project effort based on estimates of product attributes, such as size, and process characteristics, such as experience of staff involved.

In both cases, you need to use your judgment to estimate either the effort directly, or estimate the project and product characteristics. In the startup phase of a project, these estimates have a wide margin of error. Based on data collected from a large number of projects, Boehm, et al. (1995) discovered that startup estimates vary significantly. If the initial estimate of effort required is x months of effort, they found that the range may be from $0.25x$ to $4x$ of the actual effort as measured when the system was delivered. During development planning, estimates become more and more accurate as the project progresses (Figure 23.9).

Experience-based techniques rely on the manager's experience of past projects and the actual effort expended in these projects on activities that are related to software development. Typically, you identify the deliverables to be produced in a project and the different software components or systems that are to be developed. You document these in a spreadsheet, estimate them individually, and compute the total effort required. It usually helps to get a group of people involved in the effort estimation and to ask each member of the group to explain their estimate. This often reveals factors that others have not considered and you then iterate towards an agreed group estimate.

The difficulty with experience-based techniques is that a new software project may not have much in common with previous projects. Software development changes very quickly and a project will often use unfamiliar techniques such as web services, COTS-based development, or AJAX. If you have not worked with these techniques, your previous experience may not help you to estimate the effort required, making it more difficult to produce accurate costs and schedule estimates.

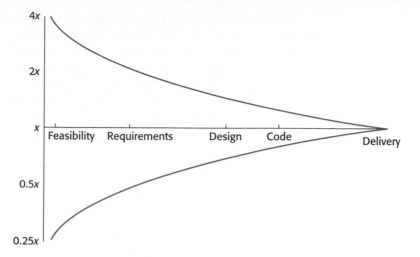

Figure 23.9
Estimate uncertainty

23.5.1 Algorithmic cost modeling

Algorithmic cost modeling uses a mathematical formula to predict project costs based on estimates of the project size; the type of software being developed; and other team, process, and product factors. An algorithmic cost model can be built by analyzing the costs and attributes of completed projects, and finding the closest-fit formula to actual experience.

Algorithmic cost models are primarily used to make estimates of software development costs. However, Boehm and his collaborators (2000) discuss a range of other uses for these models, such as the preparation of estimates for investors in software companies; alternative strategies to help assess risks; and to informed decisions about reuse, redevelopment, or outsourcing.

Algorithmic models for estimating effort in a software project are mostly based on a simple formula:

Effort = A × Size^B × M

A is a constant factor which depends on local organizational practices and the type of software that is developed. **Size** may be either an assessment of the code size of the software or a functionality estimate expressed in function or application points. The value of exponent **B** usually lies between 1 and 1.5. **M** is a multiplier made by combining process, product, and development attributes, such as the dependability requirements for the software and the experience of the development team.

The number of lines of source code (SLOC) in the delivered system is the fundamental size metric that is used in many algorithmic cost models. Size estimation may involve estimation by analogy with other projects, estimation by converting function or application points to code size, estimation by ranking the sizes of system components and using a known reference component to estimate the component size, or it may simply be a question of engineering judgment.

Most algorithmic estimation models have an exponential component (**B** in the above equation) that is related to the size and complexity of the system. This reflects the fact that costs do not usually increase linearly with project size. As the size and complexity of the software increases, extra costs are incurred because of the communication overhead of larger teams, more complex configuration management, more difficult system integration, and so on. The more complex the system, the more these factors affect the cost. Therefore, the value of **B** usually increases with the size and complexity of the system.

All algorithmic models have similar problems:

1. It is often difficult to estimate **Size** at an early stage in a project, when only the specification is available. Function-point and application-point estimates (see later) are easier to produce than estimates of code size but are still often inaccurate.

2. The estimates of the factors contributing to **B** and **M** are subjective. Estimates vary from one person to another, depending on their background and experience of the type of system that is being developed.

Accurate code size estimation is difficult at an early stage in a project because the size of the final program depends on design decisions that may not have been made when the estimate is required. For example, an application that requires high-performance data management may either implement its own data management system or use a commercial database system. In the initial cost estimation, you are unlikely to know if there is a commercial database system that performs well enough to meet the performance requirements. You therefore don't know how much data management code will be included in the system.

The programming language used for system development also affects the number of lines of code to be developed. A language like Java might mean that more lines of code are necessary than if C (say) was used. However, this extra code allows more compile-time checking so validation costs are likely to be reduced. How should this be taken into account? Furthermore, it may be possible to reuse a significant amount of code from previous projects and the size estimate has to be adjusted to take this into account.

Algorithmic cost models are a systematic way to estimate the effort required to develop a system. However, these models are complex and difficult to use. There are many attributes and considerable scope for uncertainty in estimating their values. This complexity discourages potential users and hence the practical application of algorithmic cost modeling has been limited to a small number of companies.

Another barrier that discourages the use of algorithmic models is the need for calibration. Model users should calibrate their model and the attribute values using their own historical project data, as this reflects local practice and experience. However, very few organizations have collected enough data from past projects in a form that supports model calibration. Practical use of algorithmic models, therefore, has to start with the published values for the model parameters. It is practically impossible for a modeler to know how closely these relate to their own organization.

If you use an algorithmic cost estimation model, you should develop a range of estimates (worst, expected, and best) rather than a single estimate and apply the costing

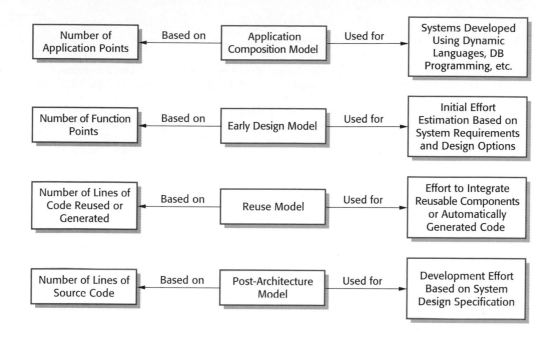

Figure 23.10
COCOMO estimation models

formula to all of them. Estimates are most likely to be accurate when you understand the type of software that is being developed, have calibrated the costing model using local data, or when programming language and hardware choices are predefined.

23.5.2 The COCOMO II model

Several similar models have been proposed to help estimate the effort, schedule, and costs of a software project. The model that I discuss here is the COCOMO II model. This is an empirical model that was derived by collecting data from a large number of software projects. These data were analyzed to discover the formulae that were the best fit to the observations. These formulae linked the size of the system and product, project and team factors to the effort to develop the system. COCOMO II is a well-documented and nonproprietary estimation model.

COCOMO II was developed from earlier COCOMO cost estimation models, which were largely based on original code development (Boehm, 1981; Boehm and Royce, 1989). The COCOMO II model takes into account more modern approaches to software development, such as rapid development using dynamic languages, development by component composition, and use of database programming. COCOMO II supports the spiral model of development, described in Chapter 2, and embeds submodels that produce increasingly detailed estimates.

The submodels (Figure 23.10) that are part of the COCOMO II model are:

1. *An application-composition model* This models the effort required to develop systems that are created from reusable components, scripting, or

Software productivity

Software productivity is an estimate of the average amount of development work that software engineers complete in a week or a month. It is therefore expressed as lines of code/month, function points/month, etc.

However, whilst productivity can be easily measured where there is a tangible outcome (e.g., a clerk processes *N* invoices/day), software productivity is more difficult to define. Different people may implement the same functionality in different ways, using different numbers of lines of code. The quality of the code is also important but is, to some extent, subjective. Productivity comparisons between software engineers are, therefore, unreliable and so are not very useful for project planning.

http://www.SoftwareEngineering-9.com/Web/Planning/productivity.html

database programming. Software size estimates are based on application points, and a simple size/productivity formula is used to estimate the effort required. The number of application points in a program is a weighted estimate of the number of separate screens that are displayed, the number of reports that are produced, the number of modules in imperative programming languages (such as Java), and the number of lines of scripting language or database programming code.

2. *An early design model* This model is used during early stages of the system design after the requirements have been established. The estimate is based on the standard estimation formula that I discussed in the introduction, with a simplified set of seven multipliers. Estimates are based on function points, which are then converted to number of lines of source code. Function points are a language-independent way of quantifying program functionality. You compute the total number of function points in a program by measuring or estimating the number of external inputs and outputs, user interactions, external interfaces, and files or database tables used by the system.

3. *A reuse model* This model is used to compute the effort required to integrate reusable components and/or automatically generated program code. It is normally used in conjunction with the post-architecture model.

4. *A post-architecture model* Once the system architecture has been designed, a more accurate estimate of the software size can be made. Again, this model uses the standard formula for cost estimation discussed above. However, it includes a more extensive set of 17 multipliers reflecting personnel capability, product, and project characteristics.

Of course, in large systems, different parts of the system may be developed using different technologies and you may not have to estimate all parts of the system to the same level of accuracy. In such cases, you can use the appropriate

Developer's experience and capability	Very low	Low	Nominal	High	Very high
ICASE maturity and capability	Very low	Low	Nominal	High	Very high
PROD (NAP/month)	4	7	13	25	50

Figure 23.11
Application-point productivity

submodel for each part of the system and combine the results to create a composite estimate.

The application-composition model

The application-composition model was introduced into COCOMO II to support the estimation of effort required for prototyping projects and for projects where the software is developed by composing existing components. It is based on an estimate of weighted application points (sometimes called object points), divided by a standard estimate of application point productivity. The estimate is then adjusted according to the difficulty of developing each application point (Boehm, et al., 2000). Productivity depends on the developer's experience and capability as well as the capabilities of the software tools (ICASE) used to support development. Figure 23.11 shows the levels of application-point productivity suggested by the COCOMO developers (Boehm, et al., 1995).

Application composition usually involves significant software reuse. It is almost certain that some of the application points in the system will be implemented using reusable components. Consequently, you have to adjust the estimate to take into account the percentage of reuse expected. Therefore, the final formula for effort computation for system prototypes is:

$$PM = (NAP \times (1 - \%reuse/100))/PROD$$

PM is the effort estimate in person-months. **NAP** is the total number of application points in the delivered system. "%reuse" is an estimate of the amount of reused code in the development. **PROD** is the application-point productivity, as shown in Figure 23.11. The model produces an approximate estimate as it does not take into account the additional effort involved in reuse.

The early design model

This model may be used during the early stages of a project, before a detailed architectural design for the system is available. Early design estimates are most useful for option exploration where you need to compare different ways of implementing the user requirements. The early design model assumes that user requirements have been agreed and initial stages of the system design process are under way. Your goal at this stage should be to make a quick and approximate cost estimate. Therefore, you have to make simplifying assumptions, for example, that the effort involved in integrating reusable code is zero.

The estimates produced at this stage are based on the standard formula for algorithmic models, namely:

$$\text{Effort} = A \times \text{Size}^B \times M$$

Based on his own large data set, Boehm proposed that the coefficient **A** should be 2.94. The size of the system is expressed in KSLOC, which is the number of thousands of lines of source code. You calculate KSLOC by estimating the number of function points in the software. You then use standard tables that relate software size to function points for different programming languages, to compute an initial estimate of the system size in KSLOC.

The exponent **B** reflects the increased effort required as the size of the project increases. This can vary from 1.1 to 1.24 depending on the novelty of the project, the development flexibility, the risk resolution processes used, the cohesion of the development team, and the process maturity level (see Chapter 26) of the organization. I discuss how the value of this exponent is calculated using these parameters in the description of the COCOMO II post-architecture model.

This results in an effort computation as follows:

$$\text{PM} = 2.94 \times \text{Size}^{(1.1\,-\,1.24)} \times M$$

where

$$M = \text{PERS} \times \text{RCPX} \times \text{RUSE} \times \text{PDIF} \times \text{PREX} \times \text{FCIL} \times \text{SCED}$$

The multiplier **M** is based on seven project and process attributes that increase or decrease the estimate. The attributes used in the early design model are product reliability and complexity (**RCPX**), reuse required (**RUSE**), platform difficulty (**PDIF**), personnel capability (**PERS**), personnel experience (**PREX**), schedule (**SCED**), and support facilities (**FCIL**). I explain these attributes on the book's webpages. You estimate values for these attributes using a six-point scale, where 1 corresponds to 'very low' and 6 corresponds to 'very high'.

The reuse model

As I have discussed in Chapter 16, software reuse is now common. Most large systems include a significant amount of code that has been reused from previous development projects. The reuse model is used to estimate the effort required to integrate reusable or generated code.

COCOMO II considers two types of reused code. 'Black-box' code is code that can be reused without understanding the code or making changes to it. The development effort for black-box code is taken to be zero. 'White box' code has to be adapted to integrate it with new code or other reused components. Development effort is required for reuse because the code has to be understood and modified before it can work correctly in the system.

Many systems include automatically generated code from system models, as discussed in Chapter 5. A model (often in UML) is analyzed and code is generated to implement the objects specified in the model. The COCOMO II reuse model includes a formula to estimate the effort required to integrate this generated code:

$$PM_{Auto} = (ASLOC \times AT/100) \text{ / ATPROD // Estimate for generated code}$$

ASLOC is the total number of lines of reused code, including code that is automatically generated.

AT is the percentage of reused code that is automatically generated.

ATPROD is the productivity of engineers in integrating such code.

Boehm, et al. (2000) have measured **ATPROD** to be about 2,400 source statements per month. Therefore, if there are a total of 20,000 lines of reused source code in a system and 30% of this is automatically generated, then the effort required to integrate the generated code is:

$$(20,000 \times 30/100) \text{ / 2400} = 2.5 \text{ person-months // Generated code}$$

A separate effort computation is used to estimate the effort required to integrate the reused code from other systems. The reuse model does not compute the effort directly from an estimate of the number of reused components. Rather, based on the number of lines of code that are reused, the model provides a basis for calculating the equivalent number of lines of new code (**ESLOC**). This is based on the number of lines of reusable code that have to be changed and a multiplier that reflects the amount of work you need to do to reuse the components. The formula to compute **ESLOC** takes into account the effort required for software understanding, making changes to the reused code, and making changes to the system to integrate that code.

The following formula is used to calculate the number of equivalent lines of source code:

$$ESLOC = ASLOC \times AAM$$

ESLOC is the equivalent number of lines of new source code.

ASLOC is the number of lines of code in the components that have to be changed.

AAM is an Adaptation Adjustment Multiplier, as discussed below.

Reuse is never free and some costs are incurred even if no reuse proves to be possible. However, reuse costs decrease as the amount of code reused increases. The fixed understanding and assessment costs are spread across more lines of code. The Adaptation Adjustment Multiplier (**AAM**) adjusts the estimate to reflect

COCOMO II cost drivers

COCOMO II cost drivers are attributes that reflect some of the product, team, process, and organizational factors that affect the amount of effort needed to develop a software system. For example, if a high level of reliability is required, extra effort will be needed; if there is a need for rapid delivery, extra effort will be required; if the team members change, extra effort will be required.

There are 17 of these attributes in the COCOMO II model, which have been assigned values by the model developers.

http://www.SoftwareEngineering-9.com/Web/Planning/costdrivers.html

the additional effort required to reuse code. Simplistically, **AAM** is the sum of three components:

1. An adaptation component (referred to as **AAF**) that represents the costs of making changes to the reused code. The adaptation component includes sub-components that take into account design, code, and integration changes.

2. An understanding component (referred to as **SU**) that represents the costs of understanding the code to be reused and the familiarity of the engineer with the code. **SU** ranges from 50 for complex unstructured code to 10 for well-written, object-oriented code.

3. An assessment factor (referred to as **AA**) that represents the costs of reuse decision making. That is, some analysis is always required to decide whether or not code can be reused, and this is included in the cost as **AA**. **AA** varies from 0 to 8 depending on the amount of analysis effort required.

If some code adaptation can be done automatically, this reduces the effort required. You therefore adjust the estimate by estimating the percentage of automatically adapted code (**AT**) and using this to adjust **ASLOC**. Therefore, the final formula is:

$$\text{ESLOC} = \text{ASLOC} \times (1 - \text{AT}/100) \times \text{AAM}$$

Once **ESLOC** has been calculated, you then apply the standard estimation formula to calculate the total effort required, where the Size parameter = **ESLOC**. You then add this to the effort to integrate automatically generated code that you have already computed, thus computing the total effort required.

The post-architecture level

The post-architecture model is the most detailed of the COCOMO II models. It is used once an initial architectural design for the system is available so the subsystem structure is known. You can then make estimates for each part of the system.

The starting point for estimates produced at the post-architecture level is the same basic formula used in the early design estimates:

$$PM = A \times Size^B \times M$$

By this stage in the process, you should be able to make a more accurate estimate of the project size as you know how the system will be decomposed into objects or modules. You make this estimate of the code size using three parameters:

1. An estimate of the total number of lines of new code to be developed (**SLOC**).

2. An estimate of the reuse costs based on an equivalent number of source lines of code (**ESLOC**), calculated using the reuse model.

3. An estimate of the number of lines of code that are likely to be modified because of changes to the system requirements.

You add the values of these parameters to compute the total code size, in KSLOC, that you use in the effort computation formula. The final component in the estimate—the number of lines of modified code—reflects the fact that software requirements always change. This leads to rework and development of extra code, which you have to take into account. Of course there will often be even more uncertainty in this figure than in the estimates of new code to be developed.

The exponent term (**B**) in the effort computation formula is related to the levels of project complexity. As projects become more complex, the effects of increasing system size become more significant. However, good organizational practices and procedures can control the diseconomy of scale that is a consequence of increasing complexity. The value of the exponent **B** is therefore based on five factors, as shown in Figure 23.12. These factors are rated on a six-point scale from 0 to 5, where 0 means 'extra high' and 5 means 'very low'. To calculate **B**, you add the ratings, divide them by 100, and add the result to 1.01 to get the exponent that should be used.

For example, imagine that an organization is taking on a project in a domain in which it has little previous experience. The project client has not defined the process to be used or allowed time in the project schedule for significant risk analysis. A new development team must be put together to implement this system. The organization has recently put in place a process improvement program and has been rated as a Level 2 organization according to the SEI capability assessment, as discussed in Chapter 26. Possible values for the ratings used in exponent calculation are therefore:

1. *Precedentedness*, rated low (4). This is a new project for the organization.

2. *Development flexibility*, rated very high (1). No client involvement in the development process so there are few externally imposed changes.

Scale factor	Explanation
Precedentedness	Reflects the previous experience of the organization with this type of project. Very low means no previous experience; extra-high means that the organization is completely familiar with this application domain.
Development flexibility	Reflects the degree of flexibility in the development process. Very low means a prescribed process is used; extra-high means that the client sets only general goals.
Architecture/risk resolution	Reflects the extent of risk analysis carried out. Very low means little analysis; extra-high means a complete and thorough risk analysis.
Team cohesion	Reflects how well the development team knows each other and work together. Very low means very difficult interactions; extra-high means an integrated and effective team with no communication problems.
Process maturity	Reflects the process maturity of the organization. The computation of this value depends on the CMM Maturity Questionnaire, but an estimate can be achieved by subtracting the CMM process maturity level from 5.

Figure 23.12 Scale factors used in the exponent computation in the post-architecture model

3. *Architecture/risk resolution*, rated very low (5). There has been no risk analysis carried out.

4. *Team cohesion*, rated nominal (3). This is a new team so there is no information available on cohesion.

5. *Process maturity*, rated nominal (3). Some process control is in place.

The sum of these values is 16. You then calculate the exponent by dividing this by 100 and adding the result to 0.01. The adjusted value of **B** is therefore 1.17.

The overall effort estimate is refined using an extensive set of 17 product, process, and organizational attributes (cost drivers), rather than the seven attributes used in the early design model. You can estimate values for these attributes because you have more information about the software itself, its non-functional requirements, the development team, and the development process.

Figure 23.13 shows how the cost driver attributes can influence effort estimates. I have taken a value for the exponent of 1.17 as discussed in the previous example and assumed that **RELY**, **CPLX**, **STOR**, **TOOL**, and **SCED** are the key cost drivers in the project. All of the other cost drivers have a nominal value of 1, so they do not affect the computation of the effort.

In Figure 23.13, I have assigned maximum and minimum values to the key cost drivers to show how they influence the effort estimate. The values taken are those from the COCOMO II reference manual (Boehm, 2000). You can see that high values for the cost drivers lead an effort estimate that is more than three times the initial estimate, whereas low values reduce the estimate to about one-third of the original. This highlights the significant differences between different types of projects and the difficulties of transferring experience from one application domain to another.

Exponent value	1.17
System size (including factors for reuse and requirements volatility)	128,000 DSI
Initial COCOMO estimate without cost drivers	**730 person-months**
Reliability	Very high, multiplier = 1.39
Complexity	Very high, multiplier = 1.3
Memory constraint	High, multiplier = 1.21
Tool use	Low, multiplier = 1.12
Schedule	Accelerated, multiplier = 1.29
Adjusted COCOMO estimate	**2,306 person-months**
Reliability	Very low, multiplier = 0.75
Complexity	Very low, multiplier = 0.75
Memory constraint	None, multiplier = 1
Tool use	Very high, multiplier = 0.72
Schedule	Normal, multiplier = 1
Adjusted COCOMO estimate	**295 person-months**

Figure 23.13
The effect of cost
drivers on effort
estimates

23.5.3 Project duration and staffing

As well as estimating the overall costs of a project and the effort that is required to develop a software system, project managers must also estimate how long the software will take to develop, and when staff will be needed to work on the project. Increasingly, organizations are demanding shorter development schedules so that their products can be brought to market before their competitor's.

The COCOMO model includes a formula to estimate the calendar time required to complete a project:

$$TDEV = 3 \times (PM)^{(0.33 + 0.2*(B - 1.01))}$$

TDEV is the nominal schedule for the project, in calendar months, ignoring any multiplier that is related to the project schedule.

PM is the effort computed by the COCOMO model.

B is the complexity-related exponent, as discussed in Section 23.5.2.

If **B** = 1.17 and **PM** = 60 then

$$TDEV = 3 \times (60)^{0.36} = 13 \text{ months}$$

However, the nominal project schedule predicted by the COCOMO model and the schedule required by the project plan are not necessarily the same thing. There may be a requirement to deliver the software earlier or (more rarely) later than the date suggested by the nominal schedule. If the schedule is to be compressed, this increases the effort required for the project. This is taken into account by the **SCED** multiplier in the effort estimation computation.

Assume that a project estimated **TDEV** as 13 months, as suggested above, but the actual schedule required was 11 months. This represents a schedule compression of approximately 25%. Using the values for the **SCED** multiplier as derived by Boehm's team, the effort multiplier for such a schedule compression is 1.43. Therefore, the actual effort that will be required if this accelerated schedule is to be met is almost 50% more than the effort required to deliver the software according to the nominal schedule.

There is a complex relationship between the number of people working on a project, the effort that will be devoted to the project, and the project delivery schedule. If four people can complete a project in 13 months (i.e., 52 person-months of effort), then you might think that by adding one more person, you can complete the work in 11 months (55 person-months of effort). However, the COCOMO model suggests that you will, in fact, need six people to finish the work in 11 months (66 person-months of effort).

The reason for this is that adding people actually reduces the productivity of existing team members and so the actual increment of effort added is less than one person. As the project team increases in size, team members spend more time communicating and defining interfaces between the parts of the system developed by other people. Doubling the number of staff (for example) therefore does not mean that the duration of the project will be halved. If the development team is large, it is sometimes the case that adding more people to a project increases rather than reduces the development schedule. Myers (1989) discusses the problems of schedule acceleration. He suggests that projects are likely to run into significant problems if they try to develop software without allowing sufficient calendar time to complete the work.

You cannot simply estimate the number of people required for a project team by dividing the total effort by the required project schedule. Usually, a small number of people are needed at the start of a project to carry out the initial design. The team then builds up to a peak during the development and testing of the system, and then declines in size as the system is prepared for deployment. A very rapid buildup of project staff has been shown to correlate with project schedule slippage. Project managers should therefore avoid adding too many staff to a project early in its lifetime.

This effort buildup can be modeled by what is called a Rayleigh curve (Londeix, 1987). Putnam's estimation model (1978), which incorporates a model of project staffing, is based around these Rayleigh curves. This model also includes development time as a key factor. As development time is reduced, the effort required to develop the system grows exponentially.

KEY POINTS

■ The price charged for a system does not just depend on its estimated development costs and the profit required by the development company. Organizational factors may mean that the price is increased to compensate for increased risk or decreased to gain competitive advantage.

■ Software is often priced to gain a contract and the functionality of the system is then adjusted to meet the estimated price.

■ Plan-driven development is organized around a complete project plan that defines the project activities, the planned effort, the activity schedule, and who is responsible for each activity.

■ Project scheduling involves the creation of various graphical representations of part of the project plan. Bar charts, which show the activity duration and staffing timelines, are the most commonly used schedule representations.

■ A project milestone is a predictable outcome of an activity or set of activities. At each milestone, a formal report of progress should be presented to management. A deliverable is a work product that is delivered to the project customer.

■ The XP planning game involves the whole team in project planning. The plan is developed incrementally and, if problems arise, it is adjusted so that software functionality is reduced instead of delaying the delivery of an increment.

■ Estimation techniques for software may be experience-based, where managers judge the effort required, or algorithmic, where the effort required is computed from other estimated project parameters.

■ The COCOMO II costing model is a mature algorithmic cost model that takes project, product, hardware, and personnel attributes into account when formulating a cost estimate.

FURTHER READING

Software Cost Estimation with COCOMO II. This is the definitive book on the COCOMO II model. It provides a complete description of the model with many examples, and includes software that implements the model. It's extremely detailed and not light reading. (B. Boehm et al., Prentice Hall, 2000.)

'Ten unmyths of project estimation'. A pragmatic article that discusses the practical difficulties of project estimation and challenges some fundamental assumptions in this area. (P. Armour, *Comm. ACM*, **45** (11), November 2002.)

Agile Estimating and Planning. This book is a comprehensive description of story-based planning as used in XP, as well as a rationale for using an agile approach to project planning. However, it also includes a good, general introduction to project planning issues. (M. Cohn, Prentice Hall, 2005.)

'Achievements and Challenges in Cocomo-based Software Resource Estimation'. This article presents a history of the COCOMO models and influences on these models, and discusses the variants of these models that have been developed. It also identifies further possible developments in the COCOMO approach. (B. W. Boehm and R. Valeridi, *IEEE Software*, **25** (5), September/October 2008.) http://dx.doi.org/10.1109/MS.2008.133.

EXERCISES

23.1. Under what circumstances might a company justifiably charge a much higher price for a software system than the software cost estimate plus a reasonable profit margin?

23.2. Explain why the process of project planning is iterative and why a plan must be continually reviewed during a software project.

23.3. Briefly explain the purpose of each of the sections in a software project plan.

23.4. Cost estimates are inherently risky, irrespective of the estimation technique used. Suggest four ways in which the risk in a cost estimate can be reduced.

23.5. Figure 23.14 sets out a number of tasks, their durations, and their dependencies. Draw a bar chart showing the project schedule.

23.6. Figure 23.14 shows the task durations for software project activities. Assume that a serious, unanticipated setback occurs and instead of taking 10 days, task T5 takes 40 days. Draw up new bar charts showing how the project might be reorganized.

23.7. The XP planning game is based around the notion of planning to implement the stories that represent the system requirements. Explain the potential problems with this approach when software has high performance or dependability requirements.

23.8. A software manager is in charge of the development of a safety-critical software system, which is designed to control a radiotherapy machine to treat patients suffering from cancer. This system is embedded in the machine and must run on a special-purpose processor with a fixed amount of memory (256 Mbytes). The machine communicates with a patient database system to obtain the details of the patient and, after treatment, automatically records the radiation dose delivered and other treatment details in the database.

The COCOMO method is used to estimate the effort required to develop this system and an estimate of 26 person-months is computed. All cost driver multipliers were set to 1 when making this estimate.

Explain why this estimate should be adjusted to take project, personnel, product, and organizational factors into account. Suggest four factors that might have significant effects on the initial COCOMO estimate and propose possible values for these factors. Justify why you have included each factor.

Task	Duration (days)	Dependencies
T1	10	
T2	15	T1
T3	10	T1, T2
T4	20	
T5	10	
T6	15	T3, T4
T7	20	T3
T8	35	T7
T9	15	T6
T10	5	T5, T9
T11	10	T9
T12	20	T10
T13	35	T3, T4
T14	10	T8, T9
T15	20	T2, T14
T16	10	T15

Figure 23.14
Scheduling example

23.9. Some very large software projects involve writing millions of lines of code. Explain why the effort estimation models, such as COCOMO, might not work well when applied to very large systems.

23.10. Is it ethical for a company to quote a low price for a software contract knowing that the requirements are ambiguous and that they can charge a high price for subsequent changes requested by the customer?

REFERENCES

Beck, K. (2000). *extreme Programming Explained*. Reading, Mass.: Addison-Wesley.

Boehm, B. 2000. 'COCOMO II Model Definition Manual'. Center for Software Engineering, University of Southern California. http://csse.usc.edu/csse/research/COCOMOII/cocomo2000.0/CII_modelman2000.0.pdf.

Boehm, B., Clark, B., Horowitz, E., Westland, C., Madachy, R. and Selby, R. (1995). 'Cost models for future life cycle processes: COCOMO 2'. *Annals of Software Engineering,* **1** 57–94.

Boehm, B. and Royce, W. (1989). 'Ada COCOMO and the Ada Process Model'. *Proc. 5th COCOMO Users' Group Meeting*, Pittsburgh: Software Engineering Institute.

Boehm, B. W. (1981). *Software Engineering Economics*. Englewood Cliffs, NJ: Prentice Hall.

Boehm, B. W., Abts, C., Brown, A. W., Chulani, S., Clark, B. K., Horowitz, E., Madachy, R., Reifer, D. and Steece, B. (2000). *Software Cost Estimation with COCOMO II*. Upper Saddle River, NJ: Prentice Hall.

Londeix, B. (1987). *Cost Estimation for Software Development*. Wokingham: Addison-Wesley.

Myers, W. (1989). 'Allow Plenty of Time for Large-Scale Software'. *IEEE Software,* **6** (4), 92–9.

Putnam, L. H. (1978). 'A General Empirical Solution to the Macro Software Sizing and Estimating Problem'. *IEEE Trans. on Software Engineering.,* **SE-4** (3), 345–61.

Schwaber, K. (2004). *Agile Project Management with Scrum*. Seattle: Microsoft Press.

24

Quality management

Objectives

The objectives of this chapter are to introduce software quality management and software measurement. When you have read the chapter, you will:

■ have been introduced to the quality management process and know why quality planning is important;

■ understand that software quality is affected by the software development process used;

■ be aware of the importance of standards in the quality management process and know how standards are used in quality assurance;

■ understand how reviews and inspections are used as a mechanism for software quality assurance;

■ understand how measurement may be helpful in assessing some software quality attributes and the current limitations of software measurement.

Contents

Problems with software quality were initially discovered in the 1960s with the development of the first large software systems, and continued to plague software engineering throughout the 20th century. Delivered software was slow and unreliable, difficult to maintain and hard to reuse. Dissatisfaction with this situation led to the adoption of formal techniques of software quality management, which have been developed from methods used in the manufacturing industry. These quality management techniques, in conjunction with new software technologies and better software testing, have led to significant improvements in the general level of software quality.

Software quality management for software systems has three principal concerns:

1. At the organizational level, quality management is concerned with establishing a framework of organizational processes and standards that will lead to high-quality software. This means that the quality management team should take responsibility for defining the software development processes to be used and standards that should apply to the software and related documentation, including the system requirements, design, and code.

2. At the project level, quality management involves the application of specific quality processes, checking that these planned processes have been followed, and ensuring that the project outputs are conformant with the standards that are applicable to that project.

3. Quality management at the project level is also concerned with establishing a quality plan for a project. The quality plan should set out the quality goals for the project and define what processes and standards are to be used.

The terms 'quality assurance' and 'quality control' are widely used in manufacturing industry. Quality assurance (QA) is the definition of processes and standards that should lead to high-quality products and the introduction of quality processes into the manufacturing process. Quality control is the application of these quality processes to weed out products that are not of the required level of quality.

In the software industry, different companies and industry sectors interpret quality assurance and quality control in different ways. Sometimes, quality assurance simply means the definition of procedures, processes, and standards that are aimed at ensuring that software quality is achieved. In other cases, quality assurance also includes all configuration management, verification, and validation activities that are applied after a product has been handed over by a development team. In this chapter, I use the term 'quality assurance' to include verification and validation and the processes of checking that quality procedures have been properly applied. I have avoided the term 'quality control' as this term is not widely used in the software industry.

The QA team in most companies is responsible for managing the release testing process. As I discussed in Chapter 8, this means that they manage the testing of the software before it is released to customers. They are responsible for checking that the system tests provide coverage of the requirements and that proper records are maintained of the testing process. As I have covered release testing in Chapter 8, I do not cover this aspect of quality assurance here.

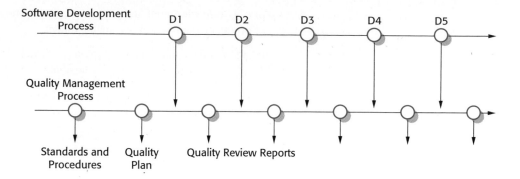

Figure 24.1 Quality management and software development

Quality management provides an independent check on the software development process. The quality management process checks the project deliverables to ensure that they are consistent with organizational standards and goals (Figure 24.1). The QA team should be independent from the development team so that they can take an objective view of the software. This allows them to report on software quality without being influenced by software development issues.

Ideally, the quality management team should not be associated with any particular development group, but should rather have organization-wide responsibility for quality management. They should be independent and report to management above the project manager level. The reason for this is that project managers have to maintain the project budget and schedule. If problems arise, they may be tempted to compromise on product quality so that they meet their schedule. An independent quality management team ensures that the organizational goals of quality are not compromised by short-term budget and schedule considerations. In smaller companies, however, this is practically impossible. Quality management and software development are inevitably intertwined with people having both development and quality responsibilities.

Quality planning is the process of developing a quality plan for a project. The quality plan should set out the desired software qualities and describe how these are to be assessed. It therefore defines what 'high-quality' software actually means for a particular system. Without this definition, engineers may make different and sometimes conflicting assumptions about which product attributes reflect the most important quality characteristics. Formalized quality planning is an integral part of plan-based development processes. Agile methods, however, adopt a less formal approach to quality management.

Humphrey (1989), in his classic book on software management, suggests an outline structure for a quality plan. This includes:

1. *Product introduction* A description of the product, its intended market, and the quality expectations for the product.

2. *Product plans* The critical release dates and responsibilities for the product, along with plans for distribution and product servicing.

3. *Process descriptions* The development and service processes and standards that should be used for product development and management.

4. *Quality goals* The quality goals and plans for the product, including an identification and justification of critical product quality attributes.

5. *Risks and risk management* The key risks that might affect product quality and the actions to be taken to address these risks.

Quality plans, which are developed as part of the general project planning process, differ in detail depending on the size and the type of system that is being developed. However, when writing quality plans, you should try to keep them as short as possible. If the document is too long, people will not read it and this will defeat the purpose of producing the quality plan.

Some people think that software quality can be achieved through prescriptive processes that are based around organizational standards and associated quality procedures that check that these standards are followed by the software development team. Their argument is that standards embody good software engineering practice and that following this good practice will lead to high-quality products. In practice, however, I think that there is much more to quality management than standards and the associated bureaucracy to ensure that these have been followed.

Standards and processes are important but quality managers should also aim to develop a 'quality culture' where everyone responsible for software development is committed to achieving a high level of product quality. They should encourage teams to take responsibility for the quality of their work and to develop new approaches to quality improvement. Although standards and procedures are the basis of quality management, good quality managers recognize that there are intangible aspects to software quality (elegance, readability, etc.) that cannot be embodied in standards. They should support people who are interested in the intangible aspects of quality and encourage professional behavior in all team members.

Formalized quality management is particularly important for teams that are developing large, long-lifetime systems that take several years to develop. Quality documentation is a record of what has been done by each subgroup in the project. It helps people check that important tasks have not been forgotten or that one group has not made incorrect assumptions about what other groups have done. The quality documentation is also a means of communication over the lifetime of a system. It allows the groups responsible for system evolution to trace the tests and checks that have been implemented by the development team.

For smaller systems, quality management is still important but a more informal approach can be adopted. Not as much paperwork is needed because a small development team can communicate informally. The key quality issue for small systems development is establishing a quality culture and ensuring that all team members have a positive approach to software quality.

24.1 Software quality

The fundamentals of quality management were established by manufacturing industry in a drive to improve the quality of the products that were being made. As part of this, they developed a definition of 'quality', which was based on conformance with a detailed product specification (Crosby, 1979) and the notion of tolerances. The underlying assumption was that products could be completely specified and procedures could be established that could check a manufactured product against its specification. Of course, products will never exactly meet a specification so some tolerance was allowed. If the product was 'almost right', it was classed as acceptable.

Software quality is not directly comparable with quality in manufacturing. The idea of tolerances is not applicable to digital systems and, for the following reasons, it may be impossible to come to an objective conclusion about whether or not a software system meets its specification:

1. As I discussed in Chapter 4, which covered requirements engineering, it is difficult to write complete and unambiguous software specifications. Software developers and customers may interpret the requirements in different ways and it may be impossible to reach agreement on whether or not software conforms to its specification.

2. Specifications usually integrate requirements from several classes of stakeholders. These requirements are inevitably a compromise and may not include the requirements of all stakeholder groups. The excluded stakeholders may therefore perceive the system as a poor quality system, even though it implements the agreed requirements.

3. It is impossible to measure certain quality characteristics (e.g., maintainability) directly and so they cannot be specified in an unambiguous way. I discuss the difficulties of measurement in Section 24.4.

Because of these problems, the assessment of software quality is a subjective process where the quality management team has to use their judgment to decide if an acceptable level of quality has been achieved. The quality management team has to consider whether or not the software is fit for its intended purpose. This involves answering questions about the system's characteristics. For example:

1. Have programming and documentation standards been followed in the development process?

2. Has the software been properly tested?

3. Is the software sufficiently dependable to be put into use?

4. Is the performance of the software acceptable for normal use?

Safety	Understandability	Portability
Security	Testability	Usability
Reliability	Adaptability	Reusability
Resilience	Modularity	Efficiency
Robustness	Complexity	Learnability

Figure 24.2 Software quality attributes

5.   Is the software usable?

6.   Is the software well structured and understandable?

There is a general assumption in software quality management that the system will be tested against its requirements. The judgment on whether or not it delivers the required functionality should be based on the results of these tests. Therefore, the QA team should review the tests that have been developed and examine the test records to check that testing has been properly carried out. In some organizations, the quality management team is responsible for system testing but, sometimes, a separate system testing group is made responsible for this.

The subjective quality of a software system is largely based on its non-functional characteristics. This reflects practical user experience—if the software's functionality is not what is expected, then users will often just work around this and find other ways to do what they want to do. However, if the software is unreliable or too slow, then it is practically impossible for them to achieve their goals.

Therefore software quality is not just about whether the software functionality has been correctly implemented, but also depends on non-functional system attributes. Boehm, et al. (1978) suggested that there were 15 important software quality attributes, as shown in Figure 24.2. These attributes relate to the software dependability, usability, efficiency, and maintainability. As I have discussed in Chapter 11, I believe that dependability attributes are usually the most important quality attributes of a system. However, the software's performance is also very important. Users will reject software that is too slow.

It is not possible for any system to be optimized for all of these attributes—for example, improving robustness may lead to loss of performance. The quality plan should therefore define the most important quality attributes for the software that is being developed. It may be that efficiency is critical and other factors have to be sacrificed to achieve this. If you have stated this in the quality plan, the engineers working on the development can cooperate to achieve this. The plan should also include a definition of the quality assessment process. This should be an agreed way of assessing whether some quality, such as maintainability or robustness, is present in the product.

An assumption that underlies software quality management is that the quality of software is directly related to the quality of the software development process. This again comes from manufacturing systems where product quality is intimately related

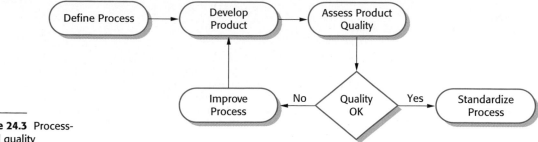

Figure 24.3 Process-based quality

to the production process. A manufacturing process involves configuring, setting up, and operating the machines involved in the process. Once the machines are operating correctly, product quality naturally follows. You measure the quality of the product and change the process until you achieve the quality level that you need. Figure 24.3 illustrates this process-based approach to achieving product quality.

There is a clear link between process and product quality in manufacturing because the process is relatively easy to standardize and monitor. Once manufacturing systems are calibrated, they can be run again and again to output high-quality products. However, software is not manufactured—it is designed. In software development, therefore, the relationship between process quality and product quality is more complex. Software development is a creative rather than a mechanical process, so the influence of individual skills and experience is significant. External factors, such as the novelty of an application or commercial pressure for an early product release, also affect product quality irrespective of the process used.

There is no doubt that the development process used has a significant influence on the quality of the software and that good processes are more likely to lead to good quality software. Process quality management and improvement can lead to fewer defects in the software being developed. However, it is difficult to assess software quality attributes, such as maintainability, without using the software for a long period. Consequently, it is hard to tell how process characteristics influence these attributes. Furthermore, because of the role of design and creativity in the software process, process standardization can sometimes stifle creativity, which leads to poorer rather than better quality software.

24.2 Software standards

Software standards play a very important role in software quality management. As I have discussed, an important part of quality assurance is the definition or selection of standards that should apply to the software development process or software product. As part of this QA process, tools and methods to support the use of these standards may also be chosen. Once standards have been selected for use, project-specific

Documentation standards

Project documents are a tangible way of describing the different representations of a software system (requirements, UML, code, etc.) and its production process. Documentation standards define the organization of different types of documents as well as the document format. They are important because they make it easier to check that important material has not been omitted from documents and ensure that project documents have a common 'look and feel'. Standards may be developed for the process of writing documents, for the documents themselves, and for document exchange.

http://www.SoftwareEngineering-9.com/Web/QualityMan/docstandards.html

processes have to be defined to monitor the use of the standards and check that they have been followed.

Software standards are important for three reasons:

1. Standards capture wisdom that is of value to the organization. They are based on knowledge about the best or most appropriate practice for the company. This knowledge is often only acquired after a great deal of trial and error. Building it into a standard helps the company reuse this experience and avoid previous mistakes.

2. Standards provide a framework for defining what 'quality' means in a particular setting. As I have discussed, software quality is subjective, and by using standards you establish a basis for deciding if a required level of quality has been achieved. Of course, this depends on setting standards that reflect user expectations for software dependability, usability, and performance.

3. Standards assist continuity when work carried out by one person is taken up and continued by another. Standards ensure that all engineers within an organization adopt the same practices. Consequently, the learning effort required when starting new work is reduced.

There are two related types of software engineering standard that may be defined and used in software quality management:

1. *Product standards* These apply to the software product being developed. They include document standards, such as the structure of requirements documents, documentation standards, such as a standard comment header for an object class definition, and coding standards, which define how a programming language should be used.

2. *Process standards* These define the processes that should be followed during software development. They should encapsulate good development practice. Process standards may include definitions of specification, design and validation processes, process support tools, and a description of the documents that should be written during these processes.

Product standards	Process standards
Design review form	Design review conduct
Requirements document structure	Submission of new code for system building
Method header format	Version release process
Java programming style	Project plan approval process
Project plan format	Change control process
Change request form	Test recording process

Figure 24.4 Product and process standards

Standards have to deliver value, in the form of increased product quality. There is no point in defining standards that are expensive in terms of time and effort to apply that only lead to marginal improvements in quality. Product standards have to be designed so that they can be applied and checked in a cost-effective way, and process standards should include the definition of processes that check that product standards have been followed.

The development of international software engineering standards is usually a prolonged process where those interested in the standard meet, produce drafts for comment, and finally agree on the standard. National and international bodies such as the U.S. DoD, ANSI, BSI, NATO, and the IEEE support the production of standards. These are general standards that can be applied across a range of projects. Bodies such as NATO and other defense organizations may require that their own standards be used in the development contracts that they place with software companies.

National and international standards have been developed covering software engineering terminology, programming languages such as Java and C++, notations such as charting symbols, procedures for deriving and writing software requirements, quality assurance procedures, and software verification and validation processes (IEEE, 2003). More specialized standards, such as IEC 61508 (IEC, 1998), have been developed for safety and security-critical systems.

Quality management teams that are developing standards for a company should normally base these company standards on national and international standards. Using international standards as a starting point, the quality assurance team should draw up a standards 'handbook'. This should define the standards that are needed by their organization. Examples of standards that could be included in such a handbook are shown in Figure 24.4.

Software engineers sometimes consider standards to be overprescriptive and not really relevant to the technical activity of software development. This is particularly likely when project standards require tedious documentation and work recording. Although they usually agree about the general need for standards, engineers often find good reasons why standards are not necessarily appropriate to their particular project. To minimize dissatisfaction and to encourage buy-in to standards, quality managers who set the standards should therefore take the following steps:

1. *Involve software engineers in the selection of product standards* If developers understand why standards have been selected, they are more likely to be committed to these standards. Ideally, the standards document should not just set out the standard to be followed, but should also include commentary explaining why standardization decisions have been made.

2. *Review and modify standards regularly to reflect changing technologies* Standards are expensive to develop and they tend to be enshrined in a company standards handbook. Because of the costs and discussion required, there is often a reluctance to change them. A standards handbook is essential but it should evolve to reflect changing circumstances and technology.

3. *Provide software tools to support standards* Developers often find standards to be a bugbear when conformance to them involves tedious manual work that could be done by a software tool. If tool support is available, very little effort is required to follow the software development standards. For example, document standards can be implemented using word processor styles.

Different types of software need different development processes so standards have to be adaptable. There is no point in prescribing a particular way of working if it is inappropriate for a project or project team. Each project manager should have the authority to modify process standards according to individual circumstances. However, when changes are made, it is important to ensure that these changes do not lead to a loss of product quality. This will affect an organization's relationship with its customers and will probably lead to increased project costs.

The project manager and the quality manager can avoid the problems of inappropriate standards by careful quality planning early in the project. They should decide which of the organizational standards should be used without change, which should be modified, and which should be ignored. New standards may have to be created in response to customer or project requirements. For example, standards for formal specifications may be required if these have not been used in previous projects.

24.2.1 The ISO 9001 standards framework

There is an international set of standards that can be used in the development of quality management systems in all industries, called ISO 9000. ISO 9000 standards can be applied to a range of organizations from manufacturing through to service industries. ISO 9001, the most general of these standards, applies to organizations that design, develop, and maintain products, including software. The ISO 9001 standard was originally developed in 1987, with its most recent revision in 2008.

The ISO 9001 standard is not itself a standard for software development but is a framework for developing software standards. It sets out general quality principles,

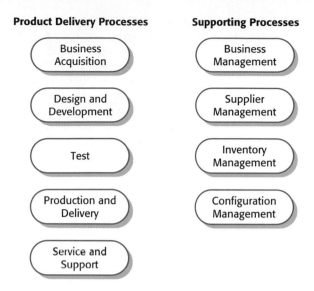

Product Delivery Processes

Business Acquisition

Design and Development

Test

Production and Delivery

Service and Support

Supporting Processes

Business Management

Supplier Management

Inventory Management

Configuration Management

Figure 24.5
ISO 9001 core processes

describes quality processes in general, and lays out the organizational standards and procedures that should be defined. These should be documented in an organizational quality manual.

The major revision of the ISO 9001 standard in 2000 reoriented the standard around nine core processes (Figure 24.5). If an organization is to be ISO 9001 conformant, it must document how its processes relate to these core processes. It must also define and maintain records that demonstrate that the defined organizational processes have been followed. The company quality manual should describe the relevant processes and the process data that has to be collected and maintained.

The ISO 9001 standard does not define or prescribe the specific quality processes that should be used in a company. To be conformant with ISO 9001, a company must have defined the types of process shown in Figure 24.5 and have procedures in place that demonstrate that its quality processes are being followed. This allows flexibility across industrial sectors and company sizes. Quality standards can be defined that are appropriate for the type of software being developed. Small companies can have unbureaucratic processes and still be ISO 9001 compliant. However, this flexibility means that you cannot make assumptions about the similarities or differences between the processes in different ISO 9001–compliant companies. Some companies may have very rigid quality processes that keep detailed records, whereas others may be much less formal, with minimal additional documentation.

The relationships between ISO 9001, organizational quality manuals, and individual project quality plans are shown in Figure 24.6. This diagram has been derived from a model given by Ince (1994), who explains how the general ISO 9001 standard can be used as a basis for software quality management processes. Bamford and Dielbler (2003) explain how the later ISO 9001: 2000 standard can be applied in software companies.

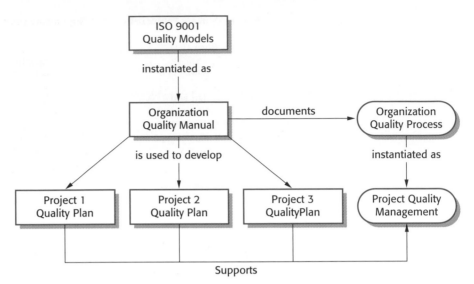

Figure 24.6
ISO 9001 and quality management

Some software customers demand that their suppliers should be ISO 9001 certified. The customers can then be confident that the software development company has an approved quality management system in place. Independent accreditation authorities examine the quality management processes and process documentation and decide if these processes cover all of the areas specified in ISO 9001. If so, they certify that a company's quality processes, as defined in the quality manual, conform to the ISO 9001 standard.

Some people think that ISO 9001 certification means that the quality of the software produced by certified companies will be better than that from uncertified companies. This is not necessarily true. The ISO 9001 standard focuses on ensuring that the organization has quality management procedures in place and it follows these procedures. There is no guarantee that ISO 9001 certified companies use the best software development practices or that their processes lead to high-quality software.

For example, a company could define test coverage standards specifying that all methods in objects must be called at least once. Unfortunately, this standard can be met by incomplete software testing, which does not run tests with different method parameters. So long as the defined testing procedures were followed and records kept of the testing carried out, the company could be ISO 9001 certified. The ISO 9001 certification defines quality to be the conformance to standards, and takes no account of the quality as experienced by users of the software.

Agile methods, which avoid documentation and focus on the code being developed, have little in common with the formal quality processes that are discussed in ISO 9001. There has been some work done on reconciling these approaches (Stalhane and Hanssen, 2008), but the agile development community is fundamentally opposed to what they see as the bureaucratic overhead of standards conformance. For this reason, companies that use agile development methods are rarely concerned with ISO 9001 certification.

24.3 Reviews and inspections

Reviews and inspections are QA activities that check the quality of project deliverables. This involves examining the software, its documentation and records of the process to discover errors and omissions and to see if quality standards have been followed. As I discussed in Chapters 8 and 15, reviews and inspections are used alongside program testing as part of the general process of software verification and validation.

During a review, a group of people examine the software and its associated documentation, looking for potential problems and non-conformance with standards. The review team makes informed judgments about the level of quality of a system or project deliverable. Project managers may then use these assessments to make planning decisions and allocate resources to the development process.

Quality reviews are based on documents that have been produced during the software development process. As well as software specifications, designs, or code, process models, test plans, configuration management procedures, process standards, and user manuals may all be reviewed. The review should check the consistency and completeness of the documents or code under review and make sure that quality standards have been followed.

However, reviews are not just about checking conformance to standards. They are also used to help discover problems and omissions in the software or project documentation. The conclusions of the review should be formally recorded as part of the quality management process. If problems have been discovered, the reviewers' comments should be passed to the author of the software or whoever is responsible for correcting errors or omissions.

The purpose of reviews and inspections is to improve software quality, not to assess the performance of people in the development team. Reviewing is a public process of error detection, compared with the more private component-testing process. Inevitably, mistakes that are made by individuals are revealed to the whole programming team. To ensure that all developers engage constructively with the review process, project managers have to be sensitive to individual concerns. They must develop a working culture that provides support without blame when errors are discovered.

Although a quality review provides information for management about the software being developed, quality reviews are not the same as management progress reviews. As I discussed in Chapter 23, progress reviews compare the actual progress in a software project against the planned progress. Their prime concern is whether or not the project will deliver useful software on time and on budget. Progress reviews take external factors into account, and changed circumstances may mean that software under development is no longer required or has to be radically changed.

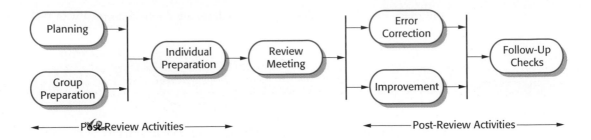

Figure 24.7 The software review process

Projects that have developed high-quality software may have to be canceled because of changes to the business or its operating environment.

24.3.1 The review process

Although there are many variations in the details of reviews, the review process (Figure 24.7) is normally structured into three phases:

1. *Pre-review activities* These are preparatory activities that are essential for the review to be effective. Typically, pre-review activities are concerned with review planning and review preparation. Review planning involves setting up a review team, arranging a time and place for the review, and distributing the documents to be reviewed. During review preparation, the team may meet to get an overview of the software to be reviewed. Individual review team members read and understand the software or documents and relevant standards. They work independently to find errors, omissions, and departures from standards. Reviewers may supply written comments on the software if they cannot attend the review meeting.

2. *The review meeting* During the review meeting, an author of the document or program being reviewed should 'walk through' the document with the review team. The review itself should be relatively short—two hours at most. One team member should chair the review and another should formally record all review decisions and actions to be taken. During the review, the chair is responsible for ensuring that all written comments are considered. The review chair should sign a record of comments and actions agreed during the review.

3. *Post-review activities* After a review meeting has finished, the issues and problems raised during the review must be addressed. This may involve fixing software bugs, refactoring software so that it conforms to quality standards, or rewriting documents. Sometimes, the problems discovered in a quality review are such that a management review is also necessary to decide if more resources should be made available to correct them. After changes have been made, the review chair may check that the review comments have all been taken into account. Sometimes, a further review will be required to check that the changes made cover all of the previous review comments.

Roles in the inspection process

When program inspection was first established in IBM (Fagan, 1976; Fagan, 1986), there were a number of formal roles defined for members of the inspection team. These included moderator, code reader, and scribe. Other users of inspections have modified these roles but it is generally accepted that an inspection should involve the code author, an inspector, and a scribe and should be chaired by a moderator.

http://www.SoftwareEngineering-9.com/Web/QualityMan/roles.html

Review teams should normally have a core of three to four people who are selected as principal reviewers. One member should be a senior designer who will take the responsibility for making significant technical decisions. The principal reviewers may invite other project members, such as the designers of related subsystems, to contribute to the review. They may not be involved in reviewing the whole document but should concentrate on those sections that affect their work. Alternatively, the review team may circulate the document and ask for written comments from a broad spectrum of project members. The project manager need not be involved in the review, unless problems are anticipated that require changes to the project plan.

The above review process relies on all members of a development team being colocated and available for a team meeting. However, project teams are now often distributed, sometimes across countries or continents, so it is often impractical for team members to meet in the same room. In such situations, document editing tools may be used to support the review process. Team members use these to annotate the document or software source code with comments. These comments are visible to other team members who may then approve or reject them. A phone discussion may only be required when disagreements between reviewers have to be resolved.

The review process in agile software development is usually informal. In Scrum, for example, there is a review meeting after each iteration of the software has been completed (a sprint review), where quality issues and problems may be discussed. In extreme programming, as I discuss in the next section, pair programming ensures that code is constantly being examined and reviewed by another team member. General quality issues are also considered at daily team meetings but XP relies on individuals taking the initiative to improve and refactor code. Agile approaches are not usually standards-driven, so issues of standards compliance are not usually considered.

The lack of formal quality procedures in agile methods means that there can be problems in using agile approaches in companies that have developed detailed quality management procedures. Quality reviews can slow down the pace of software development and they are best used within a plan-driven development process. In a plan-driven process, reviews can be planned and other work scheduled in parallel with them. This is impractical in agile approaches that focus single-mindedly on code development.

24.3.2 Program inspections

Program inspections are 'peer reviews' where team members collaborate to find bugs in the program that is being developed. As I discussed in Chapter 8, inspections may be part of the software verification and validation processes. They complement testing as they do not require the program to be executed. This means that incomplete versions of the system can be verified and that representations such as UML models can be checked. Gilb and Graham (1993) suggest that one of the most effective ways to use inspections is to review the test cases for a system. Inspections can discover problems with tests and so improve the effectiveness of these tests in detecting program bugs.

Program inspections involve team members from different backgrounds who make a careful, line-by-line review of the program source code. They look for defects and problems and describe these at an inspection meeting. Defects may be logical errors, anomalies in the code that might indicate an erroneous condition or features that have been omitted from the code. The review team examines the design models or the program code in detail and highlights anomalies and problems for repair.

During an inspection, a checklist of common programming errors is often used to focus the search for bugs. This checklist may be based on examples from books or from knowledge of defects that are common in a particular application domain. You use different checklists for different programming languages because each language has its own characteristic errors. Humphrey (1989), in a comprehensive discussion of inspections, gives a number of examples of inspection checklists.

Possible checks that might be made during the inspection process are shown in Figure 24.8. Gilb and Graham (1993) emphasize that each organization should develop its own inspection checklist based on local standards and practices. These checklists should be regularly updated, as new types of defects are found. The items in the checklist vary according to programming language because of the different levels of checking that are possible at compile-time. For example, a Java compiler checks that functions have the correct number of parameters; a C compiler does not.

Most companies that have introduced inspections have found that they are very effective in finding bugs. Fagan (1986) reported that more than 60 percent of the errors in a program can be detected using informal program inspections. Mills et al. (1987) suggest that a more formal approach to inspection, based on correctness arguments, can detect more than 90% of the errors in a program. McConnell (2004) compares unit testing, where the defect detection rate is about 25%, with inspections, where the defect detection rate was 60%. He also describes a number of case studies including an example where the introduction of peer reviews led to a 14% increase in productivity and a 90% decrease in program defects.

In spite of their well-publicized cost effectiveness, many software development companies are reluctant to use inspections or peer reviews. Software engineers with experience of program testing are sometimes unwilling to accept that inspections can

Fault class	Inspection check
Data faults	• Are all program variables initialized before their values are used? • Have all constants been named? • Should the upper bound of arrays be equal to the size of the array or Size -1? • If character strings are used, is a delimiter explicitly assigned? • Is there any possibility of buffer overflow?
Control faults	• For each conditional statement, is the condition correct? • Is each loop certain to terminate? • Are compound statements correctly bracketed? • In case statements, are all possible cases accounted for? • If a break is required after each case in case statements, has it been included?
Input/output faults	• Are all input variables used? • Are all output variables assigned a value before they are output? • Can unexpected inputs cause corruption?
Interface faults	• Do all function and method calls have the correct number of parameters? • Do formal and actual parameter types match? • Are the parameters in the right order? • If components access shared memory, do they have the same model of the shared memory structure?
Storage management faults	• If a linked structure is modified, have all links been correctly reassigned? • If dynamic storage is used, has space been allocated correctly? • Is space explicitly deallocated after it is no longer required?
Exception management faults	• Have all possible error conditions been taken into account?

Figure 24.8 An inspection checklist

be more effective for defect detection than testing. Managers may be suspicious because inspections require additional costs during design and development. They may not wish to take the risk that there will be no corresponding savings in program testing costs.

Agile processes rarely use formal inspection or peer review processes. Rather, they rely on team members cooperating to check each other's code, and informal guidelines, such as 'check before check-in', which suggest that programmers should check their own code. Extreme programming practitioners argue that pair programming is an effective substitute for inspection as this is, in effect, a continual inspection process. Two people look at every line of code and check it before it is accepted.

Pair programming leads to a deep knowledge of a program, as both programmers have to understand its working in detail to continue development. This depth of knowledge is sometimes difficult to achieve in other inspection processes and so pair programming can find bugs that sometimes would not be discovered in formal inspections. However, pair programming can also lead to mutual misunderstandings of requirements, where both members of the pair make the same mistake. Furthermore, pairs may be reluctant to look for errors because the pair does not want to slow down the progress of the project. The people involved cannot be as objective as an external inspection team and their ability to discover defects is likely to be compromised by their close working relationship.

24.4 Software measurement and metrics

Software measurement is concerned with deriving a numeric value or profile for an attribute of a software component, system, or process. By comparing these values to each other and to the standards that apply across an organization, you may be able to draw conclusions about the quality of software, or assess the effectiveness of software processes, tools, and methods.

For example, say an organization intends to introduce a new software-testing tool. Before introducing the tool, you record the number of software defects discovered in a given time. This is a baseline for assessing the effectiveness of the tool. After using the tool for some time, you repeat this process. If more defects have been found in the same amount of time, after the tool has been introduced, then you may decide that it provides useful support for the software validation process.

The long-term goal of software measurement is to use measurement in place of reviews to make judgments about software quality. Using software measurement, a system could ideally be assessed using a range of metrics and, from these measurements, a value for the quality of the system could be inferred. If the software had reached a required quality threshold, then it could be approved without review. When appropriate, the measurement tools might also highlight areas of the software that could be improved. However, we are still quite a long way from this ideal situation and, there are no signs that automated quality assessment will become a reality in the foreseeable future.

A software metric is a characteristic of a software system, system documentation, or development process that can be objectively measured. Examples of metrics include the size of a product in lines of code; the Fog index (Gunning, 1962), which is a measure of the readability of a passage of written text; the number of reported faults in a delivered software product; and the number of person-days required to develop a system component.

Software metrics may be either control metrics or predictor metrics. As the names imply, control metrics support process management, and predictor metrics help you predict characteristics of the software. Control metrics are usually associated with software processes. Examples of control or process metrics are the average effort and the time required to repair reported defects. Predictor metrics are associated with the software itself and are sometimes known as 'product metrics'. Examples of predictor metrics are the cyclomatic complexity of a module (discussed in Chapter 8),

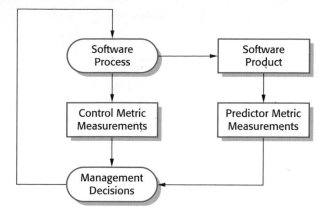

Figure 24.9 Predictor and control measurements

the average length of identifiers in a program, and the number of attributes and operations associated with object classes in a design.

Both control and predictor metrics may influence management decision making, as shown in Figure 24.9. Managers use process measurements to decide if process changes should be made, and predictor metrics to help estimate the effort required to make software changes. In this chapter, I mostly discuss predictor metrics, whose values are assessed by analyzing the code of a software system. I discuss control metrics and how they are used in process improvement in Chapter 26.

There are two ways in which measurements of a software system may be used:

1. *To assign a value to system quality attributes* By measuring the characteristics of system components, such as their cyclomatic complexity, and then aggregating these measurements, you can assess system quality attributes, such as maintainability.

2. *To identify the system components whose quality is substandard* Measurements can identify individual components with characteristics that deviate from the norm. For example, you can measure components to discover those with the highest complexity. These are most likely to contain bugs because the complexity makes them harder to understand.

Unfortunately, it is difficult to make direct measurements of many of the software quality attributes shown in Figure 24.2. Quality attributes such as maintainability, understandability, and usability are external attributes that relate to how developers and users experience the software. They are affected by subjective factors, such as user experience and education, and they cannot therefore be measured objectively. To make a judgment about these attributes, you have to measure some internal attributes of the software (such as its size, complexity, etc.) and assume that these are related to the quality characteristics that you are concerned with.

Figure 24.10 shows some external software quality attributes and internal attributes that could, intuitively, be related to them. The diagram suggests that there may be relationships between external and internal attributes, but it does not say how

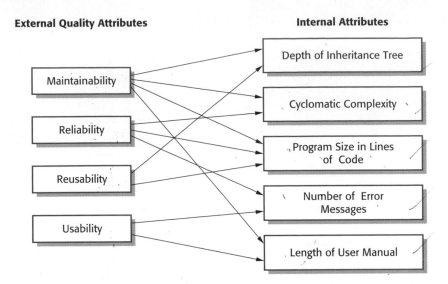

External Quality Attributes

Internal Attributes

Maintainability

Reliability

Reusability

Usability

Depth of Inheritance Tree

Cyclomatic Complexity

Program Size in Lines of Code

Number of Error Messages

Length of User Manual

Figure 24.10
Relationships between internal and external software

these attributes are related. If the measure of the internal attribute is to be a useful predictor of the external software characteristic, three conditions must hold (Kitchenham, 1990):

1. The internal attribute must be measured accurately. This is not always straightforward and it may require special-purpose tools to make the measurements.

2. A relationship must exist between the attribute that can be measured and the external quality attribute that is of interest. That is, the value of the quality attribute must be related, in some way, to the value of the attribute than can be measured.

3. This relationship between the internal and external attributes must be understood, validated, and expressed in terms of a formula or model. Model formulation involves identifying the functional form of the model (linear, exponential, etc.) by analysis of collected data, identifying the parameters that are to be included in the model, and calibrating these parameters using existing data.

Internal software attributes, such as the cyclomatic complexity of a component, are measured by using software tools that analyze the source code of the software. Open source tools are available that can be used to make these measurements. Although intuition suggests that there could be a relationship between the complexity of a software component and the number of observed failures in use, it is difficult to objectively demonstrate that this is the case. To test this hypothesis, you need failure data for a large number of components and access to the component source code for analysis. Very few companies have made a long-term commitment to collecting data about their software, so failure data for analysis is rarely available.

In the 1990s, several large companies such as Hewlett-Packard (Grady, 1993), AT&T (Barnard and Price, 1994), and Nokia (Kilpi, 2001) introduced metrics programs. They made measurements of their products and processes and used these in their quality management processes. Most of the focus was on collecting metrics on program defects and the verification and validation processes. Offen and Jeffrey (1997) and Hall and Fenton (1997) discuss the introduction of metrics programs in industry in more detail.

There is little information publicly available about the current use of systematic software measurement in industry. Many companies do collect information about their software, such as the number of requirements change requests or the number of defects discovered in testing. However, it is not clear if they then use these measurements systematically to compare software products and processes or assess the impact of changes to software processes and tools. There are several reasons why this is difficult:

1. It is impossible to quantify the return on investment of introducing an organizational metrics program. There have been significant improvements in software quality over the past few years without the use of metrics so it is difficult to justify the initial costs of introducing systematic software measurement and assessment.

2. There are no standards for software metrics or standardized processes for measurement and analysis. Many companies are reluctant to introduce measurement programs until such standards and supporting tools are available.

3. In many companies, software processes are not standardized and are poorly defined and controlled. As such, there is too much process variability within the same company for measurements to be used in a meaningful way.

4. Much of the research on software measurement and metrics has focused on code-based metrics and plan-driven development processes. However, more and more software is now developed by configuring ERP systems or COTS, or by using agile methods. We don't know, therefore, if previous research is applicable to these software development techniques.

5. Introducing measurement adds additional overhead to processes. This contradicts the aims of agile methods, which recommend the elimination of process activities that are not directly related to program development. Companies that have adopted agile methods are therefore not likely to adopt a metrics program.

Software measurement and metrics are the basis of empirical software engineering (Endres and Rombach, 2003). This is a research area in which experiments on software systems and the collection of data about real projects has been used to form and validate hypotheses about software engineering methods and techniques. Researchers working in this area argue that we can only be confident of the value of software engineering methods and techniques if we can provide concrete evidence that they actually provide the benefits that their inventors suggest.

Unfortunately, even when it is possible to make objective measurements and draw conclusions from them, these will not necessarily convince decision makers. Rather, decision making is often influenced by subjective factors, such as novelty, or the extent to which techniques are of interest to practitioners. I think, therefore, that it will be many years before the results from empirical software engineering have a significant effect on software engineering practice.

24.4.1 Product metrics

Product metrics are predictor metrics that are used to measure internal attributes of a software system. Examples of product metrics include the system size, measured in lines of code, or the number of methods associated with each object class. Unfortunately, as I have explained earlier in this section, software characteristics that can be easily measured, such as size and cyclomatic complexity, do not have a clear and consistent relationship with quality attributes such as understandability and maintainability. The relationships vary depending on the development processes and technology used and the type of system that is being developed.

Product metrics fall into two classes:

1. Dynamic metrics, which are collected by measurements made of a program in execution. These metrics can be collected during system testing or after the system has gone into use. An example might be the number of bug reports or the time taken to complete a computation.

2. Static metrics, which are collected by measurements made of representations of the system, such as the design, program, or documentation. Examples of static metrics are the code size and the average length of identifiers used.

These types of metric are related to different quality attributes. Dynamic metrics help to assess the efficiency and reliability of a program. Static metrics help assess the complexity, understandability, and maintainability of a software system or system components.

There is usually a clear relationship between dynamic metrics and software quality characteristics. It is fairly easy to measure the execution time required for particular functions and to assess the time required to start up a system. These relate directly to the system's efficiency. Similarly, the number of system failures and the type of failure can be logged and related directly to the reliability of the software, as discussed in Chapter 15.

As I have discussed, static metrics, such as those shown in Figure 24.11, have an indirect relationship with quality attributes. A large number of different metrics have been proposed and many experiments have tried to derive and validate the relationships between these metrics and attributes such as system complexity and maintainability. None of these experiments have been conclusive but program size and control complexity seem to be the most reliable predictors of understandability, system complexity, and maintainability.

The metrics in Figure 24.11 are applicable to any program but more specific object-oriented (OO) metrics have also been proposed. Figure 24.12 summarizes

Software metric	Description
Fan-in/Fan-out	Fan-in is a measure of the number of functions or methods that call another function or method (say X). Fan-out is the number of functions that are called by function X. A high value for fan-in means that X is tightly coupled to the rest of the design and changes to X will have extensive knock-on effects. A high value for fan-out suggests that the overall complexity of X may be high because of the complexity of the control logic needed to coordinate the called components.
Length of code	This is a measure of the size of a program. Generally, the larger the size of the code of a component, the more complex and error-prone that component is likely to be. Length of code has been shown to be one of the most reliable metrics for predicting error-proneness in components.
Cyclomatic complexity	This is a measure of the control complexity of a program. This control complexity may be related to program understandability. I discuss cyclomatic complexity in Chapter 8.
Length of identifiers	This is a measure of the average length of identifiers (names for variables, classes, methods, etc.) in a program. The longer the identifiers, the more likely they are to be meaningful and hence the more understandable the program.
Depth of conditional nesting	This is a measure of the depth of nesting of if-statements in a program. Deeply nested if-statements are hard to understand and potentially error-prone.
Fog index	This is a measure of the average length of words and sentences in documents. The higher the value of a document's Fog index, the more difficult the document is to understand.

Figure 24.11 Static software product metrics

Chidamber and Kemerer's suite (sometimes called the CK suite) of six object-oriented metrics (1994). Although these were originally proposed in the early 1990s, they are still the most widely used OO metrics. Some UML design tools automatically collect values for these metrics as UML diagrams are created.

El-Amam (2001), in an excellent review of object-oriented metrics, discusses the CK metrics and other OO metrics, and concludes that we do not yet have sufficient evidence to understand how these and other object-oriented metrics relate to external software qualities. This situation has not really changed since his analysis in 2001. We still don't know how to use measurements of object-oriented programs to draw reliable conclusions about their quality.

24.4.2 Software component analysis

A measurement process that may be part of a software quality assessment process is shown in Figure 24.13. Each system component can be analyzed separately using a range of metrics. The values of these metrics may then be compared for different

Object-oriented metric	Description
Weighted methods per class (WMC)	This is the number of methods in each class, weighted by the complexity of each method. Therefore, a simple method may have a complexity of 1, and a large and complex method a much higher value. The larger the value for this metric, the more complex the object class. Complex objects are more likely to be difficult to understand. They may not be logically cohesive, so cannot be reused effectively as superclasses in an inheritance tree.
Depth of inheritance tree (DIT)	This represents the number of discrete levels in the inheritance tree where subclasses inherit attributes and operations (methods) from superclasses. The deeper the inheritance tree, the more complex the design. Many object classes may have to be understood to understand the object classes at the leaves of the tree.
Number of children (NOC)	This is a measure of the number of immediate subclasses in a class. It measures the breadth of a class hierarchy, whereas DIT measures its depth. A high value for NOC may indicate greater reuse. It may mean that more effort should be made in validating base classes because of the number of subclasses that depend on them.
Coupling between object classes (CBO)	Classes are coupled when methods in one class use methods or instance variables defined in a different class. CBO is a measure of how much coupling exists. A high value for CBO means that classes are highly dependent, and therefore it is more likely that changing one class will affect other classes in the program.
Response for a class (RFC)	RFC is a measure of the number of methods that could potentially be executed in response to a message received by an object of that class. Again, RFC is related to complexity. The higher the value for RFC, the more complex a class and hence the more likely it is that it will include errors.
Lack of cohesion in methods (LCOM)	LCOM is calculated by considering pairs of methods in a class. LCOM is the difference between the number of method pairs without shared attributes and the number of method pairs with shared attributes. The value of this metric has been widely debated and it exists in several variations. It is not clear if it really adds any additional, useful information over and above that provided by other metrics.

Figure 24.12 The CK object-oriented metrics suite

components and, perhaps, with historical measurement data collected on previous projects. Anomalous measurements, which deviate significantly from the norm, may imply that there are problems with the quality of these components.

The key stages in this component measurement process are:

1. *Choose measurements to be made* The questions that the measurement is intended to answer should be formulated and the measurements required to answer these questions defined. Measurements that are not directly relevant to these questions need not be collected. Basili's GQM (Goal-Question-Metric) paradigm (Basili and Rombach, 1988), discussed in Chapter 26, is a good approach to use when deciding what data is to be collected.

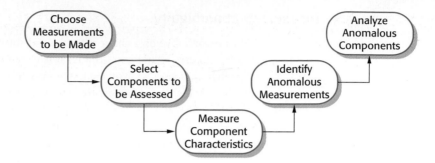

Figure 24.13 The process of product measurement

2. *Select components to be assessed* You may not need to assess metric values for all of the components in a software system. Sometimes, you can select a representative selection of components for measurement, allowing you to make an overall assessment of system quality. At other times, you may wish to focus on the core components of the system that are in almost constant use. The quality of these components is more important than the quality of components that are only rarely used.

3. *Measure component characteristics* The selected components are measured and the associated metric values computed. This normally involves processing the component representation (design, code, etc.) using an automated data collection tool. This tool may be specially written or may be a feature of design tools that are already in use.

4. *Identify anomalous measurements* After the component measurements have been made, you then compare them with each other and to previous measurements that have been recorded in a measurement database. You should look for unusually high or low values for each metric, as these suggest that there could be problems with the component exhibiting these values.

5. *Analyze anomalous components* When you have identified components that have anomalous values for your chosen metrics, you should examine them to decide whether or not these anomalous metric values mean that the quality of the component is compromised. An anomalous metric value for complexity (say) does not necessarily mean a poor quality component. There may be some other reason for the high value, so may not mean that there are component quality problems.

You should always maintain collected data as an organizational resource and keep historical records of all projects even when data has not been used during a particular project. Once a sufficiently large measurement database has been established, you can then make comparisons of software quality across projects and validate the relations between internal component attributes and quality characteristics.

24.4.3 Measurement ambiguity

When you collect quantitative data about software and software processes, you have to analyze that data to understand its meaning. It is easy to misinterpret data and to make inferences that are incorrect. You cannot simply look at the data on its own—you must also consider the context where the data is collected.

To illustrate how collected data can be interpreted in different ways, consider the scenario below, which is concerned with the number of change requests made by users of a system:

A manager decides to monitor the number of change requests submitted by customers based on an assumption that there is a relationship between these change requests and product usability and suitability. She assumes that the higher the number of change requests, the less the software meets the needs of the customer.

Handling change requests and changing the software is expensive. The organization therefore decides to modify its process with the aim of improving customer satisfaction and, at the same time, reduce the costs of making changes. The intent is that the process changes will result in better products and fewer change requests.

Process changes are initiated to increase customer involvement in the software design process. Beta testing of all products is introduced and customer-requested modifications are incorporated in the delivered product. New versions of products, developed with this modified process, are delivered. In some cases, the number of change requests is reduced. In others, it is increased. The manager is baffled and finds it impossible to assess the effects of the process changes on the product quality.

To understand why this kind of ambiguity can occur, you have to understand the reasons why users might make change requests:

1. The software is not good enough and does not do what customers want it to do. They therefore request changes to deliver the functionality that they require.

2. Alternatively, the software may be very good and so it is widely and heavily used. Change requests may be generated because there are many software users who creatively think of new things that could be done with the software.

Therefore, increasing the customer involvement in the process may reduce the number of change requests for products where the customers were unhappy. The process changes have been effective and have made the software more usable and suitable. Alternatively, however, the process changes may not have worked and customers may have decided to look for an alternative system. The number of change requests might decrease because the product has lost market share to a rival product and there are consequently fewer product users.

On the other hand, the process changes might lead to many new, happy customers who wish to participate in the product development process. They therefore generate more change requests. Changes to the process of handling change requests may contribute to this increase. If the company is more responsive to customers, they may generate more change requests because they know that these requests will be taken seriously. They believe that their suggestions will probably be incorporated in later versions of the software. Alternatively, the number of change requests might have increased because the beta-test sites were not typical of most usage of the program.

To analyze the change request data, you do not simply need to know the number of change requests. You need to know who made the request, how they use the software, and why the request was made. You also need information about external factors such as modifications to the change request procedure or market changes that might have an effect. With this information, it is then possible to find out if the process changes have been effective in increasing product quality.

This illustrates the difficulties of understanding the effects of changes and the 'scientific' approach to this problem is to reduce the number of factors that might affect the measurements made. However, processes and products that are being measured are not insulated from their environment. The business environment is constantly changing and it is impossible to avoid changes to work practice just because they may make comparisons of data invalid. As such, quantitative data about human activities cannot always be taken at face value. The reasons why a measured value changes are often ambiguous. These reasons must be investigated in detail before drawing conclusions from any measurements that have been made.

KEY POINTS

■ Software quality management is concerned with ensuring that software has a low number of defects and that it reaches the required standards of maintainability, reliability, portability, and so on. It includes defining standards for processes and products and establishing processes to check that these standards have been followed.

■ Software standards are important for quality assurance as they represent an identification of 'best practice'. When developing software, standards provide a solid foundation for building good quality software.

■ You should document a set of quality assurance procedures in an organizational quality manual. This may be based on the generic model for a quality manual suggested in the ISO 9001 standard.

■ Reviews of the software process deliverables involve a team of people who check that quality standards are being followed. Reviews are the most widely used technique for assessing quality.

■ In a program inspection or peer review, a small team systematically checks the code. They read the code in detail and look for possible errors and omissions. The problems detected are then discussed at a code review meeting.

■ Software measurement can be used to gather quantitative data about software and the software process. You may be able to use the values of the software metrics that are collected to make inferences about product and process quality.

■ Product quality metrics are particularly useful for highlighting anomalous components that may have quality problems. These components should then be analyzed in more detail.

FURTHER READING

Metrics and Models for Software Quality Engineering, 2nd edition. This is a very comprehensive discussion of software metrics covering process-, product-, and object-oriented metrics. It also includes some background on the mathematics required to develop and understand models based on software measurement. (S. H. Kan, Addison-Wesley, 2003.)

Software Quality Assurance: From Theory to Implementation. An excellent, up-to-date look at the principles and practice of software quality assurance. It includes a discussion of standards such as ISO 9001. (D. Galin, Addison-Wesley, 2004.)

'A Practical Approach for Quality-Driven Inspections'. Many articles on inspections are now rather old and do not take modern software development practice into account. This relatively recent article describes an inspection method that addresses some of the problems of using inspection and suggests how inspection can be used in a modern development environment. (C. Denger, F. Shull, *IEEE Software*, **24** (2), March–April 2007.) http://dx.doi.org/10.1109/MS.2007.31

'Misleading Metrics and Unsound Analyses'. An excellent article by leading metrics researchers that discusses the difficulties of understanding what measurements really mean. (B. Kitchenham, R. Jeffrey and C. Connaughton, *IEEE Software*, **24** (2), March–April 2007.) http://dx.doi.org/10.1109/MS.2007.49

'The Case for Quantitative Project Management'. This is an introduction to a special section in the magazine that includes two other articles on quantitative project management. It makes an argument for further research in metrics and measurement to improve software project management. (B. Curtis et al., *IEEE Software*, **25** (3), May–June 2008.) http://dx.doi.org/10.1109/MS.2008.80.

EXERCISES

24.1. Explain why a high-quality software process should lead to high-quality software products. Discuss possible problems with this system of quality management.

24.2. Explain how standards may be used to capture organizational wisdom about effective methods of software development. Suggest four types of knowledge that might be captured in organizational standards.

24.3. Discuss the assessment of software quality according to the quality attributes shown in Figure 24.2. You should consider each attribute in turn and explain how it might be assessed.

24.4. Design an electronic form that may be used to record review comments and which could be used to electronically mail comments to reviewers.

24.5. Briefly describe possible standards that might be used for:

- The use of control constructs in C, C#, or Java;
- Reports which might be submitted for a term project in a university;
- The process of making and approving program changes (see Chapter 26);
- The process of purchasing and installing a new computer.

24.6. Assume you work for an organization that develops database products for individuals and small businesses. This organization is interested in quantifying its software development. Write a report suggesting appropriate metrics and suggest how these can be collected.

24.7. Explain why program inspections are an effective technique for discovering errors in a program. What types of error are unlikely to be discovered through inspections?

24.8. Explain why design metrics are, by themselves, an inadequate method of predicting design quality.

24.9. Explain why it is difficult to validate the relationships between internal product attributes, such as cyclomatic complexity and external attributes, such as maintainability.

24.10. A colleague who is a very good programmer produces software with a low number of defects but consistently ignores organizational quality standards. How should her managers react to this behavior?

REFERENCES

Bamford, R. and Deibler, W. J. (eds.) (2003). 'ISO 9001:2000 for Software and Systems Providers: An Engineering Approach'. Boca Raton, Fla.: CRC Press.

Barnard, J. and Price, A. (1994). 'Managing Code Inspection Information'. *IEEE Software,* **11** (2), 59–69.

Basili, V. R. and Rombach, H. D. (1988). 'The TAME project: Towards Improvement-Oriented Software Environments'. *IEEE Trans. on Software Eng.,* **14** (6), 758–773.

Boehm, B. W., Brown, J. R., Kaspar, H., Lipow, M., Macleod, G. and Merrit, M. (1978). *Characteristics of Software Quality*. Amsterdam: North-Holland.

Chidamber, S. and Kemerer, C. (1994). 'A Metrics Suite for Object-Oriented Design'. *IEEE Trans. on Software Eng.,* **20** (6), 476–93.

Crosby, P. (1979). *Quality is Free*. New York: McGraw-Hill.

El-Amam, K. 2001. 'Object-oriented Metrics: A Review of Theory and Practice'. National Research Council of Canada. http://seg.iit.nrc.ca/English/abstracts/NRC44190.html .

Endres, A. and Rombach, D. (2003). *Empirical Software Engineering: A Handbook of Observations, Laws and Theories*. Harlow, UK: Addison-Wesley.

Fagan, M. E. (1976). 'Design and code inspections to reduce errors in program development'. *IBM Systems J.,* **15** (3), 182–211.

Fagan, M. E. (1986). 'Advances in Software Inspections'. *IEEE Trans. on Software Eng.,* **SE-12** (7), 744–51.

Gilb, T. and Graham, D. (1993). *Software Inspection*. Wokingham: Addison-Wesley.

Grady, R. B. (1993). 'Practical Results from Measuring Software Quality'. *Comm. ACM,* **36** (11), 62–8.

Gunning, R. (1962). *Techniques of Clear Writing*. New York: McGraw-Hill.

Hall, T. and Fenton, N. (1997). 'Implementing Effective Software Metrics Programs'. *IEEE Software,* **14** (2), 55–64.

Humphrey, W. (1989). *Managing the Software Process*. Reading, Mass.: Addison-Wesley.

IEC. 1998. 'Standard IEC 61508: Functional safety of electrical/electronic/programmable electronic safety-related systems'. International Electrotechnical Commission: Geneva.

IEEE. (2003). *IEEE Software Engineering Standards Collection on CD-ROM*. Los Alamitos, Ca.: IEEE Computer Society Press.

Ince, D. (1994). *ISO 9001 and Software Quality Assurance*. London: McGraw-Hill.

Kilpi, T. (2001). 'Implementing a Software Metrics Program at Nokia'. *IEEE Software,* **18** (6), 72–7.

Kitchenham, B. (1990). 'Measuring Software Development'. In *Software Reliability Handbook*. Rook, P. (ed.). Amsterdam: Elsevier, 303–31.

McConnell, S. (2004). *Code Complete: A Practical Handbook of Software Construction, 2nd edition*. Seattle: Microsoft Press.

Mills, H. D., Dyer, M. and Linger, R. (1987). 'Cleanroom Software Engineering'. *IEEE Software,* **4** (5), 19–25.

Offen, R. J. and Jeffrey, R. (1997). 'Establishing Software Measurement Programs'. *IEEE Software,* **14** (2), 45–54.

Stalhane, T. and Hanssen, G. K. (2008). 'The application of ISO 9001 to agile software development'. *9th International Conference on Product Focused Software Process Improvement, PROFES 2008,* Monte Porzio Catone, Italy: Springer.

25

Configuration management

Objectives

The objective of this chapter is to introduce you to configuration management processes and tools. When you have read the chapter, you will:

- understand the processes and procedures involved in software change management;

- know the essential functionality that must be provided by a version management system, and the relationships between version management and system building;

- understand the differences between a system version and a system release, and know the stages in the release management process.

Contents

Software systems always change during development and use. Bugs are discovered and have to be fixed. System requirements change, and you have to implement these changes in a new version of the system. New versions of hardware and system platforms become available and you have to adapt your systems to work with them. Competitors introduce new features in their system that you have to match. As changes are made to the software, a new version of a system is created. Most systems, therefore, can be thought of as a set of versions, each of which has to be maintained and managed.

Configuration management (CM) is concerned with the policies, processes, and tools for managing changing software systems. You need to manage evolving systems because it is easy to lose track of what changes and component versions have been incorporated into each system version. Versions implement proposals for change, corrections of faults, and adaptations for different hardware and operating systems. There may be several versions under development and in use at the same time. If you don't have effective configuration management procedures in place, you may waste effort modifying the wrong version of a system, deliver the wrong version of a system to customers, or forget where the software source code for a particular version of the system or component is stored.

Configuration management is useful for individual projects as it is easy for one person to forget what changes have been made. It is essential for team projects where several developers are working at the same time on a software system. Sometimes these developers are all working in the same place but, increasingly, development teams are distributed with members in different locations across the world. The use of a configuration management system ensures that teams have access to information about a system that is under development and do not interfere with each other's work.

The configuration management of a software system product involves four closely related activities (Figure 25.1):

1. *Change management* This involves keeping track of requests for changes to the software from customers and developers, working out the costs and impact of making these changes, and deciding if and when the changes should be implemented.

2. *Version management* This involves keeping track of the multiple versions of system components and ensuring that changes made to components by different developers do not interfere with each other.

3. *System building* This is the process of assembling program components, data, and libraries, and then compiling and linking these to create an executable system.

4. *Release management* This involves preparing software for external release and keeping track of the system versions that have been released for customer use.

Configuration management involves dealing with a large volume of information and many configuration management tools have been developed to support CM

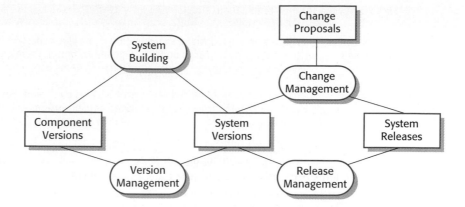

Figure 25.1
Configuration
management activities

processes. These range from simple tools that support a single configuration management task, such as bug tracking, to complex and expensive integrated toolsets that support all configuration management activities.

Configuration management policies and processes define how to record and process proposed system changes, how to decide what system components to change, how to manage different versions of the system and its components, and how to distribute changes to customers. Configuration management tools are used to keep track of change proposals, store versions of system components, build systems from these components, and track the releases of system versions to customers.

Configuration management is sometimes considered to be part of software quality management (covered in Chapter 24), with the same manager having both quality management and configuration management responsibilities. When a new version of the software has been implemented, it is handed over by the development team to the quality assurance (QA) team. The QA team checks that the system quality is acceptable. If so, it then becomes a controlled system, which means that all changes to the system have to be agreed on and recorded before they are implemented.

The definition and use of configuration management standards is essential for quality certification in both the ISO 9000 and the CMM and CMMI standards (Ahern et al., 2001; Bamford and Deibler, 2003; Paulk et al., 1995; Peach, 1996). These CM standards can be based on generic CM standards that have been developed by bodies such as the IEEE. For example, standard IEEE 828-1998 is a standard for configuration management plans. These standards focus on CM processes and the documents produced during the CM process. Using the external standards as a starting point, companies then develop more detailed, company-specific standards that are tailored to their specific needs.

One of the problems of configuration management is that different companies talk about the same concepts using different terms. There are historical

Term	Explanation
Configuration item or software configuration item (SCI)	Anything associated with a software project (design, code, test data, document, etc.) that has been placed under configuration control. There are often different versions of a configuration item. Configuration items have a unique name.
Configuration control	The process of ensuring that versions of systems and components are recorded and maintained so that changes are managed and all versions of components are identified and stored for the lifetime of the system.
Version	An instance of a configuration item that differs, in some way, from other instances of that item. Versions always have a unique identifier, which is often composed of the configuration item name plus a version number.
Baseline	A baseline is a collection of component versions that make up a system. Baselines are controlled, which means that the versions of the components making up the system cannot be changed. This means that it should always be possible to re-create a baseline from its constituent components.
Codeline	A codeline is a set of versions of a software component and other configuration items on which that component depends.
Mainline	A sequence of baselines representing different versions of a system.
Release	A version of a system that has been released to customers (or other users in an organization) for use.
Workspace	A private work area where software can be modified without affecting other developers who may be using or modifying that software.
Branching	The creation of a new codeline from a version in an existing codeline. The new codeline and the existing codeline may then develop independently.
Merging	The creation of a new version of a software component by merging separate versions in different codelines. These codelines may have been created by a previous branch of one of the codelines involved.
System building	The creation of an executable system version by compiling and linking the appropriate versions of the components and libraries making up the system.

Figure 25.2 CM terminology

reasons for this. Military software systems were probably the first systems in which configuration management was used and the terminology for these systems reflected the processes and procedures already in place for hardware configuration management. Commercial systems developers were not familiar with the military procedures or terminology and so often invented their own terms. Agile methods also have devised new terminology, sometimes introduced deliberately to distinguish the agile approach from traditional CM methods. Figure 25.2 defines the configuration management terminology that I use in this chapter.

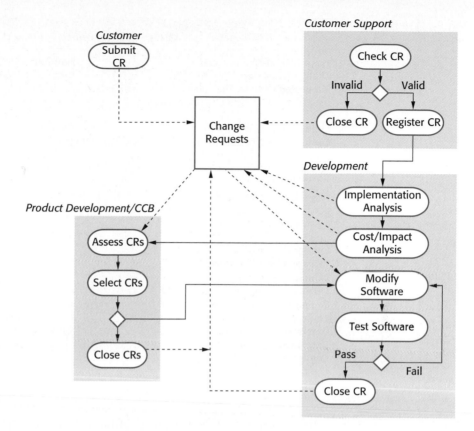

Figure 25.3 The change management process

25.1 Change management

Change is a fact of life for large software systems. Organizational needs and requirements change during the lifetime of a system, bugs have to be repaired, and systems have to adapt to changes in their environment. To ensure that the changes are applied to the system in a controlled way, you need a set of tool-supported, change management processes. Change management is intended to ensure that the evolution of the system is a managed process and that priority is given to the most urgent and cost-effective changes.

The change management process is concerned with analyzing the costs and benefits of proposed changes, approving those changes that are worthwhile, and tracking which components in the system have been changed. Figure 25.3 is a model of a change management process that shows the principal change management activities. There are many variants of this process in use but, to be effective, change management processes should always have a means of checking, costing, and approving changes. This process should come into effect when the software is handed over for release to customers or for deployment within an organization.

The change management process is initiated when a 'customer' completes and submits a change request describing the change required to the system. This could

Change Request Form

Project: SICSA/AppProcessing   **Number:** 23/02
Change requester: I. Sommerville   **Date:** 20/01/09
Requested change: The status of applicants (rejected, accepted, etc.) should be shown visually in the displayed list of applicants.

Change analyzer: R. Looek   **Analysis date:** 25/01/09
Components affected: ApplicantListDisplay, StatusUpdater

Associated components: StudentDatabase

Change assessment: Relatively simple to implement by changing the display color according to status. A table must be added to relate status to colors. No changes to associated components are required.

Change priority: Medium
Change implementation:
Estimated effort: 2 hours
Date to SGA app. team: 28/01/09   **CCB decision date:** 30/01/09
Decision: Accept change. Change to be implemented in Release 1.2
Change implementor: **Date of change:**
Date submitted to QA: **QA decision:**
Date submitted to CM:
Comments:

Figure 25.4 A partially completed change request form

be a bug report, where the symptoms of the bug are described, or a request for additional functionality to be added to the system. Some companies handle bug reports and new requirements separately but, in principle, these are both simply change requests. Change requests may be submitted using a change request form (CRF). I use the term 'customer' here to include any stakeholder who is not part of the development team, so changes may be suggested, for example, by the marketing department in a company.

Electronic change request forms record information that is shared between all groups involved in change management. As the change request is processed, information is added to the CRF to record decisions made at each stage of the process. At any time, it therefore represents a snapshot of the state of the change request. As well as recording the change required, the CRF records the recommendations regarding the change; the estimated costs of the change; and the dates when the change was requested, approved, implemented, and validated. The CRF may also include a section where a developer outlines how the change may be implemented.

An example of a partially completed change request form is shown in Figure 25.4. This is an example of a type of CRF that might be used in a large complex systems engineering project. For smaller projects, I recommend that change requests should be formally recorded and the CRF should focus on describing the change required, with less emphasis on implementation issues. As a system developer, you decide how to implement that change and estimate the time required for this.

After a change request has been submitted, it is checked to ensure that it is valid. The checker may be from a customer or application support team or, for internal requests, may be a member of the development team. Checking is necessary because not all change requests require action. If the change request is a bug report, the bug may have already been reported. Sometimes, what people believe to be problems are actually misunderstandings of what the system is expected to do. On occasions, people request features that have already been implemented but which they don't know about. If any of these are true, the change request is closed and the form is updated with the reason for closure. If it is a valid change request, it is then logged as an outstanding request for subsequent analysis.

For valid change requests, the next stage of the process is change assessment and costing. This is usually the responsibility of the development or maintenance team as they can work out what is involved in implementing the change. The impact of the change on the rest of the system must be checked. To do this, you have to identify all of the components affected by the change. If making the change means that further changes elsewhere in the system are needed, this will obviously increase the cost of change implementation. Next, the required changes to the system modules are assessed. Finally, the cost of making the change is estimated, taking into account the costs of changing related components.

Following this analysis, a separate group should then decide if it is cost-effective from a business perspective to make the change to the software. For military and government systems, this group is often called the change control board (CCB). In industry, it may be called something like a 'product development group', who is responsible for making decisions about how a software system should evolve. This group should review and approve all change requests, unless the changes simply involve correcting minor errors on screen displays, webpages, or documents. These small requests should be passed to the development team without detailed analysis, as such an analysis could cost more than implementing the change.

The CCB or product development group considers the impact of the change from a strategic and organizational rather than a technical point of view. It decides whether the change in question is economically justified and prioritizes accepted changes for implementation. Accepted changes are passed back to the development group; rejected change requests are closed and no further action is taken. Significant factors that should be taken into account in deciding whether or not a change should be approved are:

1. *The consequences of not making the change* When assessing a change request, you have to consider what will happen if the change is not implemented. If the change is associated with a reported system failure, the seriousness of that failure has to be taken into account. If the system failure causes the system to crash, this is very serious and failure to make the change may disrupt the operational use of the system. On the other hand if the failure has a minor effect, such as incorrect colors on a display, then it is not important to fix the problem quickly, so the change should have a low priority.

Customers and changes

Agile methods emphasize the importance of involving customers in the change prioritization process. The customer representative helps the team decide on the changes that should be implemented in the next development iteration. Although this can be effective for systems that are in development for a single customer, it can be a problem in product development where there is no real customer working with the team. In those cases, the team has to make their own decisions on change prioritization.

http://www.SoftwareEngineering-9.com/Web/CM/agilechanges.html

2.   *The benefits of the change* Is the change something that will benefit many users of the system or is it simply a proposal that will primarily be of benefit to the change proposer?

3.   *The number of users affected by the change* If only a few users are affected, then the change may be assigned a low priority. In fact, making the change may be inadvisable if it could have adverse effects on the majority of system users.

4.   *The costs of making the change* If making the change affects many system components (hence increasing the chances of introducing new bugs) and/or takes a lot of time to implement, then the change may be rejected, given the elevated costs involved.

5.   *The product release cycle* If a new version of the software has just been released to customers, it may make sense to delay the implementation of the change until the next planned release (see Section 25.3).

Change management for software products (e.g., a CAD system product) rather than systems that are specifically developed for a certain customer, has to be handled in a slightly different way. In software products, the customer is not directly involved in decisions about system evolution, so the relevance of the change to the customer's business is not an issue. Change requests for these products come from the customer support team, the company marketing team and the developers themselves. These requests may reflect suggestions and feedback from customers or analyses of what is offered by competing products.

The customer support team may submit change requests associated with bugs that have been discovered and reported by customers after the software has been released. Customers may use a webpage or e-mail to report bugs. A bug management team then checks that the bug reports are valid and translates them into formal system change requests. Marketing staff meet with customers and investigate competitive products. They may suggest changes that should be included to make it easier to sell a new version of a system to new and existing customers. The system developers themselves may have some good ideas about new features that can be added to the system.

The change request process shown in Figure 25.3 is used after a system has been released to customers. During development, when new versions of the system are

```
// SICSA project (XEP 6087)
//
// APP-SYSTEM/AUTH/RBAC/USER_ROLE
//
// Object: currentRole
// Author: R. Looek
// Creation date: 13/11/2009
//
// © St Andrews University 2009
//
// Modification history
// Version   Modifier   Date         Change       Reason
// 1.0       J. Jones   11/11/2009   Add header    Submitted to CM
// 1.1       R. Looek   13/11/2009   New field     Change req. R07/02
```

Figure 25.5
Derivation history

created through daily (or more frequent) system builds, a simpler change management process is normally used. Problems and changes must still be recorded, but changes that only affect individual components and modules need not be independently assessed. They are passed directly to the system developer. The system developer either accepts them or makes a case for why they are not required. However, an independent authority, such as the system architect, should assess and prioritize changes that affect those system modules that have been produced by different development teams.

In some agile methods, such as extreme programming, customers are directly involved in deciding whether a change should be implemented. When they propose a change to the system requirements, they work with the team to assess the impact of that change and then decide whether the change should take priority over the features planned for the next increment of the system. However, changes that involve software improvement are left to the discretion of the programmers working on the system. Refactoring, where the software is continually improved, is not seen as an overhead but rather as a necessary part of the development process.

As the development team changes software components, they should maintain a record of the changes made to each component. This is sometimes called the derivation history of a component. A good way to keep the derivation history is in a standardized comment at the beginning of the component source code (Figure 25.5). This comment should reference the change request that triggered the software change. You can then write simple scripts that scan all components and process the derivation histories to produce component change reports. For documents, records of changes incorporated in each version are usually maintained in a separate page at the front of the document. I discuss this in the web chapter on documentation.

Change management is usually supported by specialized software tools. These may be relatively simple web-based tools such as Bugzilla, which is used to report problems with many open source systems. Alternatively, more complex tools may be used to automate the entire process of handling change requests from initial customer proposal to change approval.

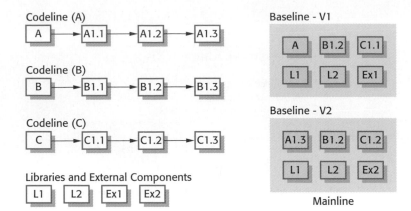

Figure 25.6 Codelines and baselines

25.2 Version management

Version management (VM) is the process of keeping track of different versions of software components or configuration items and the systems in which these components are used. It also involves ensuring that changes made by different developers to these versions do not interfere with each other. You can, therefore, think of version management as the process of managing codelines and baselines.

Figure 25.6 illustrates the differences between codelines and baselines. Essentially, a codeline is a sequence of versions of source code with later versions in the sequence derived from earlier versions. Codelines normally apply to components of systems so that there are different versions of each component. A baseline is a definition of a specific system. The baseline therefore specifies the component versions that are included in the system plus a specification of the libraries used, configuration files, etc. In Figure 25.6, you can see that different baselines use different versions of the components from each codeline. In the diagram, I have shaded the boxes representing components in the baseline definition to indicate that these are actually references to components in a codeline. The mainline is a sequence of system versions developed from an original baseline.

Baselines may be specified using a configuration language, which allows you to define what components are included in a version of a particular system. It is possible to explicitly specify a specific component version (X.1.2, say) or simply to specify the component identifier (X). If you use the identifier, this means that the most recent version of the component should be used in the baseline.

Baselines are important because you often have to re-create a specific version of a complete system. For example, a product line may be instantiated so that there are individual system versions for different customers. You may have to re-create the version delivered to a specific customer if, for example, that customer reports bugs in their system that have to be repaired.

To support version management, you should always use version management tools (sometimes called version control systems or source code control systems).

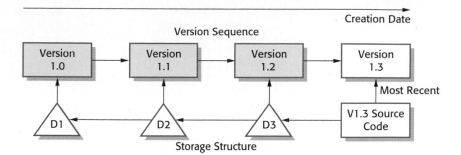

Figure 25.7 Storage management using deltas

These tools identify, store, and control access to the different versions of components. There are many different version management systems available, including widely used open source systems such as CVS and Subversion (Pilato et al., 2004; Vesperman, 2003).

Version management systems normally provide a range of features:

1. *Version and release identification* Managed versions are assigned identifiers when they are submitted to the system. These identifiers are usually based on the name of the configuration item (e.g., ButtonManager), followed by one or more numbers. So ButtonManager 1.3 means the third version in codeline 1 of the ButtonManager component. Some CM systems also allow the association of attributes with versions (e.g., mobile, smallscreen), which can also be used for version identification. A consistent identification system is important because it simplifies the problem of defining configurations. It makes it simpler to use shorthand references (e.g., *.V2 meaning version 2 of all components).

2. *Storage management* To reduce the storage space required by multiple versions of components that differ only slightly, version management systems usually provide storage management facilities. Instead of keeping a complete copy of each version, the system stores a list of differences (deltas) between one version and another. By applying these to a source version (usually the most recent version), a target version can be re-created. This is illustrated in Figure 25.7.

3. *Change history recording* All of the changes made to the code of a system or component are recorded and listed. In some systems, these changes may be used to select a particular system version. This involves tagging components with keywords describing the changes made. You then use these tags to select the components to be included in a baseline.

4. *Independent development* Different developers may be working on the same component at the same time. The version management system keeps track of components that have been checked out for editing and ensures that changes made to a component by different developers do not interfere.

5. *Project support* A version management system may support the development of several projects, which share components. In project support systems, such as

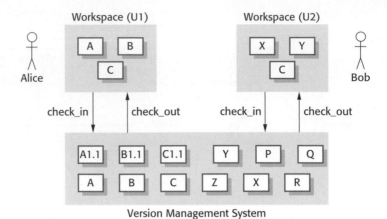

Figure 25.8 Check-in and check-out from a version repository

CVS (Vesperman, 2003), it is possible to check in and check out all of the files associated with a project rather than having to work with one file or directory at a time.

When version management systems were first developed, storage management was one of their most important functions. The storage management features in a version control system reduce the disk space required to maintain all system versions. When a new version is created, the system simply stores a delta (a list of differences) between the new version and the older version used to create that new version (shown in the bottom part of Figure 25.7). In Figure 25.7, the shaded boxes represent earlier versions of a component that are automatically re-created from the most recent component version. Deltas are usually stored as lists of changed lines and, by applying these automatically, one version of a component can be created from another. As it is most likely that the most recent version of a component will be used, most systems store that version in full. The deltas then define how to re-create earlier system versions.

Most software development is a team activity, so situations often arise where different team members work on the same component at the same time. For example, let's say Alice is making some changes to a system, which involves changing components A, B, and C. At the same time, Bob is working on changes and these require making changes to components X, Y, and C. Both Alice and Bob are therefore changing C. It's important to avoid these changes interfering with each other—Bob's changes to C overwriting Alice's or vice versa.

To support independent development without interference, version management systems use the concept of a public repository and a private workspace. Developers check out components from the public repository into their private workspace and may change these as they wish in their private workspace. When their changes are complete, they check in the components to the repository. This is illustrated in Figure 25.8. If two or more people are working on a component at the same time, each must check out the component from the repository. If a component has been checked out, the version management system will normally warn other users wanting

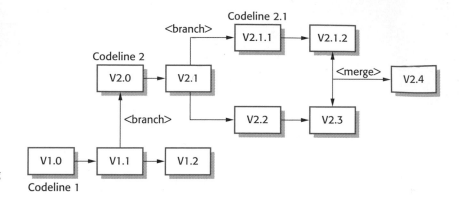

Figure 25.9 Branching and merging

to check out that component that it has been checked out by someone else. The system will also ensure that when the modified components are checked in, the different versions are assigned different version identifiers and are separately stored.

A consequence of the independent development of the same component is that codelines may branch. Rather than a linear sequence of versions that reflect changes to the component over time, there may be several independent sequences, as shown in Figure 25.9. This is normal in system development, where different developers work independently on different versions of the source code and change it in different ways.

At some stage, it may be necessary to merge codeline branches to create a new version of a component that includes all changes that have been made. This is also shown in Figure 25.9 where versions 2.1.2 and 2.3 of the component are merged to create version 2.4. If the changes made involve completely different parts of the code, the component versions may be merged automatically by the version management system by combining the deltas that apply to the code. More often, there are overlaps between the changes made and they interfere with each other. A developer has to check for clashes and modify the changes so that they are compatible.

25.3 System building

System building is the process of creating a complete, executable system by compiling and linking the system components, external libraries, configuration files, etc. System building tools and version management tools must communicate as the build process involves checking out component versions from the repository managed by the version management system. The configuration description used to identify a baseline is also used by the system building tool.

Building is a complex process, which is potentially error-prone, as there may be three different system platforms involved (Figure 25.10):

1.   The development system, which includes development tools such as compilers, source code editors, etc. Developers check out code from the version management system into a private workspace before making changes to the system.

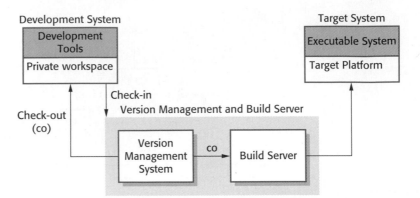

Figure 25.10
Development, build,
and target platforms

They may wish to build a version of a system for testing in their development environment before committing changes that they have made to the version management system. This involves using local build tools that use checked-out versions of components in the private workspace.

2. The build server, which is used to build definitive, executable versions of the system. This interacts closely with the version management system. Developers check in code to the version management system before it is built. The system build may rely on external libraries that are not included in the version management system.

3. The target environment, which is the platform on which the system executes. This may be the same type of computer that is used for the development and build systems. However, for real-time and embedded systems, the target environment is often smaller and simpler than the development environment (e.g., a cell phone). For large systems, the target environment may include databases and other COTS systems that cannot be installed on development machines. In both of these cases, it is not possible to build and test the system on the development computer or on the build server.

The development system and the build server may both interact with the version management system. The VM system may either be hosted on the build server or on a dedicated server. For embedded systems, a simulation environment may be installed in the development environment for testing, rather than using the actual embedded system platform. These simulators may provide better debugging support than is available on an embedded system. However, it is very difficult to simulate the behavior of an embedded system in every respect. You therefore have to run system tests on the actual platform where the system will execute, as well as the system simulator.

System building involves assembling a large amount of information about the software and its operating environment. Therefore, for anything apart from very small systems, it always makes sense to use an automated build tool to create a system build (Figure 25.11). Notice that you don't just need the source code files that are involved in the build. You may have to link these with externally provided

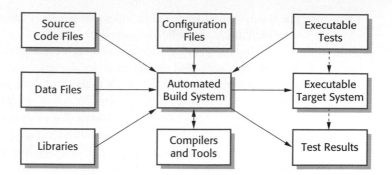

Figure 25.11 System building

libraries, data files (such as a file of error messages), and configuration files that define the target installation. You may have to specify the versions of the compiler and other software tools that are to be used in the build. Ideally, you should be able to build a complete system with a single command or mouse click.

There are many build tools available and a build system may provide some or all of the following features:

1. *Build script generation* If necessary, the build system should analyze the program that is being built, identify dependent components, and automatically generate a build script (sometimes called a configuration file). The system should also support the manual creation and editing of build scripts.

2. *Version management system integration* The build system should check out the required versions of components from the version management system.

3. *Minimal recompilation* The build system should work out what source code needs to be recompiled and set up compilations if required.

4. *Executable system creation* The build system should link the compiled object code files with each other and with other required files, such as libraries and configuration files, to create an executable system.

5. *Test automation* Some build systems can automatically run automated tests using test automation tools such as JUnit. These check that the build has not been 'broken' by changes.

6. *Reporting* The build system should provide reports about the success or failure of the build and the tests that have been run.

7. *Documentation generation* The build system may be able to generate release notes about the build and system help pages.

The build script is a definition of the system to be built. It includes information about components and their dependencies, and the versions of tools used to compile and link the system. The build script includes the configuration specification so the scripting language used is often the same as the configuration description language.

The configuration language includes constructs to describe the system components to be included in the build and their dependencies.

As compilation is a computationally intensive process, tools to support system building are usually designed to minimize the amount of compilation that is required. They do this by checking if a compiled version of a component is available. If so, there is no need to recompile that component. Therefore, there has to be a way of unambiguously linking the source code of a component with its equivalent object code.

The way that this is done is to associate a unique signature with each file where a source code component is stored. The corresponding object code, which has been compiled from the source code, has a related signature. The signature identifies each source code version and is changed when the source code is edited. By comparing the signatures on the source and object code files, it is possible to decide if the source code component was used to generate the object code component.

There are two types of signatures that may be used:

1. *Modification timestamps* The signature on the source code file is the time and date when that file was modified. If the source code file of a component has been modified after the related object code file, then the system assumes that recompilation to create a new object code file is necessary.

   For example, say components Comp.java and Comp.class have modification signatures of 17:03:05:02:14:2009 and 16:34:25:02:12:2009, respectively. This means that the Java code was modified at 3 minutes and 5 seconds past 5 on the 14th of February 2009 and the compiled version was modified at 34 minutes and 25 seconds past 4 on the 12th of February 2009. In this case, the system would automatically recompile Comp.java because the compiled version does not include changes made to the source code since 12th of February.

2. *Source code checksums* The signature on the source code file is a checksum calculated from data in the file. A checksum function calculates a unique number using the source text as input. If you change the source code (even by one character), this will generate a different checksum. You can therefore be confident that source code files with different checksums are actually different. The checksum is assigned to the source code just before compilation and uniquely identifies the source file. The build system then tags the generated object code file with the checksum signature. If there is no object code file with the same signature as the source code file to be included in a system, then recompilation of the source code is necessary.

As object code files are not normally versioned, the first approach means that only the most recently compiled object code file is maintained in the system. This is normally related to the source code file by name (i.e., it has the same name as the source code file but with a different suffix). Therefore, the source file Comp.Java may generate the object file Comp.class. Because source and object files are linked by name rather than an explicit source file signature, it is not usually possible to build different versions of a source code component into the same directory at the same time, as these would generate object files with the same name.

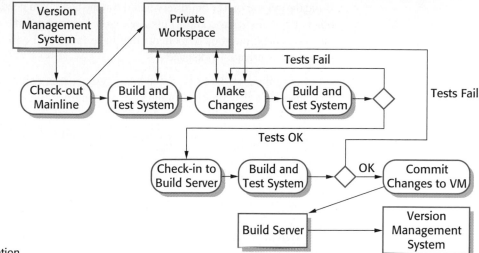

Figure 25.12
Continuous integration

The checksum approach has the advantage of allowing many different versions of the object code of a component to be maintained at the same time. The signature rather than the file name is the link between source and object code. The source code and object code files have the same signature. Therefore, when you recompile a component, it does not overwrite the object code, as would normally be the case when the timestamp is used. Rather, it generates a new object code file and tags it with the source code signature. Parallel compilation is possible and different versions of a component may be compiled at the same time.

Agile methods recommend that very frequent system builds should be carried out with automated testing (sometimes called smoke tests) to discover software problems. Frequent builds may be part of a process of continuous integration, as shown in Figure 25.12. In keeping with the agile methods notion of making many small changes, continuous integration involves rebuilding the mainline frequently, after small source code changes have been made. The steps in continuous integration are:

1. Check out the mainline system from the version management system into the developer's private workspace.

2. Build the system and run automated tests to ensure that the built system passes all tests. If not, the build is broken and you should inform whoever checked in the last baseline system. They are responsible for repairing the problem.

3. Make the changes to the system components.

4. Build the system in the private workspace and rerun system tests. If the tests fail, continue editing.

5. Once the system has passed its tests, check it into the build system but do not commit it as a new system baseline.

6. Build the system on the build server and run the tests. You need to do this in case others have modified components since you checked out the system. If this is the case, check out the components that have failed and edit these so that tests pass on your private workspace.

7. If the system passes its tests on the build system, then commit the changes you have made as a new baseline in the system mainline.

The argument for continuous integration is that it allows problems caused by the interactions between different developers to be discovered and repaired as soon as possible. The most recent system in the mainline is the definitive working system. However, although continuous integration is a good idea, it is not always possible to implement this approach to system building. The reasons for this are:

1. If the system is very large, it may take a long time to build and test. It is therefore impractical to build that system several times per day.

2. If the development platform is different from the target platform, it may not be possible to run system tests in the developer's private workspace. There may be differences in hardware, operating system, or installed software. Therefore more time is required for testing the system.

For large systems or for systems where the execution platform is not the same as the development platform, continuous integration may be impractical. In those circumstances, a daily build system may be used. Features of this are as follows:

1. The development organization sets a delivery time (say 2 P.M.) for system components. If developers have new versions of the components that they are writing, they must deliver them by that time. Components may be incomplete but should provide some basic functionality that can be tested.

2. A new version of the system is built from these components by compiling and linking them to form a complete system.

3. This system is then delivered to the testing team, which carries out a set of predefined system tests. At the same time, the developers are still working on their components, adding to the functionality and repairing faults discovered in previous tests.

4. Faults that are discovered during system testing are documented and returned to the system developers. They repair these faults in a subsequent version of the component.

The advantages of using frequent builds of software are that the chances of finding problems stemming from component interactions early in the process are increased. Frequent building encourages thorough unit testing of components. Psychologically, developers are put under pressure not to 'break the build'; that is, they try to avoid checking in versions of components that cause the whole system to fail. They are therefore reluctant to deliver new component versions that have not been properly tested. Consequently, less time is spent during system testing discovering and coping with software faults that could have been found by the developer.

25.4 Release management

A system release is a version of a software system that is distributed to customers. For mass- market software, it is usually possible to identify two types of release namely major releases, which deliver significant new functionality, and minor releases, which repair bugs and fix customer problems that have been reported. For example, this book is being written on an Apple Mac computer where the operating system is OS 10.5.8. This means minor release 8 of major release 5 of OS 10. Major releases are very important economically to the software vendor as customers have to pay for these. Minor releases are usually distributed free of charge.

For custom software or software product lines, managing system releases is a complex process. Special releases of the system may have to be produced for each customer and individual customers may be running several different releases of the system at the same time. This means that a software company selling a specialized software product may have to manage tens or even hundreds of different releases of that product. Their configuration management systems and processes have to be designed to provide information about which customers have which releases of the system and the relationship between releases and system versions. In the event of a problem, it may be necessary to reproduce exactly the software that has been delivered to a particular customer.

Therefore when a system release is produced, it must be documented to ensure that it can be re-created exactly in the future. This is particularly important for customized, long-lifetime embedded systems, such as those that control complex machines. Customers may use a single release of these systems for many years and may require specific changes to a particular software system long after its original release date.

To document a release, you have to record the specific versions of the source code components that were used to create the executable code. You must keep copies of the source code files, corresponding executables, and all data and configuration files. You should also record the versions of the operating system, libraries, compilers, and other tools used to build the software. These may be required to build exactly the same system at some later date. This may mean that you have to store copies of the platform software and the tools used to create the system in the version management system along with the source code of the target system.

Preparing and distributing a system release is an expensive process, particularly for mass-market software products. As well as the technical work involved in creating a release distribution, advertising and publicity material have to be prepared and marketing strategies put in place to convince customers to buy the new release of the

Factor	Description
Technical quality of the system	If serious system faults are reported which affect the way in which many customers use the system, it may be necessary to issue a fault repair release. Minor system faults may be repaired by issuing patches (usually distributed over the Internet) that can be applied to the current release of the system.
Platform changes	You may have to create a new release of a software application when a new version of the operating system platform is released.
Lehman's fifth law (see Chapter 9)	This 'law' suggests that if you add a lot of new functionality to a system; you will also introduce bugs that will limit the amount of functionality that may be included in the next release. Therefore, a system release with significant new functionality may have to be followed by a release that focuses on repairing problems and improving performance.
Competition	For mass-market software, a new system release may be necessary because a competing product has introduced new features and market share may be lost if these are not provided to existing customers.
Marketing requirements	The marketing department of an organization may have made a commitment for releases to be available at a particular date.
Customer change proposals	For custom systems, customers may have made and paid for a specific set of system change proposals, and they expect a system release as soon as these have been implemented.

Figure 25.13 Factors influencing system release planning

system. Careful thought must be given to release timing. If releases are too frequent or require hardware upgrades, customers may not move to the new release, especially if they have to pay for it. If system releases are too infrequent, market share may be lost as customers move to alternative systems.

The various technical and organizational factors that you should take into account when deciding on when to release a new version of a system are shown in Figure 25.13.

A system release is not just the executable code of the system. The release may also include:

• configuration files defining how the release should be configured for particular installations;

• data files, such as files of error messages, that are needed for successful system operation;

• an installation program that is used to help install the system on target hardware;

• electronic and paper documentation describing the system;

• packaging and associated publicity that have been designed for that release.

Release creation is the process of creating the collection of files and documentation that includes all of the components of the system release. The executable code of the programs and all associated data files must be identified in the version management system and tagged with the release identifier. Configuration descriptions may have to be written for different hardware and operating systems and instructions prepared for customers who need to configure their own systems. If machine-readable manuals are distributed, electronic copies must be stored with the software. Scripts for the installation program may have to be written. Finally, when all information is available, an executable master image of the software must be prepared and handed over for distribution to customers or sales outlets.

When planning the installation of new system releases, you cannot assume that customers will always install new system releases. Some system users may be happy with an existing system. They may consider that it is not worth the cost of changing to a new release. New releases of the system cannot, therefore, rely on the installation of previous releases. To illustrate this problem, consider the following scenario:

1. Release 1 of a system is distributed and put into use.

2. Release 2 requires the installation of new data files, but some customers do not need the facilities of release 2 so remain with release 1.

3. Release 3 requires the data files installed in release 2 and has no new data files of its own.

The software distributor cannot assume that the files required for release 3 have already been installed in all sites. Some sites may go directly from release 1 to release 3, skipping release 2. Some sites may have modified the data files associated with release 2 to reflect local circumstances. Therefore, the data files must be distributed and installed with release 3 of the system.

The marketing and packaging costs associated with new releases of software products are high so product vendors usually only create new releases for new platforms or to add significant new functionality. They then charge users for this new software. When problems are discovered in an existing release, the software vendors make patches to repair the existing software available on a website to be downloaded by customers.

The problem with using downloadable patches is that many customers may never discover the existence of these problem repairs and may not understand why they should be installed. They may instead continue using their existing, faulty system with the consequent risks to their business. In some situations, where the patch is designed to repair security loopholes, the risks of failing to install the patch can mean that the business is susceptible to external attacks. To avoid these problems, mass-market software vendors, such as Adobe, Apple, and Microsoft, usually implement automatic updating where systems are updated whenever a new minor release becomes available. However, this does not usually work for custom systems because these systems do not exist in a standard version for all customers.

KEY POINTS

■ Configuration management is the management of an evolving software system. When maintaining a system, a CM team is put in place to ensure that changes are incorporated into the system in a controlled way and that records are maintained with details of the changes that have been implemented.

■ The main configuration management processes are concerned with change management, version management, system building, and release management. Software tools are available to support all of these processes.

■ Change management involves assessing proposals for changes from system customers and other stakeholders and deciding if it is cost-effective to implement these in a new version of a system.

■ Version management involves keeping track of the different versions of software components that are created as changes are made to them.

■ System building is the process of assembling system components into an executable program to run on a target computer system.

■ Software should be frequently rebuilt and tested immediately after a new version has been built. This makes it easier to detect bugs and problems that have been introduced since the last build.

■ System releases include executable code, data files, configuration files, and documentation. Release management involves making decisions on system release dates, preparing all information for distribution, and documenting each system release.

FURTHER READING

Configuration Management Principles and Practice. This very comprehensive book covers standards and traditional approaches to CM as well as CM approaches that are more appropriate to modern processes, such as agile software development. (Anne Mette Jonassen Hass, Addison-Wesley, 2002.)

Software Configuration Management Patterns: Effective Teamwork, Practical Integration. A relatively short, easy-to-read book that gives good practical advice on configuration management practice, especially for agile methods of development. (S. P. Berczuk with B. Appleton, Addison-Wesley, 2003.)

'High-level Best Practices in Software Configuration Management'. This web article, written by staff at a CM tool supplier, is an excellent introduction to good practice in software configuration management (L. Wingerd and C. Seiwald, 2006.) http://www.perforce.com/perforce/papers/bestpractices.html.

'Agile Configuration Management for Large Organizations'. This web article describes configuration management practices that can be used in agile development processes, with a particular emphasis on how these can scale to large projects and companies. (P. Schuh, 2007.) http://www.ibm.com/developerworks/rational/library/mar07/schuh/index.html.

EXERCISES

25.1. Suggest five possible problems that could arise if a company does not develop effective configuration management policies and processes.

25.2. What are the benefits of using a change request form as the central document in the change management process?

25.3. Describe six essential features that should be included in a tool to support change management processes.

25.4. Explain why it is essential that every version of a component should be uniquely identified. Comment on the problems of using a version identification scheme that is simply based on version numbers.

25.5. Imagine a situation where two developers are simultaneously modifying three different software components. What difficulties might arise when they try to merge the changes that they have made?

25.6. Software is increasingly being developed by teams where the team members are working at different locations. Suggest features in a version management system that may be required to support this distributed software development.

25.7. Describe the difficulties that may arise when building a system from its components. What particular problems might occur when a system is built on a host computer for some target machine?

25.8. With reference to system building, explain why you may sometimes have to maintain obsolete computers on which large software systems were developed.

25.9. A common problem with system building occurs when physical file names are incorporated in system code and the file structure implied in these names differs from that of the target machine. Write a set of programmer's guidelines that helps avoid this and any other system-building problems that you can think of.

25.10. Describe five factors that should be taken into account by engineers during the process of building a release of a large software system.

REFERENCES

Ahern, D. M., Clouse, A. and Turner, R. (2001). *CMMI Distilled*. Reading, Mass.: Addison-Wesley.

Bamford, R. and Deibler, W. J. (2003). ' ISO 9001:2000 for Software and Systems Providers: An Engineering Approach'. Boca Raton, FL: CRC Press.

Paulk, M. C., Weber, C. V., Curtis, B. and Chrissis, M. B. (1995). *The Capability Maturity Model: Guidelines for Improving the Software Process*. Reading, Mass.: Addison-Wesley.

Peach, R. W. (1996). *The ISO 9000 Handbook, 3rd edition*. New York: Irwin Professional Pub.

Pilato, C. M., Collins-Sussman, B. and Fitzpatrick, B. W. (2004). *Version Control with Subversion*. Sebastopol, Calif.: O'Reilly Media Inc.

Vesperman, J. (2003). *Essential CVS*. Sebastopol, Calif.: O'Reilly and Associates.

26

Process improvement

Objectives

The objective of this chapter is to introduce software process improvement as a way of increasing software quality and reducing development costs. When you have read the chapter, you will:

■ understand the rationale for software process improvement as a means of improving both product quality and the efficiency and effectiveness of software processes;

■ understand the principles of software process improvement and the cyclic process improvement process;

■ know how the Goal-Question-Metric approach may be used to guide process measurement;

■ have been introduced to the ideas of process capability and process maturity, and the general form of the SEI's CMMI model for process improvement.

Contents

Nowadays, there is a constant demand from industry for cheaper, better software, which has to be delivered to ever-tighter deadlines. Consequently, many software companies have turned to software process improvement as a way of enhancing the quality of their software, reducing costs, or accelerating their development processes. Process improvement means understanding existing processes and changing these processes to increase product quality and/or reduce costs and development time.

Two quite different approaches to process improvement and change are used:

1. The process maturity approach, which has focused on improving process and project management and introducing good software engineering practice into an organization. The level of process maturity reflects the extent to which good technical and management practice has been adopted in organizational software development processes. The primary goals of this approach are improved product quality and process predictability.

2. The agile approach, which has focused on iterative development and the reduction of overheads in the software process. The primary characteristics of agile methods are rapid delivery of functionality and responsiveness to changing customer requirements.

Adherents of each of these approaches are generally skeptical of the benefits of the other. The process maturity approach is rooted in plan-driven development and usually requires increased 'overhead', in the sense that activities are introduced that are not directly relevant to programming. Agile approaches focus on the code being developed and deliberately minimize formality and documentation.

I have discussed agile methods in Chapter 3 and elsewhere in the book, so I focus in this chapter on process management and maturity-based process improvement. This does not mean that I prefer this approach to agile methods. In fact, I am convinced that, for small to medium-sized projects, adopting agile practices is likely to be the most cost-effective process improvement strategy. However for large systems, critical systems, and systems involving developers in different companies, management issues are often the reasons why projects run into problems. For companies whose business is large, complex systems engineering, a maturity-focused approach to process improvement should be considered.

As I discussed in Chapter 24, the development process that was used to create a software system influences the quality of that system. Therefore, many people believe that improving the software development process will lead to better quality software. This notion of process improvement is the brainchild of American engineer W. E. Deming, who worked with Japanese industry after World War II to help improve quality. Japanese industry has been committed to continuous process improvement for many years, which has led to the acknowledged high quality of Japanese manufactured goods.

Deming (and others) introduced the idea of statistical quality control. This is based on measuring the number of product defects and relating these defects to the process. The aim is to reduce the number of product defects by analyzing and

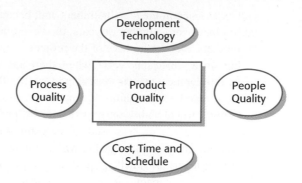

Figure 26.1 Factors affecting software product

modifying the process so that the chances of introducing defects are reduced and defect detection is improved. Once a lower defect count has been achieved, the process is standardized and a further improvement cycle then begins.

Humphrey (1988), in his seminal book on process management, argues that the same techniques can be applied to software engineering. He states:

> *"W. E. Deming, in his work with the Japanese industry after World War II, applied the concepts of statistical process control to industry. While there are important differences, these concepts are just as applicable to software as they are to automobiles, cameras, wristwatches and steel."*

Although there are clearly similarities, I do not agree with Humphrey that results from manufacturing engineering can be transferred easily to software engineering. Where manufacturing is involved, the process/product relationship is obvious. Manufacturing usually involves setting up automated tools and product checking processes. If someone makes a mistake in calibrating a machine, this will affect all of the products produced by that machine. Avoiding mistakes in setting up machines and introducing more effective checking processes clearly improves product quality.

This process quality/product quality relationship is less obvious when the product is intangible and dependent, to some extent, on intellectual processes that cannot be automated. Software quality is not influenced by its manufacturing process but by its design process, where people's skills and experience are significant. In some cases, the process used may be the most significant determinant of product quality. However, for innovative applications in particular, the people involved in the process have more influence on quality than the process used.

For software products, or any other intellectual products such as books or films where the quality of the product depends on its design, there are four important factors that affect product quality. These are shown in Figure 26.1.

The influence of each of these factors depends on the size and type of the project. For very large systems that include separate subsystems, developed by teams who may be working in different locations, the principal factor that affects product quality is the software process. The major problems with large projects are integration, project management, and communications. There is usually a mix of abilities and experience in the team members and, because the development process usually takes place over a number of years, the development team is volatile. It may change completely over the lifetime of the project.

For small projects, however, where there are only a few team members, the quality of the development team is more important than the development process used. Hence, the agile manifesto proclaims the importance of people rather than process. If the team has a high level of ability and experience, the quality of the product is likely to be high, irrespective of the process used. If the team is inexperienced and unskilled, a good process may limit the damage but will not, in itself, lead to high-quality software.

Where teams are small, good development technology is particularly important. The small team cannot devote a lot of time to tedious administrative procedures. The team members spend most of their time designing and programming the system, so good tools significantly affect their productivity. For large projects, a basic level of development technology is essential for information management. Paradoxically, however, sophisticated software tools are less important in large projects. Team members spend a smaller proportion of their time in development activities and more time communicating and understanding other parts of the system. Development tools make no difference to this. However, Web 2.0 tools that support communications, such as wikis and blogs, can significantly improve communications between members of distributed teams.

Irrespective of people, process, or tool factors, if a project has an inadequate budget or is planned with an unrealistic delivery schedule, product quality will be affected. A good process requires resources for its effective implementation. If these resources are insufficient, the process cannot be really effective. If resources are inadequate, only excellent people can save a project. Even then, if the deficit is too great, the product quality will be degraded. If there is not enough time for development, the delivered software is likely to have reduced functionality or lower levels of reliability or performance.

All too often, the real cause of software quality problems is not poor management, inadequate processes, or poor quality training. Rather, it is the fact that organizations must compete to survive. To gain a contract, a company may underestimate the effort required or promise rapid delivery of a system. In an attempt to meet these commitments, an unrealistic development schedule may be agreed upon. Consequently, the quality of the software is adversely affected.

26.1 The process improvement process

In Chapter 2, I introduced the general idea of a software process as a sequence of activities that, when executed, lead to the production of a software system. I described generic processes, such as the waterfall model and reuse-based development, and I discussed the most important process activities. These generic processes are instantiated within an organization to create the particular process that they use to develop software.

Software processes can be observed in all organizations, from one-person companies to large multinationals. These processes are of different types depending on the

Process characteristic	Key issues
Understandability	To what extent is the process explicitly defined and how easy is it to understand the process definition?
Standardization	To what extent is the process based on a standard generic process? This may be important for some customers who require conformance with a set of defined process standards. To what extent is the same process used in all parts of a company?
Visibility	Do the process activities culminate in clear results, so that the progress of the process is externally visible?
Measurability	Does the process include data collection or other activities that allow process or product characteristics to be measured?
Supportability	To what extent can software tools be used to support the process activities?
Acceptability	Is the defined process acceptable to and usable by the engineers responsible for producing the software product?
Reliability	Is the process designed in such a way that process errors are avoided or trapped before they result in product errors?
Robustness	Can the process continue in spite of unexpected problems?
Maintainability	Can the process evolve to reflect changing organizational requirements or identified process improvements?
Rapidity	How fast can the process of delivering a system from a given specification be completed?

Figure 26.2 Process attributes

degree of formality of the process, the types of products developed, the size of the organization, and so on. There is no such thing as an 'ideal' or 'standard' software process that is applicable in all organizations or for all software products of a particular type. Each company has to develop its own process depending on its size, the background and skills of its staff, the type of software being developed, customer and market requirements, and the company culture.

Process improvement, therefore, does not simply mean adopting particular methods or tools or using a published, generic process. Although organizations that develop the same type of software clearly have much in common, there are always local organizational factors, procedures, and standards that influence the process. You will rarely be successful in introducing process improvements if you simply attempt to change the process to one that is used elsewhere. You must always consider the local environment and culture and how this may be affected by process change proposals.

You also have to consider what aspects of the process that you want to improve. Your goal might be to improve software quality and so you may wish to introduce new process activities that change the way software is developed and tested. You may be interested in improving some attribute of the process itself and you have to decide which process attributes are the most important to your company. Examples of process attributes that may be targets for improvement are shown in Figure 26.2.

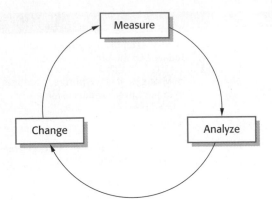

Figure 26.3 The process improvement cycle

These attributes are obviously related, sometimes positively and sometimes negatively. Therefore, a process that scores highly on the visibility attribute will probably also be understandable. A process observer can infer the existence of activities from the outputs produced. On the other hand, process visibility may be inversely related to rapidity. Making a process visible requires the people involved to produce information about the process itself. This may slow down software production because of the time it takes to produce these documents.

It is not possible to make process improvements that optimize all process attributes simultaneously. For example, if your aim is to have a rapid development process, then you may have to reduce the process visibility. If you wish to make a process more maintainable, then you may have to adopt procedures and tools that reflect broader organizational practice and that are used in different parts of the company. This may reduce the local acceptability of the process. Engineers may have introduced local procedures and non-standard tools to support their way of working. As these are effective, they may not wish to give them up in favor of a standardized process.

The process of process improvement is a cyclical process, as shown in Figure 26.3. It involves three subprocesses:

1. *Process measurement* Attributes of the current project or the product are measured. The aim is to improve the measures according to the goals of the organization involved in process improvement. This forms a baseline that helps you decide if process improvements have been effective.

2. *Process analysis* The current process is assessed, and process weaknesses and bottlenecks are identified. Process models (sometimes called process maps) that describe the process may be developed during this stage. The analysis may be focused by considering process characteristics such as rapidity and robustness.

3. *Process change* Process changes are proposed to address some of the identified process weaknesses. These are introduced and the cycle resumes to collect data about the effectiveness of the changes.

Without concrete data on a process or the software developed using that process, it is impossible to assess the value of process improvement. However, companies starting the process improvement process are unlikely to have process data available as an improvement bascline. Therefore, as part of the first cycle of changes, you may have to introduce process activities to collect data about the software process and to measure software product characteristics.

Process improvement is a long-term activity, so each of the stages in the improvement process may last several months. It is also a continuous activity as, whatever new processes are introduced, the business environment will change and the new processes will themselves have to evolve to take these changes into account.

26.2 Process measurement

Process measurements are quantitative data about the software process, such as the time taken to perform some process activity. For example, you may measure the time required to develop program test cases. Humphrey (1989), in his book on process improvement, argues that the measurement of process and product attributes is essential for process improvement. He also suggests that measurement has an important role to play in small-scale personal process improvement (Humphrey, 1995), where individuals try to become more productive.

Process measurements can be used to assess whether or not the efficiency of a process has been improved. For example, the effort and time devoted to testing can be monitored. Effective improvements to the testing process should reduce the effort and/or testing time. However, process measurements on their own cannot be used to determine if product quality has improved. Product quality data (see Chapter 24) must also be collected and related to the process activities.

Three types of process metrics can be collected:

1. *The time taken for a particular process to be completed* This can be the total time devoted to the process, calendar time, the time spent on the process by particular engineers, and so on.

2. *The resources required for a particular process* Resources might include total effort in person-days, travel costs, or computer resources.

3. *The number of occurrences of a particular event* Examples of events that might be monitored include the number of defects discovered during code inspection, the number of requirements changes requested, and the average number of lines of code modified in response to a requirements change.

The first two types of measurement can be used to discover if process changes have improved the efficiency of a process. Say there are fixed points in a software

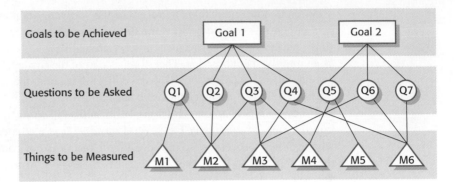

Figure 26.4 The GQM paradigm

development process, such as the acceptance of requirements, the completion of architectural design or the completion of test data generation. You may be able to measure the time and effort required to move from one of these fixed points to another. After changes have been introduced, measurements of system attributes can show if the process changes have been successful in reducing the time or effort required.

Measurements of the number of events that occur have a more direct bearing on software quality. For example, increasing the number of defects discovered by changing the program inspection process will probably be reflected in improved product quality. However, this has to be confirmed by subsequent product measurements.

A fundamental difficulty in process measurement is knowing what information about the process should be collected to support process improvement. Basili and Rombach (1988) proposed what they call the GQM (Goal-Question-Metric) paradigm, which has become widely used in software and process measurement. Basili and Green (1993) describe how this approach has been used in a long-term, measurement-based process improvement program in the U.S. space agency NASA.

The GQM paradigm (Figure 26.4) is used in process improvement to help answer three critical questions:

1. Why are we introducing process improvement?

2. What information do we need to help identify and assess improvements?

3. What process and product measurements are required to provide this information?

These questions are directly related to the abstractions (goals, questions, metrics) in the GQM paradigm:

1. *Goals* A goal is something that the organization is trying to achieve. It should not be directly concerned with process attributes but rather with how the process affects products or the organization itself. Examples of goals might be an improved

level of process maturity (see Section 26.5), shorter product development time, or increased product reliability.

2. *Questions* These are refinements of goals where specific areas of uncertainty related to the goals are identified. Normally, a goal will have a number of associated questions that need to be answered. Examples of questions related to the goal of shortening product development times might be "Where are the bottlenecks in our current process?", "How can the time required to finalize product requirements with customers be reduced?", and "How many of our tests are effective in discovering product defects?"

3. *Metrics* These are the measurements that need to be collected to help answer the questions and to confirm whether or not process improvements have achieved the desired goal. To help answer the above questions, you might collect data on the time taken to complete each process activity (normalized by system size), the number of formal communications between clients and customers for each requirements change, and the number of defects discovered per test run.

The advantage of using the GQM approach in process improvement is that it separates organizational concerns (the goals) from specific process concerns (the questions). It provides a basis for deciding what data should be collected and suggests that collected data should be analyzed in different ways, depending on the question it is intended to answer.

The GQM approach has been developed and combined with the SEI's capability maturity model (Paulk et al., 1995) in the AMI (Analyze, Measure, Improve) method of software process improvement. The developers of the AMI method propose a staged approach to process improvement, where measurement is started after an organization has introduced some standardization into its processes, as opposed to beginning measurement straight away. The AMI handbook (Pulford et al., 1996) provides guidelines and practical advice on implementing measurement-based process improvement.

As I discussed in Chapter 24, interpreting what measurements actually mean is sometimes problematic. For example, say you measure the average time taken to repair reported bugs in software that has been delivered for external testing. This is the time between the team receiving an error report and the time when this report is formally marked as 'cleared'. You introduce a new web-based tool for error reporting and, after this tool has been in use for some time, you observe that the time to repair reported bugs has been reduced.

You may then assert that the introduction of the error reporting tools has actually reduced the time to repair bugs. When you observe changes to a metric, it is always tempting to attribute these changes to the process changes that you have introduced. However, it is dangerous to make simplistic assumptions about improvements. Changes in a metric could be caused by something completely different, such as a change of the people in the project team, changes to the project

Analysis of process practice

One approach to process analysis is to use questionnaires to discover the extent to which good software engineering practices are used. Therefore, for some stage in the process, such as requirements engineering, you may identify what practices are most appropriate for the type of system being developed in a company and ask questions about how widely these are used. This is the approach that I suggested in my book on requirements engineering process improvement (Sommerville and Sawyer, 1997).

http://www.SoftwareEngineering-9.com/Web/ProcImp/goodpractice.html

schedule, or management changes. It may also be the case that the team's practice changes simply because it is being measured. In the case of the error reporting tools, some of the reasons why the change has been observed include:

1. The new system may have reduced overhead and so more time is available to repair bugs. This has led to a reduction in average 'bug repair' times. The process improvement may have made a genuine difference.

2. The new system may have made no difference to the actual time taken to fix bugs but it may have made it easier to record information. Therefore, the bug repair times are more accurately measured with the new system. There has been no actual change in the average time to fix bugs.

3. The measurements before the new system was introduced were, perhaps, made part way through the testing of a system. The bugs that were easiest and quickest to fix had already been fixed and only 'hard bugs' remained that took longer to repair. However, after the bug reporting system was introduced, measurements were made at the beginning of the testing of the new system and the bugs being fixed were the 'easy bugs', which could be repaired quickly.

4. A new manager of the testing team may have instructed team members to report user interface inconsistencies as bugs, whereas before these were ignored. This meant that many more 'easy bugs' were reported that could be fixed quickly.

Measurement is a way of generating evidence about a process and process changes. However, this evidence has to be interpreted along with other information about the process before you can be sure that process changes are effective. You should always use measurement in conjunction with qualitative assessment of changes. This involves talking to the people involved in the process about the changes that have been introduced and getting their impression of the effectiveness of these changes. Not only does this reveal other factors that may have influenced the process, it reveals the extent to which the team has adopted the proposed changes and how these have affected actual development practice.

26.3 Process analysis

Process analysis is the study of processes to help understand their key characteristics and how such processes are performed in practice by the people involved. I have suggested in Figure 26.3 that process analysis follows process measurement. This is a simplification because, in reality, these activities are intertwined. You need to carry out some analysis to know what to measure, and, when making measurements, you inevitably develop a deeper understanding of the process being measured.

Process analysis has a number of closely related objectives:

1. To understand the activities involved in the process and the relationships between these activities.

2. To understand the relationships between the process activities and the measurements that have been made.

3. To relate the specific process or processes that you are analyzing to comparable processes elsewhere in the organization, or to idealized processes of the same type.

During process analysis you are trying to understand what is going on in a process. You are looking for information about that process's problems and inefficiencies. You should also be interested in the extent that the process is used, the software tools used to support the process, and how the process is influenced by organizational constraints. Figure 26.5 shows some of the aspects of the process that you may investigate during process analysis.

The most commonly used techniques of process analysis are:

1. *Questionnaires and interviews* The engineers and managers working on a project are questioned about what actually goes on. The answers to a formal questionnaire are refined during personal interviews with those involved in the process. As I discuss below, the discussion may be structured around models of software processes.

2. *Ethnographic studies* Ethnographic studies (see Chapter 4), where process participants are observed as they work, may be used to understand the nature of software development as a human activity. Such analysis reveals subtleties and complexities that may not be revealed by questionnaires and interviews.

Each of these approaches has advantages and disadvantages. Questionnaire-based analysis can be carried out fairly quickly once the right questions have been identified. However, if the questions are badly worded or inappropriate, you may end up with an incomplete or inaccurate understanding of the process. Furthermore, questionnaire-based analysis may appear to them as a form of assessment or appraisal. The engineers being questioned may therefore give the answers that they think you want to hear rather than the truth about the process used.

Process aspect	Questions
Adoption and standardization	Is the process documented and standardized across the organization? If not, does this mean that any measurements made are specific only to a single process instance? If processes are not standardized, then changes to one process may not be transferable to comparable processes elsewhere in the company.
Software engineering practice	Are there known, good software engineering practices that are not included in the process? Why are they not included? Does the lack of these practices affect product characteristics, such as the number of defects in a delivered software system?
Organizational constraints	What are the organizational constraints that affect the process design and the ways that the process is performed? For example, if the process involves dealing with classified material, there may be activities in the process to check that classified information is not included in any material due to be released to external organizations. Organizational constraints may mean that possible process changes cannot be made.
Communications	How are communications managed in the process? How do communication issues relate to the process measurements that have been made? Communication problems are a major issue in many processes and communication bottlenecks are often the reasons for project delays.
Introspection	Is the process reflective (i.e., do the actors involved in the process explicitly think about and discuss the process and how it might be improved)? Are there mechanisms through which process actors can propose process improvements?
Learning	How do people joining a development team learn about the software processes used? Does the company have process manuals and process training programs?
Tool support	What aspects of the process are and aren't supported by software tools? For unsupported areas, are there tools that could be deployed cost-effectively to provide support? For supported areas, are the tools effective and efficient? Are better tools available?

Figure 26.5 Aspects of process analysis

Interviews with the people involved in the process are more open-ended than questionnaires. You start with a prepared script of questions but adapt these according to the responses that you get from different people. If you give participants an opportunity to discuss issues more widely, you may find that the process participants talk about process problems, the ways that the process is changed in practice, and so on.

In almost all processes, the people involved make local changes to adapt the process to suit local circumstances. Ethnographic analysis is more likely than interviews to discover the true process used. However, this type of analysis can be a prolonged activity that can last several months. It relies on external observation of the process as it is being enacted. To do a complete analysis, you have to be involved from the initial stages of a project through to product delivery and maintenance. For large projects, this could take several years, so it is clearly impractical to do a complete ethnographic analysis of the processes in a large project. Ethnographic analysis is actually most useful when an in-depth understanding of process fragments is required. Once you identify areas that need further investigation from interview material, you can then do a focused ethnographic study to discover process details.

When analyzing a process, it is often useful to start with a process model that defines the activities in the process and the inputs and outputs of these activities. The model may also include information about the process actors—the people or roles responsible for performing activities, and the critical deliverables that must be produced. You can use an informal notation to describe process models or more formal tabular notations, UML activity diagrams, or a business process modeling notation such as BPMN (discussed in Chapter 19). There are lots of examples of process models in this book that I use to present and describe software processes.

Process models are a good way of focusing attention on the activities in a process and the information transfer between these activities. These process models do not have to be formal or complete—their purpose is to provoke discussion rather than document the process in detail. Discussion with people involved in the process and observations of that process are often structured around a set of questions about the formal process model. Examples of these questions might be:

1. What activities take place in practice but are not shown in the model? Inevitably, models are incomplete but if different people identify different missing activities, this tells you that the process is not performed consistently across the organization.

2. Are there process activities, shown in the model, that you (the process actor) think are inefficient? In what ways are they inefficient and how might these be improved? How do these inefficient activities affect process measurements that may have been made?

3. What happens when things go wrong? Does the team continue to follow the process defined in the model, or is the process abandoned and emergency action taken? If the process is abandoned, this suggests that the software engineers do not believe that the process is good enough or that it does not have sufficient flexibility to handle exceptions.

4. Who are the actors involved at different stages in the process and how do they communicate? What bottlenecks commonly occur in the information exchange?

5. What tool support is used for the activities shown in the model? Is this effective and universally used? How could tool support be improved?

When you have completed an analysis of the software process, you should have a deeper understanding of that process and the potential for process improvements in the future. You should also understand the constraints on process improvement and how these can limit the scope of improvements that may be introduced.

Software process modeling

Software process modeling started in the early 1980s (Osterweil, 1987) with the long-term objective of using process models as a way of organizing and coordinating tool support for the process. A process model should include information about process activities, inputs and outputs, and the actors involved in the process. Special-purpose software process modeling notations were developed but these have been largely supplanted by notations for business process modeling such as BPMN (White, 2004) or UML activity models.

http://www.SoftwareEngineering-9.com/Web/ProcImp/spm.html

26.3.1 Process exceptions

Software processes are complex entities. There may be a defined process model in an organization but this can only represent the situation where the development team is not faced with any unanticipated problems. In reality, unanticipated problems are a fact of everyday life for project managers. The 'ideal' process model must be modified dynamically as solutions to these problems are found. Examples of the kinds of exception that a project manager may have to deal with include:

- several key people becoming ill at the same time, just before a critical project review;

- a serious breach in computer security that means all external communications are out of action for several days;

- a company reorganization, which means that managers have to spend much of their time working on organizational matters rather than on project management;

- an unanticipated request to write a proposal for a new project that means effort must be transferred from the current project to proposal writing.

Essentially, an exception will affect and usually alter, in some way, the resources, budgets, or schedules of a project. It is difficult to predict all exceptions in advance and to incorporate them into a formal process model. You therefore often have to work out how to handle exceptions and then dynamically change the 'standard' process to cope with these unexpected circumstances.

26.4 Process change

Process change involves making modifications to the existing process. As I have suggested, you may do this by introducing new practices, methods, or tools; changing the ordering of process activities; introducing or removing deliverables from the process; improving communications; or by introducing new roles and responsibilities. Process

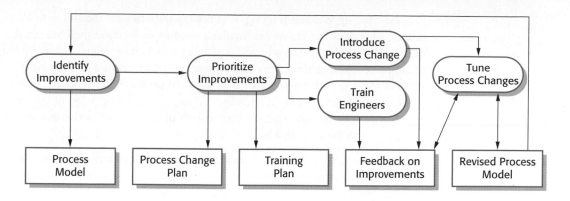

Figure 26.6 The process change process

changes should be driven by improvement goals such as 'reduce the number of defects discovered during integration testing by 25 percent'. After the changes have been implemented, you use the process measurements to assess the effectiveness of the changes.

There are five key stages in the process change process (Figure 26.6):

1. *Improvement identification* This stage is concerned with using the results of the process analysis to identify ways to tackle quality problems, schedule bottle-necks, or cost inefficiencies that have been identified during process analysis. You may propose new processes, process structures, methods, and tools to address process problems. For example, a company may believe that many of its software problems stem from requirements problems. Using a requirements engineering best practice guide (Sommerville and Sawyer, 1997), various requirements engineering practices that could be introduced or changed may then be identified.

2. *Improvement prioritization* This stage is concerned with assessing possible changes to the process, and prioritizing them for implementation. When many possible changes have been identified, it is usually impossible to introduce them all at once, and you must decide which are the most important. You may make these decisions based on the need to improve specific process areas, the costs of introducing a change, the impact of a change on the organization, or other fac-tors. For example, a company may consider the introduction of requirements management processes to manage evolving requirements to be the highest-priority process change.

3. *Process change introduction* Process change introduction means putting new procedures, methods, and tools into place and integrating them with other process activities. You must allow enough time to introduce changes and ensure that these changes are compatible with other process activities and organizational procedures and standards. This may involve acquiring tools for requirements management and designing processes to use these tools.

4. *Process training* Without training, it is not possible to gain the full benefits of process changes. The engineers involved need to understand the changes that have been proposed and how to perform the new and changed processes. All too often, process changes are imposed without adequate training and the effect of these changes is to degrade rather than improve product quality. In the case of requirements management, the training might involve a discussion of the value of requirements management, an explanation of the process activities, and an introduction to the tools that have been selected.

5. *Change tuning* Proposed process changes will never be completely effective as soon as they are introduced. You need a tuning phase where minor problems can be discovered, and modifications to the process can be proposed and introduced. This tuning phase should last for several months until the development engineers are happy with the new process.

It is generally unwise to introduce too many changes at the same time. Apart from the training difficulties that this causes, introducing too many changes makes it impossible to assess the effect of each change on the process. Once a change has been introduced, the improvement process can iterate, with further analysis used to identify process problems, propose improvements, and so on.

As well as the difficulties of assessing the effectiveness of changed processes that I have discussed, there are two major difficulties that those involved in change processes may have to face:

1. *Resistance to change* Team members or project managers may resist the introduction of process changes and propose reasons why changes will not work, or delay the introduction of changes. They may, in some cases, deliberately obstruct process changes and interpret data to show the ineffectiveness of proposed process changes.

2. *Change persistence* Although it may be possible to introduce process changes initially, it is common for process innovations to be discarded after a short time and for the processes to revert to their previous state.

Resistance to change may come from both project managers and the engineers involved in the process that is being changed. Project managers often resist process change because any innovation has unknown risks associated with it. Process changes may be intended to speed up software production or reduce software defects. However, there is always the danger that these process changes will be ineffective or that the time required to introduce the changes will be longer than the time saved. Project managers are judged according to whether or not their project produces software on time and to budget. Therefore, they may prefer an inefficient but predictable process to an improved process that has organizational benefits, but which may also have short-term risks associated with it.

Engineers may resist the introduction of new processes for similar reasons, or because they see these processes as threatening their professionalism. That is, they may feel that the new predefined process gives them less discretion and does not recognize the value of their skills and experience. They may think that the new process will mean that fewer people will be required and that they may lose their job. They may not wish to learn new skills, tools, or ways of working.

As a manager, you have to be sensitive to the feelings of the people affected when introducing process change. You have to involve the team all the way through the change process, understand their doubts, and involve them in planning the new process. By making them stakeholders in the process change, it is much more likely that they will want to make it work. Business process reengineering (Hammer, 1990; Ould, 1995), a fashion of the 1990s which involved making radical process changes, was largely unsuccessful because it failed to take the legitimate concerns of the people involved into account.

To address the concerns of project managers that process change will adversely affect project schedules and costs, you have to increase project budgets to allow for additional costs and delays resulting from the change. You also have to be realistic about the short-term benefits of the change. Changes are unlikely to lead to large-scale, immediate improvements. The benefits of process change are long term rather than short term so you have to support the process changes over several projects.

The problem of changes being introduced then subsequently discarded is a common one. Changes may be proposed by an 'evangelist' who believes strongly that the changes will lead to improvement. He or she may work hard to ensure the changes are effective and the new process is accepted. However, if the 'evangelist' leaves, then he or she may be replaced by someone who is less committed to the new process. The people involved may therefore simply revert to the previous ways of doing things. This is particularly likely if the changes that have been introduced have not been universally adopted and the full benefits of the process changes have not yet been realized.

Because of problems of change persistence, the CMMI model, discussed in Section 26.5, argues strongly for the institutionalization of process change. This means that process change is not dependent on individuals but that the changes become part of standard practice in the company, with company-wide support and training.

26.5 The CMMI process improvement framework

The U.S. Software Engineering Institute (SEI) was established to improve the capabilities of the American software industry. In the mid-1980s, the SEI initiated a study of ways to assess the capabilities of software contractors. The outcome of this capability assessment was the SEI Software Capability Maturity Model (CMM) (Paulk et al., 1993; Paulk et al., 1995). This has been tremendously influential in convincing the software engineering community to take process improvement seriously. The Software CMM was followed by a range of other capability maturity models, including the People Capability Maturity Model (P-CMM) (Curtis et al., 2001) and the Systems Engineering Capability Model (Bate, 1995).

Other organizations have also developed comparable process maturity models. The SPICE approach to capability assessment and process improvement (Paulk and Konrad, 1994) is more flexible than the SEI model. It includes maturity levels comparable with the CMM levels, but also identifies processes, such as customer-supplier processes, that cut across these levels. As the level of maturity increases, the performance of these cross-cutting processes must also improve.

The Bootstrap project in the 1990s had the goal of extending and adapting the SEI maturity model to make it applicable across a wider range of companies. This model (Haase et al., 1994; Kuvaja, et al., 1994) uses the SEI's maturity levels (discussed in Section 26.5.1). It also proposes a base process model (based on the model used in the European Space Agency) that may be used as a starting point for local process definition. It includes guidelines for developing a company-wide quality system to support process improvement.

In an attempt to integrate the plethora of capability models based on the notion of process maturity (including its own models), the SEI embarked on a new program to develop an integrated capability model (CMMI). The CMMI framework supersedes the Software and Systems Engineering CMMs and integrates other capability maturity models. It has two instantiations, staged and continuous, and addresses some of the reported weaknesses in the Software CMM.

The CMMI model (Ahern et al., 2001; Chrissis et al., 2007) is intended to be a framework for process improvement that has broad applicability across a range of companies. Its staged version is compatible with the Software CMM and allows an organization's system development and management processes to be assessed and assigned a maturity level from 1 to 5. Its continuous version allows for a finer-grain classification of process maturity. This model provides a way of rating 22 process areas (see Figure 26.7) on a scale from 0 to 5.

The CMMI model is very complex, with more than 1,000 pages of description. I have radically simplified it for discussion here. The principal model components are:

1. A set of process areas that are related to software process activities. The CMMI identifies 22 process areas that are relevant to software process capability and improvement. These are organized into four groups in the continuous CMMI model. These groups and related process areas are listed in Figure 26.7.

2. A number of goals, which are abstract descriptions of a desirable state that should be attained by an organization. The CMMI has specific goals that are associated with each process area and define the desirable state for that area. It also defines generic goals that are associated with the institutionalization of good practice. Figure 26.8 shows examples of specific and generic goals in the CMMI.

3. A set of good practices, which are descriptions of ways of achieving a goal. Several specific and generic practices may be associated with each goal within a process

Category	Process area
Process management	Organizational process definition (OPD)
	Organizational process focus (OPF)
	Organizational training (OT)
	Organizational process performance (OPP)
	Organizational innovation and deployment (OID)
Project management	Project planning (PP)
	Project monitoring and control (PMC)
	Supplier agreement management (SAM)
	Integrated project management (IPM)
	Risk management (RSKM)
	Quantitative project management (QPM)
Engineering	Requirements management (REQM)
	Requirements development (RD)
	Technical solution (TS)
	Product integration (PI)
	Verification (VER)
	Validation (VAL)
Support	Configuration management (CM)
	Process and product quality management (PPQA)
	Measurement and analysis (MA)
	Decision analysis and resolution (DAR)
	Causal analysis and resolution (CAR)

Figure 26.7 Process areas in the CMMI

area. Some examples of recommended practices are shown in Figure 26.9. However, the CMMI recognizes that it is the goal rather than the way that the goal is reached that is important. Organizations may use any appropriate practices to achieve any of the CMMI goals—they do not have to adopt the practices recommended in the CMMI.

Generic goals and practices are not technical but are associated with the institutionalization of good practice. What this means depends on the maturity of the organization. At an early stage of maturity development, institutionalization may mean ensuring that plans are established and processes are defined for all software development in the company. However, for an organization with more mature, advanced processes, institutionalization may mean introducing process control using statistical and other quantitative techniques across the organization.

Goal	Process area
Corrective actions are managed to closure when the project's performance or results deviate significantly from the plan.	Project monitoring and control (specific goal)
Actual performance and progress of the project are monitored against the project plan.	Project monitoring and control (specific goal)
The requirements are analyzed and validated, and a definition of the required functionality is developed.	Requirements development (specific goal)
Root causes of defects and other problems are systematically determined.	Causal analysis and resolution (specific goal)
The process is institutionalized as a defined process.	Generic goal

Figure 26.8 Process areas in the CMMI

A CMMI assessment involves examining the processes in an organization and rating these processes or process areas on a six-point scale that relates to the level of maturity in each process area. The idea is that the more mature a process, the better it is. The six-point scale assigns a level of maturity to a process area as follows:

1. *Incomplete* At least one of the specific goals associated with the process area is not satisfied. There are no generic goals at this level as institutionalization of an incomplete process does not make sense.

2. *Performed* The goals associated with the process area are satisfied, and for all processes the scope of the work to be performed is explicitly set out and communicated to the team members.

3. *Managed* At this level, the goals associated with the process area are met and organizational policies are in place that define when each process should be used. There must be documented project plans that define the project goals. Resource management and process monitoring procedures must be in place across the institution.

4. *Defined* This level focuses on organizational standardization and deployment of processes. Each project has a managed process that is adapted to the project requirements from a defined set of organizational processes. Process assets and process measurements must be collected and used for future process improvements.

5. *Quantitatively managed* At this level, there is an organizational responsibility to use statistical and other quantitative methods to control subprocesses; that is, collected process and product measurements must be used in process management.

6. *Optimizing* At this highest level, the organization must use the process and product measurements to drive process improvement. Trends must be analyzed and the processes adapted to changing business needs.

Goal	Associated practices
The requirements are analyzed and validated, and a definition of the required functionality is developed.	Analyze derived requirements systematically to ensure that they are necessary and sufficient.
	Validate requirements to ensure that the resulting product will perform as intended in the user's environment, using multiple techniques as appropriate.
Root causes of defects and other problems are systematically determined.	Select the critical defects and other problems for analysis.
	Perform causal analysis of selected defects and other problems and propose actions to address them.
The process is institutionalized as a defined process.	Establish and maintain an organizational policy for planning and performing the requirements development process.
	Assign responsibility and authority for performing the process, developing the work products, and providing the services of the requirements development process.

Figure 26.9 Goals and associated practices in the CMMI

This is a very simplified description of the capability levels and, to put these into practice, you need to work with more detailed descriptions. The levels are progressive, with explicit process descriptions at the lowest levels, through process standardization, to process change and improvement driven by measurements of the process and the software at the highest level. To improve its processes, a company should aim to increase the maturity level of the process groups that are relevant to its business.

26.5.1 The staged CMMI model

The staged CMMI model is comparable with the Software Capability Maturity Model in that it provides a means to assess an organization's process capability at one of five levels, and prescribes the goals that should be achieved at each of these levels. Process improvement is achieved by implementing practices at each level, moving from the lower to the higher levels in the model.

The five levels in the staged CMMI model are shown in Figure 26.10. They correspond to capability levels 1 to 5 in the continuous model. The key difference between the staged and the continuous CMMI models is that the staged model is used to assess the capability of the organization as a whole, whereas the continuous model measures the maturity of specific process areas within the organization.

Each maturity level has an associated set of process areas and generic goals. These reflect good software engineering and management practice and the institutionalization of process improvement. The lower maturity levels may be achieved by

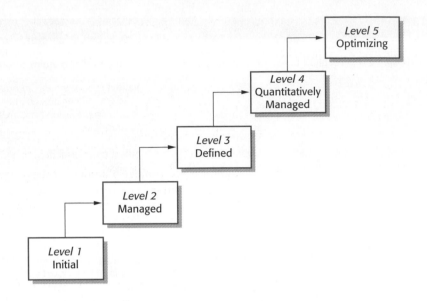

Figure 26.10 The CMMI staged maturity model

introducing good practice; however, higher levels require a commitment to process measurement and improvement.

For example, the process areas as defined in the model associated with the second level (the managed level) are:

1. *Requirements management* Manage the requirements of the project's products and product components, and identify inconsistencies between those requirements and the project's plans and work products.

2. *Project planning* Establish and maintain plans that define project activities.

3. *Project monitoring and control* Provide understanding into the project's progress so that appropriate corrective actions can be taken when the project's performance deviates significantly from the plan.

4. *Supplier agreement management* Manage the acquisition of products and services from suppliers external to the project for which a formal agreement exists.

5. *Measurement and analysis* Develop and sustain a measurement capability that is used to support management information needs.

6. *Process and product quality assurance* Provide staff and management with objective insight into the processes and associated work products.

7. *Configuration management* Establish and maintain the integrity of work products using configuration identification, configuration control, configuration status accounting, and configuration audits.

As well as these specific practices, organizations operating at the second level in the CMMI model should have achieved the generic goal of institutionalizing each of the processes as a managed process. Examples of institutional practices associated with project planning that lead to the project planning process being a managed process are:

- Establish and maintain an organizational policy for planning and performing the project planning process.

- Provide adequate resources for performing the project management process, developing the work products, and providing the services of the process.

- Monitor and control the project planning process against the plan and take appropriate corrective action.

- Review the activities, status, and results of the project planning process with high-level management, and resolve any issues.

The advantage of the staged CMMI is that it is compatible with the software capability maturity model that was proposed in the late 1980s. Many companies understand and are committed to using this model for process improvement. It is therefore straightforward for them to make a transition from this to the staged CMMI model. Furthermore, the staged model defines a clear improvement pathway for organizations. They can plan to move from the second to the third level and so on.

The major disadvantage of the staged model (and of the Software CMM), however, is its prescriptive nature. Each maturity level has its own goals and practices. The staged model assumes that all of the goals and practices at one level are implemented before the transition to the next level. However, organizational circumstances may be such that it more appropriate to implement goals and practices at higher levels before lower-level practices. When an organization does this, a maturity assessment will give a misleading picture of its capability.

26.5.2 The continuous CMMI model

Continuous maturity models do not classify an organization according to discrete levels. Rather, they are finer-grained models that consider individual or groups of practices and assess the use of good practice within each process group. The maturity assessment is not, therefore, a single value but a set of values showing the organization's maturity for each process or process group.

The continuous CMMI considers the process areas shown in Figure 26.7 and assigns a capability assessment level from 0 to 5 (as described earlier) to each process area. Normally, organizations operate at different maturity levels for different process areas. Consequently, the result of a continuous CMMI assessment is a capability profile showing each process area and its associated capability assessment. A fragment of a capability profile that shows processes at different capability levels is shown in Figure 26.11. This shows that the level of maturity in configuration management, for example, is high, but that risk management maturity is low. A company may develop

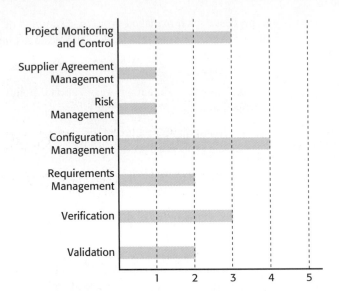

Figure 26.11 A process capability profile

actual and target capability profiles where the target profile reflects the capability level that they would like to reach for that process area.

The principal advantage of the continuous model is that companies can pick and choose processes for improvement according to their own needs and requirements. In my experience, different types of organization have different requirements for process improvement. For example, a company that develops software for the aerospace industry may focus on improvements in system specification, configuration management, and validation, whereas a web development company may be more concerned with customer-facing processes. The staged model requires companies to focus on the different stages in turn. By contrast, the continuous CMMI permits discretion and flexibility, while still allowing companies to work within the CMMI improvement framework.

KEY POINTS

■ The goals of process improvement are higher product quality, reduced process costs, and faster delivery of software.

■ The principal approaches to process improvement are agile approaches, geared to reducing process overheads, and maturity-based approaches based on better process management and the use of good software engineering practice.

■ The process improvement cycle involves process measurement, process analysis and modeling, and process change.

■ Process models, which show the activities in a process and their relationships with software products, are used for process description. In practice, however, engineers involved in software development always adapt models to their local circumstances.

■ Measurement should be used to answer specific questions about the software process used. These questions should be based on organizational improvement goals.

■ Three types of process metrics used in the measurement process are time metrics, resource utilization metrics, and event metrics.

■ The CMMI process maturity model is an integrated process improvement model that supports both staged and continuous process improvement.

■ Process improvement in the CMMI model is based on reaching a set of goals related to good software engineering practice and describing, standardizing, and controlling the practices used to achieve these goals. The CMMI model includes recommended practices that may be used, but these are not obligatory.

FURTHER READING

'Can you trust software capability evaluations?' This article takes a skeptical look at the subject of capability evaluation, where a company's process maturity is assessed, and discusses why these evaluations may not give a true picture of an organization's maturity. (E. O'Connell and H. Saiedian, *IEEE Computer*, **33** (2), February 2000) http://dx.doi.org/ 10.1109/2.820036.

Software Process Improvement: Results and Experience from the Field. This book is a collection of papers focusing on process improvement case studies in several small and medium-sized Norwegian companies. It also includes a good introduction to the general issues of process improvement. (Conradi, R., Dybå, T., Sjøberg, D., Ulsund, T. (eds.), Springer, 2006.)

CMMI: Guidelines for Process Integration and Product Improvement, 2nd edition. A comprehensive description of the CMMI. The CMMI is large and complex and it is practically impossible to make it easy to read and understand. This book does a reasonable job by including some anecdotal and historical material, but it's still sometimes tough going. (M. B. Chrissis, M. Konrad, S. Shrum, Addison-Wesley, 2007.)

EXERCISES

26.1. What are the important differences between the agile approach and the process maturity approach to software process improvement?

26.2. Under what circumstances is product quality likely to be determined by the quality of the development team? Give examples of the types of software product that are particularly dependent on individual talent and ability.

26.3. Suggest three specialized software tools that might be developed to support a process improvement program in an organization.

26.4. Assume that the goal of process improvement in an organization is to increase the number of reusable components that are produced during development. Suggest three questions in the GQM paradigm that this might lead to.

26.5. Describe three types of software process metric that may be collected as part of a process improvement process. Give one example of each type of metric.

26.6. Design a process for assessing and prioritizing process change proposals. Document this process as a process model showing the roles involved in this process. You should use UML activity diagrams or BPMN to describe the process.

26.7. Give two advantages and two disadvantages of the approach to process assessment and improvement that is embodied in the process improvement frameworks such as the CMMI.

26.8. Under what circumstances would you recommend the use of the staged representation of the CMMI?

26.9. What are the advantages and disadvantages of using a process maturity model that focuses on goals to be achieved, rather than good practices to be introduced?

26.10. Do you think that process improvement programs, which involve measuring the work of people in the process and introducing changes into that process, can be inherently dehumanizing? What resistance to a process improvement program might arise and why?

REFERENCES

Ahern, D. M., Clouse, A. and Turner, R. (2001). *CMMI Distilled*. Reading, Mass.: Addison-Wesley.

Basili, V. and Green, S. (1993). 'Software Process Improvement at the SEL'. *IEEE Software,* **11** (4), 58–66.

Basili, V. R. and Rombach, H. D. (1988). 'The TAME Project: Towards Improvement-Oriented Software Environments'. *IEEE Trans. on Software Eng.,* **14** (6), 758–773.

Bate, R. 1995. 'A Systems Engineering Capability Maturity Model Version 1.1'. Software Engineering Institute.

Chrissis, M. B., Konrad, M. and Shrum, S. (2007). *CMMI: Guidelines for Process Integration and Product Improvement, 2nd edition*. Boston: Addison-Wesley.

Curtis, B., Hefley, W. E. and Miller, S. A. (2001). *The People Capability Model: Guidelines for Improving the Workforce*. Boston: Addison-Wesley.

Haase, V., Messnarz, R., Koch, G., Kugler, H. J. and Decrinis, P. (1994). 'Bootstrap: Fine Tuning Process Assessment'. *IEEE Software,* **11** (4), 25–35.

Hammer, M. (1990). 'Reengineering Work: Don't Automate, Obliterate'. *Harvard Business Review,* July–August 1990, 104–112.

Humphrey, W. (1989). *Managing the Software Process*. Reading, Mass.: Addison-Wesley.

Humphrey, W. S. (1988). 'Characterizing the Software Process'. *IEEE Software,* **5** (2), 73–79.

Humphrey, W. S. (1995). *A Discipline for Software Engineering*. Reading, Mass.: Addison-Wesley.

Kuvaja, P., Similä, J., Krzanik, L., Bicego, A., Saukkonen, S. and Koch, G. (1994). *Software Process Assessment and Improvement: The BOOTSTRAP Approach*. Oxford: Blackwell Publishers.

Osterweil, L. (1987). 'Software Processes are Software Too'. *9th Int. Conf. on Software Engineering*, IEEE Press, 2–12.

Ould, M. A. (1995). *Business Processes: Modeling and Analysis for Re-engineering and Improvement*. Chichester: John Wiley & Sons.

Paulk, M. C., Curtis, B., Chrissis, M. B. and Weber, C. V. (1993). 'Capability Maturity Model, Version 1.1'. *IEEE Software,* **10** (4), 18–27.

Paulk, M. C. and Konrad, M. (1994). 'An Overview of ISO's SPICE Project'. *IEEE Computer,* **27** (4), 68–70.

Paulk, M. C., Weber, C. V., Curtis, B. and Chrissis, M. B. (1995). *The Capability Maturity Model: Guidelines for Improving the Software Process*. Reading, Mass.: Addison-Wesley.

Pulford, K., Kuntzmann-Combelles, A. and Shirlaw, S. (1996). *A Quantitative Approach to Software Management*. Wokingham: Addison-Wesley.

Sommerville, I. and Sawyer, P. (1997). *Requirements Engineering: A Good Practice Guide*. Chichester: John Wiley & Sons.

White, S. A. 2004. 'An Introduction to BPMN'. http://www.bpmn.org/Documents/Introduction%20to%20BPMN.

Glossary

abstract data type

A type that is defined by its operations rather than its representation. The representation is private and may only be accessed by the defined operations.

activity (PERT) chart

A chart used by project managers to show the dependencies between tasks that have to be completed. The chart shows the tasks, the time expected to complete these tasks, and the task dependencies. The critical path is the longest path (in terms of the time required to complete the tasks) through the activity chart. The critical path defines the minimum time required to complete the project.

Ada

A programming language that was developed for the U.S. Department of Defense in the 1980s as a standard language for developing military software. It is based on programming language research from the 1970s and includes constructs such as abstract data types and support for concurrency. It is still used for large, complex military and aerospace systems.

agile manifesto

A set of principles encapsulating the ideas underlying agile methods of software development.

agile methods

Methods of software development that are geared to rapid software delivery. The software is developed and delivered in increments, and process documentation and bureaucracy are minimized. The focus of development is on the code itself, rather than supporting documents.

algorithmic cost modeling

An approach to software cost estimation where a formula is used to estimate the project cost. The parameters in the formula are attributes of the project and the software itself.

application family

A set of software application programs that have a common architecture and generic functionality. These can be tailored to the needs of specific customers by modifying components and program parameters.

application framework

A set of reusable concrete and abstract classes that implement features common to many applications in a domain (e.g., user interfaces). The classes in the application framework are specialized and instantiated to create an application.

Application Program Interface (API)

An interface, generally specified as a set of operations, that allows access to an application program's functionality. This means that this functionality can be called on directly by other programs and not just accessed through the user interface.

architectural pattern (style)

An abstract description of a software architecture that has been tried and tested in a number of different software systems. The pattern description includes information about where it is appropriate to use the pattern and the organization of the components of the architecture.

aspect-oriented software development

An approach to software development that combines generative and component-based development. Cross-cutting concerns are identified in a program and the implementation of these concerns is defined as aspects. Aspects include a definition of where they are to be incorporated into a program. An aspect weaver then weaves the aspects into the appropriate places in the program.

aspect weaver

A program that is usually part of a compilation system that processes an aspect-oriented program and modifies the code to include the defined aspects at the specified points in the program.

availability

The readiness of a system to deliver services when requested. Availability is usually expressed as a decimal number, so an availability of 0.999 means that the system can deliver services for 999 out of 1,000 time units.

bar chart

A chart used by project managers to show the project tasks, the schedule associated with these tasks, and the people who will work on them. It shows the tasks' start and end dates and the staff allocations against a timeline.

BEA

A U.S. vendor of ERP systems.

black-box testing

An approach to testing where the testers have no access to the source code of a system or its components. The tests are derived from the system specification.

BPMN

Business Process Modeling Notation. A notation for defining workflows.

brownfield software development

The development of software for an environment where there are several existing systems that the software being developed must integrate with.

C

A programming language that was originally developed to implement the Unix system. C is a relatively low-level system implementation language that allows access to the system hardware and which can be compiled to efficient code. It is widely used for low-level systems programming and embedded systems development.

C++

An object-oriented programming language that is a superset of C.

C#

An object-oriented programming language, developed by Microsoft, that has much in common with C++, but which includes features that allow more compile-time type checking.

CASE (Computer-Aided Software Engineering)

The process of developing software using automated support.

CASE tool

A software tool, such as a design editor or a program debugger, used to support an activity in the software development process.

CASE workbench

An integrated set of CASE tools that work together to support a major process activity such as software design or configuration management.

change management

A process to record, check, analyze, estimate, and implement proposed changes to a software system.

class diagram

A UML diagram types that shows the object classes in a system and their relationships.

client–server architecture

An architectural model for distributed systems where the system functionality is offered as a set of services provided by a server. These are accessed by client computers that make use of the services. Variants of this approach, such as three-tier client–server architectures, use multiple servers.

Cleanroom software engineering

An approach to software development where the aim is to avoid introducing faults into the software (by analogy with a cleanroom used in semiconductor fabrication). The process involves formal software specification, structured transformation of a specification to a program, the development of correctness arguments, and statistical program testing.

cloud computing

The provision of computing and/or application services over the Internet using a 'cloud' of servers from an external provider. The 'cloud' is implemented using a large number of commodity computers and virtualization technology to make effective use of these systems.

CMM

The Software Engineering Institute's Capability Maturity Model, which is used to assess the level of software development maturity in an organization. It has now been superseded by CMMI, but is still widely used.

CMMI

An integrated approach to process capability maturity modeling based on the adoption of good software engineering practice and integrated quality management. It supports discrete and continuous maturity modeling and integrates systems and software engineering process maturity models.

code of ethics and professional practice

A set of guidelines that set out expected ethical and professional behavior for software engineers. This was defined by the major U.S. professional societies (the ACM and the IEEE) and defines ethical behavior under eight headings: public, client and employer, product, judgment, management, colleagues, profession, and self.

COM+

A component model and supporting middleware designed for use on Microsoft platforms; now superseded by .NET.

Common Request Broker Architecture (CORBA)

A set of standards proposed by the Object Management Group (OMG) that defines distributed object models and object communications; influential in the development of distributed systems but now rarely used.

component

A deployable, independent unit of software that is completely defined and accessed through a set of interfaces.

component model

A set of standards for component implementation, documentation and deployment. These cover the specific interfaces that may be provided by a component, component naming, component interoperation, and component composition. Component models provide the basis for middleware to support executing components.

component-based software engineering (CBSE)

The development of software by composing independent, deployable software components that are consistent with a component model.

configuration item

A machine-readable unit, such as a document or a source code file, that is subject to change and where the change has to be controlled by a configuration management system.

configuration management

The process of managing the changes to an evolving software product. Configuration management involves configuration planning, version management, system building, and change management.

Constructive Cost Modeling (COCOMO)

A family of algorithmic cost estimation models. COCOMO was first proposed in the early-1980s and has been modified and updated since then to reflect new technology and changing software engineering practice.

CORBA component model

A component model designed for use for the CORBA platform.

control metric

A software metric that allows managers to make planning decisions based on information about the software process or the software product that is being developed. Most control metrics are process metrics.

critical system

A computer system whose failure can result in significant economic, human, or environmental losses.

CVS

A widely-used, open source software tool used for version management.

data processing system

A system that aims to process large amounts of structured data. These systems usually process the data in batches and follow an input-process-output model. Examples of data processing systems are billing and invoicing systems, and payment systems.

denial of service attack

An attack on a web-based software system that attempts to overload the system so that it cannot provide its normal service to users.

dependability

The dependability of a system is an aggregate property that takes into account the system's safety, reliability, availability, security, and other attributes. The dependability of a system reflects the extent to which it can be trusted by its users.

dependability case

A structured document that is used to back up claims made by a system developer about the dependability of a system.

dependability requirement

A system requirement that is included to help achieve the required dependability for a system. Nonfunctional dependability requirements specify dependability attribute values; functional dependability requirements are functional requirements that specify how to avoid, detect, tolerate, or recover from system faults and failures.

design pattern

A well-tried solution to a common problem that captures experience and good practice in a form that can be reused. It is an abstract representation than can be instantiated in a number of ways.

distributed system

A software system where the software subsystems or components execute on different processors.

domain

A specific problem or business area where software systems are used. Examples of domains include real-time control, business data processing, and telecommunications switching.

domain model

A definition of domain abstractions, such as policies, procedures, objects, relationships, and events. It serves as a base of knowledge about some problem area.

DSDM

Dynamic System Development Method; claimed to be one of the first agile development methods.

embedded system

A software system that is embedded in a hardware device (e.g., the software system in a cell phone). Embedded systems are usually real-time systems and so have to respond in a timely way to events occurring in their environment.

emergent property

A property that only becomes apparent once all of the components of the system have been integrated to create the system.

enterprise Java beans (EJB)

A Java-based component model.

enterprise resource planning (ERP) system

A large-scale software system that includes a range of capabilities to support the operation of business enterprises and which provides a means of sharing information across these capabilities. For example, an ERP system may include support for supply chain management, manufacturing, and distribution. ERP systems are configured to the requirements of each company using the system.

ethnography

An observational technique that may be used in requirements elicitation and analysis. The ethnographer immerses him- or herself in the users' environment and observes their day-to-day work habits. Requirements for software support can be inferred from these observations.

event-based systems

Systems where the control of operation is determined by events that are generated in the system's environment. Most real-time systems are event-based systems.

extreme programming (XP)

A widely used agile method of software development that includes practices such as scenario-based requirements, test-first development, and pair programming.

fault avoidance

Developing software in such a way that faults are not introduced into that software.

fault detection

The use of processes and run-time checking to detect and remove faults in a program before these result in a system failure.

fault tolerance

The ability of a system to continue in execution even after faults have occurred.

formal methods

Methods of software development where the software is modeled using formal mathematical constructs such as predicates and sets. Formal transformation converts this model to code. Mostly used in the specification and development of critical systems.

Gantt chart

An alternative name for a bar chart.

incremental development

An approach to software development where the software is delivered and deployed in increments.

information hiding

Using programming language constructs to conceal the representation of data structures and to control external access to these structures.

inspection

See program inspection.

insulin pump

A software-controlled medical device that can deliver controlled doses of insulin to people suffering from diabetes. Used as a case study in several chapters in this book.

interface

A specification of the attributes and operations associated with a software component. The interface is used as the means of accessing the component's functionality.

ISO 9000/9001

A set of standards for quality management processes that is defined by the International Standards Organization (ISO). ISO 9001 is the ISO standard that is most applicable to software development. These may be used to certify the quality management processes in an organization.

iterative development

An approach to software development where the processes of specification, design, programming, and testing are interleaved.

J2EE

Java 2 Platform Enterprise Edition. A complex middleware system that supports the development of component-based web applications in Java. It includes a component model for Java components, APIs, services, etc.

Java

A widely used object-oriented programming language that was designed by Sun with the aim of platform independence.

language processing system

A system that translates one language into another. For example, a compiler is a language-processing system that translates program source code to object code.

legacy system

A sociotechnical system that is useful or essential to an organization but which has been developed using obsolete technology or methods. Because legacy systems often perform critical business functions, they have to be maintained.

Lehman's laws

A set of hypotheses about the factors that influence the evolution of complex software systems.

maintenance

The process of making changes to a system after it has been put into operation.

make

One of the first system building tools; still widely used in Unix/Linux systems.

mean time to failure (MTTF)

The average time between observed system failures; used in reliability specification.

MHC-PMS

Mental Health Care Patient Management System; used as a case study in several chapters.

middleware

The infrastructure software in a distributed system. It helps manage interactions between the distributed entities in the system and the system databases. Examples of middleware are an object request broker and a transaction management system.

model checking

A method of static verification where a state model of a system is exhaustively analyzed in an attempt to discover unreachable states.

model-driven architecture (MDA)

An approach to software development based on the construction of a set of system models, which can be automatically or semiautomatically processed to generate an executable system.

model-driven development (MDD)

An approach to software engineering centered around system models that are expressed in the UML, rather than programming language code. This extends MDA to consider activities other than development such as requirements engineering and testing.

.NET

A very extensive framework used to develop applications for Microsoft Windows systems; includes a component model that defines standards for components in Windows systems and associated middleware to support component execution.

object class

An object class defines the attributes and operations of objects. Objects are created at run-time by instantiating the class definition. The object class name can be used as a type name in some object-oriented languages.

object constraint language (OCL)

A language that is part of the UML, used to define predicates that apply to object classes and interactions in a UML model. The use of the OCL to specify components is a fundamental part of model-driven development.

Object Management Group (OMG)

A group of companies formed to develop standards for object-oriented development. Examples of standards promoted by the OMG are CORBA, UML, and MDA.

object model

A model of a software system that is structured and organized as a set of object classes and the relationships between these classes. Various different perspectives on the model may exist such as a state perspective and a sequence perspective.

object-oriented (OO) development

An approach to software development where the fundamental abstractions in the system are independent objects. The same type of abstraction is used during specification, design and development.

open source

An approach to software development where the source code for a system is made public and external users are encouraged to participate in the development of the system.

pair programming

A development situation where programmers work in pairs, rather than individually, to develop code; a fundamental part of extreme programming.

peer-to-peer system

A distributed system where there is no distinction between clients and servers. Computers in the system can act as both clients and servers. Peer-to-peer applications include file sharing, instant messaging, and cooperation support systems.

People Capability Maturity Model (P-CMM)

A process maturity model that reflects how effective an organization is at managing the skills, training, and experience of the people in that organization.

predictor metric

A software metric that is used as a basis for making predictions about the characteristics of a software system, such as its reliability or maintainability.

probability of failure on demand (POFOD)

A reliability metric that is based on the likelihood of a software system failing when a demand for its services is made.

process improvement

Changing a software development process with the aim of making that process more efficient or improving the quality of its outputs. For example, if your aim is to reduce the number of defects in the delivered software, you might improve a process by adding new validation activities.

process maturity model

A model of the extent to which a process includes good practice and reflective and measurement capabilities that are geared to process improvement.

process model

An abstract representation of a process. Process models may be developed from various perspectives and can show the activities involved in a process, the artifacts used in the process, constraints that apply to the process, and the roles of the people enacting the process.

program evolution dynamics

The study of the ways in which an evolving software system changes. It is claimed that Lehman's laws govern the dynamics of program evolution.

program generator

A program that generates another program from a high-level, abstract specification. The generator embeds knowledge that is reused in each generation activity.

program inspection

A review where a group of inspectors examine a program, line by line, with the aim of detecting program errors. Inspections are often driven by a checklist of common programming errors.

Python

A programming language with dynamic types, which is particularly well suited to the development of web-based systems; extensively used by Google.

quality assurance (QA)

The overall process of defining how software quality can be achieved and how the organization developing the software knows that the software has met the required level of quality.

quality plan

A plan that defines the quality processes and procedures that should be used. This involves selecting and instantiating standards for products and processes and defining the system quality attributes that are most important.

rapid application development (RAD)

An approach to software development aimed at rapid delivery of the software. It often involves the use of database programming and development support tools such as screen and report generators.

rate of occurrence of failure (ROCOF)

A reliability metric that is based on the number of observed failures of a system in a given time period.

Rational Unified Process (RUP)

A generic software process model that presents software development as a four-phase iterative activity, where the phases are inception, elaboration, construction, and transition. Inception establishes a business case for the system, elaboration defines the architecture, construction implements the system, and transition deploys the system in the customer's environment.

real-time system

A system that has to recognize and process external events in 'real-time'. The correctness of the system does not just depend on what it does but also on how quickly it does it. Real-time systems are usually organized as a set of cooperating sequential processes.

reengineering

The modification of a software system to make it easier to understand and change. Reengineering often involves software and data restructuring and organization, program simplification, and redocumentation.

reengineering, business process

Changing a business process to meet a new organizational objective such as reduced cost and faster execution.

reference architecture

A generic, idealized architecture that includes all the features that systems might incorporate. It is a way of informing designers about the general structure of that class of system rather than a basis for creating a specific system architecture.

release

A version of a software system that is made available to system customers.

reliability

The ability of a system to deliver services as specified. Reliability can be specified quantitatively as a probability of failure on demand or as the rate of occurrence of failure.

reliability growth modeling

The development of a model of how the reliability of a system changes (improves) as it is tested and program defects are removed.

requirement, functional

A statement of some function or feature that should be implemented in a system.

requirement, non-functional

A statement of a constraint or expected behavior that applies to a system. This constraint may refer to the emergent properties of the software that is being developed or to the development process.

requirements management

The process of managing changes to requirements to ensure that the changes made are properly analyzed and tracked through the system.

REST

REST is derived from Representational State Transfer, which is a style of development based around simply client/server interaction, and which uses the HTTP protocol. REST is based around the idea of an identifiable resource, which has a URI. All interaction with resources is based on HTTP POST, GET, PUT, and DELETE. It is now widely used for implementing low overhead web services.

risk

An undesirable outcome that poses a threat to the achievement of some objective. A process risk threatens the schedule or cost of a process; a product risk is a risk that may mean that some of the system requirements may not be achieved.

risk management

The process of identifying risks, assessing their severity, planning measures to put in place if the risks arise, and monitoring the software and the software process for risks.

Ruby

A programming language with dynamic types that is particularly well suited to web application programming.

safety

The ability of a system to operate without catastrophic failure.

safety case

A structured argument that a system is safe and/or secure. Many critical systems must have associated safety cases that are assessed and approved by external regulators before the system is certified for use.

SAP

A German company that has developed a well-known and widely used ERP system. It also refers to the name given to the ERP system itself.

scenario

A description of one typical way in which a system is used or a user carries out some activity.

Scrum

An agile method of development, which is based on sprints—short development, cycles. Scrum may be used as a basis for agile project management alongside other agile methods such as XP.

security

The ability of a system to protect itself against accidental or deliberate intrusion. Security includes confidentiality, integrity, and availability.

SEI

Software Engineering Institute. A software engineering research and technology transfer center, founded with the aim of improving the standard of software engineering in U.S. companies.

sequence diagram

A diagram that shows the sequence of interactions required to complete some operation. In the UML, sequence diagrams may be associated with use cases.

server

A program that provides a service to other (client) programs.

service

See web service.

sociotechnical system

A system, including hardware and software components, that has defined operational processes followed by human operators and which operates within an organization. It is therefore influenced by organizational policies, procedures, and structures.

software architecture

A model of the fundamental structure and organization of a software system.

software life cycle

Often used as another name for the software process; originally coined to refer to the waterfall model of the software process.

software metric

An attribute of a software system or process that can be expressed numerically and measured. Process metrics are attributes of the process such as the time taken to complete a task; product metrics are attributes of the software itself such as size or complexity.

software product line

See application family.

software process

The related set of activities and processes that is involved in developing and evolving a software system.

spiral model

A model of a development process where the process is represented as a spiral, with each round of the spiral incorporating the different stages in the process. As you move from one round of the spiral to another, you repeat all of the stages of the process.

state diagram

A UML diagram type that shows the states of a system and the events that trigger a transition from one state to another.

static analysis

Tool-based analysis of a program's source code to discover errors and anomalies. Anomalies, such as successive assignments to a variable with no intermediate use, may be indicators of programming errors.

structured method

A method of software design that defines the system models that should be developed, the rules and guidelines that should apply to these models, and a process to be followed in developing the design.

Structured Query Language (SQL)

A standard language used for relational database programming.

Subversion

A widely used, open source system building tool that is available on a range of platforms.

system building

The process of compiling the components or units that make up a system and linking these with other components to create an executable program. System building is normally automated so that recompilation is minimized. This automation may be built into the language processing system (as in Java) or may involve software tools to support system building.

systems engineering

A process that is concerned with specifying a system, integrating its components and testing that the system meets its requirements. System engineering is concerned with the whole sociotechnical system—software, hardware, and operational processes—not just the system software.

test coverage

The effectiveness of system tests in testing the code of an entire system. Some companies have standards for test coverage (e.g., the system tests shall ensure that all program statements are executed at least once).

test-driven development

An approach to software development where executable tests are written before the program code. The set of tests are run automatically after every change to the program.

transaction

A unit of interaction with a computer system. Transactions are independent and atomic (they are not broken down into smaller units) and are a fundamental unit of recovery, consistency, and concurrency.

transaction processing system

A system that ensures that transactions are processed in such a way so that they do not interfere with each other and so that individual transaction failure does not affect other transactions or the system's data.

Unified Modeling Language (UML)

A graphical language used in object-oriented development that includes several types of system models that provide different views of a system. The UML has become a de facto standard for object-oriented modeling.

use case

A specification of one type of interaction with a system.

user interface design

The process of designing the way in which system users can access system functionality, and the way that information produced by the system is displayed.

validation

The process of checking that a system meets the needs and expectations of the customer.

verification

The process of checking that a system meets its specification.

version management

The process of managing changes to a software system and its components so that it is possible to know which changes have been implemented in each version of the component/system, and also to recover/re-create previous versions of the component/system.

waterfall model

A software process model that involves discrete development stages: specification, design, implementation, testing, and maintenance. In principle, one stage must be complete before progress to the next stage is possible. In practice, there is significant iteration between stages.

web service

An independent software component that can be accessed through the Internet using standard protocols. It is completely self-contained without external dependencies. XML-based standards such as SOAP (Standard Object Access Protocol), for web service information exchange, and WSDL (Web Service Definition Language), for the definition of web service interfaces, have been developed. However, the REST approach may also be used for web service implementation.

white-box testing

An approach to program testing where the tests are based on knowledge of the structure of the program and its components. Access to source code is essential for white-box testing.

wilderness weather system

A system to collect data about the weather conditions in remote areas. Used as a case study in several chapters in this book.

workflow

A detailed definition of a business process that is intended to accomplish a certain task. The workflow is usually expressed graphically and shows the individual process activities and the information that is produced and consumed by each activity.

WSDL

An XML-based notation for defining the interface of web services.

XML

Extended Markup Language. XML is a text markup language that supports the interchange of structured data. Each data field is delimited by tags that give information about that field. XML is now very widely used and has become the basis of protocols for web services.

XP

A commonly used abbreviation for Extreme Programming.

Z

A model-based, formal specification language developed at the University of Oxford in England.

Subject Index

A

Q

R

T

Author Index

S

T

U

V